D1524552

MEANING AND HISTORY
IN SYSTEMATIC THEOLOGY

ROBERT M. DORAN, SJ

MEANING AND HISTORY
IN SYSTEMATIC THEOLOGY

ESSAYS IN HONOR OF
ROBERT M. DORAN, SJ

EDITED BY

JOHN D. DADOSKY

MARQUETTE
UNIVERSITY

PRESS

MARQUETTE STUDIES IN THEOLOGY
NO. 68
ANDREW TALLON, SERIES EDITOR

LIBRARY OF CONGRESS CATALOGING-IN-PUBLICATION DATA

Meaning and history in systematic theology : essays in honor of Robert M. Doran /
edited by John D. Dadosky.
  p. cm. — (Marquette studies in theology ; No. 68)
Includes bibliographical references and index.
ISBN-13: 978-0-87462-745-9 (hardcover : alk. paper)
ISBN-10: 0-87462-745-1 (hardcover : alk. paper)
1. Theology. 2. Doran, Robert M., 1939- 3. Lonergan, Bernard J. F. I. Dadosky, John
Daniel, 1966- II. Doran, Robert M., 1939-
  BT80.M43 2009
  230.01—dc22

                                                                    2009030243

♾The paper used in this publication meets the minimum requirements of the
American National Standard for Information Sciences—
Permanence of Paper for Printed Library Materials, ANSI Z39.48-1992.

MARQUETTE UNIVERSITY PRESS
MILWAUKEE

The Association of Jesuit University Presses

TABLE OF CONTENTS

Contents

FOREWORD

Theologian Fr. Robert Doran, SJ is a Jesuit priest I truly admire, not only as a theologian, but also for his years of compassionate care for people with HIV/AIDS. Fr. Doran is an original and significant presence as a theologian in the Roman Catholic Church.

I was honored when he asked me to write an Icon which would open people to-pray-into Fr. Bernard Lonergan's theology of the Triune God. It seems to me that while reading this profound work I was most aware of how often Fr. Lonergan stresses the word 'mystery' in approaching the Most Blessed Trinity. This word prepares the contemplative soul to come to the Triune God on bended knee in adoration as well as with the intellect.

In the Eastern Church the Trinity is most often represented as the Three Angelic Figures who appear to Abraham and Sarah in Genesis 18. With this in mind I wanted to place the figures in procession moving towards Fr. Lonergan amidst his native Canadian landscape. I chose *Decorative Landscape 1917*, a work by Lawren Harris, one of Canada's famed Group of Seven. He hoped to elevate the Canadian people to see the vast beauty of the nature around them after suffering so much from the war. Harris' own brother Howard was killed in action that year.

Both Harris and Lonergan shared in a vocation to lift our spirits towards God. And believe both succeed with their dazzling talents in leading us to pray before this great and loving mystery. It is God who gave each of them a way to instruct us so that we might be able to pray with their insights.

I know that this is why Fr. Bob Doran is also honored by his fellow colleagues and former students in this great gift of a book edited by theologian and philosopher John Dadosky.

Fr. William Hart McNichols
Ranchos de Taos, December, 2008

INTRODUCTION

B ernard Lonergan states in the Epilogue of *Insight* that he spent years reaching up to the mind of Aquinas and it was the *reaching* that changed him profoundly.[1] Robert M. Doran, SJ spent over the last 40 years of his life reaching up to the mind of Lonergan. To say that the reaching has changed him may not adequately capture the influence that Lonergan has had, not only on Doran's own life, but on the colleagues who have benefitted from the bounty of Doran's labors.

Robert Michael Doran was born in the Bronx on June 20, 1939. His family moved to Milwaukee in 1948 and resided in Whitefish Bay, Wisconsin. He entered the Wisconsin Province of the Society of Jesus in August 16, 1956. His intellectual formation in the Society took place at St. Louis University and culminated in his doctoral studies at Marquette University, which he completed in 1975. His dissertation was published as *Subject and Psyche: Ricoeur, Jung, and the Search for Foundations* (1977).[2] He was ordained to the priesthood on June 4, 1969 and took his Final Vows as a Jesuit on April 16, 1982. After spending several initial years teaching at Marquette University and Creighton University, he spent the bulk of his professional career (1979-2006) at Regis College, Toronto. During the last five years of his time in Toronto, he served as Executive Director of the Lonergan Research Institute, which he had co-founded with Frederick E. Crowe in 1985. In 2006, he returned to Marquette University in order to take up the distinguished Emmett Doerr Chair in Systematic Theology, which he currently occupies. He continues his research, writing, and editing in Milwaukee but travels widely to various conferences.

In terms of Doran's intellectual career, it is possible to identify three major movements: 1.) the appropriation of Lonergan's thought to depth psychology, 2.) the attempt to integrate history into theology and 3.) the attempt to begin a collaborative comprehensive systematic theology for our time.

---

1 Bernard Lonergan, *Insight: A Study of Human Understanding*, CWL 3, ed. F. E. Crowe and R. M. Doran (Toronto: University of Toronto Press, 1992), 769.

2 See bibliography below for complete references specific to his books.

Regarding the first, Doran developed the notion of psychic conversion as a fourth conversion to Lonergan's threefold conversions: intellectual, moral, and religious. Lonergan explicitly writes, "To these Doran has added a psychic conversion in his book on *Psychic Conversion and Theological Foundations*. He has thought the matter through very thoroughly and it fits very adroitly and snugly into my own efforts."[3]

Regarding the second, using the insights he developed in terms of psychological self-transformation, Doran works out the foundations for an integration of history into theology. This endeavor culminated after ten years of writing into his *magnum opus, Theology and the Dialectics of History* (1990). This text went to a second printing in 2001 and has been translated into Spanish.

Regarding the third, Doran is laboring to begin writing a systematic theology from the standpoint of a third stage of meaning. While editing Lonergan's treatise on the Trinity, Doran discovered the significance of the fourfold hypothesis for the future of a systematic theology.[4] His methodological foray into this systematics appears in his latest volume, *What is Systematic Theology?* (2006). He is currently writing his first volume which is tentatively titled *The Trinity in History*.

However, in addition to these three principal moments in his thought, there have been fresh discoveries and developments along the way which appear as fruitful offshoots. One such offshoot is his advance in the first level of intentional consciousness in Lonergan's philosophy when he brought it into dialogue with Heidegger's *Verstehen* and Wittgenstein's *ordinary language*.[5] There was also the helpful clarification of the fourth level operation – decision – by placing

---

3 Lonergan's Recommendation to Publisher in support of a book proposal by Robert Doran, A2280 (File 490.1/6), Archives, Lonergan Research Institute of Regis College, Toronto. Similarly in a letter to Fr. Edward Braxton (February 12, 1975) Lonergan writes: "I agree with Robert Doran on psychic conversion and his combining it with intellectual, moral, and religious conversion." File 132, p. 1, also from the Lonergan Archives.

4 Robert M. Doran, SJ, "Addressing the Four-point Hypothesis," *Theological Studies* 68 (2007): 674-82

5 Robert M. Doran, SJ, "Reception and Elemental Meaning: An Expansion of the Notion of Psychic Conversion," *Toronto Journal of Theology* 20/2 (2004): 133-57.

it within the context of Saint Ignatius of Loyola's three moments of election.[6] Such keen hermeneutic clarifications are of the kind that fall into place only after someone has been striving for years to understand one person's thought.

More recently, Doran has brought Lonergan's thought into dialogue with René Girard.[7] Doran believes the latter's theory on the origin of violence, mimetic rivalry, and scapegoating will complement Lonergan's work on the redemption. Undoubtedly, Doran's appreciation of Girard extends beyond the categories the latter offers to bring deeper theological understanding to the mystery of redemption; it resonates with Doran's own sensitivity to the victims of mimesis, violence, and scapegoating, his encounters with the general bias of common sense over the years, and his resistance to instances of unintelligent ecclesial pastoral praxis. Encountering Girard's work also confirmed his own pastoral ministry to the modern day outcasts of society – the victims of AIDS. Hence, Doran has sought to integrate theory and praxis by advancing the world of theory concretely with conjugate acts of faith, hope, and charity.

Corresponding to this intellectual vocation, and inextricably connected with it, is Doran's desire to preserve and promote the legacy of Bernard Lonergan. This has occurred over the years through 1) his General Editorship with F. E. Crowe of the entire *Collected Works* of Lonergan, 2) his work to establish a permanent center of Lonergan studies, and 3) his insistence that the promotion and development of Lonergan's thought is a collaborative venture. These three are inextricably intertwined.

Doran has felt a personal responsibility for Lonergan's legacy ever since he had the privilege of ministering to Lonergan during his last days. One of the last comments Lonergan made to him before his

---

6 Robert M. Doran, SJ, "Ignatian Themes in the Thought of Bernard Lonergan: Revisiting a Topic That Deserves Further Reflection," *Lonergan Workshop* 19, ed. Fred Lawrence (Boston College, 2006); and "Ignatian Themes in the Thought of Bernard Lonergan," *Toronto Journal of Theology* 22/1 (2006): 39-54.

7 Robert M. Doran, SJ, "Lonergan and Girard on Sacralization and Desacralization," *Revista Porguguesa de Filosofia* 63/4 (2007): 1171-1201; and "Summarizing 'Imitating the Divine Relations: A Theological Contribution to Mimetic Theory,'" *Contagion: Journal of Violence, Mimesis, and Culture* 14 (2007): 27-38.

death was, "It is in your hands now." The day before Lonergan died, having initiated and finalized a commitment from the University of Toronto Press, Doran was able to inform 'Bernie' that his entire *Collected Works* would be published. Those of us who have labored for years studying Lonergan's thought can only imagine what a sacred moment that must have been. In 1979, Lonergan had asked Doran personally to be one of the Trustees of his estate. Doran has acted as such ever since Lonergan's death on November 26, 1984.

With F. E. Crowe, Doran established the Lonergan Research Institute on April 15, 1985. Almost simultaneously, Doran and Crowe began editing the weighty critical editions of the *Collected Works*. When completed they will exceed twenty volumes. Subsequent volumes in conjunction with other Lonergan scholars throughout the world have acquired a reputation for impeccable thoroughness and detail and are considered an invaluable resource for Lonergan studies. Under Crowe's and Doran's stewardship, the Lonergan Research Institute became a focal point for the preservation, promotion, development, and dissemination of Lonergan's ideas. Throughout the years, this Institute has attracted various scholars and students to Toronto in order to study and develop Lonergan's thought.

Perhaps the epitome of what Lonergan would have hoped for in such a center occurred in the summer of 2004 when the Institute hosted the Second International Lonergan Workshop at Regis College, Toronto. The Lonergan Workshop has become a staple institution hosted annually by Fred and Sue Lawrence at Boston College. This Workshop has been an invaluable forum for the creative exchange of ideas throughout the years from a diverse range of scholars; it continues to be a vital organ in the Lonergan legacy. This meeting in the summer 2004 symbolized the hope for a future of collaboration not only between scholars but between institutions.

Doran has always called for collaboration among scholars in the vital exchange of ideas and the development of Lonergan's thought, but more recently he has actively encouraged the various Lonergan institutions to collaborate with each other. In the summer of 2007, after a meeting of such centers, Doran, supported by Marquette University, began working on a major electronic resource that would make much of the primary data of Lonergan's personal papers available online. On the feast of the Queenship of Mary, exactly 50 years to the date of his first Jesuit vows in 1958, Doran launched the website through

Marquette University. While the original Lonergan and Crowe papers housed at Regis College will continue to have a vital hermeneutic importance in the future of Lonergan research, the website www.bernardlonergan.com makes his personal papers available to the entire world. This launching is unprecedented in that it makes Lonergan's thought available to those who may not have the resources to travel, such as Jesuits belonging to provinces in developing parts of the world. For those of us who labor to promote the mentality and social structures of *cosmopolis*, the world-city Lonergan writes about in Chapter 7 of *Insight*, the website places Lonergan's legacy 'in everyone's hands now.'

There was a robust response to calls for contributions to this tribute to Professor Doran. It is a challenge for any editor to find a title that accurately speaks to the range of topics contained in a volume of this nature. I settled on a title *a posteriori* after receiving the manuscripts. I believe the diverse range of subjects has been captured in the title *Meaning and History in Systematic Theology: Essays in Honor of Robert M. Doran, SJ* Rather than trying to force the range of topics into various parts or themes, I chose to keep it simple by putting the authors' contributions alphabetically.

Such achievements can be carried out expeditiously only when there exists a single-mindedness of support from the contributors, the editors, the publisher, community members, and colleagues that flows from a communal and immediate grasp of value for someone who is so worthy of honor. I would like to thank specifically Andrew Tallon and the Marquette University Press for their willingness, patience, and flexibility in the publication process. I thank Fr. James Flaherty (Rector) and the Marquette Jesuit Community for their moral and financial support for this project. I thank Dorothy Cummings who meticulously copy edited the entire collection of essays. Finally, I would like to thank Regis College for giving me the time to see this project through from its inception to its completion.

It is with a deep spirit of gratitude for these people and for the life's work of Robert Doran that this volume goes from our hands into the reader's hands.

WORKS OF ROBERT M. DORAN, sj

A. BOOKS

2006 *Psychic Conversion and Theological Foundations*. Second, revised edition. Milwaukee: Marquette University Press, 2006.

2005 *What Is Systematic Theology?* Toronto: University of Toronto Press, 2005.

2001 *Theology and the Dialectics of History*. Toronto: University of Toronto Press, 2001 (Second printing).

1995 *Theological Foundations, vol. 1: Intentionality and Psyche*. Milwaukee: Marquette University Press, 1995.

    Theological Foundations, vol. 2: Theology and Culture. Milwaukee: Marquette University Press, 1995.

1995 *Libertad, Sociedad e Historia: Antología de textos de Bernard Lonergan y Robert Doran*. Mexico City: Universidad Iberoamericana, 1995

1994 *Subject and Psyche*. Second, revised edition. Milwaukee: Marquette University Press, 1994.

1993 *La Teologia y Las Dialecticas de la Historia*. Spanish translation of *Theology and the Dialectics of History*. Mexico City: Universidad Iberoamericana, 1993.

1990 *Theology and the Dialectics of History*. Toronto: University of Toronto Press, 1990.

2006 *Collected Works of Bernard Lonergan*. General Editor of entire series of twenty-five volumes. Thirteen published to date. Particular editor of ten of these twelve. Toronto: University of Toronto Press, 1988-2007.

1981 *Psychic Conversion and the Theological Foundations*. Chico, CA: Scholars Press, 1981.

1977 *Subject and Psyche: Ricoeur, Jung, and the Search for Foundations*. Washington, D.C.: University Press of America, 1977.

B. CHAPTERS IN BOOKS

2007 'Empirical Consciousness in *Insight*: Is Our Conception Too Narrow?' in *The Importance of Insight*, ed. John Liptay and David Liptay (Toronto: University of Toronto Press, 2007), 49-63.

2006 'System Seeking Method: Reconciling System and History,' in *Il Teologo e la Storia: Lonergan's Centenary*, ed. Natalino Spaccapelo and Paul Gilbert (Rome: Gregorian University, 2006), 275-99.

1998 AIDS Ministry as a Praxis of Hope,' in *Jesus Crucified and Risen: Essays in Spirituality and Theology*, ed. William P. Loewe and Vernon J. Gregson (Collegeville, MN: The Liturgical Press, 1998), 177-93.

1993 'Foreword: Common Ground,' in *Communication and Lonergan: Common Ground for Forging the New Age*, ed. Thomas J. Farrell and Paul A. Soukup (Kansas City, MO: Sheed & Ward, 1993), ix-xvi.

1989 'Psychic Conversion and Lonergan's Hermeneutics,' in *Lonergan's Hermeneutics: Its Development and Application*, ed. Sean E. McEvenue and Ben F. Meyer (Washington, D.C.: The Catholic University of America Press, 1989), 161-216.

1988 'Bernard Lonergan: An Appreciation,' in *The Desires of the Human Heart*, ed. Vernon Gregson (Mahwah, NJ: Paulist Press, 1988), 1-15.

1988 'The Analogy of Dialectic and the Systematics of History,' in *Religion in Context: Recent Studies in Lonergan*, ed. Timothy P. Fallon, SJ, and Philip Boo Riley (Lanham, MD: University Press of America, 1988), 35-57.

1988 'Jung and Catholic Theology,' in *Catholicism and Jungian Psychology*, ed. J. Marvin Spiegelman (Phoenix: Falcon Press, 1988), 41-73.

1984 'Report on a Work in Progress,' in *Searching for Cultural Foundations*, ed. Philip McShane (Lanham, MD: University Press of America, 1984), 44-64.

1981 'Theological Grounds for a World-Cultural Humanity,' in *Creativity and Method: Essays in Honor of Bernard Lonergan*, ed. Matthew L. Lamb (Milwaukee: Marquette University Press, 1981), 105-22.

1977 'Christ and the Psyche,' in *Trinification of the World*, ed. Thomas A. Dunne and Jean-Marc Laporte (Toronto: Regis College Press, 1977), 112-43.

C. ARTICLES

2008 'Envisioning a Systematic Theology,' *Lonergan Workshop* 20, ed. Fred Lawrence (Boston College, 2008): 101-26.

2008 'Being in Love with God: A Source of Analogies for Theological Understanding,' *Irish Theological Quarterly* 73 (2008): 227-42.

2008 'Lonergan and Girard on Sacralization and Desacralization,' *Revista Porguguesa de Filosofia* 63/4 (2007): 1171-1201.

2008 'Summarizing "Imitating the Divine Relations: A Theological Contribution to Mimetic Theory,"' *Contagion: Journal of Violence, Mimesis, and Culture* 14 (2007): 27-38.

2007 'Addressing the Four-point Hypothesis,' *Theological Studies* 68 (2007): 674-82.

2006 'Ignatian Themes in the Thought of Bernard Lonergan: Revisiting a Topic That Deserves Further Reflection,' *Lonergan Workshop* 19, ed. Fred Lawrence (Boston College, 2006).

2006 'Ignatian Themes in the Thought of Bernard Lonergan,' *Toronto Journal of Theology* 22/1 (2006): 39-54.

2006 'The Starting Point of Systematic Theology, *Theological Studies* 67 (2006): 750-76.

2004 'Insight and Language: Steps toward the Resolution of a Problem,' *Divyadaan: Journal of Philosophy and Education* 15/3 (2004): 405-26.

2004 'Reception and Elemental Meaning: An Expansion of the Notion of Psychic Conversion,' *Toronto Journal of Theology* 20/2 (2004): 133-57.

2003 'Implementation in Systematics: The Structure,' *Journal of Macrodynamic Analysis* 3 (2003): 264-72.

2002 'Reflections on Method in Systematic Theology,' *Lonergan Workshop* 17 (2002): 23-51.

2002 'The Truth of Theological Understanding in *Divinarum Personarum* and *De Deo Trino, Pars Systematica,' Method: Journal of Lonergan Studies* 20: 1 (2002): 33-75.

2001 'Intelligentia Fidei in *De Deo Trino, Pars Systematica,' Method: Journal of Lonergan Studies* 19/1 (2001): 35-83.

2000 'The First Chapter of *De Deo Trino, Pars Systematica: The Issues,' Method: Journal of Lonergan Studies* 18/1 (2000): 27-48.

1999 'System and History: The Challenge to Catholic Systematic Theology,' *Theological Studies* 60/4 (1999): 652-78.

1998 'Bernard Lonergan and the Functions of Systematic Theology,' *Theological Studies* 59/4 (1998): 569-607.

1997 '"Complacency and Concern" and a Basic Thesis on Grace,' *Lonergan Workshop* 13 (1997): 57-78.

1997 'Lonergan and Balthasar: Methodological Considerations,' *Theological Studies* 58/1 (1997): 569-607.

1996 'Response to Helminiak's "A Scientific Spirituality: The Interface of Psychology and Theology,' *The International Journal for the Psychology of Religion* 6/1 (1996): 21-25.

1995 'Revisiting "Consciousness and Grace,"' *Method: Journal of Lonergan Studies* 13/2 (1995): 151-59.

1994 'Prolegomenon for a New Systematics,' *Grail: An Ecumenical Journal* 10/3 (1994): 75-87.

1993 'Jung, Gnosis and Faith Refused,' *Cross Currents* 43/3 (1993): 307-23.

1993 'Consciousness and Grace,' *Method: Journal of Lonergan Studies* 11/1 (1993): 51-75.

1988 'Duality and Dialectic,' *Lonergan Workshop* 7 (1988): 59-84.

1986 'Self-Knowledge and the Interpretation of Imaginal Expression,' *Method: Journal of Lonergan Studies* 4 (1986): 55-84.

1986 'From Psychic Conversion to the Dialectic of Community,' *Lonergan Workshop* 6 (1986): 84-107.

1985 'Primary Process and the Spiritual Unconscious,' *Lonergan Workshop* 5 (1985): 23-47.

1984 'Theology's Situation: Questions to Eric Voegelin,' *Lonergan Workshop* 4 Supplement (1984): 69-91.

1983 'Suffering Servanthood and the Scale of Values,' *Lonergan Workshop* 4 (1983): 41-67.

1983 'Education for Cosmopolis,' *Method: Journal of Lonergan Studies* 1 (1983): 134-57.

1981 'Dramatic Artistry in the Third Stage of Meaning,' *Lonergan Workshop* 1 (1981): 147-99.

1979 'Jungian Psychology and Christian Spirituality: III,' *Review for Religious* 38/6 (1979): 857-66.

1979 'Jungian Psychology and Christian Spirituality: II,' *Review for Religious* 38/5 (1979): 742-52.

1979 'Jungian Psychology and Christian Spirituality: I,' *Review for Religious* 38/4 (1979): 497-510.

1979 'Jungian Psychology and Lonergan's Foundations: A Methodological Proposal,' *Journal of the American Academy of Religion* 47/1 Supplement (1979): 23-45.

1979 'Psyche, Evil, and Grace,' *Communio* 6/2 (1979): 192-211

1979 'Aesthetic Subjectivity and Generalized Empirical Method,' *The Thomist* 43/2 (1979): 257-78.

1978 'The Theologian's Psyche: Notes toward a Reconstruction of Depth Psychology,' *Lonergan Workshop* 1 (1978): 93-141.

1977 'Subject, Psyche, and Theology's Foundations,' *The Journal of Religion* 57/3 (1977): 267-87.

1977 'Aesthetics and the Opposites,' *Thought* 52 (1977): 117-33.

1977 'Psychic Conversion,' *The Thomist* 41/2 (1977): 200-36.

1973 'Paul Ricoeur: Toward the Restoration of Meaning,' *Anglican Theological Review* 55/4 (1973): 443-58.

1967 'Sartre's Critique of the Husserlian Ego,' *The Modern Schoolman* 44/4 (1967): 307-17.

WHICH SCALE OF VALUE PREFERENCE?
LONERGAN, SCHELER, VON HILDEBRAND, AND DORAN

Patrick H. Byrne

I. INTRODUCTION

In his masterwork *Method in Theology*, Bernard Lonergan set forth his account of the scale of value preference in the following terms: "Not only do feelings respond to values. They do so in accord with some scale of preference. So we may distinguish vital, social, cultural, personal, and religious values in an ascending order."[1] I have been struck by the number of people who have been attracted to Bernard Lonergan's account of the scale of value preference. Many have put his scale to fruitful use in a remarkable variety of ways.[2] What people seem to find especially attractive is Lonergan's version of the ascending order or hierarchy of values. Lonergan's account of the scale of values has struck a chord with me as well. It feels just right. Yet it is very sketchy–only five levels of values are identified. Surely the realm of values is richer and more diverse than that. In addition, Lonergan offered no arguments or rationales in support of his version of this scale of value preference. I suspect that he arrived at it after a long and perhaps difficult period of reflecting on the matter. It would have been helpful to know how he came to his own version, especially for knowing how to flesh out the thin structure of that scale.

Absent of such explanations, we may well ask: Why should we accept Lonergan's account of the scale of value preference instead of the accounts by the many others who have written on this subject of value

---

1 Bernard Lonergan, *Method in Theology* (NY: Herder and Herder, 1972), 31; cited hereafter as *MT*.

2 To cite only one very recent example, see Gerard Whelan, SJ, "Robert Doran and Pastoral Theology: Reflections from Nairobi, Kenya," *Lonergan Workshop*, 20 (2008): 357-390.

priorities? This is an important question, for without an explicit and adequate answer, Lonergan's account will likely come to be regarded as merely another subjective opinion about value priorities. This would be lamentable for Lonergan's scale meets an important need for our own times, and likely for some time to come. Therefore, if Lonergan's account of the scale is to be taken seriously by a wider audience, and to have the important influence that it ought to have, then some explicit justification of it is called for.

In this essay I attempt to work out an explanation for Lonergan's scale of value preference. I begin with a review of the pioneering work on this problem by Robert Doran, SJ, and it is fitting that this *Festschrift* is dedicated to him. I then survey the discussions of scales of values by Max Scheler and Dietrich von Hildebrand. I turn to Scheler and von Hildebrand because Lonergan read works by or about them on this topic, and these works profoundly influenced his thinking about the scale of value preference. Even so, Lonergan diverged in significant ways from both of their versions of the scale – and they also differed from each other. Exploring these differences will enable us both to flesh out Lonergan's scale and to deepen the rationale. Finally, I suggest some sources in Lonergan's work that address difficulties in the work of Scheler and von Hildebrand and show how these sources contribute to an explanation for Lonergan's departure from their accounts.

2. DORAN'S TWO EXPLANATIONS OF THE SCALE OF VALUE PREFERENCE

Robert Doran has offered two explanations in support of Lonergan's account of the scale of value preference. The first correlates the levels of the scale with levels of consciousness.[3] In this essay, however, I will explore the implications of his second explanation. Along those lines Doran writes: "[F]rom below, more basic levels [of value] are required for the emergence of higher levels...whereas from above, these

---

3 Robert M. Doran, *What is Systematic Theology?* (Toronto: University of Toronto Press, 2005), 181; hereafter cited as *WST*. See also Robert M. Doran, *Theology and the Dialectics of History* (Toronto: University of Toronto Press, 1990), 88; hereafter cited as *TDH*. Elsewhere I have pointed to some difficulties in this approach to grounding Lonergan's account of the scale.

proportionate developments are the condition of possibility of the appropriate schemes of recurrent events at the more basic levels."[4]

This is a very subtle but very important distinction. A less sophisticated thinker would see the conditioning in only one direction, from below: we must eat in order to paint or to pray. While conditioning from below is certainly a reality, it overlooks the further reality of the reciprocal form of conditioning from above: when people lose all sense of higher purpose, they abandon their plows in the fields and stop eating.

Doran illustrates his keen observation with examples from all four of the interfaces between the five levels of values. For example, says Doran, the health and strength (vital values) of a multiplicity of people are needed to implement new social organizations. Yet on the other hand, once technological, economic, and political institutions are functioning actually and recurrently, they become the indispensable conditions for the effective and regular continuation of the values of health and strength of members of the society. Likewise, as Doran further notes, "the social order is a direct function of the cultural values that inform the everyday life of the community," so that the maintenance of the social order becomes crucially dependent upon cultural institutions and values. He continues, making strong arguments that this reciprocal relationship of the conditioning of the lower from above applies also to the relationships between cultural values and personal integrity and virtues, and between personal integrity and religious values.[5]

We may generalize Doran's second approach to explaining Lonergan's scale as follows: What makes one level of value higher than another is its capacity, once it emerges, to operate "from above" and to set the conditions for the sustained and continued recurrence of a whole series of values at the lower levels. This does not negate the fact that the values at lower levels also provide the indispensable "materials" or conditions for the emergence of higher level values. But it does point toward an explanatory criterion for distinguishing between lower and higher levels of values.

This is a possible explanation that I personally find more promising, and one that I wish to explore in the remainder of this article. In doing so, I will draw upon the writings of Scheler and von Hildebrand, as

---

4 *WST*, 190. See also *TDH*, 89.

5 *WST*, 190.

well as some of Lonergan's own reflections – not only from *Method in Theology*,[6] but also from "The Ontology of the Good" in *Insight*.[7]

3. SCHELER, VON HILDEBRAND, AND LONERGAN ON THE SCALE OF VALUES

Each person has his or her own, individual scale of value preference.[8] This scale is a fundamental dimension of feelings that intend and apprehend values. As Lonergan observes, "Not only do feelings respond to values. They do so in accord with some scale of preference."[9] Perhaps he was influenced by von Hildebrand's parallel remark: "The pure value response will always be imparted in a degree corresponding to the rank of the value."[10] Scheler is even more emphatic:

> One must not assume that the height of a value is *"felt"* in the same manner as the value itself, and that the higher value is *subsequently* "preferred" or "placed after." Rather, the height of a value is "given," by virtue of its essence, only *in* the act of preferring.[11]

This value preference as felt is prior to our evaluating, deliberating, or choosing among comparative values. As such, it guides and channels those activities of evaluating and deliberating with regard to questions of greater and lesser value. Our own, existential felt scale of value preference settles for us what further questions will be pertinent as we proceed toward grasping the virtually unconditioned grounds for making comparative judgments of value and for choosing the best value or best course of action.

---

6 *MT*, 31-32.

7 Bernard Lonergan, *Insight: A Study in Human Understanding*, ed. Frederick E. Crowe and Robert M. Doran (Toronto: University of Toronto Press, 1992), 628-29.

8 Elsewhere I have explored this issue in detail in a companion article. See "What is Our Scale of Value Preference?" forthcoming, *Lonergan Workshop*, 22 (2009); cited hereafter as "What is Our Scale?"

9 MT, 31.

10 Dietrich von Hildebrand, *Christian Ethics* (NY: David McKay Company, Inc.), 239; cited hereafter as *CE*.

11 Max Scheler, *Formalism in Ethics and Non-Formal Ethics of Values*, trans. Manfred S. Frings and Roger L. Funk, (Evanston, IL: Northwestern University Press, 1973), 87; hereafter cited as *Formalism/Values*.

This of course implies that *objectivity in judgments and decisions re-garding comparative values rests upon the normativity of the feeling-scale of value preference.* That is to say, we can only be as authentic and ob-jective in making comparative judgments of value and choices as our own existential felt scale of value preference enables us to be. If our actual, existential scale is biased or otherwise distorted, so also will be our judgments and choices. Hence, the questions of the utmost im-portance are: What is *the* normative scale of value preference? *Why* is that the normative scale? And, *how* can one best bring oneself into harmony with that scale? The remainder of this article probes these important questions.

3.1 THE SCALE THAT UNDERLIES THE SCALES

Each of us, therefore, has her or his own individual existential scale of value preference. As Scheler observes, "He who 'prefers' the noble to the agreeable will end up in an...experience of a *world of goods* very dif-ferent from the one in which he who does not do so will find himself."[12] However, this does *not* mean that all such scales are equivalent and ar-bitrary. To the contrary, as Scheler claims emphatically:

> ...if the height of a value is given "in" preferring, this height is nev-ertheless a relation in the *essence* of the values concerned. Therefore, the *"ordered ranks of values"* are themselves absolutely *invariable* whereas the "rules of preferring" are in principle variable through-out history.[13]

In his book *Ressentiment*, Scheler offers a keen phenomenological observation in support of this strong position.[14] In this extended re-ply to Nietzsche, Scheler says that *ressentiment* is a distortion of the normative scale of values itself. In *ressentiment*, value A comes to be felt as lower than B, even though value A is normally and spontane-ously felt as "higher" than value B. According to Nietzsche, the values of independence, strength, robust health, wealth, and physical beauty are naturally felt as higher than the values of servitude, weakness, and poverty. Out of *ressentiment*, however, slave morality, "creatively" intro-duces virtues such as humility, self-renunciation and love of the poor

12 *Formalism/Values*, 88.

13 *Formalism/Values*, 88.

14 Max Scheler, *Ressentiment*, trans., ed. Lewis A. Coser (New York: Scho-ken Books, 1961); hereafter cited as *Ressentiment*.

as "higher" values. Scheler adds his own examples, arguing that the elevation of uniquely modern values – such as measuring worth by effort alone (e.g., the value of the "self-made" person), materialism, and utilitarianism – are all the results of the distortions that grow from *ressentiment.*[15]

Ressentiment unnaturally elevates these lower values to an abnormally higher rank in the value scale. A person of *ressentiment* does this in order to denigrate – to "put down" – the genuinely higher values. According to Scheler, resentful people denigrate these higher values because they feel impotent to attain them. Nevertheless, *ressentiment* is not primarily a product of evaluation, deliberation, or choice. Rather, almost unconsciously, the actual, existential scale of felt preference is altered and distorted. Once this happens, *ressentiment* takes over and directs subsequent deliberating and choosing. Scheler captures the dark spirit of this force in the following remarks:

Ressentiment man, on the other hand, now feels "good," "pure," and "human" – at least in the conscious layers of his mind. He is delivered from hatred, from the tormenting desire of an impossible revenge, *though deep down his poisoned sense of life and the true values may still shine through the illusory ones.*[16]

Scheler held unambiguously that there is a normative scale of value preference. This is the basis for his claim that *ressentiment* is a distortion of this scale. It is also noteworthy that the true and normative scale of values "may still shine through the illusory" distorted scale. This is analogous to the manner in which for Lonergan unanswered further questions linger around the periphery of our consciousnesses, no matter how strong our biases. Just as the pure, unrestricted desire to know cannot be completely repressed, neither can the normative scale of values.

There is then a unique, normative scale of value preference. Individual, existential scales are more or less in harmony with the normative scale. Lonergan and von Hildebrand are in agreement with Scheler's claim. They differ, however, in their accounts of the details of this underlying invariant scale of value preference. Let us proceed, therefore, to a comparison of these three accounts.

---

15 *Ressentiment,* 138-74.

16 *Ressentiment,* 77. Emphasis added.

3.2 SCHELER'S ACCOUNT OF THE SCALE

Earlier I pointed out that Lonergan's account is a mere sketch that would profit from additional detail. In his lengthy account Scheler adds a wealth of details that is absent from Lonergan's account.[17] Scheler adds these details by means of a kind of multi-dimensional co-ordinate axis system of scales, rather than by expanding a single, one-dimensional linear scale. He distinguishes between *bearers* of values and value *qualities* (or "value-modalities"),[18] each forming something like a distinct axis within the realm of values. It is Scheler's scale of qualitative values that is most similar to that of Lonergan's. Yet Scheler also identifies further *subdivisions* among the qualitative values themselves, which Lonergan does not attempt to do.

Scheler's scale of qualitative values is basically as follows: In ascending order, there are the values of the useful, the agreeable (i.e. the pleasant or enjoyable), the vital, and the spiritual. He also speaks of the value of the "infinitely holy person – the *divine*,"[19] somewhat ambiguously, as the foundation of all other values. The divine does not really correspond to the category of spiritual values, which are principally values of the *human* spirit. But unlike Lonergan, Scheler does not explicitly identify a distinct value-quality that would properly correspond to the divine.

Scheler explores subdivisions within the qualitative values in extensive but sometimes confusing detail. For example, he includes the following as subdivisions of spiritual values: cognition, beauty and other aesthetic values, cultural values (which are said to include science and art), ethical/moral values, and holiness. He further draws a keen distinction between the cultural value of the *"pure cognition of truth"* in philosophy and that of "positive 'science,' which is guided by the aim of controlling natural appearances."[20] In addition, Scheler groups utility and pleasantness together as "material values," but pleasantness is still ranked higher than utility with this grouping.[21]

Though rich in details, Scheler is not as clear or forthright as Lonergan in his formulation of the exact hierarchical ordering of this scale

17 *Formalism/Values*, 81-110.

18 *Formalism/Values*, 100.

19 *Formalism/Values*, 94.

20 *Formalism/Values*, 108.

21 *Formalism/Values*, 93.

of qualitative values and subdivisions. He nowhere gives a precise, un-
ambiguous statement of this ordering. His convoluted account makes
it difficult to derive a single, consistent account. I summarize Scheler's
discussions of the scale (or ranking) of values in Figure 1. This chart,
however, should be regarded as only approximate because of the many
ambiguities in his discussion. In a later section I will return to the
criteria that Scheler offers in support of his formulation of the scale of
value preference.

SCHELER'S SCALE (RANK) OF VALUES

Bearers of Values	Scale of Qualitative Values	Subdivisons
Persons/Things/Living Beings	Infinitely Personified Spirit	
Oneself/Others	Spiritual	Spiritual values: (holiness, cogni-tion, moral, beauty, cultural, social)
Acts/Functions/Reac-tions		
	Vital	Vital values: (economic)
Moral Tenor/Deeds/ Success	Material: Agreeable	
Intentional Feelings/ States of Feelings	Material: Useful	
Terms/Relations/ Forms of Relations		
Individual/Collective		
"Self-Values"/Consecu-tive Values		

FIGURE I

Lonergan seems to have gotten most of his impressions of Scheler
from Manfred Frings's book rather than directly from Scheler's writings themselves. Frings summarizes Scheler's ascending scale of values
and feelings as sensible values (agreeable/disagreeable, sensible plea-
sure/pain), vital values, spiritual values (beautiful/ugly, right/wrong,
philosophical truth and falsity but not scientific truth and falsity),

and values of the holy/unholy.[22] Certainly many of the important nuances (and confusing details) to be found in Scheler's own words are missing from Frings's summary. There is no doubt much more to be learned from studying how Frings's account may have affected Lonergan. Perhaps even more importantly, a more detailed study of Scheler's own writings could lead to nuances in Lonergan's account of the scale. However the preceding discussion of the Scheler's view of the scale will have to suffice for the present context.

3.3 VON HILDEBRAND'S ACCOUNT OF THE SCALE

While there are clear similarities between Lonergan's and Scheler's formulations of the scale of value preference, there are also notable differences. In all likelihood this is because Lonergan relied far more heavily upon the formulation set forth by Dietrich von Hildebrand. Von Hildebrand was greatly influenced by Scheler but deviated from him in significant ways. Still, like Scheler and Lonergan, von Hildebrand is emphatic that there is a unique, normative scale of feelings of value preference and that it is foundational in our consciousness of values.[23]

In formulating the details of his scale, von Hildebrand offers a more nuanced account than Lonergan. Von Hildebrand also offers a multi-dimensional schema with something like three or four axes: ontological values, "capacities" or "parts" of entities, "domains" or "families" of qualitative values, and "types" of values within families.

His discussion of these axes of the scale is complicated but much more straightforward than that of Scheler. According to von Hildebrand, in ascending order the scale of ontological values runs: things, plants, animals, and persons (including God). The scale of qualitative values likewise arranges the families or domains in the hierarchy: vital, aesthetic, intellectual, and moral. He further claims there is also a hierarchy within each of these families or domains: within vital values, sight is higher than taste; within intellectual values, depth is higher than acuteness; and within moral values, humility is higher than reliability. Unfortunately he offers only a few examples such as these, and

---

22 Manfred S. Frings, *Max Scheler* (Pittsburgh, PA: Duquesne University Press, 1965), 114-117.

23 See for example CE, 237, 239.

he does not propose any rules or criteria for thinking about why one of these pairs is higher than the other.[24]

Interestingly, von Hildebrand does not explicitly include religious values in his scale although they permeate his discussions in *Christian Ethics*. In addition, he also drops from his scale Scheler's qualitative value of the useful. He apparently does so because he regards the useful as an equivocal term, a point he makes in a lengthy discussion.[25] That is to say, whatever item or skill is deemed "useful" derives its value-meaning from the more fundamental value that it serves. Hence, usefulness would be, so to speak, everywhere and nowhere on the scale.

In perhaps his most significant deviation from Scheler's scale, von Hildebrand also drops its lowest level – that of the pleasant/unpleasant or the agreeable/disagreeable. Von Hildebrand insists that the difference between satisfactions and the agreeable/disagreeable on the one hand and values on the other is *not* at all a matter of value rank. By way of illustration, he says that the choice between saving someone from a moral danger and attending an entertaining social affair is not a choice between two values. The satisfaction derived from a party, he says, is merely subjective satisfaction and not at all "comparable" to a value. Thus he contends that there is no real choosing between values involved in such a case. This would instead be a matter of choosing between radically opposed orientations, a choice between value and non-value.[26] Therefore, what is agreeable or satisfying is not the lowest on the scale of values. The agreeable or satisfying is simply not on that scale of values at all – not in any way whatsoever. Von Hildebrand chastises Scheler for missing this fundamental difference – for even including at all "the agreeable" within his rank order of value preferring.[27] According to von Hildebrand, a person oriented toward what is "merely subjectively satisfying" is "not even interested in the question of whether something is important [i.e., of value] in itself or not."[28] Later he writes, "The great and decisive difference in man's moral life

---

24 CE, 136.

25 CE, 64-71.

26 CE, 42.

27 CE, 40.

28 CE, 40; 43.

lies precisely in whether he approaches the universe from the point of view of value or of the merely subjectively satisfying."[29]

So for von Hildebrand there is a radical difference between orientation toward value and orientation toward satisfaction. He further illustrates his claim with the example of a person who kills another out of revenge: "There is a simple decision to satisfy his desire for revenge, without in any way bothering about the value of a human life."[30] This he says is "an indifference in the point of view of value."[31] It is a "value blindness."[32]

When it comes to the realm of values as such, von Hildebrand identifies several kinds of hierarchies:

1.) First, he claims that there is a hierarchy among the ontological values that pertain to different kinds of existents (especially persons). Among ontological values, "the ontological value of a living organism ranks higher than that of dead matter; that of an animal higher than that of a plant; that of a human person higher than an animal."[33]

2.) In addition, he points to a hierarchy of values of the "capacities" or "parts" of those existing entities. In illustration of the hierarchy among capacities and parts, von Hildebrand claims that "intellect ranks higher than the sense; the will ranks higher than mere instinct … sight is nobler than taste."[34]

3.) Third, he identifies the vital, aesthetic, intellectual and moral as distinct and hierarchically arrayed domains (or families) of value. These correspond to the qualitative values in Scheler's account.[35] These domains or families of values are "somewhat like" the hierarchy among ontological values although each ontological value is completely

---

29 CE, 61.

30 CE, 44.

31 CE, 44.

32 CE, 46.

33 CE, 135.

34 CE, 136.

35 CE, 129-31. Von Hildebrand explicitly says that intellectual values are higher than vital values (129) and moral values are higher than intellectual (130), but the exact place of aesthetic values is left implicit. However, he repeats the order "moral, intellectual, or aesthetic," suggesting this is the objective order as he understands it – presumably with vital falling below aesthetic values.

identified with its specific entity, unlike the values from the domains, which can be instantiated in many entities.[36]

4.) Lastly, within each of the value domains there is said to be a hierarchy of "value types": humility is said to rank higher than reliability in the moral domain while intellectual depth is said to be higher than acuteness within their intellectual domain.[37]

Figure 2 presents a summary of von Hildebrand's discussion of the scale of values.

VON HILDEBRAND'S SCALE OF VALUES

Ontological Values (values of existing entities)	Capacities and Parts	Qualitative Values (Domains/ Families)	Types within Domains/Families
Persons (including God) Animals Plants Non-living Material Things	Will > Instinct Intellect > Sensation	Moral Intellectual Aesthetic Vital	Humility > Reliability "Depth" > Acuteness Sight > Taste
		Agreeable*	

* Not in the scale of values at all.

FIGURE 2

4. LONERGAN, VON HILDEBRAND, & SCHELER COMPARED

Even though Lonergan relied heavily upon von Hildebrand's discussions, his formulation clearly differs from that of von Hildebrand and Scheler. While all three authors include vital values, Lonergan gives both a prominence to and a differentiation among values pertaining

---

36 "The ontological value is so much embodied in a being, so much included in it, that we are tempted to form one concept embracing the whole – the specific being as well as its value," CE, 138.

37 CE, 130.

to the structure of the human good (social and cultural values) that is missing from the formulations of his predecessors. Likewise, he explicitly includes personal values on one and the same linear scale while Scheler and von Hildebrand treat these values as belonging to an axis ("bearers" of "ontological values") different from the axis of qualitative values in their complex coordinate systems. Lonergan places religious values highest on the scale, unlike both Scheler and von Hildebrand, who do not carve out a definite place for religious values. These three thinkers all emphatically agree that there is one normative scale of value despite the many human deviations from that norm. Yet they differ significantly from one another as to the details of this scale. This of course raises the question, which, if any of these, is the correct or at least the most accurate formulation, and why is that the correct one? The question of justifications for the various formulations are the topics of subsequent sections.

SCALES OF VALUES COMPARED

Lonergan	Von Hildebrand	Scheler
Religious Personal Cultural Social Vital	 Moral Intellectual Aesthetic Vital	Infinitely Personified Spirit Spiritual Vital Agreeable Useful
Agreeable*	Agreeable*	

* Not in the scale of values at all.

FIGURE 3

4.1 SATISFACTION, MORAL CONVERSION, AND THE SCALE OF VALUES

Knowing of von Hildebrand's influence is quite helpful in understanding Lonergan's remarks about satisfaction in *Method in Theology*. In particular, I am convinced that von Hildebrand's discussion is the origin of Lonergan's way of speaking about moral conversion: "Moral conversion changes the criterion of one's decisions and choices from satisfactions to values."[38] Within the horizon of von Hildebrand's terminology, concern with the satisfying and the agreeable is simply

38 *MT*, 240.

incompatible with concern for values of any kind. Satisfaction is not even in the same universe as values. Given this terminology, moral conversion would be the shift from a consciousness that is without any care about values whatsoever to a consciousness for whom values suddenly begin to play a role. At first the morally converted person might well be confused about true *versus* apparent values and about what is objectively higher *versus* lower on the scale of values. A neophyte in moral conversion may well stand in need of much development and dialectical correction with respect to valuing and choosing. But such a person would have radically changed her or his orientation and living in the world.

Still, I am not convinced that there really are any persons who are so radically and completely without any concern for values at all although extreme sociopaths might qualify. Even a Mafioso values his "family" although he shows complete disregard for other vital, social, cultural, personal, and religious values. Moral conversion would be a very rare phenomenon indeed if it only meant a shift away from a complete absence of concern for values. But von Hildebrand certainly is emphatic on this score. On the other hand, if such radical apathy regarding all values is as rare as I think, then perhaps we need to look once again at the nature of moral conversion with an eye for more nuanced criteria.

I propose that instead of thinking of moral conversion as the break of satisfaction from value that it would be more accurate to think about moral conversion in terms of the normative scale of value preference. That is to say, moral conversion should be regarded not as a shift away from absolute indifference in feelings regarding all values but as a shift within an individual's actual, felt structure of value preference. It would be a shift toward the normative scale of value preference within one's intentional feelings. So conceived, moral conversion would overcome partial or distorted value blindness, and it would not be exclusively a matter of overcoming absolute value indifference. This shift in the scale of value preference can come about in at least two ways.

The first kind of moral conversion would be from a truncated to a full scale of value preference. For example, a fitness fanatic can be totally preoccupied with vital values and have no effective feeling for social, cultural, personal, or religious values. A religious fanatic might be indifferent to vital and social values. A business mogul might have intense feelings for the economic good of his or her corporation with no appreciation for cultural values. A certain kind of economist might value market efficiency to the exclusion of all else. The feelings of such people would be truncated in their effective capacity to feel the values in other ranks within the scale. These, of course, are stereotypes; no one's actual scale of value preference is so simplistic or quite so crude. These stereotypes are offered solely to indicate what I mean by a truncated scale of value preference, and how moral conversion could be thought of as an expansion of one's actual feelings of value preferring to encompass the full scale.

The second kind of moral conversion would be a conversion of a person's actual felt sense of preference from a distorted to the normative scale of values. In the most profound cases, this would involve turning away from *ressentiment* and becoming free to feel the goodness even of values that one is not personally able to attain. In lesser cases, this might mean a shift in feelings from orientation to lesser level values toward values at a higher level. Perhaps the most common examples of this are people once driven by ambition to reach the highest utilitarian values (e.g., wealth) who suddenly become profoundly committed to what Lonergan calls social and personal values.[39]

In the first kind of moral conversion there is an expansion of the actual scale of someone's feelings of value preference, e.g., adding proper felt preference for social and cultural values to a truncated, pre-existing scale of preference for vital values over comfort. In the second kind of moral conversion, there would be a reorientation of a whole scale of values. Prior to this kind of moral conversion, a person's felt preferring might already include, say, social and cultural values but as inauthentically subordinated to vital values. The second kind of moral conversion would involve a transformation of the feelings of preference that restore the normative order. The differences between these two types of moral conversion are no doubt subtle, and careful attention to particular cases would be required in order to discern these differences. Nevertheless, I think both diseases of value preference may be familiar to most readers. Hopefully instances of moral conversion in which both kinds of distortions have been overcome are also familiar.

---

39 For but one of numerous examples, see Robert N. Bellah, et al., *Habits of the Heart: Individualism and Commitment in American Life* (Berkeley: University of California Press, 1996), 3-8. Of course, by "personal values" Lonergan does not mean individualism – that something is of value merely because an individual arbitrarily chooses it. Rather, he means the values that pertain to persons qua "originating values," *MT*, 51 and *Insight*, 601.

Before closing this section, I wish to draw an analogy between the phenomena of scales of value preference and Lonergan's discussion of essential and effective freedom. As Lonergan puts it, human beings are:

> ...free essentially inasmuch as possible courses of action are grasped by practical insight, motivated by reflection, and executed by decision. But man is free effectively to a greater or less extent inasmuch as this dynamic structure is open to grasping, motivating, and executing a broad or a narrow range of otherwise possible courses of action.[40]

I think something similar is to be said regarding felt scales of value preference. Each and every person has his or her individual, existential, and actual felt scale of value preference. These individual scales can be truncated or comprehensive. They may be crude or they may be refined and include many felt discernments within the broad generic categories of values. They may be inverted, distorted, *ressentiful*, or they may be normative, generous, and at peace. These actual existential felt scales of value preference correspond to what in the realm of choosing Lonergan calls effective freedom. A person is able to effectively feel value preference only according to her or his own existential scale. This means, of course, that she or he is able to evaluate, judge, deliberate, and choose only among comparative values within the limits defined by this existential scale. On the other hand, within the feeling horizon of every human being, *the* normative scale of value preference perdures. As Scheler says, it "shines through" even the truncations, inversions, distortions, or *ressentiments* of actual, individual felt scales of preference. This corresponds to what Lonergan calls essential freedom.

Therefore, individual scales of felt preferring are not the whole story. The normative, essential scale of value preference underlies and permeates the conscious, feeling horizon of every person. Cognitional biases, by their creative attempts to subvert it, nevertheless give witness to the persistence of the pure, unrestricted desire to know which underlies them. Likewise, even distorted existential scales of value preference are secondary reactions to the normative scale. That normative scale is always immanent and operative within consciousness. As such,

---

40 *Insight*, 643.

it is the ground of the possibility and normativity of authentic moral conversion.

4.2. SCHELER AND VON HILDEBRAND'S CRITERIA FOR PREFERENCE

Scheler and von Hildebrand not only state the respective hierarchical orderings of values in their scale; they also offer some criteria for this ordering although Scheler is far more detailed than von Hildebrand. This section considers their criteria. This consideration has two goals. The first is to point to difficulties in Scheler and von Hildebrand's criteria, which in turn raise questions about the adequacy of their formulations of the scales of preference. The second is to derive some clues as to a set of criteria for Lonergan's formulation of the scale.

Scheler proceeds by using a phenomenological method. He sets forth his criteria as qualities that will be discerned through methodical attention to the feelings of value preference. These qualities inhere in the feelings themselves. These qualities are also indices of the objective orders among the values themselves, since there are "essential connections" among the values as well as between the values and the feelings which apprehend them. Hence the feelings will show forth the essential criteria that constitute hierarchies among the values themselves.

Scheler succinctly states five criteria for distinguishing higher from lower values as follows:

> It appears that values are "higher" [1] the *more* they *endure* and [2] the *less* they partake in *extension* and *divisibility*. They are higher [3] the *less they are "founded"* through other values and [4] the *"deeper"* the [contentment] connected with feeling them. Moreover, they are higher [5] the *less* the feeling of them is *relative* to the *positing* of a specific bearer of "feeling" and "preferring."[41]

Scheler's first two criteria find an interesting parallel with Lonergan's criterion that the "spiritual neither is constituted, nor is conditioned intrinsically, by the empirical residue."[42] Lonergan observes

---

41 *Formalism/Values*, 90; emphasis is Scheler's own; bracketed numbering is added. Scheler actually uses the term 'satisfaction' in this quotation, but his meaning is exactly the opposite of Lonergan's. In his detailed discussion of this criterion, Scheler consistently uses the word 'contentment' where he might have used 'satisfaction.' In order to avoid mistaken associations, I substituted the word 'contentment' for 'satisfaction' in this passage.

42 *Insight*, 541.

that ultimately the distinctions among particular places and particular times are merely empirically residual. Because these differences are empirically residual, they lack any intrinsic intelligibility of their own. This fact makes the particular places and times open to all sorts of intelligible formations – what can be "made of" or done in particular places and times.[43] By way of contrast, that which is spiritual is not tied down by particularities of space or time.

Scheler is doing something similar with regard to values. He explicitly tags utility and the agreeable as material values precisely because they are localized in space and because it is possible to participate in these goods only by dividing them up spatially. For example, a piece of cloth cannot be useful to everyone unless cut, and the sweetness of sugar cannot be savored unless distributed and tasted. By way of contrast, Scheler cites the value of a work of art, which not only can be felt by many without subdivision, but whose value would be destroyed if it were cut up. Likewise, he contrasts "endurance" with temporal "succession." The rolling of a rock down a hill in itself is a succession of changes; it would not be what it is without those differences at different successive times. By way of contrast, according to Scheler, endurance of a value means something like its invariance with respect to changes in times. Once one has had an insight, this emergent understanding endures while time flows past it, so to speak. Scheler himself uses the act of love to illustrate endurance. He remarks that it would be very strange to say "I love you *now*" or "for a certain time" because true love (*versus* its many illusions) is in no way intrinsically conditioned by material time. This amounts, then, to saying something like material values are lower than spiritual values. However, these criterion for distinguishing higher and lower values are not very differentiated and are not helpful in explaining why vital values stand where they do in Scheler's scale. Are vital values material or spiritual, and why? Are vital values a little bit but not entirely independent of the spatial extension and temporal succession? If so, by how much, and how is this to be determined? While there is some phenomenological evidence for Scheler's criteria for distinguishing material from spiritual values, these criteria cannot be applied unambiguously to all value differences. These criteria lack the fine-tuning needed to really understand why every one of the values in the scale reside at the rank that Scheler assigns to them.

---

43 *Insight*, 50-52.

Scheler's third criterion is much more helpful. In its general form, the criterion is that 1.) if value *B* is the foundation of value *A*, then *B* is higher than *A*; and 2.) *B* is the foundation of *A* if "*A* can only be given on the condition of the givenness of … *B*."[44] But the "givenness" in question is more subtle than would first come to mind. Within the humanistic psychology and "human potential" movements of the late twentieth century, there was a tendency to say that one must first attend to the most basic needs (food, drink, shelter, sexual release) as the condition of the possibility of moving to a higher level of values (artistic, intellectual, moral, spiritual, etc.)[45] Scheler, on the other hand, exactly reverses this simple-minded ordering. Values of utility are founded in values of the agreeable, for what is useful "reveals itself as a '*means*' to something agreeable." (Think of labor-saving appliances). Again, the agreeable is founded in the vital values needed by living beings. No agreeable feelings can occur unless there are vital, living beings. Scheler continues his analysis, saying that spiritual acts "are not vitally conditioned" and that "life *simpliciter* has a value, apart from the differentiations among vital value-qualities, only insofar as there are spiritual values and spiritual acts through which they are grasped."[46] Finally, he concludes that all possible values are founded "in the *value of an infinitely personified spirit*."[47]

Scheler's criterion that the founding value is higher than the founded value has a ring of truth to it. However, his examples justifying this claim are quite tenuous, especially as he ascends the scale. Increasingly his claims regarding value superiority seem merely stipulated rather than explained. Yet this third criterion of Scheler also finds an important parallel in Lonergan's writings. Lonergan's account provides

---

44 *Formalism/Values*, 94.

45 Abraham H. Maslow's formulation hierarchy of needs played a major role in this movement although the fault is that of his readers whose existential scales of preference were quite truncated in comparison to Maslow's. See his *Motivation and Personality* (NY: Harper and Row Publishers, 1954), 80-106.

46 *Formalism/Values*, 95.

47 *Formalism/Values*, 96. It is worth noting that Scheler avoids connecting this infinitely personified spirit with the word 'God'; indeed he seldom uses that word in his own voice, most often using it only when speaking of what others say about God.

both nuances and justifications that would shore up Scheler's claims. I return to this issue in the next section.

Concerning his fourth criterion, Scheler asserts that the "restless search for [the lower values of] pleasures" can never give the degree of contentment that is enjoyed in the feeling of the deeper values "at the more central sphere of our life." The degree of contentment in the feeling of a value therefore reveals the relative depth of the value felt, "if the former proves to be *independent* of the latter while the latter remains dependent on the former."[48] Clearly, then, Scheler's fourth criterion is closely related to his third, since both are ultimately concerned with what is grounded and what does the grounding.

Scheler sees the need for a fifth criterion because, he says, the four previous criteria "do not give us the *ultimate* meaning of value-heights."[49] This fifth criterion is of that of the fundamental quality of relativity or absoluteness *"given in emotive immediacy."* This fundamental felt sense always "silently tells [us] what the 'relativity' of felt values is, no matter how much [we] may seek to cover it up." He claims that the other four criteria can be derived from this most fundamental criterion. This criterion becomes clearer through his examples. A sweet pear cannot be an agreeable value for non-sentient being (e.g., an angel or God), which cannot feel the agreeableness. Such beings can know about agreeableness, but agreeableness is not a value *for them.* Hence the agreeable can only be a value *relative* to certain kinds of beings who are able to experience agreeableness. A value like agreeableness will be lower than values felt to be absolute.

By way of contrast, Scheler asserts that higher values (e.g., beauty and truth) and the feelings which apprehend them have a *"phenomenal detachment"* from sensation and even from the feeling of life. Hence, he says, these detachable values are higher than the agreeable and even higher than vital values. Finally, highest of all among Scheler's values is the value of the person. The value of the person is an absolute value. This is because the value of the person is given in an act of pure love, which is detached from all other "felt-values of our own personal world of values."[50]

---

48 *Formalism/Values,* 96-97.

49 *Formalism/Values,* 97.

50 *Formalism/Values,* 97-98.

Although von Hildebrand devotes a great many pages to the criteria that distinguish satisfaction from value, he says very little about the criteria that differentiate lower from higher values.[51] He presents his observations about the nature of the scale more as pronouncements than as judgments with justifications. One of the few things von Hildebrand does say in this regard is: "The higher a being ranks, the more it is able to actualize different and distanced values." The example that seems to illustrate this criterion is the Christian's capacity to simultaneously embrace strength and meekness, but he says little more on this score.[52] Elsewhere he writes that "higher values have to a higher degree the character of a 'message from above,'" meaning that they more fully reflect "God who is the infinite goodness and sum of all values."[53] True as von Hildebrand's claims may be, they are not especially helpful in comprehending *why*, say, aesthetic values of beauty are higher than vital values but lower than moral values.

Like Scheler, von Hildebrand seems to be attending to the data of normative feelings of value preference and simply reporting what he finds to be given. His approach is vulnerable because actual felt scales of value preference vary from one person to another, due to various kinds of distortions. Von Hildebrand's reports will not be persuasive to those with distorted scales. Nor is he in a position to offer reasons why the data from his own scale of values should be regarded as free from such distortions. Why should reports from von Hildebrand's data on his feelings of value preference be privileged? Nietzsche and his many contemporary followers, after all, would regard von Hildebrand's formulation of the scale with contempt as yet another pathetic version of the slave morality of Christian *ressentiment*.

The writings of both Scheler and von Hildebrand are filled with important phenomenological insights into feelings of value preference. To a greater or lesser extent, their extensive comments could serve as "rules for discernment" in reflecting on one's own existential scale of value preference. Yet each (apart from von Hildebrand's extensive

---

51 He comes close to providing such criteria in his discussion of the special and exalted value of the human person. However, these comments come in the context of his discussion of the "marks" that distinguish ontological from qualitative values, rather than what makes one value higher than another. See CE, 135.

52 CE, 143-44.

53 CE, 165, 162; see also 134.

discussion of the radical difference between satisfaction and value) is frustrating when it comes to explaining why these are the levels, and why one level is higher than the other. Scheler's discussions do reveal in different ways that the conditioning and the conditioned figure as a central frame of reference for higher over lower values. If empirical residues of space and time intrinsically condition a value, it is lower; if not, it is higher. If a value is the foundation of another value, the former conditions the latter and is therefore higher. If a value is felt to have greater depth through contentment, this is because it is higher. Still, in every case Scheler's discussions suffer from degrees of vagueness. This vagueness causes difficulties in knowing how to apply his criteria, especially in cases where one may be confused about one's feelings. This vagueness also undermines an attempt of providing a convincing rationale for the scale as a whole. These difficulties are even more pronounced in von Hildebrand's writings. As I hope to show in the next section, Lonergan's discussion of the ontology of the good preserves the basic core of Scheler's and von Hildebrand's insights, while at the same time bringing greater clarity and nuance as well as a more adequate formulation and rationale for the scale.

4.3 WHY LONERGAN'S SCALE OF VALUE PREFERENCE?

We may now return to the question posed at the beginning of this essay: Why should we accept Lonergan's account of the scale of value preference instead of those of Scheler, von Hildebrand, or the many others who have written on this subject of value priorities? Notice the question here is not whether there is an invariable scale of values. The question asks why, upon what basis, does Lonergan's *formulation* of that scale have the advantage over others?

Ultimately, the question of a sound grounding of the scale of value preference will receive an adequate answer only by turning to the foundational realities of the conversions. Lonergan's eight functional specialties[54] are designed to face this challenge among others. The eight functional specialties can be used to sort through the many expressions of value priorities and value preference and to discern among them those expressions that are compatible with the conversions – as well as those that are not – and then to pass along that discernment to new generations. Since those expressions extend not only across millennia in Western culture, but also across all world cultures, this will

---

54 See *MT*, 125-45.

be a massive scholarly project.[55] Clearly Lonergan's own formulation of the scale is but an infinitesimal contribution to that project.

Still, I believe that his formulation will remain a lasting and basic contribution to that project. To say that conversion is the foundation of the proper understanding and formulation of the scale of value preference includes all the conversions. By moral conversion people begin to live in accord with the normative scale of value preference. Religious conversion will "transform, magnify, [and] glorify" that natural scale of value preference by the entry of the supernatural originating and terminal values of unconditional love.[56] But intellectual conversion is required in order to give a positional explanation for that scale. The last section of this essay endeavors to explain why.

Prior to his discovery of the eight functional specialties of theological method, Lonergan was still influenced to an extent by an older tradition where metaphysics provided the grounding for ethics and the theory of values. For example, at the time he wrote *Insight*, Lonergan intended to develop "a method of ethics that parallels the method of metaphysics."[57] Certainly von Hildebrand, and to some extent Scheler, also thought along similar lines. Both granted a priority to things over other categories of values in their discussions of the scale, just as substance was considered basic in traditional metaphysics. Von Hildebrand devotes an entire chapter to "Being and Value." He also explicitly draws a connection between value levels and metaphysical genera and species saying: "the ontological value of a species or genus represents each time a new type of value, such as the value of animal life, the value of a human being or the value of an angel."[58]

Unfortunately, neither von Hildebrand nor Scheler was able to offer a sound grounding for their versions of the scale of values because of counter-positions in their conceptions of metaphysics.[59] In particular, their ways of understanding things, qualities, genera, and species lack the sophistication needed to meet the task at hand. It is not possible here to set forth the evidence that would be needed to support this

---

55 See "What is Our Scale?"

56 *MT*, 116.

57 *Insight*, 618.

58 *CE*, 136.

59 Regarding positions and counter-positions, see *Insight*, 413-14.

criticism. Instead I must limit myself to indicating how Lonergan's approach to metaphysics would allow him to overcome these limitations.

In the wake of Heidegger's destruction of metaphysics and the parallel shift that takes place in *Method in Theology*, metaphysics can no longer be understood as the science that grounds ethics and the theory of values. Nevertheless, there is *a relationship* between metaphysics and the theory of values even though that relationship is no longer the relationship of founding to founded. Lonergan argues for that relationship by means of his intentionality analysis of what we are doing when we are choosing. As he puts it:

> If the intelligible orders of human invention are a good because they systematically assure the satisfaction of desires, then so also are the intelligible orders that underlie, condition, precede, and include man's invention. Finally, intelligible orders and their contents, as possible objects of rational choice, are values; but the universal order which is generalized emergent probability conditions and penetrates, corrects and develops every particular order; and rational self-consciousness cannot consistently choose the conditioned and reject the condition, choose the part and reject the whole, choose the consequent and reject the antecedent. Accordingly, since [humans are] involved in choosing, and since every consistent choice, at least implicitly, is a choice of universal order, the realization of universal order is a true value.[60]

Notice that in Lonergan's argument the starting points are not metaphysical principles; rather they are actual conscious activities of *choosing*. Lonergan's argument is directed toward the affirmation of the value and goodness of the whole of proportionate being (the "universal order" of generalized emergent probability). Yet his argument also implies a further affirmation of the hierarchy of values. That is to say, whenever human beings authentically evaluate, deliberate, and choose something, they implicitly choose it in all its concreteness. Objects of desire, for example, do not occur in vacuums. Such objects of desire may *look* simple and self-contained, but concretely they are what they are through the massive sets of conditions that constitute them in their very being. If I choose a meal at a nice restaurant, implicitly I am choosing the complex economic and social patterns of cooperation which are the concrete conditions of that meal being grown, transported, prepared, and financed. As Lonergan repeatedly said, the

---

60 *Insight*, 628–29.

good is concrete, and the concrete means the conditioned combined with all of its conditions.

The key to Lonergan's account of the structure of proportionate being is his conception of the "intelligible orders." These orders (or ecosystems) comprise numerous schemes of recurrence. Among these schemes of recurrence, some are conditioned by others. Schemes that come earlier in time initially set the conditions for the emergence of later schemes. But once the later schemes emerge and begin to concretely function as higher integrations of the lower schemes, the conditioned-conditioning relationship is reversed. The lower schemes can no longer survive without the conditioning provided by the higher schemes. For example, hemoglobin cannot be chemically re-oxygenated if the respiratory and circulatory biological systems fail.

Lonergan looks more closely at these conditioning-conditioned relationships among orders of schemes of recurrence. In particular, he focuses upon the relationships among explanatory genera. An explanatory genus comprises all the schemes of recurrence and sequences of events whose regularities can be systematized by one science and its set of explanatory "laws" and conjugates.[61] A second, higher explanatory genus comprises those further regular recurrences that cannot be systematized by the first science.[62] Likewise, a third explanatory genus systematizes regularities that escape the explanatory resources of the first two, and so on. The structural relationship between two genera is isomorphic to that of higher and lower viewpoints.[63] More broadly, the hierarchical structure of the whole sequence of all explanatory genera results from the unfolding dynamism of emergent probability.[64] That is to say, once a sufficiently large and diverse range of lower events and schemes collects into the same region of space and time, schemes of a higher order genus will emerge and incorporate those lower schemes and events as their own constituents.

Thus, the ontological hierarchy of explanatory genera becomes for Lonergan the standard for value hierarchy: "within terminal values

---

61 I have temporarily omitted mention of the things that are also constituents of an explanatory genus. This is because for Lonergan the orders and genera are metaphysically prior. I return to this point later in this section.

62 See *Insight*, 280-83, 463-67.

63 *Insight*, 281-82, 464-65.

64 *Insight*, 284-86.

themselves there is a hierarchy; for each is an intelligible order, but some of these orders include others, some are conditioning and others conditioned, some conditions are more general and others less."[65] This is because whenever converted subjects respond authentically through their feelings of value preference to the realities that they encounter, those realities are always already ordered within the conditioning structure of explanatory genera within proportionate being. Likewise, when converted human beings choose something, they choose it as it stands in the hierarchy of that structure. Finally, when converted subjects deliberate, choose and act, they bring about new realities within that structure of explanatory genera. Therefore, when choosing a value, we implicitly choose all the higher orders of value genera that condition our choices, as well as all the lower genera of values that are conditioned by the objects of our choosing. In this fashion Lonergan laid out the basis for an intimate correspondence between the scale of values and the structure of explanatory genera. In so doing, he provided a set of criteria and a rationale for those criteria that are grounded in intellectual conversion.

Lonergan worked out this framework for thinking about a scale of values prior to his breakthrough to a distinct, transcendental notion of value. At the time of *Insight*, the standard for responsible choosing was the "exigence for self-consistency in knowing and doing."[66] But Lonergan left very unclear the exact nature of the knowing with which doing ought to be consistent. I have argued that Lonergan's attempt to develop his "ontology of the good" (including the hierarchy of values) was flawed. However, its problems can be overcome once the transcendental notion of value is grasped and its implications worked out.[67]

For the present, I wish to draw attention to the fact that even in *Insight* Lonergan's case for the scale of values is based only upon the human act of choosing. In choosing *anything* as truly valuable, human beings implicitly choose a hierarchy of values. In *Insight* Lonergan had not yet arrived at a refined understanding of the deliberative process that leads up to choosing something as truly valuable. He had neglected the roles played by the transcendental notion of value, by the virtu-

---

65 *Insight*, 625.

66 *Insight*, 622.

67 See Patrick H. Byrne, "The Goodness of Being in Lonergan's *Insight*," *American Catholic Philosophical Quarterly* (2007): 43-72.

ally unconditioned grasp of value, by feelings that apprehend values, and by the felt scale of value preference. But to add these features in no way undermines his argument. When we choose what is truly good, we implicitly but really are simultaneously choosing a normative order of values that corresponds to the metaphysical hierarchy of explanatory genera. This in no way makes metaphysics the foundation of ethics. Instead, it makes intentionality analysis of *choosing* foundational and draws upon metaphysics to clarify the implications of what we are doing when we are choosing.

One of the greatest differences after *Insight* concerns the intentionality analysis of choosing. *Method in Theology* reveals that humans can *neither* fully know *nor* choose what is truly valuable unless they are morally converted. That is to say, our deliberations result in knowing and choosing what is truly good only insofar as we are guided by a felt scale of value preference that is in accord with the normative scale, a scale that is isomorphic to the metaphysical scale of explanatory genera.

In *Insight* Lonergan sketches an ascending metaphysical sequence of higher genera of the physical, chemical, biological, psychic, and human.[68] This would imply that there is also a hierarchy of value genera, where the values of the human order are highest of all in the realm of proportionate being, followed by values proper to the psychic/animal order, then the biological/botanical order, and finally the chemical and physical orders. This hierarchy of what might be called the pre-human scale of natural values provides a framework that can be extended to the differentiations among values within the human realm itself: social, cultural, personal, and religious. This of course brings us back to Doran's second approach to answering the question of why Lonergan's scale of values is arrayed the way it is. As Doran observed, social institutions are the indispensable conditions for the maintenance of the vital values of nutrition and health of the society. Likewise, cultural institutions educate members into the values that underpin the maintenance of the social order and its institutions. Hence, the same structure of *conditioning and conditioned* that was key to the scale of pre-human values seems to be continued into the scale of properly human values. Of course, it would be necessary to show that social schemes assure the regular realization of values that biological and animal-psychic schemes alone are incapable of doing systematically,

68 *Insight*, 280-81.

and that cultural schemes of recurrence likewise systematically realize values that social schemes alone cannot achieve. It is beyond the scope of this article to undertake this type of argument in full. Hence, my claim must remain provisional for the present.

If this can be shown, then there remains the task of connecting Lonergan's pre-human scale of values in *Insight* with his properly human scale in *Method in Theology*. That is, what is the proper way to mesh the scale of physical, chemical, biological, and psychic values with the scale of vital, social, cultural, personal, and religious values? For example, if vital values are identified with biological values, are vital values, then, properly human or pre-human? And what becomes of the level of values corresponding to the psychic genus, which includes all sensate animals and their schemes of behavior? Part of the problem, I believe, may be Lonergan's reliance on Scheler and von Hildebrand's understanding of vital values. Consider Scheler's comment: "the values of 'noble and vulgar' are relative to 'living beings' in general."[69] Among horses, people do speak of "a noble steed," but surely this value is generically different from the person who endures suffering nobly. But it does not seem that either nobility or vulgarity is commonly attributed to plants although plants as well as animals surely manifest vital values. Nietzsche does use "life" as a criterion for nobility, and this identification does seem deeply rooted in the German language and in the ancient Greek language as well.[70] This tendency to conflate animal, aesthetic, and ethical values does suggest the need to move from descriptive to differentiated explanatory language. This is a place where Lonergan's account of explanatory genera can be especially helpful. If so, and if this lack of differentiation has crept into Lonergan's thinking in *Method in Theology*, perhaps there is a need for some greater differentiation within the category of vital values from the vitalities of bacterial and plant life to the greater vitalities that accompany the capacities and behaviors of sensate animals and then on to the still greater, perhaps metaphorical, vitalities of thriving cultures. Then a full scale of values would run something like: physical, chemical, biological, psychic, social, cultural, personal, and religious. However, a fuller exploration of this suggestion will have to be deferred to another time.

69 *Formalism/Values*, 97-98.

70 See for example the use of *kalon* for both vital beauty and moral nobility in Plato's *Gorgias*, 474C–475D and Aristotle, *Nicomachean Ethics*, IV.2, 1122b6–7.

Finally, we may now compare Lonergan's account of the scale of values with those of Scheler and von Hildebrand. Von Hildebrand was right in his intuition that genera and species had something to do with the scale of values, but he needed Lonergan's positional and heuristic conception of metaphysics in order to deliver on that hunch. Scheler and von Hildebrand differ from Lonergan in their approach to metaphysics in two important ways. First, both grant a priority to things over and above their qualities. As a consequence, the schemes and orders (which are the concrete ontological setting for things, qualities, and events) barely register in their discussions. Hence, their ways of conceiving of the conditioning-conditioned relationships are beset with the vagaries that were identified previously. Second, Scheler and von Hildebrand are also too dependent upon commonsense and descriptive ways of characterizing metaphysical categories. This often leaves them in the position of having to merely assert (often rightly) value priorities without being able to give clear arguments or justified rationales for their assertions. Lonergan's way of clarifying values by their correspondence with explanatory genera and species gives his approach distinct advantages over Scheler and von Hildebrand.

5. CONCLUSION

When Lonergan articulated his own account of the scale of value preference, I believe that he was effectively engaging in the functional specialty of Foundations and asserting that intellectually, morally, and religiously converted subjects spontaneously prefer values according to the ascending order that parallels the explanatory genera. His way of articulating the scale of value preference is heuristic but no more than heuristic. It makes strong claims about the proper axiological priority among value-genera but leaves the fine-tuning of value-species within the value-genera to be worked out. As Lonergan observes, the explanatory species are a "series of solutions" to the problem of living as posed by the concrete conditions in the environment.[71] Insofar as the problem of living pertains to bacteria and plants, these are species-differentiations within the biological genus. Insofar as it pertains to animal living, they are species within the higher genus of the psychic. Insofar as it pertains to the problems of human living, this means that the spe-

---

71 More precisely, Lonergan writes: "The biological species are a series of solutions to the problem of systematizing coincidental aggregates of chemical processes," *Insight*, 288-289. See also *Insight*, 463.

cies of social, cultural, personal, and religious values need to be worked out under their proper historical conditions. As Scheler observes, "the *ordered ranks of values*' are themselves absolutely *invariable* [but] the 'rules of preferring' are in principle variable throughout history."[72] In Lonergan's context, it is the scale of genera that is invariable. On the other hand, the value-species will be worked out by converted human beings as they ask and answer questions for evaluation, deliberation, and choice under the guidance of the generic felt structure of value preferences. Within a given generic level of values, one value-species would be higher than another by using the same criterion: a value-species is higher if it is the condition for the lower value-species. In all this, the methodical use of Lonergan's eight functional specialties will enhance human progress toward authentic values.[73]

Lonergan's heuristic, generic scale of value preference leaves almost all of the details of specific value preferences to be filled out by converted people as they live their lives. It offers no more than a heuristic for the global orientation of the life of human feelings. In effect Lonergan seems to be asking, "Is the *whole* of your feeling scale of preference attuned to this scale of values, or is it in rebellion against this scale?" He appears to be assuming that when the generic heuristic scale is intact, the other dimensions of people's feelings of preference will gradually develop normatively.[74] The judgments and decisions of converted people concerning comparative values will grow in authenticity and objectivity because the generic scale of value preferences upon which they rest is properly oriented. This need not mean, of course, that people for whom the scale of value preference is properly oriented will be completely free of biases or value distortions. But, in effect, Lonergan seems to be inferring that such distortions can be overcome when human subjects are converted. The greatest danger comes when *ressentiment* has grabbed hold and distorted the generic order as such. It is for this reason, I believe, that Lonergan devoted his attention to getting right the generic scale of value preference.

---

72 *Formalism/Values*, 88.

73 See "What is Our Scale?"

74 A scale is intact, of course, when religious conversion as well as moral conversion is operative; religious conversion is the existential foundation for the level of religious values being properly preferred in one's own individual scale of value preference.

In formulating this heuristic account of the scale of values, therefore, Lonergan intended to offer an important heuristic tool. Methodical use of this scale of value can enhance the capacity of individual persons, of cultural traditions, and of traditions of spiritual practices to notice and rectify distortions in value preference. It will provide them with anticipations of growth and development in valuing. Such, I believe, is the role that Lonergan's scale is meant to play.

ROBERT DORAN'S
THEOLOGY OF HISTORY AND THE
LIBERATION OF THE POOR

Rohan M. Curnow

REGIS COLLEGE, UNIVERSITY OF TORONTO

I. INTRODUCTION

Robert Doran recently gave of his time to listen to my 'nascent' thoughts on dissertation topics. During this meeting, he noted as an aside that he would be very pleased to help the Church and theology on the issue of the preferential option for the poor. It appears to me that he has done just this. *Prima facie*, Doran's *Theology and the Dialectics of History* (*TDH*) may seem an unlikely text to focus upon when considering the preferential option.[1] Even to those who have worked through it, it can appear highly technical, dense, and seemingly more suited for an ivory tower than a slum or barrio. Moreover, *TDH* may seem doubly irrelevant to liberationist thought if one has encountered comments like José Comblin's suggestion that the Lonergan corpus was tailor-made to supporting the ideologies of Latin America's juntas and dictatorships.[2] However, I think a quote from Lonergan's early writings on history sheds some light on the relevance of Doran's work:

> a metaphysic of history is not only imperative for the church to meet the attack of the Marxian materialist conception of history and its realization in apostolic Bolshevism: it is imperative if [humans are] to solve the modern politico-economic entanglement, if political and economic forces are to be subjected to the rule of

---

1 Robert Doran, *Theology and the Dialectics of History* (Toronto: University of Toronto Press, 1990).

2 Enrique Ruiz Maldonado (ed.), *Liberación y cautiverio: Debates en torno al método de la teología en América Latina* (México Cita: Comité Organizador, 1975), 518–19.

reason, if cultural values and all the achievement of the past is to be saved both from the onslaughts of the purblind statesmen and from the perfidious diplomacy of the merely destructive power of communism.[3]

This seventy-year-old quotation takes on a new relevance when read in conjunction with the recent statement made by the Superior General of the Society of Jesus – Fr. Aldofo Nicolas, SJ – that the "courageous and creative" work of liberation theology needs more time to mature.[4] In light of Fr. Nicolas's claim, we can ask how – if at all – Doran's work might assist liberation theologians. If at all, can his ideas help exactly where engagement with Marxism proved problematic in liberation theology? Though I lean towards an affirmative answer to these questions, they are clearly too large to be answered in such a short essay.[5] I hope it suffices to present an outline of how Doran's work can be useful in developing a comprehensive understanding of the doctrine of the preferential option for the poor.

2. THE DOCTRINE OF THE PREFERENTIAL OPTION FOR THE POOR

The Latin American Catholic Bishops' Conference, CELAM, at Puebla (1979) reaffirmed the stance taken at Medellín (1968) when it asserted "the need for conversion on the part of the whole Church to a preferential option for the poor, an option aimed at their integral liberation."[6] In doing so, the document bore witness to the first Ro-

---

3 Bernard Lonergan, "Pantôn Anakephalaiôsis: A Theory of Human Solidarity," (1935), 17–18. As cited in Michael Shute, *The Origins of Lonergan's Notion of the Dialectic of History: A Study of Lonergan's Early Writings on History* (New York: University Press of American, 1993), 75.

4 Jordi Casabella, "Adolfo Nicolás: 'No sé si abrir fosas y beatificar mártires ayudará a reconciliar,'" *El periódico*, November 14, 2008, http://www.el-periodico.com/default.asp?idpublicacio_PK=46&idioma=CAS& idnoticia_PK=561824&idseccio_PK=1021 (accessed November 28, 2008).

5 This essay is necessarily selective and brief. But in manuscripts under development I am seeking to compare Doran's work with known proponents of liberation theology, as well as develop a fuller presentation of Doran's stance.

6 CELAM, "Evangelization in Latin America's Present and Future" in *Puebla and Beyond*, ed. J. Eagleson and P. Scharper, trans. J. Drury (Maryknoll, NY: Orbis, 1979), §1134.

man Catholic episcopal sanction of the phrase 'preferential option for the poor'. Although it was in use among Latin American theologians for years before the meeting of CELAM in Mexico,[7] the terminology was not as readily used in Vatican documents. It received passing treatment in 1981 in John Paul II's Apostolic Exhortation on the Family, *Familiaris consortio*.[8] Not until 1985 was there more than a peripheral use of the phrase, when a section in the final report of the Extraordinary Synod was titled "Preferential Option for the Poor and Human Promotion."[9] This signaled a watershed in official use of the expression. Pope John Paul II then explicitly employed it in his social encyclicals *Sollicitudo rei socialis* (1987) and *Centesimus annus* (1991).

But the use of a common phrase did not signal the common use of a phrase. And despite employing the terminology, John Paul II was clear that in his mind the term was not to be understood in terms of sociological analysis and active class struggle. Rather, it indicates "a special form of primacy in the exercise of Christian charity."[10] By contrast, for liberation theologies the preferential option is not solely a matter of ethical emphasis within ministry.[11] To be sure, it certainly does refer to the exercise of charity. But many liberation theologians will further contend that the option for the poor "constitutes the hermeneutic and epistemological locus of faith and theology."[12] A nonexhaustive explication of the preferential option's role in Christian

7   See Justo González, "The Option for the Poor in Latin American Theology" in *Poverty and Ecclesiology*, ed. A. Dunnavant, (Collegeville, MN: The Liturgical Press, 1992), 9–26. P. Hebblethwaite claims that the first use of the phrase "option for the poor" occurred in a letter from Pedro Arrupe, SJ, to the Jesuits of Latin America in 1968. See Peter Hebblethwaite, "Liberation Theology and the Roman Catholic Church" in *The Cambridge Companion to Liberation Theology*, ed. C. Rowland (Cambridge: CUP, 1999), 179.

8   *Familiaris consortio*, §47.

9   "The Church, in the Word of God, Celebrates the Mysteries of Christ for the Salvation of the World" *The Final Report of the 1985 Extraordinary Synod*, §D6

10 *Sollicitudo rei socialis*, §42. See also *Centesimus annus*, §57.

11 Juan José Tamayo, "Reception of the Theology of Liberation" in *Mysterium Liberationis: Fundamental Concepts of Liberation Theology*, ed. I. Ellacuría and J. Sobrino (Maryknoll, NY: Orbis, 1993), 53.

12 Ibid.

thought could arguably note its functioning in Trinitarian theology,[13] Christology,[14] ecclesiology,[15] soteriology,[16] spirituality,[17] and Christian ethics.[18] Moreover, the term 'poor' can be taken to refer not simply to the economically marginalized but to all those suffering injustice – whether it is race, gender, age, religious belief, or sexual orientation that is at the root of their oppression. Caution is clearly needed when speaking of the preferential option.

In this essay I understand the option for the poor in a precise sense. Firstly, I understand 'the poor' as the materially poor. Material poverty is not the only form of oppression, but it is foundational. As Clodovis Boff notes:

> The socioeconomically oppressed (the poor) do not simply exist alongside the other oppressed, like the black, the Indian, or the woman (to restrict ourselves to the most significant categories of the oppressed in the Third World). No, the oppression of a class – socioeconomic poverty – is precisely the infrastructural expression of the process of oppression. The other types represent mere superstructural expressions of oppression. As such, they are profoundly conditioned by the infrastructural. A black taxi driver and a black soccer star are not the same thing. Similarly, a female domestic servant and the first lady of the land are not the same. An

---

13 Leonardo Boff, *Trinity and Society*, trans. P. Burns (Tunbridge Wells, UK: Burns & Oates, 1988).

14 There is, rightly, a litany of liberation Christology stressing the link between poverty and Christ as Lord and Saviour. See, for example, Jon Sobrino, *Christ the Liberator: A View from the Victims*, trans. P. Burns (Maryknoll, NY: Orbis, 2001).

15 See, for example, Jon Sobrino, *The True Church and the Poor* (Maryknoll, NY: Orbis Books, 1984); or, Marcello Azevedo, *Basic Ecclesial Communities* (Washington, DC: Georgetown University Press, 1987).

16 See, for example, Jon Sobrino, *No Salvation Outside the Poor: Prophetic-Utopian Articles* (Maryknoll, NY: Orbis, 2008).

17 See, for example, Gustavo Gutiérrez, "Faith as Freedom: Solidarity with the Alienated and Confidence in the Future" in *Living with Change, Experience, Faith*, ed. F. Eigo (Villanova, PA: Villanova University Press, 1976), 15–54. It contains a clear sense of the preferential option for the poor as conversion.

18 See, for example, Enrique Dussel, *Ethics and the Theology of Liberation*, trans. B. McWilliams (Maryknoll, NY: Orbis, 1978).

Indian whose land is stolen and an Indian still in possession of it are not the same.[19]

Bracketing the issue of what may be labeled a Marxist understanding of the infrastructure and superstructure of society, Boff's point is clear. While non-economic oppression can – and does – aggravate economic oppression, economic oppression is the most basic form of societal injustice. Secondly, in this essay I limit the understanding of the option for the poor to two of its main emphases: (a) the option is an hermeneutical principle which facilitates a (re-)reading of the Christian tradition from the underside of history, and (b) the option focuses Christian praxis upon the needs of the victimized. It is this bifold nature of the preferential option that I intend in this essay.[20]

3. ROBERT DORAN'S THEOLOGICAL FOUNDATIONS: A SYSTEMATIC THEOLOGY OF HISTORY

Building on Lonergan's work, Doran also employs a transcendental approach that involves a critical turn to the subject.[21] But we should note with Lonergan that "the withdrawal into interiority is not an end in itself."[22] If we can understand the properties of the key, we can acquire some understanding of the lock. Doran refined Lonergan's stance on the human subject (the key) and employed it to construct a

---

19 Clodovis Boff, "Epistemology and Method of the Theology of Liberation" in *Mysterium Liberationis: Fundamental Concepts of Liberation Theology*, ed. I. Ellacuría and J. Sobrino. (Maryknoll, NY: Orbis, 1993), 77.

20 It is clear that this is not an exhaustive understanding of the option for the poor. Again, in a manuscript under development I am exploring the role of the option in the functional specialization of Communications. Many elements of the preferential option not addressed in Doran's understanding of Foundations become apparent in a consideration of its complexity in Communications.

21 It ought to be noted that Doran's early works involve a detailed engagement with the human sciences as much as they do the work of Lonergan. See Robert Doran, *Subject and Psyche: Ricoeur, Jung and the Search for Foundations* (Washington, DC: University Press of America, 1971). See also Robert Doran, *Psychic Conversion and Theological Foundations: Toward a Reorientation of the Human Sciences* (Chico, CA: Scholars Press, 1981).

22 Lonergan, *Method in Theology* (Toronto: University of Toronto Press, 1996), 83.

heuristic structure for developing an understanding of historical process (the lock). In this section I sketch Doran's approach.

3.1 ROBERT DORAN: FOUNDATIONS FOR SYSTEMATIC THEOLOGY AND PRAXIS

Doran's *TDH* is not an exercise in systematic theology *per se* – that is, in faith seeking understanding – but rather it "is a work more of foundations than of systematics."[23] Theological foundations, in this sense, are the framework within which all doctrinal theology, systematic theology, and practical theology have their meaning. Doran intends these foundations to facilitate the theologian's task of constructing "the meanings constitutive of that praxis of the Reign of God through which the human world itself is changed."[24] His view of theology is grounded in "a theory of history elaborated with a theological end in view" which is thereby able to "specify just what the reign of God in this world would be."[25] Doran draws on three key elements of Lonergan's thought to achieve this aim: the scale of values, the vectors of healing and creating in the human subject, and dialectic.

3.2 THE SCALE OF VALUES

Essential to Doran's project is the scale of values. It is our feelings that respond to values. But as feelings need to be discerned, all values are not equal. Lonergan notes that the converted Christian subject responds to values in an order of preference. It is worth quoting Lonergan on this scale:

> ... we may distinguish vital, social, cultural, personal and religious values in ascending order. Vital values, such as health and strength, grace and vigor, normally are preferred to avoiding the work, privations, pains involved in acquiring, maintaining, restoring them. Social values, such as the good of order which conditions the vital values of the whole community, have to be preferred to the vital values of individual members of the community. Cultural values do not exist without the underpinning of vital and social values, but none the less they rank higher. Not on bread alone doth man live. Over and above mere living and operating, men have to find a meaning and value in their living and operating. It is the function

---

23   Doran, *Theology and the Dialectics of History*, 7.

24   Ibid., 5.

25   Ibid., 12.

of culture to discover, express, validate, criticize, correct, develop, improve such meaning and value. Personal value is the person in his self – transcendence, as loving and being loved, as originator of values in himself and in his milieu, as an inspiration and invitation to others to do likewise. Religious values, finally, are at the heart of the meaning and value of man's living and man's world.[26]

Vital values are those goods essential to the quality of physical life such as food, health, and shelter. Social values are concerned with the good of order, the distribution of power, and communal identity. Cultural values provide the meaning to life, and they can be mediated through story, myth, philosophy, science, art, or many other systems of meaning. Personal values deal with issues of individual integrity and self-transcendence. But the mover of all things, God, initiates and sustains personal integrity by the gift of grace at the level of religious value. These five interrelated levels of values that Lonergan identified are the foundation of Doran's project.

3.3 THE VECTORS OF CREATING AND HEALING IN THE HUMAN SUBJECT

Lonergan has identified a two-fold movement within the human spirit. Doran describes the first 'upward' vector when he writes of the movement that begins before consciousness and unfolds through the levels of consciousness – through sensitivity, intelligence, rationality, and responsibility – to find its fulfillment at the apex of human consciousness.[27] Yet there is also a complementary movement downward. Lonergan writes:

> There is development from below upwards, from experience to understanding, from growing understanding to balanced judgment, from balanced judgment to fruitful courses of action, and from fruitful courses of action to new situations that call for further understanding, profounder judgment, richer courses of action. But there also is development from above downwards. There is the transformation of falling in love: the domestic love of the family; the human love of one's tribe, one's country, [humanity]; the divine

---

26 Lonergan, *Method in Theology*, 31–32.

27 Doran, *Theology and the Dialectics of History*, 31. Bernard Lonergan, "Natural Right and Historical Mindedness," in *A Third Collection*, ed. F.E. Crowe (Mahwah, N.J.: Paulist Press, 1985), 174–75.

love that orientates man in his cosmos and expresses itself in worship.[28]

This second healing vector is rooted in love and it complements the achievements of the human spirit. Lonergan believes that development from above (downwards) conditions our development from below (upwards). Ideally – specifically, when the human subject is in love with God – the vectors are concurrently operative and the corrosive effect of bias upon human achievement is overcome by divine grace. A transformation rooted in being-in-love then guides the creative process of the human subject. There are thus two vectors in human history, that of human achievement (progress) and that of divine healing (redemption).

3.4 THE NOTION OF DIALECTIC

Doran suggests that there are two forms of dialectic based on distinct kinds of opposition.[29] These are the 'dialectic of contradictories'

---

28 Bernard Lonergan "Healing and Creating in History," in A Third Collection, 106.

29 For Lonergan, dialectic refers to "a concrete unfolding of linked but opposed principles of change. Thus there will be a dialectic if (1) there is an aggregate of events of a determinate character, (2) the events may be traced to either or both of the two principles, (3) the principles are opposed yet bound together, and (4) they are modified by the changes that successively result from them." Bernard Lonergan, Insight: A Study of Human Understanding, Vol. 3 in Collected Works of Bernard Lonergan, ed. F.E. Crowe and R.M. Doran (Toronto: University of Toronto Press, 1992), 242. And further, "For dialectic is a pure form with general implications; it is applicable to any concrete unfolding of linked but opposed principles that are modified cumulatively by the unfolding; it can envisage at once the conscious and the non-conscious either in a single subject or in an aggregate and succession of subjects; it is adjustable to any course of events, from an ideal line of pure progress resulting from the harmonious working of the opposed principles, to any degree of conflict, aberration, break-down, and disintegration; it constitutes a principle of integration for specialized studies that concentrate on this or that aspect of human living, and it can integrate not only theoretical work but also factual reports; finally, by its distinction between insight and bias, progress and decline, it contains in a general form the combination of the empirical and the critical attitudes essential to human science." Lonergan, Insight, 268–69.

and the 'dialectic of contraries'.[30] The dialectic of contradictories takes the form of an opposition of exclusion. In a dialectic of contradictories these opposed principles are mutually exclusive – a case of either/or – and can only be resolved by a choice of one pole.[31] Unlike the dialectic of contradictories in which the tension is broken and transcended in favor of one pole, dialectics of contraries function by virtue of the creative tension of the dialectic relationship.[32] A dialectic of contraries represents an opposition between opposed principles that is reconcilable in higher synthesis. Doran refers to the first of these as a principle of transcendence (the operator), and the other is a principle of limitation (the integrator). The operator transforms the integrator – in a dialectic of contraries – as they work together in an inclusive manner.

3.5 THE HEURISTIC STRUCTURE OF SOCIETY WITHIN HISTORY

These elements – the scale of values, the creating and healing vectors, and dialectic – combine to provide a heuristic structure that enables the understanding of historical process and also any given

---

30 Robert Doran, *What Is Systematic Theology?* (Toronto, University of Toronto Press, 2005), 185. See also Lonergan, *Insight*, 11–24. The dialectic of contradictories is evident in the relationship between what Lonergan identifies as the two kinds of human knowing. This is Lonergan's more prevalent usage of the term 'dialectic'. The two types of knowledge are the sensate knowledge humans have in common with all animals and the rational and spiritual intelligence that are unique to humans. For Lonergan, sensing is not knowing. One resolves this dialectic by breaking it and affirming that one is a knower who understands correctly only by a composite performance of experiencing, understanding, and judging.

31 Doran, *Theology and the Dialectics of History*, 64–92. Good and evil is an obvious instance of a dialectic of contradictories. Ibid., 46.

32 A dialectic of contraries is manifest in what Lonergan identifies as the tension between the two types of consciousness. In Doran's terminology such a dialectic arises from this duality of consciousness, that is, in the tension between intentionality and psyche. The psyche is the experienced flow of life, the sensitive representation of the underlying neural demand functions. It is comprised of the flow of our sensations, memories, images, emotions, conations, associations, bodily movements, spontaneous intersubjective responses, and of the symbolic integrations of these that are our dreams. But the intentional operations of understanding, judgment and decision re-patterns, organizes and arranges our experiences. See Doran, *Theology and the Dialectics of History*, 46–47.

situation within historical process including the social situation.[33] Doran identifies a dialectic functioning as the principle of integrity at the level of personal value, and by analogy he suggests that one is operative at each of the levels of cultural and social value.[34] Further-more, the creating and healing vectors are employed to account for the unity and movement from level-to-level of the scale of values. In this manner, history can be conceived as a complex network of dialectics of subjects, cultures, and communities.[35] Sketching Doran's understand-ing of 'society' – as understood within his theory of history – may help

---

33 Ibid., 10. See also Robert Doran, "The Analogy of Dialectic and The Sys-tematics of History" in *Religion in Context: Recent Studies in Lonergan*, ed. T.P. Fallon and P.B. Riley (Lanham: University Press of America, 1988), 37.

34 The integrity of the human person is a function of the successful naviga-tion of the dialectic between bodiliness (integrator) and spirit (operator). The integrity of the cultural level of society is constituted by a dialectic between cosmological culture (integrator) and anthropological culture (operator). The integrity of the social level of value resides in the successful functioning of a dialectic between spontaneous intersubjectivity (integra-tor) and practical intelligence (operator). To quote Doran at some length, "Cosmological symbolizations of the experience of life as a movement with a direction that can be found or missed find the paradigm of order in the cosmic rhythms. This order is analogously realized in the society, and social order determines individual rectitude. Cosmological insight thus moves from the cosmos, through the society, to the individual. As such it is more compact than anthropological insight, where the measure of integrity is recognized as world-transcendent and as providing the standard first for the individual whose ordered attunement to the world-transcendent mea-sure is itself the measure of the integrity of the society. Anthropological insight moves from God through the individual to the society. The dialectic of culture, like every dialectic of contraries, is a concrete unfolding of these linked but opposed principles of change." Doran, "The Analogy of Dialec-tic," 54–55. And again, "There is a dialectic of community internally con-stituted by the linked but opposed principles of spontaneous intersubjec-tivity [communal sense] and practical intelligence. ... The integrity of the dialectic, and so of the society that it informs, 'rests on the concrete unity of opposed principles; the dominance of either principle results in a distor-tion, and the distortion both weakens the dominance and strengthens the opposed principle to restore an equilibrium.'" The parenthetical comment is added. Doran, "The Analogy of Dialectic," 40. The internal quote is from Lonergan, *Insight*, 258.

35 Doran, *Theology and the Dialectics of History*, 144.

to clarify his system. It will also emerge that it is highly relevant to liberation concerns.

For Doran, 'society' is a generic term.[36] With more precision, he claims that a society is comprised of five distinct but interrelated elements: intersubjective spontaneity, technological institutions, the economic system, the political order and culture.[37] Culture has two dimensions: the every day infrastructural level that informs a given way of life and the reflexive superstructural level that arises from scientific, philosophic, scholarly, and theological objectifications. Doran sets forth the interrelationship of these components in six points.[38]

Firstly, the spontaneous intersubjectivity – the communal sense that bonds family, friends, and nation – functions on its own as one of the elements of society in the dialectic of community. Secondly, practical intelligence, which is the other constitutive principle of the dialectic of community, gives rise to three constitutive elements of society, viz., technological institutions, the economic order, and the political-legal echelon of society. Thirdly, in a society operating along an optimum line of progress, these three elements must be kept in dialectical tension with spontaneous intersubjectivity. Fourthly, the integrity – and inversely the distortion – of the dialectic of community is a function, proximately of the infrastructural level of culture and, more remotely, of the reflexive superstructural level of culture. Fifthly, spontaneous intersubjectivity, technological institutions, economic systems, political-legal institutions, and everyday culture constitute the infrastructure of a healthy society. Moreover, the reflexive level of culture constitutes society's superstructure, and culture at *both* levels is a limit-condition upon the possible existence of an integral dialectic of community. Sixthly, there is needed at the superstructural level an orientation that takes responsibility for the dialectic of community. This orientation addresses the integrity of cultural values at both the superstructural and infrastructural levels. (Lonergan refers to this specialization of intelligence as cosmopolis)[39]

---

36 Ibid., 359.

37 Ibid., 361.

38 This is the more concise presentation taken from Doran, *What Is Systematic Theology?*, 174–75.

39 Doran, *Theology and the Dialectics of History*, 361.

In terms of progress and decline as measured by this structure, Doran offers a helpful summary:[40]

> From above, then, religious values condition the possibility of personal integrity; personal integrity conditions the possibility of authentic cultural values; at the reflexive level of culture, such integrity will promote an authentic superstructural collaboration that assumes responsibility for the integrity not only of scientific and scholarly disciplines, but even of everyday culture; cultural integrity at both levels conditions the possibility of a just social order; and a just social order conditions the possibility of the equitable distribution of vital goods. Conversely, problems in the effective and recurrent distribution of vital goods can be met only by a reversal of distortions in the social order; the proportions of the needed reversal are set by the scope and range of the real or potential maldistribution; the social change demands a transformation at the everyday level of culture proportionate to the dimensions of the social problem; this transformation frequently depends on reflexive theoretical and scientific developments at the superstructural level; new cultural values at both levels call for proportionate changes at the level of personal integrity; and these depend for their emergence, sustenance, and consistency on the religious development of the person.[41]

The dialectics at the levels of social and cultural value are of most relevance to our present discussion, for these are levels of value that constitute society. Society is proceeding along a line of pure progress inasmuch as the dialectics at the levels of culture and society function as dialectics of contraries. So, for Doran, social schemes that are responsible for the just distribution of vital goods can in fact result in an unjust distribution of vital goods. In such a case, new technological institutions, economic systems, and politico-legal structures are required to promote the just distribution of vital goods. New social schemes are possible only if new cultural values emerge to motivate and sustain the existence of these new values. And the new cultural values informing the transformed social structures are a function of individuals' conversion and their originating values. So it is these aforementioned components that combine to form Doran's understanding of the complexion of a theory of history of society.

---

40 Ibid., 96.

41 Ibid., 96–97.

4. THE PREFERENTIAL OPTION FOR THE POOR: A DISCUSSION OF DORAN'S STANCE

As I noted above, the understanding of the preferential option employed in this essay has two key elements: (a) the hermeneutical privileged position occupied by the poor in terms of the Church's retrieval of the tradition, and (b) the concentration of praxis upon the needs of the victims of history. In this section I discuss the manner in which these elements function in Doran's *TDH*.

4.1 THE PREFERENTIAL OPTION FOR THE POOR AS A HERMENEUTICAL PRINCIPLE

In *TDH*, the framework for analysis of the social situation presented above is conducted from within an horizon that identifies – and responds to – the integral scale of values. Apropos this observation, with respect to the hermeneutically privileged position of the oppressed in the retrieval of the tradition, one can also note that the scale of values becomes a permanent heuristic element of any retrieval of any historical situation. As the converted theologian engages in the retrieval of the tradition – remembering that it is the converted subject who responds to the scale of values – he/she will possess an heuristic anticipation that incorporates a priority position for those who are oppressed. It helps here to recall that, especially from below upwards along the scale, the social situation is being evaluated by its capacity to distribute vital goods. A cultural system is likewise appraised – not solely but at a foundational level – on its ability to create and sustain meanings that can underpin social structures that ensure equitable distribution of vital values across the community. Regardless of the socio-cultural situation being appraised – from the Gospel world of first-century Palestine to Chile under General Augusto Pinochet – the issue of the distribution of vital goods is the primary hermeneutical principle that sets conditions by which the adequacy of all three dialectics are judged.

In terms of the hermeneutic nature of the option for the poor, Doran's use of the scale of values and dialectic to ground the option stands in marked contrast to those approaches that employ conflictualist theories, and then theologize using the results.[42] In a critical real-

---

42 See, for example, this methodological suggestion by Clodovis Boff, *Theology and Praxis: Epistemological Foundations* (Maryknoll: Orbis, 1987). The

ist approach, values are essential to the scientific nature of social theory because – in the limit case – complete understanding is the goal of all scientific disciplines. If reality is the world mediated by meaning and motivated by value,[43] to exclude values is to bracket elements of reality and thus produce a truncated and erroneous scientific theory. One would need to possess a view of sociology that is in some sense positivist to bracket values. Yet this is precisely what Boff suggests liberation theology does.[44] The process of social analysis is 'Christianized'; values are introduced only by referring to the preferential option. By contrast, Doran's use of the scale of values to ground the option gives rise to fewer problems from a Christian, and ultimately scientific, perspective. Theologically, Doran recognizes that the social situation is characterized by matters of sin (when dialectics are distorted or broken) and grace (when the dialectics function as contraries), and he thus develops a system with the potential to anticipate such data. Philosophically, Doran recognizes that the ultimate motivations for actions are values and that any theory of society must take values into account. To allow a sociology with no anticipation of sin or grace a priority of access to the data is to distort the data and perhaps normalize sin.[45]

For Doran, as noted, the preferential option enters the heuristic anticipation of historical (and therefore social) analysis as part of the

---

shorter summary of the method contained in *Mysterium Liberationis* is also used. Boff, "Epistemology and Method of the Theology of Liberation," 57–102.

43 Lonergan, *Method*, 265.

44 Boff is aware of these limitations and uses the notion of the 'popular' understanding of society to import values into the socio-analytic mediation. This would not need to be done if the sociology was adequate. See Boff, "Epistemology and Method of the Theology of Liberation," 78.

45 Conflictualist social theorists readily admit that their analyses are motivated by ethical concerns. But in adopting its hermeneutic of suspicion, conflictualism employs an heuristic anticipation of conflict with a limited conception of progress. The genuinely constructive elements of society – those that promote genuine progress – are often reduced to the issue of competing interests. In this manner, conflictualist social theory can normalize conflict and even promote violence that simply compounds decline in a society. This is not to argue against the morality of armed resistance under some situations, merely to assert that a social theory needs to be able to appraise the difference between progress and decline.

scale of values. It is, in this sense, potentially transcultural and not solely a Christian doctrine received by faith. Doran derives these categories from analysis of human consciousness without. The option for the poor is in some way knowable not simply because of Biblical revelation. Thus, if one builds on the foundation provided by *TDH*, the preferential option is not 'tacked on' to studies of social reality by virtue of appeal to specific Christian revelation. The option for the poor can be understood by referring to general non-religious categories, not by reference to a special religious set. It is beyond the scope of this essay to explore fully the ramifications of this understanding of the preferential option. But it is reasonable to conclude that this is a radical stance with sweeping relevance for socio-cultural analysis at the micro- and macro-societal levels, for both religious and non-religious social institutions. Can a parish, diocese, or Church be called Christian if it does not implement social structures proportionate to the demands of the option for the poor? Can the option be included in a more strident Charter of Human Rights on the basis of its *a priori* status? Whilst liberation theologians have been wrongly accused of holding fringe positions in their dedication to the poor, the option – according to *TDH* – can be transcendentally grounded as fundamental and universal without reference to Marxism.[46]

---

46 Furthermore, in Doran's approach in *TDH* the criticism that the option for the poor is partisan and divisive can be avoided without compromising its demands of preference for God's anawim. The Congregation for the Doctrine of the Faith (CDF) expressed some disquiet in its second document aimed at warning against the 'dangers' of the Liberation Theology movement. The CDF was concerned that theologians who used conflictualist social theory were interpreting the preferential option in a manner that pitted Christians against both each other and non-Christians:

The special option for the poor, far from being a sign of particularism or sectarianism, manifests the universality of the Church's being and mission. This option excludes no one. This is the reason why the Church cannot express this option by means of reductive sociological and ideological categories which would make this preference a partisan choice and a source of conflict. (Congregation for the Doctrine of the Faith, Instruction on Christian Freedom and Liberation, §68).

From the perspective of *TDH*, the option for the poor can be understood in a manner that does not gloss over conflict – there are dialectics of contradictories – but also avoids positing conflict as a primordial reality in which the option is (naïvely) dismissed as a call to arms.

4.2 THE PREFERENTIAL OPTION FOR THE POOR AND THE CHURCH'S PRAXIS

From the perspective of *TDH*, with respect to the mission of the Church, the relations that obtain within the scale of values – when considered from below upwards – reveal the preferential option for the poor as grounded in transcendental method. Global injustice is *the* foundational problem by which the adequate functioning of all other dialectics is measured. Implicit in this social analysis stemming from *TDH* is the notion of a line of pure progress. And a line of progress implies a goal or an endpoint. In theological terms it was noted that Doran derived categories for understanding the *approximation* of the Kingdom that humans can construct on earth. Having a specific end in mind – comparing the historical/current situation with an understanding of the Kingdom – is not to project onto the social situation. Rather, the end point of the Kingdom illuminates all historical situations and indicates where they have deviated from the ideal line of history. Teleology has fallen out of favor in the social sciences including sociology. However, contrary to the Humean fact-value distinction, Alasdair MacIntyre has illustrated that one can derive an 'ought' from an 'is' when considering teleological realities.[47] *TDH* incorporates this understanding of teleology, and the preferential option is built into this *telos*. Doran's stance directs praxis because it is empirical (it is an heuristic structure that needs to be filled by concrete socio-cultural data), critical (it is conscious of its own assumptions), normative (complete human flourishing in the Kingdom is its goal), dialectic (it is aware of the vagaries of human freedom), and practical (it suggests paths to return to the normal line of pure progress).[48]

Doran's work is able to suggest an interpretation of the option for the poor that presents it in the terms of an account of a line of pure historical progress. It provides a means of comprehending deviation from that progress, specifically, when that which ought to function as dialectics of contraries function as dialectics of contradictories. Moreover, being able to distinguish between dialectics of contraries and

47 Alasdair MacIntyre, *After Virtue: A Study in Moral Theory* (Guildford: Duckworth, 1985), 51–61.

48 These categories – empirical, critical, normative, dialectic, and practical – are identified by Ormerod in his consideration of the relevance of Doran's work for systematic ecclesiology. See Neil Ormerod, "The Structure of a Systematic Ecclesiology," *Theological Studies* 63, no. 1 (2002): 3.

contradictories, and having these function as part of one's heuristic anticipation, permits Doran to distinguish between constructive dialectical relationships and destructive ones in a way that conflictualism – and certainly functionalism – cannot.

Neil Ormerod begins to demonstrate what Doran's heuristic structure of history is capable of in practice. Specifically, Ormerod has adopted a critical-realist sociological approach to the Christian Church. Akin to a Weberian attempt to distinguish a Church from a sect, Ormerod has used Doran's framework to develop a typology that permits him to identify socio-cultural deviation from the line of pure progress. As noted above, when dialectics break down, distortion results. Distortion manifests as a bias towards the poles of the dialectics, and these distortions can be represented as anti-types. Two sets of values (social and cultural), multiplied by two sets of dialectic, results in there being four anti-types of Church:[49]

> *Type 1: Social limitation and cultural limitation.*

> At the social level, there is focus upon the bond of the group at the expense of new ways of doing things. At the cultural level, there is a strong emphasis on tradition. Integration holds priority over new innovations, which are seen as suspect.

> *Type 2: Cultural limitation and social transcendence.*

> At the cultural level, as per type 1, integration is upheld at the expense of new cultural developments. At the social level, practical intelligence is prioritized resulting in a willingness to adopt new ideas, but conversely the inter-subjectivity may be compromised. This is an inherently unstable type as the compromise of the social bond can lead to an attitude of mobility.

> *Type 3: Social limitation and cultural transcendence.*

> At the social level, as per type 1, the bond of the group is prioritized over practical intelligence. At the cultural level, the past is eschewed so new ideas and systems can be adopted very quickly. They can "have enduring social organizations coupled with a non-traditional approach to the gospel."[50]

---

49 Neil Ormerod, "Church, Anti-Types and Ordained Ministry: Systematic Perspectives," *Pacifica* 10 (October 1997): 336.

50 Ibid., 339.

Type 4: Social transcendence and cultural transcendence.

At the social level, this is as per type 2: practical intelligence is prioritized. At the cultural level, this distortion is similar to type 3: the anthropological alignment is preferred. New developments, social and cultural, are quickly adopted rendering this type inherently unstable.

Ormerod is measuring these anti-types against a line of pure progress; in this manner he is both diagnosing the situation and suggesting that alternative schemes are required. The specific policies to act as a corrective to these distortions depend on the situation, but their need and shape is demanded by the analysis. Although this is a brief outline of Ormerod's position, the typology allows possible limitations of Church on the socio-cultural levels to be identified, addressed, and rectified. But they also provide a means by which any socio-cultural system can be appraised. It does not have to be the Church that is studied by Doran's heuristic device; any socio-cultural situation can be assessed for its distortion or destruction of the integral dialectics.

5. CONCLUSION

This essay sought to indicate the liberative capability of Doran's theological foundations. Specifically, as a means of controlling the scope of the discussion, I focused upon the role of the option for the poor – taken to refer to the economically poor – and its hermeneutical and praxis facets in *TDH*. Doran's theory of history is able to accord the preferential option an *a priori* status that grounds the option as truly universal. It is operative in the retrieval of the Church's tradition, in the reading of all history, and it is included in an account of pure progress that is able to direct praxis whereby the poor are the measure of its adequacy.

It can certainly be argued that Doran's stance appears more methodologically complete than some liberation theology. However, when the first wave of liberation theology was being formulated, the need was for tools of social analysis then and there, and conflictualist social theories served this purpose well. Criticisms of liberationist perspectives that do not suggest a viable alternative are facile. Doran grounds the option for the poor in a manner that sates the need – at a foundational level, at least – for a means of dialectical social analysis. This is not to claim that there is any substitute for theologians getting their hands dirty' in both the social sciences and the social situation. Without such involvement by theologians, theology as Doran conceives it will remain a heuristic anticipation that is never filled by data and is unable to transform unjust social structures. Ormerod's work is instructive in this regard, but it is still very much in its early stages.[51] Doran's understanding of theology demands praxis oriented towards the poor, but those whom his foundations convince must now demonstrate this in transformative action.

Nonetheless, the key intention of this essay was to indicate that Doran's method grounds a highly potent understanding of the preferential option in terms of both the hermeneutics of the poor and Church praxis. Doran certainly provides a cogent Christian, indeed potentially deeply inter-religious, foundation that permits an understanding of exactly what constitutes progress toward the Reign and deviation from the realization of the Reign. He is able to understand the Reign of God such that, from above, what moves all goodness is God's gracious gift of God's self. But from below, in *TDH*, the litmus test of all authenticity – social, cultural, and personal – is the treatment of the poor. Doran has constructed a theology of history that facilitates the irruption of the poor into history and can help reorient history to deliver justice for the poor. Whether or not this fact can help liberation theologians remains to be seen.

---

51 Doran notes that unless history is transformed, theology is incomplete. But it is an emphasis that can be lost in such a dense text. It is perhaps clearer in his shorter work *What is Systematic Theology?* though at this stage he is largely re-expressing the foundations of *TDH*. Doran, *What Is Systematic Theology?*, 197–203

MIDWIVING THE FOURTH STAGE OF MEANING: LONERGAN AND DORAN

John D. Dadosky
REGIS COLLEGE/UNIVERSITY OF TORONTO

I. INTRODUCTION

In 1995 I was working as a high school teacher in the Midwestern United States when I began to think about doctoral studies in theology. Since Lonergan had been at Regis College and Doran was now there advancing his legacy, Regis was the natural place to study. I visited Bob in Toronto and asked him if I could study with him. I especially wanted to take his course on Lonergan's *Insight*. That was a distinctive moment in my career. Since arriving at Regis in the fall of 1996, I have had the opportunity to know Bob as a teacher, thesis director, mentor, colleague, and friend. I have also been fortunate to sit in on subsequent courses that he taught on Lonergan's *Insight*.

Of pertinence to this paper is his introductory lecture on Lonergan's *Insight* during the 2003-2004 academic year. I quote from his notes:

> [T]here is emerging a new period of Lonergan studies, where the major themes are community, dialogue, otherness, mediation, and plurality. Some characteristics of Lonergan's early writings made some people regard him as only remotely concerned about such themes, perhaps intellectually concerned but not existentially so. And yet perhaps that is a misreading. To state upfront in a preface to a major work in philosophy, to a work that in effect attempts to redraw the map of the discipline and in my estimation largely succeeds in doing so, that one is seeking a common ground on which people can meet is to evince a concern for these themes – for community, dialogue, otherness, mediation, and plurality – that is more than simply intellectual.[1]

---

1 Robert M. Doran, "Notes on Insight: 2003-2004." September 11, 2003. Unpublished, 1.

Two other noteworthy things occurred in that initial lecture. First, Bob used the phrase, 'the midwiving of meaning.' Second, quite separate from his use of that phrase, I raised the question of whether there was a fourth stage of meaning. At that time Bob was too immersed in trying to explain to his students the third stage of meaning to try to speculate about a fourth stage. However, while recently listening to those recorded lectures in preparing my own course on Lonergan's *Insight*, it occurred to me that Bob had already answered the question, that is, in his intuition of a new era in Lonergan studies as emphasizing the aforementioned themes.

In the summer of 2008 I presented a paper entitled "Is there a Fourth Stage of Meaning?" at the Lonergan Workshop in Boston. I received surprisingly positive feedback from several respected experts in Lonergan's thought. Moreover, I did not realize it at the time, but the fruits of what I was proposing in identifying a fourth stage pertained, as I was only to later discover, to the themes Doran identified: community, dialogue, mediation, and plurality.

In this paper I would like to reframe and summarize the argument for a fourth stage of meaning in light of the themes that Doran suggested. I believe in that intuiting these five elements, he was unwittingly anticipating an explication of a fourth stage of meaning.

Lonergan explicitly identified three stages of meaning: common sense, theory, and interiority. It may be that Doran implicitly began intuiting a fourth stage when he suggested that *mutual self-mediation* in Lonergan's article "The Mediation of Christ in Prayer" pertained to communities, where heretofore, Lonergan had only associated *self-mediation* with communities.[2] One can say they have both been integral in midwiving an understanding of a fourth stage of meaning.

2. ANTICIPATING A FOURTH STAGE

Although we may never know if Lonergan would approve of a fourth stage of meaning, I argue that the idea is implicit in his later works, especially in an essay titled "Prolegomena to the Study of the Emerg-

---

2 Bernard Lonergan, 'Mediation of Christ in Prayer', in *Philosophical and Theological Papers 1958-1964* CWL Vol. 6, ed. R. Croken, F. Crowe and R. Doran (Toronto, University of Toronto Press, 2004), 160-82; Robert Doran, *What Is Systematic Theology?* (Toronto, University of Toronto Press, 2005), 45, 57-58.

ing Religious Consciousness of our Time."[3] Therein he speaks of an
infrastructure or inner word spoken to the heart in religious experience which is habituated and integrated within the life of the mystic.[4]
He also speaks of Robley Whitson's book *The Coming Convergence of
World Religions* which, as the title suggests, anticipates a new cooperation among the world's religions as the fruit of interreligious dialogue
and engagement.[5] Additionally, he speaks about a 'new sacralization to
be fostered.'[6] I have argued elsewhere that the latter anticipates a higher integration of relating between religions and cultures, one in which
mutuality and difference grounds the principal relationship between
the two. I have also suggested that it anticipates a genetic unfolding
towards what Lonergan referred to in *Insight: A Study of Human Understanding* as *cosmopolis* and has as its theological correlate the Reign
of God on Earth.[7]

There may be additional references in other parts of his corpus, but
in this paper I will argue that the notion of a fourth stage of meaning
is implicit in his thought in that it follows logically from his theory
of consciousness as unearthed in *Insight* and later in the chapter on
meaning in *Method in Theology*. This can be further developed in light
of the chapter on religion in the latter text.

---

3 Lonergan does explicitly mention a fourth stage in the drafts of *Method
in Theology* and seems to indicate that it pertains to chapter 4. "The nature
of the fourth stage will be indicated in the next chapter." Page 42 MiT V
(Meaning) discards 732, by Lonergan, B., Language(s): English, Decade:
1960, 73200DTE060 / A732. www.Bernardlonergan.com. The question
remains why he did not explicate it in the published manuscript.

4 Bernard Lonergan, *A Third Collection*, ed. F. E. Crowe (Mahwah, NJ: Paulist Press, 1985), 55-73.

5 Robley Whitson, *The Coming Convergence of World Religions* (New York:
Newman, 1971).

6 Bernard Lonergan, "Sacralization and Secularization," in *Philosophical and
Theological Papers: 1965-1980*, CWL 17, ed. R. Croken and R. Doran,
(Toronto, University of Toronto Press, 2004), 265.

7 John Dadosky, "Sacralization, Secularization, and Religious Fundamentalism," *Studies in Religious/Sciences Religieuses*, 36.3-4 (Fall, 2007): 513–529.
On cosmopolis, see Bernard Lonergan, *Insight: A Study in Human Understanding*, CWL, Vol. 3 (Toronto, University of Toronto Press, 1992), 263-
267.

Lonergan admits that the stages are ideal constructs and also that they are not strictly chronological, that various members of a culture can be in different stages simultaneously. Still, as constructs, the stages give us some insight into our current philosophical context and where we might be going.[8]

Lonergan never formally spoke of a fourth stage of meaning. He labored chiefly to provide a philosophical response for a third stage of meaning – the turn to conscious interiority. However, let us take some liberty and speculate what it might entail if he in fact would acknowledge it. For example, we can ask if the task of the third stage of meaning is the critical appropriation of one's intentional conscious-ness – the basic task of philosophy, what might be the comparable task of theology in a fourth stage of meaning? I will return to this question below, but first let us presume for a moment that there is a fourth stage of meaning. The transition from the first to the second stage of meaning is brought about by a *systematic exigence* which results in the possibility of theoretically differentiated consciousnesses, one that correlates with the level of understanding for Lonergan. The transi-tion from the second to the third stage of meaning comes about as the result of a *critical exigence* in order to relate the seemingly disparate worlds of common sense and theory. Likewise, the turn to interiority enables the critical grounding of this relationship between common sense and theory and further yields the possibility of interiorly dif-ferentiated consciousness. This stage can be correlated with the level of judgment for Lonergan in that this is the basic task of philosophy. Here the philosophers' object of inquiry becomes consciousness and their main task becomes critical reflection, i.e. to ask "What are we doing when…?"

Admittedly, Lonergan identifies these exigencies when he speaks of the realms of meaning rather than the stages of meaning. How-ever, they are pertinent to the stages because it is possible to locate their emergence concretely in history. For example, Descartes' *cogito* comes about as the result of a critical exigence, not just in Descartes' own intellectual questioning, but insofar as Western philosophy was in need of it as well. Descartes inaugurates the *zeitgeist* of the turn to the subject.

---

8 I will be referring to the chapter on meaning in *Method*, specifically the sections on the realms and the stages of meaning from Bernard Lonergan, *Method in Theology* (Toronto: University of Toronto Press, 1990), 81-99.

Therefore, if we are to presume that there is a fourth stage of meaning, then we can take as a clue what Lonergan refers to as a *transcendental exigence*. He writes:

> There is to human inquiry an unrestricted demand for intelligibility. There is to human judgment a demand for the unconditioned. There is to human deliberation a criterion that criticizes every finite good. So it is – as we shall attempt to show in the next chapter [Religion] – that [humans] can reach basic fulfillment, peace, joy, only by moving beyond the realms of common sense, theory, interiority and into the realm in which God is known and loved.[9]

Lonergan implies that the transcendental exigence takes us beyond realms of common sense, theory, and interiority, each of which are characterized by the three stages of meaning respectively. Therefore, we can logically deduce, consonant with his mention of the other differentiations of consciousness, that the transcendental exigence gives rise to religiously differentiated consciousness – a consciousness that speaks to a person who is habituated into the dynamic state of being-in-love in an unrestricted manner. In this way, we can surmise that a fourth stage of meaning would bring about an emphasis on religiously differentiated consciousness including a general heightened desire for a basic fulfillment in reality as transcendent. This unrestricted being-in-love is the basic fulfillment for which all human beings long whether their conscious intending occurs within the world of common sense, theory, interiority, or some combination thereof. It is the *basic* fulfillment, but I presume Lonergan chose his words carefully, so we can say that it is not the complete fulfillment. Such fulfillment would pertain to the finality of human longing for the beatific vision.

Much of what Lonergan says about unrestricted being-in-love pertains to what he identifies in religious conversion. The latter concerns a transformation such that one's being becomes a dynamic state of *being*-in-love. There follows a desire to surrender and commit to that love, which has a content but no apprehended object.

> Religious conversion is being grasped by ultimate concern. It is other-worldly falling in love. It is total and permanent self-surrender without conditions, qualifications, reservations. But it is such a surrender, not as an act, but as a dynamic state that is prior to and principle of subsequent acts. It is revealed in retrospect as an under-tow

9 Lonergan, *Method in Theology*, 83-4.

of existential consciousness, as a fated acceptance of a vocation to holiness, as perhaps an increasing simplicity and passivity in prayer. It is interpreted differently in the context of different religious traditions. For Christians it is God's love flooding our hearts through the Holy Spirit given to us.[10]

In this way, we can surmise that where interiority provides the conditions for the self-appropriation of the human person to affirm oneself as a knower at the level of judgment, being-in-love in an unrestricted manner implies the affirmation of a transcendent Other. This, in turn, demands a commitment and self-surrender, a constitutive act such as the choice Ignatius calls for in the *Two Standards*. In this way, a fourth stage of meaning would correspond to the level of decision, the way in which interiority corresponds to the level of judgment.

Moreover, the unrestricted being-in-love is not just the recognition of a transcendent Other of whom one is conscious but does not know; it also includes the love which flows over into one's family, one's neighbor and the general desire to contribute to the well-being of humankind. In his later writings Lonergan often speaks of religious conversion in the context of family, society, and of God. We can derive from this, therefore, that the fruits of unrestricted loving include not just a recognition and response to a transcendent Other in a vertical sense but also horizontally to the Other – family, friends, neighbors, society and, perhaps most importantly, one's enemies.

As unrestricted loving demands complete and total self-surrender, the fruits of such self-surrender entail a complete re-ordering and re-orientation of one's knowing and choosing. In terms of knowing, the realms of commonsense, theory, and interiority are re-oriented and re-directed in line with this unrestricted being-in-love. In terms of choosing, one commits oneself to self-surrender in light of this basic horizon of loving. One comes to the resolve that being attentive to one's experience, being intelligent in one's understanding, and being reasonable in one's judgments – of not restricting the unrestricted desire to know – is the responsible and loving way in which to act. Moreover, one accepts responsibility for one's neighbor; one chooses to love one's enemy. Nor is this simply the license of Christianity, as the Dalai Lama demonstrates in his ongoing non-violent responses to the Chinese government.

---

10 Lonergan, *Method in Theology*, 240-1

3. OTHERNESS: VERTICAL AND HORIZONTAL

The fourth stage of meaning involves a turn to the Other – alterity. This alterity includes a horizontal commitment to one's neighbor that is intertwined with a vertical relation with a transcendent Other.

3.1 HORIZONTAL ALTERITY

The 'turn to the subject' inaugurated by Descartes' *Meditations* involves a shift to the notion of person. A person is an individual *in relation* to others. As an individual, a person mediates oneself to another. This self-mediation comprises the person's self-presence and self-constitution to oneself and to another. In the editorial notes of Lonergan's *Verbum: Word and Idea in Aquinas*, the following note states: "It might be said that in *Insight*, despite some remarkable passages on intersubjectivity, one's encounter is objectively with the real and subjectively with oneself, rather than with persons, but in the Gonzaga University lecture of 1963 on Mediation (the institute Knowledge and Learning), the occasion of mutual self-mediation is asserted to be 'the encounter, the meeting, keeping company, living together,' and that ties in with encountering in Augustine..."[11]

This note indicates that Lonergan's earlier work focused on the subject as present to oneself as a knower but that later Lonergan acknowledged that alterity was implied in the notion of mutual self-mediation.[12] This relation with the Other is not a one-way street or strict self-mediation, rather it is a mutual self-mediation between individuals and communities.

I suspect that this movement from *presence to oneself as knower* to *presence to the Other* through mutual self-mediation is consonant with a work by Paul Ricoeur titled *Oneself as Another*. In this text, published as the Gifford Lectures, Ricoeur argues that there is a philosophical sense of alterity inherent in the subject's consciousness, a sense in which the person is present to oneself as another. "[S]elfhood

---

11 Bernard Lonergan, *Verbum: Word and Idea in Aquinas*, CWL Vol. 2, ed. F. E. Crowe and R. M. Doran (Toronto: University of Toronto Press, 1997), 254.

12 The recent publication of *The Triune God* and its treatment of the divine relations will no doubt add to this understanding of relations, the details of which remain to be worked out. Bernard J. F. Lonergan, *The Triune God: Systematics*, CWL. Vol. 12, ed. R. Doran and H. D. Monsour, trans. M. Shields (Toronto, University of Toronto Press: 2007).

of oneself implies otherness to such an intimate degree that one cannot be thought of without the other....."[13] From here he can analogize
to the person as present to another, outside of oneself. "The autonomy
of the self... [appears] to be tightly bound up with the solicitude for
one's neighbor and with justice for each individual."[14] Further, Emmanuel Levinas develops this line of thinking where the ethics of the
Other precedes ontology or, in the words of Lonergan, a spontaneous intersubjectivity implies at a rudimentary level a responsibility for
the Other, in a non-reflective way. The transcendence Levinas refers to
does not necessarily speak of God but, rather, from one's turn from the
self to the Other. He refers to the work of Martin Buber's *I and Thou*
in order to emphasize the inextricable relationship between the self
and the Other.[15] In a sense, one could say the *I-Thou* relationship is
descriptive language for what can be articulated in a more explanatory
way in the technical language of mutual self-mediation.

In terms of being-in-love in an unrestricted manner, the re-orientation and transvaluation of values which are the fruits of unrestricted
loving, reinforce and redirect one's intersubjectivity in a heightened
and spontaneous way. This enables free and creative acts of charity
that often the saints and holy people exemplify. Without giving it a
second thought, Dorothy Day gave away a diamond ring to a homeless
woman who was admiring it. When asked why she would do such a
thing Day replied, "The poor need beauty." Such acts of charity are not
only acts of dramatic artistry and are likewise beautiful in themselves,
but they are also required to further advance the creation of a social
order that lends itself to the spontaneous reception of the Other as
opposed to the red tape of bureaucracy.

Hence, to posit a fourth stage of meaning would include the turn
from the subject's intentional consciousness to the subject's awareness
of the Other. I believe that Ricouer has provided that bridge from the
selfhood of oneself to the self of the Other by articulating how the
self is present to the self as another. In addition, I believe Levinas has
further articulated this turn by expounding upon the responsibility

---

13 Paul Ricoeur, *Oneself as Another*, trans. Kathleen Blamey (Chicago: University of Chicago Press, 1992), 3.

14 Ibid., 18.

15 Emmanuel Levinas, *Alterity and Transcendence*, trans. Michael B. Smith
(New York: Columbia University Press, 1999).

for the Other that precedes all self-reflection. In turn, Lonergan's work can further articulate the dynamism of this relationship in terms of mutuality, difference, and discernment, to which I will return below. At this point, I turn to vertical alterity and how it would pertain to the fourth stage of meaning.

3.2 VERTICAL ALTERITY

The transition from a third stage of meaning to a fourth stage would occur as the result of a transcendental exigence. I have argued that the turn to the Other (one's neighbor) is part of the fruit of this exigence manifesting itself, for example, in the work of Levinas, especially as represented by his work *Alterity and Transcendence*. Similarly, the transcendental exigence would issue in a turn to vertical alterity in the recognition of a transcendent Other as a first principle. I would like to draw on some of the spiritual theology of Catherine of Siena as an example of this transition.

Self knowledge for Catherine is foundational in her spiritual theology. In one of her key mystical revelations from one she identifies as the Eternal Father, she is told: "You are she who is not, and I AM HE WHO IS."[16] Thomas McDermott identifies this as the *basic maxim* of self-knowledge in her thinking. Interestingly, the mystical revelation informs Catherine of her identity by way of negation. Her creatureliness reminds her of her absolute dependence on God and that all of this existence is a gift.[17]

According to McDermott, Catherine's understanding of this maxim develops over time and deepens. From the initial revelation of complete dependence on and participation in the life of God, there is the recognition of the limits of self-knowledge. The Eternal Father further reveals to her, "So, as I told you in the beginning, knowledge of the truth comes through self-knowledge; not pure self-knowledge, but seasoned (*condito*) and united with the knowledge of me in you

---

16 Thomas McDermott, OP. "Catherine of Siena's Teaching on Self-Knowledge," *New Blackfriars*, 88, (November 2007): 637-648, at 639.

17 Ibid., 640. "[F]or I am she who is not. And if I should claim to be anything of myself, I should be lying through my teeth. . . . For you alone are who are, and whatever being I have and every other gift of mine I have from you, and you have given it all to me for love, not because it was my due (*Dialogue*, 134, 273)." Quoted in ibid., 640

(*cognoscimento di me in te*)."[18] Hence, the second dimension of self-knowledge is the knowledge of God within or the knowledge of God's goodness within. McDermott notes that knowledge of God refers to a biblical notion referring to the awareness of a transcendent Other.[19]

From these revelations, Catherine speaks of two dimensions of self-knowledge, and she will often use images to capture the difference between them. One image is a well that includes earth and water. The earth symbolizes the first truth of the maxim: it highlights our own poverty. The living water symbolizes the second truth of God's goodness dwelling within us. McDermott states, "we pass through the dry earth of self-knowledge to the living water of knowledge of God."[20]

The second image Catherine draws upon is that of a 'cell of two rooms' or a 'cell within a cell.' Self-knowledge of our own imperfection and creatureliness abides with the knowledge of God's life within us. To dwell in the cell of self-knowledge alone would lead to spiritual confusion. To dwell only in the cell of the knowledge of God would lead to 'presumption.' We must dwell in both cells. "The existence of a second dimension of self-knowledge conveys the fact that knowledge of self invariably includes knowledge of God (and his goodness) in oneself, '[j]ust as the fish is in the sea and the sea in the fish.'"[21]

According to McDermott, Catherine's view of self-knowledge comes to maturity in the image of the *peaceful sea*. Therein one is attracted to the beauty of the sea (God) and in gazing upon its beauty one sees one's own image in the sea. Importantly one is drawn not to love the image reflected by the sea but to love the sea itself and to this one could add all its creatures. In doing so, one increasingly becomes aware of one's own imperfections in correspondence with this awareness of one's own love.[22]

Admittedly, the self-knowledge that Catherine speaks about, especially in the maxim, is not the philosophical knowledge one acquires when one makes one's own conscious operations the object of one's intentional consciousness. Indeed, she is speaking about the knowledge of our own imperfections and moral limitations, perhaps along the

18 Cited in ibid, 641.

19 Ibid., 641, n. 19.

20 Ibid., 641.

21 Ibid., 643, quoting *Dialogue* 112, 211.

22 Ibid., 644.

lines of what Ignatius calls for in the *examine*. However, the two are not unrelated if one recalls the comments by Lonergan in an archival letter to Thomas O'Malley where he declares a transposition of the Ignatian *examination of conscience* to that of the *examination of consciousness* which follows, one could surmise, from the "anthropological turn" in the third stage of meaning.[23]

I will explore the specifically Ignatian contribution to a fourth stage of meaning below, but for now I would suggest that there is an analogy to be drawn in the doctrine of self-knowledge in Catherine, which helps us to understand the transition from the third to a fourth stage of meaning. As has been suggested, this transition has been marked by a transcendental exigence that moves the subject beyond interiorly differentiated consciousness to the world of the Other, both vertically and horizontally, as being-in-relation and in love. The mystical revelations of Catherine reveal that the entire Western tradition of philosophy that begins with the Socratic maxim 'know thyself' is not in vain although of itself it is incomplete. The revelation from the Eternal Father tells Catherine that 'pure self-knowledge' is not sufficient; there is the need to recognize 1) that she is completely dependent upon God and nothing without him, and 2) that the image of God or God's goodness dwells within her. The self-knowledge of the philosophers is transcended and even completed by this twofold realization. Analogously, we can compare this to the history of Western philosophy that culminates in the third stage of meaning.

I believe that Lonergan's argument in *Insight* is the appropriate response to and completion of the philosophical turn to the subject, at least epistemologically, as an attempt to 'know thyself' more adequately through the turn to one's interiority and one's conscious operations. Lonergan's *Insight* crests on chapters 9 and 10 and the self-affirmation of the knower in chapter 11, i.e., the knowing in oneself that one is a knower. This affirmation corrects the aberrant and incomplete turns in the 'wrong' turns to the subject which have yielded what Michael Polanyi has described as the doctrine of doubt.[24] However, the self-knowledge yielded in the self-affirmation of the knower is not enough in and of itself. In fact, it is the beginning of articulating the critical

---

23 Bernard Lonergan, "Letter to Thomas O'Malley," ed. Gordon Rixon, *Method: Journal of Lonergan Studies* 22/1 (Spring, 2002): 77-86, at 81.

24 Michael Polanyi, *Personal Knowledge* (London: Routledge & Kegan Paul, 1962), 269-272.

ground of one's knowing in which an epistemology, metaphysics, and ethics can be further established. Nevertheless, the transcendental exigence demands that we ask further questions that philosophers will not be able to answer. For example, philosophers raise the question 'why is there something and not nothing?,' but they cannot answer it without entering into either explicit or implicit theological speculations regardless of how adequate their answers may be.

The dynamic state of unrestricted loving is the basic fulfillment of our conscious intentionality. It re-orients human knowing and trans-values one's values with respect to one's family, one's neighbor and, unrestrictedly, with God. The habituation of this dynamic state into one's horizon of intentionality gives rise to religiously differentiated consciousness. However, this habituation rests upon a prior decision or a fundamental commitment wherein one chooses to love in return in response to the gift of love that has been freely given.

To summarize, the doctrine of self-knowledge in Catherine serves as an analogy to understand the transition from the third stage to a fourth stage of meaning wherein the self-knowledge of the affirming knower, which is the culmination of the turn to interiority in the third stage of meaning, of itself is incomplete. There is the further longing for, and encounter with, a transcendent Other who in turn re-orients our knowing and choosing in a fundamental way. This demands a committed response, the fruits of which are demonstrated in loving God with one's mind, heart, strength and the love of one's neighbor as oneself.

4. MEDIATION AND DIALOGUE

The fourth stage of meaning brings with it a new emphasis on mediation and dialogue where the mediation reflects a two-way relation or mutual self-mediation and such mediation contributes to a new method for interreligious dialogue.

The turn to vertical and horizontal alterity characterizing the fourth stage of meaning brings with it a heightened sense of relatedness to the Other and the need for a method in order to guide such relations. One cannot afford to isolate within oneself, on the one hand, or to try to strictly mediate oneself to another without consideration for the Other, on the other hand. Hence, while several factors converge to bring about a heightened need for dialogue in the fourth stage of meaning, the principle of mutuality, or non-biased mutual self-mediation[25], will be the principle for guiding such relations. I would like to say something about this as it pertains to inter-religious dialogue.

In the 1991 joint pontifical statement *Dialogue and Proclamation*, it is clear that dialogue is now to be considered a part of the mission of the church. Moreover, recently, Pope Benedict declared, "I repeat with insistence [that] research and interreligious and intercultural dialogue are not an option but a vital necessity for our time."[26] Therefore, the question is not whether dialogue is important; rather, the question is one of method. How do we carry out dialogue without compromising our religious identity or imposing our view upon another? I believe the method of dialogue is best represented by mutual self-mediation, but it will need a fuller component – discernment.[27] The heuristic structure for articulating the multifarious relations with the Other in- volves: 1) the recognition of mutual self-mediation, 2) the encounter of different types of differences in that relationship, and 3) the need to discern which differences are complementary, which are contradictory, and which are genetic. The interreligious engagement with the Other will be mutually enriching as well as mutually challenging. The iden- tification of genetic differences would highlight the higher integration of interreligious relating as well as clarify how religions are to relate with culture, including secular culture. That is, the fruit of authentic dialogue may give way to something greater than the sum of the dia- logue partners, that is, a fuller integration of what Lonergan implies as a 'new sacralization to be fostered'. In the authentic dialogue between people from other religions who are 'unrestrictedly in love' with the transcendent as understood from within their respective traditions, it is possible that a further difference will emerge – the genetic differ- ence, and with this perhaps, even a theology of theologies.[28] That is,

25 I am indebted to Robert Doran for the clarification of 'unbiased' mutual relations.

26 Pope Benedict, *Zenit News Service*, February 1, 2007.

27 I have developed this argument in two articles. See John Dadosky "The Church and the Other: Mediation and Friendship in Post-Vatican II Ro- man Catholic Ecclesiology," *Pacifica: Australian Journal of Theology* (Octo- ber, 2005): 302-322; and "Towards a Fundamental RE-Interpretation of Vatican II." *Heythrop Journal*, 49/5 (September, 2008): 742-63.

28 Dadosky, "Sacralization, Secularization, and Religious Fundamentalism"; Robert M. Doran, "Bernard Lonergan and the Functions of Systematic Theology," *Theological Studies* 59/4 (December 1998), 574.

there is the possibility of a genetic unfolding in such a manner hinted at by what Lonergan called a "new sacralization to be fostered."[29] The fruit of such sacralization would be the recognition of non-biased mutual self-mediation between religion and cultures in such a way as to issue in the promise of what Lewis Mumford calls a 'world cultural humanity,' that is, a global culture of 'citizens of the world' (*cosmopolites*) which is a development beyond the violence of totalitarian regimes and terrorist/counter-terrorist violence.[30]

In terms of interreligious dialogue, Lonergan's fascination with Whitson's *Coming Convergence of World Religions* anticipates a relationship, not of conformism or separate co-existence, but what Whitson calls convergence. For Whitson, the question of convergence concerns "not one *or* many, but one *and* many," and this seemingly "unresolvable paradox" contains the seeds of convergence.[31] The goal of such convergence is not a syncretization of religious belief systems but an integration and inter-relationship through the emergence of a common theological understanding. While a detailed analysis of Whitson's proposal is beyond the scope of this paper, one thing seems clear: This potential higher integration of interfaith relating would be an advance beyond the intolerance and triumphalism fostered by many religious fundamentalisms of our day.

Therefore, while there may be a broad agreement on the importance of dialogue in the current context of the Church, we have yet to tease out the methodological issues and realize the importance of discernment within this dialogue.

5. DISCERNMENT, DELIBERATION AND COMMITMENT

Before speaking to role of plurality and community in the fourth stage, it is necessary to say something about the role of discernment and commitment in such a stage. This new emphasis on dialogue and mutuality brings with it a fresh problem that has not existed historically within the Church. Once the Church recognizes that it has mutual relations with the Other, a fresh problem occurs. How does

---

29 See Bernard Lonergan, "Sacralization and Secularization," 265.

30 See Lewis Mumford, *The Transformations of Man* (New York: Harper and Row, 1956), Chapters 7 and 8.

31 Whitson, *Coming Convergence of World Religions*, 23-26.

one distinguish between the different types of differences that one encounters in the dialogue with the Other? Naïve approaches to dialogue assume that differences are complementary or that there really are no differences. But, in fact, many differences are contradictory, and some of those might even be the difference between good and evil. The wisdom of the Ignatian tradition reminds us that we can be deceived, and so the rules of discernment ensure our path in the midst of the darkness of desolation and confusion. For example, in 1985 the Synod of Bishops in their *Final Report* admitted that it was their own lack of discernment to distinguish between the Vatican Council's call to openness to the world, on the one hand, and the suspicion of the world, on the other hand, which led falsely to the perception that the Church was a pure institution.[32]

The idea of a mutual relationship with the world is certainly not universal to Christian theology: it would have hardly been envisaged by John's Gospel. But Ignatius' ability 'to find God in all things' is not naïve because his affirmation of the world goes hand-in-hand with the practice of discernment. This might also have enabled the Jesuit order to chiefly avoid participation in the Inquisition, a legacy the Dominicans did not escape. It is discernment that will be necessary for dialogue with the Other because discernment allows us to distinguish between the different types of differences we meet within the dialogical encounter. In contrast, undifferentiated consciousness fails to recognize these distinct types of differences so it tends to fall back on either a naïve acceptance of the Other, or its opposite, a default stance of suspicion.

I have argued elsewhere that the affirmation of mutuality – an unprecedented development in the Church's self-understanding at Vatican II – is Ignatian in spirit. It is an ecclesiology of friendship.[33] It addresses ecclesial relations *ad extra* – with the Other. This affirmation was pre-figured by the non-systematic divergences of the successful methods of Matteo Ricci and Robert de Nobili in their engagement with 16th century Chinese and Indian cultures. The subsequent Jesuit suppression would thwart the attempts of mutual engagement for years to come.

---

32 Extraordinary Synod of 1985, *The Final Report*, I, 4.

33 See Dadosky, "Towards a Fundamental RE-Interpretation of Vatican II".

The model of mutual engagement with cultures and religions pioneered by these two 16th century Jesuits flows naturally from the spirituality of the *Exercises*. Indeed, the engagement with the *Spiritual Exercises* contains the recognition of mutuality and the principles of discernment in order to guide such mutuality.

In terms of how the *Spiritual Exercises* demonstrate both mutual horizontal and vertical alterity, I turn to the famous essay by Roland Barthes titled "Loyola".[34] This essay unlocks an important hermeneutical key in the theology of the *Exercises*, one that demonstrates the principle of mutuality at the heart of the *Exercises*. That is, one finds in the dynamic of the practice of *Spiritual Exercises* an interplay of horizontal and vertical alterity as the exercitant moves towards a fundamental commitment and prepares to live out that response subsequently.

Barthes examines the *Spiritual Exercises* in terms of its multiple 'texts' or layers of meaning reflected in the traditional four senses of scripture: literal, semantic, allegorical, and anagogic. Each text contains an interlocution between a donor, or sender, and receiver. In the literal text, Ignatius communicates with the director, didactically. Although Barthes does not state this, it already presupposes a previous encounter of Ignatius, one of vertical alterity in which the Exercises were developed within the laboratory of Ignatius' own psyche and interiority during his personal communicative encounter with the Divine. In the semantic text, the director communicates with the exercitant in the directives to the exercises. In the allegorical, the exercitant communicates with the Divinity through the imagination of the prayer periods. Finally, in the anagogical is the communication of the Divinity to the exercitant.

We have in this interlocution of multiple texts of the *Spiritual Exercises* an interplay between sender and receiver both pertaining to vertical and horizontal alterity – horizontal in the communication between Ignatius and the director and between the director and exercitant. Vertical alterity exists in the exercitant's communication with the Divine and vice versa. In the anagogic text, the Divinity communicates with the exercitant, providing a direction which orients the exercitant during the fourth week to live out the commitment made during the

---

34 Roland Barthes, *Sade, Fourier, Loyola*, trans. Richard Miller (New York: Hill and Wang, 1976), 38-75. I am grateful to my student Guia Sambonet for bringing this article to my attention.

second week with the election. Indeed this is all very rich and worthy of further study; for now, I wish to emphasize only that mutuality is grounded by the sender-receiver interplay in each of the texts of the *Exercises*. I shall turn to the importance of discernment and commitment in this process.

The election, that precipice in which one chooses vertical alterity and to live out of the unrestricted being-in-love which is the animating principle of that alterity, can be clouded by desolation and deception. Such deception can come from another person, from one's own ego and weaknesses, or from 'the Enemy.'

Doran has helpfully clarified Lonergan's fourth level of operations, *decision*, by drawing on what Ignatius describes as the three times of election.[35] The first time involves an immediate grasp of value where one's path is clear, almost as given directly and immediately by the Divinity. In the second time of election, one's feelings may conflict, prompting discernment of the various pulls of one's intrasubjective affectivity in order to discern properly the voice of the Divinity or, in the words of Lonergan, to discern true value from the apparent value. Here Ignatius has helpfully set out rules for the discernment of spirits in order to discover the true voice of the Divinity. In the third time of election, the affectivity is flat, one could say, in that one is neither pulled strongly in one direction or another. As a result, the exercitant draws up a list of pros and cons with respect to the election and chooses accordingly towards the greater weighted list.

Doran applies this process to Lonergan's fourth level of operations and in so doing has recovered an important hermeneutic for Lonergan's theory of intentional consciousness. This analysis is also pertinent for speculation about a fourth stage of meaning. The latter, as we have stated, will require discernment in order to acknowledge and clarify the different types of differences that one encounters within the intersubjective relations, horizontally. However, because discernment pertains to deliberation at the fourth level of operations, it will also pertain to a fundamental self-constitutive choice and commitment. In other words, the dynamic state of being-in-love in an unrestricted manner is sustained by a commitment on the part of the beloved. Within the context of one's faith tradition, this means that one has to

---

35 Robert M. Doran, "Ignatian Themes in the Thought of Bernard Lonergan: Revisiting a Theme that Deserves Further Reflection," *Journal of the Lonergan Workshop* 19 (2006): 83-106.

discern the true spirit within it from the aberrant or outmoded teachings within that tradition. Such questioning marks the difference between, to use Kierkegaard's taxonomy, the believers in religion A and
those in the more authentic religion B. For Kierkegaard, those in religion A were like the nominal Danish Christians of his day who were
not really committed to Christianity in their hearts but rather only in
name as expected by the State.[36]

6. PLURALITY AND COMMUNITY

In this final section, I venture two final speculations about the
fourth stage of meaning pertaining to plurality and community. Some
things have already been said concerning plurality and the Christian's
engagement with Other religions. Moreover, while community is a
broad notion, I limit my comments to community as the Church's self-
understanding emerging from Vatican II as a community of believers
(*ad intra*) and in relation to the Other (*ad extra*) in friendship.

6.1 PLURALITY

We can deduce that just as interior consciousness and philosophy
are inextricably linked to a critical exigence for Lonergan, so faith and
its expression in religious beliefs and practices are inextricably linked
to a transcendental exigence. In this way, we can postulate that where
the third stage of meaning calls for a critical appropriation of one's
consciousness, the fourth stage of meaning would entail a critical appropriation of one's own faith tradition. Such appropriation would
be spearheaded by the questions that one encounters when learning
about and living out of one's faith tradition.

The unrestricted desire to know is foundational to Lonergan's entire
philosophy. Questions that arise naturally from one's curiosity cannot
simply be brushed aside. If serious questions arise within a believer
concerning his/her faith tradition, the questions must be allowed to
be raised and taken seriously. The person as unrestrictedly in love
must be willing to critically enquire into one's own tradition in order
to make it his or her own, that is, to appropriate the tradition to oneself. Moreover, the principles of discernment would go hand-in-hand
with this critical appropriation of one's faith tradition as two sides of
the same coin. I would add that the failure or refusal to critically ap-

36 See George Price, *The Narrow Pass: A Study of Kierkegaard's Concept of
Man* (London: Hutchinson, 1963).

propriate one's own faith tradition leads to a fundamentalism (where fundamentalism might be defined in Lonergan's terminology as a 'radical restriction of the unrestricted desire to know'). This perpetuates a refusal to question one's faith tradition. For Catholics, the critical appropriation of one's faith tradition would certainly bring a renewed emphasis and meaning to the sacrament of confirmation. It also means that, technically, there can be no 'fundamentalisms' in the fourth stage of meaning. However, just as the principles of discernment would be applied in the dialogical encounter with the Other, so they would also be applied to one's own faith tradition in order to avoid the two extremes Lonergan cautions against, 'the solid right' and 'the scattered left.'[37] In so doing, one can distinguish clearly between the authentic riches of the tradition and the distortions of it through human bias and sin. Hence, the fourth stage of meaning embraces plurality in a critical appropriation of one's faith tradition that transcends obscurantism and likewise resists fundamentalist attitudes while simultaneously enabling a fuller embrace of the Other.

6.2 COMMUNITY

In terms of community, I will limit my comments to the Church's self-understanding as it continues to develop in the wake of Vatican II. In 2007, the Congregation for the Doctrine of the Faith declared that Vatican II did not change or intend to change its doctrine of the Church, but "rather it developed, deepened and more fully explained it."[38] For the most part I would agree with this statement; however, I would argue that the major development in the Church's self-understanding has yet to be accounted for in a systematic ecclesiology. The debate surrounding the hermeneutics of Vatican II continues with respect to the significance of the Council. Nevertheless, what is unique about Vatican II, among other things, is that for the first time in its history the Church officially recognizes it has mutual relations with the Other. This is exemplified by the final chapter of *Gaudium et Spes* which is entitled "The Church and the World as Mutually Related."

---

37 Bernard Lonergan, "Dimensions of Meaning," in *Collection*, CWL Vol. 4, ed. F. Crowe and R. Doran (Toronto: University of Toronto Press, 1993), 245.

38 Congregation for the Doctrine of the Faith, "Responses to Some Questions Regarding Certain Aspects of the Doctrine of the Church", June 29, 2007.

Moreover, *Nostra Aetate* called for a relationship of mutuality between Muslims and Jews respectively. I have argued this point elsewhere; suffice it to say that the recognition of mutuality is a permanent achievement of Vatican II, and this mutuality is lived out in dialogue with the Other.[39]

In terms of the Church's self-understanding, one can speculate that a fourth stage of meaning will bring with it a transposition in terms of such understanding, *ad intra* and *ad extra*. In terms *ad intra*, the fourth stage of meaning will call for a critical appropriation of one's faith tradition so as to prevent obscurantism and the abuses of power related to undifferentiated consciousness and strict self-mediation. In terms of the Church's self-understanding *ad extra*, there will be the recognition of mutual relations with the Other, the recognition and identification of different types of differences, and the principles of discernment in order to identify and distinguish those differences properly.

I mentioned at the beginning of this article that Lonergan distinguished between self-mediation and mutual self-mediation, and while he did not explicitly ascribe to communities the latter type of mediation, Doran has helpfully clarified that it does belong to them.[40] Indeed, communities in and of themselves are not isolated groups but are constituted in part by their multifaceted relations *ad intra* and *ad extra*. From these insights, I have argued elsewhere that it is appropriate to speak of two conceptions of the Church, *ad intra* and *ad extra*, emerging from Vatican II. The *ecclesia ad intra* pertains to the authentic self-mediation of the Church in terms of her distinctive identity, mission, and goal within salvation history. Conversely, *ecclesia ad extra* pertains to the authentic mutually self-mediating conception of the Church. I have used the adjective 'authentic' in front of each conception in order to distinguish these from the aberrant forms that can flow from the distortions of each of these self-understandings respectively. In terms of the Church's self-mediating understanding, the distortion occurs when the relationship between the Church is construed as a one-way relationship with the Other. Historically, such strict self-mediation has led to the triumphalism, juridicism, and clericalism that were called into question at Vatican II. There is also a distortion that can follow from mutual relations if the approach to the Other is naïve

39 Dadosky, "Towards a Fundamental RE-Interpretation of Vatican II," 742-63.

40 Robert Doran, *What is Systematic Theology?*, 45, 57-58.

and does not acknowledge that differences exist and/or fails to distinguish the different types of differences. Therefore, the ecclesiology of friendship is also based on a method of relating with the Other and must include mutual self-mediation, the different types of differences, and discernment in order to distinguish those differences.

To conclude, there are two basic ecclesial understandings emerging at Vatican II. The first, *communio*, has been affirmed by the bishops at the Extraordinary Synod of 1985 and recognized by various other officials and theologians. The second speaks to the Church's relations *ad extra* and accounts for the Church's mutual relations with the Other. It refers to an ecclesiology of friendship, and it complements the *ecclesia ad intra*, or communion ecclesiology of Vatican II. These two ecclesial understandings are complementary of each other, and their unity is grounded in the visible mission of the Son as it ensures the unity within the mystical body of Christ (communion) and the mission of the Spirit who is greeted in the encounter with the Other in the fellowship of the Spirit (friendship). Moreover, there is a sense in which these two conceptions of Church interpenetrate so that mutuality can be incorporated and integrated into the life of the Church's self-mediating identity, *ad intra*.[41] Likewise, the self-mediating identity is fully present within mutual encounters with the Other and represents the integrity and authentic spirit of the tradition. In this way, the identity is not compromised within a dialogical encounter with the Other.

The perichoresis of the divine persons in the life of the Trinity serves as the analogy for understanding the dynamic relationship between the two dimensions of the Church as self-mediating and as mutually self-mediating. One can say there is a sense that the missions of the Son and the Spirit are inextricably intertwined together within the life of the Church and invisibly outside of the explicit Church. The two basic conceptions of Church may speak to the both of these.

7. CONCLUSION

I have been arguing for the possibility of a fourth stage of meaning based on Lonergan's suggestion of a transcendental exigence in his chapter "Meaning" in *Method in Theology*. I have drawn on the five themes that Doran speculates need to be developed in Lonergan's

---

41 See John Dadosky: "The Official Church and the Church of Love in Balthasar's Reading of John: An Exploration in Post-Vatican II Ecclesiology," *Studia Canonica*, 41 (2007): 453-471.

thought: community, dialogue, otherness, mediation, and plurality. I hope to have demonstrated that the fruits of a fourth stage of meaning will speak to such themes. I suspect that these themes will be included in the systematic theology Doran not only envisions, but for which he continually labors. He is not alone in these endeavors.

THE EMERGENCE OF A SYSTEMATICS OF RELIGIOUS DIVERSITY: CONTRIBUTIONS FROM ROBERT M. DORAN

Darren Dias, OP

UNIVERSITY OF ST. MICHAEL'S COLLEGE, TORONTO

> The question of the 'other religions' can no longer be left
> until the end of a Christian systematic theology but
> should enter at the very beginning[1]
> —David Tracy

I. INTRODUCTION

Religious diversity, the simultaneous presence of multiple religions, has become a topic of sustained and serious reflection in recent years in theological circles, in the wider academy, and in the pluralistic societies in which we live.[2] The task of constructing a systematic theology that includes from its inception, and at least heuristically or anticipatorily, a consideration of the world's religions and their relationships is one of the most pressing issues facing theology today. Robert Doran's proposal for a unified field structure offers systematic theology a mechanism to appropriate, organize, and direct the emerging meanings and significance of religious diversity into the life and history of the church.

---

1 David Tracy, "Christianity in the Wider Context: Demands and Transformations," *Religion and Intellectual Life* 4 (1987): 8.

2 For examples, see Terrence W. Tilley, *Religious Diversity and the American Experience: A Theological Approach* (New York: Continuum, 2007); David Basinger, *Religious Diversity: A Philosophical Assessment* (Burlington: Ashgate, 2002); Gilles Paquet, *Deep Cultural Diversity: A Governance Challenge* (Ottawa: University of Ottawa Press, 2008).

2. DIFFERENCE IN CONVERSATION

One of the central features of the current context for doing theology is the acknowledged reality of diversity and plurality whether
religious, cultural, linguistic, political, sexual, biological, ecological,
etc. While David Tracy affirms that "Plurality is a fact,"[3] he also draws
a distinction between the facticity of this affirmation and the subsequent task of its evaluation.

Diversity, plurality, otherness, and related terms and concepts are
predicated upon a basic notion that differences exist. In general, writes
M. Shawn Copeland, two understandings of difference are currently
operative. The first is a common sense approach where "difference in-
sinuates not merely variance, but deviation, division, discrepancy, discord, incongruity, incompatibility, inconsistency, anomaly, contrariety,
aberration, and misunderstanding."[4] An alternate understanding is
hard-won but rewarding where "difference carries forward the struggle
for life in its uniqueness, variation and fullness; difference is a celebra-
tive option for life in all its integrity, in all its distinctiveness."[5] The
former understanding results in a negative evaluation of difference and
diversity as something to be overcome in favour of some kind of unity
(read: uniformity). The latter "challenges us to overcome the societal
conditioning that would have us ignore our differences or treat them
with suspicion or contempt, arrogance or conceit. Difference instigates
a new pedagogy by which to educate ourselves critically about ourselves, about 'other' and different women [people, religions, cultures],
about our inter-relations."[6]

Difference is too important to be reified or reduced into a category
that functions like Aristotle's *hyle* or Lonergan's empirical residue, as

3 Tracy, "Christianity in the Wider Context," 8.

4 M. Shawn Copeland, "Difference as a Category in Critical Theologies for
   the Liberation of Women," in *Feminist Theology in Different Contexts*, ed.
   Elisabeth Schussler Fiorenza and M. Shawn Copeland (Maryknoll: Orbis
   Books, 1996), 143.

5 Copeland, "Difference as a Category in Critical Theologies for the Liberation of Women," 143.

6 Copeland, "Difference as a Category in Critical Theologies for the Liberation of Women," 146.

it does for some postmodern theorists of difference.[7] Such a function, writes Frederick Lawrence, "stands outside the context of intelligibility," and thus is a contingency without a cause.[8] Difference is the condition of possibility for dialectical and dialogical encounter as well as interdependence and mutuality among peoples, cultures, and religions. Difference need not function as a barrier to relationality, "an unbridgeable and absolute chasm,"[9] or as a concept that reduces otherness to really just the same, where "under the banner of difference, the 'same' secretly rules."[10] Difference is not absolute and outside the context of intelligibility but relational and relative, meaningful and intelligible.

It is through "conversation" that differences are neither reified nor reduced and that their relational and relative identity can be navigated and negotiated. Conversation demands some "hard rules": accuracy and rigour, respectful listening and spirited debate, confrontation and conflict, and the willingness to change.[11] It provides the opportunity to better understand and account for differences. According to John Dadosky, religious differences may be contradictory differences that challenge conversation partners to change, or they may be complementary and mutually enriching, or else differences may be genetically related, reflecting differentiations in the one Divine plan.[12] Tracy describes conversation as a strategy for recognizing and appreciating the positive potential of difference: "where the question or subject matter is allowed to 'take over,' we learn to abjure our constant temptation to control all reality by reducing all difference to the 'same' (viz., what 'we' already believe)…we learn to allow the other, the different to become other *for us*."[13] Through conversation, differences are better understood

---

7 Frederick Lawrence, "The Fragility of Consciousness: Lonergan and the Postmodern Concern for the Other," *Theological Studies* 54 (1993): 82.

8 Lawrence, "The Fragility of Consciousness," 82.

9 James B. Wiggins, *In Praise of Religious Diversity* (New York: Routledge, 1996), 13.

10 Tracy, "Christianity in the Wider Context," 12.

11 Paul Mojzes, "The What and How of Dialogue," in *Interreligious Dialogue: Voices from a New Frontier*, ed. M. Darrol Bryant and Frank Flinn (New York: Paragon House, 1989), 19.

12 John D. Dadosky, "Toward a Fundamental Theological Re-interpretation of Vatican II," *The Heythrop Journal* XLIX (2008): 747.

13 Tracy, "Christianity in the Wider Context," 18.

and new possibilities arise: the recognition of the Other as a possible mode-of-being-in-the-world that is different from one's own as well as indicative of an alternate way of being-in-the-world for oneself.

Recognizing alternate ways of being-in-the-world both as *different from* one's own and *possible for* one's self is the existentially transformative aspect of conversation. Through conversation "we develop better ways as selves, as communities of inquirers, as societies, as cultures, as an inchoately global culture to allow for more possibilities to enrich our personal and communal lives."[14] The rules of conversation encourage the establishment of authentic community that struggles "to understand common and different experiences; to interrogate those differences, commonalties and different experiences rigorously; to reach common judgments; to realize and sustain interdependent commitment. As community in difference is a hard-won achievement, so too is difference in community."[15] The possibilities emerging from inter-religious conversations are in ways of relating to God and one another, in understanding the nature of these relationships, and in what they disclose about the divine in history, in the possibility of community rooted in diversity.

3. HISTORICAL APPROACHES TO OTHER RELIGIONS

The simultaneous presence of many religions is not a new fact, but understanding, evaluating and responsibly engaging with this reality takes on new meanings and directions in a postmodern world. From its beginnings, Christianity has had complex relationships with the Jewish community in which it was born and with the Greco-Roman culture in which it grew. Relationships were marked variously by exclusion and persecution but also by continuity and inculturation and eventually a growing sense of uniqueness and privilege as Christianity became the official religion of the Roman Empire. Once firmly ensconced in the religious, social, cultural, and political fabric of Europe, the Christian Church believed itself to be the sole conduit of grace and salvation and engendered the confident declaration, "Outside the Church, no salvation."

---

14 Tracy, "Christianity in the Wider Context," 9.

15 Copeland, "Difference as a Category in Critical Theologies for the Liberation of Women," 149.

With the intensification of European imperialism in the 16th century, Christendom faced a new challenge: the world was much more
expansive than previously imagined and the majority of its inhabitants
were not members of the Church. In light of the teaching "Outside
the Church, no salvation," theories abounded to reconcile the salvific
love of God with the fact that most of humanity had neither heard
nor accepted the Gospel.[16] One theory held that those on the road to
salvation secretly and unknowingly desired baptism and were, therefore, implicitly members of the Church. Another theory was that the
possibility of salvation by accepting Jesus could be offered to non-
Christians immediately before their deaths in a supernatural death-
bed intervention. Still another was that the opportunity to accept the
Gospel would be afforded at the final judgement. All these theories
shared the belief that membership in the body of Christ was necessary for salvation and that the content of non-Christian religions was
deficient and inferior.

Christian theology, praxis, and missiology developed from within
the mindset of Western colonialism that repressed, often violently and
irreparably, other cultures (non-European) and other religions (non-
Christian). Western Christianity constructed a non-factual, imagined
religious Other: "a projection of ... fears, hopes and desires," the contrasting image, idea, personality, experience of the Western self-imag-
ination.[17] The stories of the religious Other have been either excluded
or subsumed into the meta-narrative of Western culture, reduced to
mere accidentals of Christian history and theology. Attempts to sup-
press diversity in favour of a single culture and religion lasted well into
the last days of official colonialism in the mid-twentieth century, and
its effects are still evident today.

Various approaches to religious diversity have developed since
Vatican II when the language of "Outside the Church, no salvation"
disappeared from official literature, and Roman Catholic Christians
were charged with establishing positive relationships with non-Chris-

---

16 For a history of theological opinions regarding the salvation of non-
   Christians, see Francis A. Sullivan, *Salvation Outside the Church: Teaching
   the History of the Catholic Response* (Eugene, OR: Wipf and Stock Publishers, 2002), 63-103.

17 David Tracy, *Dialogue with the Other: The Inter-Religious Dialogue* (Louvain: Peeters Press, 1990), 49.

tians.[18] Since then theological discussions around religious diversity have been circumscribed by issues of Christology and ecclesiology as they relate to questions of soteriology. Approaches to religious diversity have resulted in three principal and general typologies:[19] the exclusivist typology that holds an ecclesiocentric paradigm for salvation with Jesus Christ as the exclusive and constitutive way of salvation; the inclusivist typology that holds Jesus Christ as the constitutive but not exclusive way (with differing views on the role of the Church in the explicitation of divine grace); and the pluralist typology that holds Jesus Christ as either normative but not constitutive of salvation or perhaps as one of many saving figures. These typologies or a combination thereof permit theologians to speak of Christocentric, theocentric, regnocentric, and pneumatocentric theories of salvation upon which models that order Christianity within the wider history of religions are constructed.[20]

Indian theologians involved in interfaith encounters maintain that these typologies "do not make sense" in the context of the Indian subcontinent.[21] Felix Wilfred claims that these theological discussions are "a debate of Western factions" that cannot be meaningfully transposed easily to other cultural contexts.[22] A document produced at the 1989 Annual Meeting of the Indian Theological Association highlights the limitations of approaches that issue "from a monoreligiocultural society and a mere academic and speculative point of view."[23] The Indian theologians suggest that Christians, from their unique faith perspective, should strive to "understand the purpose and meaning of the

---

18 *Nostra Aetate*, 5.

19 J. Peter Schineller, "Christ and Church: A Spectrum of Views," *Theological Studies* 37 (1976): 545- 66.

20 Examples of these models are the replacement, fulfillment, mutuality, and acceptance models as enumerated by Paul F. Knitter, *Introducing Theologies of Religions* (Maryknoll, NY: Orbis Books, 2002).

21 Aloysius Pieris, "An Asian Paradigm: Interreligious Dialogue and Theology of Religions," *Month* 26 (1993): 130.

22 Felix Wilfred, "Some Tentative Reflections on the Language of Christian Uniqueness: An Indian Perspective," *Pro Dialogo Bulletin* 85/86 (1994): 57.

23 Indian Theological Association, "Towards an Indian Christian Theology of Religious Pluralism," quoted in Jacques Dupuis, *Toward a Christian Theology of Religious Pluralism* (Maryknoll: Orbis Books, 2002), 199.

wonderful religious variety around us and its role and function in the attainment of salvation."[24]

To this effect, theologians such as Jacques Dupuis, Gavin D'Costa, and S. Mark Heim[25] have attempted to transcend the limitations of these various typologies in an approach to religious diversity that retrieves the place of the Trinity in Christian theologizing. However, they do so in a combination of the Christological-soteriological typologies. For example, Dupuis calls for a "pluralistic inclusivism" or "inclusive pluralism;"[26] Heim argues as a "convinced inclusivist."[27] Thus, while they outline a schema for a trinitarian understanding of salvation, they "do not offer a full-scale Trinitarian programme" for understanding religious diversity in history.[28]

The theological approaches to religious diversity that proved useful in the wake of Vatican II no longer suffice if they are circumscribed by discussions of Christology and soteriology because they are unable to integrate the data of diversity gleaned throughout the past forty years of inter-religious relationships. These approaches are rooted in a theoretical theology – how non-Christians are saved (or not saved) in relation to Jesus Christ. Lonergan's methodical theology and its development by Robert Doran respond to the contemporary challenge that aims at understanding the meaning of religious diversity. Doran's unified field structure provides the necessary mechanism to appropri-

---

24 Ibid.

25 See Gavin D'Costa, *The Meeting of Religions and the Trinity* (Maryknoll, NY: Orbis Books, 2000); Gavin D'Costa, "Christ, the Trinity and Religious Plurality," in *Christian Uniqueness Reconsidered*, ed. Gavin D'Costa (Maryknoll: Orbis Books, 1990); S. Mark Heim, *The Depth of the Riches, A Trinitarian Theology of Religious Ends* (Cambridge: Wm. B. Eermans Publishing, 2001); Jacques Dupuis, SJ, *Toward a Christian Theology of Religious Pluralism* (Maryknoll, NY: Orbis Books, 2002); Jacques Dupuis, SJ, *Jesus Christ at the Encounter of World Religions*, trans., Robert R. Barr, (Maryknoll, NY: Orbis Books, 1991); Jacques Dupuis, *Christianity and the Religions: from Confrontation to Dialogue*, trans. Phillip Berryman (Maryknoll, NY: Orbis, 2002).

26 Jacques Dupuis, *Christianity and the Religions, From Confrontation to Dialogue*, trans. Phillip Berryman (Maryknoll: Orbis Books, 2001), 255.

27 Heim, *The Depth of the Riches*, 8.

28 Veli-Matti Karkkainen, *Trinity and Religious Pluralism* (Burlington, VT: Ashgate, 2004), 7.

ate and integrate the experience of inter-religious encounter and the insights of other religions into the life and meaning of the Church. It offers both the structural element and the theological content that a systematics of religious diversity requires: a trinitarian core found in Lonergan's four-point hypothesis and an explanatory, synthetic theory of history poised to understand stages and sequences of meaning past, present and future.

4. THE UNIFIED FIELD STRUCTURE

A systematics of religious diversity requires a heuristic that can accommodate, organize, and integrate new data gleaned in the encounter of the world's religions. A heuristic that takes into account the reality of other religions "at the very beginning"[29] is open to ongoing development. In the task of constructing a systematics of religious diversity, the doctrine of the Trinity plays a decisive role as *the* Christian doctrine of God. In the words of the *Catechism of the Catholic Church*:

> The mystery of the Most Holy Trinity is the central mystery of Christian faith and life. It is the mystery of God in himself. It is therefore the source of all the other mysteries of faith, the light that enlightens them. It is the most fundamental and essential teaching in the "hierarchy of truths of faith." The whole history of salvation is identical with the history of the way and the means by which the one true God, Father, Son, and Holy Spirit, reveals himself to men "and reconciles and unites with himself those who turn away from sin."[30]

The central mystery of the Christian faith, the doctrine[31] of the Trinity, is found latently in scripture, in more developed and explicit conciliar statements and dogmatic definitions, and in theological doctrines that "put order and coherence" to the tradition "and have been received as either entering into or explicating the meaning constitutive of the community."[32] The psychological analogy is an example of a

---

29 Tracy, "Christianity in the Wider Context," 8.

30 *Catechism of the Catholic Church* (1995) no. 234.

31 On what constitutes doctrines see Lonergan, *Method in Theology*, 295-297.

32 Robert M. Doran, *What Is Systematic Theology?* (Toronto: University of Toronto Press, 2005), 28. On why the psychological analogy for understanding the Trinity may be considered a 'theological doctrine' see 28-40.

'theological doctrine' regarding the Trinity. Peter Phan postulates that "the doctrine of the Trinity can function as the architectonic principle with which to build the cathedral of faith, or to vary the metaphor, as the thread to weave all the Christian doctrines into a patterned tapestry."[33]

Doran proposes a unified field structure that has as its "architectonic principle" the doctrine of the Trinity, understood through the psychological analogy, toward the construction of a contemporary systematics that "aims at an understanding of the religious realities affirmed by doctrines" that are constitutive in the meaning of the community.[34] Doran describes the unified field structure:

> The unified field structure would not be some finished system but an open heuristic set of conceptions that embraces the field of issues presently to be accounted for and presently foreseeable in that discipline or functional speciality of theology whose task it is to give a synthetic understanding of the realities that are and ought to be providing the meaning constitutive of the community called church.[35]

The unified field structure would not only be a summation of the current "dogmatic-theological" context that takes into account historical developments thus far, but also a heuristic for "an intelligent, faith-filled anticipation of where theology must go."[36]

According to Doran, a unified field structure would function in theology in a manner analogous to the periodic table in chemistry; it would "mediate the relation of *every* less comprehensive conception in the whole of systematics."[37] The unified field structure would be open to further development through systematic syntheses and transpositions "in the light of new questions and exigencies"[38] while simultaneously preserving its permanent achievements of the past. Doran states:

---

33 Peter C. Phan, *Being Religious Interreligiously, Asian Perspectives on Interfaith Dialogue* (Maryknoll NY: Orbis Books, 2004), 24.

34 Lonergan, *Method in Theology*, 349.

35 Doran, *What is Systematic Theology?*, 62.

36 Doran, *What Is Systematic Theology?*, 63.

37 Doran, *What Is Systematic Theology?*, 67.

38 Doran, *What Is Systematic Theology?*, 67.

Eventually, every system will give rise to questions that cannot be answered on the basis of the resources provided by that system. Every system is an open system, that is, one in which it is anticipated that questions will arise from within the system itself that the system is not able to answer, that will demand the move to a higher viewpoint perhaps a paradigm shift, before satisfactory hypotheses can be provided. Any system that claims not to be open in this way is an idol.[39]

The unified field structure provides the necessary heuristic for systematic theology to approach the question of religious diversity. Unlike approaches that are unable to take into account new questions and anticipate further developments, Doran's approach is inherently open to further developments because of its methodical and historical character.

Lonergan's four-point hypothesis[40] provides understanding of the doctrine of the Trinity according to the psychological analogy. Following Lonergan, Doran writes:

> The hypothesis differentiates the theorem of the supernatural into a set of connections between the four divine relations – what the tradition calls paternity, filiation, active spiration, and passive spiration – and created supernatural participations in those relations. Thus, (1) the secondary act of existence of the Incarnation, the assumed humanity of the Incarnate Word, is a created participation in paternity...In the immanent Trinitarian relations, the Word does not speak; the Word is spoken by the Father. But the Incarnate Word speaks. However, he speaks only what he has heard from the Father. Again, (2) sanctifying grace as the dynamic state of being in love is a created participation in the active spiration *by* the Father and the Son *of* the Holy Spirit, so that as the Father and the Son together breathe the Holy Spirit as uncreated term, sanctifying grace as created participation in the active spiration of Father and Son – that active spiration that is really identical with paternity and filiation taken together as one principle – 'breathes' some created participation in the same Holy Spirit. (3) The habit of charity is that created participation in the third person of the Blessed Trinity. And (4) the

---

39 Doran, *What Is Systematic Theology?*, 71-72.

40 Bernard J.F. Lonergan, *The Triune God: Systematics*, vol. 12 of Collected Works of Bernard Lonergan, trans. Michael Shields, ed. Robert M. Doran and H. Daniel Monsour (Toronto: University of Toronto Press, 2007), 471, 473.

light of glory that is the consequent created contingent condition of
the beatific vision is a created participation in the Sonship of the divine Word. And so the hypothesis enables a synthetic understanding of the four mysteries of the Trinity, the Incarnation, grace, and
the last things…There is in Lonergan's hypothesis a coordination
of the divine processions with the processions of word and love in
authentic human performance, a coordination that, in Lonergan's
beautiful words, almost brings God too close to us.[41]

The four-point hypothesis for understanding the trinitarian relations *ad intra* and *ad extra* provide the "core categories to which all
other categories must be referred"[42] but is not, according to Doran,
enough for the construction of a contemporary systematics. The other
constitutive ingredient is a theory of history.[43]

The four-point hypothesis indeed provides the core categories, but
it cannot account for and organize all theological categories that depend also on some theory of history without falsely reducing those
categories into the four-point hypothesis. Doran writes:

> The four-point hypothesis does not itself tell us anything about
> what the Incarnation and the Indwelling of the Holy Spirit have
> to do with historical progress and decline, whereas creation, revela-
> tion, redemption, the church, the sacraments, and Christian praxis
> cannot be understood apart from historical progress or decline.[44]

Doran's advancement of Lonergan's thought on history into a more
expansive explanatory theology of history is based on his development
of the interrelations of values.[45] These values are religious, personal,
cultural, social, and vital, and are located in the recurrent emanation
of the word of authentic value judgments and acts of love in human

41 Doran, *What Is Systematic Theology?*, 65; Lonergan, *The Triune God: Systematics*, 417.

42 Doran, *What Is Systematic Theology?*, 70. See also Robert M. Doran, "The Starting Point of Systematic Theology," *Theological Studies* 67 (2006): 750-776.

43 For an account of why the four-point hypothesis on its own is not enough to constitute a unified field structure, see Doran, *What Is Systematic Theology?*, 72-74.

44 Doran, *What Is Systematic Theology?*, 74.

45 Robert M. Doran, *Theology and the Dialectics of History* (Toronto: University of Toronto Press, 1990), 88-90.

consciousness (personal value) due to the grace of mission of the Holy Spirit (religious value). Religious value is the source of history-making, of progress through schemes of recurrence in realms of cultural, social, and vital values, and wherever genuine and authentic progress takes place, the Holy Spirit is present.[46] Personal and cultural transformation through relationships with other religions is measured according to a scale of values[47] in order to evaluate and direct the ongoing evolution in relational transformation. Doran writes:

> The combination of the four-point hypothesis with the theory of history thus enables us to relate Trinitarian theology, and even the theology of the immanent Trinity, directly to the process not only of individual sanctification but also of human historical unfolding. The discernment of the mission of the Holy Spirit thus becomes the most important ingredient in humankind's taking responsibility for the guidance of history.[48]

Doran names the "dialogue of world religions as a *principal arena* for the cross-cultural generation of world-cultural values."[49] Thus, grace is not linked exclusively to one or another individual religious tradition but to the network of inter-religious relationships: authentic community rooted in religious diversity.

Due to the divine missions, Christians can "*expect* to find meanings and values"[50] outside of a narrow conception of history precisely in what Christians consider other: non-Christian religions. Any attempts to domesticate otherness may be tantamount to extinguishing the Spirit. The theological shortcoming of Christianity's relationship with the religious Other has been an underdeveloped theology of the Spirit: "Failure on the part of the church to recognize the varieties of grace in history, the fact of the gift of the Holy Spirit beyond the boundaries of church affiliation, has resulted in some of the most con-

---

46 Doran, *What Is Systematic Theology?*, 77, 204-205.

47 There are five levels in the scale of values: first, vital, social, cultural, and personal which correspond respectively to the four levels of consciousness; the fifth level in the scale of values is religious and corresponds to a fifth level of consciousness relating to the dimension of love. See Doran, *Theology and the Dialectics of History*, 30-31, 88-90.

48 Doran, *What Is Systematic Theology?*, 77.

49 Doran, *What Is Systematic Theology?*, 193. Italics added.

50 Doran, *What Is Systematic Theology?*, 56.

spicuous mistakes in the mission of the church throughout the course of Christian history. These mistakes continue into our own day."[51]

5. NEW HISTORICAL VISTAS

Lonergan's trinitarian thought proposes a pneumatology in which the Spirit is God's love given as the first and foundational divine gift to all humanity. All subsequent divine initiatives in history, including the ensuing mission of the Son, take place within the context of the one divine plan revealed in the economy of salvation that begins and is in continuity with this first and foundational gift. Imitation of, and participation in, the divine life is made possible through the divine missions which are the eternal processions linked to contingent external terms and so located in creation and history. The gift of God's love, the Holy Spirit, floods our hearts and results in our being beings-in-love. According to Doran, being-in-love in an unrestricted manner is a created participation in the active spiration that is the Father and the Son in God. It is sanctifying grace. It flows from divine knowledge and love and not from human love. The gift of God's love and the horizon born of it that together constitute sanctifying grace ground the acts of loving that cumulatively coalesce into an ever more firmly rooted habit of charity. Therefore, sanctifying grace is the created graced analogue of the active spiration of the Father and Son while the habit of charity is the graced created analogue for the passive spiration that is the Holy Spirit.[52]

Neither the gift of God's love nor its apprehension in human living is conditioned by any particular culture or religion. As much as the gift is universal, so is the human "spiritual nature," the capacity to receive and respond to it.[53] This is evidenced in the myriad of responses to the divine found in the history of the world's religion. The same Spirit that breaks down barriers between different people – Jews and Greeks, slaves and free[54] – is the source of the positive moments of all the

---

51 Doran, *What Is Systematic Theology?*, 199.

52 Robert M. Doran, "Addressing the Four-Point Hypothesis," *Theological Studies* 68 (2007): 678-679.

53 Robert M. Doran, "Summarizing the Divine Relations: A Theological Contribution to Mimetic Theory," *Contagion: Journal of Violence Mimesis, and Culture*, vol. 14, (2007): 37.

54 1 Corinthians 12: 12-14

world's religions and reorients the "relation, attitude, and approach" to the religious Other.[55] Frederick Crowe asks, "How will our understanding of non-Christians as gifted with the Spirit affect our general attitude and relation to them?"[56] Christians need to examine their own attitudes and behaviours and make "agonizing reappraisals"[57] in the face of the Spirit-filled religious Other.

An understanding of religious diversity within a view of history structured by the threefold divine self-giving raises different questions from the past. They no longer centre around Christology and soteriology but are contextualized within some "total view of history"[58] in which the missions of the Spirit and the Son are given equal attention as both are intensely historical, the former being experienced and known through the data of sense, and the latter through the data of consciousness. Crowe enumerates some of these new questions: "What is God doing in the divine economy of the twofold mission, an economy that extends over all ages? What was God doing in past ages? What is God doing now? What can we discern of the possibilities the future holds and of the actualities God's intentions may have already determined for us?"[59]

Crowe outlines two approaches to this series of questions. Both approaches explore how human history is constituted and how freedom and responsibility are exercised in light of the divine missions. Both approaches affirm Doran's assertion that the Holy Spirit "becomes the most important ingredient in humankind's taking responsibility for the guidance of history."[60] The first approach is based on Lonergan's structure of history: progress, decline, and redemption. These are simultaneously present in varying degrees at any given moment,

---

55 Frederick E. Crowe, "Son of God, Holy Spirit, and World Religions," in *Appropriating the Lonergan Idea*, ed. Michael Vertin (Washington D.C.: The Catholic University of America Press, 1989), 325-326.

56 Crowe, "Son of God, Holy Spirit, and World Religions," 333.

57 Crowe, "Son of God, Holy Spirit, and World Religions," 334.

58 Frederick E. Crowe, "Lonergan's Universalist View of Religion," *Method: Journal of Lonergan Studies* 12 (1994): 174.

59 Frederick E. Crowe, SJ, *Christ and History, the Christology of Bernard J.F. Lonergan, 1935-1982* (Ottawa: Novalis, 2004), 218. See also "Lonergan's Universalist View of Religion," 174.

60 Doran, *What Is Systematic Theology?*, 77.

"though emphases may vary in different sequences, we are always progressing in some way, always in some degree declining, and equally always being redeemed."[61] This *synchronic* view of history perceives "the simultaneous presence among us of the many religions, each with its fidelity to the Spirit present in them (progress), each with its infidelity to the promptings of the Spirit (decline), and each being led to the ultimate end of all creation (redemption)."[62] This first approach has to do with the authenticity or inauthenticity of the various religions according to their own self-understanding and criteria to what Christians would call the promptings of the Holy Spirit.

The second approach to "some total view of history" is *diachronic* and refers to the structure of historical sequences: "sequences in meaning and expression, in social institutions and culture, in all that pertains to human living, and this, whether it be question of progress or question of decline."[63] In the diachronic scenario:

> God has seen fit to allow – and promote – the simultaneous existence of many religions[;] has God a 'plan' also for the sequences in the various roles of the various religions? Are some transient, and others meant to endure to the end, if there is to be an end? What is the rationale of the appearance at a particular time in the Judaic religion, when Augustus was Roman Emperor, of the birth of Jesus of Nazareth? Was the appearance of Jesus 'timed' not only in relation to Augustus but also in relation to the stage of development reached by the world religions?[64]

Such a view of history explores "the role of the Holy Spirit to the order of universal history" and asks, "How should we conceive of the overarching order of a universe when we give equal attention to the presence of Son and to the presence of Spirit?"[65] It explores the meaning of concrete events in the history of a particular religion as they may relate to the shared history of religions.

If initial reflection is on the divine initiative in history (the gift of the Spirit) then secondary reflection has to do with contingency and

---

61 Crowe, *Christ and History*, 219.

62 Crowe, *Christ and History*, 219.

63 Crowe, "Lonergan's Universalist View of Religion," 175.

64 Crowe, *Christ and History*, 219 and "Lonergan's Universalist View of Religion," 176.

65 Crowe, *Christ and History*, 220.

freedom. This is significant in thinking about the future and the role human decision plays in its constitution since "God has no will for tomorrow, or anything else that is not."[66] Crowe explains:

> If God's 'plan' is already in place for us, that is, in the 'already' of our 'now,' then to that extent we are no longer free. And if God has a determinate 'plan' in place for Christianity and the world religions, then we will let be what must be. But suppose God has no such plan, suppose that God loves a slow-learning people enough to allow them long ages to learn what they have to learn, suppose that the destiny of the world religions is contingent on what we all learn and do – say, on Christians being authentically Christian, Hindus being authentically Hindu, and so on – then responsibility returns to us with a vengeance, and the answer to the question of the final relationship of Christianity and the world religions is that there is no answer yet.[67]

The authenticity of each religion and what they learn from one another affects "the destiny of the world religions" and so the destiny of the world is contingent upon the "actual realization of future possibilities."[68] If divine interaction with human history were determinate in the form of a set plan, then not only would humankind not be free, but it would have no responsibility in the unfolding and construction of history. On the other hand, if there is no determinate plan for human history in place then meaning-making in the world and the direction history takes includes human responsibility. The Holy Spirit remains "the most important ingredient" in the construction of history.[69]

6. EMERGING POSSIBILITIES

The application of the unified field structure to the reality of religious diversity is a concrete development of the four emphases in

---

66 Crowe, "Lonergan's Universalist View of Religion," 178. For Lonergan there is no contingent decision on God's part without a created counterpart; for example, it is true to say that God creates only if the universe exists.

67 Crowe, "Lonergan's Universalist View of Religion," 178.

68 Donna Teevan, *Lonergan, Hermeneutics, & Theological Method* (Milwaukee: Marquette University Press, 2005), 151.

69 Doran, *What Is Systematic Theology?*, 77

Lonergan's notion of systematic theology.[70] First, systematics begins with those mysteries affirmed as doctrinal. The unified field structure has as its "architectonic principle" the doctrine of the Trinity, the central Christian God-doctrine affirmed in the Nicene-Constantinople creed. Secondly, the principal function of systematics is a hypothetical and analogical understanding of the mysteries of faith. The psychological analogy for understanding the consubstantial unity of the three-personed God necessitates a transposition of metaphysical categories derived from theoretical theology to a methodical theology grounded in interiority, in subjective existential states, from which the analogy is drawn. Next, as systematics proceeds in the way of teaching and not of discovery, the unified field structure calls for reflection on the historical and theological meanings regarding the doctrinally affirmed missions of the Son *and the Spirit* as equal, unique, non-superfluous, and complementary in the one divine plan conceived by the Father. Lastly, systematics moves beyond the descriptive to an explanatory history that seeks to understand the stages and sequences of meaning in the history of religious diversity.

In *What Is Systematic Theology?*, Doran examines the relationship between the systematic ideal and the reality of historical consciousness relevant to the unified field structure. He enunciates two methodological issues that have serious implications for understanding and organizing the data of religious diversity. The first posits that theology in contemporary culture[71] is an ongoing process. That later theology grasps better what an earlier theology grasps less reflects the emergence of higher viewpoints that are more inclusive and comprehensive and "call for a shift in the basic terms and relations."[72] These higher viewpoints are sometimes "occasioned by cultural developments that are relatively independent of theology, while at other times they are the fruit of deepened insight into the mysteries of faith themselves."[73] The emerging systematics of religious diversity is an example of a

---

70 Doran, *What Is Systematic Theology?*, 7-12.

71 In the older, classicist view of culture, theology is conceived of as a static, permanent achievement. Contemporary culture is empirical: "a set of meanings and values informing a common way of life." Lonergan, *Method in Theology*, 301.

72 Doran, *What Is Systematic Theology?*, 145.

73 Doran, *What Is Systematic Theology?*, 145.

higher viewpoint occasioned by recent postmodern and postcolonial cultural developments.

The second methodological issue is the anticipation of something new in the history of Christian constitutive meaning that results from "a historical exegesis that *no longer omits the accidentals but includes them in a synthetic manner*" toward "*a more concrete and comprehensive theology that considers and seeks to understand the economy of salvation in its historical development.*"[74] Such a task requires "a principle, something that is first in some order, that will make possible an understanding of religious and theological history that is not only narrative and descriptive but also synthetic, systematic, and explanatory."[75] The unified field structure provides this principle that anticipates something new in heuristic notions capable of relating the world's religions to one another, as an 'upper blade' that organizes, evaluates and integrates the data of diversity into Christian history and consciousness. Thus, differences in religious beliefs are no longer marginal accidentals in the history of Christianity but significant factors informing Christian constitutive meaning. What it means to be a Christian today cannot be ascertained without reflection on what it means to be Christian in a religiously diverse world.

The shift in terms and relations that results from a better grasp of the divine meaning in history reorients theological discussions previously circumscribed by the double foci of Christology and soteriology. A methodical theology grounded in conscious operations resolves debates related to causality into wider discussions about meaning. The recognition of the entry of divine meaning in history, outside the Judeo-Christian dispensation, and the discovery of this myriad of meanings in the encounter of religions, reveals the theological character of the actual situation of religious diversity. The typologies of exclusivism or pluralism no longer suffice because these respectively reify or reduce difference. Even the 'via media' of inclusivism captured in the famous notion of the 'anonymous Christian' incorporates the religious Other into a Christian framework, rendering the Other a deficient-same,

---

74 Bernard Lonergan, *Divinarum Personarum* (Rome: Gregorian University, 1959), 19, quoted in Doran, *What Is Systematic Theology?* Italics added in Doran's translation.

75 Doran, *What Is Systematic Theology?*, 147.

erasing differences through an evaluation of what is positive and salvific in the Other merely as an imperfect reflection of what is Christian.[76]

If different religions are not obstructions to the divine plan but constitutive elements in it, then in the intelligibility of historical process
what may otherwise have been considered "accidents" of history are
significant aspects in the discernment of how history is constituted.
Reflection on the stages and sequences of meaning in our shared history draws attention to what is theological about the contemporary
situation toward the construction of inter-religious communities of
shared meaning. The evolving and emerging meanings of religious
diversity, what they disclose about each religion singly and together,
and the appropriation of these meanings into the life and praxis of the
Church, reflect the ongoing process that is systematic theology. It is
from within the context of community-in-difference and difference-
in-community that a systematics of religious diversity emerges.

---

76 Jeanine Hill Fletcher, "As long as we wonder: possibilities in the impossibility of interreligious dialogue," *Theological Studies* 68 (2007): 533-534.

LONERGAN'S PHILOSOPHY OF ART: FROM VERBUM TO TOPICS IN EDUCATION

JOSEPH FLANAGAN, SJ
BOSTON COLLEGE

I. INTRODUCTION

Lonergan's first major publication, *Insight*, was written from a moving viewpoint, which implies that the meanings of the later chapters presume and incorporate the context of the earlier chapters. The same is true of all Lonergan's major writings so that to appreciate and correctly interpret later texts requires that the reader must have some understanding of the earlier writings. Lonergan's first major treatise on art was not composed until six years after he finished *Insight*, yet the foundational context for the treatise had already been established in a series of articles published under the title *Verbum: Word and Idea in Aquinas* published a number of years before *Insight*. As a result, to appreciate fully the wealth of meanings that were expressed in Lonergan's philosophy of art, it is necessary to go back to earlier writings and study how the context for his theory on art evolved. In the light of this reading of Lonergan, I will begin this paper by examining the *Verbum* articles where Lonergan lays the groundwork for his later work. In the second section, I will examine *Insight* and analyze from *Insight* Lonergan's notion of "patterns of experience" which set the context for his first explicit treatment of art. In the third section, I will examine the major developments that emerged in Lonergan's thinking during his research into phenomenology and existentialism. It was this research that facilitated Lonergan's ongoing shift from the scholastic language of faculty psychology to the language of intentionality analysis that was first explored in the philosophy of phenomenology. Finally, in the fourth section we shall see how this background of the earlier writings set the context for Lonergan's philosophy of art.[1]

2. KNOWING BY IDENTITY

In the fifth *Verbum* article, Lonergan makes a basic distinction and contrast between the cognitional theory of Aristotle and Plato. For Plato knowing is primarily a confrontation and presumes a duality between the knower and the known, which implies that knowing requires an added movement from knower to known. If knowing implies a movement, then, this leaves Plato with the problem that the subsistent idea of being cannot be both a knower and immutable. Plato struggles with this problem in the *Sophist*, whereas for Aristotle this is not a problem. For Aristotle confrontation is not an essential quality of knowing. Just the opposite, knowing is by act, identity, and perfection. In a perfect knower there would be no difference between the knower and the known. For Aristotle knowing does not presuppose a duality between knower and known; knowing is a perfection of the knower and the more perfect the knower is, the more perfect is the identity between knower and known. There is no need of the knower moving to or merging with the known, which means that Aristotle's unmoved mover can be both a perfect knower and immutable. However, Aristotle has a problem that Plato does not have.

If you assume with Plato that knowing assumes a duality and that knowing is by confrontation, then there is no major problem in knowing an object as an object; but if you assume with Aristotle that knowing is by act, identity, and perfection, then knowing another as other is a serious problem since knower and known are identical and, if identical, how can they be different and distinguishable? If the knower becomes the known, then how does the knower know this? Aristotle therefore has a serious problem with the objectivity of knowing, whereas Plato does not because he begins with a duality, a confrontation of knower and known. For Plato the knower and the known

---

1 I am dealing with the question of Lonergan's Philosophy of Art as articulated in *Topics in Education*, as it developed from his early writings up until 1959. To trace the further developments that took place up until the publication of *Method in Theology* would involve a second major paper. Collected Works of Bernard Lonergan, vol. 10, *Topics in Education*, ed. Robert M. Doran and Frederick E. Crowe (Toronto: University of Toronto Press, 1993).

are already distinct, and for the knower to become a known he or she must make contact with the known. The known for Plato is the idea or form, and that form is grasped or perceived by the knower. No doubt for Plato, as also for Augustine, knowing occurs through an inner vision of the idea or form, but that idea is distinct from the knower. For Aristotle, on the other hand, form is not an idea; it is an act and a perfection of the knower's own being. Knowing by identity makes the known one with the knower; that is why for Aristotle a perfect knower would be identical with perfect being. Aristotle's "unmoved mover" is unmoved because it contains all perfection and all act within itself. For Plato an "unmoved mover" would not be a knower since knowing involves a movement or contact with the known. For Plato knowing is what the mind does, but for Aristotle we do knowing because that is what we are. But how do we know that? If we are perfectly identical with whatever object we know, then, how can we be certain that we know that object? There are a number of ways this question may be answered, but for the purpose of this paper I will select Lonergan's distinction between immediately given experiences as opposed to the mediation of immediate experience through the various cognitional operations.

For Lonergan there are two quite different classes of data to be considered. There is the immediate sensible data that we mediate through our different language systems, and there is the immediate conscious data of our own operating subject. In the *Verbum* articles Lonergan focuses his attention on the conscious, cognitional operations of his own consciously operating self in order to appropriate and differentiate the different operating levels of his own knowing. A central discovery is the way his own wondering initiates and sustains the different operations, urging them on to their final objective of knowing being. But because the wondering, which underlies and directs the different but related operations of knowing, is unrestricted and because every judgment is a restricted affirmation, our wondering keeps recurring, seeking to understand and judge more and more about its ultimate objective, namely, being.

By focusing on the operations by which the subject knows, and putting aside the object or content that is known, Lonergan was able to make a basic distinction between the immediate object that is consciously intended in knowing and the mediating operations by which that object becomes understood and judged. This distinction revealed the fundamental problem in all knowing, namely, the tendency to assume that reality is known immediately before the mediating operations of wondering, understanding, and judging have taken place. Even more misleading and mistaken is the assumption that the subject doing the knowing and the sensible objects that are intended to be known are already and immediately known in the sense that their reality is known in their givenness, in their unmediated presence to our wondering. Furthermore, the conscious subject doing the knowing and the objects intended to be known are really different. The knowing subject is really different from the object to be known, and this difference is immediately known. The subject is real, the object is real, and there is a real difference between subjects and objects, and those three realities are immediately given. From these assumptions, the operations of wondering, understanding, and judging are primarily intended to confirm that the immediately given realities of subjects, objects, and differences are actually given and are not imagined or supposed. Such a set of assumptions is the exact opposite of what Lonergan proposed in the *Verbum* articles. For Lonergan the immediate awareness of your own consciously operating subject is not knowing yourself but merely experiencing or being aware of yourself. Awareness or consciousness is not knowing but a quality or characteristic that makes cognitional operations possible. As conscious you can begin to wonder or inquire into who you are and what you are, but unless you mediate your unmediated awareness of yourself by understanding and correctly judging, you cannot know your own reality. The same is true of the sensible objects that we speak about in ordinary language. Before we can name sensible objects such as persons, plants, and animals, we have to learn how to name and speak about them. Language mediates our ability to talk about sensible objects. Even more surprising is the need to mediate the immediately given differences between knowing subjects and known objects. We spontaneously sense that we are here and objects are out-there in front of us. However, sensing the difference between a knowing subject and the known objects is not knowing the real difference between subject and objects. Sensing differences is not knowing differences. The reality of differences, of subjects, or of objects, is known only by combining the three different and related operations of experiencing, and understanding, and reasoning or judging, their respective realities. These statements, which are based on the distinction between the immediate and mediated awareness, underscore and explain Lonergan's insistence that there is a basic difference between Plato and Aristotle's theory of knowing.

Plato's theory of knowing, as stated before, assumes a "duality between knower and known," and the knowing involves a subsequent movement from the knower to the known, thereby creating the problem of the bridge between subject and object. The same position leads Plato to assume that because we know ideas, these ideas must subsist. Aristotle, on the other hand, assumes that knowing begins with an identity of the subject with the object to be known and that the subsequent mediating of the immediate identity of knower and known reveals a limited identity of knower and known because our knowing is not a perfect and complete comprehension of reality but only a limited act or perfection. If we were perfect knowers in a perfect act, there would be no limit to our identity with reality, which is why Aristotle's perfect knower is not only a perfect knower but a perfect being. It is also why Aquinas could follow Aristotle in asserting that God is a perfect and complete act without any limit or potency. As one denies potency, one denies limit or distinction. The perfect knower is the perfect being and is identical with all the beings that can be. In human beings knowing is primarily a potency to know, and while our being is a knowing being, we are primarily beings by becoming more and better knowers. As just stated, this may sound like a difficult but assumable argument which would result in a shift from Plato's to Aristotle's and Aquinas's positions on knowing and its relation to being. The problem is much more difficult than it appears because, first, it involves understanding the sort of conversion that Plato described in the famous parable of the cave in the *Republic*, and second, it involves a conversion of the type that Lonergan describes in the fourteenth chapter of *Insight*. We need to identify the sources of these difficulties, which means it is necessary to move to our second section and describe this context as it is found in Lonergan's *Insight*.

3. PATTERNS OF EXPERIENCE

Our central topic is Lonergan's philosophy of art, and our first step in articulating Lonergan's position has been to explore Lonergan's cognitional theory as it was first articulated in the *Verbum* articles. The major methodological achievement of this work was to reverse the relation between metaphysics and cognitional theory. Traditionally metaphysics was first philosophy, epistemology was second philosophy, and cognitional theory was third philosophy. In this traditional context, metaphysical terms were extended and adapted to express epistemological and cognitional meanings. Why did Lonergan reverse the order? He did so for reasons of method, and method for Lonergan is a set of procedures that guide a knower toward his or her objective. The method does not guarantee results as a recipe or a set of rules would do, but it does make it more probable that in the long run the method will produce results.

Lonergan's method proposes that a metaphysical theory depends on and is determined by the assumed, epistemological theory, and the epistemological theory depends on the prior, assumed, cognitional theory. Lonergan agrees with Kant that metaphysical questions cannot be addressed until you have answered the prior epistemological question concerning the objectivity of knowing. But Lonergan points out that the way you answer questions about the objectivity of knowing depends on what you are presently assuming about what knowing itself is, and so Lonergan reasons that if you want to do philosophy in a methodical way, then, begin with the problem of knowing knowing, and then move on to the epistemological problem concerning the objectivity of knowing, and finally take up the metaphysical problems. This is the way Lonergan structured his text *Insight*.

The first eleven chapters focus on what a knower is doing when he or she is doing knowing, and then chapter twelve and thirteen take up the problem of the objectivity of knowing. Only in chapter fourteen does Lonergan begin dealing with a theory of metaphysics. The key to the book, then, is for the readers to appropriate what they are doing when they are knowing because that will determine what they assume objective knowing is, which in turn will ground their position on metaphysics.

In *Verbum* the major problem of knowing was formulated in the contrast between Plato's confrontational theory of knowing and Aristotle's theory of knowing by act or identity. In *Insight* Lonergan traces the roots of the problem of differences in philosophical positions on knowing to the different patterns of experience in which human subjects operate, and he identified five different patterns of experience. For the purpose of this paper I will consider four of these patterns: biological, aesthetic, practical, and intellectual.

As we have seen in the first section, Lonergan differentiated the activity of knowing into three distinct and dynamically oriented op-

erations of experiencing, understanding, and judging. These operations are consciously linked and dynamically oriented by the desire
to know which is revealed in the operation of wondering and which
directs these different activities of knowing to their ultimate objective of knowing what is real. Equally important, each of these three
operations involves three successive levels of consciousness with the
second level sublating the first level, transforming those lower activities and making them part of the higher operations and of the objective intended by that higher operation. The same is true as the knower
moves his or her conscious subject from being an understander of
possible ideas to the critical problem of verifying the reality of these
possible ideas.

As a first indication of what Lonergan means by the term "patterns
of experience," consider the way that wondering orients and directs the
three operations of knowing toward their final objective. Each level
of operation has its own partial objective, but these partial objectives
are brought together and integrated into a final objective unity. The
ultimate objective of all knowing is being or reality, but that final objective can be differentiated and parceled out into subordinate objectives within the more comprehensive objective – the concrete universe
of being. Thus the knower may seek pragmatic or theoretical realities
by directing and patterning his or her cognitional operations toward
these more limited pragmatic or theoretical objectives. A second, more
complex meaning of pattern emerges when we consider not only the
purposeful direction of our knowing operations but also the contents
of those operations.

A major achievement of Lonergan in *Verbum* was to differentiate
the knowing operations from their respective contents. In this way he
was able to distinguish between the invariant acts of the cognitional
operations and the variable contents that become known though those
operations. Further, by establishing being as the final and ultimate objective of all knowing, the knower was free to pursue more limited
goals which were partial aspects of being. Thus, we may distinguish
between the invariant pattern of experiencing, understanding, and
judging that is oriented to the full and final knowing of being and the
more limited, pragmatic patterns of knowing directed to a limited objective within the concrete universe of being. This gives us a preliminary understanding of the notion of patterning as a recurring order or
design of the three dynamically related operations of knowing.

A more complicated understanding of patterns of experience can be gained if we consider the more limited forms of pragmatic and theoretical knowing and the contents that become known through these limited forms of knowing as directed by different patterns of questioning. In such patterns, while the underlying operations may be the same, the contents that become known are understandably different. For example, in the ordinary practical pattern of knowing, the sun rises and sets, but in pursuing the theoretical or intellectual pattern, a new world-order emerges in which the supposedly stable earth is discovered to rotate a thousand miles an hour while at the same time it circles the sun at eighteen miles a second. Such dramatic contrasts reveal that the wondering or questioning in these different patterns reaches down even into the concrete subject's sensible experiences and, as will be shown, permeates even below all sensory-motor experiences into our subconscious, organic movements.

To speak of knowing as a structured operation of experiencing, understanding, and judging can be somewhat misleading since the spatial metaphors of different levels of the operating subject leave us with a somewhat static image of knowing. A better image is that of a song that moves up and down and at the same time flows back and forth as the melodic pattern cycles forward, moving horizontally and vertically and, at the same time, repeating the past cycles in ever changing ways. An even more serious limitation of the structural metaphor applied to knowing is its failure to include the subjective and objective aspects of our experiencing.

When we are asleep and dreaming, our consciousness is fragmentary and intermittent with little or no interaction or exchange with the outer sensible world. But as we begin to wake, the flow of our subjective experience begins to organize itself into a more directed and selective flow of inner and outer sensible experiences, and we begin to see, hear, smell, feel, and move about in our surroundings. This continuous engagement with the outer environment stimulates steady changes in our inner, conscious experiences. As the subject wakes up and begins his or her practical routines, the flow of conscious experience begins to be patterned by his or her practical interests. Such routine schemes of practical tasks require that the inner activities of memory, imagination, and effort also be directed toward the performance of these practical tasks. Thus, the pragmatic patterning of our conscious activities involves ordering both our inner and outer experiences. This same subject could shift from a practical pattern of experience into an intellectual pattern by changing the basic orientations of his wondering from a limited pattern of experience to a fully unrestricted and comprehensive understanding and judging of the concrete universe.

To make such a shift requires a fundamental change in the subject and the objects he or she intends to know. In explaining the intellectual pattern or flow of conscious activity, Lonergan frequently uses the example of Thales falling in the well because he is so absorbed with the stars above, while the milkmaid, who is operating in the practical pattern of experience, cannot understand how anyone could be so absent-minded that he could not see a hole in the ground. The example illustrates the key characteristic of the intellectual pattern since it requires that you withdraw from practical interests and results and surrender yourself to the goal dictated by disinterested wonder. The knower has to put aside his or her ordinary practical interests and submit to the demands and directions of unrestricted wondering and its objective. In such a pattern the knower wants to know the what and why of things, especially if the knower's answers to the what and why are actually true. It is the normative objectivity of truth that takes over the subject who ought to submit himself or herself to its demands. So impartial and strong is this desire to know that it directs and orders all the other conscious operations to serve its objective as memory yields related facts that support or even contradict proposed judgments. So persistent is this desire to know that it perdures even when we cease to operate in the intellectual pattern and shift to practical matters. Thus we may be trying to forget a problem when suddenly some sight or other sensible experience unexpectedly triggers an insight. Not only Archimedes relaxing in the baths of Syracuse illustrates the mind's perduring search for truth, but many scientists in strange circumstances report similar incidents. This disinterested desire to know seems to reach down into subconscious levels of the subject preparing and stirring up images that will release the desired insights.

While we operate in the practical pattern of experience, we ourselves and our everyday concerns tend to regulate the flow of our consciousness and conscious operations, but when we let go of our practical, ordinary pattern of experience, we decenter ourselves and our private world seems to disappear as we become only one small being within the vast, unlimited universe of being. The wonder released in the intellectual pattern reveals our ability, as Aristotle says, to do and become all things.

In addition to the practical and theoretical patterns of experience, Lonergan also invites us to appropriate the more spontaneous and primal flow of consciousness which he identifies as the aesthetic pattern of experience. Prior to our practical and theoretical experience of our surroundings, there is the simple joy of being alive, the wonderful delight of a sunny day, a walk in the woods, or the welcome relief from work. Or there is even the more strenuous experience of sports, or the pleasure of performing gymnastics. While we may have a purpose in playing the game, yet we can also play the game just for the sake of the game. The game has a certain autonomy, and when we decide to play games such as cards or tennis we give ourselves over to the game. Such entertainment or exercise has no practical or theoretical goal but seems to contain within itself a self-justifying satisfaction.

Finally and quite paradoxically, Lonergan calls our attention to the biological pattern of experience which we share with both plants and animals. I say paradoxically because this biological pattern reveals the source of the basic, philosophical problem of knowing which we discussed in the first section, namely, the Platonic confrontational theory of knowing as opposed to the Aristotelian theory that knowing is primarily by identity. In plants, of course, there is no conscious patterning of activities, but there is the organic, recurring pattern of cellular activities by which plants are able to draw their nourishment from the surrounding environment as they interact with earth, air, sunlight, and water in order to establish and sustain their own inner environment in the face of changes in their outer surroundings. Animals, on the other hand, satisfy the same needs of plants to establish and maintain their internal environment by elevating and transforming organic activities through their various psychobiological operations. Animals link their internal activities of sensing, remembering, imagining, and feeling with their outer activities of sensing and motoring in order to satisfy the basic needs of securing food and water, mating, and self-preservation. Lonergan refers to these inner and outer activities as the biological pattern of experience because the focus of all these operations is on satisfying the animal's need to sustain its internal environment. However, while the animal is able to seek out and satisfy its lower organic needs through its higher conscious operations, still the conscious living of the animal seems to be dominated by the lower, unconscious, cellular activity. It is as if, Lonergan notes, the lower, un-conscious, organic needs summoned the psychic, animal operator into conscious behavior in order to satisfy its organic needs, and when the lower, organic, purposive needs are met, then, the lower organic opera-tor releases the higher, psychic operator and the animal dozes off. A similar restriction of psychic consciousness can be seen in the way ani-mals pattern their outer sensible experience. Animals see, hear, smell, touch, and move about in a sensible environment, but their interest in that environment is primarily in the opportunity it provides to satisfy their inner, biological needs. Thus, while animals have many and var-ied inner and outer experiences, the pattern that orders these experi-ences is biological and extroverted. The dynamic drives of the animals are outward and immediate, which explains why sensitive conscious-ness is so confrontational and alert to objects that face it and stimulate its various responses. What focuses the animal responses is the drive to satisfy its vital needs. Beyond such satisfactions the animal does not seem to search. Animals do not wonder about the reality of the objects that satisfy their needs because reality for animals is given by the ob-ject's ability to assuage their appetites. To get beyond satisfaction an animal would have to free itself from its own sensible appetites and wonder about the reality of the sensible objects surrounding it. Such wondering assumes an ability to focus on the sights, sounds, shapes, smells, and touches that characterize an object. But such wondering also assumes an open-ended objective about what and why objects are the way they are. Animals are curious, but their curiosity seems to be directed by and motivated by their sensible and organic needs. They seem unable to abstract from their neurophysiological needs and to seek objects for their own sake as a scientist or artist might do.

To appreciate Lonergan's position, it is important to underscore the dynamic meaning of patterns of consciousness. To speak of seeing or hearing as sensible operations is to speak abstractly since sensible operations like seeing or feeling occur within a flow of consciousness which is determined by the orientation, background, and motivation of the concretely conscious subject at any given time. This concrete, conscious flow involves both the outer senses and the inner activities of remembering, imagining, striving, and feeling. All these activities are related and directed by the motivating interest and intentions of the operating subject.

To clarify further how these different operations cooperate and move together, consider the example Lonergan gives of a predator chasing a prey – a fox chasing a rabbit. The fox focuses all his attention on the position of the rabbit, concentrating his bodily movements in seizing the rabbit and, as the rabbit flees and twists his path of flight, the fox focuses and directs sensations, imagination, anticipations, memories, and movements into a single flow of conscious experiences organized by the concrete pursuit of a biological purpose. The fox does not just see or hear or smell or move or remember or imagine or seek the rabbit; rather, all the activities cooperate and flow into a purposeful pattern of capturing the rabbit. The flow is dynamic as the outer sensible environment of the fox keeps changing as does its inner conscious environment which adapts to the outer movements of the rabbit. There is a continuous interchange between the outer and inner environment of the fox as it directs the chase. Even more significant, this flow of conscious engagement of the changing inner experiences of the fox corresponding to the outer awareness takes place in the fox's sensory system. Thus the nerve endings of the fox receive the various stimuli and are carried to the central nervous system in the brain where they elicit the suddenly changing responses in the fox's skeletal-muscular system as the chase goes on. This means that we have two different cooperating systems, one conscious, the other unconscious.

In the pursuit of the rabbit there is a flow of observable experiences that are conditioned by and dependant on lower unconscious neural systems just as the animal's unconscious cellular system is conditioned by and dependant on the lower chemical processes. However, while the neural and psychic refer to two different levels of activities with their respective, autonomous goals, they are not separate levels; rather, the conscious psychic level subsumes and elevates the lower, unconscious organic level so that it participates in the higher, conscious psychic level. Thus the appetite for food, sex, and self-preservation which operate unconsciously in organic beings likes grasses, plants, and trees become conscious dynamic needs in animals. Plants and animals are alive, but in the animal some aspects of living like foraging, stalking, mating, and striving occur consciously which permits animals to adapt their inner needs to the outer changing environments in more flexible and subtle ways, expanding the biological pattern of living in unexpected ways.

Somewhat surprising organic diversity is much more evident in animals than in plants. We do not find highly sophisticated organs like eyes and ears in plants. The tropisms and irritability of certain species of organism or plants seem to be on the verge of conscious, sensitive living, but such conscious possibilities remain undeveloped. Similarly, while there is considerable difference in the sensible experiences of elephants and whales, neither species can detach themselves from their sensible environments and consider what it would be like living in another kind of sensory-motor pattern of experience. The human biologist, however, can explore a vast variety of sensory-motor experiences, not by becoming or taking on the sensory-motor experiences of an animal, but by patterning his or her own sights and sounds and other sensations in a strictly intelligible conscious pattern of the sensibly given experiences. The biologist does this by withdrawing from simply sensing the world to focus on the sensible contents and patterning these contents by a new patterning interest and wonder. Just as the elephant can transform and sublate unconscious organic appetites, so biologists can take sensibly conscious experiences and explore their potentially intelligible reality over and beyond their sensible reality. Biologists do this by liberating themselves from the biological pattern of living and not only entering into a strictly intelligible patterning of sensible data but into a pattern where their own interests must be put aside. In fact, as noted earlier, to enter into the intellectual pattern the biologist has to submit his own interests to those of the theoretical objective, letting his own subject disappear as the subject enters an objective universe where he or she becomes one small item in a universe of objects, where even the subject must also be considered as an object to be explained. Animals cannot pattern and mediate sensible data in this intellectual way because they cannot release themselves from the immediate conscious sensible data and begin to mediate that same data in a pattern that is not serving biologically pressing needs and drives. Lions don't wonder about the diet they consume and whether they ought to consider a different diet or even better ways of ordering the pursuit of their prey. Once the person shifts from actually eating and focuses on what they are eating, then the food becomes a variable. Having been freed from the biological pattern of needs, the food can become a variable content that may be considered in different patterns including a strictly intellectual one.

The same, or similar, sensible data that the scientist considers and mediates in order to fully understand them can also be considered from an aesthetic point of view. For example, consider a biologist, a real estate developer, and an artist considering the same broad, fertile meadow. For the biologist, the meadow is the possible locus of an ecological system which can be studied and observed in accord with accepted scientific procedures. For the real estate dealer, the same meadow is experienced as an opportunity for a housing development or real estate purchase. For the artist, the same meadow may evoke his aesthetic interest and provide a model that could make for an interesting landscape painting. All three persons are considering the same sensible realities, but they are doing so from three quite different perspectives, and their different perspectives are determined by the different interests that they bring to the same sensible data. These differences can be clarified if we shift from the sensible data they are sensing and perceiving to the internal conscious experiences of the three subjects.

While they observe and examine the same field, all these subjects are remembering, expecting, feeling, imagining, and wondering. It is misleading to think of those activities as separate since they are all related, and not only do they unite in different patterns but the patterns flow under the direction of differently motivated desires and fears. Thus all three persons will be sensing, remembering, anticipating, feeling, imagining, but their operations are all directed to different goals. The scientist will put aside the practical concerns that preoccupy the real estate agent and concentrate instead on the flow of memories, expectancies, and images that will assist him in achieving the kind of results that his profession will accept. The practical real estate dealer, on the other hand, expects to make a profit and will pattern and organize his conscious operations in accord with this very different goal. Finally the artist, like the scientist, is not totally detached from his objective and may expect to profit from his work, but if the artist is to succeed and reach his objective, then, like the scientist and the entrepreneur, he must pattern his internal conscious operations in accord with the autonomous objective of art. Unlike the scientist or business man, the artist does not attempt to restrict his experiences as he observes the wealth of colors, shapes, sizes of the variety of things in his sensible surroundings. His purpose is not theoretical or practical but something more elemental and comprehensive. Just what this objective of the artist actually is remains obscure and hidden. This is so because before we wonder in practical or theoretical patterns, there is a more elemental wondering that emerges from the more primordial awareness that precedes practical and pragmatic interests, and while it transforms and elevates the artist from sensible, biological needs, it also seems to reach down and sublimate our lower appetites to bring sensible needs and spiritual desires into a harmonious, higher integration.

For the artist observing the flowering meadow, the field seems to be flooded with feelings and filled with secret, hidden meanings. The inner play of the artist's memories, images, and feelings united with this surplus of sensible experiences provide the artist with a rich range of possibilities to initiate and sustain a variety of artistic explorations. We shall examine this pattern in more detail in the final section.

This completes our summary of Lonergan's philosophy of art as articulated in *Insight*, and so I will now turn to the first attempt by Lonergan to work out a full treatise on philosophy of art, which can be found in volume 10 of his Collected Works under the title of *Topics in Education*. While the treatment of art in this volume is confined to one chapter, the material is so condensed and original that it could be expanded into an entire volume.

4. THE SUBJECT'S WORLD

Between the completion of *Insight* and the presentation of Lonergan's treatise on art, there were a series of remarkable developments, and among these his research in existentialism, phenomenology, and the study of the subject as a symbolic operator were especially significant in the development of his philosophy of art. From existentialism Lonergan was able to complete his shift from the language of faculty psychology to the language of intentionality analysis which permitted him to be much more concrete in his analysis of the human person. Not only does the language of intentionality lead beyond knowing to deciding and doing, but it also initiates the shift from substance to subject. The person as unconscious is actually a substance but potentially a subject, and when he or she begins to dream, she or he becomes an actual subject, and his or her consciousness begins to flow. This flow has a direction and orientation given to it by the interests and concerns of the subject. It is the dynamic interest of the subject that directs his or her conscious operations to their desired objective. The subject gradually learns to combine these various operations required to reach his or her desired objective. Beside the operating subject, there is also the "world" of objects that is mediated through and by the operating subject.

The introduction of the notion of "world" is a key step for Lonergan because it correlates simultaneously the conscious, operating subject to the objects that the subject is operating on or could be operating on. "World" is the totality of objects that fall within the horizon of the subject's operational range. A further advantage to introducing the term "world" is that it allows Lonergan to distinguish between the immediate conscious objects that can be sensed and the different ways those immediate experiences can be mediated by the subject's operating range. A further advantage is that it allows the subject to differentiate different worlds according to different patterns of operations and the different orienting interests that control these patternings. Consider as a first example the world of the infant before he or she has learned a language. The infant's world is restricted to the immediate sensible world of sights, sounds, smells, tastes, felts, and sensory-motor movements. Once children learn a language, their world begins to expand as they begin to mediate their immediate experiences linguistically and begin to enter into the sociocultural world of their parents, leaving behind the former, immediate sensible world of the child.

It is difficult to exaggerate the importance of the emergence of speaking and listening in the lives of children since language is one of the main sources of the child's development. As the child begins interacting with others through speech, he or she begins to assimilate the cultural world into which he or she was born. Not only does the language mediate this cultural world to the subject, but it also sets the conditions under which the self-constituting subject freely chooses his or her orientation in and to that world. It is important to emphasize that the subject freely commits himself or herself to this world since Lonergan distinguishes between the world itself and the world constituted by the consciously intending subject. The world itself is not changed by knowing or meaning that world, but the world of human subjects does change and develop as the conscious subject changes and develops. The reason is, as noted, the subject's world is correlated to and mediated by the subject. This world that the subject lives in may be a fictional or imaginative world as in the case of the child who does not distinguish between fanciful characters who live in stories and real people. In such a situation, the child cannot yet differentiate the world of fact and fiction, but as the child develops so does the world within which the child lives. Again, there is the subject's world that changes and the world that does not change by being known or by being mediated by meaning.

The child's world or horizon expands as he or she develops and then gradually assimilates the sociocultural context in which he or she is born. It is important to note that not all changes of world or horizon bring about a development. A person changes jobs or neighborhoods and thereby brings about changes in the objects within their world, but there is no development of their world or horizon; there is only a change of objects within their horizon. Take the example of a person learning to play the piano who has acquired the skills to perform a certain range of musical compositions. To extend the range of performance, the pianist will have to add to his or her acquired skills a much more sophisticated range of performances. With the development of such new skills, the musical horizon and world of the pianist will dramatically increase. The same is true of the development of language skills as the child masters the more advanced grammatical skills and extends his or her vocabulary. With such developments, the child enters more fully into the world mediated by meaning. Such development gradually leads to a clear distinction between the fictional world and the concrete, actual world. This actual world is for the maturing person a sociocultural world of meanings, but it is not a world simply mediated by meanings as is the world of plants and animals; rather, the human world of concrete subjects is a world that is both mediated and constituted by meaning. This distinction between *mediated by meaning* and *mediated and constituted by meaning* has quite remarkable implications because it distinguishes and relates the human and the natural sciences. The distinction can be illustrated in the composition of different languages.

If you listen to two people speaking Chinese, and you have no knowledge of this language, then you can hear the sounds, and you can know that they are speaking a language, but you cannot understand what they are saying. The meanings that they are exchanging are being carried in sonic waves that the human ear can receive and respond to quite naturally, but you cannot understand and interpret the meanings with your ears. To speak is not just the making of sounds, but it *is* the making of meanings in and through the mediation of sounds. The biologist can mediate the reality of trees through specialized, organic meanings, but human beings are meaning makers and they not only learn to freely mediate the sensible and social world surrounding them, but in the process they constitute themselves as intending these meanings. For human beings to know themselves is to know the self as a "meaning maker." In self-knowledge the subject is both the meant and the meaner who constitutes the meant. Such a subject is a self-constituting self, and that is why Lonergan insists that the world made by the subject is correlated with the subject freely making that world and also why he distinguishes the world that does not change by being known from the subject's world that is changed by his or her knowing.

Before considering whether the subject's world is authentically grounded, there is the prior topic of relating the subject's world to the communal world into which the subject is born and the history of that communal world. The subject is born into a physical world which the subject immediately experiences through his or her sensory-motor system of receiving and responding to the various internal and external sensible stimuli, but once the changing subject begins to talk and listen, then he or she begins to enter into a sociocultural context of meanings which both mediate the physical and cultural meanings to the subject and also mediate the history of that sociocultural world. No doubt individual subjects may initiate or reject the commonly shared meanings that make up the communities into which subjects are born, but most of the meanings that constitute the community in which we live have been inherited from past generations, which means that the development of the world of meanings in which we are living depends on those previously achieved and inherited meanings. Moreover, the choices made by the individual subject about his or her own vocation or roles to be played are also dependant on the historical, sociocultural context into which subjects are born. Thus the sociocultural context into which we are born provides us with opportunities to assimilate past achievements, but at the same time the same culture sets certain boundaries to future advances. The question now arises as to the authenticity of those inherited and lived meanings and values.

Lonergan distinguishes two types of authenticity – major and minor authenticity. Minor authenticity regards the subject's critical reflection and deliberate choices to live in a world with the meanings and values that have been inherited from past traditions. To understand major authenticity it is necessary to understand the conscious operating structures that generated this cultural tradition. This includes not only the operational structures of the subject as knower but also the operating structure of the deciding and doing subject or what Lonergan names the existential subject. This includes a focus on feelings and the role they play in symbolic modes of expression and the need to work out how the cognitional and affective elements interact and blend. Such considerations gradually placed the cognitive wonder of *Insight* into the more primordial and comprehensive context of moral and religious wonder that precedes and conditions the willingness we bring to cognitional wonder. This means that the relation between knowing as leading to deliberating and deciding is reversed as deliberating and deciding are found to orient the direction of our cognitive wondering.

This reversal of knowing and deciding also brings the role of the subject's feelings into the foreground, and so Lonergan began exploring the intentionality of feelings and the values to which they respond and by which people are oriented to pursue these values. Thus in the case of knowing, the subject's intention is oriented by the value of knowing the truth; truth becomes an ultimate value and that value initiates, permeates, and sustains the dynamic search through the successive operational levels and their respective ends that lead the subject to the discovery of a particular, probable, possible, or actual truth. This further implies that the search for truth is a moral quest as well as cognitive and thereby involves a moral obligation on the part of the knower to find and tell the truth. The quest for truth is a moral, dynamic drive in which you are personally involved. Lonergan summed up this reversal of knowing and choosing under four dynamic imperatives – be attentive, be intelligent, be reasonable, be responsible. (Later he would add "be in love.") These imperatives or moral commands are not communicated to the subject by the community but are conscious, spontaneous, and immanent norms orienting subjects to their natural ends. Moreover, because these imperatives are grounded in the natural dynamic of the conscious subject, they include, beyond moral knowing, moral doing and living. These dynamic, transcending imperatives or precepts provide the immanent norms for judging the value of alternative courses of action that a subject may initiate or choose to cooperate with others in pursuing these common goals. However, we do not begin our lives by initiating a specific way to live. We are born into a way of life, and that way of life may be authentic or inauthentic or more likely some combination of the two.

On the assumption that the sociocultural mode of living into which we are born is pursuing its destiny in authentic and inauthentic ways, the subject who lives according to these inherited cultural norms will probably be living authentically an inauthentic way of life. There will be, therefore, a dialectical tension within the concrete, consciously operating subject, a dialectic between the inauthentic cultural norms the subject has inherited and is practicing and the natural, immanent, conscious norms that the subject received at birth. This is so because there is no separation between the subject's own existential choices and the practical actions by which the subject cooperates with others in the community. As the infant matures, he or she tends to develop a sociocultural character that is more or less in tune with the meanings and values of that culture. These values are communicated to the members of the community by means of the various media which carry the cultural norms and values that make up the sociocultural customs and practices of the participating subjects. For example, learning the language of your native sociocultural community not only mediates, orders, and orients your presence to the world and to the people around you, but it also simultaneously makes you present to yourself in authentic or inauthentic ways.

In *Insight*, Lonergan introduced the reader to the method of appropriating yourself as a knowing being, but the concrete, existential, and practical subject is not only a knower, but also a chooser and performer within a sociocultural context that sets the conditions under which you become an authentic or inauthentic human being. This means that the method of self-appropriation which Lonergan developed has to be expanded into appropriating oneself as an existential and practical subject. This is not the place to explore this dimension, but it does set the stage for Lonergan's theory of art as he expresses it in chapter nine of *Topics in Education*.

5. ART AS ULTERIOR SIGNIFICANCE

In the first eight chapters of *Topics in Education* Lonergan spends considerable time explaining various specialized patterns of experience such as mathematics, science, philosophy, and psychology. While such pursuits are very valuable and can be integrated into our concrete living, still, such specialized pursuits do not embrace the full reality of life. This does not diminish the remarkable significance and progress we have made in differentiating these specialized worlds of inquiry, but it does underscore the problem of thinking in more concrete ways.

For Lonergan, the concrete is always particular and contingent, but it is also comprehensive. Further, the concrete is contingent and dynamic; life does not stand still, nor does the consciousness of the concrete subject whose awareness is also always changing. Thus your present experience is constantly shifting into the past while the future keeps changing from the future into your present. It is not just the concrete subject's flow of consciousness that keeps changing, but also the world correlated to the subject's consciousness keeps changing. Recall the example of the fox chasing the rabbit. The rabbit continually changes his path of escape while the fox's sensible awareness continually changes as the rabbit tries to escape. The fox's eyes and ears and inner senses do not change, but the contents of these senses do. The sights, sounds, felts and other sensations continually change, and the pattern of these changes is directed by the animal operators as they seek to satisfy their biological needs. This example of a predator pursuing a prey illustrates how the internal flow of consciousness of the operator matches the external changes in the operator's environment. If we shift to the human, conscious operator, we can set the stage for Lonergan's definition of art.

Lonergan frequently refers to Binswanger's use of Heidegger's thought to give a new perspective to depth psychology.[2] Binswanger distinguished dreams of night and day in terms of the way that the flow of memories and images were directed. The dreams of night seemed to be related to lower digestive and organic activities while the dreams closer to the beginning of the subject's day seemed to be preparing the subject to play his or her role in their respective sociocultural world of meanings and values. The dreams of night lack the intentional ordering or patterning that begins to emerge as the subject wakes up and prepares to enter into and participate in his or her cultural world. In the dreams of night the intending subject is barely conscious, but as the subject awakens the existential subject begins to sense, remember, imagine, judge, and decide. With this background we may now turn to Lonergan's definition of art.

---

2 See Bernard Lonergan, *Topics in Education*, 210. See also Bernard Lonergan, "The Philosophy of History," in *Philosophical and Theological Papers 1958-1964*, CWL 6, ed. Robert C. Croken, Frederick C. Crowe and Robert M. Doran (University of Toronto Press, 1996), 72-73.

Lonergan defines art as "the objectification of the purely experiential pattern."[3] Lonergan interprets this definition beginning with the last term contrasting abstract and concrete patterns which may be exemplified by the contrast between reading a musical score and listening to the same score being performed by an orchestra. It is also important to contrast the flow of musical tones as sensibly experienced and as meaningfully ordered tones. We do not hear a flow of musical tones. What we hear is a song or symphony. The sounds or musical tones are patterned by the composer into a musical composition. Thus the ordering of tones shape a recurring

melodic pattern. Or take the example of a dance in which we sense the outer movements of the dancers, but we do not simply see the dancers moving; rather, what we perceive is a dance which is present in and through the recurring pattern of bodily movements. Dance consists in the pattern of an order of relations within the movements. In a painting, painters pattern the shapes and colors into an ordered whole which we interpret as a picture. In a movie, we do not see moving pictures; rather, what we see is an ordering of the pictures into a story that patterns or plots the events into a narrative whole. The key point for Lonergan is that ordering or patterning is intrinsic to the story or pictures or dance. The picture may also be imitative or representative or have external relations to a situation or scene external to the story or picture, but such external relations or representative functions are not essential. Only the internal relations of the pattern are essential for art. By rendering representations nonessential to art, Lonergan thereby established the autonomy of the artistic objective.

Lonergan next applies the pattern of relations to consciousness or experience. Again, the contrast between the dreams of night and day illustrate the point. Dreams of the night are more chaotic and diffuse than the dreams of the morning which reveal the subject awakening and organizing his or her experience with some sort of initial patterning. The same point is exemplified in listening to a friend in a noisy room where you select from the total sound data only the meaningful sounds of your friend's words. To be conscious of something requires that your consciousness or experiences must be patterned. Patterns can make words memorable as we notice in rhyming patterns or make surfaces of walls or rugs more visible as we discover in their surfaces decorative patterns. As we have already seen, there are different ways

3 *Topics in Education*, 211.

to pattern our conscious operations, but for Lonergan art is a "purely" experiential pattern.

By a purely experiential pattern Lonergan intends to eliminate all alien patterns that tend to instrumentalize our sensible experiences. Thus when one is driving in highway traffic the subject must pay close attention to the sights and sounds around his or her car, or when a biologist is studying a specimen under a microscope, then his or her sensible experiences are serving as a tool for careful observation, interpretation, and verification. The same is true of a person who is sizing up a situation as a practical opportunity for his or her own economic advantage. In all these examples, sensible experiences are serving as instruments for some purpose or motive other than that of the senses themselves whereas when the painter looks at a field of orange poppies she is not limiting her sensible experience to any predetermined purpose or pattern. On the contrary, sensing and feeling are encouraged to seek their own objectives, establish their own rhythm, and follow their own kind of expansion and organization.

Most important is that this purely experiential pattern has a meaning. Here we return to the first section to identify the sort of meaning that is present in this purely experiential pattern before it becomes objectified in art. That prior meaning is primordial and elemental. The most important characteristic of this elemental meaning is that within this field of experience there is no difference between the meaning and the meant. Not only is there no difference, but there is an identity in the subject that is doing the meaning and the meant that is intended. Lonergan, as we saw, explains this identity between meaning and meant or what in modern philosophy becomes subject and object by Aristotle's axiom that knowing is by identity. The sense in act is identical with the sensible in act, and the intelligent in act is identical with intelligible in act. This implies that the knowing subject is identical with the known object. In other words, when we know something we become what we know, but if this were so there would be an identity without any difference or limit. In this case there would be identity but no knowing. This is why Aristotle goes onto explain that the identity of the knower is a limited but real identity or that in knowing it is the knower who is changed, not the known. Knowing is a perfection of the knower or intender or meaner. Or again it is the knower who is transformed, and this is why, when we immerse ourselves into the realm of elemental meanings, we are transported from the ordinary world of practical affairs and enter into the strange, different, remote, novel, uncanny, and intimate world of art. For some this world of art is fictional and illusory, but for others it is even more real than our familiar world. We are all familiar how a great novel or film can remove us from our ordinary life and set us up with a new horizon of interest, with a new world of people, places, and things. Elemental meaning then invokes both the subject and the object and can take the subject out of his or her ordinary world and reveal to you a free, open, original, even ecstatic self in an unfamiliar world.

In clarifying the notion of elemental meaning Lonergan makes an important comparison between the world of mathematics and the world of art. This comparison becomes manifest as we trace the general history of these two disciplines. Mathematics begins in the numbering and measuring of sensible data, but gradually it is incorporated into the science of physics. Then in the nineteenth century mathematics breaks free from physics and the mediation of the physical world and seems to be more and more interested in its own pursuits, precipitating the problem as to just what mathematics is and what is its foundation. Turning to the history of art we find a similar development.

Art begins not as an autonomous discipline but as embedded in the contextual life of a historical community. Art functions as a description or moral critique of a people's practical living. It also may serve as a historical explanation of a people's institutional living as it communicates to its people, values, and motives that ground their way of life. Critical commentaries on art stress how art imitates, resembles, and represents the manners and mores of a people and their surrounding places and things. It is not until the nineteenth century when critical commentaries begin to focus on the author's creativity that the autonomy of art emerges into focus as critical attention shifted to the internal relations within the works of art; the traditional external reference of art as realistic or representative becomes much less important. When this happens, art loses its traditional grounding in the cultural life of a community, and the foundations of art, like the foundations of mathematics, become problematic. Before establishing the new foundations for art, we must consider the defining characteristics of art as the symbolic mediation of the purely experiential pattern of meaning.

It is one thing to have an artistic experience and quite a different issue to be able to objectify or express that experience in convincing and effective ways. In examining this issue, Lonergan quotes Wordsworth's definition of poetry as "emotion recollected in tranquility."[4] While the objectification of art evokes emotion in the audience, still that emotion is not simply the artist expressing his emotion in spontaneous or instinctive modes of expression. The emotional experience must be carefully interpreted and articulated, but how does this happen? As we have already noted, it is not through any kind of theoretical or practical mode of expression. In a theoretical pattern of experience, theoretical wonder leads to theoretical understanding and conceiving, which is then followed by critical reflection and judging. But in artistic objectification, artistic wonder leads to understanding but not to conceptualization and critical reflection. Artistic insights are embedded in the material that serves as the medium of expression, such as pigments for ordering different styles of drawing and coloring patterns. Without the material conditions, the artistic patterns cease to be since the pattern penetrates and orders the material as an independent work of art. Furthermore, this artistic intelligibility or meaning is not conceptual and cannot be conceptualized since it is a more concrete and more primordial form of intelligibility.

The critic can comment on the various meanings of artistic expression and translate these artistic meanings into theoretical conceptual meanings, but such critical commentaries on stories and songs are not the same as the artistic expression of those meanings any more than reading the score of a symphony is the same as listening to a performance of that symphony. Artistic expression and meanings involve a more concrete form of communication than theoretical expressions do. It is comparable to the differences between studying books on how to play golf and actually playing golf. But there is an even more important character to artistic expression that needs to be emphasized, and that is the role that symbols play in artistic expression.

Up to this point I have stressed the way artistic experiences are more primordial and elemental than other patterns of experiences. This primordial aspect of artistic experience can be readily established by noting that art and literature existed long before philosophy and theoretical reasoning emerged in human culture. The reason this has not been described and explored is that our Western tradition, culminating in the period of the Enlightenment, has left us with an impoverished notion of reason and, more importantly, that artistic or symbolic reasoning involves imagining and feeling in a variety of unfamiliar ways.

4 Ibid., 218.

To explain symbolic reasoning we can begin with Lonergan's definition of a symbol as an "image of a real or imaginary object that evokes feelings or is evoked by a feeling."[5] Authors and artists reason with images while mathematicians and theoreticians reason with ideas or concepts. This does not mean that poets do not sense, wonder, remember, imagine, feel, understand, judge, and choose as theoreticians and scientists do, but they do so in a very different pattern and for a different purpose. Socrates and Euclid spent endless hours and energy trying to find and fix the precise meaning of certain words because they were initiating a new mode of human reasoning, namely, systematic reasoning. Euclid established the exact meaning of a point, line, and plane in Book One of his geometry, and those meanings have stayed the same for over two thousand years, whereas what Homer and the poets meant by the "sky" and the "earth" cannot be rigorously and exactly established because the meanings of these two terms are almost endless. This does not make poets unreasonable and irrational. Even more surprising, some of the poets' meanings are contradictory. Earth may symbolize life, fertility, growth, and regeneration, but it may also symbolize death, burial, descent, and barrenness. And the same words may take on these opposite meanings at the same time. This does not mean the poet is illogical and that he does not follow the laws of non-contradiction, identity, and the excluded middle. Rather, the poet operates according to the older and more primordial logic – the logic of the image or feeling.

In the logic of image the author is not attempting to argue with the reader by setting down a series of syllogisms that prove his position; the author is dealing with what people do and how they live. People's lives are full of tensions, conflicts, and contradictions which cannot be expressed in any logical way because a great deal of human life is illogical. The philosophers invented the dialectical method to deal with such oppositions and interactions in people's reasoning, but long before the philosophers invented these logical and dialectical methods to control and correct reasoning, authors and artists employed a more primal mode of logic and dialect of images and feelings.

Lonergan provides a number of characteristics of these more primal symbolic modes of meaning. First, in place of the philosophers' classification of different things, the symbolist thinks in terms of types that

---

5 Bernard Lonergan, *Method in Theology* (University of Toronto Press, 1996), 64.

are representative figures of the whole class. Thus a rose symbolizes not a particular species of flower but all the different classes of flowers simultaneously. Second, the poet or artist does not try to prove to you the theme of his plot but instead overwhelms you with an exuberance of emotional images and meanings. "If I say it three times," the symbolist says, "then it's true." The symbolist thus creates the illusion of logical thinking, but in fact the poet may embrace opposite meanings, and instead of asserting X or Y the poet may insist on love and hate, thereby expressing the complexities of our emotional lives. Lonergan describes a number of other aspects of symbolic reasoning but finally focuses on what he considers to be the key characteristic of symbols, namely, the way they provide a person with the power to integrate and unify his or her mind and body.[6]

Lonergan refers to this character of symbols as "an internal communication" between the lower levels of organic and psychic activities with the higher levels of cognitional and volitional operations.[7] The lower levels need to reveal their vital needs to a person's higher intentional activities, which in turn require the cooperation of the organic and psychic energies as motives to carry out and execute a person's higher intentional goals. In this way symbols allow the mind to speak to the heart, and the heart to communicate to the mind, and both to communicate to our bodies. While Euclid's treatise on geometry speaks to your mind, Sophocles's *Antigone* speaks to your mind and heart. Euclid intends to teach us geometrical proofs about the truth of sets of mathematical propositions. In the context of traditional rhetorical criticism, Sophocles may be interpreted as intending to "instruct and delight" his audience, but such a traditional interpretation of the purpose of art can be misleading. The purpose of rhetoric is to learn the various devices and ways in which an orator may effectively persuade an audience to think or act in certain intended ways. This leads to a distinction between the message or meaning to be expressed and the ornaments, figures of speech, and other decorative devices which are traditionally considered as figurative meanings surrounding the literal or cultural or historical meaning. Such a distinction is basically misleading in the light of Lonergan's analysis of symbolic patterns of meaning.

---

6 See *Method in Theology*, 64-69.

7 Ibid., 66.

Lonergan quotes the familiar saying, "Let me write a nation's songs, and I care not who writes her laws."[8] This saying underscores Lonergan's position on the primacy of symbolic modes of expression in the life of a community. The "laws" in this saying refer to the institutional, cooperative patterns of a community while the songs refer to the cultural or symbolic level of that same community. In the light of this interpretation, we may rephrase the saying, "Let me create the culture of a people, and I care not who shapes and structures its institutions." By rephrasing the familiar saying this way, we may say that institutions refer to what people do and culture is why they do it. Cultural symbols provide the meanings and motives of a people's way of life while the purpose of poets and artists is to explore the concrete possibilities of new ways that people might live together. As past poets, painters, architects, and songwriters have provided present cultures and communities with the symbolic expressions that give the meanings and values that motivate a common way of life, so present poets and artists can expand and further develop these past symbolic modes of expression as well as originate new symbolic meanings and values.

Finally Lonergan draws our attention to the defining essence of art. All art has an "ulterior significance,"[9] which means that art reveals something strange and startling about ourselves and our world. Art reveals that our ordinary world has a concealed dimension; hidden in our everyday world there is the splendor and mystery, the dark and demonic, waiting to be revealed and shown to us, and it is the artist who discloses this unsuspected majesty and mystery of our everyday world. There is in everything in our world a secluded surplus of meaning, a primordial, elemental meaning that will evoke within us transcendent feelings and values when they are given genuine symbolic expression by the artist. Not all expression has this extra dimension, this "ulterior significance," and when it is lacking, art tends to be clever, brilliant, even ingenious, but in the final analysis it is not art but an expression of aesthetic enjoyment without "ulterior significance."

8 *Topics in Education,* 221.
9 Ibid., 221.

6. SUMMARY

In summarizing Lonergan's philosophy of art I will focus on what I think are the most difficult aspects of Lonergan's theory as I have presented it. I will briefly discuss six difficulties.

In the first place, art is relevant to concrete living, and to understand the significance of the concrete is remarkably difficult. To illustrate the point, consider the contrast between the formal, classroom education we receive and the cultural education we acquire by being born into a particular culture and gradually growing up and assimilating its sociocultural meanings and values by actually living those values and meanings. The formal classroom education tends to be abstract and specialized in comparison to the concrete, lived meanings and values of practical, everyday, lived experience. To understand Lonergan's theory of art we must understand this distinction because for Lonergan art involves the concrete, lived meanings and values of a people, but art is not about the actual lived meanings and values of a people but about the concretely possible or idealized meanings and values.

The second problem in understanding Lonergan's theory is to understand how the "purely experiential pattern" operates as a "release" or liberation from other patterns of experience. The problem here is twofold: first, the reader must understand that there are different patterns of experience and that these patterns have different objectives which are controlled by the orienting interest and wonder that directs the operating subject's pursuits. Second, the pattern involves simultaneously both the subject and objects as correlated to one another and as comprising the subject's horizon or world of objects. This means that we not only operate in different patterns but in different worlds, and the artistic pattern has its own horizon or world. The word "release" suggests that the artist's move to a purely experiential pattern is a liberation from a prior world that is restricted or limited in some special way. For example, the scientist operating in the scientific pattern of sensible experiences does not deal with these experiences for their own sake but rather is interested in a systematic mediation of this sensible data, and therefore the scientist instrumentalizes and restricts his own sensible spontaneities. To shift from this restricted use of our sensible experiences to the pure, artistic pattern releases our sensible spontaneities and permits the artist to follow these natural tendencies in whatever direction they may lead. Or take the example of the way people use words to talk to one another while the poet liberates language, permitting it to evoke its full retinue of emotions and associations. Or consider the way the scientist uses words as tools for mediating critical judgments. Scientists do not use words to provoke a range of emotions but insist on limiting linguistic meanings to precise, clear, and rigorous meanings. Artists, then, free us, release us from making judgments about what is practical or scientifically significant and invite us to step out of our ready-made world or to withdraw from the wearying pursuit of scientific knowledge and enter into the strange, uncanny, intimate, or remote realms of possible realities.

The third problem is to understand the notion of "elemental meaning." For Lonergan, the pure pattern of experience has a meaning which he refers to as "elemental" or primordial meaning. It may be more understandable if we consider elemental meaning as undifferentiated meaning which all human beings experience before they discover the differences among things including their own difference from other things. Human babies begin life with an undifferentiated identity of themselves with their sensible surroundings and only gradually learn that there are differences between self and others. Our first infantile experiences are of a spontaneous, pervasive intersubjectivity; our lives begin as a "we" and only gradually do we discover our individuality, our "I." Or, to repeat, we begin with an identity immediate to our surroundings and gradually mediate the differences among things. The crucial distinction, then, is between spontaneous, immediate meanings and acquired, mediated meanings. This difference between mediate and immediate pervades the history of philosophy, beginning with Aristotle, who assumes this undifferentiated or unmediated identity, and Plato, who assumes an immediate duality. Lonergan's theory of art, therefore, is foundationally different from Plato and foundationally similar to Aristotle.

In explaining the meaning of "elemental meaning," Lonergan quotes Aristotle's text which he refers to as Aristotle's axiom: "Sense in act is the sensible in act and intellect in act is the intelligible in act."[10] This means that a perfect knower would have a perfect identity with all beings, but we are only potential knowers with a potential identity that must be actualized or mediated or differentiated so that in actual knowing we acquire a limited identity with different kinds of beings. Artists explore this "elemental meaning," and they have symbolically

10 Ibid., 215.

objectified it during the long course of historical works of art and literature.

The fourth problem in understanding Lonergan's theory of art is the role that symbols play in the artists' objectifications of elemental meaning. The problem here is that we have such an impoverished grasp of the pervasive and fundamental role that symbols play in our concrete daily lives. Long before the Greeks attempted to learn how to reason in logically correct ways, human beings had been making, speaking, and listening symbolically. Human beings have to learn how to reason correctly, but they begin symbolizing spontaneously before they even learn how to converse linguistically. Babies who can hardly speak can learn to read image books. It was only in the nineteenth century that art criticism began to attempt to study and probe the logic of symbols, and it was not until the twentieth century that the philosopher Ernst Cassirer redefined the human being as a symbol-making animal.

In studying the process of symbolizing, the critic must realize that symbolizing is pre-conceptual and rather than abstracting a meaning from sensible conditions, as takes place in conceptual reasoning, the symbolizer must incarnate meaning in the sensible materials. Further, because symbolizing is pre-conceptual, it is also pre-reflective. The thinker or reasoner will keep testing or critiquing his or her meanings in order to be certain that they are not incoherent or contradictory, but that is not what poets or painters do. Life is filled with conflicts and contradictions, and so are the plots of stories and dramas that explore in symbolic form the concrete, contingent, particular possibilities of human living in this and other possible similar universes.

The fifth problem to be explained is the reversal in the history of art criticism between our imaginative and sensible experiences or between the literal and figurative meanings in interpreting artistic and literary works. Traditionally, ever since the Latin poet Horace had proposed that the aim of the poet was to "instruct and delight," the tendency has been to interpret literature as primarily intending to communicate a moral or religious message and that the various decorative devices of art were intended to enhance and to make more lively and persuasive the literal, moral, and historical meaning in works of art. In this context the final meaning of the work of art seems to be found in its references to realities outside of the poem or painting. In the nineteenth century with the "turn to the symbol," art critics discovered the autonomy of literature and art and found the meaning of artistic works were within the poem or picture itself. At the same time, artists discovered the plasticity and malleability of the natural world which they could transform and thereby then reveal the hidden dimensions of our surrounding nature, including the subterranean levels of the human consciousness. Suddenly the "underground man" emerged in the writings of Dostoevsky, the surrealist poets and artists began exploring the dark recesses of human thought, and Henri Matisse kept transforming the different appearances of our three-dimensional world into wonderfully two-dimensional, decorative patterns. Art took over the sensible world and metamorphosed it into a world governed by the logic of the symbol, thereby reversing the traditional relation of literal and figurative meanings. But this reversal left the critic wondering about the ultimate purpose of art. This brings us to the sixth and last aspect of Lonergan's theory of art.

Lonergan's answer is that the purpose of art is to communicate some "ulterior significance" or meaning through the symbolic mediation of the purely experiential pattern. For Lonergan, art creates a break away from ordinary living, from the ready-made world; art is a sudden or sustained opening into another world. In our concrete, everyday living there is always the possibility of a further, undisclosed dimension, some ulterior significance, some new concrete possibility, and it is the artist who reveals and communicates that hidden, undisclosed dimension in the concrete particular things that surround us. Lonergan speaks of humanity as "nature's priest" and "nature as God's silent communion" with humanity. In this context we may speak of the artist as the potential priest or prophet who reveals in surrounding substances a sudden epiphany of an unsuspected presence of another social world. Brancusi, the Romanian sculptor, restores the mystery hidden in a simple stone, that strange, sacred presence long forgotten in our modern world. For Lonergan, all genuine art has this special plus, this further meaning, this remote and obscure meaning.[11] Without this transcendental dimension, art becomes some form of aestheticism and, however brilliant or inventive it may be, it fails to evoke the timeless present within our passing lives.

---

11 Ibid., 222.

LONERGAN'S *CUR DEUS HOMO*: REVISITING THE 'LAW OF THE CROSS'

CHARLES HEFLING
BOSTON COLLEGE

I. INTRODUCTION

Whatever Lonergan meant by calling systematic theology 'quite a homely affair,'[1] he was certainly not commending slapdash amateurism. The enterprise he envisioned is at once meticulous and thoroughgoing, broad and deep. Perhaps for that reason it has not, as yet, many practitioners. Systematics, as functionally specialized, presents a daunting set of challenges. No one has done more to meet these than Robert Doran, whose work shows in concrete fashion what is required of a systematic theologian who would speak at the level of his times. To honor him with a small investigation that contributes, indirectly, to the functional specialty he has been practicing so admirably for so long is a delight.

My investigation has to do with what I take to be the central concern of Systematics, which is to shed light on 'mysteries.' For Lonergan mysteries, properly so called, belong to a 'supernatural' order, a *Heilsgeschichte* that can be summed up in his words as God's taking part in 'man's making of man.' One component of this 'taking part' is the advent of Christ, the mystery of his 'person' and 'work.' Among the statements or assertions or judgments of belief that Systematics might endeavor to understand is the belief that God has *become* a human being: 'the Word was made flesh and dwelt among us.' Understanding this statement is not a matter of determining *whether* it is true – that belongs to a different functional specialty – but instead a matter of asking *why*. In general, to ask *why* is to ask for an explanation, and there are a number of things about the Incarnation that need, argu-

---

1 Bernard Lonergan, *Method in Theology* (Toronto: University of Toronto Press, 1996), 350.

ably, to be explained. Three of these, three specifications of *why*, are especially relevant here.

(1) What does the Incarnation itself consist in? What is the constitution of the one who is the incarnate Word?

(2) What does being the incarnate Word entail as regards his abilities and actions? Why does it take being constituted as Christ was, to do what Christ did?

(3) What was the purpose of his doing what he did? What did his becoming human happen *for*? Why were actions needed that require the abilities of a 'God-man' to perform them?

To draw a rough parallel, the first of these questions is like the one at the beginning of Lonergan's *Insight*. It asks something like 'Why is a cartwheel round?' To ask the second question is like asking, 'How do cartwheels behave in virtue of their roundness?' And the third question asks: 'Why cartwheels? What purpose is served by something which, being constituted as a cartwheel is, does what cartwheels do?'

When this third sort of question is posed with respect to the Incarnation, answering it involves understanding *inter alia* how the Incarnation fits intelligibly with other 'mysteries' comprised in the supernatural order. This can be an awkward question for the Augustinian tradition of theology in so far as that tradition is anchored in a different mystery. Augustinianism has stressed above all the supernatural *grace* that justifies or sanctifies, especially in its relation to human freedom. God 'plucks out the heart of stone and puts in a heart of flesh'; he gives both good will and good performance. What more could be needed? Granted, in other words, that God takes part in 'man's making of man' by giving the supernatural gift of grace, it becomes a question why God has *also* taken part by becoming human. Why a God-man when the interior renovation effected by grace evidently accomplishes everything required for reconciling the human race with God?

To such questions Augustine himself cannot be said to have provided much in the way of an answer although the idea that he has no Christology at all is a caricature. As for that notable Augustinian theologian Thomas Aquinas, it is not immediately obvious just how the Christology in the third part of his *Summa theologiae* is related to the two preceding parts, if it is related at all. There are critics who think that after explaining how rational creatures make their way homeward to God, guided by law and pre-eminently by grace, the *Summa* could just as well have stopped. The third part that Thomas went on to write appears to be an appendage. Then there is Lonergan. In the book *Insight* he proposes that God's supernatural solution to the human problem can be expected to consist in faith, hope, and charity – to consist, that is, in what Thomas would call habits directly 'infused' by God. Similarly, the pivot on which Lonergan's *Method in Theology* turns is conversion, religious conversion in particular, which he speaks of as 'the love of God flooding our hearts' and which he identifies with sanctifying grace. This unmediated entry of God into 'man's making of man' would seem to be the supernatural *par excellence*. So once more the question arises: Why a God-man as well? *Cur Deus homo?*

2. THE EQUIVOCAL LAUNCHING OF 'SYSTEMATIC' CHRISTOLOGY: ANSELM

Cur Deus homo is, of course, the title of Anselm's famous book, and it was Anselm, more than anyone else, who set the course that Western Christology has taken. The influence of *Cur Deus homo*, for better and for worse, can hardly be exaggerated. It is all the more regrettable, then, that Anselm did not revise it, as he says he would have liked to do. As it stands, the book is a magnificent failure. Since this is not primarily an essay on Anselm, it will be enough to mention one reason why, according to Lonergan, *Cur Deus homo* fails. Anselm made a noble attempt to do something that cannot be done properly without adopting an intellectual perspective he was not in a position to adopt. He needed the 'theorem of the supernatural,' which had not yet been discovered. His attempt, as Lonergan once put it, was an attempt to make bricks without straw.

The attempt itself was not misguided, in so far as its aim was to control meaning. Anselm was trying to bring Christian belief into the 'second stage' of meaning, as Lonergan names it, trying, that is, to sort out, criticize, and grasp the intelligibility of the kaleidoscopic imagery that Christian tradition was using to speak about what Christ, the incarnate Word, has done *propter nos homines et propter nostram salutem*, as the Creed puts it – 'for us and for our salvation.' In that regard, Anselm's aim was to *understand*, which is the aim of Systematic theology. Methodologically speaking, however, his lack of a coherent notion of the supernatural order led to problems. Two of these, one more general and the other more specific, are worth mentioning.

The general problem is well known: Anselm thought (or anyhow said) that control of meaning was a matter of discovering *necessary* reasons. The second problem, which appears specifically in *Cur Deus homo*, is that Anselm tried to conceive what was super*natural* about Christ's saving work in terms of super*erogation*. Stated briefly, his argument is that Christ exceeded the call of duty, doing more to uphold justice than he was obliged to do, and by so doing earned a reward that was transferred, at his own request, from himself to his human 'kindred.' The gift he gave by 'giving his life' was not so much the payment of a debt as it was an *overpayment*, a supplement to the honor that is justly due to God. It was meritorious because it was excessive. The difficulty with such an argument (and the difficulty with the whole idea of supererogation) is that excess implies that what exceeds and what is exceeded share a common measure. A supplement can be only 'more of the same.' Thus the honor that Christ rendered by giving his life was not essentially different from the honor everyone owes to God. To say, as Anselm does, that rendering it earned God's reward is to say that merit before God, at least in this case, does not depend on grace.

Here is not the place to pursue the convolutions of Anselm's reasoning. Suffice to say that, according to Lonergan, the ultimately incoherent idea that merit has its ground in supererogation began to pass away once the theorem of the supernatural began to take hold. The important thing, for present purposes, is that Anselm had the right *question* and that he was the first to address it in something like a systematic way. Moreover, *Cur Deus homo* has the formal layout of a cogent answer once it is recognized that Anselm's question is really not one question but two – though whether he recognized the difference between them is doubtful. I have already hinted at both of these questions. 'Why a God-man?' can mean: What was the *purpose* of the Incarnation? This is rather like asking what good it is for a cart to have wheels. But 'Why a God-man?' can also mean: Why is God's becoming human a condition of realizing that purpose? This is rather like asking what it is about cartwheels that meets the relevant requirements. Now, cartwheels are known to be round, and similarly Anselm knows what he means by the Incarnation; he means that Christ is a divine person with a human and a divine nature. What he asks in the first place, then, is what purpose was served by Christ's being at once human and divine. But he also asks, more particularly, why the fact of being at once human and divine fulfilled the conditions set by the purpose for which God became human.

All this can be put a little more technically. Anselm's project is to grasp two *if–then* relations, which are themselves related. Let X stand for the incarnate Word, constituted as the council of Chalcedon defined. Let Y stand for whatever it was that his being so constituted made possible. Let Z stand for the end or purpose for which he became incarnate. Very broadly stated, what Anselm sets out to show is that Z depends on Y and that Y in turn depends on X. In other words:

If X, then Y; and if Y, then Z.

There is a connection between who Christ was and what he did, and there is a connection between what he did and why he did it. *Cur Deus homo* is an endeavor to grasp all three of those in a single view.

The argument begins from Z, the purpose. This purpose Anselm conceives eschatologically as the glory of God, which includes the everlasting felicity of rational beings, human and angelic. The image for Z in *Cur Deus homo* is the celestial City of God, fully populated according to God's intentions in creating the universe. What Anselm thinks about Y, the condition on which Z depends, I have already mentioned. He conceives this condition as a supererogatory deed, the God-man's 'gift' of his life, which was more pleasing to God than the whole universe. The logic of Anselm's argument, then, is as follows: *If* there is a God-man, *then* there can be a work of supererogation that honors God; *and if* God is so honored, *then* he can justly welcome into the celestial City those on whose behalf Christ gave his life, and who would otherwise be excluded.

Two qualifications need to be added. First, these two *if–then* relations, as stated, raise further questions. Anselm is aware of the fact that they do. The link he forges between Y and Z is consequently more complex than I have suggested, but to expound Anselm's way of dealing with the complexity would take us too far afield without changing the overall structure of his logic. Secondly, however, if Anselm himself had schematized his own argument, as he regards it, he would have put it this way: If *and only if* X, then Y; and if *and only if* Y, then Z. In other words, as I have mentioned, he thinks that the links between X and Y, and between Y and Z, are *necessary* links. For thinking so, or at least saying so, he has a number of reasons. One reason is that he wants his argument to be such as will convince unbelievers. Intelligent reasoning, with or without faith, is enough to generate assent to his conclusion – or so he says. Another reason, closely related, is Anselm's assumption that there is something counter-intuitive about the Incarnation. Why would any self-respecting God become human and suffer and die unless doing so was the *only* way to achieve some purpose? Thus Anselm's strategy involves eliminating every alternative means by showing that it is unfitting and thus 'impossible,' so that Incarnation, which alone remains, is in that sense 'necessary.'

How seriously and strictly Anselm's methodological asides are to be construed is a difficult question on which interpreters disagree wildly. What is true is that he deduces the fact of the Incarnation from the 'necessity' of a supererogatory gift, X from Y, on the basis of premises that are not, in fact, necessary, and the same is true of the reasoning that takes him from Z to the 'necessity' of Y. In other words, there is some disparity between what Anselm actually does and what he (sometimes) says he is doing. Not that his effort is wasted on that account. True, an attempt to demonstrate the necessity of a supernatural reality is bound to fail if the supernatural itself is not necessary. According to the theorem of the supernatural, it is not. It can be understood, but understanding is not a matter of deductive proof. It is not surprising, then, that Anselm's proofs do not *demonstrate* what they purport to prove. Nevertheless, it does not follow that they shed no light on the question he addresses. What is interesting, important, and original in *Cur Deus homo* is that it proposes an intelligible (though not a necessary) link between X and Y. *If* there is a God-man, *then* something can happen; more exactly, *if* there is a divine person who has a human as well as a divine nature – if God has become human, not in some unspecified sense, but in the sense defined at Chalcedon – *then* what needed to happen *could* happen.

That *if–then* relation would seem to be significant, and understanding it would seem to belong to theology working in the functional specialty Systematics. Even if the 'hypostatic union' (to use the technical phrase) was not necessary, what made it fitting or appropriate or 'convenient' is still a legitimate and worthwhile question. Why was such a union required in order for Christ to do what he did, granted that there were other ways of achieving the purpose he achieved by doing it? That is the question posed in the title of this essay. By 'Lonergan's *Cur Deus homo*' I mean his way of answering a question that Anselm introduced into the theological conversation in an incipiently systematic way. More exactly, I am interested in understanding what

Lonergan said or might have said about the reason for the Incarnation, taking into account everything that a truly 'methodical' theology has to take account of, including, among other things, the theorem of the supernatural.

3. WHY (ACCORDING TO LONERGAN) A GOD-MAN?

So far, I have drawn on Anselm's Christology, making the best of a not altogether satisfactory argument, to pose a question: How can the hypostatic union, the constitution of Christ the incarnate Word, X in my scheme, best be understood in relation to its purpose, to Z in my scheme, so that what Christ has done – so that Y, whatever it turns out to be – is intelligible *both* as congruent with his constitution *and* as an appropriate (not necessary) way of bringing about the purpose? How can those three items be grasped as an intelligible whole?

The first of the three, Christ's constitution, is the one to which Lonergan devoted the most attention. On the second item, the 'work' of Christ, and especially its relation to how he was constituted, ontologically and psychologically, Lonergan had less to say. The only extensive treatments are to be found, not surprisingly, in the theology he wrote while he was teaching at the Gregorian University in Rome. There are two of these.

(1) In his textbook on *The Incarnate Word*, the fifth and final part, which is headed 'Redemption,' concludes with a thesis on the 'Law of the Cross.' This thesis, which Lonergan mentioned once or twice in later essays,[2] has been discussed and appropriated by his students, Robert Doran among them, and so is at least somewhat familiar.

(2) Less widely known is a book that Lonergan began to write but evidently never completed. It would have been a big book. The six finished chapters, in English translation, come to eighty thousand words. About its original purpose, its date, and even its title there are a number of unanswered and probably unanswerable questions, which Fred-

---

2 See Lonergan, 'Transition from a Classicist World-View to Historical-Mindedness' (1966), in *A Second Collection*, ed. Wm. F. J. Ryan and Bernard J. Tyrell (Toronto: University of Toronto Press, 1974), 7; and 'Moral Theology and the Human Sciences' (1974), in *Collected Works of Bernard Lonergan*, vol. 17, Philosophical and Theological Papers 1965-1980, ed. Robert C. Croken and Robert M. Doran (Toronto: University of Toronto Press, 2004), 309.

erick Crowe has discussed[3] and which are not directly relevant here. I shall refer to it as Lonergan's *Redemption* book. Possibly it was meant to replace the whole fifth part of *The Incarnate Word* although there are some weighty arguments against that hypothesis. What is interesting about the book, in any case, is the last section of its last chapter, which in the original typescript bears the title *Cur Deus homo?* I find it all but inconceivable that Lonergan did not intend to evoke comparison with Anselm.

Moreover, my best judgment would be that it is in this section, rather than in the textbook on *The Incarnate Word*, that Lonergan offers his most complete and illuminating answer to the question Anselm attempted to address. This is not to say that the two texts are at odds. On the contrary, they cover much of the same ground in the same way and sometimes in the same words. The textbook, however, is the less satisfactory of the two. In some ways it represents Lonergan's rewriting of the textbook by Charles Boyer that he had used in teaching Christology.[4] Like Boyer's, Lonergan's textbook puts redemption at the end, and like Boyer's it gives pride of place to 'satisfaction,' the idea that Anselm is famous (or notorious) for introducing into Christian theology. The *Redemption* book by no means abandons satisfaction any more than it abandons the Law of the Cross. Both, however, are put in a different and wider context.

Let me now consider each of these two sources in greater detail. First, the textbook on *The Incarnate Word*. Here Lonergan never quite answers the question 'Why a God-man?' On the face of it, his thesis on the Law of the Cross might seem to provide an answer:

> This is why the Son of God became man, suffered, died, and was raised again: Because divine wisdom has ordained and divine goodness has willed, not to do away with the evils of the human race by force, but to convert those evils into a supreme good in keeping with the just and mysterious Law of the Cross.

But in fact the thesis is concerned with a somewhat different question. Lonergan gave it a title of its own: 'Understanding the Mystery.' The mystery to be understood, however, is not the Incarnation in the specific sense of Christ's constitution as God-man; it is the mystery of

3 See Frederick E. Crowe, *Christ and History: The Christology of Bernard Lonergan from 1935 to 1982* (Ottawa: Novalis, 2005), chapter 9.

4 See Crowe, *Christ and History*, 135.

redemption. The title, in other words, refers directly to the fifth part
of *The Incarnate Word*, and only indirectly to the four preceding parts,
which explain the hypostatic union and its consequences. Why did
the Son of God become human, suffer, die, and rise? Because of what
redemption *is* – because it has the 'nature,' the essence, the intrinsic
intelligibility that the Law of the Cross expresses.

Now, the Law of the Cross is a completely general law, as Lonergan
emphasizes. That is so for two reasons. In the first place, the Law of
the Cross presupposes the human problem of moral impotence and
longer-cycle decline. But when Lonergan says that this problem is permanent, he fairly clearly means it is permanent with respect to the
past as well as the future. It is a problem for the concrete universal
that is 'man,' humankind in its space-time solidarity.[5] In the second
place, then, any solution that God provides will likewise pertain to
'man's making of man' in its totality. The solution that has, in fact,
been provided is a supernatural order. To that order the Law of the
Cross belongs inasmuch as it includes elements that exceed the grasp
of human intelligence as such. The supernatural, however, is within
the world-order which actually exists. It follows that the creative act
by which God has ordained and chosen the existing world-order is
identical with the act by which he has ordained and chosen the Law of
the Cross. In other words, the Law of the Cross is not a divine after-
thought. There are no divine afterthoughts.

What the complete generality of the Law of the Cross implies for
Christology – and what Lonergan says more or less explicitly in the
textbook on *The Incarnate Word* – is that Jesus Christ did not invent
it. The Law of the Cross has always pertained to the existing world-
order. Christ *knew* the Law of the Cross. Moreover, he knew what it
presupposes and what it implies; he knew that it is by divine wisdom
that this law has been ordained, and by divine goodness that it has
been willed, and, knowing all this, Christ *chose* it, made his own the
essence of redemption, and did so freely. *Why* did he do this? Not, according to Lonergan, so as to cancel or abrogate the Law of the Cross,

5 It does not follow that it is a 'natural' problem. What does follow is that,
as for Thomas Aquinas, 'fallen human nature and nature as such *coincide*';
see Lonergan, CWL 1, *Grace and Freedom*, ed. Frederick E. Crowe and
Robert M. Doran (Toronto: University of Toronto Press, 2000), 351, n.
63. Emphasis added.

so that we would no longer have to choose it ourselves. On the contrary, he chose it so that we might choose it too.

In terms of my $X–Y–Z$ scheme, then, Lonergan's thesis on 'Understanding the Mystery' is a thesis about Y and Z, where Z is the 'supreme good' that Y, the mystery of redemption, brings about. What the thesis does not explain is any connection between Christ's specific role in Y, his having made the 'form' or 'essence' of redemption his own, and on the other hand X, his ontological and psychological constitution. It *was* the incarnate Word who suffered, died, and was raised; it *was* his Incarnation, passion, and resurrection that conformed with the Law of the Cross and brought about a supreme good. *Why* it was the incarnate Word, as such, the thesis does not explain.

At least, the thesis does not explain it in a way that avoids difficulties. An explanation, of sorts, there is. Lonergan draws an analogy between a builder, who introduces the form of a house into the 'matter' of building materials, and Christ, who introduces the form of redemption into the 'matter' of the sinful human race. The argument is that Christ's constitution qualified him to effect the introduction. The question that arises is exactly what 'introducing' this form consists in and what it accordingly achieves. Nor is it an unimportant question. On the interpretation of the Chalcedonian definition that Lonergan himself follows, the divinity and the humanity that are united in the one Person of the Word are united 'without confusion, without change.' Christ's humanity is a created reality. It remains human and finite, whatever supernatural gifts and graces the man Christ Jesus may have had. It follows that what he does, precisely as the *incarnate* Word, he does in a human and finite way – not immediately, but through the mediation of physical, chemical, biological, sensitive, and intellectual conjugates. What he does, he does inasmuch as he is a secondary cause, metaphysically speaking. No secondary cause, however, can reorient or convert the human will. That is metaphysical Pelagianism, so to say. It follows that, whatever Lonergan may have meant by 'introducing the form of redemption,' he cannot have meant that Christ *as* man, a divine person subsisting in a human nature, bestowed the supernatural conjugate form that is sanctifying grace.[6]

---

6 It is true that Christ bestows sanctifying grace because it is he who, together with the Father, sends the Spirit. It is just conceivable that it was this aspect of Christ's constitution – his being a divine Person – that Lonergan

Exactly what Lonergan did mean is a question that need not be pursued here. Since his main intention in the thesis on the Law of the Cross is not to answer Anselm's question, the brief and somewhat ambiguous answer he does give should not be made to carry more weight than it can bear. When he wrote it, Lonergan may or may not have been aware of the difficulty I have mentioned. In any case, the final section of the *Redemption* book abandons the analogy of the housebuilder, and the difficulty is dealt with head–on. To that point I will return at the end of this essay. More important at present is the explicit answer given in the *Redemption* book to the question of what Christ does, not only *as* human, but because he *is* a divine person.

Why a God-man? In the *Redemption* book Lonergan divides the question as follows:

> The intrinsic causes of Christ are dealt with in the treatise on his ontological constitution. His extrinsic *agent* cause is the triune God in his external operation. The [extrinsic] *final* cause or end ... is divided into primary and secondary, the primary end being the divine goodness itself, and the secondary end the external glory of God, the order of the universe, and the body of Christ, wherein all things are brought together and reconciled in him. ... About this end or purpose, we may ask this further question: why was a divine person required to accomplish it...?

> The answer is: The Son of God became a human *so that divine friendship might be communicated in orderly fashion to the unfriendly.*[7]

Again it will be useful to put this in terms of the alphabetic scheme introduced earlier. What Lonergan here refers to as 'the intrinsic causes of Christ,' his ontological constitution, corresponds to X. As for Z, there is agreement with Anselm. Primarily, Z is the divine goodness, but secondarily it is the external glory of God. It consists, that is, in *pantôn anakephalaiosis*, the 'recapitulation' of all things, which is also the 'supreme good' referred to in the thesis on the Law of the Cross. Lonergan's question, then, is why a divine person (X) was required to accomplish Z. In other words, as for Anselm, *Cur Deus homo?* is first of all a question about Y. Anselm, as we have seen, thinks that X was

had in mind. The point, however, is that this Person sends the Spirit inasmuch as he is himself God, not inasmuch as he has become human.

7 The emphasis is original: 'Respondetur ergo ideo Dei Filium esse hominem factum *ut amicitia divina inimicis ordinate communicetur.*'

required necessarily because Y, as he conceives it, was the one and only way in which Z could be accomplished. Lonergan, in keeping with the theorem of the supernatural, does not think Y was necessary. Consequently there is no question of deducing X, like a rabbit pulled from a hat, as Anselm purports to do. Nevertheless it *is* possible to reason from Z through Y to X, not by way of proving that there must have been a God-man, but by way of showing that the hypostatic union was an altogether appropriate way of promoting God's glory. That is what Lonergan proceeds to show.

Since X, Y, and Z are all three supernatural, the only option for understanding them is recourse to analogies drawn from the natural order. That recourse, however, includes natural knowledge *of God*. The point should be emphasized. It explains why Lonergan, in his later writings, proposed that chapter XIX of *Insight*, his own 'philosophy of God,' should be included in the functional specialty Systematics. Natural knowledge of God may or may not play a part in previous functional specialties. Systematics, however, cannot do without it precisely because, as I said at the outset, Systematics endeavors to understand mysteries. There are, then, two things that can be known about God on a philosophical basis such as chapter XIX:

(1) God commonly acts through secondary causes; say, through a man or a woman.

(2) God commonly preserves natural laws, including the statistical laws that pertain to 'man's making of man.'

To these two principles, the section of the *Redemption* book I am discussing adds a third, which could be said to be derived from a 'philosophy of the human,' and which is the most interesting of the three. Lonergan calls it the principle of diffusion, or perhaps extension, of friendship. It is:

(3) Friends love, take delight in, each other's *other* friends.[8]

Now, by friendship Lonergan means mutual, benevolent love, committed to some common good. By extrapolation, the *divine* friendship that God became human to communicate is mutual, benevolent love, committed to divine goodness, or to what might be thought of in 'later Lonergan' terms as analogous to the higher integration of intellectual,

8 'Principium diffundendae amicitiae dicimus secundum quod amicus amici amicos diligit.'

rational, and moral consciousness that is the state of being-in-love. From that definition it follows that there are, properly speaking, just three friends of God, three who enjoy divine friendship, three who are unrestrictedly in love with unrestricted loving. God *are* those friends: the Father, the Son, and the Spirit. To say this is, of course, to go beyond a philosophy of God to the theology of God's Trinity, but that is to be expected. Understanding the mystery of the incarnate Word depends not only on 'natural' analogies, but also on grasping its relation to other elements of the supernatural order.

Suppose then that Z, the end for the sake of which God takes part in 'man's making of man,' is conceived in interpersonal terms as a community of friends. Suppose too that it is God's intention to diffuse or extend to finite friends the friendship that characterizes the Trinity. This diffusion or extension would correspond to Y. In keeping with the first principle listed above, it would be appropriate, though not necessary, for God to act through a secondary cause, a finite being. In order to mediate divine friendship, such a secondary cause would have to be a friend of God in his or her own right; otherwise, this friendship would have to be mediated *to* him or her, and so on *ad infinitum*. The alternative, that is, to an infinite regress, which explains nothing, is an *intermediate friend*. But the right to be God's friend belongs to no created being, no finite person, because commitment to infinite good is by definition supernatural. Humans have no claim to it, no exigence for it. It is natural only to divine persons.

Before taking the argument further, let me pause to compare it with Anselm's procedure.

Anselm asks 'Why a God-man?' and frames his answer in terms of the order of the universe, the end for which God created it. This order depends – 'necessarily' depends, according to Anselm – on a work of supererogation, performed by someone who *ought* to perform it and who at the same time *can* perform it. That is the sound-bite summary of Anselm's *Cur Deus homo*: only God *can* and only man *should*. The required work of supererogation 'must' therefore be performed by someone who is God *and* man.

Lonergan similarly asks 'Why a God-man?' and similarly frames his answer in terms of the order of the universe, the end for which God created it. But he conceives this end in terms of mutual benevolent love, that is, in terms of friendship, with the common good to which all the friends are committed being the goodness of God. This friendship is appropriately, but not necessarily, mediated by an intermediate friend, and what is required of this intermediate friend is that he or she *can* mediate divine friendship and that he or she *ought* to enjoy it in the first place. Thus the corresponding sound-bite summary of Lonergan's *Cur Deus homo*, compared with Anselm's, would interchange 'can' and 'ought.' For Anselm, someone divine *can* perform a work of supererogation, while only someone human *should*. For Lonergan it is the other way around. Someone human *can* mediate to other humans, but only someone divine *should*, by right, have what is mediated, namely commitment to the love that God is.

Formally speaking, then, Lonergan has deduced the constitution of the incarnate Word, just as Anselm did. The difference, which is important, is that the three premises from which Lonergan argues are not themselves necessary. As to the first of them, God is not bound to work through secondary causes; as to the second, God is quite capable of suspending scientific or psychological or historical laws. He could, therefore, have achieved his eschatological purpose in an apocalyptic manner. To judge by the New Testament, there were many who expected him to do so. As it happens, he did not. As it happens, he chose the Incarnation.

4. SOME FURTHER DETERMINATIONS OF LONERGAN'S ANSWER

In its basic shape, the answer to 'Why a God-man?' that Lonergan presents in his unfinished *Redemption* book is quite straightforward. It admits, however, of further explication and refinement. For present purposes, three points may be added.

(1) The advent of the Son, who became human, was for the sake of mediating divine friendship in a human way, which is to say, mediating it 'incarnately.' To affirm that divine friendship *can* be so mediated is, by definition, to affirm that it can be mediated by conscious human acts. The mediation could, no doubt, occur spontaneously and unreflectively. Humans make friends by mutually mediating the meaning and value they live by, whether or not they understand this meaning and value, and whether they know they are mediating it. The same *could* be true of the incarnate Word, who according to Chalcedon was 'like us in all things apart from sin.' He *could* have done what he was sent to do but without knowing, in so far as he was human, what he was doing. On the other hand, it would surely be appropriate or

suitable or fitting for the incarnate Word, in his role as intermediate friend, to be expressly aware of that role and expressly aware as well of his identity, his aims, and his motivations. It would be 'convenient,' in the technical sense, for this friend to understand and conceive whose friend he is, who God is, and what God has in mind for the created universe, including 'man's making of man,' since the universe and its history manifest the goodness on the basis of which he *is* God's friend.

In brief, it would be appropriate for the intermediate friend, *as* human, to exercise in his temporal life the supernatural knowing that theology calls the 'beatific vision' of God. Towards the end of his professorship in Rome, Lonergan became interested in working out a coherent understanding of what it would mean for the man Christ Jesus, in his human, historical life, to enjoy the eschatological blessedness of knowing God. The account of Christ's *consciousness* set out in the little textbook on *The Ontological and Psychological Constitution of Christ* did not change, but the account of Christ's conscious *acts*, and in particular his cognitive acts, did. No small part of Christ's work as mediator, as historical agent, as intermediate friend, lay in his communicating through humanly intelligible language a 'vision' that is in itself ineffable. And as I have argued elsewhere, this communication can be seen as the principal or definitive occurrence of 'revelation.'[9]

(2) As I mentioned earlier, Anselm appears to have thought that it was somehow unbecoming or base or degrading for God to become human. *Cur Deus homo* makes it seem as though the Almighty was faced with a Hobson's choice: *either* he must be unjust to himself, which is unthinkable, *or* he must augment his own honor by performing an act of supererogation such as humans, by reason of their sinfulness, are incapable of performing. Were it not for this sinfulness, there would have been no reason to become human. From Anselm's emphasis on sin as 'necessitating' the Incarnation, a long and complicated history of theological dispute has followed down to the present. It need not be rehearsed here. The one point which should be noted is that in my X–Y–Z scheme, as Anselm works it out, Y entails remitting the punishment that is the just consequence of sin. That remission is the

---

9 Charles Hefling, 'Revelation and/as Insight,' in *The Importance of Insight: Essays in Honour of Michael Vertin*, ed. John J. Liptay Jr. and David S. Liptay (Toronto: University of Toronto Press, 2007), 97–115; and 'Another Perhaps Permanently Valid Achievement: Lonergan on Christ's (Self-) Knowledge,' *Lonergan Workshop* 20 (2008): 127–164.

reward that God gives to Christ's 'kindred' because of the supererogatory act that Christ performed, and it was for the sake of earning such
a reward that Christ performed it. Thus Y amounts to redemption in
the sense of 'atonement' – and that is all it amounts to. God became
human so that humans need not be punished and for no other reason.
That is one baleful aspect of Anselm's legacy.

Now Lonergan by no means denies that Y is redemption in that
sense. He does hold, in his *Redemption* book, that Y is not *only* redemption in that sense, and that it is not *primarily* redemption in that
sense. Primarily, Y is the mediation of friendship. What calls for God's
Incarnation is not, in the first instance, the sinfulness of those whom
God would befriend. In the first instance it is the self-diffusiveness of
the divine friendship that God would share. That being said, however,
it is true *de facto* that those whom God would befriend *are* sinners.
'Man's making of man,' in which God takes part by becoming human,
is no neutral country, as it were. It is enemy territory. There is un-
friendliness, decline, the objective social surd. But one of the principles
from which Lonergan argues for the 'fittingness' of the Incarnation
states that friends love their friends' other friends. If P is friends with
Q, and Q is friends with R, and R is P's enemy, P will nevertheless love
R, if not for R's own sake, then for the sake of Q. Similarly, someone
who is a friend of God will love God's enemies for God's sake – and
vice versa.

Now add to this what has already been said under the first point
above. Suppose there is an intermediate friend, someone who loves
God and therefore loves God's enemies, and someone who also knows
the whole of God's plan for the universe and therefore knows how God
brings good out of evil. Suppose, in other words, that the intermediate
friend grasps the 'essence' of redemption as expressed in the Law of the
Cross. It would be reasonable to expect that this intermediate friend
would teach and exhort and live according to that intelligible law, even
to the point of laying down his life. My suggestion, then, is that in the
context of the *Redemption* book and its answer to 'Why a God-man?'
redemption in the sense of 'atonement' belongs to Y as a special case.
Every genuine friend wants for his or her friends what is best for them,
as Aristotle pointed out. The intermediate friend of God will want for
his friends, who happen to be God's enemies, what is best for them,
namely that they should repent and be converted.

Here is another way to put the same hypothesis. In the context of Lonergan's *Redemption* book, I think there is an isomorphism between the 'outer' function of the incarnate Word, *Y* that is, and the 'inner' gift of grace as analyzed in *Grace and Freedom*. The *general* function of grace is to 'elevate' or 'divinize' human nature. Because it does that, and in the process of doing it, so to say, grace heals – if it so happens that there is anything to heal. The fact that it does heal has been, at least in Western, Augustinian theology, the obvious thing about grace, and Western theologians have tended at times to think that what is most obvious about grace is what grace obviously is. Not so. Similarly, Western theology has concentrated on the cross as though what is most obvious about the work of Christ is what the work of Christ obviously consists in. Lonergan's interpretation of what it meant for Christ to *choose* the Law of the Cross does something to redress this imbalance. God became human to befriend humankind, and in the process of befriending them, expressed his sorrow and hatred for their sin.[10]

(3) This leads to a further point. In the larger context of the *Redemption* book, Lonergan ties together the various components of *Y*, Christ's work, by proposing that the Word was made flesh so as to function as an 'expressive sign.' It would take a good deal of space to expound the meaning of that phrase. Very briefly stated, it seems evident that it means what Lonergan would later, in *Method in Theology*, mean by 'symbol' although at the same time he is moving towards the notion that *Method* refers to as 'incarnate meaning.' In any case, 'expressive signification' is the basic mode in which the incarnate Word, as intermediate friend, goes about making friends. He manifests the love of God that is his by right.

An interesting consequence follows. Abelard was not mistaken after all, at least not entirely. Historical theology in the twentieth century has rather consistently presented Anselm and Abelard as opposed and as exemplifying in their opposition the only two routes, 'objective' and 'subjective' respectively, that an understanding of Christ's work can possibly take. Where Abelard is concerned, the passage that is rou-

---

10 This is the gist of Lonergan's interpretation of the Anselmian term 'satisfaction.' See Charles Hefling, "A Perhaps Permanently Valid Achievement: Lonergan on Christ's Satisfaction," *METHOD: Journal of Lonergan Studies* 10 (1992): 51–74.

tinely quoted is this one from his commentary on the Epistle to the Romans:

> Our redemption through Christ's suffering is that deeper affection in us which not only frees us from slavery to sin but also wins for us the true liberty of sons of God, so that we do all things out of love rather than fear – love to him who has shown us such grace that no greater can be found, as he himself asserts, saying 'Greater love than this no man hath, that a man lay down his life for his friends.'[11]

Lonergan quotes the same passage in his textbook on *The Incarnate Word*. He does not entirely approve of it, but his disapproval is notably mild. All he says about Abelard's view is that it is a rather serious oversimplification[12] – not that it is simply wrong. Moreover, the source of Abelard's mistake is the same as the source of Anselm's: both of them wrote before the theorem of the supernatural was discovered. By 'deeper affection' and 'love' Abelard is evidently referring to *charity*, since it is charity that 'frees us from slavery to sin.' But to recognize that charity is supernatural is to recognize that no secondary cause can produce or elicit it. Charity is not mediated; God causes it immediately. The incarnate Word, however, *is* a secondary cause. That is simply one way of stating the mystery of the hypostatic union. Consequently, no matter how great the love is that the incarnate Word displays, even if 'greater love hath no man than this,' it remains that the display is finite. As such it is not proportionate to inducing in anyone the supernatural love that is charity.

In brief, the difficulty with Abelard's view is on all fours with the difficulty that arises from Lonergan's own house-building analogy. It may sound *un*fitting to say that the incarnate Word, precisely *as* incarnate, 'could not' call forth unrestricted love. But Lonergan does say it. He says it rather explicitly in the *Redemption* book. It is one thing to love a divine person who has become human. To love him as a divine person is something else. The first is natural, the second supernatural. The difference is that loving a divine person *as* divine can only be loving that person as another divine person does. To love the person of

---

11 Peter Abelard, *Exposition of the Epistle to the Romans*, book 2, §3 (on Romans 3:19-26), quoting John 15:13. Translation adapted from Eugene R. Fairweather, ed., *A Scholastic Miscellany: Anselm to Ockham* (New York: The Macmillan Company, 1970), 284.

12 Lonergan, *De Verbo Incarnato* (Rome: Gregorian University Press, 1964), 450: *gravior simplificatio*.

Christ requires the indwelling of the Holy Spirit and requires the love for God which is participation in the Spirit, and which is poured by the Spirit into human hearts. Stated in the biblical terms that Lonergan uses on occasion, Christ draws everyone to himself when he is 'lifted up.' Being so drawn is loving a divine person in the human nature he assumed. But to Christ the divine person no one comes 'unless the Father draws him,' and Lonergan identified the Father's drawing with the gift of the Spirit.

5. OBSERVATIONS IN CONCLUSION

There is a case to be made, then, that Lonergan's appropriation of the theorem of the supernatural makes it possible for him to outline, at least, an intelligible account of Christ's person and work that 'sublates' the accounts given by Anselm and Abelard – an account, that is, which includes what is valid in both but does so from a higher viewpoint. Moreover, a case could be made that this viewpoint also includes, in a more synthetic fashion, Thomas Aquinas's views on Christ's work in particular. In the *Summa theologiae*, Thomas seems content simply to list a number of different ways in which the life and death of Christ were beneficial, including Anselm's explanation. These reasons for the Incarnation are not simply disconnected *sententiae*, but neither do they have a clearly intelligible unity. It was Lonergan's aspiration, as Frederick Crowe has observed, to find and articulate such an intelligible unity – a single explanation capable of grounding all the traditional images and theories. As the present essay has tried to suggest, I agree that this is the direction in which Lonergan's thought was moving. Crowe, however, seems inclined to judge that the Law of the Cross in *The Incarnate Word* represents Lonergan's solution to the problem of integrating in a 'total view' the various components of Christ's work.[13] I would say that he found a comprehensive viewpoint, not in the Law of the Cross *per se*, but in the answer his *Redemption* book gives to the question 'Why a God-man?' As I have already pointed out, the Law of the Cross is no less significant in the *Redemption* book than in *The In-*

---

13 See Bernard Lonergan, CWL 6, *Philosophical and Theological Papers 1958-1964*, ed. Robert C. Croken, Frederick E. Crowe, and Robert M. Doran (Toronto: University of Toronto, 1996), 14, n. 26. This long editorial note is of course anonymous, but both its manner and its matter strongly suggest Crowe's authorship. *Ex pede Herculem.*

carnate Word. It is, however, included within what I take to be a wider and more integrated 'systematic' context.

One important aspect of the integration is that the answer to Anselm's question proposed in the *Redemption* book links not only that book but also two others, *The Incarnate Word* and the earlier *Constitution of Christ*, with the most estimable of Lonergan's theological treatises, *The Triune God*. Judging only by the two books on Christology that he finished, it might be supposed that Lonergan thought of their subject matter as more or less independent of Trinitarian theology. No doubt the 'impossible conditions' under which he taught his course on the incarnate Word are partly to blame in so far as they encouraged the atomization of the various theological 'tracts.' In any case, the *Redemption* book – which, significantly, does not follow the scholastic thesis–format used in *The Triune God* and *The Incarnate Word* – sets the systematic conception of Christ's constitution in a context that is congruent with what Lonergan says elsewhere about the purpose of the divine 'missions.' As those who are familiar with *The Triune God* will recognize, the invisible mission of the Spirit and the visible mission of the Son have, according to Lonergan, a common purpose, which is to establish and confirm new interpersonal relations – relations, as he puts it in the *Redemption* book, of friendship.

A further, somewhat tentative observation follows on this. Lonergan speaks of loving a divine person made man – which is to say loving the man Jesus of Nazareth – *as* divine. What it would be, concretely, to love another member of the human species as divine, the *Redemption* book does not say. Arguably, however, it would be to *worship* him.

Worship is a topic on which Lonergan had little if anything to say. There is one *obiter dictum* to the effect that religious conversion consists in transferring oneself into 'the world of worship.'[14] To describe this 'transfer' would be to describe something that is on the one hand intensely personal, and on the other hand thoroughly concrete – and therefore complex. To move from such a description to analysis and explanation would be a task at once delicate and monumental. It would depend on self-appropriation in answer to some such question as 'What am I doing when I am worshiping?' It would be to distinguish and relate 'inner' and the 'outer' components of an ongoing process, to distinguish between the immediate and the mediated, to distinguish knowledge born of religious love and expressed beliefs that further de-

---

14 Lonergan, *A Second Collection*, 217.

termine such knowledge. It would be to pay attention to an exercise of the friendship that is at once mediated, through the mission of a friend who is the Son, and immediate, in the gift of a friend who is the Spirit.

The key to *theological* account of Christian worship would perhaps be Lonergan's definition of a symbol as an image that evokes or is evoked by feeling.[15] His idea that the Incarnation can be understood in functional terms as a symbol has already been mentioned. To ask what this symbol *means*, what Christ was and is a symbol *of*, is to begin to do theology. Here the point to be made is simply that symbols mediate. Considered as images, real or imagined, they are 'carriers' of meaning. On the other hand, neither the feeling that a symbol evokes nor the feeling that evokes it is itself an image. Feelings *mean*, in the sense that they have objects that are consciously present. Such objects, however, may be either 'agent objects,' which awaken affectivity, or objects in the 'passive' sense that feeling *makes* them present. To ask which of the two, feeling or symbol, is prior is to ask a question that Lonergan does not regard as especially important. The relationship is not static. It runs in both directions.

Now love is, among other things, feeling. When Lonergan insists that it is a mistake to think that nothing is loved unless it is already known, he is proposing that love can arise spontaneously with no determinate object – no symbol – to evoke it. Such is 'the love of God flooding our hearts.' Theologically speaking, there is nothing in the universe of proportionate being that *can* evoke this love, not even a divine person made man. At the same time, Lonergan identifies such unrestricted love with sanctifying grace, and grace is always cooperative as well as operative. It could perhaps be said, then, that the Word was made flesh so that grace, the immediate love of God, might have something to cooperate with, an 'outer word' adequate to express 'what is congruent with the gift of love that God works within us.'[16] In that case worship, as love for Jesus Christ as a divine person, could be conceived as an instance, perhaps in some sense the principal instance, of human cooperation with divine grace. In so far as it consists in loving God, worship depends on the unmediated gift of the Spirit. In so far as it has as its mediated object, directly or indirectly, the 'expressive sign' who was Jesus Christ, it depends on the Incarnation of the Word.

---

15 Lonergan, *Method in Theology*, 64.

16 Lonergan, *Method in Theology*, 113.

The cooperation may take the form of 'sighs too deep for words'; it may take the form of crying, 'Abba! Father!'; it may take the form of eucharistic *anamnesis* of the Lord's death 'until he come.'[17]

My suggestion then, briefly stated, is that Christian worship is a kind of definitive microcosm of Christian living as supernatural. It involves the 'ontic present' of God's love; it involves the 'objective past in which God's revelation of his love...through Christ Jesus has been mediated...by the ongoing Christian community', and the result of co-operation between these 'inner' and 'outer' moments is an eschatological attitude and orientation that issues 'from above downwards' in a transformation of existential ethics.[18] To be anyone's friend is to share his or her commitments and the judgments of value they are based on. To be a friend of the incarnate Word, and to love him as his Father does, is at the same time to be committed to a terminal value that transcends the human good. Of such an eschatological commitment, Christian worship is – or ought to be – not only an expressive but an effectual sign, a sacrament. It has always been recognized that sacramental theology depends on Christology. To work out an account of sacraments derived from Lonergan's Christology would be a project well worth the enormous effort that undertaking it would call for.

---

17 Romans 8:26; Romans 8:15; 1 Corinthians 11:26.

18 See Lonergan's remarkable account of this 'economic Trinity' in his response to a questionnaire on philosophy, CWL 17, *Philosophical and Theological Papers 1965-1980*, 358.

FROM A SYSTEMATICS OF
HISTORY TO COMMUNICATIONS:
TRANSITION, DIFFERENCE, OPTIONS

Thomas Hughson, SJ
MARQUETTE UNIVERSITY

I. INTRODUCTION

Robert Doran proposes a unified field structure for systematic theology.[1] The proposal correlates four real relations in the Trinity (paternity, filiation, active spiration, and passive spiration) with four created participations (*esse secundarium* of the Incarnation, the light of glory, sanctifying grace, and the habit of charity).[2] This is the four-point hypothesis. Joining the correlation to a theological theory of history completes the unified field structure that "would stand to a contemporary systematics as the periodic table of elements stands to contemporary chemistry."[3] The structure serves as a method "capable of guiding for the present and the foreseeable future the ongoing genetic development of the entire synthetic understanding of the

---

1 Robert Doran, "Bernard Lonergan and the Functions of Systematic Theology," *Theological Studies* 59, 4 (1998): 569-607, "System and History: The Challenge to Catholic Systematic Theology," *Theological Studies* 60 (1999), *What Is Systematic Theology?* (Toronto: University of Toronto Press, 2005), and "The Starting-Point of Systematic Theology," *Theological Studies* 67 (2006): 750-76. Doran's *Theology and the Dialectics of History* (Toronto: University of Toronto Press, 1990) lays the groundwork.

2 In page 18 of *What Is Systematic Theology?*, Doran translates and quotes the four-point hypothesis from Lonergan's *De Deo trino: Pars systematica* (Rome: Gregorian University, 1964): 234/5. See English translation, Bernard J.F. Lonergan, Collected Works of Bernard Lonergan, vol. 12, *The Triune God: Systematics*, ed. Robert M. Doran and H. Daniel Monsour, tr. Michael Shields (Toronto: University of Toronto Press, 2007).

3 Doran, *What Is Systematic Theology?* 63.

mysteries of faith and of the other elements."[4] The structure develops and refines Bernard Lonergan's method for systematic theology.[5]

Recent discussion of Doran's complex heuristic has addressed the four-point hypothesis.[6] But Doran also conceives the human making of history in the mode of constitutive meaning, no less than the cognitive meaning of dogma and doctrine, as the content or object of systematics. Accordingly, "history is the mediated object of systematics."[7] Doran's "systematics of history"[8] proceeds in light of Lonergan's theory of history amplified with analytic concepts contributed by Doran: psychic conversion, the dialectic of culture along with person and community, and a distinction between a dialectic of contraries and a dialectic of contradictories.[9] Connecting the theory of history to the four-point hypothesis will yield a theological theory of history.

In considering Doran's proposal I would like to move in a different direction from a discussion of the four-point hypothesis. Looking more to Doran's approach to history, yet not confining attention to systematics, I will ask how Doran's theological theory of history affects other functional specialties besides systematics. I will address *communications* in particular. Expectation of further clarity from the continuing debate on the four-point hypothesis notwithstanding, and in advance of a substantial application of Doran's methodological

---

4 Ibid., 62.

5 Bernard Lonergan, *Method in Theology* (New York: Seabury Press, 1972).

6 In 1993 Frederick E. Crowe, SJ, drew attention to Lonergan's correlation of the four divine relations in the Trinity with "four divine graces par excellence" in "The Spectrum of 'Communication' in Lonergan," ed. Thomas J. Farrell and Paul A. Soukup, *Communication and Lonergan: Common Ground for Forging the New Age* (Kansas City: Sheed & Ward, 1993), 67-86 at 85. Crowe's survey and summary of communication as a theme in Lonergan's writings are invaluable.

See recent responses by Charles Hefling, "On the (Economic) Trinity: An Argument in Conversation with Robert Doran," *Theological Studies* 68 (2007): 642-60, and Neil J. Ormerod, "Two Points or Four – Rahner and Lonergan on Trinity, Incarnation, Grace, and Beatific Vision," *Theological Studies* 68 (2007): 661-73. Robert Doran replies in "Addressing the Four-Point Hypothesis," *Theological Studies* 68 (2007): 674-82.

7 Doran, *What Is Systematic Theology?*, 147.

8 Ibid., 156.

9 See Doran, *Theology and the Dialectics of History*, 70-77.

proposal, questions about its wider implications are unavoidable.[10] A modification in the application of the seventh functional specialty cannot help but affect the successor specialty that at once depends on and crowns not only systematics but the whole task of theology. I hazard the view that it is not too soon to ask how Doran's modification of Lonergan's systematics leads into adjustments in receiving and applying Lonergan's functional specialty of communications. Change initiates consequences. Hence, what consequences occur for communications following from the proposed changes in systematics?

One consequence involves the goal of systematics. Doran's modification touches *Method in Theology*'s stated goal for this specialty. Lonergan said that systematics seeks an "understanding of the realities affirmed in the previous specialty, doctrines."[11] When attained, this understanding becomes available to the next and final specialty, communications. But Doran broadens "the realities affirmed" by dogmas and doctrines to those also meant in (non-dogmatic) Christian constitutive meaning.[12] This calls for an adjustment in the overall goal of systematics. A re-statement of what systematics seeks in light of Doran's proposal could read: an "understanding of the realities affirmed in the previous specialty, doctrines, ["and an understanding of the realities intended in the community's constitutive meaning"].[13] Expansion of the scope of systematics from dogma to constitutive meaning directs systematics to a broader goal. The fact and formulation of a reformulated goal flows from a modification in method.

Incorporating history and constitutive meaning into the object of systematics changes the goal and content of systematics. The altered content in turn impinges on the tasks for communications outlined in chapter 14 of *Method*. To explain how, I will comment on chapter 14

---

10 Doran anticipates substantive application in reference to the mission of the Holy Spirit in *What Is Systematic Theology?*, 76-77. Ivo Coelho, SDB reflects fruitfully on applying Lonergan's whole approach in "Applying Lonergan's Method: The Case of an Indian Theology," *METHOD: Journal of Lonergan Studies* 22 (2004): 1-22. He remarks that "communication is mediated not only by understanding [systematics] but also by love," 16.

11 Ibid., 335.

12 See especially, Doran, "Bernard Lonergan and the Functions of Systematic Theology," and *What Is Systematic Theology?*, Chapter 3, 'Dogma and Mystery'.

13 Ibid., 148.

and then will consider how Doran's work on systematics affects it. My interest stems from a conviction that the importance and potential of communications in reference to Doran's work merits extensive discussion. I hope my contribution will resonate with others and further the discussion.

2. COMMUNICATIONS

Chapter 14, "Communications", lays out a path that articulates theology's mediation between a cultural matrix and the significance and role of religion in that matrix. Doran emphasizes that communications occurs through the "mutual self-mediation" between religion and its cultural context.[14] Lonergan removed this crowning specialty from simply being a direct implementation of the determinate content taken over from systematics.[15] Similarly, communications is not about "a band of preachers sermonizing the passive congregation."[16] The eighth specialty is more than how to speak about, write on, teach and preach the meaning of dogmas and doctrines attained in systematics. That is, Lonergan did not title the eighth specialty ethics, homiletics, or mission. Nevertheless, Christian commitment to the common good of society, the witnessing to and preaching of the gospel, mission, and inculturation are all important objectives.[17]

First of all, Lonergan emphasizes that it is the church that does the communicating. Therefore, communications has a strong ecclesial di-

---

14 Robert Doran in *What Is Systematic Theology?*, especially in pages 202-203, distinguishes the church's self-mediation accomplished in the first seven specialties from the mutual self-mediation between religion and culture carried out in the eighth. See also Francisco Sierra-Gutiérrez, "Communication: Mutual Self-Mediation in Context," in Farrell and Soukup, eds., *Communication and Lonergan*, 269-293.

15 *The Handbuch der Pastoraltheologie* takes the same approach.

16 Frederick E. Crowe, SJ, *The Lonergan Enterprise* (USA: Cowley Publications, 1980), 99.

17 On preaching, see Carla Mae Streeter, OP, "Preaching as a Form of Theological Communication: An Instance of Lonergan's Evaluative Hermeneutics," in *Communication and Lonergan*, 48-66. Streeter remarks, "Teaching intends ordered information. Preaching pushes on to the behavioral transformation we identify as conversion," 58. Attention to the link between communications, here instantiated in preaching, and conversion is important.

mension. As Lonergan pointed out subsequent to *Method*: "communications is not simply about one person doing something. What is the church? The church is a process of communication ...of the message of the Gospel, of that message that is what the Christian knows, of the content that informs his life, and of the precepts that guide his actions."[18] Frederick E. Crowe states succinctly that the specialty described in chapter 14 of *Method* is about "the church constituting herself."[19] Communications brings within its ambit preaching, inculturation, evangelization, the church's handing on of faith within itself, the self-constitution of the church, the reconstitution of society, ecumenism, interreligious relations, and integral human studies. Communications is a pastoral or practical theology as exemplified in the Arnold, Rahner, et al. *Handbuch der Pastoraltheologie* to which Lonergan refers.[20]

The *Handbuch* concentrates on the life and activity of the church as the material object; that life and activity precisely as conditioned by

---

18 Bernard Lonergan, *The Philosophy of God, and Theology* (London: Darton, Longman, & Todd, 1973) 65/6, quoted by Crowe, *The Lonergan Enterprise*, 99/100.

19 Crowe, *The Lonergan Enterprise*, 100.

20 Lonergan, *Method*, 355/6. Herausgegeben von Franz Xavier Arnold, Karl Rahner, Viktor Schurr, Leonhard M. Weber, Ferdinand Klostermann, *Handbuch der Pastoraltheologie: Praktische Theologie der Kirche in ihrer Gegenwart*, zweite, überarbeitete Auflage, Bände I-5 (Freiburg: Herder, 1970-72). Volume 5 is a *Lexikon der Praktische Theologie*, herausgegeben von Ferdinand Klostermann, Karl Rahner, Hansjörg Schild. An entry by K. Gastgeber at 421 under "Praktische Theologie" explains that what Catholic theology called pastoral theology, Protestant theology has designated practical theology. An entry on "Pastoraltheologie" at 393-395 by Rahner agrees that practical theology is a preferable title.

Today there is a tendency to redefine practical theology as public theology. See for example William F. Storrar and Andrew R. Morton, *Public Theology for the 21ˢᵗ Century: Essays in Honour of Duncan B. Forrester* (London: T & T Clark, 2004) and Elaine Graham and Anna Rowlands, editors, *Pathways to the Public Square: Practical Theology in an Age of Pluralism* (Münster: Lit Verlag, 2005). See also Michael J. Himes and Kenneth R. Himes, *Fullness of Faith: the Public Significance of Theology* (New York: Paulist Press, 1993) and Mary Doak, *Reclaiming Narrative for Public Theology* (Albany: State University of New York Press, 2004).

the present situation are the formal perspective.[21] Nevertheless, because of Vatican II the *Handbuch* moved beyond being simply a model for pastoral theology meant specifically for seminaries which followed dogmatic theology and concluded the sequence of seminary courses by instructing future pastors in the ways and means of parish ministry. In contrast, Lonergan's communications, as it presupposes the analysis of operations in intentional consciousness and the account of meaning in social existence, pushes past the ecclesiocentric perspective of the earlier *Handbuch*. Lonergan sets communications in the direction not only of a contribution to renewal in the life and work of the church, but also of a contribution to progress in society in those dimensions of social existence – political life, social movements, economic life, and cultural life – outside church authority but not separate from the Reign of God.

The final 'crowning' specialty in theology, communications, is not to be understood primarily as theology coming back full circle to common sense. However, it is true that engaging common sense in church and society eventually plays a significant role in the renewal of both insofar as teaching and preaching, on the one hand, and policy-formation, on the other hand, both introduce changes and elicit feed-back in church as well as in society. Moreover, communications takes up the labor of transposing and translating religious beliefs in order to make them accessible to people from various cultures on diverse levels, and this includes using mass media effectively. Such a return to common sense, however, is not the first immediate step or operation in communications, as if all theology had been wrapped up in systematics, leaving communications with, as it were, the job of marketing the systematic product. For this would be to revert to the obsolete idea of praxis as the mute vessel or agent of theory. Communications is "theology in its external relations."[22] Communications returns theology to the level of experience, not only in a noetic mode, but also as active experience in actions that make history and produce further data.

---

21 H. Schüster, Part One, chapter 3 "Wesen und Aufgabe der Pastoraltheologie als praktischer Theologie," *Handbuch der Pastoraltheologie* I 93-117. In the entry on "Pastoraltheologie," Rahner says the key question is, what must the church do today? This question "encompasses the whole task of practical theology" 394.

22 Lonergan, *Method*, 132. See Streeter, "Preaching as a Form of Communication," 61.

However, there are specific tasks of a theological nature proper to communications. Communications takes the content of systematics a further step towards contextualization. In doing so, communications allows for advances in the understanding attained in systematics and should not be construed simply as an addition to or transmission of what systematics already understands. Lonergan spoke of communications as "concerned with the task of preaching and teaching the doctrines to all men [sic] in every culture and in every class of each culture," and there is a sense, one could say, that systematics hands over the clarification of doctrines to preachers and teachers.[23] Understanding of the mysteries of faith does not come to fruition in systematics alone. For instance, Lonergan remarks that, "communications is concerned with...interdisciplinary relations with art, language, literature, and other religions, with the natural and the human sciences, with philosophy and history...."[24] Interdisciplinary relations are not strictly matters of common sense although personal relations between exponents of the various disciplines likely involves common sense as well as their respective expertise. A method promoting interdisciplinary relations between theology and other disciplines already prolongs the theological position on the Athens/Jerusalem debate, likewise supporting their interchange and resisting the temptation to view them as simply antithetical. In Lonergan's terms, these interdisciplinary relations involve the theological task of combining the general categories that theology has in common with other disciplines with the special categories proper to theology. This is in contrast with a position that prefers that theology stay exclusively with special categories, as tends to be the case with Karl Barth and Hans Urs von Balthasar.

Another theological task proper to communications has to do with theology's contribution to the Christian mission. Communications brings together theological analysis of a cultural context with systematic-theological understanding of the missions of Son and Spirit, of participation in them by the church and other Christians, of the sending of the Gospel to all nations, and to the growth of the church. This is needed within and between cultures since, as Lonergan states about communications, "there are the transpositions that theological

---

23 Bernard Lonergan, *Philosophy of God, and Theology: The Relationship between Philosophy of God and the Functional Specialty, Systematics* (London: Darton, Longman & Todd, 1973), 23.

24 Lonergan, *Method*, 132.

thought has to develop if religion is to retain its identity and yet at the same time find access into the minds and hearts of men [sic] of all cultures and classes."[25] Communications has to combine those special categories gained from its specific traditions within a particular language and for a culture or subculture in a given stage of development, with the general categories derived from the dynamic and operations of intentional consciousness.

Still another theological task in communications consists in promoting common meaning in the church and in society. The orientation in communications toward common meaning, whether in church or society, does not derive only from the tendency inherent in the intentional consciousness and from socially situated persons to expression, language, and intersubjective communication. Rather, subsuming that tendency, the orientation toward common meaning flows from and expresses the finality inherent in the mission and message of Christ toward communication in all functions of meaning to all peoples. This depends on the church's own prior hearing and receiving of Christ's message, as understood to some degree in systematics. Communications involves theological analysis of the contemporary situation of the church and identifying specific needs of renewal in the church's common Christian meaning. On that basis communications then puts a more nuanced systematic understanding into motion toward church renewal.

3. THE TRANSITION FROM SYSTEMATICS TO COMMUNICATIONS

With chapter 14 of *Method* in mind let us take up a second issue, the consequences of Doran's unified field structure for communications. How would accepting at least the main lines of Doran's complex argument for a theological theory of history affect the reception and application of Lonergan's final specialty, communications? This question parallels one raised and answered in the *Handbuch der Pastoraltheologie* in a section defining the material and formal object of pastoral theology.[26] There may be implications in this parallel, but the purpose for describing it here is simply to note that altering one aspect

---

25 Ibid.

26 See H. Schuster, "3 Kapitel: Wesen und Aufgabe der Pastoraltheologie als praktisher Theologie," in *Handbuch der Pastoraltheologie*, Bd. I 93-117.

of systematic theology affects not only other parts of systematics but other parts that are dependent upon systematics and in this case communications.

H. Schuster explains that Vatican II's ecclesiology as a whole, and not only the structures, offices, and official ministries, modified dogmatic ecclesiology. This, in turn, prepared for a renewal in pastoral theology, one no longer centered in the official exercise of clerical ministries. This altered dogmatic ecclesiology led to questions about pastoral theology which had been defined in reference to pre-conciliar dogmatic ecclesiology. By identifying pastoral theology anew, Schuster defines its material object as the church. However, he is not referring simply to the church's sacramental life and essential structures but to the event of manifesting the Gospel's divine truth and love in the concrete human dimensions of the church's actual, contemporary life and work. In his view dogmatic ecclesiology (still unfinished) and pastoral theology cannot be separated because dogmatic ecclesiology has an element of pastoral theology within it and likewise pastoral theology carries principles of dogmatic ecclesiology. What then is distinctive about pastoral theology?

The answer is that it is to become practical theology, an existential ecclesiology. The event-character of the church as such is also an element in dogmatic ecclesiology. While ecclesiology can say on the basis of scripture and tradition what the church is and does, these sources by themselves do not suffice to interpret the present situation as the condition within which the church realizes itself. What distinguishes a practical-theological approach to the church as actualizing itself, that which is its formal object or viewpoint, is the qualification and conditioning of the church-event by the present situation.[27] The church's realization in and interaction with the contemporary situation reflects its participation in the mission of Jesus Christ and likewise constitutes part of its historicity. Practical theology analyzes the church in relation to the ever changing contemporary situation that enters into both the web and woof of the church. It also contains a call from God which the social sciences alone cannot enable practical theology to discern.

The parallel between pastoral theology and communications arises from the fact that a change in systematic theology, whether by the ecclesiology of Vatican II or in systematics as with Doran's integration of history into it, initiates the rethinking of a dependent yet distinct

27 Ibid., 100-102.

theological discipline. It is with this respect for change now underway in systematic theology, and without wanting to foreclose further
debate on it, that I raise the question about how accepting history as
the mediated object of systematics goes on to affect the method, tasks,
and perspectives of communications. What is the impact of Doran's
systematics on communications? Summarily, history as the mediated
object of systematics brings increased clarity to the transition from
systematics to communications and opens up the difference between
systematics and communications with new options for communications.

First, the matter of the transition from systematics to communications arises for discussion because of the lexical sequence through
the specialties, from research, interpretation, history, and dialectic
to foundations, doctrines, and systematics. After the specialty of research, each subsequent specialty in one way or another takes over
content arrived at by the operations of its predecessor. The opening
paragraph of chapter 14 of *Method* recapitulates this sequence and
then "finally comes our present concern with the eighth functional
specialty, communications."[28] Like its predecessors, communications
takes over content, in this case from systematics. Earlier, in chapter 5
on the functional specialties, Lonergan set forth a direct purpose for
the last specialty by stating, "communications is concerned with theology in its external relations."[29]

However, there is no statement at the start of communications
about its relation to systematics analogously comparable in clarity
to the first sentence in the chapter on systematics about systematics
relation to doctrines ("...systematics is concerned with promoting
an understanding of the realities affirmed in the previous specialty,
doctrines.")[30] Given the sequence of specialties, one would expect that
communications would open with a similar programmatic statement.
There is one, but it occurs in section 4: "Since God can be counted on
to bestow his grace, practical theology [chapter 14] is concerned with
the effective communication of Christ's message."[31] This declaration of
the parameters and focus of the specialty occurs halfway through the

---

28　Lonergan, *Method*, 355.

29　Ibid., 132.

30　Ibid., 335.

31　Ibid., 359/60.

chapter in the section titled 'The Christian Church and Its Contemporary Situation'. Yet it seems to be a transitional statement offering a clear point of departure for a method in service of such apostolic labors on behalf of Christ's message as witness, that is, the witness through preaching, inculturation, and assisting local churches to develop, insofar as evangelization or mission is understood to include a collaboration with those seeking the renewal of society. One wonders why sections 1-3 precede sections 4 and 5. In other words, there seems to be a jagged edge at the outset of chapter 14 rather than a clear, smooth transition.

There are advantages to this abrupt turn to the topic of meaning insofar as sections 1-3 protect the 'message of Christ' from being misunderstood, that is, as if only kerygmatic formulas or verbal formulations sum up the New Testament witness to Christ. However, Lonergan's breadth and depth of perspective removes the pre-eminence assigned to dogmas as stated in chapter 13. Therein, the cognitive meaning of Nicaea and Chalcedon, for example, could be stable even though the formulations develop and change. However in sections 1-3 on communications, the kind and function of meaning emphasized the most is not the cognitive meaning proper to dogmas. Rather, and in line with "the church constituting herself," it is especially the constitutive and effective meaning Lonergan emphasizes in chapter 14.[32]

The constitutive function of meaning has a prominent role in chapter 14. Meaning, Lonergan notes, "constitutes part of the reality of the one who means."[33] As common, meaning "constitutes community," and community as the achievement of common meaning "is the ideal basis of society"[34] that constantly needs repair and healing to reverse the decline ever introduced by bias. The message of Christ, broadly understood to include his person, deeds, initiatives, and impact, is common Christian meaning. As common, it is "constitutive inasmuch as it crystallizes the hidden inner gift of love into overt Christian fellowship."[35] The church is "a process of self-constitution occurring within world-

---

32 See Note 10 above.

33 Lonergan, *Method*, 356.

34 Ibid., 360-61.

35 Ibid., 362.

wide society."[36]Lonergan framed and initiated chapter 14 in terms of chapter 3 on meaning, especially constitutive and effective meaning.

Section 1 on 'The Ontology of Meaning', section 2 on 'Common Meaning and Ontology', and section 3 on 'Society, State, Church' proceed from a starting-point more closely associated with chapter 3 on meaning(s) than with that of chapter 13's goal of "an ultimate clarification of the meaning of doctrine."[37] An alternative, conceivable possibility would have been to frame chapter 14 in terms of chapter 2 on the human good, which figures among the objectives aimed at by communications but only within the priority of meaning.[38] The effect of a return to meaning at the beginning of chapter 14, and especially to constitutive and effective meaning, is to undermine the singular preeminence that chapter 13 accorded to dogma and the cognitive function of meaning. Lonergan's transition to chapter 14 becomes clearer and smoother in light of Doran's analysis of Christian constitutive meaning and his theory of history. Guided by Doran's refined method, systematics will have explored and articulated some Christian constitutive meaning and not only the meaning of dogmas. This wider goal for systematics provides a smooth passage to sections 1-3 of communications.

Communications as a specialty flows thematically and with greater clarity from the systematics undertaken in light of Doran's heuristic than from Lonergan's centering systematics on dogma. Doran's historical focus more easily surfaces the multi-dimensional aspects of Lonergan's 'message of Christ'. The historical focus likewise more clearly links the message of Christ with Christian constitutive meaning and with the Church's mission understood as a participation in the divine missions of God's self-communication. Doran's development of Lonergan succeeds in opening a direct path from systematics to communications, a path that without history becomes construed solely as constitutive meaning already part of systematics. The significance of this improved transition lies not only in the clearer logic of the sequence of the specialties but also in its evidentiary value as supporting the validity of Doran's revision as a genuine development and not a departure from Lonergan's overall thought.

---

36 Ibid., 363-64.

37 Ibid.

38 On the human good in communications see Lonergan, *Method*, 359-361.

4. COMMUNICATIONS:
DIFFERENCE AND OPTIONS

Another consequence of Doran's proposed unified field structure pertains to the difference between systematics and communications. The specialties laid out in chapters 13 and 14 respectively are unmistakably distinct, and the distinction pertains to a division of labor that divides each task into manageable functional specialties. The difficulty is that Doran's methodological development already establishes the proximity of human decision and action into systematics. Indeed he states that "…there is a praxis orientation to systematic theology…a relation to 'historical action', to 'the data as produced', that is the concern of communications."[39] He expects that "this component will be more pronounced in future systematic theologies than has been the case in the past."[40] This placing of praxis within systematics also blurs a difference from communications, not only as the return to experience, but as active in making history.

In Chapter 10 of *What Is Systematic Theology?*, Doran addresses topics such as 'The Constitution of Society', 'Collective Responsibility and Social Grace', and 'Theology as Praxis', all which might seem to better fit communications than systematics. Since history is potentially all-encompassing and its theological analysis equally comprehensive and oriented toward making as well as interpreting history, one may wonder what is left for communications to do. Does Doran's systematics insofar as it incorporates history as mediated object overtake and extend into communications, thereby losing the benefit of a division of labor? Once systematic theology identifies Christian constitutive meaning, along with the church dogmas, as subject-matter for systematics, and once it has begun to interpret history from a Christian perspective as the locus of divine presence, it becomes clear that the mediated object of systematics has no boundary to divide it from the contemporary context, an arena of human decision and action – the arena of communications.

The result is that Doran's systematics changes, but does not replace, communications. For the purpose of discussion, a proposal on several aspects of that change follows without claiming to have exhausted the possibilities. The proposal addresses the question "What is the basic

---

39 Ibid., 197.

40 Ibid.

task of communications once history has become the mediated object of systematics according to the analytic method Doran develops from Lonergan's theory of history?" First, I think communications does everything Lonergan spells out in chapter 14 of *Method* but in such a way that it is prioritized by three options that underline certain themes in chapter 14. I do not argue that these options are logically necessary consequences of a systematics of history, or that they simply extend Doran's heuristic from systematics to communications. Rather, each option is like an elective affinity between Doran's development of systematics and a specific theme in Lonergan's communications.[41] What guides the option in each case is Doran's methodological advance.

In light of Doran's work, the affinities between themes then steer communications in a certain direction by establishing priorities for its many tasks. The options prepare a contemporary agenda for communications. The three options are: 1.) communications, informed by systematic understandings, relating theology to determinate cultural contexts; 2.) communications informed by systematics, adopting a pragmatic orientation that contributes a theological perspective to theoretical and practical problems blocking progress and redemption; and 3.) communications, competent in systematics, engaging in interdisciplinary dialectic/dialogue with historiography, the social sciences, philosophy, and the natural sciences.

The first option highlights *Method in Theology*'s change from the revelational vocabulary of chapter 13, the 'mysteries of faith,' to the missionary language of chapter 14, 'the message of Christ,' as content directed to all nations and not simply an object for theological exploration and the church's contemplation. In *The Dialectics of History* and *What Is Systematic Theology?*, Doran develops Lonergan's situating of systematic theology within a cultural matrix and context. Doran emphasizes mutuality in the mediation between the contemporary

---

41 In sociology an elective affinity is a nondeterministic coinciding of components from different socio-cultural systems (e.g. the protestant ethic and the spirit of capitalism) favorable to each and generative of social change. See William H. Swatos, Jr., "Elective Affinity," in William H. Swatos, Jr., ed., *Encyclopedia of Religion and Society* (Walnut Creek, CA: Altamira Press,1998), 163. Analogy here means a contingent, not logically compulsory though not arbitrary, linking of themes from systematics in light of Doran and themes in communications.

situation and the Christian heritage, with theology learning from the analyses of the situation as well as offering insights to it.

The second option draws attention to the schema of progress/ decline/redemption in sections 3 and 4 of chapter 14. Doran made the redemptive purpose of the divine economy a motif in his development of systematics. That purpose is a reason why understanding the mysteries of faith does not come to fruition in systematics. The mysteries of faith have a redemptive finality as divine initiatives *pro nobis*; while not all dogmas explicitly affirm, they all presuppose it. This finality, biblically expressed in Acts by the pouring out of the Holy Spirit on the church at Pentecost, belongs to the constitutive meaning of Christ's message continually received into the church, lived through the centuries, and functioning as an effective meaning in Christian mission.[42] Without this finality the mysteries of faith are less completely understood by systematics. The focus on redemption in communications with the implication of *pro nobis* fulfills systematic understandings.

The third option picks up the description in chapter 5 of communications as interdisciplinary and links it to what chapter 14 says about integrated studies and collaboration for the common good of both church and society. In *What Is Systematic Theology?*, Doran went into greater detail than Lonergan about how and why systematic theology has an obligation to work with both general and special categories. Doran's treatment of general and special categories offers communications an invaluable impetus toward the characteristically theological priority of revelation and faith in yoking general with special categories. Theology need not adopt a method of correlation in order to carry out this combination and Doran explains how to avoid reductionism.[43]

These three options complement Doran's proposal for systematic theology. His analytic of three dialectics (person, community, and culture) has a universal and comprehensive scope as part of an approach grounded in the universal human operations of intentional consciousness. Each dialectic is open to divine transcendence and, in fact, the divine potentially enables each to be and become an integral dialectic,

---

42 On the constitutive, not dogmatic, meaning of the *pro nobis*, see Doran, *What Is Systematic Theology?*, 19-27.

43 Applying the method of correlation sometimes neglects the priority of the special categories. See *What Is Systematic Theology?*, 47-51, 82-88.

thus preventing a one-sided distortion of the person, the community, or the culture. Hence, it would seem that systematics more or less has to work through the dialectic of community (developed by Lonergan) and the dialectic of culture (a contribution of Doran) at the universal level of intentional consciousness and, religiously, in terms of divine presence. However, people live within various concrete contexts, i.e., specific languages, cultures, eras, conditions, etc. This is where Doran's methodology bears fruit especially for communications.

5. A DETERMINATE LOCAL CONTEXT

It does not seem feasible or productive for systematics to develop a theological theory of history for every local, cultural context of church and society, and after that go on to seek the integration of all their diverse insights for the whole church. Such might be an ideal, but it would be a Herculean task. One way of limiting the task of systematics in regard to history is for systematics to retain a formal connection with: 1) the unity of the church amid the evident, blessed diversity, 2) the unity of the manifold gospel, 3) the unity within historically-conditioned church teachings, and 4) the unity-to-be-discovered among systematic theologies originating in many contexts. That would delineate a main task for communications as moving back and forth between systematic theology and the local context. It would leave detailed, local specification and interpretation in light of Doran's three dialectics to communications. It also would respect dogma, doctrine, and the four-point hypothesis as important to the life and thought of the whole church.

An example clarifies this division of labor. In anticipating a substantive application of dialectical analysis, Doran looks to the mission of the Holy Spirit. In a brief synopsis he states:

> The theory of history based on the interrelations of the levels of value – from above, religious, personal, cultural, social, vital – proposes that the recurrent intelligent emanation of the word of authentic value judgments and of acts of love in human consciousness (personal value) is due to the grace of the mission of the Holy Spirit (religious value) and is also the source of the making of history, of historical progress through schemes of recurrence in the realms of cultural, social and vital values.[44]

---

44 Doran, *What Is Systematic Theology?*, 77.

The Holy Spirit influencing people toward authentic value judgments and acts of love thereby continually acts in history to affect human agency in the making of history.

Systematic theology can elucidate and articulate the presence and
influence of the Holy Spirit, but it need not monopolize such reflection on the Spirit as active in local cultural and historical contexts.
Demarcating more clearly how systematics differs from communications lets systematics concentrate on the universal reality of the mission of the Spirit, so that communications can focus primarily on the
charismatic element in the local church and on the divine influence
on human authenticity and cooperation in each specific cultural context. For example, systematics would bring the three dialectics to bear
on Vatican II as an event of the whole church while communications
would examine the appropriation of the multi-dimensional meanings
of the Council from within local churches and contexts. This would
alter the agenda of chapter 14, elevating theological reflection on the
mission of the Spirit as "the inner gift of God's love" to a task for communications.[45]

The difference is one of moving the Spirit from the background
to the foreground. Lonergan states in chapter 14, "The Christian
church is the community that results from the outer communication of Christ's message and the inner gift of God's love [Holy Spirit
poured out]." When it comes to defining the scope of communications, however, he urges that "practical theology is concerned with the
effective communication of Christ's message rather than the inner gift
of God's love that opens hearts to the message."[46] The reason for a
certain Christocentrism is that "God can be counted on to bestow his
grace [the Holy Spirit poured out]," so this can be taken for granted
while human efficacy in communication cannot be thought to be independent of education and theology. This understandable selection of
priority has the effect of removing the mission of the Holy Spirit from
among the realities with which practical theology (communications) is
concerned except insofar as the dogmas on, and a systematic theology
of, the Holy Spirit belong to Christ's message.

However, as Doran argues, the mission of the Spirit is coextensive
with history and has not come to a temporal end within the church

---

45 Lonergan, *Method*, 361/2.

46 Lonergan, *Method*, 361/2.

and within other religions and in humanity at large. He states concerning his theory of history, "The discernment of the mission of the Holy Spirit thus becomes the most important ingredient in humankind's taking responsibility for the guidance of history." [47] Presuming that this discernment has a theological as well as an existential dimension, in which specialty does theological discernment occur? The task of discernment seems unable to be fulfilled solely by systematic theology. While the latter can objectify, test, and think through the sending of the Spirit on the basis of the religious experience of receiving the gift of the Spirit poured out, it is too much to charge systematics with the burden of a theology of the Holy Spirit that can take into account each cultural context of the church and the wider global society as well.

6. A PRAGMATIC ORIENTATION

Another change in communications due to Doran's development of systematics concerns the promise of theological reflection with a pragmatic turn within a determinate cultural context. This does not refer to the pragmatic criterion for truth, where the criterion of the truth and reality is one of practicality. Nor does it refer to the skills and logistics needed for the management of church facilities, nor to the common sense overcoming of theory, but rather it refers to giving priority to a theological contribution to problem-solving. The problems I have in mind are not especially those already defined as theological but rather, to locate them in reference to the scale of values operative in history, those that present themselves as vital, social, cultural, personal, and religious values. Moreover, the three dialectics move within a progress/decline/redemption dynamic in regard to person, community, and culture. Problems arise when persons, communities, and cultures do not integrate progress in one set of values with progress in other values, or from acute decline in any one set of values, and from ignorance as to how to encourage the love enabling redemption.

Due to its methodological nature and universal scope, Doran's proposal attends to the three dialectics without applying them in detail. Systematics could most easily apply them in regard to large-scale progress/decline/redemption in church and society. That would leave to communications the tasks of attending to concrete, particular, local

---

47 Doran, *What Is Systematic Theology?*, 77. I am grateful to John Dadosky for the suggestion that discerning the presence of the Spirit in the Other has a place among the tasks of communications.

problems (speaking for the moment to society) such as distinguishing and engaging each variety of secularization in the West, contributing to support for international cooperation through institutions such as the United Nations and the European Union, and altering the self-understanding operative within the reduction of nonhuman nature to a purely instrumental status in North America.

In particular, Doran's application of Lonergan's insight that problems of decline in social value (the structure of the human good) depend for their solution upon the positive influence of cultural values, rather than only upon changes in social structures, has immense significance for the cause of social justice.[48] However, working this out for a determinate cultural context in consultation with other disciplines probably exceeds what even a praxis-oriented systematics of history can do if it also has the agenda of synthesizing insights from *ressourcement*, Thomistic, and liberation theologies. Theological entry into social problem-solving at the local level could be handed over to the task of communications, thus dividing the labor between the two. Equally, communications would be in a stronger position if systematics made available a systematics of history that dealt with constitutive meaning in light of the three dialectics as well as with the four-point hypothesis. Systematics as proposed by Doran already would have identified the large-scale problems in terms especially of the dialectics of community and of culture, pointing further to the basic dimensions of redemption as well. But communications could handle the fuller more determinate context in detail, and facilitate in a more concrete way the process for love and redemption. Thus, in light of Doran's work, when Lonergan states that the notion of dialectic "can be an instrument for the analysis of social process and the social situation," this can be directed to the local context and situation with a pragmatic orientation.[49]

7. INTERDISCIPLINARY DIALECTIC/DIALOGUE

Since historical situations, contexts, and problems are marked by specific social, linguistic, cultural, political, and economic meanings, and these predispose potential parties to such interdisciplinary dialogue, this means that dialogue has to be conceived as a flexible process with stages, of which the first is dialectic and the last is dialogue.

---

48 Doran, *What Is Systematic Theology?*, 188-201.

49 Lonergan, *Method*, 365.

The third option opened up by Doran's work has to do with interdisciplinary dialogue. The history of interdisciplinary scholarship indicates that crossing disciplinary boundaries occurs with two goals in mind: 1) the unity of knowledge and 2) to solve a problem that exceeds the capacity of a single discipline.[50] For example, whereas a systematics of history engages historiography for the sake of incorporating the knowledge of history into a theological synthesis, I have suggested that communications offers the staging area from which theology can relate to other disciplines with an eye to the alternative goal of solving problems of church and society within local contexts.

This approach finds support in *Method in Theology*. One of the beauties in *Method* on communications is the provision Lonergan makes for combining general categories shared with other disciplines with special (theological) categories without necessarily having to integrate or synthesize them. Integrative studies undertaken by theology do serve the redemptive process in the church, and it goes without saying that some integration or synthesis would be indispensable. However, parallel to this and looking to the human good in society at large, another sort of integrative studies is needed for the sake of generating "well-informed and continuously revised policies and plans for promoting good and undoing evil...[also] in society generally."[51] This cooperation includes the tasks of exchanging information, defining and addressing problems, multiple investigations, coordination, and collaboration that are not compatible simply with the model of integrative studies as a synthesis by one discipline alone (i.e., philosophy, theology, historiography, sociology, etc.) either as carried out by an individual or a team in that discipline.[52]

Instead, the implied model is some version of cooperation, dialogue, and consensus formation across disciplinary boundaries that lead the participating experts to find solutions in the form of policy recommendations. Something more could be said about the dialogue be-

---

50 See Julie Klein Thompson's *Interdisciplinarity: History, Theory & Practice* (Detroit: Wayne State University Press, 1990) and *Crossing Boundaries: Knowledge, Disciplinarities, and Interdisciplinarities* (Charlottesville: University of Virginia Press, 1996). This record does not include interdisciplinary work between theology and other disciplines but is enlightening nonetheless.

51 Lonergan, *Method*, 366.

52 Ibid.

tween theology and historiography as a way of keeping a systematics of history conversant with the theory and practice of historiography. However, here I will take up briefly how Doran's work could pass from a methodological guidance to a more substantive contribution to problem-solving by inquiring as to how his appropriation of Lonergan's thought can be brought into discussion with post modernity in the work of Gianni Vattimo.[53] Doran's heuristic for a systematics of history contains an extraordinarily rich starting-point for what many might think an improbable dialogue. Though other problems such as marginalization or religious fundamentalism would be equally eligible for consideration, the problem I have in mind is the tension between nationalism and international cooperation in a geo-political world scarred by terrorism. Vattimo is an important contemporary philosopher who, like Doran, looks to a more humane quality of social existence at all levels and supports cross-cultural, international, and multidisciplinary cooperation.

Bringing the works of Doran and Vattimo into closer proximity has a precedent in the unlikely pairing of Joseph Cardinal Ratzinger and Jürgen Habermas in *The Dialectics of Secularization: On Reason and Religion.*[54] Calling this a precedent does not imply that either Doran and Ratzinger or Vattimo and Habermas hold the same positions. Vattimo, for example, represents an idea of postmodernity at considerable distance from and in disagreement with Habermas. Doran's participation in the tradition of Aquinas differs in certain ways from an Augustinian tendency in Ratzinger.[55]

---

53 See among others Gianni Vattimo, *The End of Modernity: Nihilism and Hermeneutics in Postmodern Culture*, trans. Jon R. Snyder (Baltimore: Johns Hopkins Press, 1991; Italian original, *La fine della modernita*, 1985) and Gianni Vattimo, *Nihilism & Emancipation: Ethics, Politics, and Law*, ed. Santiago Zaba, trans. William McCuaig, (New York: Columbia University Press, 2004; Italian original *Nichilismo ed emanzipazione: Etica, politica, diritto*, 2003).

54 Joseph Cardinal Ratzinger and Jürgen Habermas, *The Dialectics of Secularization: On Reason and Religion*, ed. Florian Schuller, trans. Brian McNeil, CRV (San Francisco: Ignatius Press, 2006). The work was first published as *Dialektik der Säkulasierung: Über Vernunft und Religion* (Freiburg im Bresigau: Herder, 2005).

55 It should be said that one of Doran's concerns is to prevent fruitless conflict between Augustinian and Thomist positions. See *What Is Systematic Theology?*, 82-88.

Why would such a dialogue be sought and how could it proceed? There is a possibility from Doran's side. His work displays an interest in the work of Martin Heidegger, one not found in Lonergan. In *What Is Systematic Theology?* Doran set aside the "self-mediating advantages in dialogues between Lonergan and, say Gadamer, Heidegger, and Ricoeur" to devote himself to systematic theology.[56] Nevertheless, in subsequent pages of his book (pp.139-143) Doran briefly explores a convergence between his concept of psychic conversion and Heidegger's theme of *Verstehen*, and in so doing Doran is able to mediate between the contrasting positions of Lonergan and Heidegger on truth. My reading of Vattimo is limited. However, his appropriation of Friedrich Nietzsche and Heidegger on nihilism as the dissolution of first principles does not rule out, it seems to me, another way of being and thinking that starts from interiority as opposed to the first principles of theory and theoretical understanding. It is a methodological starting point that respects feelings, art, and empirical facts while also thinking about the decisive significance of the contemporary postmodern context. Both Doran's respect for liberation theology and Vattimo's commitment to the European Union indicate their common hope for a more humane social existence which includes a priority for responding to human suffering.

How might an interdisciplinary dialogue between Doran's theology and Vattimo's philosophy begin? First, I would not presume the universal validity and instantaneous productivity of *dialogue* unless it occurs as a dynamic process. While it may be at times suspected of harboring a pre-commitment that overrides points of substantive conflict or of ratifying the lack of parity between partners, the possibility of dialogue remains a hoped for challenge. Preferably, the initial framework, in order to begin the process, would respect the integrity in the respective thinkers' contrasting statements on metaphysics (e.g., Lonergan's integral heuristic structure of proportionate being and Heidegger's 'overcoming' of metaphysics, humanism, science, and technology), on God (e.g., Christian faith/atheism) and on culture (e.g., redemption/constructive nihilism). I would suggest conceiving the initial relationship between their respective positions not as a dialogue *per se*, but as a dialectic of opposed views, with the view perhaps

---

56 Doran, *What Is Systematic Theology?*, 6. In *Theology and the Dialectics of History*, he remembers, "Twenty years ago I was haunted by the question of the relation of Lonergan's work to Martin Heidegger," 11.

of what Lonergan called "an ecumenical spirit, aiming ultimately at a comprehensive viewpoint…."[57] This would be an interdisciplinary dialectic out of which dialogue may or may not come to fruition.

However, the "ecumenical spirit" and "comprehensive viewpoint" I have in mind would differ from Lonergan's by virtue of a location in civil society and in view of religious and philosophical pluralism. The "ecumenical spirit" can be transposed to civil amity, and the "comprehensive viewpoint" can be that of a pluralistic democracy wherein sincere contradictions may not move toward resolution by intellectual, moral, or religious conversion. This would mean adopting postmodern recognition that an irresolvable plurality of interpretations exists as the factual and legally protected condition of most societies if not also the truest situation of human thought. An outright declaration of adhesion to the pragmatic yet ethical principle of democratic social peace would be the most appropriate starting-point for the interdisciplinary dialectic/dialogue. Doran's dialectic also could underscore democratic initiatives toward cooperation in the common good, especially on behalf of those presently marginalized or oppressed.

The Doran/Vattimo dialectic would likely lead to dialogue away from any narrow nationalism but without dissolving cultural heritages, and to thought about how cultures affect cooperation among nations. However, I do not refer primarily to a *viva voce* dialogue between the two thinkers but more to a way of studying their work which seeks guidance from both perspectives as to what changes in social, cultural, political, and religious life are most needed in order to prevent nationalistic attitudes from corroding international cooperative efforts that can benefit the marginalized.

In sum, Doran's development of Lonergan's method for systematics affects systematics delineation from, its transition to, and the options for, the functional specialty communications. The delineation is marked by mutuality, the transition between the two becomes clearer, and the options include the priority of a determinate local context, a pragmatic orientation, and interdisciplinary dialectic/dialogue.

---

57 Lonergan, *Method*, 130.

THE HERMENEUTICS OF INTERIORITY:
TRANSPOSITIONS IN THE
THIRD STAGE OF MEANING

CHRISTIAAN JACOBS-VANDEGEER
SALVE REGINA UNIVERSITY

Systematics currently stands at a crossroad. Major transpositions and massive transformations of both method and content are required. It may take several decades before a new tradition in Catholic systematics is underway in a consolidated and not merely coincidental fashion, a tradition in essential continuity with past achievements but responding as well to contemporary exigences.[1]

Robert M. Doran, SJ

I. INTRODUCTION

This article seeks to clarify the meaning of the task of transposition, a task that Lonergan acknowledged as crucial for the renewal of Catholic intellectual life.[2] It begins with a biographical sketch of Lonergan's intellectual conversion to underscore the existential dimension of genuine transpositions of older insights into newer theologies. I happily dedicate this article in honor of my teacher Robert M. Doran, SJ, who has contributed enormously not only to my personal intellectual and existential growth but also to the fields of Lonergan studies and Catholic systematic theology.

---

1 Robert M. Doran, "Bernard Lonergan and the Functions of Systematic Theology," *Theological Studies* 59 (1998): 569-607, at 572.

2 Bernard J.F. Lonergan, "The Scope of Renewal," in *Philosophical and Theological Papers 1965-1980*, CWL 17, ed. Robert C. Croken and Robert M. Doran (Toronto: University of Toronto, 2004) 282-98; Lamb, "Lonergan's Transpositions," 4.

2. THE HERITAGE OF
INTELLECTUAL CONVERSION

When Lonergan finished his coursework in philosophy at Heythrop in 1929, he had a farewell conversation with Fr. Joseph Bolland who encouraged him to consider further studies in philosophy and theology. As Lonergan recounted it: "I answered that there was no question of that since I was a nominalist. He in turn said, 'Oh! No one remains a nominalist very long.' It was, in current parlance, a quite 'cool' reply from a high member of the establishment at a time when anti-modernist regulations were still in full force."[3]

Like most, if not all, scholars Lonergan benefited from conversations with several of the people he met during his academic journey and formation. Fr. Bolland predicted what a reading of J.A. Stewart's *Plato's Doctrine of Ideas* effected for Lonergan.[4] Later, while studying theology in Rome, Lonergan met Stefanos Stefanu, an Athenian Jesuit and fellow student, who studied with Maréchal in Belgium and taught Lonergan to recognize the discursive character of knowledge and its decisive component in judgment.[5] While Lonergan's familiarity with Augustinian *veritas* confirmed Stefanu's view, a course with Bernard Leeming on the Incarnate Word helped him to appreciate the real distinction between essence and existence. "This, of course, was all the more acceptable," he noted, "since Aquinas' *esse* corresponded to Augustine's *veritas* and both harmonized with Maréchal's view of judgment."[6]

Lonergan's account of his academic and intellectual journey verifies the prescience of Fr. Bolland's remark. Of course, Fr. Bolland predicted more than a shift in philosophical commitment. He predicted growth. The influences of Plato and Augustine, Stefano and Leeming partly shaped Lonergan's understanding of himself and his world. He delighted in the familial resonances of Aquinas' *esse*, Augustine's *veritas*, and Maréchal's view of judgment because of his desire to know, not a catalogue of philosophical and theological history, but the truth

---

3 Bernard J.F. Lonergan, *"Insight* Revisited," in *A Second Collection: Papers by Bernard J.F. Lonergan, SJ*, ed. William F. J. Ryan and Bernard J. Tyrell (Toronto: University of Toronto, 1974), 263-78, at 264.

4 Ibid.

5 Ibid., 265.

6 Ibid.

of his own knowing and being. Most philosophy students probably can identify with having such a desire to some degree, but their philosophical preoccupations and commitments may or may not consistently align with that desire.

Much of Lonergan's work throughout his scholarly career aims at helping others to experience the intellectual conversion that Leeming's course brought to fruition for him.[7] His work invites readers to embrace rather than flee or disparage their intellectual desire and to use it to govern their cognitive enterprises – whether in philosophy and theology, the natural or human sciences, or in practical living. His early book *Insight* (1957) represents, perhaps, the paradigmatic instance of that invitation in all his writings.[8] In fact, Lonergan recounted the events I cited above in a paper titled *"Insight Revisited,"* which he opened by suggesting that he "narrate briefly how *Insight* came to be written."[9] He understood his unique philosophical contributions in close proximity to his own intellectual conversion.

How do Lonergan's developments in philosophy and theology relate to Augustine's *veritas*, Aquinas' *esse*, or Maréchal's view of judgment? Lonergan's work resists the view that would reduce it to a novel combination of great ideas in the history of philosophy and theology. He acknowledged his influences, but his work does not aspire to rank under another author's or genre's mantle; for example, he denied the label of "transcendental Thomism" that still often attaches itself to his work. It seems to me that his resistance to such labels did not originate in any self-aggrandizing need to stake out intellectual independence or uniqueness. His understanding of how his most influential teachers (e.g., Augustine and Aquinas) impacted his thought may not differ much from how he assessed the increasing significance of his own philosophical and theological contributions. Of a "Lonerganian" framework or perspective, he once remarked: "The word *Lonerganian*

7 For an informative discussion of Leeming's influence on Lonergan's intellectual conversion, see William A. Matthews, *Lonergan's Quest: A Study of Desire in the Authoring of* Insight (Toronto: University of Toronto, 2005) 81-85.

8 Bernard J.F. Lonergan, *Insight: A Study of Human Understanding*, CWL 2, ed. Frederick E. Crowe and Robert M. Doran (Toronto: University of Toronto, 1997).

9 Lonergan, "Insight Revisited," 263.

has come up in recent days. In a sense there is no such thing. Because what I'm asking people is to discover themselves and be themselves."[10]

I tend to think that what Lonergan asks of his readers differs little from what he learned from his most valued teachers, especially Augustine and Aquinas. Not only did those teachers assist in his self-discovery, but their texts also taught him the importance of genuine self-discovery for correctly interpreting their valid insights and theories. Likewise, Lonergan stressed the importance of his readers' intellectual conversions as the hermeneutical entry points to his central proposals. His work places the existential quest for meaning at the centre of a philosophical and theological inquiry that mines the past for genuine insights into human living and anticipates the continual enrichment of those older findings with ever newer discoveries.

In many ways, Lonergan's work represents a series of transpositions. His analyses maintain continuity with several past achievements while developing those achievements within a contemporary context. Matthew Lamb says that "Lonergan always – both before and after *Method in Theology* – emphasized that his work was a transposition rather than a rejection of the achievements of the great Catholic theologians, especially Augustine and Aquinas."[11] Lonergan's transpositions unfold in the creative tension of continuity and development that defines the growth of theological reflection in a living religious tradition. His approach to ancient, patristic, and medieval authors partly begins with the invitation to intellectual conversion that echoes interiorly in all of us and resounds in the classic texts of the Church's theological heritage.

3. TRANSPOSITION: ITS NATURE AND TASK

In a 1979 lecture given at the Lonergan Workshop at Boston College, Lonergan addressed the nature of transposition. Relating it to a change in horizon, he said: "Now a change of horizon takes us out of the field of deductive logic. As long as one is simply logical, one remains within the same horizon. As soon as one changes one's horizon,

---

10 Bernard J. F. Lonergan, "An Interview with Fr. Bernard Lonergan, SJ," ed. Philip McShane, *A Second Collection*, 213.

11 Matthew Lamb, "Lonergan's Transpositions of Augustine and Aquinas: Exploratory Suggestions," in *The Importance of Insight: Essays in Honour of Michael Vertin*, ed. John J. Liptay and David S. Liptay (Toronto: University of Toronto, 2007), 3-21, at 5.

one begins to operate in virtue of a minor or major change in one's basic assumptions. Such a change may be just a jump, but also *it may be a genuine transposition, a restatement of an earlier position in a new and broader context*."[12]

Let us begin by noting a few implications of the notion of transposition. If a genuine transposition restates an earlier position in a new and broader context, still it implies a change of horizon, a shift in perspective. It implies that standpoints move, that interests and knowledge vary according to personal development, education, and larger socio-historical factors.[13] It implies that distinct horizons – the ranges of interests and knowledge that select or determine worlds of meaning – contextualize the positions or achievements emerging within them without imprisoning those achievements.[14] The notion of transposition eschews the varieties of relativism that would totally relegate validity to the social, historical, or linguistic materials used in the construction of knowledge. The notion of transposition implies that validity has a guarantor in the universe of being, that genuine knowledge has more than social currency. It implies that valid insights authored in a past horizon may take root in the richer field of a newer and broader context because the very possibility of a horizon originates with self-transcendence.[15]

Only with the subject's capacity for going beyond him or herself to what exists independently of him or herself does the possibility arise for the subject to have a *horizon* – a range of interests and knowledge that determines the totality of intelligibly varying objects that engage

---

12 Bernard J.F. Lonergan, "Horizons and Transpositions," in *Philosophical and Theological Papers 1965-1980*, CWL 17, ed. Robert C. Croken and Robert M. Doran (Toronto: University of Toronto, 2004), 409-32, at 410 (emphasis added); also cited in Lamb, "Lonergan's Transpositions," 5.

13 For more on how "horizon" pertains to a range of interests and knowledge that may vary according to several factors, see Bernard J.F. Lonergan, "The Human Good as the Developing Subject," in *Topics in Education: The Cincinnati Lectures of 1959 on the Philosophy of Education*, CWL 10, ed. Robert M. Doran and Frederick E. Crowe (Toronto: University of Toronto, 1993), 79-106, at 83-86, 88-92.

14 Ibid., 85, 90.

15 Bernard J.F. Lonergan, "Horizons," in *Philosophical and Theological Papers 1965-1980*, CWL 17, ed. Robert C. Croken and Robert M. Doran (Toronto: University of Toronto, 2004), 10-29, at 10-13.

one's concern.[16] "One can live in a world," Lonergan said, "[and] have a horizon, just in the measure that one is not locked up totally within oneself."[17] Horizons denote limits for engagements with a world, but the principle of self-transcendence in human consciousness – the principle of moving beyond oneself and having a horizon – has no limits or restrictions.[18] Its reach extends to the whole universe of being. Its anticipatory intention corresponds to the totality. It establishes the possibility for a supremely meaningful engagement with one's world by transcending the narrow concerns that shape particular horizons. Lonergan identified this principle with the pure desire to know – the dynamism of questioning – and recognized it as the standard for personal development and progress in history.[19] What makes a horizon possible also makes it capable of changing and developing.

By self-transcendence, then, the subject lives in a world with ever expanding possibilities for authentically meaningful engagement. Lonergan differentiated the unrestricted dynamism of questioning from the determinate horizons that contextualize particular answers. The former makes possible the latter, but it also marks the constitutive principle of genuine objectivity.[20] It relates intentionality to being immediately and sets the standard for knowledge by its immanent exigencies for intelligence and reasonability.[21] For Lonergan, horizons originate and expand according to a principle of self-transcendence that generates and safeguards authentic achievements of the human spirit. His analysis helps to clarify a crucial meaning of transposition.

---

16 Ibid., 11.

17 Ibid.

18 Ibid. See also Bernard J.F. Lonergan, *Method in Theology* (Toronto: University of Toronto, 1990), 104-5.

19 "Broadening the horizon cannot appeal to attained or developed interests, but has to appeal to more fundamental potentialities represented, for example, by the wonder of desiring to understand, a wonder which is unlimited in its scope, and by its corollaries in the affective field and in the field of the will" (Lonergan, "The Human Good as the Developing Subject," 105).

20 "Our position, then…discerns in self-transcendence both genuine subjectivity and the principle of genuine objectivity" (Lonergan, "Horizons," 13).

21 On the intrinsic relation of knowing to being, see Bernard J. F. Lonergan, "Cognitional Structure," in *Collection*, CWL 4, ed. Frederick E. Crowe and Robert M. Doran (Toronto: University of Toronto, 1988), 205-21, at 211-14.

The genuine restatement of an earlier position in a newer and broader context hinges on the self-transcending subject who integrates the valid insights of an earlier age into the contemporary effort for ongoing advance. On the genuineness of transpositions Lonergan wrote:

> [B]e it observed that a change of horizon cannot be demonstrated from a previous horizon. So the genuineness of transpositions cannot be a simple logical conclusion. What is basic is authenticity. It is a summit towards which one may strive, and only through such striving may one come to some imperfect participation of what Augustine and Aquinas named Uncreated Light.[22]

Before illustrating a change of horizon, I want to emphasize the point that authenticity in self-transcendence – faithfully responding to the exigencies of human consciousness – measures the genuineness of transpositions. By referring to authenticity as basic, Lonergan linked the task of transposition to the capacity for self-transcendence in all cognitional and intentional endeavors. He understood transpositions as more than translations of categories or transliterations of texts.[23] He identified the foundational aspect of transposition with the principle of genuine objectivity, namely, authentic subjectivity. His reference to an "imperfect participation" in "Uncreated Light" confirms and illustrates the point that transpositions primarily penetrate realities.

The reference confirms that transpositions require genuine insights into realities rather than only the conventions or linguistic habits of older theories because "imperfect participations" in "Uncreated Light" denote genuine exercises of human knowing.[24] The reference also illustrates the point because Augustine and Aquinas used the language

---

22 Lonergan, "Horizons and Transpositions," 410.

23 Lamb, "Lonergan's Transpositions," 6.

24 Interpreting Aquinas' views, Lonergan wrote: "The ultimate ground of our knowing is indeed God, the eternal Light; but the reason why we know is within us. It is the light of our own intellects; and by it we can know because 'ipsum enim lumen intellectuale quod est in nobis, nihil est aliud quam quaedam participata similitudo luminis increati' ['the intellectual light itself which we have within us is nothing else than a certain participated likeness of the uncreated light']" (Bernard J.F. Lonergan, *Verbum: Word and Idea in Aquinas*, CWL 2, ed. Frederick E. Crowe and Robert M. Doran [Toronto: University of Toronto, 1997] 85; Lonergan cited Aquinas, *ST* 1, q. 84, a. 5, c.).

of "intellectual light" to speak of a reality that Lonergan understood and named according to the legitimate trends and progress of his milieu: "the unrestricted desire to know."[25] His transpositions invite readers to recreate for themselves the genuine insights that once inspired the great philosophers and theologians of the past. Lamb nicely summarizes the point:

> Thus, transposition is not a translation or transliteration from one set of texts to another. Rather it involves judgment and thus knowledge of the realities referred to in the texts one is studying. Reaching up to the mind of an Augustine or an Aquinas means reaching up to the realities they knew.[26]

If genuine transpositions require knowledge of realities, still they also entail the insertion of previously attained knowledge into richer, broader contexts. The task of transposition implies navigating a change of horizons.

4. CHANGING HORIZONS:
REALMS AND STAGES OF MEANING

A "horizon" denotes a field or range of interests and knowledge that determines a world of meaning.[27] Such a field or range may expand or contract. It may contract by the intervention of a narrower concern as, for example, when self-interest overwhelms one's attention and pursuits. It may also admit a material expansion by the accumulation of new experiences (e.g., travels to new places and encounters with different kinds of people).[28] However, horizons may also undergo genuine development, which, Lonergan said, "depends upon, and is measured by, not so much the external objects with respect to which one operates as the organization of one's operations, their reach, their implications, the orientation of one's living, of one's concern."[29]

The notion of development in horizons highlights another key aspect of transposition, for transpositions operate out of the broader

25 Bernard J.F. Lonergan, *Understanding and Being: An Introduction and Companion to Insight: The Halifax Lectures*, CWL 5, ed. Elizabeth A. Morelli et al. (Toronto: University of Toronto, 1990), 389-90.

26 Lamb, "Lonergan's Transpositions," 6.

27 Lonergan, "Horizons and Transpositions," 425-26.

28 Ibid. See also, "The Human Good as the Developing Subject," 92.

29 Lonergan, "The Human Good as the Developing Subject," 92.

contexts defined by shifts in the organization of intentional dynamics and in the orientation of living and concern. The task of transposition entails navigating the changes that occur with the development of a horizon. It demands sufficient facility with the newer context and adequate familiarity with the older. But the task does not treat the two contexts as disparate or opposed because it recognizes that with horizons no less than with the valid positions formulated within them, development "retains all that was had before and adds to it, and it can add to it enormously."[30]

Lonergan explicated the principal divisions of developing horizons in terms of realms and stages of meaning.[31] His analysis differentiates four realms of meaning – common sense, theory, interiority, and transcendence – according to their correspondences with varying modes of conscious intentional operations.[32] He also identified three stages of meaning that arise successively with the differing modes of intentionality that generate the distinct realms of meaning.[33] The stages illustrate the notion of development as applied to horizons, for development pertains more to the organization of intentional operations than to the intended objects. The task of transposition thus requires the ability to transition among the realms of meaning that distinguish the different horizons or contexts of earlier and later formulations of valid philosophical and theological positions.

The realm of common sense characterizes the horizon of theology in its earliest, if not incipient, phase.[34] It dominates the first stage of meaning. Lonergan defined the realm of common sense by the mode of understanding persons and things in their relations to us.[35] Such a mode of understanding relies on description and uses ordinary, everyday language to express its meanings. Of course, people across the

---

30 Ibid.

31 Lonergan, *Method*, 257.

32 For explications of the four realms, see Lonergan, *Method*, 81-85.

33 On the stages of meaning, see Lonergan, *Method*, 85-99.

34 Lonergan, *Method*, 85, 93. For an example of theology in the first stage of meaning, see Lonergan's description of Augustinian reflection on grace in, Bernard J.F. Lonergan, *Grace and Freedom: Operative Grace in the Thought of St. Thomas Aquinas*, CWL 1, ed. Frederick E. Crowe and Robert M. Doran (Toronto: University of Toronto, 2000), 194-96.

35 Lonergan, *Method*, 81.

globe use varieties of common sense to understand rather uniquely an endless list of things in practical living, but Lonergan pointed out that several notable thinkers used their particular brands to shed significant light on the perennial question of the human subject: "Augustine's penetrating reflections on knowledge and consciousness, Descartes' *Regulae ad directionem ingenii*, Pascal's *Pensées*, Newman's *Grammar of Ascent* all remain within the world of commonsense apprehension and speech yet contribute enormously to our understanding of ourselves."[36] Common sense attains genuine knowledge of reality, but its specific manner of operation limits the questions it can adequately satisfy.

By the intrusion of a systematic exigence into the realm of common sense, there arises the explanatory mode of understanding that grounds the realm of theory. "The systematic exigence not merely raises questions that common sense cannot answer but also demands a context for its answers, a context that common sense cannot supply or comprehend. This context is theory, and the objects to which it refers are in the realm of theory."[37] The systematic exigence separates the realms of theory and common sense by demanding the mode of cognitional apprehension that conceives things in their relations to one another rather than to us. The realm of theory corresponds to explanatory efforts to know objects by their "internal relations, their congruences, and differences, the functions they fulfill in their interactions."[38] It uses a specialized, technical language to express its meanings.

The theoretical mode of theology develops in the second stage of meaning.[39] In the second stage, subjects continue to operate in the realm of common sense when dealing with particulars and concrete problems, but they can advert to the theoretical mode of operating when their inquiries require abstraction. By its explanatory mode of understanding, theoretical discourse approximates the logical ideals of clarity, rigor, and coherence.[40] Its technical language consists mainly in

---

36 Ibid., 261.

37 Ibid., 82.

38 Ibid.

39 For a discussion of theology in the second stage of meaning, see Lonergan's description of Thomism in Bernard J. F. Lonergan, "The Future of Thomism," in *A Second Collection*, 43-53.

40 Lonergan, *Method*, 258.

objective reference and thus tends to conceive things in metaphysical terms.[41] While a philosopher or theologian operating in the realm of theory "may advert to the subject and his operations, still any systematic treatment, as in Aristotle and in Aquinas, is of the subject and the operations as objectified and, indeed, conceived metaphysically in terms of matter and form, of potency, habit, and act, of efficient and final causes."[42]

The theories of Aristotle and Aquinas may address the same realities as do Augustine's *Confessions* or Pascal's *Pensées*, but the modes of understanding markedly differ. Still, the systematic discourses of theory do not negate the valid insights of a culturally stylized prose. In a second stage of meaning, theory intervenes to organize data in a mode of cognitional apprehension that by its explanatory potential surpasses common sense. Standpoints of earlier and later stages of meaning significantly change even when the actual referents of disparate texts stay the same. If genuine apprehension of the referent ensures continuity, still the manner of apprehending largely characterizes the development.

The task of transposing the valid insights of an earlier age hinges on the subject's ability to understand the intended reality and to integrate the achievement into the context of the later stage of meaning. Aquinas offers a clear example of the task. Lonergan explained that "[i]n working out his concept of *verbum* [word] Aquinas was engaged not merely in fitting an original Augustinian creation into an Aristotelian framework but also in attempting, however remotely and implicitly, to fuse together what to us may seem so disparate: a phenomenology of the subject with a psychology of the soul."[43] Aquinas creatively synthesized Greek and Arabic thought with Christian doctrine.[44] His insertion of Augustinian insights into Aristotelian theory illustrates how genuine understanding of various positions sometimes requires navigating the realms of meaning that partly distinguish a change in horizon between texts.

Navigating shifts in realms of meaning can occur "remotely and implicitly" or explicitly and methodically. The systematic exigence

---

41 Ibid., 95-96.

42 Ibid., 259.

43 Lonergan, *Verbum*, 3.

44 Lonergan, "The Future of Thomism," 43-47.

separates the realms of common sense and theory but falls short of making the distinction explicit or thematic. It effectively expands only the subject's ability to perform as a knower; it does not attain a critical perspective on subjectivity. The biologist, for example, can look at a giraffe and see "skeletal, locomotive, digestive, vascular, and nervous systems combine and interlock," and she can easily respond to her son's questions about what the giraffe eats and why it kicks.[45] But the ability to operate in different realms of meaning does not necessitate or imply the additional ability to thematize the cognitional performance and its implications.

Rather, the performance provokes the questions that anticipate the thematization. The cognitional performance highlights the critical exigence that demands an account of human knowing, its modes, and the realms of meaning it generates. Lonergan explained that "to meet fully the systematic exigence only reinforces the critical exigence. Is common sense just primitive ignorance to be brushed aside with an acclaim to science as the dawn of intelligence and reason? Or is science of merely pragmatic value, teaching us how to control nature, but failing to reveal what nature is? Or, for that matter, is there any such thing as human knowing?"[46]

The critical exigence confronts the subject with basic questions about the validity of human knowing and the nature of intended objects in varying modes of intentionality. Such foundational questions turn the subject's attention away from the outer realms of common sense and theory to the inner realm of the subject's interiority.[47] Lonergan distinguished interiority as a distinct realm of meaning. He explained that it corresponds to the heightening of intentional consciousness that constitutes the evidence for a verifiable account of human knowing. By adverting to interiority, the subject attends not merely to objects but also to the intending subject and his or her acts and operations. By heightening intentional consciousness, the subject can appropriate and thematize the structure, norms, and potentialities of his or her conscious intentional performance in terms and relations derived from consciousness itself. In short, the realm of interiority

45 Lonergan, *Method*, 82-83.

46 Ibid., 83.

47 Ibid.

contextualizes the meanings generated by a critical self-appropriation of conscious intentionality.

Such a critical self-appropriation allows the subject to meet the methodical exigency for relating the procedures of common sense and theory.[48] For Lonergan, the realm of interiority offers a critical reference point that severely reduces the potential for antagonism between the world of everyday affairs (common sense) and the increasingly exclusive world of specialized sciences (theory) because it allows the subject to define the differing modes of understanding and to affirm their validity. Interiority essentially bridges the divide between common sense and theory. Self-appropriation thus enables the subject to navigate methodically the shifts in realms of meaning that correspond to the varied transitions of his or her cognitional performance. It engenders what Lonergan called "interiorly differentiated consciousness," the unity of which he described as "the self-knowledge that understands the different realms and knows how to switch from any one to any other."[49]

The examples of common sense and theoretical modes of understanding cited above all pertain to self-knowledge. Lonergan recognized that philosophers and theologians operating in the realms of common sense and theory may attain tremendous insight into the nature of the subject. He also recognized that transpositions may occur in the second stage of meaning; Aquinas, for example, navigated differing realms of meaning, "however remotely and implicitly," to transpose Augustinian positions into an Aristotelian framework. Lonergan did not invent the task of transposition, but he defined the context in knowledge for explaining the nature of transposition. Where Aquinas performed with an exceptionally developed consciousness, Lonergan thematized the performance and the structure of the development. The thematization of the cognitional performance requires and partly constitutes interiorly differentiated consciousness, which, as Lonergan explained, "appears when the critical exigence turns attention upon interiority, when self-appropriation is achieved, when the subject relates his different procedures to the several realms, relates the several realms

48 Ibid.
49 Ibid., 84.

to one another, and consciously shifts from one realm to another by consciously changing his procedures."[50]

By the methodical exigence for interiorly differentiated consciousness, a culture enters the third stage of meaning.[51] Such an entrance marks for theology the beginning of its methodical mode. Lonergan defined methodical theology as theology grounded in the conscious operations and states of the existential subject.[52] In the third stage of meaning, the subject continues to operate in the realms of common sense and theory, but methodically adverts to interiority to establish a critical perspective for controlling the cognitional performance throughout its variations. The adoption of a critical perspective enriches theology with a transcultural base (i.e., a foundation in interiority), which promotes ecumenism and interreligious dialogue by enabling theologians to identify the conscious intentional dynamics that generate the varieties of religious expressions.[53] Such critical control over knowledge also allows theologians to understand, relate, and reconcile the various expressions that may significantly diversify their particular religious traditions.

Religious expression has its source in an experience of deep fulfillment that pertains to a fourth realm of meaning, which Lonergan named "the realm of transcendence."[54] He recognized a transcendent exigence that arises with the pure desire to know, which by its unrestricted reach orients the subject to the transcendent reality of the divine.[55] But only with the religious experience that inchoately fulfills transcendental intending (i.e., the unrestricted dynamism of questioning) does the ground of genuine religious expression appear in consciousness. Not corresponding to the emergence of a distinct stage of meaning, the realm of transcendence pertains to each of the three stages mentioned above, for religious expression speaks in the different realms of meaning and moves through all of the stages.

The second stage of meaning allows for tensions and conflicts to arise among distinct kinds of religious utterance. The culturally spe-

---

50 Ibid.

51 Ibid., 85, 94-99.

52 Ibid., 289.

53 Ibid., 119, 114.

54 Ibid., 83-84, 113-15.

55 Ibid., 83-84; 101-3.

cific, symbolic, aesthetic, and dramatic expressions of common sense may contrast sharply with the definitions, objectifications, and logical arguments of religion in the realm of theory. "So the God of Abraham, Isaac, and Jacob is set against the God of the philosophers and theologians."[56] But in the third stage of meaning, theologians advert to interiority to understand their own conscious intentional operations "and so explain the nature and the complementary purposes of different patterns of cognitional activity."[57] The methodical differentiation of the realms of meaning allows theologians to understand and reconcile the diversity of religious utterance. "For," as Lonergan explained, "its source and core is in the experience of the mystery of love and awe, and that pertains to the realm of transcendence. Its foundations, its basic terms and relationships, its method are derived from the realm of interiority. Its technical unfolding is in the realm of theory. Its preaching and teaching are in the realm of common sense."[58] Methodical theology possesses the critical perspective for recognizing the validity of seemingly disparate positions and affirming their complementary purposes.

Only when theology reaches the third stage of meaning does it have the ability to explain adequately the nature and task of transposition. Aquinas completed several transpositions for an *aggiornamento* ("bringing up to date") of Christian theology in his contemporary milieu, but an explanatory account of his performance requires explanations of the differing modes of cognitional activity and the realms of meaning that characterize the shifts in horizon relevant to his transpositions. The task of transposition in the third stage of meaning presupposes the personal achievement of interiorly differentiated consciousness. It implies the philosophical commitments in epistemology and metaphysics that rely on a critical self-appropriation. For Lonergan, interiorly differentiated consciousness establishes the critical base for affirming the validity of human knowing and constructing a verifiable metaphysics. Genuine transpositions presuppose the heuristic structures of knowing and being associated with these philosophical views.

The use of a verifiable base for constructing metaphysical categories distinguishes the methodical mode of theology and establishes direc-

56 Ibid., 115.

57 Ibid.

58 Ibid., 114.

tives for the task of transposition in the third stage of meaning. Lonergan recognized that a lack of recourse to methods for concretely proving the basic premises of logical arguments in theoretical theologies led to "vast arid wastes of theological controversy."[59] Metaphysics assumes priority for theologies of theory in the second stage of meaning, but it lacks the critical basis to substantiate valid claims and resolve disagreements. By contrast, methodical theology constructs a genuinely critical metaphysics by deriving its categories from the concrete realm of interiority. "For every [metaphysical] term and relation," Lonergan said, "there will exist a corresponding element in intentional consciousness. Accordingly, empty or misleading terms and relations can be eliminated, while valid ones can be elucidated by the conscious intention from which they are derived."[60]

Lonergan said that "a change of horizon cannot be demonstrated from a previous horizon." The shifts that demarcate the stages of meaning illustrate his point. The potentialities of common sense simply cannot generate theoretical or interiorly differentiated consciousness; and the logic of theory does not foresee the foundational primacy of interiority. Only interiorly differentiated consciousness thoroughly understands itself and the distinct realms of meaning that characterize earlier and later horizons. When theology enters its methodical phase, the task of transposition also responds to the methodical exigence. The task fixes its point of reference in the realm of interiority to pronounce the validity of earlier positions and to restate them in the later context of a third stage of meaning.

5. DEVELOPMENT AND CONTINUITY: TRANSPOSITIONS AND DIFFERENCES

Lonergan identified different kinds of differences: genetic, complementary, and dialectical.[61] Our overview of horizons emphasizes the former two. It acknowledges *genetically* distinct stages of meaning and explains how the realms of meaning correspond to the *complementary* purposes of different modes or patterns of cognitional activity. Dialectical differences denote absolute oppositions such as "right and wrong"

---

59 Ibid., 343.

60 Ibid.

61 Ibid., 236-37.

or "true and false." The task of transposition requires identifying and distinguishing all three kinds of differences.

The effort to identify differences within the living tradition of religion pertains to the creative tension of continuity and development in theology. Again, transpositions establish continuity with the past by preserving the valid insights of earlier theologies; they recognize continuity in the valid apprehensions of common referents. But transpositions also promote development by integrating older insights into the contemporary theological horizon; they recognize progress in the enriched contexts generated by diverse manners of apprehending. Self-transcendence serves as the unifying force that spans changes in horizons and safeguards the healthy tension of continuity and development because it attains the objectivity of diverse insights and grounds the hermeneutic for creative and accurate reformulations. It governs the task of transposition. Not only does interiorly differentiated consciousness then explicitly identify self-transcendence as the principle of genuine transpositions, but it also enhances transpositions with the methodical procedure that uses interiority explicitly to verify or eliminate the categories of older theologies.

Methodical theology derives its basic terms and relations from the interior realm of human consciousness.[62] It begins neither with a particular variety of common sense nor with the metaphysical framework of theory. Its basic categories may not primarily appeal to the concrete wisdom of the day or to the syllogistic force of logic, but they allow theologians to recognize genuine insight within the limits of common sense and to verify the achievements of theory. Methodical theology gains the critical perspective needed to identify the complementary relations of diverse religious expressions and to adjudicate the competing metaphysics of medieval theologies. Its critical perspective allows theologians to recognize the genetic, complementary, and dialectical differences among older and newer theologies. The task of transposition in the third stage of meaning uses interiorly differentiated consciousness as a key hermeneutical entry point to diverse texts.

Still, methodical theology does not claim exclusive rights to either self-knowledge or introspection. The first and second stages of meaning contextualize various theologies which offer incisive insights into the nature of human knowing and choosing. Lonergan showed in his *Verbum* articles that Aquinas controlled his use of metaphysi-

62 Ibid., 343.

cal categories with insights into psychological facts.[63] He also claimed that Augustine used introspection to grasp the reality of *verbum*, a non-linguistic inner word.[64] Both the medieval and patristic authors understood the importance of introspection for correctly interpreting interior realities. Their achievements stand as genetic precursors to Lonergan's explicit development of an introspective method. On Augustine's contribution, Lonergan wrote:

> Naturally enough, as Augustine's discovery was part and parcel of his own mind's knowledge of itself, so he begged his readers to look within themselves and there to discover the speech of spirit within spirit, an inner *verbum* prior to any use of language, yet distinct both from the mind itself and from its memory or its present apprehension of objects.[65]

Both Augustine and Aquinas recognized the importance of introspection for true self-knowledge. Lonergan, however, elevated it to a reflectively elaborated technique and fully developed its methodological potential. He explained how introspection offers the controls for distinguishing and relating the specialized fields and tasks of theology.[66] His notion of theological method structures theological contents according to the critical perspective of interiorly differentiated consciousness. It prepares theologians to reflectively control their retrievals of the religious tradition and their responses to the questions and concrete problems of their contemporary context.

Method and transposition are intimately intertwined tasks. Both are ongoing. Both rely on self-transcendence for their principle. And thus both anticipate the fuller realization of authentic subjectivity that unlocks the door to the past and meets the challenges of the contemporary life of the Church with the creative synthesis that maintains genuine continuity in the currents of a developing tradition.

---

63 Lonergan, *Verbum*, 5-6, 104-5. References to "psychological facts" denote verifiable intentions and events of consciousness.

64 Ibid., 6.

65 Ibid.

66 For Lonergan's explanation of functional specializations in theology, see *Method*, 125-45.

6. FROM THEORETICAL TO
METHODICAL THEOLOGY

Contemporary systematic theologies unavoidably bear genetic, complementary, and dialectical relationships to older theologies. If the task of constructing a methodical theology should take full advantage of Lonergan's contributions to the project, then it should emulate his effort to transpose rather than neglect or discard the past achievements of the Catholic theological tradition, especially those of Augustine and Aquinas. On the permanent value of Thomist achievements, Lonergan wrote:

> I have done two studies of the writings of St. Thomas Aquinas. One on *Grace and Freedom*, the other on *Verbum*. Were I to write on these topics today, the method I am proposing would lead to several significant differences from the presentation by Aquinas. But there also would exist profound affinities. For Aquinas' thought on grace and freedom and his thought on cognitional theory and on the Trinity were genuine achievements of the human spirit. Such achievement has a permanence of its own. It can be improved upon. It can be inserted in larger and richer contexts. But unless its substance is incorporated in subsequent work, the subsequent work will be a substantially poorer affair.[67]

Lonergan esteemed the permanent value of Aquinas' achievements, but the question of how methodical theologians should incorporate those achievements into the context of contemporary theological reflection remains somewhat unclear. Where does the task of transposition begin? Methodical theology relies on contemporary foundations for its appropriation of the religious tradition as well as its constructive response to the current situation of the Church. But if modern theologies govern retrievals of past insights, how do methodical theologians mitigate the risk of discarding an older achievement on the basis of a new oversight? Does the task of transposition start with modern developments? Or does it begin with older achievements?

The understanding of "transposition" I propose in the remainder of this article accounts for why methodical theology does not fix a strict starting point for transpositions. My proposal approaches transposition as a performance and thus allows us to explain what a methodical theologian such as Doran does when he incorporates theoretical

---

67 Ibid., 352.

insights into his methodically oriented work in systematic theology. Elsewhere, I referred to Doran's work as exemplary because of his sustained effort to integrate the permanently valuable achievements that Lonergan praised in Thomist theory.[68] Whereas Doran often begins with theoretical rather than methodical categories in his transpositions, I suggest that his approach conforms to the norms of methodical theology.[69] Still, there are places in Lonergan's texts which seem to prescribe the opposite procedure of "starting" with intentionality analysis rather than theory. Does Doran's approach contradict Lonergan's direction for the task? I do not think so. In what follows, I argue that Lonergan emphasizes intentionality analysis as to underscore the need to discover the conscious intention that controls the use of a valid metaphysical term. Such emphasis does not translate into a rigid procedure for transposing theologies of theory. Rather, it highlights the richness that a methodical context adds to theology, a richness that retains all that was had before and adds to it enormously.

6.1 THE STRUCTURE OF TRANSPOSING THOMIST THEORIES: DEVELOPMENT

The task of transposing Thomist theories of intellect and will requires consideration of the fact that Aquinas studied the subject in objective terms.[70] He used metaphysics to analyze the human person and the activities of knowing and choosing. The transposition of his analysis entails navigating the shifts in horizon that characterize the second and third stages of meaning. It involves effecting the transition from theory to method in the study of the subject. As Lonergan instructed: "Now to effect the transition from theoretical to methodical

---

68 See Christiaan Jacobs-Vandegeer, "Sanctifying Grace in a 'Methodical Theology,'" *Theological Studies* 68 (2007): 52-76, at 53-57. The next three sections of this article elaborate on those pages.

69 In "Consciousness and Grace," Doran says: "I have made a general decision that wherever possible, I will begin my own treatment of systematic issues by attempting to transpose Lonergan's systematic achievements into categories derived from religiously and interiorly differentiated consciousness" (Robert M. Doran, "Consciousness and Grace," *Method: Journal of Lonergan Studies* 11 [1993] 51-75, at 51).

70 Lonergan, *Method*, 258-59.

theology one must start, not from a metaphysical psychology, but from intentionality analysis and, indeed, from transcendental method."[71]

The transposition begins with intentionality analysis and method rather than theory because interiority offers the critical basis for verifying the valid categories of theoretical achievements. The task of transposition in the third stage of meaning shares the same foundations as methodical theology, namely, the self-appropriation of authentic subjectivity. Lonergan held Aquinas' cognitional theory in high regard, but he also acknowledged that his presentation of cognition markedly differed according to the method he implemented. His transposition of Thomist theory does not precede his method. It does not begin with the metaphysical psychology of theory and arrive at intentionality analysis. Rather, the transposition begins with method and uses the critical perspective of interiorly differentiated consciousness to retrieve Thomist achievements with reflective control.

6.2 THE STRUCTURE OF TRANSPOSING THOMIST THEORIES: CONTINUITY

Lonergan recognized a shift from the primacy of logic to the primacy of method in the transition from a theoretical to a methodical theology. The development of method affects the foundations of theological reflection.[72] Still, he also recognized the shift as a change in structure rather than content.[73] Logic continues to operate in methodical theology, but it operates under the governance of a method that unites logical operations (e.g., formulating hypotheses and deducing implications) with non-logical operations (e.g., inquiry, observation, discovery, experiment, synthesis, verification) to comprise an open, ongoing, progressive, and cumulative process rather than a rigorous deduction of necessary and immutable truths.[74] Likewise, the shift from metaphysical or faculty psychology to intentionality analysis does not negate the validity of the theoretical understanding of the subject. It changes the structure of the analysis but does not necessarily contra-

---

71 Ibid., 289.

72 Bernard J. F. Lonergan, "Theology in its New Context," in *A Second Collection*, 55-67; see also "The Future of Thomism," 49-53.

73 Bernard J .F. Lonergan, "Aquinas Today: Tradition and Innovation," in *A Third Collection: Papers by Bernard J. F. Lonergan*, ed. Frederick E. Crowe (New York: Paulist, 1985), 35-54, at 45.

74 Lonergan, *Method*, 6.

dict or render irrelevant the content. Clarifying his shift to the primacy of intentionality analysis, Lonergan said: "I do not mean that the metaphysical notion of the soul and its properties is to be dropped, any more than I mean that logic is to be dropped."[75]

Such comments underscore the continuity with theoretical theologies that Lonergan recognized in his development of theological method. But nowhere does that continuity appear more clearly than in Lonergan's interpretation of Aquinas. He showed in the *Verbum* articles that a core of psychological fact grounds the metaphysical categories of Thomist theory.[76] Aquinas analyzed human knowing in terms of apprehensive potencies, habits, and acts, but he also grasped the interior event of insight and used that grasp to reflectively control his metaphysics. In fact, Lonergan acknowledged at the end of the first *Verbum* article that he began with the psychological content of Thomist theory rather than its metaphysical framework, admitting that "logic might favor the opposite procedure but, after attempting it in a variety of ways, I found it unmanageable."[77] Lonergan also had to make the shift to the primacy of introspective method in order to present Aquinas' cognitional theory in the clearest light.[78]

The continuity of Lonergan with Aquinas extends beyond the content of their cognitional theories to the procedures of their analyses. Lonergan not only regarded Thomist intellectualism as a genuine achievement of the human spirit, he also recognized an incisive introspective perspective that permeates the Thomist metaphysical framework. He recognized a similar perspective in Aristotle. "But," Lonergan said, "if Aristotle and Aquinas used introspection and did so brilliantly, it remains that they did not thematize their use, did not elevate it into a reflectively elaborated technique, did not work out a proper method for psychology, and thereby lay the groundwork for the contemporary distinctions between nature and spirit and between the natural and the human sciences."[79]

---

75 Lonergan, "The Future of Thomism," 51.

76 Lonergan, *Verbum*, 59, 104-5.

77 Ibid., 59.

78 Crowe commented on Lonergan's personal transition from a faculty psychology to intentionality analysis in this context; see Frederick E. Crowe, "Editor's Preface," in *Verbum: Word and Idea in Aquinas*, xvii.

79 Lonergan, *Verbum*, 6.

The development of method defines the limits of a remarkable continuity with the faculty psychology of Thomist theory. Insight into insight occurred well before the emergence of the third stage of meaning and effectively controlled its attendant theoretical frameworks.[80] But its possessors did not thematize their self-appropriation.[81] Aquinas performed largely in consonance with the norms of a methodical construction of metaphysics, but he did not thematize his performance and work out its methodological implications. By developing the method he recognized in Thomist theory, Lonergan established for theological reflection a radically enriched context that preserves and develops Aquinas' achievements in cognitional theory.

6.3 THE STRUCTURE OF TRANSPOSING THOMIST THEORIES: THE CIRCLE OF METAPHYSICS AND COGNITIONAL THEORY

The strong affirmation of the core of psychological fact in Thomist theory validates the achievement. It illustrates why the task of transposition relies on intentionality analysis and method to implement a critical procedure. But it also illustrates why transpositions do not begin with the assumption that introspection and its reflective perspective belong solely to the third stage of meaning. Aquinas' achievements demonstrate that transpositions may discover introspective acumen in an earlier stage. Such discovery affects the procedure of the transposition by allowing methodical theologians to use the valid categories of an older theology to enrich or at times control contemporary theological development.

Lonergan instructed theologians to effect the transition from a theoretical to a methodical theology by starting with intentionality analysis and method rather than a metaphysical psychology. His instruction rightly serves to safeguard the primacy of interiority for establishing the validity of theoretical achievement. But it does not imply a strict recipe for the task of transposition. It does not suggest that methodical theologians should transpose older theories by ignoring medieval thinkers and constructing theological foundations through solitary

---

80 Jacobs-Vandegeer, "Sanctifying Grace in a 'Methodical Theology,'" 55.

81 "Finally, while Aristotle and St. Thomas did not elaborate a transcendental method, they understood its point" (Lonergan, "The Future of Thomism," 53).

advertence to interiority.[82] Such a procedure would not allow for the mind of an Aquinas to teach to our contemporary horizon.

Where, then, does the task of transposition begin? I suggest that Lonergan's instruction for beginning with intentionality analysis and method underscores the importance of discovering the conscious intention that controls the use of a valid metaphysical term. The instruction aims to safeguard the methodical primacy of interiority, but it does not settle or prescribe a strict starting point for the task of transposition. The following passage suggests that recognizing the methodical primacy of introspection allows a theologian to start with either metaphysics or cognitional theory:

> The point is to complete the circle [of cognitional theory and metaphysics]. One way to complete the circle is to begin from knowing. But one can begin with the metaphysics of the object, proceed to the metaphysical structure of the knower and to the metaphysics of knowing, and move on to complement the metaphysics of knowing with the further psychological determinations that can be had from consciousness. From those psychological determinations one can move on to objectivity and arrive at a metaphysics. One will be completing the same circle, except that one with be starting at a different point....*As long as one completes the circle, the same thing will be said, but it will be said at different points along the line.*[83]

The task of transposing theoretical theology into a methodical context consists in linking a valid metaphysical category to the corresponding element in the field of intentional consciousness. But the task may begin with either metaphysics or interiority; the critical problem consists in making the link between the two. The empirical base of interiority, which allows theologians to verify their terms and relations, explains the import of linking metaphysics to intentionality analysis. But the primacy of generalized empirical method only establishes the circle of metaphysics and cognitional theory because it verifies the isomorphism of knowing and being. The isomorphism relates the two modes of inquiry (i.e., critical metaphysics and cognitional theory) regardless of the starting point. Hence, the task of transposing Thomist theory into a methodical theology becomes the task of completing the circle of metaphysics and cognitional theory.

---

82 Jacobs-Vandegeer, "Sanctifying Grace in a 'Methodical Theology,'" 55.

83 Lonergan, *Understanding and Being*, 178. Emphasis added.

The circle of metaphysics and cognitional theory offers the view-point for understanding how introspective method allows methodical theologians to verify or eliminate the categories of older theologies and to use medieval achievement to enhance or correct a contemporary proposal. It offers the structure for transposing the valid insights of theory into a methodical context.

Lonergan offered the explanatory framework for understanding how the task of transposition sustains the creative tension of continuity and development that characterizes the living tradition of theological reflection. My article has dealt less with the content of theology and more with its method of retrieving the valid insights of the past for the needs of the contemporary life of the Church. It has attempted to explain what a methodical theologian such as Doran does when he develops our knowledge of the structure of conscious intentionality – whether at the level of the psyche through dialogue with depth psychology or at the *apex animae* (peak of the soul) – or when he relates Lonergan's differing analyses of choosing the good to Ignatius' distinct times of election.[84] Doran's transpositions perform what Lonergan called the "third possibility," the possibility of contributing creatively and faithfully to the larger and ongoing task of renewal for Catholic intellectual life.

> As yet, issues are unsettled. There is the danger that new notions in science, scholarship, philosophy can be exploited in the manner Karl Rahner would name substantial heresy. There is the opposite danger that the whole effort of renewal give rise to a panic that now, as on earlier occasions, would close doors, and shut eyes, and stop ears. But there exists the third possibility that the new can be analogous to the old, that it can preserve all that is valid in the old, that it can achieve the higher synthesis mentioned by Leo XIII in his bull *Aeterni Patris: vetera novis augere et perficere*, augmenting and perfecting the old by what is new. To that end we must labor and for it we must pray.[85]

---

84 Robert M. Doran, "Ignatian Themes in the Thought of Bernard Lonergan," *Toronto Journal of Theology* 22/1 (2006): 39-54.

85 Lonergan, "The Scope of Renewal," 298.

VALUE, ACTIVE MEANING, AND THE
METHOD OF PRAXIS:
SOUNDINGS IN LONERGAN'S THOUGHT

Paul Joseph LaChance

COLLEGE OF ST. ELIZABETH

I. INTRODUCTION

In this essay, I have chosen to write on what I believe is of utmost importance in Lonergan's later thought. I owe a great debt to the tireless and thoughtful work of Fr. Robert Doran in coming to this conclusion. At the heart of Fr. Doran's analysis of theology and history is his concern for theology's task of "mediating through theological understanding the passage from the prevailing situation in the world to an alternative situation that approximates more closely the rule of God in every department of human affairs..."[1] Theologians fulfill this mediating role when their efforts at understanding and judgment are sublated to the "*telos* of the development of the Christian person and of the self-constitutive process that is the church."[2] To speak of the church as a self-constitutive process is to speak of the church in its human dimension – not of the church in its human as distinct from its divine element. Rather we must recognize that the church is self-constitutive if we want to affirm that the church is truly human.

In 1965 Lonergan interpreted the Vatican Council's openness to the modern world as an embrace of the existential challenge to accept responsibility for our lives and for the world in which we live them. He wrote that "the free and responsible self-constituting subject can exist only in a freely constituted world."[3] Thus, the church as self-

---

1 Robert Doran, *Theology and the Dialectics of History* (Toronto: University of Toronto Press, 1990), 111.

2 Ibid., 112.

3 Bernard F. J. Lonergan, "*Existenz* and *Aggiornamento*" in *Collection*, ed. Frederick E. Crowe and Robert M. Doran (Toronto: University of To-

constitutive is the church as fully, and not merely apparently, a human community constituted in response to and in cooperation with the love of the Divine Trinity. To understand, affirm, and implement this is, as Lonergan held, central to a theology of the development of doctrine and to authentic dogmatic and ecclesial development itself.[4] I am deeply grateful for Fr. Doran's constant admonishment to recognize the importance of full human and Christian development for theology as praxis.

In this paper, I will explore Lonergan's understanding of value in terms of what he called active meaning: "Active meanings come with judgments of value, decisions, actions," and they are treated under the headings of "effective and constitutive functions of meaning in the individual and the community."[5] The fullest explanation of active meanings would naturally be in the context of an explicit philosophy of action. This paper will simply trace elements of Lonergan's thought from his earliest writings to his clearest statements on value as active meaning. The cognitive, communicative, effective, and constitutive functions of meaning are distinguished by the orientations of consciousness and the acts by which subjects mean in the flowering of human development in self-transcendence. Effective and constitutive meanings pertain to those acts of consciousness oriented to real self-transcendence in moral action. For this reason, Lonergan's regularly employed phrase

---

ronto Press, 1988), 226.

4 Lonergan explained his position thusly: "It would be a long and very complex task to list all the ways in which change – *aggiornamento* – is possible and permissible and desirable, and all the other ways in which it is not. To do so would be beyond the scope of the present discussion. The present question rather is what kind of men we have to be if we are to implement the *aggiornamento* that the Council decrees, if we are to discuss what future degrees are to be desired, if we are to do so without doing more harm than good, without projecting into the Catholic community and the world any unauthenticity we have imbibed from others or created on our own. In brief, we have to ask what it is for a Catholic, a religious, a priest, to be himself today. There is the modern secularist world with all its riches and all its potentialities. There is the possibility of despoiling the Egyptians. But that possibility will not be realized unless Catholics, religious, priests, exist, and exist not as drifters but creatively and authentically ("*Existenz* and *Aggiornamento*", 229)".

5 Bernard Lonergan, *Method in Theology*, 2nd ed. (New York: Herder and Herder, 1973), 74.

"mediated by meaning and motivated by value" appears as shorthand inviting readers to further reflection. Grasping the relationship between meaning and value would mean coming to grips with a philosophy of action, yet this in itself is a tremendous task. Lonergan believed that as theologians rise to the level of their time, the emphasis in their work "will shift from the levels of experiencing, understanding, and judging, to the level of deliberating, evaluating, deciding, loving."[6] However, rising to the level of one's time is no easy matter. Hence, Lonergan's phraseology in light of his explicit statements invites wonder and signals an important next step in the Lonergan enterprise.

In this paper, I will first provide a short description of Lonergan's fullest statements on the topic in *Method in Theology* and then bring forth some data in aid of an explanation of the development of Lonergan's thought on constitutive meaning, specifically its differentiation from effective meaning. The emergence of active meaning belongs to the development of Lonergan's own ideas on a philosophy of action.[7]

2. LONERGAN ON VALUE

Lonergan's most explicit treatment of the question "What is a value?" frames the question along the same intellectualist lines of his

---

6 Bernard Lonergan, "Revolution in Catholic Theology," in *Second Collection*, ed. William F.J. Ryan and Bernard J. Tyrell (Toronto: University of Toronto Press, 1974), 237.

7 The specification of the precise nature of value would seem to depend, in part, on a careful examination of the lower processes that lie beyond the reach of intentional consciousness. The action we are talking about is not the action of a disembodied mind but the action of an incarnate being. It therefore has conditions that are extrinsic to the spirit including the physical, biochemical, and physiological conditions of feelings and of insights into feelings. Hence, any explanatory discussion of value as meaning would need to include an interdisciplinary approach to symbol. Lonergan argued that symbol is the mode of communication between spirit and the lower processes. As such, it is a carrier of effective and constitutive meaning and plays an important role in motivation and individual development: "It is through symbol that mind and body, mind and heart, heart and body communicate." (*Method*, 67) Lonergan's highly descriptive language here indicates that he is far from offering a technical account of symbol and feeling. What he does is provide an all too brief summary of a multiplicity of interpretive contexts. Lonergan's interest in the insights into symbol offered by physiologists, literary theorists, depth psychology, and existentialists, among others, indicates the ground that one would have to cover.

treatment of the question "What is being?", forestalling conceptualist answers and yielding heuristic responses. Value is what is intended in questions for deliberation. It is what answers the question for responsibility, "What am I to do about it?" What is intended in these questions is action. Thus, value as a basic term pertains to meaning in the realm of action. What distinguishes value from other meanings is the orientation of the subject and the specific operations.

The realm of action is not isolated from the realm of intellection. Lonergan stated that there is a unity to the levels of consciousness preserved in the sublation of lower levels by the successively higher levels of consciousness.[8] This unity of the subject is isomorphic with the unity of the intended object.[9] Decision, an operation of fourth level consciousness, takes up the content of the lower levels.[10] As one moves from understanding and judgment through the questions for deliberation to decision, one appropriates in a higher or deeper way the same objects intended at the other levels.

2.I VALUE AS A NOTION

Value is, first of all, a notion that constitutes the self-transcending dynamism of the human subject. As such, it is again heuristic – the heuristic that, in some sense, is the human person as a question: "as the notion of being is dynamic principle that keeps us moving toward ever fuller knowledge of being, so the notion of value is the fuller flowering of the same dynamic principle that now keeps us moving toward ever fuller realization of the good, of what is worth while".[11] The notion of value or of the good is not itself a concept of value or the good.[12]

---

8 Lonergan, "The Subject," in *Second Collection*, 81.

9 Ibid., 84.

10 Bernard Lonergan, "Natural Knowledge of God," in *Second Collection*, 128.

11 "The Subject," 82.

12 "Value is a transcendental notion. It is what is intended in questions for deliberation, just as the intelligible is what is intended in questions for intelligence, and just as truth and being are what are intended in questions for reflection. Such intending is not knowing. When I ask what, or why, or how, or what for, I do not know the answers, but already I am intending what would be known if I knew the answers. When I ask whether this or that is so, I do not as yet know whether or not either is so, but already I am intending what would be known if I did know the answers. So when I

Rather it is an intending and a reaching that is constitutive of the human subject as a dynamism.

The notion of value is also a principle of development. It not only relates individuals to goods, it also promotes the subject from the level of reasonable to responsible consciousness, from merely intentional to real self-transcendence: "Then we can be principles of benevolence and of beneficence, capable of genuine collaboration and of true love."[13] If responsibility is a matter of the achievement of adulthood, still such an achievement operates as a final cause in human development. The human being is from the very beginning self-constituting.

On authentic development stands the fortress of objectivity. The notion of value supplies the criterion for judgments concerning that which is truly good or truly better than something else. That criterion is given in the notion of value as transcendental inasmuch as it "heads for a goodness that is beyond criticism."[14]

At the summit of such development "the supreme value is God, and other values are God's expression of his love in this world, in its aspirations, and in its goals. In the measure that one's love of God is complete, then values are whatever one loves, and evils are whatever one hates so that, in Augustine's phrase, if one loves God, one may do as one pleases, *Ama Deum et fac quod vis.*"[15] It is "only by reaching the sustained self-transcendence of the virtuous man that one becomes a good judge, not on this or that human act, but on the whole range of human goodness."[16] Thus, the notion of value promotes the subject to a responsible level of consciousness, directs subjects to their goals, and thereby, supplies the criteria that determine whether the goals have been met.[17]

---

ask whether this is truly and not merely apparently good, whether that is or is not worth while, I do not yet know value but I am intending value." *Method*, 34.

13 Ibid., 35.

14 Ibid., 36.

15 Ibid., 39.

16 Ibid., 35.

17 Ibid.

2.2 APPREHENSION OF VALUE

Between judgments of fact and judgments of value, Lonergan argued, lay apprehensions of value. It is at this point, between the two judgments, that Lonergan introduced the topic of feelings, and his concern seems to have been to expand the domain of intentionality to include the dynamic state of being in love that is prior to particular acts of loving[18] and to incorporate into his concept of human development the appropriation, healing, and proper development of affectivity.[19] The state of being in love emerges as a new horizon and affects the scale of preference for other values related to the object of one's love.[20] Values are apprehended in feelings, which respond to apprehended goods according to a scale of preference. This relationship among intentional responses constitutes an *a priori* structure of intentional responses. It is heuristic and akin to knowing how to ask good questions. As apprehensions of value prior to judgments and to action, feelings may be ordered to self-transcendence or operate at cross-purposes with one's dynamic structure in violation of the law of one's own nature. The tension that exists in the subject's consciousness between fully conscious love and a spontaneous scale of preference may be objectified in psychological insight, may reveal the direction of one's personal and spiritual development, and may indicate the particular skills and conversions for which to pray and to work.

Of particular relevance to our discussion is that intentional response arising with the apprehension of the possibility of moral self-transcendence. [21] The stirring in response to the possibility of moral authenticity and the awakening of existential subjectivity need not be accompanied by an intellectual or religious conversion. It may lie at the heart of a secular or spiritual enthusiasm that nonetheless claims to

---

18 "But there are in full consciousness feelings so deep and strong, especially when deliberately reinforced, that they channel attention, shape one's horizon, direct one's life. Here the supreme illustration is loving. ... Besides particular acts of loving, there is the prior state of being in love, and that prior state is, as it were, the fount of all one's actions." Ibid., 32-33.

19 In respect of this Lonergan wrote: "More generally, it is much better to take full cognizance of one's feelings, however deplorable they may be, than to brush them aside, overrule them, ignore them." Ibid., 240.

20 Here the conflict between essential and effective freedom is transposed to a new context.

21 See ibid., 38.

eschew religious commitment. We are moved by another's conviction, but whether one was right to give oneself in response to a moral calling to a particular cause is, for better or worse, often seen in retrospect. This apprehension of the possibility of moral development is a matter of getting to know concretely a human nature that is one's own. It is an affective response to ideas about human nature that in Lonergan's thought is deeply constitutive of individuals and of societies.

2.3 JUDGMENTS OF VALUE

It is with judgments of value that we arrive at a crucial question in a philosophy of action, for the criterion of a true judgment of value is given not in intentional consciousness but in action itself. The notion of value grounds judgments of value, which are similar to judgments of fact. They are similar in that we may distinguish in both kinds of judgment criterion and content: "the criterion is the self-transcendence of the subject" and "the meaning is or claims to be independent of the subject".[22] Here we have an application of the basic principle that objectivity is authentic subjectivity. However, judgments of value and of fact differ in significant ways.[23] A judgment of value may be true prior to action, but its criterion is constituted by action. One may know for certain what would be worthwhile and yet not do it. The criterion, moral-self-transcendence, has not yet been met. The correct judgment in the absence of moral follow-through reveals the failure of the human subject.[24] The subject is not yet a principle of benevolence and a source of value.

The fundamental disjunction between knowing and doing re-emerges in a new context with a new emphasis. In this new context it would be a mistake to imagine the human subject subsisting at a developmental plateau on which knowledge is stable while one works on bringing the will into alignment. Human subjects are constituted as centers of benevolence and of beneficence through the achievement of real self-transcendence. Shortly, we will look at the role that practice plays in patterning one's consciousness, in the artistry of self-making, and in becoming a good judge of the true and the worthwhile. Just as

---

22 Ibid., 37.

23 Ibid.

24 The concept of 'moral follow-through' here is descriptive and refers to the exercise of responsibility, whatever that may turn out to be in the concrete.

rationalization has a deteriorating effect on one's mind and heart by blocking the subject's intellectual dynamism and preventing authentic development, so the failure to act well separates the human dynamism from its goal and establishes in the subject a contradictory principle of decline. Given the unity of human life and living, it is unlikely that this principle of decline can remain compartmentalized. Rather, we should expect its effect to be corrosive throughout.

The difference between the criteria of judgments of truth and of value is the occasion for my question here about the nature of value itself. My concern in the next two parts of the paper is to examine Lonergan's efforts to objectify the meaningful content of human action as a moment in the evaluation of active meanings and his identification of the method of praxis as it relates to the authenticity of those meanings.

3. EMERGING DISTINCTION BETWEEN EFFECTIVE AND CONSTITUTIVE MEANING

Lonergan distinguished between the effective and constitutive functions of meaning, and it is best to conceive of the functions of meaning on the analogy of the functional distinction between producer goods and consumer goods in Lonergan's circulation analysis.[25] The distinction accounts for the point-to-point, point-to-line, and point-to-surface or point-to-volume relationships that elements in the production process have to the standard of living. As the same producer, product, or action may fulfill now a lower, now a higher surplus function, so the same idea, thought, or meaning may fulfill a diversity of functions. That diversity is founded on the several acts of meaning.[26] Effective meaning guides action; constitutive meaning informs one's living, knowing, and doing.[27] Effective meaning is analogous to a point-to-

---

25 "The division [among the various relationships between elements in productive process and the standard of living] is, then, neither proprietary nor technical. It is a functional division of the structure of the productive process: it reveals the possibilities of the process as a dynamic system..." *Macroeconomic Dynamics: An Essay in Circulation Analysis*, ed. Frederick G. Lawrence, Patrick H. Byrne, and Charles C. Hefling, Jr. (Toronto: University of Toronto Press, 1999), 26-27.

26 *Method*, 74.

27 Ibid., 298.

point or point-to-line relationship between meaning and action. Constitutive meaning is analogous to a point-to-surface relationship.[28]

It is possible to discern in Lonergan's writings two concerns that emerge together but which mark two areas of difference between effective and constitutive meaning. The first area of difference between effective and constitutive meaning lies in the existential import of the two functions. Active meanings are those that pertain to the human person as a source of benevolence and love. They are originating values, and Lonergan's idea of active meaning developed from ideas about the human person operative in rational consciousness to constitutive principles at the fourth level. The second area of difference is rooted in Lonergan's concept of the artistry of self-making. Active meaning is personally constitutive at the fourth level in the sublation of lower processes in the service of human deliberative action. Thus, the artistry of self-making refers to the way in which one works out a functioning synthesis of the exigencies of body and spirit. The authenticity of this functioning synthesis determines the authenticity of a person's deliberations.

Human work is not mindless but is thoughtful and intentional.[29] Meanings are effective as guides to action. Human work also occurs within and creates a human world. Meanings as constitutive create the world within which human action occurs and shape the individuals who act.[30]

The emergence of a distinction between effective and constitutive meaning is a function of Lonergan's growing awareness of the unique criterion of real authenticity and his entry into the realm of a philosophy of action. Thus Lonergan disengaged constitutive meaning at the point at which he recognized that the criteria of true judgments of value are given in good actions. Further, he advanced his own understanding of the role of meaning in self-making as he shifted his focus from the operations of reasonableness to those of responsibility.[31]

---

28 The elegance of Lonergan's concept of function is that it insists on the variability of the concrete: "The analysis that insists on the indeterminacy is the analysis that insists on the present fact…" *Macroeconomic Dynamics*, 28.

29 *Method*, 78.

30 Ibid.

31 A note on communication: In *Method* Lonergan differentiated this constitutive function from the communicative function. Changes in social

3.1 THE EMERGENCE OF ORIGINATING VALUE

Lonergan's early writings on ideas that govern actions occurred in the context of faculty psychology in which effective and constitutive functions are not thematized and differentiated. Lonergan explained history in terms of ideas that specify the will and of the will that enacts the ideas specified by the intellect. A single idea governs many actions. "[E]very act of intellect," Lonergan wrote in 1935, "is a universal...We are here at the root of the philosophy of history, the one act of intellect guides a man's many actions until it is replaced by a contradictory idea."[32] In his essay "Analytic Concept of History", Lonergan conceived of the dialectic of history again in terms of "thought that goes into

---

institutions and the resultant human communal self-making are accomplished largely through the communicative processes of education, socialization, and the passing on of tradition. However, at an earlier period the communicative was not yet fully disengaged from the constitutive function of meaning as in the 1965 essay "*Existenz* and *Aggiornamento*" (233-234). This communicative function may be accomplished in as many ways as there are carriers of meaning (intersubjective, artistic, symbolic, linguistic, and incarnate). Whereas from a more compact perspective the communication of meaning and the constitution of the human world may seem to be one thing, from a differentiated perspective there are differences. There may be the intersubjective communication of meaning in a community of feeling and through fellow-feeling (*Method*, 58), but such meaning is potential rather than active (*Method*, 74). To feeling must be added the formality of symbolic interpretation and also action by which meaning becomes constitutive. Similarly, the meaning communicated in works or art may be potential, or else formal or full, as when the works are interpreted by a social or art critic. But the constitutive function is fulfilled in the act itself, for "performative meaning is constitutive or effective meaning linguistically expressed." (*Method*, 75, note 19) However, Lonergan's comment here is far more a suggestion and an invitation to investigation than it is a critical judgment. Finally, new ideas, judgments or evaluations may be 'caught' in an encounter with a good person. Lonergan seemed to accord incarnate meaning a privileged place in his understanding of active meaning. I will say no more here, but the reader should keep in mind that whereas education and inculturation seem to have both a communicative and constitutive function in Lonergan's early writings, they are susceptible to differentiation.

32 Bernard Lonergan, "*Pantôn anakephalaiôsis*," *Method: Journal of Lonergan Studies* 9.2 (1991): 134-172, at 143-144.

action."[33] That thought is not merely the idea of a particular action, for a single idea governs a multiplicity of actions. At this point the effective and the constitutive roles merge. Thought "produces the social situation with its problems."

> If the thought is good, the problems will be small and few; thus the situation will require but slight modifications of previous thought and leave man opportunity to advance and develop. If, on the other hand, the thought is poor, then its concrete results will be manifestly evil and call for a new attitude of mind.[34]

From the perspective of Lonergan's later writing, thought that produces the situation in which individuals act is meaning as constitutive of the social world. By our actions we not only transform the world, but, in doing so, we also shape ourselves. This is what Lonergan meant by the "making of man by man":

> The proximate end of man is the making of man: giving him his body, the conditions of his life, the premotions to which he will respond in the fashioning of his soul. Essentially history is the making [by actions in accordance with nature] and unmaking [by actions contrary to nature – i.e. sin] and remaking [by actions in grace] of man…[35]

Lonergan centered his thinking on the idea that a single sin establishes a predisposition in the soul and expanded this notion in a fuller context to articulate a concept of value as originating (*Insight*), and finally to implicate the full range of artistic self-making in individual actions (the lectures on Existentialism).

The problem with which Lonergan was wrestling was, of course, history. The emerging distinction between the effective and constitutive functions of meaning is tied to Lonergan's emerging ideas about history. At its most basic, the way in which meanings both direct our actions and give shape to our lives is reflected in Lonergan's concern for the large scale experiments on human living represented by mod-

---

33 Bernard Lonergan, "Analytic Concept of History," *Method: Journal of Lonergan Studies* 11.1 (1993): 5-35, at 13.

34 Ibid.

35 Ibid., 16. Lonergan's articulation of the metaphysical concept of premotion and of its role in the operations of intellect and will occupies an important place in his dissertation.

ern states.[36] Oppressive regimes engender a sense of helplessness, yet this helplessness simply magnifies and exacerbates the limited range of effective freedom that characterizes all people everywhere. Ideas govern action, bind individuals together in community, and shape the relationship between intellectual and lower operations. In this context what Lonergan means by unities is conditioned by a metaphysical inquiry. Only in the context of intentionality analysis and of his mature understanding of meaning and of history was Lonergan able to disengage and interrelate the functions meaning operative in human moral self-transcendence. Still, this did not occur all at once.

In *Insight* Lonergan began to conceive of value as a link between knowing and doing, and as possessing a uniquely self-constituting function as originating value. However, value is awkwardly founded on rational rather than on existential operations. The functions of meaning are not yet differentiated, and there is a notable blend of the cognitive and constitutive functions. A value itself is the product of practical intelligence. Values are the objects of rational choice and are subject to the criteria of rationality rather than of responsibility. Lonergan's identification of the criteria of judgments of fact and of value is a singular feature of the treatment of value in *Insight*. Judgments of value are said to proceed with a rational necessity from a grasp of a virtually unconditioned.[37]

Values are distinct from other acts of meaning in that values are determined by rational operations but are embraced by a suitably habituated will. A value is a unity of knowing and feeling that issues in an action. Further, values are terminal insofar as they are objects of choice, but they are originating insofar as the act of choosing contributes to the habituation of the will. Originating values ground and sub-

---

36 Bernard Lonergan, "The Mystical Body and the Sacraments," in *Shorter Papers*, ed. Robert C. Croken, Robert M. Doran, and H. Daniel Monsour (Toronto: University of Toronto Press, 2007), 77.

37 Bernard Lonergan, *Insight: A Study of Human Understanding*, ed. Frederick C. Crowe and Robert M. Doran (Toronto: University of Toronto Press, 1992), 730. Let me say that I appreciate and fundamentally agree with Doran's clarification of the difference between the analyses of the good in *Insight* and *Method* in terms of the distinction and relationship among Ignatius' three times of discernment in *What is Systematic Theology?* (Toronto: University of Toronto Press, 2005), 103-107. My point here is different and relates to the question not of antecedent willingness but of the criterion of the judgment of value.

ordinate terminal values. As we will see, these elements provide some warrant for adopting a terminological distinction between thoughts present in consciousness seeking understanding or truth and those present in consciousness oriented toward action.

Originating value is the central link between knowledge and will. It may be said to be related to particular goods in a point-to-volume correspondence. It is originating value that conditions the choice of an order in which particular goods are desired and enjoyed. Value is "the good as the possible object of rational choice."[38] Particular goods may be desired, and goods of order apprehended by intelligence. The good of order is grasped intellectually and governs a host of operations. Value is affirmed rationally and willed by a good will. So, individualism and socialism are both "constructions of human intelligence, possible systems for ordering the satisfaction of human desires."[39] The choice is a function of the subject's grasp of the reasonableness of one system over the other and of the subject's antecedent willingness and the act of choosing. Given what Lonergan had written about economics and culture, it would have been possible for him to approach the question of individualism and socialism from the perspective of higher ideas or the good of order at the level of culture. In weighing the reasonableness of a particular economic system, one would have to take into account the ideas of human nature implied or actualized by the system. In this way, the determining value would seem to be a higher idea that one also finds appealing. However, Lonergan in *Insight* articulated a different hierarchy. He was aiming at something different from his previous articulations of thought governing action or moving into action. That towards which he was aiming is founded on the dynamism toward self-consistency that provides the 'ought' for ethicists, that results in an easy or uneasy conscience, and that may be subverted in a flight from moral self-consciousness. However, what Lonergan was aiming at seems at times to be lost in the text. To the extent it is lost the account of responsibility is founded on rationality.

In drawing the distinction among empirical, intelligent, and reasonable consciousness, Lonergan argued that the rationality of a course of productive action is founded on a grasp of some really or apparently sufficient reason that makes the sequence worthwhile. Lonergan

---

38 *Insight*, 624.
39 Ibid., 621.

concluded, "In the thing there is the groundedness that consists in its existence being accounted for by a sequence of operations, but in the entrepreneur there was not only the groundedness of his judgment in the reasons that led to it but also the rational consciousness that required reasons to reach judgment."[40] The governing idea is not simply the image in the mind of the artisan, but the rationale for making the potential into a reality. In the fullest analysis the reasonableness of a course of action would be grounded on a grasp of the effect of the action on the habitual character of the will. Yet, this fullest analysis is sometimes lost in the text. The fact that responsibility is not an independent schema in *Insight* means that the reader would have to recall the principle that terminal values are subordinate to originating values and recognize that the choice is determined by the reasonableness of the kind of person the entrepreneur is becoming in the act of choosing and the operations of production. In the context of the book this would be warranted by the fact that judgments of value are defined as the products of practical intelligence that also shape future choices and so future values:

> The detached, disinterested, unrestricted desire to know grasps intelligently and affirms reasonably not only the facts of the universe of being but also its practical possibilities. Such practical possibilities include intelligent transformations not only of the environment in which man lives, but also of man's own spontaneous living.[41]

Still, the existential moment is not explicit in the example of the entrepreneur, and even in the quotation, the practical possibilities of intelligent transformations of environments and of lives seem to be parallel rather than interconnected.[42]

---

40 Ibid., 347.

41 Ibid., 622.

42 Performatively, the text of *Insight* itself may tell a slightly different story, and the elements of existential consciousness may emerge a bit more clearly. The salient example of responsibility and of a judgment of value lies in Lonergan's analysis of belief. Belief is defined as the willing acceptance of a responsible communication. Lonergan argued that the reasonableness of belief is founded on the role belief plays in human collaboration and on the good of the intellect present in a particular proposition. In belief we thus have a particular good (a statement), a good of order (human collaboration), and a value in light of which one freely participates in collaboration for the sake of progress in history. The subject's decision to believe

It seems likely that Lonergan's lectures on Existentialism mark a liminal time in the development of his ideas on constitutive meaning, and much more needs to be said about the content of those lectures. At the time of these lectures, the constitutive function appears to be emerging apart from the cognitive function of meaning. However, Lonergan's notes and lectures suggest that the context is still predominately faculty psychology and that he still tended to objectify the existential moment in terms of ideas about human nature. Thus, human communal self-making in the modern world is largely in terms of technical, social, and cultural institutions, and "in the field of the technical, the social, and the cultural it is man's ideas upon man that will determine the fabric of human living."[43] What is necessary is an objectification of the most important ideas that give rise to current situations, for "defects in the thinking result in defects in the situation."[44] The philosopher can effectively communicate an awareness of those defects by pointing out the evils commonly acknowledged and interpreting them as the result of defective thinking. This task is principally disclosive or revelatory.[45] For this reason values are still founded on acts of

---

is implicated in and implicates the decision to live according to the norms immanent and operative in his or her own nature as empirical, intelligent, and reasonable. Lonergan's defense of belief emerges as an act of communication aimed at communal self-making.

43 Bernard Lonergan, *Phenomenology and Logic: The Boston College Lectures on Mathematical Logic and Existentialism*, ed. Phil McShane (Toronto: University of Toronto Press, 2001), 302.

44 *Insight*, 307.

45 Lonergan noted and even affirmed, albeit conditionally, the importance of the disclosure and revelation in his lectures on Existentialism. However, he was pointedly critical of the phenomenological method's eclipse of judgment insofar as it reduces truth to disclosure and the articulation of what is revealed. Nevertheless, his account of philosophical intervention in the dialectic of history is, at this point, directed at the correction of leading ideas. Brian Braman in *Meaning and Authenticity: Bernard Lonergan & Charles Taylor on the Drama of Authentic Human Existence* (Toronto: University of Toronto Press, 2008) also points out this hermeneutic character of the historical dialectic: "Through our decisions, choices, and the risks taken, we reveal ourselves to others. We reveal the type of person we are at the moment; we reveal the ideal that informs our way of living; we reveal what we consider to be worthwhile, true, real, and valuable in terms of human living (56)." He adds also that "to speak about moral conversion, therefore,

intelligent and rational consciousness rather than on existential consciousness. 'Ideas upon man' operate at a more fundamental level than other ideas governing human activity and fulfill a function analogous to originating value in the choice of a particular social order.

At this point Lonergan had not yet distinguished judgments of fact from judgments of value. He was still thinking about value as founded on acts of practical reason. However, what begins to distinguish value from other meanings is the existential aspect of value as originating. It is the elaboration of this idea after *Insight* that gave rise to his mature understanding and enabled the differentiation of effective and constitutive functions of meanings. It seems that Lonergan began to think about value as a category distinct from intellectual meaning in 1968. He raised the question "What is a value?" in his lecture "The Subject". In that lecture he first treated value as a transcendental notion like the notion of being and identified a meaning of the good that is appropriate to the subject's existential insight. The good as value is not the good as object of appetite (Aristotle) or the good of order (Thomas). It is the sense of 'good' "that constitutes the emergence of the existential subject".[46] From this point on Lonergan's use of the tag 'mediated by meaning and motivated by value' seems to possess a new clarity founded on the emergence of the priority of freedom. The human world founded on meaning "is a world of existential subjects and it objectifies the values that they originate in their creativity and their freedom."[47] During this period he wrote that what distinguishes nature and history is the constitutive role of meaning:

> It is the fact that acts of meaning inform human living, that such acts proceed from a free and responsible subject incarnate, that meanings differ from nation to nation, from culture to culture, and that, over time, they develop and go astray. Besides the meanings by which man apprehends nature and the meanings by which he transforms it, there are the meanings by which man thinks out the possibilities of his own living and makes his choice among them. In this realm of freedom and creativity, of solidarity and responsibil-

---

necessitates that we speak about our understanding of what it is that we are choosing in each and every situation. This involves the articulation of transcendental value..." (64).

46 "The Subject," in *A Second Collection*, 84.

47 Ibid., 85.

ity, of dazzling achievement and pitiable madness, there ever occurs man's making of man.[48]

Lonergan concluded that "meaning is the stuff of man's making of man".[49] Human persons are not simply constituted by freedom; in freedom they constitute themselves and their world. They actively constitute themselves as principles of benevolence and love. Lonergan wrote,

> Men ask not only about facts but also about values. They are not content with satisfactions. They distinguish between what truly is good and what only apparently is good. They are stopped by the question: Is what I have achieved really worthwhile? Is what I hope for really worthwhile? Because men can raise such questions, and answer them, and live by the answers, they can be principles of benevolence and beneficence, of genuine co-operation, of true love.[50]

Meaning as constitutive emerges out of a constant reflection on thought and intention in relation to the action of conscious subjects and, notably, in the context of Lonergan's efforts to understand the place of history in theology. In *Method* he wrote, "Meaning, then, is a constitutive element in the conscious flow that is the normally controlling side of human action. It is this constitutive role of meaning in the controlling side of human action that grounds the peculiarity of the historical field of investigation."[51]

Lonergan defined divine revelation in similar terms: "a divine revelation is God's entry and his taking part in man's making of man. It is God's claim to have a say in the aims and purposes, the direction and development of human lives, human societies, human cultures, human history."[52] In the mission of the Word, God has taken part in human

48 "Theology in its New Context," in *A Second Collection*, 61.

49 Ibid., 62.

50 Bernard Lonergan, "Theology and Man's Future," in *A Second Collection*, 144.

51 *Method*, 178. Perhaps the caveat "normally controlling" reflects a recurring theme. Even at the early point, Lonergan did not simply reduce the historical dynamic to the operations of the intellect. He noted the crucial caveat that purely intellectual progress would not be human. See "Analytic Concept of History," 20.

52 "Theology in Its New Context," in *A Second Collection*, 62.

self-making as both constitutive and redemptive.[53] Thus in the fourth realm of transcendent or religious meaning, revelation becomes the determinative constitutive meaning in individual and communal self-making: "To communicate the Christian message is to lead another to share in one's cognitive, constitutive, effective meaning."[54] The communication of active meanings is the creation of community in the achievement of common meaning through socialization, education, and enculturation.[55]

Thus Lonergan arrived at a differentiation among the cognitive, effective, and constitutive functions of meaning with respect to the subject's quest for responsibility. The fourth level is practical and existential: "practical inasmuch as [the subject] is concerned with concrete courses of action; existential inasmuch as control includes self-control, and the possibility of self-control involves responsibility for the effects of his actions on others and, more basically, on himself. The topmost level of human consciousness is conscience."[56] The practical function pertains to the fourth level as practical, the constitutive to the fourth level as existential. Both are higher sublations of the cognitive function in intelligent and rational consciousness.

3.2 CONSTITUTIVE MEANING AND THE ARTISTRY OF SELF-MAKING

The second area of difference between effective and constitutive meaning pertains to the relationship between constitutive meaning and the artistry of self-constitution. Whereas in *Insight* rational deliberation proceeds in the context of a willingness to give free reign to the exigencies of human knowing and the problem becomes one of motivation, Lonergan faced squarely the fact that the authenticity that *Insight* assumes cannot be taken for granted. As Lonergan developed in his understanding of the self as a principle of benevolence and love, he likewise articulated the mechanism by which the existential subject shapes him or herself as a heuristic in anticipation of the achievement of the criterion of real self-transcendence. In the quotation from "The Mystical Body of Christ," we see that there is a hint at the interrela-

---

53 Bernard Lonergan, "Mission and Spirit," *A Third Collection*, 32.

54 *Method*, 362.

55 *Method*, 79.

56 Bernard Lonergan, "The Response of the Jesuit," *A Second Collection*, 168.

tionship of mind and body, heart and soul in the incarnate and social human person. The unities effected through economic, political, and cultural institutions inform the feelings, thoughts, and actions of individuals. This sense of the pluriform nature of human living is related to the category of premotions from Lonergan's dissertation, and it provides the fecund ground for the emergence of an idea of constitutive meaning related to objects that command our respect, hold our allegiance, and fire our loyalty.[57]

Lonergan's dissertation contains two important ideas that develop into his later thought on value. The first is the idea of premotion. In the first instance premotion is physical. It serves to set the conditions from the movement from being able to act to actually acting. For instance, the heat of the equator is a potential actor: it may melt an iceberg if the two are brought into proximity by a distinct movement – a physical premotion.[58] Premotion also concerns the order of secondary causes in the created universe. In this way, Lonergan distinguished providence from fate.[59] Providence is the divine intention, present in the mind of God that orders all things. Fate is the ordering of all secondary causes or the divine application of all things to their acts.

The second idea follows from this first. In order for the will to move from a state of rest and potentiality to one of actually willing, some premotion is required to bring the will and its object into relation and to establish a proper disposition. Lonergan explores two categories of premotion related to the will, external and internal premotion: "By external premotion is meant the reduction of the will from accidental potency to act, either by the presentation of an object or by a change of mood, disposition, or circumstance..."[60] Internal premotion is constituted in so far as a single action establishes an inclination in the will.[61]

The two forms of premotion come together in St. Thomas' concept of the relationship between intellect and will.[62] The intellect specifies

57 Method, 78.

58 Bernard Lonergan, Grace and Freedom: Operative Grace in the Thought of St Thomas Aquinas, ed. Frederick M. Crowe and Robert E. Doran (Toronto: University of Toronto Press, 2000), 277.

59 Ibid., 291-296.

60 Ibid., 370.

61 Ibid., 374.

62 Ibid., 94-98, 378.

the object of the will through deliberation. However, the will is not determined to follow the counsel of the intellect and must move itself by an internal premotion. This internal premotion is the volition of the end in virtue of which the will moves itself to choose a means. Further the external premotion remains an instrumental element in the movement of the agent. Thus the idea determined by the process of deliberation guides the movements of the body and "because the idea is somehow immanent in the motions, it is eventually realized in the effect."[63] Here we have a basic statement of effective meaning in a metaphysical context. Setting the evident problem of sin aside, internal premotion does not suffice to explain the motion of the will in the physical and temporal order of the created universe.[64] The concepts of premotion and secondary causality establish a heuristic for the investigation of lower manifolds which serve instrumentally in the emergence of higher actions. For example, biochemical and physiological elements that are extrinsic to intentional consciousness can serve to establish the required relationship and disposition between conscious operations and their objects. Thus, the physics of phantasms and of feelings has a place in an explanation of meaning and value.

In *Insight* Lonergan expressed similar concern for the integration of lower processes in conscious living. Effective collaboration requires that meanings proposed for belief be presented in symbols that expand effective freedom by marshaling the support of sensitive processes.[65] In this way values serve as a link between knowing and doing on the one hand, and between knowing and feeling on the other. Further, meanings function constitutively inasmuch as differences among civilizations are explained by differentiations of common sense[66] and the artistry with which people transform the lower manifolds of human life by granting the exigencies of underlying materials, psychic representation and conscious integration.[67]

Returning to Lonergan's lectures on Existentialism, we see the task of self-making described in terms of the creation of a flow of consciousness, which effects a concrete synthesis in the conscious living of

---

63 Ibid., 288.

64 Ibid., 378.

65 Ibid., 744-745.

66 Ibid., 203.

67 Ibid., 211.

underlying manifolds of neural complexes in a set of modes of dealing with persons and things. Here Lonergan transposed the metaphysical concept of premotion into an existential context. He writes:

> Marcel's thought is essentially a movement from mere existence to being, and it is the being of the self-constituting subject that he is concerned with....This concern with the good is a concern with improving my operative solution, my functioning synthesis in concrete living; with the transition from freedom of images to freedom of enlightened responsible choice; with the question, the possibility, the possible need of some conversion that will bring with it a broadening of the horizon. It is a concern with improvement not in general, not for the other fellow, but with *my own* improvement. It is a concern not with truths in general but with the truths that I live by, the truths involved in my self-constitution.[68]

The transposition of the concept of unities from a metaphysical to an intentional context and the emerging view of human beings as subjects enlarged Lonergan's understanding of meaning in terms of self-constitution. Truths to live by include those meanings whereby the subject integrates lower manifolds in a pattern of consciousness that includes the whole of conscious intentionality from attention, through understanding and judgment, to action.

In *Method*, Lonergan wrote that "deliberation sublates and thereby unifies knowing and feeling."[69] What deliberation yields is an active meaning that brings together lower manifolds and the drive to real self-transcendence. Lonergan wrote, "Besides potential, formal, and full acts of meaning, there are also constitutive and effective acts of meaning. Now the apprehension of values and disvalues is the task not of understanding but of intentional response."[70] Those intentional responses are feelings which are sublated together with knowledge in deliberation, decision, and action. Apart from this bringing together, one is left with mere resolutions or lofty ideas that do not issue in action. Active meanings may overcome inertia in an otherwise willing actor. Alternatively, disvalues as meanings realized in human action may alienate affectivity, as in the case of totalitarian practices, or render affect disordered or underdeveloped.

---

68 *Phenomenology and Logic*, 294-295.
69 "Revolution in Catholic Theology," in *A Second Collection*, 277.
70 *Method*, 245.

This aspect of the constitutive function of meaning in the artistry of self-making is perhaps best explored in terms of the symbolic carriers of meaning in internal communication:

> Organic and psychic vitality have to reveal themselves to intentional consciousness and, inversely, the intentional consciousness has to secure the collaboration of organism and psyche. Again, our apprehensions of values occur in intentional responses, in feelings: here too it is necessary for feelings to reveal their objects and, inversely, for objects to awaken feelings. It is through symbols that mind and body, mind and heart, heart and body communicate.[71]

Symbols here play a central role in intentional self-transcendence, and the context is internal communication "with its associated images and feelings, memories and tendencies that the interpreter has to appeal if he would explain the symbol."[72] Nevertheless, this internal communication in intentional self-transcendence transposes from metaphysics the concept of premotions that bring agents into proximity with their objects and establish between them and their objects a proper disposition.[73]

4. EVALUATION, MEANINGS AND THE METHOD OF PRAXIS

I would like to make a few suggestions about the evaluation of active meanings, for it appears to be the focus of much of Lonergan's thought in the period after *Method in Theology*. The importance of dialectic

---

71 Ibid., 66-67.

72 Ibid., 67.

73 This transposition merely marks out a field of investigation. Lonergan considered many possible systems of interpretation without affirming any one of them, but he did comment that "most significant from a basic viewpoint, there is the existential approach that thinks of the dream, not as the twilight of life, but as its dawn, the beginning of the transition from impersonal existence to presence in the world, to constitution of one's self in one's world" (*Method*, 69). In this way, the dream and the oft repeated difference between the dreams of the night and those of the morning appear to point toward the symbolic function of meaning operative in consciousness as self-constitutive and as oriented on real self-transcendence. At the dawn of consciousness, the subject positing him- or herself in the world symbolically re-presents both the self and the world in which he or she will become an actor.

and of foundations in Lonergan's theological method is directly tied
to the notion of value as constitutive meaning. Pointing out in explicit
terms the role of religious living in dialectic and foundations, Lonergan comments pointed that "[f]undamental theology becomes lived
religion."[74] In fact, Christian living is and all along has been praxis alive
but not thematized: "It lives by its discernment between the authenticity of a good conscience and the unauthenticity of an unhappy conscience. It devotes its efforts to overcoming unauthenticity and promoting authenticity."[75]

Out of the unity of human consciousness, decision follows from attention, understanding, judgment, and deliberation and concerns the
same object appropriated or engaged at a fuller level of human subjectivity. Again, given that unity, the subject's attention, understanding, judgment, and deliberation are patterned by the meanings of the
subject's actions as self-constituting. Personal development therefore
emerges as a central concern for any science, especially theology. Lonergan argued that to conceive of theology as praxis "is to ask whether
there are basic theological questions whose solution depends on the
personal development of theologians."[76] The method of praxis is carried out in two steps. In the first, one seeks to discern authentic and
inauthentic meanings in human action and history through the application of a twofold hermeneutic of suspicion and recovery. However,
Lonergan notes:

> ...this is just a first step, for any given operator of discernment may
> well suffer from a bias of his own; a certain amount of ideology will
> function in his discernment, and consequently a certain amount
> of objective ideology will pass for real, fine gold. At this point the
> problem takes the form of the function of the complex variable, the
> function of $x + iy$. Only in this case you don't exactly know what the
> i means. There is no clear notion of which is the source of complex-

---

74 Bernard Lonergan, "Variations in Fundamental Theology," in *Philosophical and Theological Papers: 1965-1980*, ed. Robert C. Croken and Robert
M. Doran (Toronto: University of Toronto Press, 2004), 255.

75 Bernard Lonergan, "Ongoing Genesis of Methods," in *A Third Collection*,
61.

76 Bernard Lonergan, "Theology and Praxis," in *A Third Collection*, 185.

ity in the variables because the judges, discerners, also can be subject to the error.[77]

For this reason the theologian must be attentive to both vectors of human development: "while empirical method moves, so to speak, from below upwards, praxis moves from above downwards".[78] For, as Lonergan noted, "Deciding is one thing, doing is another. One has yet to uncover and root out one's individual, group, and general bias."[79] The task of uncovering appears to be the basic hermeneutic task, but the task of rooting out engages one in the praxis of Christian living. For this reason, orthopraxis obtains for the adequately differentiated consciousness a certain priority over orthodoxy without any disparagement to the latter.[80]

In the twofold movement of theological method from research toward dialectic and from foundations toward communications, there is a priority of practice and of living over reflection on living, with a special emphasis on communal living (which one can recognize as having been present from the beginning of Lonergan's career). Lonergan's own account of the emergence and development of method itself signals such a priority. There exists the incompleteness of an intellectualist theology "that is not subordinated to a deliberately chosen method."[81] Nevertheless, method is not simply an object of choice resulting from the unfolding of consciousness from below upward, for "method begins with an apprenticeship, with doing what others have done, or advise, or demand." And along the way there is shift of emphasis from what one knows or can do to the kind of person one is becoming. For there will be variations in methods, "but ultimate issues rest on ultimate options, and ultimate options are existential. By them men and women deliberately decide – when they do not inadvertently drift into – the kind of men and women they are to be. Being a scientist is an aspect of being human, nor has any method been found

---

77 Bernard Lonergan, "The Human Good," in *Philosophical and Theological Papers: 1965-1980*, 345.

78 "Ongoing Genesis of Methods," in *A Third Collection*, 160.

79 *Method*, 240.

80 Bernard Lonergan, "Philosophy and the Religious Phenomenon," in *Philosophical and Theological Papers: 1965-1980*, 398. See also, "A New Pastoral Theology" in the same volume, 238.

81 "Philosophy and the Religious Phenomenon," 398.

that makes one authentically scientific without heading one into being authentically human."[82] The shift moves philosophy and theology into the realm of responsibility and of action, and further into the realm of the interpersonal. Cognitional theory is sublated to praxis and the philosophy of action to the unique criterion of moral judgments.[83] Yet if the shift does not occur in the theologian, it cannot become an object of reflection. Out of his disengagement of interpersonal relations with their own exigencies and course of development, Lonergan began to speak of dialogue and dialectic in the method of praxis. Christian living is communal, and Lonergan's ultimate concern was not simply for the individual self-constitution and development of the theologian but for that of the theological community.

5. CONCLUSION

The emerging awareness and self-understanding in the church today would seem to rest on the communal appropriation and implementation of a methodical theology which appreciates the priority of Christian life and practice without in any way devaluing the systematic elements of Christian thought. Perhaps the most important objects of theological investigation and discernment today are the active meanings by which theologians constitute themselves and their communities and by which they give shape and direction to their lives. But these topics can only become objects of reflection in so far as theologians themselves are governed by the exigencies of knowing and loving in collaboration with the redeeming and constituting missions of Word and Spirit.

---

82 "Method: Trend and Variations," in *A Third Collection*, 21.

83 "Variations in Fundamental Theology," in *Philosophical and Theological Papers: 1965-1980*, 247.

EMERGING PROBABILITIES AND THE
OPERATORS OF MUSICAL EVOLUTION

GREG LAUZON

MUSICIAN AND AUDIO ENGINEER, TORONTO

I would like to thank Bob Doran for encouraging me to explore the relationship between Lonergan and music. I had been exploring experimental music for a few years when I was invited by the *Lonergan on the Edge* committee to present a paper at their workshop in 2006. It was both an honor and a challenge. I had developed some theories of my own about music and was wondering if they could be correlated with Lonergan's work. Most of my knowledge of Lonergan's thought came through listening to his recorded lectures which I had been restoring but also through conversations with Bob over the years. He is an erudite thinker without the stereotypical scholarly airs of superiority. I feel fortunate to have had him as a mentor. It was meaningful to me to have someone of his stature help me believe in my ideas and teach me that we can all play a role in the evolution of culture.

I. OPERATORS

There is a dynamism that pushes music forward. Parameters within a given musical system have a finite range of variables. The more these variables are explored, the harder it becomes to create music that sounds innovative. That thirst for the "new sound" compels the artist to explore new frontiers for how music is made.

There are numerous operators in the evolution of music. I have chosen four as being most relevant to this paper: 1) new technology, 2) development of new playing methods, 3) a radical combination of seemingly unrelated musical styles, and 4) the role of the audience.[1] I thought the first three operators were my own ideas. However, through my subsequent research I found examples that were similar to these three. I also found the fourth and many others. But I chose to

---

1 Herbert Weinstock, *What Music Is* (Garden City, NY: Doubleday & Company, Inc, 1966), 330-332.

focus on these four because they seem most relevant to what I would like to contribute to music at this time through the development of new instrument designs and playing methods: 1) Polyrhythmic Knob Twiddling, 2) the Spring Dulcimer, and 3) the Tabludu Kit.[2]

Composer Burt Bacharach once said, "My hands are my worst enemies." What he meant by this statement was that it is difficult to avoid revisiting the same parameters with which you are most oriented. The hands of the composer tend to want to go to the places on the instrument where they are most comfortable. They form habits. However, experimentation with new parameters can foster insights into new developments. Musicians and composers must face these challenges in order to grow. And through these struggles new ideas are born. Carl Jung once said, "We need difficulties; they are necessary for our health."

2. POLYRHYTHMIC KNOB TWIDDLING

The ability of drummers to play a rhythm with one hand while playing another rhythm with the other hand is a foundational skill. The drum rudiments associated with this skill are called polyrhythms. A common example of this is the paradiddle, which combines single and double strokes alternated between the left (L) and right (R) hands. For example, consider the following pattern:

R   L   R   R   L   R   L   L

Traditionally the art of drumming is thought of in terms of the up and down motions of drumsticks or hands striking surfaces. There is a familiarity within the range of these motions and the percussive sounds associated with them. What if the parameters of these motions were expanded or adapted to a new form of instrumentation? Instead of a simple up and down motion, what if the pattern was left and right, back and forth, or a circular clockwise/counterclockwise motion? Within these motions lie a new range of sensory affects to be discovered. The familiarity with the motions can change. An example of this can be found in what I have been trying to develop as a playing method by rhythmically manipulating the control knobs of effects

2   Pictures and sound bite demonstrations of instruments and playing techniques that I have been developing can be found at www.greglauzon.com. The Spring Dulcimer and Tabludu Kit are my own inventions.

modules. Hence, I have given it the name Polyrhythmic Knob Twiddling.

To illustrate this method, imagine a sound generated by an oscillator (an electronic circuit that produces a repetitive signal) plugged into a pitch shifter controlled by the left hand, which is then plugged into a manual Jet Phaser controlled by the right hand. A Jet Phaser simulates the phasing sound associated with a jet taking off or a race car coming and going. The paradiddle described above is played through alternating turns of these modules' knobs. There is also the option of different knob rotation patterns within the same polyrhythm. The pattern can start with both knobs set to the left, to the right, pointing toward each other, or away from each other.

L = Left hand

R = Right hand

< or > = Direction of knob rotation

Rotation Pattern 1

R	L	R	R	L	R	L	L
>	<	<	>	>	<	<	>

Rotation Pattern 2

R	L	R	R	L	R	L	L
<	<	>	<	>	>	<	>

Rotation Pattern 3

R	L	R	R	L	R	L	L
>	>	<	>	<	<	>	<

Rotation Pattern 4

R	L	R	R	L	R	L	L
<	>	>	<	<	>	>	<

This is the transposition of rhythmic patterns that evolved from one form of instrumentation to a new form. A new gestalt emerges within the musician's method mediated by the limitations and parameters of the new instrumental form. And from this new gestalt can emerge a new set of patterns that may be more suitable for that instrument. The primary operator of Polyrhythmic Knob Twiddling as a contribution to music is that it offers a new playing method.

Most electronic music such as Techno and Industrial has become very computer based. Compositions are often a collection of electronically produced drumbeats and samples. The sounds are manipulated by a programmed computer sequencer. Sounds that are manually manipulated through effects are often brief slap-shot samples strung together via computer sequencing as well. A rudimentary system of manually manipulated knob rotation patterns provides the option of including more performance-based parts to electronic music.

One might wonder what advantage there is to learning this new performance skill if these rotation patterns could easily be programmed with computer sequencing. The issue is not one of practicality but of creativity and knowledge. Non-musicians could theoretically create and program their own polyrhythmic rotation patterns via computer sequencing and then deliberate their artistic merit and what changes to make when listening to the sequencer play them back. This process is much slower and mechanical than manual performance. Meanwhile, the creative process influences the outcome. Performance bears different fruit from sequencing. It is a matter of an artistically differentiated consciousness.[3]

3. SPRING DULCIMER

Percussion can be either tonal or atonal but is usually one or the other exclusively. A hammered dulcimer is played strictly for melody while a tabla set is operated strictly for rhythm. However, what if a percussion instrument could combine tonality and atonality as a kind of semi-inharmonic sound that could go either way depending on the application? This question moved me to create the Spring Dulcimer.

I chose springs for my new dulcimer because they have a unique tonal fuzziness. Proper selection of spring type based on the coil diam-

---

3 See Bernard Lonergan, *Method in Theology* (Toronto: University of Toronto Press, 1990), 272 and Robert M. Doran, *Theology and the Dialectics of History* (Toronto: University of Toronto Press, 1990), 232-33.

eter, wire thickness and length brings the spring into a tunable tonal range when stretched across a soundboard. It is the antithesis of a traditional hammered dulcimer, which has a sweet, ethereal sound with long bridge pieces in fixed positions. The variable tension of the wire strings is tuned with pegs. The Spring Dulcimer, however, has a heavy, dirty sound. The springs have a fixed tension. Adjustable bridge pieces for each spring assist tuning by creating nodes within the spring.

The tonal fuzziness of the springs influences how the Spring Dulcimer can be played. Unlike a traditional hammered dulcimer, the Spring Dulcimer cannot be used to play a rapid succession of notes. The characteristics of its timbre are such that it would sound too undefined. It is more suitable for slower note progressions. A similar example can be found with distortion and the electric guitar. A distorted guitar will work for certain applications in Rock music including power chords and lead solos. However, unmuffled strumming of dissonant chords often lacks clarity when played through distortion. A clean guitar sound would seem more appropriate. The parameters of limitation help define an instrument's place in musical style.

The trade-off to this partial tonal vagueness of the Spring Dulcimer is that it is appropriate for certain types of music such as performance-based industrial music. Stefan Weisser from California is credited for pioneering a metallic-sounding form of percussion as a high art in the early 1970s. But as a distinct musical style, the industrial sound emerged in pop culture around 1980 in Europe and has often been referred to as Noise music. The most notable acts from this period were Test Department from Britain and Einsturzende Neubauten from Germany. Performances were often very percussion based and involved scraping and bashing of metal, clanging pipes and any other form of found percussion or unconventional instrumentation.

The prehistory of this approach to music dates back to the early twentieth century Italian composer and Futurist painter Luigi Russolo and his 1913 manifesto *l'arte di rumori* (The Art of Noise).[4] He wanted to find the music hidden in the elemental sounds of nature and modern urban environments. He believed that the use of "pure sounds" in music placed too many restrictions on emotional expression. It certainly has been the case that there has always been an aesthetic appeal to some inharmonic sounds. Gongs have been used for thousands

---

4 Luigi Russolo, *The Art of Noise*, trans. Robert Filliou (New York: Something Else Press, 1967), 5-6.

of years in spiritual practices, for example. Russolo's reverence for all sounds as having musical potential was later echoed by twentieth century experimental composers such as John Cage. Many of Cage's early compositions were purely percussive involving the use of various objects found at the junk yard such as brake drums, hub caps, and spring coils.

But at what point is this approach considered musical and at what point is it considered a kind of quasi-conceptual performance art or even merely sound exploration? For music to be present there must be the apprehension of a rhythmic or melodic gestalt or pattern. John Cage attempted to give form to the dissonant chord structures of twelve tone music by using moments of silence as markings in the composition. Whereas other composers relied on harmony and consonance to give music its form, Cage used innovative time-based structures which he referred to as "micro/macrocosmic rhythms."[5]

In 1983 came the advent of MIDI (Musical Instrument Digital Interface), a binary protocol that allowed instruments to communicate with each other and computers. Widespread use of digital sequencing and sampling soon followed. Sounds could now be manipulated by computers in ways that were previously not possible. This gave industrial music the potential for greater musical coherence and to incorporate more melody blended with industrial sounds. This technology allowed commonly heard everyday sounds, such as clanging pipes or electric drills, for example, to be recorded or "sampled" and then played on a keyboard. The pitch of the sound could be either lowered or raised by pressing a lower or higher key on the keyboard. Many Industrial musicians as well as film composers and post-production engineers responsible for film sound effects adopted this technology which continues to this day. Performance-based industrial music was eclipsed. Whereas MIDI has touched other forms of performance music in some way, it has not become their foremost tool of creation to the same extent. Perhaps this result could have been offset for Industrial music had there developed a more systematic method of performance-based instrumentation. Enter in, the Spring Dulcimer.

Established forms of performance music are closely identified with instruments which are played with specific methods and within rudimentary systems, i.e., the guitar and blues or the violin and clas-

5 David Revill, *The Roaring Silence* (New York: Arcade Publishing, 1992), 61.

sical music. Early Industrial music never reached that stage of development before it became digitized. This is not to imply that the Spring Dulcimer is destined to be the savior of early Industrial music. But every development in music needs an audience for its acceptance. It is from the audience that new players emerge, bringing their own talents and ideas to further develop the style. The audience, the musical style, the playing method and the instrument become closely identified with each other. The Spring Dulcimer would likely be embraced by an Industrial music audience because of the instrument's sound. But it need not be limited to this. The double bass, which was used in classical music, was adopted by jazz musicians. A new playing method emerged. The hands instead of the bow were used, giving jazz its characteristic walking bass line. And from this a new audience emerged.

4. TABLUDU KIT

The integration of two established musical traditions into one requires the creation of a new musical language. This includes not only the development of new playing techniques but also a new form of instrumentation. The Tabludu enables Eastern and Western drumming techniques to be incorporated into one drum kit. I chose to call my invention the Tabludu kit because it combines the tabla from India for hand percussion and the *udu* from Nigeria as a kick drum. The idea of fusing these two radically different traditions was the main operator for the Tabludu because that is what set its development in motion. The sequence of events determines the operator's status.

The Western drum kit is a combination of drums from various cultures and traditions. The kick pedal for the bass drum was a key component because it made it possible to play several drums at one time. It was first used by the early trap drummers or the one-person bands in the late nineteenth century. Traditionally the bass drum, cymbals and snare were each played by separate people in early ragtime bands. The kick pedal allowed one person to do the job of two or three. Additional drums were added and modified to form what eventually became the modern drum kit. From this evolved traditions of playing techniques that co-developed with the music of the times along with additional modifications to the drum kit design and set up. Jazz drum kits and rock drum kits are designed differently from one another because the playing techniques associated with them are different from each other.

In India there is a family of cylindrical drums called the *mridang*. They have skins on either side that are played with the drum in a horizontal position. Over the course of several thousand years there evolved many variations of cylindrical drums with different tonal qualities and names. Each of these designs was associated with specific musical traditions. Playing techniques vary between traditions, but the hand strokes bear some basic similarities. The tabla is believed to have evolved from the *pakhawaj*, which was from the cylindrical family of drums. The tabla is unique because it is two drums, each with one skin, which are played in a vertical position. The design and tonal quality of the tabla influenced how the playing techniques were adapted from the cylindrical family of drums. The most notable characteristic of the tabla is the technique for bending the sound of the lower tones.

The udu drum is a clay pot with a hole in the side. It produces a round bass sound that rises in pitch when the hole is struck with the hand and then released. The sound is similar to the bending of the pitch sound produced by the tabla. The tabla originated from Nigeria as a standard water jug that evolved into an instrument when its musical potential was discovered.

Integrating Eastern tabla playing with Western kit drumming into one style poses interesting challenges. Each style has its own rhythmic syntax. Certain combinations of strokes and rhythmic phrases particular to each style need to be adjusted in order to work for the Tabludu. The groups of operations within the tabla player's style are mediated by the addition of the udu as a kick drum. The groups of operations within the kit drummer's style are mediated by the parameters of playing techniques of the tabla as a form of hand percussion but also slightly by the sound of the udu because of its ability to bend pitch. The udu is used as a kick drum because its sound is more compatible with the tabla. A custom floor-level stand keeps the udu in a stationary position. A silicon gel pad attached to a flat beater mallet is used with a kick pedal attached to the udu stand. The use of the gel pad kick pedal simulates the traditional hand slapping technique.

There are factors that could impede the acceptance of the Tabludu. Most percussionists do not know both Eastern and Western styles of drumming. Western kit drumming is often learned by ear, making it accessible to most. However, the tablas have a variety of strokes that need to be learned before rhythms can be played effectively. This often requires some basic training with a teacher to get the proper technique down. Tabla teachers are not as widely available in the West as they are in India.

5. EMERGING PROBABILITIES

Successful schemes set the stage for further development of new schemes. Such is the process of emerging probabilities. The modern drum kit as an instrument and polyrhythms as a playing method are two examples of successful schemes in percussion. It is inevitable that these schemes foster insight into the creation of new forms of instrumentation and playing methods.

Polyrhythmic Knob Twiddling is a method that has yet to find a home in an instrument. The present form of instrumentation is a bit crude and underdeveloped. Audience response has hitherto been either lukewarm or downright negative. However, there have been developments in recent years with the CD player scratchers used by some DJs as an alternative to turntable scratching. This would allow CDs with customized sounds to be used for what could be called "polyrhythmic scratching" or "scratch and twiddle." CD player scratchers are examples of a technology that has already been established as an instrument. It can be used for a polyrhythmic method of playing when used in tandem with effects modules. This would be the entry point for acceptance. Modifications could be made to make the technology more suitable for that style of playing.

The Spring Dulcimer as an instrument is an operator in musical evolution because it is a new technology. This sets it apart from a traditional hammered dulcimer both in sound and playing method. It is best suited as a one-handed accompaniment to another percussive instrument such as a steel pan drum. The pan drum could have a metallic-sounding snare plate among its notes. A customized bass pan drum could be used as a kick drum. This set-up could be an Industrial-sounding steel drum kit used for both rhythm and melody within the same instrument. The adjustable bridge pieces of the Spring Dulcimer along with the fixed tension of the springs make tuning easy and stable. This makes the new instrument a suitable candidate for exploring micro-tuning schemes such as quarter tones or, as American composer Charles Ives put it, "the notes between the cracks of the piano keys."

Tabludu performance could include the use of cylindrical drums such as the khol drum instead of the tabla. The khol drum produces sounds that are similar to the tablas but was designed to be played in an elevated horizontal position. The tablas were meant to be played sitting down. The Tabludu set-up requires that the tablas be elevated, which results in the loss of some bass. Perhaps a tabla skin could be fitted onto a drum with a funnel protruding down to the floor such as a Dumbek or Djembe drum. This could help reclaim some of the lost bass. The result of this modification would be a new kind of drum. It is difficult to accurately speculate how this would affect the sound or whether modifications to playing technique would be required. The technique is closely linked to various tones the tablas produce. However, as Albert Einstein once said, "We can't solve problems by using the same kind of thinking we used when we created them."

Thus continues the journey into emerging probabilities. Some things for possible exploration in the future are warranted: 1) microphone feedback, 2) urban sound exploration, 3) elemental meaning in music.

6. MICROPHONE FEEDBACK

Some years ago during an improvisational jam session with some friends, I ran the vocalist's microphone through various effects devices. This caused the microphone to feedback terribly; it was quite unpleasant to listen to. This happened to be recorded on tape. I later took this recording and decided to smooth out the loud volume spikes. Upon doing this I discovered that the feedback mixed with the voice and the effects sounded rather pleasant and interesting. It was then that I decided to find a way to use microphone feedback musically. I subsequently began experimenting with various methods and equipment to control and manipulate feedback to create melodies. The results were unpredictable and difficult to replicate, but I did manage to record a handful of melodies successfully. I have some ideas that I would like to explore to possibly improve the method.

I like to compare this experience to the process of evolution in nature. Mutations and accidents that are unsuccessful in one environment may adapt very well to a new set of circumstances. The microphone feedback was an accident that occurred when I was looking for something different. When I transferred the recording of the microphone feedback to an environment where I was able to control the volume spikes, I was able to look at it in a different way. And from this I was able to experience new insights. This Darwinian process can also be found in science. Many paradigm shifts in science have occurred as the result of these happy accidents. This evolutionary process in science has been illustrated in Thomas S. Kuhn's monumental book *The Structure of Scientific Revolutions*.[6]

7. URBAN SOUND EXPLORATION

Another area of interest that I have discovered is the exploration of old abandoned factories and their acoustic properties. With the exception of theaters and cathedrals, modern architecture tends to focus on the visual appearance and/or functional purpose of buildings. What I would like to explore is the overlooked artistic potential for industrial sounds to be found in factories.

On a visit to an abandoned brick factory in Toronto, I found several objects within its walls that had great potential as percussion instruments. These included large networks of air ducts and large metal kiln doors. What I also discovered was the influence that these objects had on the types of rhythms I played on them. I had brought with me a bass drum kick pedal with a modified rubber ball beater mallet to make it more suitable for beating on metal. I had brought also modified drumsticks that were covered with a rubbery plastic, again to make them more suitable for beating on metal objects.

Some of the rhythms that I felt moved to play seemed to have a temporal ambiguity uncharacteristic of the rhythms that I often played on a traditional drum kit. At times it was difficult to tell whether the rhythm had a standard 4/4 time signature or a triplet groove. This temporal ambiguity was similar to that found in many African rhythms. It is for this reason that African rhythms do not easily fit into linear Western classical time signatures. These are often referred to as groove based rhythms because of the "ground up" approach in which they are created.

African drumming by and large uses the hands instead of drum sticks. This tends to make the rhythms seem more temporally organic, reflecting the natural rhythmic inclination of the player. Drumsticks behave according to exact laws of physics as far as how they strike surfaces and bounce. The player's natural rhythmic inclination is me-

6 Thomas S. Kuhn, *The Structure of Scientific Revolutions* (Chicago: University of Chicago Press, 1996), 57.

diated through the exact behavior of the drumstick and so result in less temporal ambiguity. The drumsticks that I used in the factory had less bounce because of their plastic rubbery covering and so simulated some of the temporally ambiguous qualities found in hand percussion.

8. ELEMENTAL MEANING IN MUSIC

I was once asked to explain how one knows when they have it right when creating music. I was a bit stumped by this question, and so I decided to explore it. In the course of my search I came across some articles on the relationship between music and language. Both language and music share some similarities in the way they are processed by the brain for the recognition and appreciation of sound manipulation.[7]

When speaking, the pitch of one's voice rises and falls. This appears to be isomorphic with one's emotional responses. In this there is what Lonergan called elemental meaning – the apprehension of an experiential pattern that has not yet been fully transformed into objective meaning. An example of this is the feeling that people get when they have a word on the tip of their tongue. They know what they want to convey prior to formulating a way of expressing it.[8] Emotional responses to music are the result of tension and release created by the relationship between notes in melodic progression as well as tonal quality and rhythm.[9]

Examples of elemental meaning in music can be found in *interspecial* communication, in the recorded sounds of living organisms. We are all familiar with the comical experience of a dog howling to music. A more sophisticated example can be found in attempts to communicate with whales through music. An organization called 'Interspecies' (www.interspecies.com) has successfully used music to communicate with Orcas using underwater speakers through which guitar music was played. The Orcas' responses seemed to indicate that they were trying to imitate the notes. This would seem to be indicative of elemental meaning in the relationship between music and language. Whales have a fairly sophisticated form of oral communication compared to most other species.

---

7 Oliver Sacks, *Musicophilia* (Toronto: Alfred A. Knopf, 2007), 216.

8 See Lonergan, *Method in Theology*, 74.

9 Victor Zuckerkandl, *The Sense of Music* (Princeton, N.J.: Princeton University Press, 1971), 30.

Eugene Gendlin developed a process called *Focusing* as a way of identifying the true nature of one's feelings. According to Gendlin, we feel emotion throughout our bodies. He refers to this state as "felt sense."[10] Through focusing on the subtleties that we feel in our bodies during this state we gain greater clarity about why we feel the way we do. This state of "felt sense" as a form of elemental meaning is akin to the creative process by which a musician knows when he has it right.

9. CONCLUSION

Significant developments in the evolution of popular music are often sporadic. New music that is marketed as having revolutionary qualities might be better described as a variation on a theme if it does not deviate significantly from its original scheme. What I am proposing are applicable evolutionary models for creating paradigm shifts in music.

There is a flux between inert musical schemes and the operators that drive the emerging probabilities of new schemes. For Polyrhythmic Knob Twiddling, the schemes are the polyrhythms. The operator is the use of effects modules to play the rhythms. For the Spring Dulcimer, the scheme is the hammered dulcimer. The operator is the use of springs rather than wire strings to create a new sound that in turn influences playing style and an instrument that allows for easy experimentation of alternate tuning schemes. For the Tabludu Kit, the schemes are the tablas and the udu drum. The operator is the combined use of these drums in a novel way to unite two drumming traditions in order to create a new tradition. It is my hope that one day these developments will lead to new and exciting frontiers in music.

---

10 Eugene Gendlin, *Focusing* (New York: Everest House, 1978), 11.

THE PROBLEMATIC OF CHRISTIAN
SELF-UNDERSTANDING AND THEOLOGY:
TODAY'S CHALLENGE TO THE THEOLOGICAL COMMUNITY

FREDERICK G. LAWRENCE
BOSTON COLLEGE

It is an honor to be writing for a collection to honor Robert M. Doran, SJ, General Editor with Fr. Fred Crowe of the *Collected Works of Bernard Lonergan* and past Director of the Lonergan Research Institute in Toronto. Bob is surely the most innovative and productive of theologians following Lonergan's lead, and a dear friend, collaborator, and colleague to my wife Sue and me. The idea for my paper comes from his ideas on the integration of Balthasar's theology into a Lonergan-inspired systematics and on the possibility of a permanently valid component of elemental meaning within a systematic theology.[1] These fertile ideas probing the integration of feelings into systematic theology proper gave me the impetus to start thinking about a closer general relationship among Christian self-understanding, spirituality, and the kind of intelligibility sought by systematic theology.

GERMAN IDEALIST VS. CHRISTIAN
SELF-UNDERSTANDING

Hans-Georg Gadamer tells us that the concept of *Selbstverständnis* was coined originally in an objection J. G. Hamann made in his correspondence with his friend Jacobi. The objection was based on the Christian experience (classically presented by St Augustine) that human beings cannot understand themselves on the basis of their own capacities or on that of the world as the proper object of their knowledge:

> Whoever attains to true self-understanding has something happen to them, and something has happened. So modern discourse about

---

1 Doran's ideas and personal encouragement were keys to a recent Boston College doctoral dissertation by Randy Rosenberg.

the self-understanding of faith means that the believer becomes aware of his having been related to God. He achieves the insight into the impossibility of understanding himself from whatever is at his disposal (*sich aus dem Verfügbaren zu verstehen*).[2]

However, in modern times this construal of self-understanding has been compromised, if not eliminated, by German Idealism, where self-understanding refers to a process towards complete self-transparency achieved by absolute knowledge. According to Gadamer, Johann Gottlieb Fichte's *Wissenschaftslehre* held that "at the basis of the concept of self-understanding lies the idea that all dogmatic assumptions will be dissolved by the inner self-production of reason, so that at the end of this self-construction of the transcendental subject stands total self-transparency."[3] This idea was elaborated at length in Hegel's *Phänomenologie des Geistes*, in which the beginning of all being resides in the Spirit, which unfolds all of reality from its own creative power. By the absolute Spirit's diremption, matter becomes that in which the absolute Spirit appears and attains what Hegel believed his own philosophy to have accomplished, so that the unity of both God and world in the unconditioned Spirit achieves its self-actuation in the *absolutes Begriff*.

2. SELF-UNDERSTANDING IN SCHLEIERMACHER AND DILTHEY

A new chapter began when Heidegger took over the notion of *sich selbst-Verstehen* from Wilhelm Dilthey, who developed the Romantic Hermeneutics of Friedrich David Ernst Schleiermacher. While rejecting Hegel's claim that reason has direct access to a comprehensive understanding of being in its totality, where self-understanding was conceived on the model of perfect self-consciousness, Schleiermacher acknowledged the universal epistemological relevance of *Verstehen*, which means at once understanding, interpretation, and the expression of interpretation. His hermeneutics as "the art of understanding" grew precisely out of the recognition that, as regards the historical differences between text and interpreter, interpretation is systematically

---

2 Hans-Georg Gadamer, "Die Marburger Theologie (1964)," *Neuere Philosophie I*, GW 3 (Tübingen: J.C.B. Mohr (Paul Siebeck, 1999), 197-208 at 204.

3 Gadamer, "Die Marburger Theologie (1964)," *Neuere Philosophie I*, GW 3, 203.

liable to misunderstanding.[4] Hermeneutics had to be transformed from an auxiliary discipline in theology and law into a universal device that turned methodically disciplined understanding into the most secure means of overcoming the strangeness of the content to be grasped from the past. "Psychological-historical understanding enters in place of direct insight into the subject matter as the genuine methodically-scientific attitude."[5] The psychological interpretation implies that full understanding of an author's thought in a text depends on tracing it back to the living moment in the author's personal life-context. In theology past or present the key is always the "self-consciousness of the faith."

Besides grammatical skills together with the resources for the individualized interpretation of an author offered in his writings on dialectics and aesthetics, Schleiermacher introduced into hermeneutics the novel psychological notion of "divination." Divination is, according to John Wilson, "the point where interpretation has no choice but to make conjectures, to try in some sense to place itself in the situation of the author, based on everything that can possibly be learned by historical analysis."[6] However, according to Schleiermacher, "*Alle kommunikation ist das Wiedererkennen des Gefühls*"[7] – an insight dependent upon Kant's aesthetics of genius in the third Critique. Gadamer held that for Schleiermacher, then, "*Verstehen* is reproductive repetition of the original production of thought and the basis of the congeniality of the spirits."[8] Paving the way for liberal theology and for historicism,

---

4 Friedrich David Ernst Schleiermacher, *Hermeneutics and Criticism and Other Writings*, trans. Andrew Bowie (Cambridge: Cambridge University Press, 1998), 5.

5 Hans-Georg Gadamer, "Zur Problematik des Selbstverständnisses. Ein hermeneutischer Beitrag zur Frage der »Entmythologisierung« (1961)," *Gesammelte Werke* 2 (Tübingen: J.C.B. Mohr (Paul Siebeck), 1999), 121-132 at 123.

6 See the entire section on "Schleiermacher: His Mature Thought," in John E. Wilson's *Introduction to Modern Theology. Trajectories in the German Tradition* (Louisville, KY: Westminster John Knox Press, 2007), 84-94, cited at 86.

7 See footnote 21 in Hans-Georg Gadamer, "Zwischen Phänomenologie und Dialektik," *GW* 2, 3-23 at 15.

8 Hans-Georg Gadamer, "Klassische und philosophische Hermeneutik," *GW* 2, 92-117 at 98.

Schleiermacher's subjective hermeneutics displaced the basic normative meaning of the text implied by the traditional Christian doctrines
of scriptural inspiration, the canonization of Holy Scripture, and the
regula fidei – all originally considered to be grounded in the reality
expressed in the text.

Dilthey relocated Schleiermacher's hermeneutics in the borderland
between the epistemologically oriented question regarding the possibility of historical knowledge and Lebensphilosophie, which was oriented to life as the basic character of human existence. It focused on the
objective character originated not by the epistemological subject but
by the "thought-forming labor of human living." Nevertheless, under
the influence of John Stuart Mill's idea of "inductive logic" and Neo-
Kantian preoccupations with the critical grounding of the sciences,
Dilthey expanded Schleiermacher's psychological approach to hermeneutics into a full-blown epistemological foundation for the humanities and the human sciences, the Geisteswissenschaften.

3. RUDOLF BULTMANN

It remains that the critique of historical consciousness achieved by
Dilthey was not able to come adequately to terms with anything like
a historical life-context of meaning (Sinnzusammenhang or Leben-
szusammenhang). He began to realize this himself as he became familiar with Husserl's critique of psychologism. The problematic at issue
here bears upon the theological one concerning the relationship between the historical-critical method of biblical exegesis and the theological task of accounting for what is moving in and through the series
of the subjective viewpoints of authors over time, as well as upon the
tension (in both Protestant and Catholic theology) between historical
interpretation and dogmatic/systematic theology. As Gadamer noted
about the issue as framed by liberal theology, "The dilemma between
historical-individualizing analysis and carrying the kerygma forward
remains of course theoretically insoluble."[9]

We are all now familiar with liberal theology's use of modern historical research to reconstruct the picture of the person of Jesus by
discarding the dogmatic image of Christ: the Son of God, eternally
'pre-existent' Son, present to God the Father and the Holy Spirit, who
became man is replaced by the teacher of simple faith in God as Father and of a high-minded humanity. Besides the major contribution

9 Gadamer, "Klassische und philosophische Hermeneutik," GW 2, 101.

of revealing how its environment conditioned primitive Christianity, as Ernst Troeltsch made clear, historical research also had the effect of both dissolving Christianity's absolute truth-claims and of relativizing Christianity into one among many modes of religious expression – the kinds of issues so problematic to Pope Benedict XVI/Joseph Ratzinger.

Rudolf Bultmann[10] was schooled in such liberal theology by Hermann Günkel, Adolf Harnack, Adolf Jülicher, and Johannes Weiss, and by the Kantian systematic theologian, Wilhelm Hermann. In 1921 Bultmann published his first work, *The History of the Synoptic Tradition*, under the historicist auspices of liberal theology's use of Form Criticism. However, not long afterwards, he was convinced by Karl Barth, Friedrich Gogarten, and Eduard Thurneyson of the need for dialectical theology's decisive overcoming of the crisis of theological historicism. The main thrust of this often misunderstood correction was not a despair-motivated flight from total historical skepticism to a dogmatic edifice, but the exclusion of psychologism from both textual interpretation and theology by a *Sachkritik* that presupposed that the reality or mystery set forth by the texts should never be reduced to the interpreter's imaginary reconstruction of the meaning of the author.[11]

Bultmann understood that "Christian faith is not a phenomenon of the history of religion… it does not rest on a 'religious a priori' (Troeltsch), and … therefore theologians do not have to look upon it as a phenomenon of religious or cultural history."[12] Bultmann was convinced that Jesus of Nazareth existed in history. His theology began not from the putative 'historical' Jesus, but from Christ as alive today. Even if he cannot be said to have succeeded, Bultmann's aim was to mediate historical (the historical-critical interpretation of the Bible and authoritative sources) with systematic theology (the exposition

---

10 See Rudolf Bultmann, "Autobiographical Reflections," *Existence and Faith. Shorter Writings of Rudolf Bultmann*, translated and edited by Schubert Ogden (Cleveland, OH: World Publishing Co.: Meridian Books, 1960), 283-288.

11 See Rudolf Bultmann, "Die liberale Theologie und die jüngste theologische Bewegung (1924)," and "Die Bedeutung der 'dialektischen Theologie' für die neutestamentliche Wissenschaft (1927)," *Glauben und Verstehen, Gesammelte Aufsätze, Erster Band* (Tübingen: J.C.B. Mohr (Paul Siebeck), 1966), 1-25 and 114-133.

12 Bultmann, "Autobiographical Reflections," 288.

of the self-understanding of the faith). In his NT studies he intended
to expose the self-understanding of those whose Easter faith was reflected in the stories and mythological thought forms of the texts, and
to show their contemporary relevance.[13]

As he gradually distanced himself from Barth, Bultmann opposed
both the liberal orientation toward making the 'historical' Jesus the
object of theology and all conservative attempts – to which dialectical theology was also opposed – to save faith by protecting it against
historical criticism. His rigorous literary critique of the gospels and of
primitive Christianity was done to increase historical understanding
of the Easter faith of the disciples; he intended to bring to light the
historical character of the original proclamations of faith: the Bible
is the Word of God *as* the word of human beings. At the same time,
he knew that Christian faith is grounded in the resurrection of Jesus,
which cannot be known as a result of historical investigation by the
light of reason alone. Because it is otherworldly, the resurrection is
not just another general phenomenon in the world into which one can
achieve direct insight and verification. For Bultmann the resurrection
is an event of revelation disclosed to faith alone, where faith is a matter
of self-understanding, entailing an understanding of revelation and of
one's own existence at once. With Barth, Bultmann contended that
there is no support for the Christian self-understanding of the cross
and resurrection outside of these realities themselves, and that to subject revelation to this-worldly criteria of judgment is a mistake.

Bultmann thought the parallelism between the terms of Heidegger's
fundamental-ontological analysis of existence in *Sein und Zeit* (1927)
and Paul's understanding of the natural human being would help him
solve the modern theological question of *Reden über Gott*. Heidegger's
contrast between authenticity and unauthenticity, which Bultmann
developed especially in terms of what is *verfügbar* (i.e., at our disposal
or manipulable) and what is *unverfügbar*, was perfect for opposing the
Christian message of grace to the Stoic ideal of self-sufficiency (*au-
tarky*).

As Gadamer noted, "The future character of *Dasein* in the mode of
authenticity and, conversely, fallenness with respect to the world, can
be theologically interpreted by the concepts of faith and sin."[14] And

13 See Paul Ricoeur, "Préface à Bultmann," *Le conflit des interprétations: essays d'herméneutique* (Paris: Éditions du Seuil, 1969), 373-392.

14 Gadamer, "Klassische und philosophische Hermeneutik," *GW* 2, 102.

so Bultmann would have Heidegger's existential ontology ground a modern self-understanding of faith, making possible a contemporary presentation of the self-evidence of revelation and faith by means of the 'self-understanding' opened up by revelation. The person would no longer be confronted with the universal entity, "Christianity," – as in Harnack's *Das Wesen des Christentums* – but with the Word immediately addressing the sinner as justified. In accord with the Lutheran understanding that faith does not entail an ontological transformation of existence, Bultmann held that neutral ontological structures were needed to present the substance of faith. The believer lives in the same ontological state-of-mind (*Befindlichkeit*) as the unbeliever but with a new self-understanding granted by the justifying Word. Faith makes human beings radically uncertain because in virtue of the communication of God the Christian's sole privilege is the Cross. Any certainty would amount to sealing oneself off from God by some sort of self-justification; therefore, it is liberating to be overtaken by God's salvific act.

As a student and young *Privatdozent* Gadamer was Bultmann's colleague in Marburg. Later on he often claimed that Bultmann's use of Heidegger shifted the meaning of the hermeneutics of facticity into an anthropology. This also entailed a difference in Bultmann's construal of self-understanding. Bultmann was not, of course, using the term in the sense of German Idealism, but his usage still bore the marks of the modern subjectivism to which Heidegger was so opposed. Nevertheless, Gadamer credits Bultmann for emphasizing the historicity (*Geschichtlichkeit*) both of human existence and of the experience of Christian faith, and for developing hermeneutic theory by insisting that scholars acknowledge "the prior relationship-to-being of the one understanding to the text he is understanding, inasmuch as, in relation to the Holy Scripture, he taught that a *Vorverständnis* is posed regarding human existence itself in its aspect of having been moved (*Bewegtheit*) by the question of God."[15]

4. MARTIN HEIDEGGER

Gadamer recalled that Heidegger participated actively in the visits to Marburg by the leaders of dialectical theology, recalling especially

---

15 Hans-Georg Gadamer, "Hermeneutik (1969)," second Appendix to *Wahrheit und Methode, Hermeneutik II*, Gesammelte Werke 2, 425-436 at 429-430.

his response to a guest lecture by Thurneyson. Like Thurneyson, Heidegger had been deeply affected by Franz Overbeck's critique of the theology of the day, and he formulated Overbeck's challenge as follows: "it is the true task of theology, to which it must find its way back, to seek the Word that is capable of calling to faith and to preserve in the faith."[16] Like Bultmann, Heidegger knew that the most genuine clue to the nature of self-understanding came neither from Hegel's ideal of complete self-transparency nor from Schleiermacher's or Dilthey's subjectivity-based and epistemologically-oriented hermeneutics as technique for overcoming historical alienation from the past. It came from concrete religious experience.

During the years 1919 through 1921, Heidegger was making a twofold transition at the same time: first, from what he called "the Catholic system" to what he hoped would be a more authentic form of Christianity, and, second, from Edmund Husserl's reflective phenomenology to hermeneutic phenomenology. So it was not entirely fortuitous that it proved decisive for the switch from reflective to hermeneutic phenomenology when Heidegger interpreted Book X of Augustine's *Confessions*.

This book contains the bishop of Hippo's retrospective account, almost a decade afterwards, of his performance of writing Books I to IX, the story of his life up to and immediately following his conversion to Christianity. Augustine begins with the prayer, "May I know you, who know me. May I 'know as I also am known' (1 Cor 13: 12) [X.1.1]."[17] Heidegger interprets Augustine as saying that when he becomes a question to himself (*quaestio mihi sum*), he asks about God in order to discover that his seeking is constitutive of his facticity:

> That means, in seeking this Something as God, I thereby come myself into a completely different role. I become not only *the one from whom* the seeking emanates and is moved ahead somehow, or *in* whom the seeking occurs, but the performance of the seeking itself is something from the self.[18]

---

16 Gadamer, "Die Marburger Theologie (1964)," *Neuere Philosophie I*, GW 3, 197.

17 St Augustine, *Confessions*, trans. Henry Chadwick (Oxford: Oxford University Press, 1992), 179.

18 Martin Heidegger, *GA* 60, 192.

But according to Augustine, the human quest has "fallen in relation to what it itself has been capable of doing, what was at its disposal, what was comfortably attainable as regards surrounding and various other meanings pertaining to the world and to itself."[19] Thus the radical questionability that should naturally be the core of the life of the self becomes fragmented, dispersed into the world, and sealed off against the truth. Augustine came to realize that only the humiliated Word Incarnate could save him. Heidegger commented: "The Christian possesses the consciousness that [his proper] facticity can be gained not through its own power, but stems from God – a phenomenon of the causality of grace."[20]

The three dimensions of human facticity featured in Heidegger's analysis of Book X – the seeking born of radical questionability, the experience of fallenness, the recovery caused by grace – are Christian experiences that Heidegger then formalized into basic human experiences that determined his grasp of self-understanding. An approach such as Husserl's could not adequately account for conscious experience as performative. If one begins from the presupposition of the primordiality of the subject/object split that flows inevitably from intentional acts of perception, reflection can only gain access to the subject's performative awareness as an *object*. Thus Heidegger emphasized the limitations of objectification in philosophy. He knew that if one conceives of conscious intentionality (as Husserl chiefly did) in terms of the perception of a circumscribed, already-out-there-now object, one must also think of being in terms of *Vorhandenheit* by privileging 'presence' *ad instar* spatio-temporal proximity, and this leads to the forgetfulness of being. Therefore Heidegger's strategy was to focus on the 'performative meaning' (*Sinnvollzug*) enacted in the circle of experiencing and the experienced in order to heighten his awareness of consciousness as performative.

Gadamer wondered whether "in the end the Word of faith could also find a new philosophical legitimation by reason of (Heidegger's) critique of the Logos [i.e., reflective, objectified, abstract, and universal meaning] and of the understanding of being in terms of

---

19 Heidegger, *GA* 60, 197.
20 Heidegger, *GA* 60, 121.

Vorhandenheit."[21] *Sein und Zeit* broke out of the horizon of *Vorhandenheit* by portraying being from the perspective of human consciousness
as performative in terms of its unobtrusive, unimportunate, unrefrac-
tory character (*Unauffälligkeit, Unaufdringlichkeit, Unaufsässigkeit*).
Heidegger famously ascribed these traits to the *Zuhandenheit* proper to a master craftsman's tools-in-use and set them off against the
need to focus one's perceptual attention on a tool that is broken or
not functioning well (*Vorhandenheit*). In the hermeneutics of facticity,
Verstehen (rather than perception) is *Dasein*'s basic structure; asking
the question of its own existence permits being to come to light as distinct from finite beings. For Heidegger, then, every case of *Verstehen*
involves understanding oneself – self-understanding.

   In his trajectory out of the transcendental standpoint of Kant, Fichte, and Husserl, Heidegger's overall thrust led him even before the
Kehre to speak of *Sein als Erfahrung* rather than of human consciousness. Gadamer pointed out Heidegger's earlier evocation of the scholastic distinction between *actus exercitus* and *actus signatus* to indicate
implicit and performative awareness as distinct from thematic and
reflective awareness.[22] His point was that, if correctly understood, the
term consciousness, which Heidegger thought he should discard, is in
agreement with *Sein und Zeit*'s phenomenology of *Verstehen* as the key
to the hermeneutics of facticity. Consciousness correctly understood
is what Bernard Lonergan has called "consciousness as experience"
as distinct from "consciousness as perception."[23] This is 'hermeneutic'
consciousness because once one understands the correct meaning of

---

21 Gadamer, "Die Marburger Theologie (1964)," *Neuere Philosophie I*, GW
    3, 200.

22 Gadamer, "Die Marburger Theologie (1964)," *Neuere Philosophie I*, GW
    3, 200-202.

23 Bernard Lonergan, *Collected Works of Bernard Lonergan*, vol. 7, *The On-
    tological and Psychological Constitution of Christ*, trans. Michael G. Shields
    (Toronto: University of Toronto Press, 2002), 255:

    Consciousness-as-experience is a broader notion than conscious-
    ness-as-perception. For consciousness, conceived as experience
    on the side of the subject, accompanies every operation, whether
    sensitive or intellectual, cognitive or appetitive; nor does it matter
    what the object of the operation may be, since it is always the same
    subject that is operating. But if consciousness is conceived as per-
    ception of oneself on the side of the object, then there is no con-

consciousness, one is in a position to grapple with human historicity and with the contingency both of human *Verstehen* and of what can be adequately known by human beings. One also realizes that the measure of being beyond finite entities cannot be taken by human representations (picture thinking), categories, or concepts.

Understanding hermeneutic consciousness allows one to deconstruct fundamental myths concerning knowing: (1) that knowing the truth is like taking a look at and seeing what is there to be seen while not seeing what is not there; (2) that what is known in knowing the truth is the perception of what is 'already-out-there-now'. Moreover, in light of implications drawn from consciousness as experience Heidegger recognized the ultimately unsustainable character of the typically unquestioned assumptions of modern epistemology – (a) of the subject as the privileged and first object of awareness, (b) the reduction of consciousness to its intentional dimension, (c) the primordiality of the subject-object split.

---

sciousness except in those operations in which the object is the very subject operating.

Again, from *The Triune God: Systematics*, CWL 12, trans. Michael G. Shields, ed. Robert M. Doran and H. Daniel Monsour (Toronto: University of Toronto Press, 2007), 315, 317:

> It is one thing to be conscious, but it is quite another to know, through knowledge in the proper sense, that one is conscious. To be conscious belongs to everyone, for consciousness is simply the presence of the mind to itself. This self-presence is effected by the very fact that our sensitive and intellectual nature is actuated by both apprehending and desiring. It does not matter what object is apprehended or desired, since we as conscious subjects consciously apprehend and desire different things. Nor do we become conscious by adverting to ourselves, since consciousness is on the side of the adverting subject and not on the side of the object adverted to. But when this adverting to ourselves is done, we begin the second step, namely, knowing that we are conscious. For one who is conscious places oneself on the side of the object inasmuch as one understands and conceives consciousness and truly affirms that one is conscious... But unless we define what consciousness is, and unless we truly affirm that we are conscious in the sense of the definition, we do not attain knowledge, properly speaking, of our own consciousness.

Heidegger surmounted the horizon of *Vorhandenheit* by asking about the *Sein* of *Verstehen* to uncover the dynamisms of performative consciousness, from whose perspective alone the urgent modern issues of historicity and contingency could be dealt with adequately. To counter prevailing positivism, naïve realism, and idealism, he developed a radical fundamental ontology, which, although confined to the horizon of what is intrinsically conditioned by space and time, opens human self-understanding to its own historicity. This at least breaks through crucial obstacles to rightly understanding and living in light of the human relationship to transcendent being, and it also is susceptible of experiences of transcendence both natural and supernatural.

Indeed, asking the question about the being of understanding as interpretative (and therefore beyond the capacity for sense perception or intuition) is significantly similar to Lonergan's strategy of not asking the epistemological question (How do we know we are really knowing?) before first asking and attaining a phenomenologically ostensible answer to the question, What are we doing when we think we are knowing? Then the question of being is in both cases recovered and framed in terms of the *meaning* of being. Similarly, Heidegger's criticism of Logos is a criticism of the logical ideal of knowledge's all-encompassing ultimacy, especially in so far as it would either bypass or at least take for granted the *enactment* of understanding. Perhaps this is not unlike Lonergan's criticism of conceptualism as both oblivious of the act of insight and incapable of fully acknowledging Giambattista Vico's famous *aperçu* regarding the priority of poetry, so that the limits of the model of the natural sciences and of mathematics for these overarching questions are recognized. Again, Heidegger's break with the horizon of *Vorhandenheit* is not unlike Lonergan's overcoming of the dominance in spontaneous human imagination of "the already-out-there-now" in philosophical issues concerning knowledge, objectivity, and being.

Heidegger's exposition of the historicity of human self-understanding completely overturns the idealist presuppositions about the transparency of human consciousness, and about the immanentist implications drawn by idealism from Vico's dictum (which also is adopted by René Descartes, Francis Bacon, and Thomas Hobbes) that *verum et factum convertuntur*, namely, that truth is convertible with what the knower has constituted, constructed, or produced by freely instituted, fully transparent, and logically explicit procedures.[24] Heidegger refuted the assumption that being is only known inasmuch as it is *object*, an assumption that eliminates the way in which human-presence-to-self is in fact present-to-world by being actuated in operations of sensing and understanding, grasping the sufficiency of evidence, deliberating, and having practical insights. None of these basic kinds of enactment are to be thought of as human actions initiated by the human will to power, but are *suffered by* the human subject as extrinsically conditioned by space and time. And even when the human being is responsible for its decision, "historical truth is the irrevocability of the unrepeatable decision."[25] Thus, even in the natural human order that prescinds from supernatural grace and sin, human self-understanding has the basic character of gift.

Heidegger's emphasis on the historicity of *Verstehen* not only indicated its transitory nature and conditionedness, but also demonstrated that at any given time the intelligibility illumined or the truth established can always only be partial, falling short of the absolutely unconditioned; in like manner, human authenticity is never so pure or perfect that it is altogether untroubled by unauthenticity, so that, in its precariousness, it is ever something to be sought in "fear and trembling."

These ideas in their ambiguity can be given a valid Christian interpretation. Think of John Henry Newman's hymn "Lead, Kindly Light" or of the following statement from an early sermon: "We attempt great things with the certainty of failing, and yet the necessity of attempting, and so while we attempt, [we] need continual forgiveness for the failure of the attempt."[26] Nevertheless, in the course on Aristotle immediately following his Augustine course, Heidegger conflated the

---

24 On what he calls the *"verum-factum* principle" see Robert Miner, *Truth in the Making: Creative Knowledge in Theology and Philosophy* (New York: Routledge, 2004), xii, xvi, 96-97, 105. Miner makes the best of the principle, believing that both Thomas Aquinas and Nicholas of Cusa share the idea – something with which I disagree.

25 Hans-Georg Gadamer, "Das Problem der Geschichte (1943)," *Hermeneutik II*, GW 2, 27-36 at 35.

26 John Henry Newman, "Sermon 7", in *Parochial and Plain Sermons*, Volume 1 (National Institute for Newman Studies, 2007), http://www.newmanreader.org/works/parochial/volume1/sermon7.html, accessed December 1, 2008.

fallenness due to sin with the *Geworfenheit* related to human finitude's *Faktizität*. As a result, the ambiguity attending the inseparability of human authenticity and unauthenticity is connected with a lack of clarity on the part of Heidegger and Gadamer (in the role of chief interpreter he plays here) about human self-understanding's vulnerability to the individual and collective renunciation of moral responsibility and the refusal to be attentive, intelligent, reasonable, responsible and loving. If Heidegger was too ambiguous about human *Geworfenheit* or thrownness and fallenness or sin, he correctly emphasized two things: first, that the positivist and/or idealist assumptions regarding the ultimate efficacy of science and the possibilities of human engineering can only exacerbate the consequences of what Lonergan has called basic sin, and second, that although the intent of his philosophy was to reverse the falsity and the devastating effects of the assumptions listed above, he did acknowledge that human beings are morally impotent. As he proclaimed in his famous *Spiegel* interview, "Only a god can save us! (*Nur ein Gott kann uns retten!*)"

5. HANS-GEORG GADAMER

Gadamer used Heidegger on *Verstehen* in a philosophical hermeneutics that culminated in a hermeneutic ontology. In this way he arrived at an interpretation of self-understanding that went beyond Bultmann's 'existentialist' use of Heidegger in his existential interpretation of the subversion of vaunted human self-sufficiency by Christian faith. Gadamer does not deny the validity of Bultmann's point, but he believed Bultmann was still caught up in the subjectivism or immanentism that Heidegger's hermeneutics of facticity had striven to overcome.

By inquiring into the manner in which *Verstehen* is *Sein*, the human being's understanding of *Sein* becomes his or her chief existential characteristic. Thus being is not the product of the operations of self-consciousness, but of the inadequately conceivable or never properly thematizable (*Unvordenkliche*) condition for the actualization of conscious operations, which does not fit into the transcendental schema, and which after the "*Kehre*" Heidegger began to express in language such as 'Seinsgeschehen', the 'Da' as being's 'Lichtung', and human being as 'the shepherd of Being', and so on.

That for *Sein und Zeit*, *Verstehen* is the way in which historicity is actuated for *Dasein* itself profoundly affected Gadamer, who had been

trained earlier in Marburg Neo-Kantianism. In its temporal character
Verstehen projects possibilities into the future out of its *Geworfenheit*
from the past. There is no question here of sovereign self-possession
because from the ontological perspective of being, the focus shifts
from "the self-mediatedness of self-consciousness" to "the experience
of oneself, which occurs to the person and in particular, considered
theologically, happens in the address of proclamation," so that it "can
deliver the self-understanding of faith from the false claims of Gnostic
self-certainty."[27]

Gadamer adopted this standpoint from which both self-consciousness and the self are displaced from the center of consideration. Concentrating on *Verstehen* as an event of being brings out the priority of
the relationship between the one doing the understanding and what
is understood over either side of the relationship. This same priority of the relationship between the one speaking and what is spoken
distinguishes the performance of conversation: neither member of the
relationship furnishes the fixed basis. In each of these examples, self-
understanding occurs in virtue of the paradoxical self-less-ness enacted in self-transcendence.[28] The displacement of self-consciousness
and of the self from the center of one's understanding of *Verstehen*
also corrects the naïve presuppositions of historical consciousness regarding the historical retrieval of meanings or truths from the past by
hermeneutical consciousness. The thrownness or situatedness of the
historical subject is not only a limitation vis-à-vis the past meaning, or
truth, or value, but also an empowerment because both subjects enacting the past and subjects re-enacting the past in the present through
Verstehen are *participating in* a whole that is moving in and through
their self-understandings. Gadamer's phenomenology of the experience of the artwork and his phenomenology of the working out of interpretation in the humanities or the *Geisteswissenschaften* through the
dialectic of question and answer constitute paradigms for the meaning
of self-understanding that are even more relevant to the tasks of theology than Bultmann's meaning.

27 Gadamer, "Zur Problematik des Selbstverständnisses. Ein hermeneutischer Beitrag zur Frage der »Entmythologisierung« (1961)," *Gesammelte
Werke* 2, 125.

28 Gadamer, "Zur Problematik des Selbstverständnisses. Ein hermeneutischer Beitrag zur Frage der »Entmythologisierung« (1961)," *Gesammelte
Werke* 2, 126.

Against the widespread positivist and historicist misunderstand-
ings of historical consciousness, which share a distorted notion of
what reflection can accomplish, Gadamer employed the notion of the
'hermeneutical situation.' It contrasts this truncated understanding of
historical consciousness with historical consciousness thought out adequately:

> When our historical consciousness transposes itself into historical
> horizons, this does not entail passing into alien worlds unconnected
> in any way with our own; instead, they together constitute the one
> great horizon that moves from within and that, beyond the fron-
> tiers of the present, embraces the historical depths of our self-con-
> sciousness. Everything contained in historical consciousness is in
> fact embraced by a single historical horizon. Our own past and that
> other past toward which our historical consciousness is directed
> help to shape this moving horizon out of which human life always
> lives and which determines it as heritage and tradition.[29]

So, as regards the interpretation of a text, the coming to light of
the text is identical with the coming to light of the self in this non-
subjectivist sense.

Gadamer's central analogy for human attunement to the being moving in and through its operations is his phenomenology of *Spiel* – play,
or game, or game-play.[30] This is how human beings participate in being. Gadamer wrote in *Wahrheit und Methode*: "It made sense to bring
the game-play of language into closer connection with the game-play
of art in which I had contemplated the parade example of the hermeneutical. Now to consider the universal linguistic constitution of our
experience of the world in terms of the model of game-play certainly
does suggest itself."[31] When people first learn to speak, it is not so
much a learning process as a "game of imitation and exchange." Thus,
Gadamer tells us, "In the receptive child's drive to imitate the forming
of sounds, the enjoyment in such forming of sounds is paired with
the illumination of meaning. No one can really answer reasonably the

29 Gadamer, "Das Prinzip der Wirkungsgeschichte," *Wahrheit und Methode*,
    288; "The Principle of History of Effect," *Truth and Method*, 304.

30 See Gadamer, "Spiel als Leitfaden der ontologischen Explikation," *Wah-
    rheit und Methode*, 97-127, "Play as the clue to ontological explanation,"
    Truth and Method, 101-134.

31 See Hans-Georg Gadamer, "Zwischen Phänomenologie und Dialektik,"
    Hermeneutik II, 5.

question when their first understanding of meaning occurred." Theologian Austin Farrer put this beautifully when he wrote:

> Our humanity is itself a cultural heritage; the talking animal is talked into talk by those who talk at him.... His mind is not at first his own, but the echo of his elders. The echo turns into a voice, the painted portrait steps down from the frame, and each of us becomes himself. Yet by the time we are aware of our independence, we are what others have made us. We can never unweave the web to the very bottom .... Nor is it only parental impresses of which we are the helpless victims. How many persons, how many conditions have made us what we are; and, in making us so, may have undone us.[32]

Gadamer's claim that we learn everything in language-games has nothing to do with the subjective attitude of 'just playing' or not being serious. In general, game-play really starts only when players become serious, in the sense that they do not hold themselves back as 'just playing' and not being serious.[33] Language is not a set of tools – vocabulary, grammar, syntax, and so on. For Gadamer it is always language-in-use, as concretely occurring in conversation. If conversation has the structure of game-play, language exists concretely in language-games.[34] "The life of language consists ... in the constant further playing out of the game we started when we learned to speak.... It is this continuously played game in which the mutual life together of people is played out."[35] Again, if it has the structure of game-play, conversation also displays the spirit of game-play with its characteristic

---

32 See Austin Farrer, *Love Almighty and Ills Unlimited* (London: Collins/ Fontana 1967/1966), 114.

33 Hans-Georg Gadamer, "Mensch und Sprache," *Hermeneutik II* 152; ET: "Man and Language," *Philosophical Hermeneutics* trans. David Lingis (Berkeley: University of California, 197), 66.

34 So Gadamer finds himself in agreement with Wittgenstein, who hit upon the same insight completely independently. See "Die phänomenologische Bewegung," *Neuere Philosophie I: Hegel·Husserl·Heidegger* Gesammelte Werke 3 (Tübingen: J.C.B. Mohr (Paul Siebeck), 1999), 150-189, esp. 185-189/ "The Phenomenological Movement (1963), 42-146, *Philosophical Hermeneutics*, 173-177.

35 Gadamer, "Mensch und Sprache," *Hermeneutik II*, 152/"Man and Language," *Philosophical Hermeneutics*, 66.

"lightness, freedom, and the luck of success – of being fulfilling, and of fulfilling those who are playing."[36]

Heidegger's critique of the 'subjectivistic objectivism' of modernity liberated Gadamer to orient himself in the direction of the epigraph Gadamer selected from Martin Luther's *Tischreden* for the central second part of *Wahrheit und Methode*: "*Qui non intelligit res, non potest ex verbis sensum elicere.*" Whoever does not understand the realities (referred to by the words) cannot elicit the meaning from the words (by themselves)." And so Gadamer translates Heidegger's concern for being into a concern for reality. The *raison d'etre* of questions and answers is knowledge of the subject matter. For this reason, dogma is legitimate for Gadamer because it is a species of *Vorurteil*, prejudgment, prejudice, or belief that embraces truth to which we more or less tacitly assent without having, by our own immanently generated acts of understanding and checking, verified the reality in which we believe. So even though Part II of Gadamer's *Wahrheit und Methode* chose to prescind from the dogmatic considerations so central to Augustine's *De doctrina Christiana*,[37] Gadamer understood that the notion of a dogmatic tradition was in no way antithetical to intellectual probity in either theological or legal hermeneutics, as we see in his discussion of the role played by modern *Rechtsdogmatik* in the literature on German jurisprudence of his day.[38]

Once again, his preoccupation with the *Sache* enabled Gadamer to demonstrate just how the idea of the *mens auctoris* could not possibly be the norm or standard either in legal or in biblical exegesis. As he put the matter trenchantly in the case of the latter: "If we understand under the meaning of the text the *mens auctoris*, i.e., the 'verifiable' horizon of understanding of any given Christian writer, then we accord the authors of the New Testament a false honor. Their proper honor ought to lie in the fact that they announce the tidings about something

---

36 Gadamer, "Mensch und Sprache," *Hermeneutik II*, 152/"Man and Language," *Philosophical Hermeneutics*, 66.

37 See Hans-Georg Gadamer, *Wahrheit und Methode. Grundzüge einer philosophischen Hermeneutik*. Gesammelte Werke 1, Hermeneutik I, 177.

38 Gadamer, "Klassische und philosophische Hermeneutik," *GW* 2, 106-108, where one of Gadamer's references is to Erich Rothacker's classic, *Die dogmatische Denkform in den Geisteswissenschaften* (Mainz: 1954).

that surpasses the horizon of their own understanding – even if they happen to be named John or Paul."[39]

Gadamer realized that Heidegger's salient point that every case of *Verstehen* always also involves self-understanding is quintessentially at stake in the area of theology. In the essay, "Language and Understanding," Gadamer appealed to the concrete experience of 'hearing the Word':

> When I say 'word' (*das Wort*), I do not mean the word whose plural are the words (*die Wörter*) as they stand in the dictionary. Nor do I mean the word whose plural is the words (*die Worte*), which with other words go to make up the context of a statement. Rather I mean the word that is a *singularetantum*. That means the word that strikes one, the word one allows to be said to oneself, the word that enters into a determinate and unique life-situation; and it is good to be reminded that behind this *singularetantum* stands ultimately the linguistic usage of the New Testament.[40]

For Gadamer's hermeneutics generally this theological reference was a clue to his discussion of *application* (in a correction of the separation of *subtilitas intelligendi* from *subtilitas applicandi* – that had been systematically misunderstood by Emilio Betti). For Gadamer it is mistaken to think that in our interpretive endeavors we first understand the meaning of the text 'in itself,' as it were, and then apply that meaning to 'ourselves' or to 'our situation.' It follows from the fact that self-understanding is integral to every act of *Verstehen* that the dimension of application is also integral to understanding and interpreting a text from the past.

In precisely this connection, Gadamer contributed notably to the effective history of Heidegger's retrieval of Aristotle on *phronesis*. Generalized, *phronesis* in act confirms the indissolubility of the link between understanding, interpretation, and application to oneself and one's situation. Heidegger's course on Aristotle was altogether more significant for Gadamer than the Augustine course we have discussed above.

---

39 See "Die Marburger Theologie," *Neuere Philosophie I*, 207/ ET: "Martin Heidegger and Marburg Theology (1964)," *Philosophical Hermeneutics* 198-212 at 210. On the issue of self-understanding, see also Gadamer, "Hermeneutik und Historismus," *Hermeneutik II*, 403-412 and "Zur Problematik des Selbstverständnisses: Ein hermeneutischer Beitrag zur Frage der 'Entmythologisierung'," 121-132.

40 Hans-Georg Gadamer, "Sprache und Verstehen," *Hermeneutik II*, 192.

Gadamer always stressed that Heidegger's reappropriation of Aristotle's critique of Plato's Idea of the Good (as present in the Academy) and of the Aristotelian notion of *phronesis* was a model for his own endeavor to raise the question about being as distinct from beings.[41] As possessing the characteristics of a this-worldly, already-out-there-now object projected into the beyond, the idea of the Good criticized by Aristotle epitomized the inauthentic *Vorhandenheit* that needed to be resisted and overcome by the hermeneutics of facticity. As such, this ontology based on unauthentic *Vohandenheit* "asks the question of metaphysics about the highest being (God) and about the being in every being."[42] Similarly, Aristotle's analysis of *phronesis* as an *allo genos gnoseos*, and therefore as distinct both from *techne*'s concern for the particular and the concrete involved in production, and from *nous*, *sophia*, and *episteme* as oriented toward necessity and immutability,[43] became the centerpiece in Gadamer's "Broadening of the Truth Question to the Realm of the *Geisteswissenschaften*," – the title of the central part of *Wahrheit und Methode*. As Gadamer explained:

> The elucidation of the modes of being true in Book VI of 'Nicomachean Ethics' had for Heidegger this significance above all, that the primacy of judgment, of logic, and of 'science' for the understanding of the facticity of human living reached a decisive delimitation in this text. An *allo genos gnoseos* came into its own right, which does not know objects and does not wish to be objective knowledge, but rather intends the clarity proper to factically lived Dasein. So besides Aristotle's Ethics the Rhetoric was important for Heidegger, because it knows about pragmata and pathemata – and not about objects.[44]

Phronesis, then, is a habitual sense for the doable, a caring for what is practically good here and now, whose mode of "being truthful" (*aletheuein*) cannot be adequately represented either in terms of looking

41 See Hans-Georg Gadamer, "Selbstdarstllung Hans-Georg Gadamer (1975)," *Hermeneutik II. Gesammelte Werke*, Bd. 2 (Tübingen: Mohr (Siebeck) 1986) 477-508 at 484-487.

42 Hans-Georg Gadamer, "Martin Heidegger 75 Jahre," *Neuere Philosophie I*, Gesammelte Werke 3 (Tübingen: J.C.B. Mohr (Paul Siebeck), 1999), 186- 196 at 195.

43 See Aristotle, *Nicomachean Ethics* VI, 5 1140a 24ff; 9, 1141b 33ff.

44 See Hans-Georg Gadamer, "Die religiöse Dimension," *Neuere Philosophie I. Hegel, Husserl, Heidegger. Gesammelte Werke* Bd. 3, 308-319 at 312.

CHRISTIAN SELF-UNDERSTANDING & THEOLOGY

at the already-out-there-now or from the horizon of producing some artifact. The standpoint of production locates the overall form of being-in-the-world in the will that in willing itself proleptically projects the "world." From the standpoint of *phronesis*, we make preferential choices in light of the *hou heneka* – the that-for-the-sake-of-which everything and anything is chosen by us.[45] This standpoint signals the radicality of Heidegger's departure from Aristotle in the first Freiburg and early Marburg periods: the realization that comprehensive reflection on being is inextricably tied up with our habitual prudential sense for the doable. According to Heidegger we have to make an *Urentscheidung*, a fundamental option for the 'one thing needful,' in order to find our direction in the realm of our passions and of our practical ends in accord with the mean.

Thus the point of departure for the hermeneutics of facticity as directly inspired by Aristotle is the dianoetic virtue that both settles the issue of and enables us to be faithful to a decisive orientation. This establishes our basic disposition in relation to the striving and desiring that moves us to action according to the right *logos*.[46] This combination of knowing and deciding that relates our personal orientation in life to the concrete situation of action becomes the hallmark for Gadamer's sense of self-understanding.

Drawing upon the tradition of hermeneutic philosophy, Calvin Schrag writes that "an existence 'between' the poles of activity and passivity comprising a self as a dialectic of initiating and receiving action, is a defining feature of the finitude that is characteristic of the self as mortal" – yet another way of expressing Gadamer's analogy of *Spiel* as the basic mode of human participation in being.[47] Schrag delineates the social dimension of the famous middle-voice by which Gadamer characterizes human self-understanding:

---

45 See Riedel, "Hermeneutik und Gesprächsdialektik," *Hören auf die Sprache* 127-128; *Being and Time's* transposition of this is "resoluteness" toward oneself, the proleptical projecting of "wanting to have a conscience" that first provides one's ability to be a whole (in the anticipation of death) its full "transparency" (128).

46 See Aristotle, *Nicomachean Ethics* II, 2, 1103b 32, 34; 1106a 1-4.

47 Calvin O. Schrag, *The Self after Postmodernity* (New Haven: Yale University Press, 1997), 60-61, citing Paul Ricoeur, *Freedom and Nature: The Voluntary and the Involuntary*, trans. E. Kohak (Evanston: Northwestern University Press, 1966), 58.

This limitation within the very structure of human finitude does not, however, diminish the importance and urgency of choice in the odyssey of self-constitution and self-understanding. The who of action exercises a genuine freedom as she or he is implicated as a seat and source of empowerment within the wider economy of prior and contemporary co-actors. And here one is able to take a line from Ricoeur's phenomenology of will, reinforcing the notion of a hermeneutical self-implicature through action. Ricoeur tracks the self-recognition of the agentive subject by exploring what he calls the phenomenon of a 'pre-reflexive imputation of myself' in the act of deciding. An imputation of self is at work in the throes of decision making. 'Je me decide,' reads the French. 'Ich entscheide mich,' reads the German. In English, and probably somewhat cumbersomely, it recalls ours as 'I make up my mind in the act of deciding.' At any event, at issue in this multilingual exposé is the recognition that in the dynamics of decision-making the who of action is called into being as an agentive subject.

Thus, although the subject implicated in and called into being by its deliberation, decision, and action is not a sovereign and autonomous subject, secure in an abiding and monadic self-identity, it is a genuine agent of change in its consensual and dissensual responses to prior action upon it. The who of action can make a difference in the world of communicative praxis. The who is implicated as the source of empowerment and the agency of epistemological zero-point origin, the self as an implicate of action exhibits the power to become an effective agent of social change and cultural transformation.

6. SELF-UNDERSTANDING AND CHRISTIAN LIVING: THE ROLE OF THEOLOGY

The entry under 'self-understanding' in Van A. Harvey's *A Handbook of Theological Terms* tells us that it "refers to the basic interpretation a man has of himself and his relationship to all of life, an interpretation that 'stands under' and expresses itself in his action and speech."[48] The usage places great weight on the role of basic decision: it is existential. In this sense, self-understanding is roughly equivalent to Hans Urs von Balthasar's definition of 'spirituality': "the way a person understands his or her own ethically and religiously commit-

---

48 Van A. Harvey, *A Handbook of Theological Terms* (New York: Collier Books-Macmillan Publishing, 1964), 218.

ted existence, and the way he or she habitually acts and reacts to this understanding."[49]

Rowan Williams has written that Christian self-understanding is "bound *always* to be something evolving and acquiring definition in the conversations of history: it offers a direction for historical construction of meaning, but it does not offer an end to history." He associates Christian self-understanding with "the humane Trotskyism of Raymond Williams," who envisaged a "long revolution." Williams then invoked (with an important modification) the vision of Jürgen Habermas (who is in turn dependent on the American Christian pragmatist Josiah Royce) concerning an "at best ... asymptotic approach to a condition that history by itself (by definition) is incapable of realizing – a perfect communality of language and action free from the distortions imposed on understanding by the clash of group interests and the self-defense of the powerful." More importantly, Williams contrasted Christian self-understanding with the contemporary debasement of the idea of *style* that has become all-pervasive via the Nietzschean derivative, "personal life-style":

> Societies like (ours) ... have no problem in tolerating a "chaos of personal life-styles" in practice, even where there may be varieties of public rhetoric that commend some lifestyles more than others. In the context of these societies, indeed, *style* is everything: with massive commercial support, cultural options – even when their roots are in would-be dissident groupings – are developed and presented as consumer goods. Religious belief is no exception, whether this process of consumerization appears in the naked crudity of fundamentalist broadcasting or in the subtler ways in which secular media dictate the tone and agenda of the behavior and utterances of religious leaders; and religious commitment is reduced to a private matter of style, unconnected with the nature of a person's membership in his or her society. And concern with style notoriously detracts from seriousness about what is to be said (a point noted long ago by Augustine and others): a recent series in the London *Guardian* about postmodernism in the arts noted with anxiety the rising popularity of pastiche and pseudo-traditionalism alongside

---

49 I cannot now locate the reference for this definition in Balthasar's works. But see Hans Urs von Balthasar, "Spirituality," *Word and Redemption*. Essays in Theology 2, translated by A.V. Littledale in cooperation with Alexander Dru (New York: Herder & Herder, 1965), 87-108.

anarchic and parodic idioms, a kind of new baroque – two sides of the same coin.[50]

Such are the pitfalls to which Christian self-understanding – whether individual or communal – is prey. As Schrag reminds us:

[C]ommunity is not a pure, value-free description of a societal state of affairs. The very notion of a communal being-with-others is linked to normative and evaluative signifiers. This should come as no surprise, because the discourse that is operative is a mixed discourse, in which the descriptive and the prescriptive, the denotative and evaluative, commingle and become entwined. One of the tasks of philosophical analysis is to monitor the effects of this commingling and entwinement on the project of self-understanding within a communal existence.[51]

Not only philosophical analysis, but also Christian theology must perform this task which follows from the fact that "[s]elf-understanding entails an understanding of oneself as a citizen of a polis, a player in an ongoing tradition of beliefs and commitments, a participant in an expanding range of institutions and traditions."[52] Thus Gadamer's notion of self-understanding corresponds quite well with Christian self-understanding as inseparable from concrete communities of worship and witness.

According to Lonergan, theology has to mediate between the meanings and values of Christian religious institutions and the cultural matrix in which they are embedded.[53] Quite noticeable in culture today is the way academic culture – what used to be called 'the ivory tower' – has isolated itself from the concrete life of religious communities and churches, and also the way ideals of scholarly detachment have led to a perhaps too powerful separation of theology as scholarship and science from both religious self-understanding and spirituality. Here I would like to consider the interconnections among Christian self-understanding, spirituality, and the kind of intelligibilities sought by

50 Rowan D. Williams, "Postmodern Theology and the Judgment of the World," *Postmodern Theology: Christian Faith in a Pluralist World*, ed. Frederic B. Burnham (San Francisco: Harper & Row, 1989), 92-112 at 100.

51 Schrag, *The Self after Postmodernity*, 88.

52 Schrag, *The Self after Postmodernity*, 86.

53 See Bernard Lonergan, *Method in Theology* (New York: Herder & Herder, 1972), xi.

systematic theology, the understandings that Thomas Aquinas called *rationes convenientiae*, and that the First Vatican Council's constitution, *Dei Filius*, reformulated in terms of an "imperfect but very fruitful understanding of the mystery (*DS 3016*)."[54]

7. CHRISTIAN SELF-UNDERSTANDING, SPIRITUALITY, AND SYSTEMATIC INTELLIGIBILITY

Contemporary Catholic philosophical, systematic, or dogmatic theology – to use the common parlance that finds these terms virtually exchangeable – is bedeviled by rather unfriendly divisions among theologians marked by *parti pris*: if you are for the theology of Karl Rahner or Bernard Lonergan, then you must be against that of Hans Urs von Balthasar, or perhaps against the theology of liberation such as that of Gustavo Gutierrez, Leonardo Boff, Juan Luis Segundo, or Ignacio Ellacuria. Balthasar fans frequently object to Rahner's correlations between theology and anthropology or Lonergan's recondite abstractions, holding that Rahner's transcendental viewpoint or Lonergan's theorizing are utterly divorced from Christian spirituality,[55] and liberation theologians say they are well-nigh irrelevant for the Christian commitment to social justice.

As a student in Rome in the early 1960s who for the first time was learning the significance of systematic or speculative theology expressed in Lonergan's *De Deo Trino* (which is divided into a dogmatic part and a systematic part), I also read Lonergan's jocular comment in *De methodo theologiae* (his notes for one of his *exercitatio* courses of the same title) about an approach he named "*theologia magis genuflectans*" in a humorous contrast between the global and compact idea of theologizing 'on one's knees' and the more differentiated quest for explanatory understanding sought by Thomas Aquinas's theology as a "subordinated science." Anyone interested in Lonergan would be unlikely to forget the remark in his article "Theology and Understanding" pointing out that "just as the equations of thermodynamics make no one feel warmer or cooler, and, much less, evoke the sentiments associated with the drowsy heat of the summer sun or with the refreshing

---

54 Lonergan, *Method in Theology*, 309.

55 Hans Urs von Balthasar, "Theology and Sanctity," *Word and Redemption.* Essays in Theology 2, trans. A.V. Littledale in cooperation with Alexander Dru (New York: Herder & Herder, 1965), 49-86.

coolness of evening breezes, so also speculative theology is not immediately relevant to the stimulation of religious feeling."[56]

When challenged head-on, defenses of Lonergan's way of doing systematics – both in his pre-1965 phase of emphasis on the indispens-
ability of explanatory understanding (as the solution to the transcultural problem of bridging the gap between past and present cultural
contexts) and in the post-1965 phase of discovering the implications
of feelings and of the transcendental notion of value along with the
breakthrough to functional specialization – took one of three distinct
directions (each with its own legitimacy). First, there is the appeal to
Christian community's need for (in Georg Simmel's phrase) *die Wend-
ung zur Idee*, i.e., to have recourse to the intellectual pattern of experience in order to respond to ever more differentiated questions raised by
either believers or unbelievers. Faithful people or people either searching for or having lost their faith desire to have an adult apprehension
of beliefs comparable to what they have learned through modern science or modern scholarship in the humanities. Second might be an
appeal to Lonergan's oft-rehearsed evocations of Toynbee's metaphors
of withdrawal for the sake of return and of the creative minority. The
systematic theologian withdraws into the differentiated understandings and expressions proper to the world of theory in order to make
an enriching return to the communication of the Christian message
in contemporary terms. And third, appealing to a more explanatory,
methodological argument, one might try to show that by fulfilling specifically different theological tasks at different times, and by moving
from one to another of the diverse differentiations of consciousness
required by each task, one brings about both better outcomes for each
distinct field of inquiry, while also enhancing all the other differentiations, since performing one specialized task well directly or indirectly
affects all the others by way of the feedback made possible by the unity
of differentiated human consciousness. For instance, a comprehensible
systematic understanding of the Trinity would aid one to pray more
meaningfully the doxologies that come up regularly in the liturgy.

For the most part, I believe many students – even those sympathetic
to Lonergan – have in general not responded very well to any of these
lines of argument. Perhaps this is because the arguments presuppose a

56 Bernard Lonergan, "Theology and Understanding," *Collection*, CWL 4,
    ed. Frederick E. Crowe and Robert M. Doran (Toronto: University of To-
    ronto Press, 1988), 114-132 at 127.

fairly robust personal appreciation of the systematic exigence in order to be convincing. Be that as it may, the rampant allegation of a 'gaping abyss' between systematic intelligibility – at least in Lonergan's theological work proper – and personal spirituality has never rung true to me.

Fortunately, our knowledge of Lonergan's writings and the state of Lonergan scholarship have changed dramatically over the years. For example, the incessant labors of Frederick E. Crowe, SJ, (co-founder of the Lonergan Research Institute at Regis College, Toronto), presentations at diverse Lonergan Workshops by Robert Doran, SJ, (now at Marquette University), by Regis College's Gilles Mongeau, SJ, and papers on Christology – and the paper on revelation contributed to the Vertin *Festschrift*[57] – by Boston College's Charles Hefling have shed light on many of the luminous intricacies of Lonergan's theology. In addition, such writings as Lonergan's early devotional essay on the Mystical Body of Christ[58] and an unpublished Latin manuscript from the Roman years on the redemption have come to light.[59] Then, too, under the guidance of Natalino Spaccapelo, SJ, and with the help of the Lonergan Archive he established at the Gregorian University, Perugian scholar Massimiliano Marianelli recently published a work on *convenientia*,[60] together with an Appendix containing another of Lonergan's previously unpublished Latin *scripta*, redacted by Lonergan for use in his Roman *De Verbo Incarnato* course in the academic

---

57 Charles Hefling, "Revelation and/as Insight," *The Importance of* IN-SIGHT: *Essays in Honor of Michael Vertin*," ed. John J. Liptay, Jr. and David S. Liptay (Toronto: University of Toronto Press, 2007), 97-115.

58 See Bernard Lonergan, "The Mystical Body of Christ," *Shorter Papers*, CWL 20, ed. Robert Croken, Robert M. Doran, and H. Daniel Monsour (Toronto: University of Toronto Press, 2007), 106-111.

59 Bernard Lonergan, *De Verbo Incarnato: Supplementum de Redemptione*. According to translator Michael G. Shields, SJ, this document was originally composed in 1963-1964 under the title "*Bono et Malo*" as an additional thesis in *De Verbo Incarnato* (Rome: Pontifical Gregorian University, 1964, 3rd ed.) but never actually added.

60 Massimiliano Marianelli, *Ontologia della Relazione: la convenientia in figure e momenti del pensiero filosofico* (Roma: Città Nuova Editrice, *IDEE/ Filosofia*, 2008).

year 1953-1954 when he was just starting out at the Gregorian, on *"De ratione convenientiae"* with a parallel translation by Marianelli.[61]

The following proposal about the interconnectedness of the explanatory intelligibility proper to systematic theology with the self-understanding and spirituality of the Christian theological community in service to the church would not have been possible without this constantly expanding new situation for theological research in Lonergan studies.

8. CONVENIENTIA, SPIRITUALITY, AND CHRISTIAN SELF-UNDERSTANDING

8.1 MARIANELLI ON LONERGAN'S NOTION OF *CONVENIENTIA*

Marianelli's book confirms my understanding of the integral relationship between Christian self-understanding, spirituality, and *rationes convenientiae* in systematic theology. Far from being a default position by way of resignation to theology's inability to meet the requirements of the logical ideal of science, the *convenientia* proper to adequate human analogical discourse not only speaks to one's head but represents an expression of attunement to the order of the universe that Thomas Aquinas argued is the highest good of creation in a way that speaks to one's heart.

Marianelli's "Introduction" clarifies the teaching of Lonergan (and of Simone Weil) on the notion of *convenientia* by contrasting it with that of Gotthold Leibniz, who equated the "principle of *convenientia*" with the "principle of the best." Those familiar with Voltaire's *Candide* will recall the critical parody of Leibniz's "best of all possible worlds." Accordingly, for Marianelli, Leibniz's theory of the relationship between possibility and existence presupposes that "*nihil est sine ratione*," and therefore God's choice among possible competing worlds has to be motivated by both a "logical convenience" and a "moral convenience"

---

61 Lonergan's full title is, *"Supplementum schematicum. De ratione convenientiae eiusque radice, de excellentia ordinis, de signis rationis systematice et universaliter ordinatis, denique de convenientia, et fine incarnationis,"* published in Marianelli's "Appendice," *Ontologia della Relazione: la "convenientia in figure e momenti del pensiero filosofico,* 109-179.

in view of realizing the best possible world.[62] This is a case of God's matching means with a pre-established end in a putative exercise of divine instrumental reason oriented toward utility-maximization! In contrast, the line of *convenientia* pursued by Marianelli's book is that of Augustine, Aquinas, Lonergan, and Simone Weil.[63] Unlike Leibniz, who subscribed to the *verum/factum* principle dominated by technical expertise, the authors in the alternative series think of *convenientia* in terms of the ordered relationship of parts to whole within an ontology of participation.

Marianelli's Chapter 1, "*Convenientia e aptum* in Agostino d'Ippone [13-28]," considers Augustine's mention in *Confessions* of a youthful (no longer extant) work named *De pulchro et apto*. It explains Augustine's adaptation of Cicero's use of the term in the context of a theology of creation. The emphasis is on "fittingness" in relation to the beautiful, the good, and the one. A parallel with Balthasar's theological aesthetics in *Herrlichkeit* is not fanciful because in a footnote Marianelli remarks Balthasar's description of Augustine's conversion as "a conversion from an inferior aesthetics to a superior aesthetics" inasmuch as Augustine had to go beyond the opposition between *pulchrum* and *aptum* centered on the forms of material entities to the perfect beauty of the absolutely simple God as reflected in the congruence of the Son with the Father.[64]

His second chapter entitled, "*Convenientia* e Relazione di Adaequatio in Tommaso d'Aquino [29-59]," starts from a treatment of the soul's *convenire* in the disputed questions *de Veritate*, which places *convenientia* in the context of *adaequatio* and of truth, where of course "truth is founded upon being (*supra ens fundaturi*)." Whether the notion of 'appropriateness' or 'fittingness' is treated in the context of beauty and goodness or in that of truth, it is completely removed from Leibniz's framework of mere utility and production.

The next chapter, "*Convenance* comme *Accordo* e *Armonia* in Simone Weil [60-78]," Marianelli shows how Weil dealt with the issue

---

62 Marianelli, "Introduzione," *Ontologia della Relazione: la convenientia in figure e momenti del pensiero filosofico*, 10-11, where the author refers to V. Agosti, "Principio della Convenienza" in *Enciclopedia filosofica*, vol. 3, 2267.

63 About Weil Marianelli had published, *La metafora ritrovata. Miti e simboli nella filosofia di Simone Weil*, for which he was awarded a prize of the Pontifical Academy.

64 See Marianelli, *Ontologia della Relazione*, note 12, 95.

in terms of Pythagorean thought. This chapter sets the stage for the book's culmination in *"Convenientia e Ordine* in Bernard Lonergan [79-91]" and "Conclusioni [92-108]," which is a succinct and insightful commentary on Lonergan's schematic supplement, "De ratione convenientiae eiusque radice," printed and translated in the appendix.

It would not be an exaggeration to say that Marianelli presents Lonergan as gathering all the positive contributions of Augustine, Aquinas, and Weil into a compendious explanatory discourse on *convenientia* as the intelligibility that permeates the totality of the actual order of the created universe. This supplement is focused on the specific intelligibility proper to the end of the Incarnation or, in other words, on the adequate explanatory response to Anselm's question, *Cur Deus homo?* Lonergan, then, has articulated the theory of *convenientia* at the heart of all his theological work.

8.2. LONERGAN ON *CONVENIENTIA*

In part one of the Supplement, Lonergan defines the *conveniens* as "a certain kind of intelligibility properly speaking, which nevertheless is not necessary, either in relation to existence, or in relation to essence, and which in theological matters cannot be perfectly apprehended by us in this life."[65] Proper intelligibility is grasped by insight, whereas improper intelligibility includes what can be conceived, including such things as God, angels, human beings, as well as privation, nothingness, and sin. Lonergan then specifies the kinds of proper intelligibility both ontologically, in terms of potency, form, and act, and in terms of the dynamism of conscious intentionality that relates operations on the levels of experience, understanding, and judgment to each other. In the course of the latter breakdown, a first key issue is the priority of acts of understanding over concepts, clarifying the fact that one act of understanding can ground a multiplicity of concepts. A second main issue focuses on the sense in which the grasp of the sufficiency of the evidence for affirming the truth of a possibly relevant understanding can reach no more than the *virtually* unconditioned as the ground for judgment, and never attains the *formally* unconditioned that is proper only to God. Because of the structured parallelism between the elements of being proportionate to the finite human capacity to know and the cognitional structure of the dynamism of conscious intentionality, Lonergan can either treat the *convenientia* proper to the actual order of

65 Marianelli, "Appendice," *Ontologia della Relazione*, 110.

the created universe in terms of ontology or prescind from ontological causes and treat the *conveniens* in terms of cognitional reasons without begging the question of ontological presuppositions.

These matters clarified, Lonergan first explains the difference between the absolute and merely hypothetical necessity, which has to do with the contingency of the created order in its natural or supernatural components. He then links contingency to the different meanings of mystery because "the *conveniens*, finally, in matters theological, cannot be perfectly grasped by us in this life."[66] Two types of mystery are decisive for the Supplement: first, the mystery grounded in the excess of intelligibility, which is proper to both God and the mysteries of the faith whose intelligibility is grounded only in God as God really is in an infinite way; human beings cannot understand and know the mysteries of faith in this sense without divine revelation. Second, there is the mystery grounded in the lack or privation of intelligibility, of which the salient example is sin, which is a refusal to act in accord with the dictates of reason.

The second part of the Supplement handles the root of *convenientia*, which is God's wisdom and goodness. Lonergan wants us to understand why theologians are accustomed to appeal to so-called indications of reason (*signa rationis*), and how one should investigate these kinds of indications. Noteworthy from the outset is that the priority of the divine wisdom over the divine will in this account does not prejudice either the freedom of God's will or the love of infinite goodness that motivates it. The explanation of the indications pivots on the contrast between the order of human knowing and the order of divine knowledge, to the extent that we can understand it by analogy:

> We start from sensible things, advance to an understanding of quiddities and properties, and finally arrive at some understanding of the order of the universe. God however begins as it were from an understanding of himself; in his essence he grasps the whole series of orders according to which all possible worlds as a whole in accord with each one of its determinations are able to exist; and within this totality of orders he grasps all possible natures, properties, acts, and circumstances… For in this way the divine wisdom extends as far as the divine power. For everything that is possible according to the

66 Marianelli, "Appendice," *Ontologia della Relazione*, 116.

rationale of non-contradiction is found in at least one definite order of all the possible worlds.[67]

After referring to a multitude of Aquinas's writings that confirm this approach, Lonergan makes the point in part three that the intelligibility of the actual order regards not so much the logical non-repugnance of each entity in the order (which seems to have been a chief concern of Scotus, Ockham, and Suarez) as the relationship both of the entire order and of its parts to the divine wisdom. What God pre-understands and wills to create, then, is the good of order identical with the universe of created being. The good of order, therefore, grounds the excellence of *convenientia*.

No wonder the idea of the good of order loomed so significantly for Lonergan throughout his career. He understood it to be the heart of Aquinas's understanding of the common good, which (as a theologian) he could add to Aristotle's account of that notion. Thus,

> At any rate, true rest is not obtained by satisfactions of any appetites you please. For besides material satisfactions, there is also desired a certain *conveniens* measure, a right seriation of things, an order, a *convenientia* with the nature of the human being. For just as intelligence grasps an order in other things, so too it imposes an order and measure on satisfactions. Therefore besides the good that consists in satisfactions, there is also another good that can be called the good of order.

Lonergan points out that once the demands of the good of order are met, it "will shine forth both *in single individuals* and *in the entire community*."[68] *Individual* moral activity requires an order of acts in conformity with the dictates of right reason. This specifies the *formal* aspect of the good of order imposed on the *material* dimension of satisfactions. From the perspective of *community*, he uses an example drawn from his long-time personal concern for economics and politics:

> For example, what is lacking in an economic depression? The materials are still there. The workers are still there and they want to work. The managers who would like to manage workers are still there. The human desires that want to be satisfied remain. *Materi-*

---

67   Marianelli, "Appendice," *Ontologia della Relazione*, 126.

68   Marianelli, "Appendice," *Ontologia della Relazione*, 126, where the italics are Lonergan's.

ally, everything is the same as in the expansion of the real economy. But *formally* there is the greatest difference, for in an expansion the economic order thrives, and in a depression the same order is disrupted, disaggregated…Whence you may draw the conclusion: the good of order is that which formally is good, for, once that order holds sway, apparent goods become true goods, and disaggregated and unutilized goods are gathered into that greatest common good, namely, into the fruitful economic order and into the peaceful political order.

Lonergan both understands and reaffirms Thomas Aquinas's teaching that in created things the good of order of the whole universe is the greatest good.

The **fourth part** delineates six indications of reason, whose *raison d'etre* is that all theological problems that arise regarding *convenientia* may be resolved from the perspective of the order of things shaped by the divine wisdom and chosen by the divine goodness:

1) God himself knows himself;
2) God necessarily loves the divine goodness;
3) God grasps in his essence all possibilities ordered in every possible manner by divine wisdom with the knowledge proper to simple intelligence;
4) because God knows to the greatest extent the infallibility of his own intelligence, the efficaciousness of his own will, the irresistibility of his own power, he therefore knows before every act of his free will, that if he should select a certain order, all things are already completely ordered in the same manner as they are through his wisdom;
5) God selects some order, namely, the order of the actual world;
6) once the selection has been accomplished, the selected part of the knowledge proper to his simple intelligence passes into the knowledge proper to vision.[69]

According to Lonergan, because these indications of reason are both required and sufficient, human knowledge of and attunement to *convenientia* may occur from above downwards through God's revelation that divine wisdom foreknew and divine goodness selected the actual order of the universe; and it can occur from below upwards as by experiencing, understanding, and judging the actual order of things

---

69 Marianelli, "Appendice," *Ontologia della Relazione*, 136.

one gradually arrives at the order of the divine wisdom and the divine goodness. This startling proportion expresses this symmetry: as the divine wisdom stands to God's free election, so the hypotheses of empirical science stand to their verification.[70]

After these four preparatory parts, in the **fifth part** Lonergan treats the *convenientia* of the Incarnation, whose fuller explanation occurs within the scope of the order of the universe and makes explicit the drama of humanity, i.e., the historical order of the universe. He begins with an analysis of human action, which grounds the principles encompassing the total movement of history: *the intellectual nature of humanity*, from which an analysis of the wheel of progress on the levels of common (*vulgaris*) human praxis, of reflective scientific or methodical theory, and of philosophy or religion can be derived; *the defectible human will*, from which cycles of decline on the levels of common (*vulgaris*) human praxis, reflective scientific or methodical theory, and of philosophy or religion are derived; and *the divine aid of a merciful God*, from which the detailed dimensions of the redemption from sin are derived.

A first approach to the appropriateness of the Incarnation considers the merciful God's divine help from the perspective of God *as principle and source* of the actual order of the universe. These divine aids include, first, the set of three supernatural gifts: *faith*, which corrects and overcomes evil on the level of the unintelligibility and irrationality of sin; *hope*, which corrects and overcomes the demoralization, discouragement, and despair of the will; and *charity*, which by self-sacrificial love makes up for the inability of justice to correct and overcome both the objective surd and the subjective sinfulness of human beings. Second, Lonergan speaks of *mystery in the broad sense* that includes the excess of intelligibility but also involves sensible representations, exemplified by the meditations on scenes from the life of Jesus Christ in *The Spiritual Exercises* and the mysteries of the rosary. These sensible or imaginal representations convey what one has to learn by insight into the sensible or the imaginable; they mean what one has already grasped; they invite one to a fuller understanding; and they evoke appropriate feelings and emotions. Not only are such images the source of human knowledge, but whatever human beings know and decide to do is carried out more promptly and easily the more their sensibilities are affected by appropriate images and affections. Note here how

70 Marianelli, "Appendice," *Ontologia della Relazione*, 138.

much *convenientia* has to do with symbols, or images that call forth or are evoked by feelings.

A second approach considers the merciful God's divine help from the perspective of God *as the ultimate end* of the actual order of the universe. From this perspective, sin, besides being a rejection of the dictates of reason, is an offense against God, ringing down further implications regarding the supernatural virtues: *faith* has to include obedience to the God of truth and veracity; *hope* has to cure the will's attachment to this-worldly things, and keep it focused on eternal life; and *charity* has to transform our love for private goods into a love of one's neighbor.

Even more significantly from the viewpoint considering God as ultimate end, although Lonergan seems to concede that effectual hope in immortality and natural beatitude and natural love of God above all things might have sufficed to destroy sin, as a matter of fact, in the actual order of the universe humanity's end – to see and know God through his essence – is absolutely supernatural; this end is disproportionate to the human capacity by its own power. So in order for the natural human proportion to be transformed, the human being needs the supernatural love of God bestowed by the Holy Spirit, and for this, the human person needs to be loved by God the Father with the love by which the Father loves his divine Son.

Hence, it is *conveniens* that the divine Son of God should become incarnate as a human being, who by his merits, becomes the source of the communication of God's self to human beings through his life, death, and resurrection. This communication also occurs by humanity's justification through the uncreated gift of the inhabiting Spirit in this life, and in the next life, by the infusion of the supernatural intelligible species that effects the gift of vision.

However, this is only treating the *convenientia* of the Incarnation according to the order of justice. Add to that order the order of the divine law of love, by which the Father loves us as friends of the Son with the Holy Spirit, who is the love with which the Father loves the Son both as God and as human, thereby making us adoptive children, temples of the Holy Spirit, and inheritors of the vision of God. Moreover, we have to think out *convenientia* further in the context not only of elevating humanity to receive the end it desires and cannot of itself attain, but also that of rectifying human beings and restoring the original order of friendship that has been deformed by human sin. Then, in order to love God above all and to love one's neighbor as oneself (instead of one's private good alone), one needs both the justifying grace and the grace of charity, which constitutes friendship with God.

However, in relation to sin as an offence against God, it becomes even more *conveniens* that the incarnate Word redeems us through his passion and makes satisfaction to God for our offenses against him. From within the reign of sin, Jesus inaugurates the reign of God by the New Testament mysteries "prefigured in the Old Testament and imitated by the saints" in such a way as to draw out and set human sensibilities afire so that *faith* roots out falsehoods, *hope* strengthens our moral weakness, and *charity* eradicates the irrational objectivity of the reign of sin. The probability of sin foments the expedient lie of atheism, confirms one's hopes for temporal goods, and promotes hatred and envy through discord. In relation to the order of the universe and in relation to that order's function and purpose of manifesting the divine goodness, Lonergan states the following concerning the *convenientia* of the Incarnation:

> For the Incarnation is the principle of the restoration of that very order, since through him both sinners are reconciled with God and the reign of sin is conquered, and nature is elevated to its supreme perfection and God's very self is communicated justly and most lovingly to his creatures. Hence, the order thus restored manifests the goodness of God *ad extra* to the greatest degree, both because it perfects nature beyond the powers of nature, and because it communicates the very divine goodness itself, and because this communication occurs to sinners and those unworthy of it by the highest degree of mercy.[71]

In the **sixth part**, we recall that *convenientia*, besides being intelligible in the proper sense, is also unnecessary either in fact or in kind. So the necessity of the Incarnation is a matter that only supposes the existence of the Incarnation itself and hence its non-contradictory character, and the possibility that redemption from sin and elevation of human beings might either not have occurred at all, or, in God's wisdom and goodness, have occurred in another manner. The revealed fact of the Incarnation itself entails either implicitly or explicitly, either condign satisfaction for sin, or that God wills the restoration of the original order by means of an agent proportionate to the task.

---

71 Marianelli, "Appendice," *Ontologia della Relazione,* 164.

Then Lonergan asks in **part seven** about the end or purpose of the Incarnation, specifically the end of Jesus the man: Why did God become a man? The end is a good and a good is by definition something willed or chosen. As reasonable, such a choice must have a motive that can embrace many objects, be they principal, secondary, or means to the end. Moreover, if the fundamental act of the will is love, and to love is to will the good for someone, there is a parallelism between the degree of the one loved and the good willed. What motivates the divine will is the divine goodness, and as we know, the divine wisdom foreknew and the divine goodness selected (1) the actual order of the universe and (2) all the realities ordered within it; however (3) Adam's sin and the reign of sin it set in train were permitted (not willed) by God. For Lonergan, then, understanding the end of the Incarnation as the foundation of the restoration of order entails relating it to each of these three factors.

In any whole, the part is for the sake of the whole. As a part of the order of the universe, the Incarnation is for the sake of the order of the universe in relation to all of its detailed, concrete determinations, and especially in relation to the facts of the distortion of sin and the restorative divine mercy. Lonergan stresses how the order of the universe is for the good of every creature inasmuch as it adds the formal good of order (discussed in part three) to the material whole. But as a part of the actual order of the universe, the Incarnation is the most important part because it grounds and determines all the other parts within a supernatural order according to both the law of justice and the law of love.

In addition, as regards the disorder brought about by sin, the Incarnation, as the principle cause of both the restoration of the original order and the vanquishing of sin, constitutes the greatest benefit for human beings, who are subordinated to Christ incarnate as the chief part and leader. To be sure, within the present order decreed by God, restoration by Christ presupposes the loss of order due to the sin of Adam, the divine permission for which is both mysterious and, in the end, a good because of the way the infinite abyss between the reign of God willed by God and the permitted reign of sin reveals the glory of God in a way that any finite being could not possibly achieve. But this supposition of the loss of order due to sin is not what mainly makes the Incarnation *conveniens*.

At the heart of this understanding of the end of the Incarnation is the distinction between particular goods and the good of order. According to Lonergan, theologians such as Scotus, Suarez, and Molina overlooked the good of order and confined their accounts of the end of the Incarnation to the level of particular goods. With Thomas Aquinas, Lonergan holds that the good, which is the end (*finis*) pre-understood by divine wisdom and willed by divine goodness in willing the Incarnation, is the restored good of order of the universe; that object is willed for the sake of (*finis cui*) Christ and of all those who are redeemed, but it is willed mainly for Christ who is far better than the others, and who is loved by God more than the others, in accord with both the parallelism between the degree of the one loved and the good willed, and the fact that what ultimately motivates the divine will is the divine goodness.[72]

Convenientia is such a pivotal idea for Lonergan (and, as he believed, for Thomas Aquinas) that in this account we see it functioning as what he would later call both a general and a special category in his theology. Now *convenientia* as an intelligibility in the proper sense that is not necessary but, like the actual order of the universe pre-understood by divine wisdom and chosen by divine goodness, is contingent and utterly mysterious, is perhaps the chief quality of the explanatory hypotheses proper to systematic theology. As such, its centrality for systematics is not simply a matter of the acuity of the theologian's intelligence as it operates from above downwards in the indirect discourse by which it receives God's revelation, and from below upwards in the course of working out natural analogies and noting intelligibly related interconnections among the mysteries of faith; but it is also clearly related to the theologian's overall self-understanding and spirituality – or, in other words, the theologian's holiness. This is evident in the work of another theologian I will briefly consider, that of the late Austrian Jesuit, Raymund Schwager.

9. *CONVENIENTIA* IN THE THEOLOGY OF RAYMUND SCHWAGER

Although I have read many of his works, I am not an expert on Raymund Schwager's thought. One of his many students, Nikolaus Wandinger (who like Schwager has studied Lonergan's thought), has

---

72 Marianelli, "Appendice," *Ontologia della Relazione*, 176-177.

taught us that Schwager, an Innsbruck student of Karl Rahner, also learned from the works of Swiss theologian Hans Urs von Balthasar and from those of the biblical anthropologist and literary critic, René Girard. He had used the idea of drama in his dissertation, *Das dramatische Kirchenverständnis bei Ignatius von Loyola*. Balthasar's *Theodramatik*[73] further helped him think through the significance of the dramatic dimension of the life of Jesus of Nazareth. Of Girard he has written:

> Already with my first encounter with the thought of the French literary scholar René Girard (1973) the suspicion arose in me that his analyses in the fields of literary, anthropological, and religious studies could be fruitful for theology. In my study, *Do We Need Scapegoats? Violence and Redemption in the Biblical Writings* (1978) I tried to test this impression by confronting the basic ideas of his anthropological and religious scholarship with the biblical texts. This work arose parallel to Girard's work, *Things Hidden from the Foundation of the World*, in which for the first time he expressly went into biblical texts. Both works brought me to the conviction that his analyses in fact do help us to see important biblical themes and connections anew. Especially the problematic of the scapegoat becomes more concrete from this perspective and the lines that run from the entire Old and New Testament message to the event of the cross come out more clearly.[74]

Schwager summarized Girard's analysis of conflict concisely:

> People are fundamentally creatures of desire, and their aspirations are not autonomous but are determined, as if by osmosis, by a desire that fastens on models so that they act out of imitation. Consequently, if the aspirations are instinctively directed toward something which another person's desire, mediated by a model, is already longing for, then two appetites are "unintentionally" aiming over

---

73 Raymund Schwager, *Das dramatische Kirchenverständnis bei Ignatius von Loyola. Historisch-pastoraltheologische Studie über die Stellung der Kirche in den Exerzitien und im Leben des Ignatius* (Zürich-Einsiedeln-Köln: Benzinger Verlag, 1970).

74 Raymund Schwager, "Einleitung," *Der wunderbare Tausch Zur Geschichte und Deutung der Erlösungslehre* (Munich: Kösel Verlag, 1986), 5.

and over again at the same object, which must awaken reinforced desire, rivalry, and finally aggression.[75]

Similarly, with Girard's analysis of the scapegoat mechanism:

> ... R. Girard also understands sacrifice first of all from the point of view of the act of killing, and he too sees the rites in connection with a fundamental human and societal issue. However, what ... becomes for him central [is] the problematic of human rivalry and aggression. In accordance with his theory of mimesis, conflicts arise spontaneously from human desire, and this is why peaceful living together is anything but self-explanatory. The hidden factor for order in pre-civilized societies was for him the scapegoat mechanism. Aggression had to be ... diverted outward; a member of the society had to be sacrificed, so that the others should have peace again. This process was played out in a state of ecstatic and violent excitement and remained for that reason hidden from those taking part. They were aware of it only in that distortion which is mirrored in the myths. In order to maintain the healing power of the original spontaneous driving out, it was regularly repeated in a controlled form – as a ritual sacrifice. ... The phenomenon of transformation ... is important ... since through the scapegoat mechanism – and through the sacrifices which imitate it – the aggression which is within the group and therefore dangerous is transformed into a frightening and salvation-bringing external force, into the sacral reality which protects the community of the tribe by means of their fear.[76]

In *Jesus in the Drama of Salvation*, the final stage of his evolving thought on salvation before his death, Schwager went even further than he hitherto had gone in applying both the significance of the mimetic theory of human sinfulness and the primordial religious scapegoat theory of sacrifice to an understanding Christ's work of reconciling the world with God and reestablishing the divine order of love on earth. His application of a systematic framework to the interpretation of the Bible also engages in a continuous conversation with the historical critical retrieval of the Bible at the time he wrote it. The result is an original comprehension of the *convenientia* of the Incarnation different from, and perhaps complementary to, Lonergan's.

75 Raymund Schwager, *Jesus and the Drama of Salvation. Toward a Biblical Doctrine of Redemption*, trans. James G. Williams and Paul Haddon (New York: Herder & Herder/Crossroad Publishing Company, 1999), 42.

76 Schwager, *Jesus and the Drama of Salvation*, 176-177.

Balthasar's dramatic approach to Christology[77] gave Schwager the clues he needed to articulate an intelligible pattern to be grasped in the gospel accounts of Jesus's 'biography' in terms of acts in a dramatic play in which God directs the Gospel characters. And so Schwager discerned the basic structure of the Gospel message and of Jesus's destiny in terms of a dramatic story: to paraphrase Aristotle's definition of 'plot' – a set of actions and passions leading toward a point.[78] The five acts in this drama are: First Act: The Dawning of the Kingdom of God; Second Act: The Rejection of the Kingdom of God and Judgment; Third Act: The Bringer of Salvation Brought to Judgment; Fourth Act: Resurrection of the Son as Judgment of the Heavenly Father; Fifth Act: The Holy Spirit and the New Gathering. Let us rehearse these briefly.

9.1 THE NEW GATHERING AND ANNOUNCEMENT OF THE KINGDOM OF GOD

Jesus the Messiah sets out to call Israel as the eschatological people of God to join in the "new gathering" inaugurated by the kingdom of God made present in his own person, his activities, and his words. Through such symbolic deeds as meal fellowship with the lost and outcast, the many healings performed to communicate the fulfillment of God's promises and the reality of God's offer of forgiveness and love, and the special calling of the twelve disciples, Jesus calls the people of the covenant into a new gathering. Announcing the advent of the kingdom of God, he invites Israel into the eschatological kingdom. Jesus's proclamation of God's unconditional love and the utter lack of vindictiveness of God's forgiveness overturned the usual Old Testament order of repentance and conversion. The Sermon on the Mount states the terms of God's regime, neither as a kind of new moral servitude, nor as an unattainable ideal, but as what life has to be like should the new order of the kingdom take hold.[79] The Sermon on the Mount

---

77 Hans Urs von Balthasar, *Theodramatik*. 4 vols. (Einsiedeln: Johannes Verlag, 1973-8=1983). Vol. 1: *Prologomena* (1973); vol. 2: *Die Personen des Spiels*, part 1, 1976; part 2, 1978; vol. 3: *Die Handlung* (1980); *Das Endspiel* (1983).

78 Raymund Schwager, "Part Two: Drama in the Destiny of Jesus," *Jesus and the Drama of Salvation*, 27-158.

79 Raymund Schwager, *Für Gerechtigkeit und Frieden. Der Glaube als Antwort auf die Anliegen der Gegenwart* (Innsbruck: Tyrolia Verlag, 1986), 40-41.

makes it unmistakable that reversal of unfaithfulness to God's covenant – chiefly by unbelief, violence, and lying (Mt 5: 19), and by the
will to be "number one" and "have it all" in the satanic mode of rivalry
– demands not just a new set of rules but an inward conversion of
heart and the transvaluation of values as proclaimed in the Beatitudes.
According to the Sermon, the essential requirements for living out the
command to love God above all things and to love one's neighbor as
oneself (something that can only be achieved with the utmost trust in
the heavenly Father) include the refusal of the lustful gaze that lays
the seeds for adultery; the rejection of the inclination to be judgmental
that leads to murder; the denial of the desire for revenge and outrage
as an unconditional requirement for breaking the circle of violence;
and the culminating demand for a higher love than the gentiles practice when they love only those that love them: to pray for and love one's
enemy.

9.2 THE JUDGMENT ON THOSE
WHO REJECT THE KINGDOM

When he discerned the general rejection of the meaning of his deeds
and his preaching, Jesus responded with judgment, the second great
moment in the drama of Christ. Schwager's argument about judgment
is inspired by such texts as Matthew 23 :37 – "Jerusalem, Jerusalem,
you that kill the prophets and stone those who are sent to you! How
often have I longed to gather your children together as a hen gath-
ers her chicks under her wings, and you refused!"; the parable of the
wicked winegrowers (Mark 12: 1-12 and parallels); and Luke 11: 49-
51: "therefore also the Wisdom of God said, 'I will send them prophets and apostles, some of whom they will kill and persecute,' that the
blood of all the prophets, shed from the foundation of the world, may
be required of this generation – from the blood of Abel to the blood
of Zechariah, who perished between the altar and the sanctuary. Yes, I
tell you, it will be requited to this generation."

Jesus's judgment is not an act of vindictiveness or revenge against
those who do not accept or even oppose his divine offer of unconditional love and forgiveness. "If the kingdom of God was dawning in
his activity and his proclamation, then any human will which opposed
Jesus's will for a new gathering blocked the fate of the *basileia* itself."[80]
Schwager explained:

---

80 Schwager, *Jesus and the Drama of Salvation*, 58.

There corresponds to Jesus's greater offer – in case it is refused – a deeper inner destruction of life by a complete separation from God as the source of life, a destruction whose final consequence is hell. In no way did Jesus want to say by his preaching that hidden behind the God who anticipates human response with blessings is another God of wrath. Rather, in all seriousness did he want to make clear that no salvation can exist without free human consent. Wherever people close themselves, there they condemn themselves to a downfall and to ultimate despair.[81]

Thus, "punishment is not an arbitrary divine sanction, but only the intrinsic consequence of those deeds and forces to which human beings abandon themselves when they repel the divine offer."

Furthermore, as so many texts from both Old and New Testaments attest, "a negative decision has an effect on the one who makes it,"[82] typically, repetition and obduracy as in the cases of the Egyptian pharaoh's hardening of the heart (Exod. 5-11) and the obstinate resistance that met the prophets Isaiah and Jeremiah. God's absolute love and forgiveness having been rejected, a person has no recourse but to self-judgment. The hardening of the heart of those turning down God's offer of forgiveness climaxes in the judgment and execution of Jesus on the cross, in which Jesus suffers the effects of the self-judgment of his accusers and murders.

9.3 THE CROSS

The third great moment in the drama of Christ is the judgment of condemnation received by the one who is faultless and his execution on the cross. "Everything Jesus had exposed by his words of judgment he underwent himself. He had convicted human beings (first) of lying, (second) of murder, and (third) of possessing a satanic spirit, and he himself was (first) condemned by lies, (second) violently executed, and (third) decried as a satanic person. – This event was a farce, to be sure, but even so there was enacted in it, and the NT writings stress in many ways, a divine judgment about sin (John, 12: 31, Romans 8: 3)."[83]

Here the picture of the Suffering Servant of Isaiah (especially Isaiah 53: 5-9) is the interpretive key. Just as in their desire to usurp the

---

81 Schwager, *Für Gerechtigkeit und Frieden*, 46.

82 Schwager, *Jesus and the Drama of Salvation*, 63.

83 Schwager, *Für Gerechtigkeit und Frieden*, 49.

true ownership of the vineyard the vineyard stewards in the parable murder even the owner's son, so Christ accepts his condemnation and death, as 1 Peter 2: 22-24 tells us: "He had done nothing wrong, *and had spoken no deceit.* He was insulted and did not retaliate with insults; when he was suffering he made no threats but put his trust in the upright judge; he was *bearing our sins* in his own body on the cross, so that we might die to our sins and live for uprightness; *through his bruises you have been healed."* As John the Baptist said in John's Gospel (1: 29), "Look, there is the Lamb of God that takes away the sins of the world." So the cross is the sign that runs counter to conduct under the reign of sin. Schwager expressed it concisely: "The cross is the Sermon on the Mount lived out."[84] What the cross also accomplished at the same time is stated in the words of Paul's Letter to the Romans (5: 8-10): "So it is proof of God's own love for us, that Christ died for us while we were still sinners. How much more can we be sure, therefore, now that we have been justified by his death, we shall be saved through him from the retribution of God. For if, while we were enemies, we were reconciled to God through the death of his Son, how much more can we be sure that, being now reconciled, we shall be saved by his life."

9.4 THE RESURRECTION AND THE JUDGMENT OF THE HEAVENLY FATHER

The resurrection is the fourth great moment in the drama of Christ's life. The quotation from 1 Peter above said, "when he was suffering he made no threats but put his trust in the upright judge." The 'upright judge' is Jesus's heavenly Father. Jesus, according to Schwager, "had not spoken the words of judgment in order to push people into hell, but to manifest how seriously God takes human freedom. After the refusal of God's initial anticipatory performance (forgiveness), he took the judgment about sin upon himself, and thereby doubled that anticipatory initiative. He did not bring cruelty into the world, but took both – human freedom and God's love – with the utmost seriousness. His bitter destiny shows how God found a way to help hardened and refusing human beings without impinging on their freedom."[85] If Jesus's passion and death reconciled human beings while it made clear how horrible sin is to God, by raising Jesus on Easter, the Father vindicated Jesus's way of countering violence not with violence or insults

84 Schwager, *Für Gerechtigkeit und Frieden,* 51.

85 Schwager, *Für Gerechtigkeit und Frieden,* 50.

or threats, but by handing himself over to become a victim of violence instead. Schwager wanted to emphasize that the Father's verdict in favor of his Son, who died for his enemies and opponents, is also for all those who have turned against God, his love, and his forgiveness.

> The opponents of the kingdom of God, closing themselves off, had the way to salvation opened for them by the Son, who allowed himself to be drawn into their darkness and distance from God. Although they had already turned their backs, as far as they were concerned, the self-giving of the Son got around this hardening of hearts once more, insofar as he allowed himself to be made the victim of their self-condemnation.[86]

This verdict of the Father in favor of sinners was underlined when Jesus, returning from the Father after being raised from the dead, speaks to his disciples for the first time: "My peace be with you!"

> [This greeting] went out from the one who had endured the whole world of lies and violence, and addressed those disciples who out of human respect had betrayed their Lord and fled. In the hour of darkness, sin was so dominant that even the disciples were complicit in guilt. Yet precisely because the peace greeting went out to these guilty ones, it was manifested as a word of forgiveness. The Easter greeting not only wished peace, but *established peace*, because the very ones who had abandoned and betrayed him were once again accepted fully by the Risen One. In the forgiving Easter greeting, the ultimate depths of the divine initiative in relation to the human beings who rejected it is revealed.[87]

9.5 THE HOLY SPIRIT AND THE NEW GATHERING

The rejection of the kingdom of God had a further unintended outcome: the still more radically efficacious saving outpouring of God's mercy when the crucified and risen Lord together with his Father sent the Spirit of Pentecost "by which the church as a new people was definitively constituted from Jews and gentiles."[88] If the NT writings describe the time of the post-Easter appearances between Easter and Pentecost as a period dominated by uncertainty and even fear, because love casts out fear, this pneumatic experience inspired the apostles and

---

86 Schwager, *Jesus and the Drama of Salvation*, 135.

87 Schwager, *Für Gerechtigkeit und Frieden*, 53.

88 Schwager, *Für Gerechtigkeit und Frieden*, 63.

disciples to go out and, with a spontaneous outburst of praise, to begin the mission at the heart of the church as the new gathering of God's eschatological people.[89] Schwager also noted that the coming of the Holy Spirit made a new universality possible, as shown when on Pentecost the apostles were enabled to speak in all the languages of the pilgrims to the Jewish feast. From many diverse ethnic groups the Holy Spirit was creating a new gathering (assembly, *ekklesia*) without eliminating their mother tongues or native cultures.

I hope this very brief summary of Schwager's construction of the New Testament message captures the principal themes of his biblical account of redemption. Balthasar's dramatic principle governs the unfolding of the story of Jesus's destiny in a five-act drama. This thematization of scriptural meanings uses Girard's key ideas as an upper blade for understanding the data while engaging in a critically reasoned conversation with then current German historical-critical studies. It is important to remember here that, in addition to the influence of Girard and Balthasar upon Schwager, there was the impact of the meditations on the mysteries of the life of Jesus prescribed by Ignatius Loyola's *Spiritual Exercises*. This is significant for locating Schwager's understanding of the *convenientia* of the Incarnation.

In this respect, it is tempting to compare Schwager's accomplishment to Lonergan's use of "schemata" (each consisting in a name, a sensible presentation, an act of understanding, and the assent of the act of faith) in thesis 1 of *De Verbo Incarnato*.[90] Thus, Lonergan found: (1) the prospective scheme with the name 'Son of Man' and images relating to Jesus's earthly life, his passion and death, and his coming as judge in the future; (2) the retrospective scheme common in Paul, linked with the names Lord, Christ, Son of God in power, and including images ranging from the risen one sitting at the right hand of the Father to those connected with his post-Easter appearances, his earthly life, and going back to the pre-existent one who plays a role in creation; and (3) the inverse-retrospective scheme that begins with the pre-existent Word who became flesh, suffered, died, and was glorified to rule in heaven (e.g., the Philippians hymn in 2: 6-11, or John's Gospel taken as a whole). This was a way to organize whatever is contained in the NT documents "as they stand, i.e., what was meant

89 Schwager, *Jesus and the Drama of Salvation*, 142-143.

90 See Bernard Lonergan, *De Verbo Incarnato* (ad usum auditorum), (Rome: Gregorian University, 1964, editio tertia), 2-102.

by authors of Mark, Matthew, Luke, John, Epistles" as witnesses to the faith in their time and place instead of the common practice of Catholic theologians, which was "to argue about what Our Lord meant …" as a source of doctrine.[91] It took the historicity of the evidence seriously by trying to show the Church's learning processes, while bringing several elements into unity, and it did so with a specifically apologetic purpose.

This is not what Schwager was doing. A first context from Lonergan's thought that may be relevant for understanding what Schwager was doing is *Method in Theology's* chapter on the functional specialty of Interpretation,[92] where Lonergan disparaged the "principle of the empty head" and did so chiefly from the perspective that understanding requires an anticipatory understanding of the reality to which the text refers. He wrote trenchantly about *Vorverständnis* (pre-understanding), *Fragestellung* (framing the question), and *Wirkungsgeschichte* (effective history), and of how all these things enter into understanding oneself and conversion. A second relevant context for grasping Schwager's performance is History and Historians,[93] where Lonergan discussed the importance of "linguistic categories" for asking questions. Such categories (he wrote) "carry with them their host of presuppositions and implications." As he went on to say:

> They are colored by a retinue of concerns, interests, tastes, feelings, suggestions, evocations. Inevitably the historian operates under the influence of his language, his education, his milieu, and these with the passage of time inevitably change to give rise to a demand for and supply of rewritten history.[94]

Next Lonergan's discussion of the role of heuristic structures focused especially on the role of the "ideal type": "not a description of reality or a hypothesis about reality" but "a theoretical construct" whose "utility is heuristic and expository, that is, it can be useful inasmuch

---

91 This important letter is quoted by its addressee, Frederick E. Crowe, *Christ and History. The Christology of Bernard Lonergan from 1935 to 1982* (Ottawa: Novalis, 2005), 236-237.

92 Bernard Lonergan, "Interpretation," *Method in Theology*, 153-173.

93 Bernard Lonergan, "History and Historians," *Method in Theology*, 197-234.

94 Bernard Lonergan, "History and Historians," *Method in Theology*, 215-216.

as it suggests and helps formulate hypotheses and, again, when a concrete situation approximates to the theoretical construct, it can guide an analysis of the situation and promote a clear understanding of it."[95] All of these considerations, of course, are inseparable from self-understanding and spirituality, which pervasively influence all the tasks of theology whenever it encounters the Word in the past, whether in exegesis, history, or dialectics. Schwager's use of Girard's thought certainly concretizes Lonergan's discussion of these matters.

A final (already mentioned) context is Robert Doran's writings on the possible permanent role of elemental meaning in systematic theology, pointing to its pertinence for the theology of the cross, and suggesting that the work of Balthasar and Lonergan in this connection may be complementary. Because Balthasar probably goes beyond the data of scripture to accord Adrienne von Speyer's vision too much theological weight, I suggest that Schwager's use of Girard's theoretical construction of the dynamics of conflict and sacrifice for thematizing the different stages of Jesus's destiny on the basis of critically assessed scriptural evidence as a more well-grounded interpretation of the redemption than Balthasar's theology of the *triduum*. However, by applying Balthasar's and Girard's best insights, Schwager was able not only to portray Jesus in the drama of redemption in a way that illuminates concrete human existence in the tension between the effects of sin and the offer and the acceptance or rejection of God's grace, but to do so in the form of a story conveying an elemental meaning whose possibly relevant understanding of the *convenientia* of the Incarnation combines religious, moral, and aesthetic aspects.

10. *CONVENIENTIA*/APPROPRIATENESS, SELF-APPROPRIATION, AND THEOLOGY

Bernard Lonergan's notion of *convenientia* or appropriateness, as we have seen, is saturated with the idea linking the mysterious proper intelligibility emerging from the divine wisdom and goodness with the universal good of order. In one of his summer lecture courses on *Insight*, he noted that in the *Summa contra Gentiles* Thomas Aquinas's notion tended to conceive the plan of the good of order of the

---

95 Bernard Lonergan, "History and Historians," *Method in Theology*, 227.

universe as the best thing in God's creation; the idea of persons became prominent in the *Summa theologiae*. Once this personal dimension was explicit, according to Lonergan, "the order of the universe
and interpersonal relations are two notions that tend lightly to cover
each other, when the order of the universe is considered concretely."[96]
Lonergan's emphasized interpersonal relations in formulations of the
human good in "Finality, Love, Marriage" (from the early 1940s)[97] and
"The Role of the Catholic University in the Modern World" (1951),[98]
in contrast to the accent on the good of order in *Insight* and in the
Supplementum. In "Finality ..." Lonergan noted explanatory parallels
among the components in the human good, so that (a) living (→par-
ticular good), (b) the good life (→good of order), and (c) eternal life
(→terminal values) correspond to (*a*) 'nature' ("understood in the current restricted sense of physical, vital, sensitive spontaneity"), (*b*) reason and rational appetitite, and (*c*) divine grace.[99] These parallels agree
with Aquinas in the *Summa theologiae*. The Catholic University essay
added distinctions among the levels of the human good as intersubjective, civil, and cultural communities, where the levels correspond
to the empirical (sensing, imagining, representing), intelligent (asking
the *quid sit* questions), and rational (asking *an sit* questions) levels of
human consciousness.[100] Here Lonergan also adopted and adapted
the distinction between *civilization*, encompassing all the results of human intelligence's inventiveness, and *culture*, which expresses human
"reflection, appreciation, criticism." This formulation prescinds from
the supernatural dimension of the intervention of divine grace.

In fact, however, we know that the interpersonal relations congruent with the universal good of order are above all those eternal rela-

---

96 Bernard Lonergan, *Conocimento y Aprendizaje, Reconstrucción interpretative de Armando J. Bravo de las conferencias de Spokane in 1963*, trans. and
ed. Armando J. Bravo (México City: Universidad Iberoamericana, 2008),
103.

97 Bernard Lonergan, "Finality, Love, Marriage," *Collection*, 17-52.

98 Bernard Lonergan, "The Role of the Catholic University in the Modern
World," *Collection*, 108-113.

99 Lonergan, "Finality, Love, Marriage," *Collection*, 38-39.

100 Lonergan, "The Role of the Catholic University in the Modern World,"
Collection, 109.

tions among the persons of the Trinity.[101] As we have seen, the good of order of the universe in the Supplementum has both natural and supernatural components. Lonergan always followed Aquinas in holding that the universe as natural is the contingent term that the divine wisdom and goodness created as a participation in the intelligibility and goodness of God **as one**.[102] In the Supplementum, the Incarnation's assumption of human nature is a sublation of the human good by reason of the absolutely supernatural component into the good of order. As supernatural, the universe's order is a participation in the intelligibility and the goodness of God **as three Persons** inasmuch as the contingent supernatural terms constitutive of grace are created participations in the relations among Father, Son, and Spirit.[103] As divine, these interpersonal relations embrace the universal good of order in the theologies of both Aquinas and Lonergan.

Again, greater prominence expressly accorded the dimension of interpersonal relations underlines how even in the Supplementum the incarnate Word is the created principle of the transformation of the universal good of order by God's self-communication.[104] This means the at least implicit acknowledgment of friendship as the central factor in both the human good and in salvation. In relation to the human good, Lonergan wrote in "Finality …",

> Now it is not by organistic spontaneity but by mutual esteem and mutual good will that reason sets up its comparable union of friendship; and … we may note that human friendship is to be found not only the urbanity and collaboration of contemporaries but much more in the great republic of culture, in contemporaries' esteem for the great men of the past, on whose shoulders they stand, and in their devotion to the men of the future, for whom they set the stage of history for better or for worse.[105]

---

101 See Lonergan, *The Triune God: Systematics*, 497.

102 This is already clear in the *Supplementum*. On the analogy of contingent predication as regards both creation as natural and the supernatural divine missions, see Assertions 15 & 16, *The Triune God: Systematics*, 439-447.

103 See Lonergan, "The Divine Missions," *The Triune God: Systematics*, 437-528.

104 Marianelli, "Appendice," *Ontologia della Relazione*, 160-164.

105 Lonergan, "Finality, Love, Marriage," *Collection*, 39.

At the heart of this passage may be discerned Aquinas's point in *Summa theologiae* I, q. 23, a. 1 in using friendship for the analogy of the grace of charity:

> not any love has the nature of friendship, except love that has benevolence, namely, when we so love someone that we will the good for them. … [N]or does benevolence suffice for the nature of friendship, but there is also required mutual love … However, such mutual benevolence is founded on some communication.

Lonergan's mature explanatory theology of the Trinity is based on the Augustinian and Thomist interpretation that human beings are made in the image and likeness of the God, in which the *singularetantum* of the Word proceeds from the infinite act of loving understanding as uttering because of understanding and knowing, and in which the Father's Word spirates the love that is the Holy Spirit because of the Son's Yes! (judgment of value) to the goodness of the infinite act of loving understanding that is God.[106] Here, then, the *convenientia* or appropriateness of the universe in relation to the divine wisdom and goodness intersects Lonergan's theme of self-appropriation.[107] Self-appropriation is normally actualized in virtue of intellectual, moral, and religious conversion.[108] It is not only the prime analog for the relations of origin in the Trinity, but it also provides the basis for a methodically grounded systematic theology as a whole. This Trinitarian and conversational orientation constitutes the heart of Lonergan's self-understanding and spirituality.[109]

Raymund Schwager presented his systematic considerations in part three of *Jesus in the Drama of Salvation*. His theology of redemption[110] was derived from the drama in the destiny of Jesus. The intelligibility of the redemption corresponds for the most part to chief elements of Lonergan's theses on redemption in *De Verbo Incarnato*. Schwager liberates redemption from atonement theories (based on a caricature of

---

106 See Lonergan, "An Analogical Conception of the Divine Processions," *The Triune God: Systematics*, 125-229.

107 Recall that the original subtitle of *Insight* was "An Essay in Aid of Self-Appropriation".

108 See Lonergan, *Method in Theology*, 217, 243.

109 See Tad Dunne, *Lonergan and Spirituality. Towards a Spiritual Integration* (Chicago, IL: Loyola University Press, 1985).

110 See Schwager, *Jesus in the Drama of Salvation*, 159-196.

St Anselm) that make God's Wrath the motive for the Incarnation; inspired by Karl Barth and Hans Urs von Balthasar, Schwager redeems (so to speak) Anselm's willingness to integrate God's justice into his mercy. This is also true of *Der wunderbare Tausch* where Schwager examined the theological tradition on redemption in light of Girard's ideal type.

However, a problem with Schwager's systematics (as dependent on Girard) is the tendency to conflate the two distinguishable aspects in the theology of grace – grace as *salvans* and *elevans*. To do justice to both aspects of grace, one needs all three of the principles set forth by Lonergan in the Supplementum for considering the specifically *historical* dimension of appropriateness (there expressed in classical terms: the intellectual nature of humanity, the defectible human will, and the divine aid of a merciful God). The mimetic theory of Girard and Schwager, unlike the biblical revelation, tends to naturalize human sin. This confines redemption (1) to overcoming the deficient veracity and the violence resulting from mimetic rivalry and (2) to reversing the distortion of sacrifice by displaced vengeance and magical protection from a monstrous external and divinized force. According to this understanding of divine grace, friendship plays a less central role in redemption through God's self-communication than it does for Aquinas and for Lonergan.

Again, in the central section of that third part in *Jesus in the Drama of Salvation*, "The Revelation of the Triune God in the Redemption event,"[111] the contrast between Schwager's and Lonergan's fundamental self-understanding and spirituality as theologians becomes clear when Schwager transposes the pattern of temporal interpersonal transactions in the Jesus drama (traditionally known as the 'economic' Trinity) into the immanent Trinity. This is related to a lack of differentiation between what is 'first for us' (the *priora quoad nos*, the *causae cognoscendi*) and the 'first in itself' (the *priora quoad se*, the *causae essendi*).[112] In contrast, Lonergan – who adopts Aquinas's noetic differentiation – moves from the hypothesis of intelligible emanations as the analogy for the Trinitarian processions (what is 'first in itself') to conceive the relations, the persons, the notional acts, and the relations among the persons, and only then returns to the Trinitarian missions

111 See Schwager, *Jesus in the Drama of Salvation*, 197-217.

112 See Bernard Lonergan, "*Insight*: A Preface to a Discussion," and "Theology and Understanding," *Collection*, 142-152 and 114-132.

(what is 'first for us'). His Christology, which includes a methodically controlled metaphysics capable of doing justice to Chalcedon,[113] focuses on the communicative dimensions of Jesus' knowing and doing in a systematic understanding of the redemption in which friendship is the pivotal idea and reality.[114]

None of these explanatory contexts adduced by Lonergan exclude the possibility of not only integrating into a theology of history what Schwager achieved in working out the drama of salvation, but also of "making the best" of Schwager's achievement both in the theology of the divine missions and in the theology of grace. This will involve a more differentiated and adequate account of the relationships between God's grace and human free will[115] than Schwager or Lonergan had time to finish. It is left for theologians like Robert Doran to complete this task.

In conclusion, we may relate this account of the relationships among self-understanding, spirituality, and systematic intelligibility to the deeper underlying criterion for theology made completely explicit by Innsbruck theologian Roman Siebenrock, namely, the harmony between the theology and the life of the theologian. Siebenrock formulated this criterion in his work for his *Habilitation: Wahrheit, Gewissen, und Geschichte. Eine systematisch-theologische Rekonstruktion des Wirkens John Henry Kardinal Newmans.*[116] Newman's *Essay in Aid of a*

113 See Lonergan, "The Notion of Person," "The Constitution of a Finite Person," and "The Ontological Constitution of Christ," *The Ontological and Psychological Constitution of Christ*, CWL 7, 9-43, 45-75, and 107-155; also Lonergan, *De Verbo Incarnato*, 105-310.

114 Lonergan, "Theses 11-17," *De Verbo Incarnato*, 313-593.

115 See Lonergan's retrieval of St Thomas's theology of grace in *Grace and Freedom: Operative Grace in the Thought of St. Thomas Aquinas*, CWL 1, ed. Frederick E. Crowe and Robert M. Doran (Toronto: University of Toronto Press, 2000), and his personal transposition of key terms and relations into psychological terms and relations in *Method in Theology*, passim.

116 This immense yet groundbreaking work of 590 pages (including the indications of abbreviations, bibliography, and index) appearing as *Internationale Cardinal Newman Studien*, Folge XV was published in Sigmaringendorf by regio Verlag Glock und Lutz. It includes an account of the context of Newman's life and times, a reconstruction of the development of his thought; it is in a sense a symphony based on the implications in Newman's life and thought of one of Lonergan's favorite themes in Newman, namely, the distinction between real and notional apprehension and assent.

Grammar of Assent pivoted on the difference between 'real' as opposed to merely 'notional' apprehension and assent. The gravamen of this essay is that 'real' rather than 'notional' apprehension of and assent to *convenientia* or appropriateness in Christian theology demands what Gadamer claims Plato required for philosophy: "the Doric harmony between *logos* and *ergon*."[117] This is the existential challenge of religious, moral, and intellectual conversion in the theological community in our, and in any, day.

---

117 See Hans-Georg Gadamer, "*Logos* and *Ergon* in Plato's *Lysis*," *Dialogue and Dialectic. Eight Hermeneutical Studies on Plato,* trans. Christopher Smith (New Haven, CT: Yale University Press, 1980), 19-20.

SELF-APPROPRIATION AS A WAY OF LIFE

JAMES L. MARSH

FORDHAM UNIVERSITY

I. INTRODUCTION

A s is well-known to most of us, self-appropriation is an important notion in Lonergan's thought, maybe the most important. In various places, especially in the Introduction to
Insight, Lonergan has testified to its importance. *Insight*, he tells us, is
an invitation to a decisive, personal act, the intellectual and volitional
taking possession of oneself. All other disciplines and sub-disciplines
in philosophy are, in *Insight*, simply indications or manifestations or
examples of self-appropriation.[1] I am on record in a recent article in a
book of collected articles on Lonergan and post-modernism, *In Deference to the Other*, as testifying to the importance of self-appropriation.
In "Self-appropriation: Lonergan's Pearl of Great Price," I show how
important that notion is in itself and for my own development as a
philosopher.[2]

Nonetheless, Lonergan's emphasis in his work and my own orientation in the article address self-appropriation as a basis for the doing of
philosophy and theology. What remains in the background and less
emphasized is the relationship between self-appropriation and the
rest of one's non-professional, non-philosophical, non-theological life.
This is not to say that Lonergan leaves such issues totally unaddressed
but simply to say that his main attention is directed elsewhere.

Consequently the question I would like to address today is this:
What is the relationship of self-appropriation to the rest of human

---

1 Bernard Lonergan, *Insight A Study of Human Understanding*, ed. Frederick Rowe and Robert Doran (Toronto: The University of Toronto Press,
1992), 12-14.

2 James L. Marsh, "Self-appropriation: Lonergan's Pearl of Great Price." *In
Deference to the Other*, ed. Jim Kanaris and Mark Doorley (Albany: SUNY
Press, 2004), 53-63.

life? Does it make sense to talk about a back-and-forth reciprocal movement between ordinary life and philosophical life? In addition to seeing self-appropriation as a basis of and core of philosophy and theology as professional vocations, do we not also have to see it as a way of life, as a modern version of the examined life? I am reminded here of a claim by one of my first great teachers: 2% of people think, 4% think that that they think, and 94% would rather die than think. Self-appropriation is a very contemporary, sophisticated approach to enabling us to enter that elite category, the 2% who think.[3]

What I come up with in my preliminary reflection on this issue is that we can discover a general or universal relationship of self-appropriation to daily life as a whole and at least four different sub-levels or aspects: self-appropriation and non-professional intellectual life, aesthetic life or aesthetic conversion, ethical-political praxis, and the religiously converted subject in the world and the Church. I will treat each of these issues in turn and then in my conclusion reflect on the relationship between and among these levels and aspects.

2. FROM SELF-APPROPRIATION TO ORDINARY HUMAN LIFE

As I conceive self-appropriation, it is the deliberate, conscious experiencing, understanding, judging, and choosing of myself as an experiencing, understanding, judging, and choosing subject in relation to being. One of the best discussions of this theme occurs in *Method in Theology* in Chapter One on transcendental method. Transcendental method is the explicit expression and formulation of self-appropriation, and it leads, of course, to epistemology, ethics, and metaphysics as its immediate consequences.[4]

One way to think about extending self-appropriation into daily life is to ask, "Why do that?" And one argument that occurs to me is to see such extension as based on the general imperative that doing in the rest of my life should conform to knowing. This imperative is like the ethical imperative that Lonergan develops in *Insight* [5] but goes beyond

---

3 The teacher was William Weller, a Jesuit in the philosophy department at Seattle University.

4 Bernard Lonergan, *Method in Theology* (New York: Herder and Herder, 1972), 3-25.

5 Lonergan, *Insight*, 621-622.

it and includes it as a moment of itself. Let us imagine, then, that we have gone through intellectual conversion, that we have moved from the world of the child to the world of the adult, the world mediated by meaning, that we have moved from the late industrial capitalist or state socialist cave into the sunlight illuminating being. As such people, we are literally and figuratively in love with meaning, being, and the good, and what, therefore, is more natural than to extend that love everywhere and to everything we do. As Lonerganian lovers, we are so in love with our beloved, being, that we seek it everywhere and are on the look-out everywhere. "As a hart longs for flowing streams…"[6]

As I envision this extension, this search is both a desire and an imperative. I link Aristotle and Kant because it is right to do so and because Lonergan does so. Because I am a Lonerganian lover of being animated by the desire to know and grounded in a deeply-rooted decision to follow that out, I seek intelligibility everywhere. Because I am intellectually converted, I experienced a demand in myself to allow my whole self to fall under this imperative. I sense, in other words, an imperative to be consistent in my professional and private, non-professional life.[7]

Now we should note that Lonergan has already said some things explicitly about the relationship between self-appropriation and ordinary life. One such place is in *Method in Theology*. Though religious conversion sublates moral conversion and moral conversion sublates intellectual conversion, one is not to infer that generally intellectual conversion comes first chronologically. First is the gift of God's love, and then the eye of this love illumines moral values in their splendor and helps bring about their realization, and finally among the values discerned is that of believing the truths taught by the religious tradition, which contains the seed of intellectual conversion. The mature adult man or woman, then, pursuing and deepening intellectual conversion is already doing that in a life that is religiously and morally informed and grounded and providing a solidity, security, and habitually willingness in his or her pursuit of intellectual conversion.[8]

---

6 "Psalm 42," *Psalms for Praying*, ed. Nan Merrill (New York: Continuum, 1996), 81.

7 For this union of desire and demand in Lonergan, see the whole of his chapter on ethics in *Insight*, 618-56.

8 Lonergan, *Method in Theology*, 241-243.

Second, in *Insight* is found Lonergan's discussion of genuineness as it emerges at the climax of his treatment of genetic method. Genuineness as such is a requirement and an aspect of human development, which includes philosophy, of course, but goes beyond that and is more inclusive. Genuineness as law admits the tension between limitation and transcendence into consciousness. As a requirement, the law of genuineness is both conditional and analogous. It is conditional because it arises only insofar as development occurs in human consciousness. It is analogous because the content is different in different cases. There is the development of a simple soul, a St. Therese of Lisieux, for example; there is also another kind of genuineness "that has to be won back through a self-scrutiny that expels illusion and pretense, and as this enterprise is difficult and its issue doubtful, we do not think of its successful outcome when we cast about for obvious illustrations of genuineness."[9] But in our world of self-appropriated knowers, choosers, and lovers in Lonergan's sense, it is only this latter kind of genuineness that is open to most of us. There is a simplicity that we can attain, but it is a complex, mediated simplicity attained at the end of a long process of differentiation. There is an innocence that can be won, but it is a second innocence, if you like, a second naïveté.

A third place in which the interplay between philosophy and ordinary life occurs is in the discussion of the appropriation of truth in *Insight*. To appropriate the truth is to make it my own authentically, not just repeating the pronouncements of the crowd. I stand on my own intellectually, stand somewhere; I step up to the plate. The sensitive appropriation of truth is cognitional. Because reasonableness demands consistency between what we know and what we do, there is a volitional appropriation of truth that consists in our willingness to live up to it and a sensitive appropriation consisting of an adaptation of our sensibility to the requirements of our knowledge and our decisions. By "sensibility" here, I take it that Lonergan means our feelings, psyche, memories, and unconscious. Psychic conversion, therefore, as Bob Doran defines it, my becoming aware of, understanding, affirming, choosing, and integrating my psyche with my intelligence, becomes crucial. Without such psychic conversion, I remain or run the risk of remaining one-sidedly intellectual or volitional, tempted by a

---

9 Lonergan, *Insight*, 500.

false idealism about myself and the world that can block both effective practical living and cognitive, philosophical performance.[10]

There are many fascinating aspects and implications about what we have been discussing. I have, for example, in the essay already noted, drawn attention to the way self-appropriation as Lonergan understands it is not the affair of any generalized Tom, Dick, or Harry but is an affair of my knowing and my choosing as the individual self that I am. Lonergan picks up here and integrates insights from Kierkegaard and Heidegger on the existential self as individual but also links such understanding to our universal, cognitive, transcendental structure. We are all unique individuals, but we are also experiencing, understanding, judging, and choosing subjects in community.[11]

When such individuality is translated into daily life, then we can affirm a personal style of the subject, a dramatic artistry and aesthetics of living that approximates some insights of Nietzsche and Foucault but links these to cognitive and moral normativity more than they did. The subject as cognitive-volitional and as psychic expresses itself in the world in aesthetic self-creation in the way this subject speaks, dresses, eats, laughs, walks, runs, and tells jokes. I am a transcendental subject and have that in common with other transcendental subjects, but as incarnate, self-expressive, and aesthetic in the world, I am a different, individual transcendental subject.[12]

What has also helped me in thinking about this relationship between philosophy and daily life is that Lonergan has already articulated a notion of philosophy performed by the subject as having both subjective and objective poles. The subjective, existential pole is the experience of the philosopher as a lover of wisdom and incarnation of the desire to know oriented to experience, understanding, and judgment. But because philosophy is a search for complete intelligibility, the objective, systematic imperative arises. Even within the objective pole, there is a distinction between subjective and objective. In the former case (subject as object), we have cognitional theory and tran-

10 Lonergan, *Insight*, 581-85. Robert Doran, *Theology and the Dialectics of History* (Toronto: The University of Toronto Press, 1990), 8-9.

11 Marsh, "Self-appropriation: Lonergan's Pearl of Great Price," 54, 60-61.

12 On self-creation as aesthetic self-creation, see Michel Foucault, *The Use of Pleasure: The History of Sexuality, Vol. II*, trans. Robert Hurley (New York: Vintage Books, 1986). For a more nuanced discussion of this issue, see Doran, *Theology and the Dialectics of History*, 85-86.

scendental method. In the latter case (object as object), we have epistemology, ethics, and metaphysics along with related domains such as theology and the physical and social sciences. Because the subject as operative subject in the subjective pole already is himself more than a "plaster cast of a man," then the subject more easily moves into daily life. Indeed philosophy as philosophy and the engagement in daily life are just two different modes of the subject as subject in which he moves in and out of different patterns of experience in a more and more accomplished manner. He has become a differentiated subject who has distinguished, related, and verified in himself the distinctions among common sense, theory, interiority, and religious transcendence. More of that anon.[13]

3. FROM PROFESSIONAL TO INTELLECTUAL

Let us imagine a self-appropriated, Lonerganian philosopher who has been working at her desk for several hours and needs to take a break. Let us imagine the person in mid-afternoon in a city like Toronto or Boston or Los Angeles or New York City. The philosopher takes a walk.

Let us imagine further that because such a person is on her way to self-appropriation and its consequences, she is more and more animated by a sense of second innocence or complex simplicity or second naïveté. More and more she feels her life being taken over not by a primitive wonder, the wonder of a child, but by a subsequent or consequent wonder more and more open to the mystery and gift of being as manifest in daily life. For her wonder can no longer be confined to the study but insists on spilling over into daily life. At this point the philosopher as professional becomes the philosopher as intellectual, excited by and nourished by the wonder of ordinary life.

I confess in this formulation to being influenced by an older, more traditional book, *The Intellectual Life*, by A.G. Sertillanges, OP. I was introduced to it many years ago when I was just getting started as a philosopher and intellectual and return to it regularly for insight and inspiration. And I do this even though Sertillanges is not my kind of Thomist. He is pre-transcendental, conservative, and more one-sidedly contemplative in that he has not linked theory to practice in the way that both Lonergan and I have tried to do. Also, his definition

13 Thomas McPartland, *Lonergan and the Philosophy of Historical Existence* (Columbia: University of Missouri Press, 2001), 147-54.

of "intellectual" includes both the thinker as specialist and as engaged in daily life. While I do not reject that definition, the notion of "Intellectual" that I am defending here is that of the intellectual as non-specialist, as open to and excited by daily life.[14]

Thus the philosopher leaving his study and taking his walk sees "his walks as voyages of discovery."[15] He is not leaving his desire to know the truth behind but broadening it to include everyone and everything and every event he encounters. No person is too insignificant, no place too boring, and no event too banal to evoke wonder. I have had great conversations with salespersons in my neighborhood deli and convenience store; I look forward to meeting again my friends in Mr. Donut when I go there to replenish my supply. A waitress working in a restaurant on 57th street in Manhattan, struggling in her own way to lead an authentic, moral life, has been to me the source of stunning insights about how to do that; a male waiter and manager in the same place has become a model to me of combining strength with restrained gentleness in dealing with unruly customers.

Sertillanges can be remarkably eloquent on this issue:

> So acquire the habit of being present at this activity of the natural and moral universe. Learn to look; compare what is before you with your familiar or secret ideas. Do not see in a town merely houses, but human life and history. Let a gallery or museum show you something more than a collection of objects, let it show you schools of art and of life, conceptions of destiny and of nature, successive or varied tendencies of technique, of inspiration, of feeling. Let a workshop speak to you not only of iron and wood, but of man's estate, of work, of ancient and modern social economy, of class relationships....If you cannot look thus, you will become, or be, a man of only commonplace mind. A thinker is like a filter, in which truths as they pass through leave their best substance.[16]

Learn to listen, Sertillanges urges us, to everyone. The whole of the human is in everyone, and we can receive a deep-reaching imitation from him. The greatest novelist is found on doorsteps or in the streets,

14 A.G. Sertillanges, *The Intellectual Life: Its Spirit, Conditions, Methods*, trans. Mary Ryan (Washington, D.C.: Catholic University of American Press, 1987).

15 Ibid., 81.

16 Ibid., 74.

the least in the Sorbonne or the New York Public Library. The thinker is truly a thinker only if he finds in the least external stimulus the occasion of a limitless interior urge. "It is his character to keep all his life the curiosity of childhood, to retain its vivacity of impression, its tendency to see everything under an aspect of mystery, the happy faculty of everywhere finding wonderment full of consequences."[17]

The thinker should be perpetually ready to see, to hear, "to shoot the bird as it flies, like a good sportsman."[18] We should carry our problems about with us. "The hackney horse does his run and goes back to his stall; the free courser always has his nostrils to the wind."[19] We cultivate an attitude of open, wondering, reverent receptivity because of which we see as enlightening what others find only banal, problematic what others take to be obvious, stimulating what others find to be only boring. "Everyone looks at what I am looking at," says Lamennais, as quoted by Sertillanges, "but nobody sees what I see."[20]

For those who have undergone religious conversion, who have fallen in love with God, there is an additional motivation. For one genuinely in love with God is constantly striving to live in the presence of God, thirsting for God, treading the highways and byways for signs of his presence. Similarly, Sertillanges asks, should not the Christian who is an intellectual live in the presence of truth? For the self-appropriated philosopher, why cannot the presence of God for him take the form of intelligibility or truth? If we are Christians all the time, why cannot we be philosophers or intellectuals all the time? "Truth is, as it were, the special divinity of the thinker."[21] Have we approached here, in this sense of philosopher as a contemplative in action, what Ignatius envisions?

4. FROM INTELLECTUAL CONVERSION TO AESTHETIC CONVERSION

To some extent the discussion here is rooted in the distinction in *Insight* between the intellectual and aesthetic patterns of experience. In the intellectual pattern of experience, operative in formal logic, the sci-

17 Ibid., 74-75, quotation from 75.

18 Ibid., 77.

19 Ibid., 77.

20 Ibid., 73.

21 Ibid., 78.

ences, philosophy, and theology, we are oriented to knowledge for its own sake and animated by the criteria of evidence, rigor, and logicality. In the aesthetic pattern of experience, we are enriched by experience for its own sake, lifted up and liberated from the pragmatic orientation of common sense – only the useful is true – as well as from the serious striving of intellectual inquiry of moral life. Aesthetic experience is "useless," a value in itself and for its own sake, and as such, challenges the "seriousness" of philosophy, morality, and religious faith.[22]

Let us imagine somebody who has gone through or is on the way to intellectual, moral, and religious conversion. Why, such a person might ask, when we consider the state of the world, should we bother with aesthetic experience? Do not the hungry have to be fed, the naked clothed, and the homeless housed? Do not men and women throughout the world have need for intellectual, moral, and religious truth? Why waste time lingering before a Picasso, a Matisse, or a Kandinsky? What good does that do anybody? Thus the troubled philosopher may end up in an art museum, perhaps the Museum of Modern Art.

There is a good Lonerganian answer to such a question. It is the very uselessness of art that as an end in itself constitutes its value. Aesthetic experience, Lonergan says, promises a twofold liberation, from rigid biological or common sense purposiveness in which my nose is always focused on the grindstone and from the seriousness of intellectual inquiry ordered to truth, evidence, and systematicity. The playfulness of art reveals to me to my freedom as a subject. Art opens us up to an elemental wonder that is prior to systematic inquiry, and this openness to the non-functional on that elemental level prepares us to accept philosophy in its uselessness and non-functionality. "Philosophy," Heidegger tells us, "...is that thinking with which one can start nothing and about which housemaids necessarily laugh."[23]

When we reflect on the historically specific kind of society we are, the role of art is even more salient and important. For is it not the character of capitalistic society to take a capitalized common sense, in which financial profit is the goal of all economic striving, and extend that to the whole of society? And rather than the useful being subordinated to the useless, to the intrinsically valuable, as would be the case in a truly sane, ethical society, do we not have a systematic ordering

22 Lonergan, *Insight*, 207-210.

23 Martin Heidegger, *What is a Thing?*, tr. W. Barton and Vera Deutsch (Chicago: Henry Regnery, 1967), 3.

of the intrinsically valuable to the useful, the reign of money? And does art not legitimately challenge the absurd tyranny of the useful, in which means becomes ends and ends means? (Beckett and the theater of the absurd could only arise in a capitalistic society.) When I view Matisse's *Red Studio*, I become aware of dimensions in myself and the world that cannot be easily, legitimately subordinated to the reign of money. "Wasting time," tarrying before the work of art becomes a form of liberation from such tyranny.

Lonergan reminds us that the presence of intelligence is not just formal, the ordering of lines or sounds or color by the artist in a pleasing, challenging aesthetic form, which is also worth contemplating in itself, but also content that can be symbolized. And as Adorno tells us, part of that content is social. Art is both in-itself and for-others and produced by and for others and, as such, in an alienated, totally or mostly administered society can testify to these aspects. Thus the dissonance of a Bartok or the dark, twelve tone harmony of Schoenberg, Webern, and Berg can alert us to the dissonant, unhappy, and unjust suffering of millions in capitalist society. Such works give the Lonerganian inquirer other images and possible insights that he might not otherwise have. Maybe he has too easily learned to live with late capitalism and loves it. The power of Arthur Miller's *Death of a Salesman* can alert us to the possible nightmare hidden behind The American Dream, the unhappiness lurking underneath the superficial happiness promoted by Madison Avenue, and the ugliness behind the pleasing, commodified images of Hollywood. Great art makes trouble for an unjust, alienated society in different ways, either by calling it into questions through images of dissonance or suffering, or by introducing us to the value of the intrinsically valuable, the useless, in such a way that we see the truth of the paradox that the most valuable elements in human life are useless.[24] Moreover, as those committed to Lonergan's philosophy we know that objectivity is the fruit of authentic subjectivity and that objectivity lies in self-transcendence. Good art, really good, challenging art, not the junk on most American television, invites us into its own kind of self-transcendence and objectivity. For to properly respond to a work like Picasso's *Guernica* or Stravinsky's *Rite of Spring*, I have to give myself to it for its own sake and be receptive to it on its own terms in a kind of disposability or hospitality. The question to

---

24 Theodore Adorno, *Aesthetic Theory*, trans. Robert Hullot-Kentor (Minneapolis: University of Minnesota Press, 1997), 3-8.

ask, according to Adorno, is not "What do I get out of it?" but "what do I give to it?" Asking what I can get out of it, like the typical bourgeois consumer of art, is to misuse the work of art, to turn it into another utilitarian object. That which by its purpose and structure transcends utility is turned into a utilitarian object.[25] "Insofar as a function is to be ascribed to artworks," Adorno says, "it is their functionlessness."[26] And again, "Artworks are the plenipotentiaries of things beyond the motivating sway of exchange, profit, and the false needs of a degraded humanity."[27]

5. FROM THE IVORY TOWER TO THE STREETS

In the last two sections, I have been stressing the role of contemplation in daily life and aesthetics. But thought and freedom are also practical, critical, and transformative, and indeed Lonergan himself helps to overcome any false conflict or dichotomy between contemplation and action. In *Method in Theology*, he argues that freedom as a fourth moment sublates cognition and that the priority of intellect is just the priority of the first three levels of experience, understanding, and judgment. It also follows that speculative intellect or pure reason is just an abstraction. Scientific and philosophical understanding do not occur in a vacuum but are the operations of an existential subject who has decided to devote himself to the pursuit of understanding and truth. This would be true also of the contemplative lover of beauty in nature as well as of the intellectual pursuing truth in ordinary life. And then, of course, there is the famous sentence from *Method*: "A life of pure intellect or pure reason without the control of deliberation, evaluation, responsible choice is less than the life of a psychopath."[28]

Consequently, and I take myself to be agreeing with Lonergan here, self-appropriation and transcendental method that follows upon it is contemplation because I am committing myself to philosophical knowledge for its own sake and to a kind of praxis, indeed the most basic praxis, because I choose myself as an experiencing, understanding, judging, and choosing subject. Other kinds of praxis, such as ethical or political action in the world, although they precede self-

25 Ibid., 13, 17.
26 Ibid., 227.
27 Ibid.
28 Lonergan, *Method in Theology*, 122.

appropriation psychologically and historically, are derivative from it as founding and giving clarity and direction to these activities. And such activities, although based on knowledge, are dominantly practical and transformative. I aim, to refer to the words of a great thinker, to change the world and not simply to know it.[29]

Let us imagine, then, the self-appropriated philosopher not simply going for a walk but going for a walk to an anti-war demonstration. And let us imagine that that demonstration is organized to protest a war in the Middle East carried out by our government for reasons that are manifestly false. There is no demonstrated presence of weapons of mass destruction, there is no link of Saddam Hussein to al Qaeda or bin Laden, and there is no serious commitment to democracy. What kind of sense does it make to spend hundreds of billions of dollars, lay waste a country, and lose, so far, over a thousand of our men and women, and see thousands more of them wounded, and endanger hundreds of thousands of Iraqis, to impose a democracy that we directly or indirectly deny to dozens of countries throughout the world and even, in the Middle East, to nations such as Turkey or Egypt or the Palestinian people. Something else has to be going on here, functioning as the real reasons for intervention, such as, possibly, more adequate control of oil, securing water resources for Israel, and establishing a stronger, more permanent U.S. military and political presence in the region.

Let us imagine the Lonerganian activist operating on grounds of consistency between knowing and doing. She is offended intellectually by the lies, morally by the sheer injustice of the war, which does not come even close to the criteria of just war theory (violation of the last resort criterion is the most obvious), and religiously by the tendency of the American empire to function as a fetish, a God substitute, and by President Bush's fundamentalist use of religion in the service of empire. The Lonerganian activist, in other words, is confronted by the contradiction between her own self-appropriation and its intellectual, moral, and religious implications, and the war. And the reasons for her opposition do not necessarily have to be radical – opposition to capitalism and imperialism in principle – although I think radicalism is the most adequate moral and political response and interpretation. She can oppose the war for conservative reasons – because it violates

---

29 James L. Marsh, *Post-Cartesian Mediations* (New York: Fordham University Press, 1988), 110-112.

the U.N. Charter and the U.S. Constitution – and she can oppose it for liberal reasons – because it is unjust.

The experience of the Lonerganian activist in this kind of illegal, unjust, and imperial context is one of legitimate offense. She experiences the necessity to speak out, act out, resist, protest, or, to be a little more blunt, raise hell. There is or could be a kind of "not being able to look at myself in the mirror" unless I engage in this kind of direct action. The necessarily prophetic nature of philosophy in bad times is striking here and something I have been acutely aware of as I have been traveling around the country speaking out and acting out against this war and the occupation, as well as the war on terror begun in 2001, something equally or more problematic in my opinion. And such speaking and acting out do not have to take the form of direct action but can be carried out by philosophers and other intellectuals in a forum of public intellectuals named "cosmopolis" by Lonergan in *Insight*. "Cosmopolis" seems to be nothing more than Lonergan's heuristic projection of the way a self-appropriated community of philosophers, scientists, theologians, and artists could carry out a practical-theoretical discourse about policies and actions that can help or harm our nation and the world.[30]

What I am trying to suggest here is the necessity to combine a professional commitment to philosophy with the role of a public intellectual and activist *as essential to my vocation as philosopher*. Moreover, unlike Sertillanges, the Lonerganian intellectual in the world is practical and critical as well as wondering and contemplative. Staying in the ivory tower is not enough in bad and increasingly worse times such as our own but maybe also in all times. Such a conviction was brought home to me and reinforced in the wake of the events of 9-11when I was engaged in my usual teaching duties at Fordham. I discussed the event in all three of my classes, inviting students to reflect with me on the following kinds of questions. If we grant that the attack on the World Trade Center was unjustified morally, indefensible in the light of any moral or political theory that would be worth defending, do we not need to think about the imperial context created by our own national and international policies that could make people angry enough to strike out against us? This context includes the first Iraq War in 1990-1991, equally as destructive and unjustified in my opinion as the recent war; the sanctions against Iraq leading to the deaths

30 Lonergan, *Insight*, 263-67.

of hundreds of thousands of children, several thousand a month; U.S. bases in Saudi Arabia enraging millions in the Middle East; and U.S. support for Israel in its dispossession and persecution of the Palestinians, denying them rights of nationhood proclaimed by many U.N. resolutions.

Now what really surprised me was that after the last class that I taught that week, a graduate class, several students came up to me, thanked me for discussing the event and informed me that no other professor had even mentioned it in class. How could one be silent about an event that was at least as important in the lives of these students as the Kennedy or King assassinations were in mine? What would it take to motivate my esteemed colleagues to depart from academic business as usual? An earthquake? A nuclear attack that directly hit Fordham? A student riot? In any event, I concluded by noting that probably operative here was a notion of academic professionalism that may have briefly tempted me two or three seconds out of the womb, which I then rejected as inadequate. There had to be something less narrow, more progressive, more radical, a model of professionalism that could motivate me to speak out, demonstrate, resist, and even at times run the risk of arrest. "Why were you arrested?" "Because I read *Insight*."

Now I am on record elsewhere as arguing for radical political conversion as flowing from intellectual, moral, and religious conversion. I have not been able to do more than allude to that here and indicate some of its motivation, but I offer it as a possible complement to Doran's psychic conversion and as a possible addition to the Lonerganian pantheon of conversions. And, to conclude this section here, it does seem to me that there is a fruitful complementary relationship between the two conversions helping to constitute a legitimate Lonerganian "materialism." Freud and Marx are appropriated by both myself and Doran here, but sublated non-reductionistically. One way that such complementarity can operate is that awareness of my own psychic victimization can allow me to be open to and compassionate with and in solidarity with the victims of capitalism, militarism, imperialism, racism, sexism, and heterosexism. Here I have affirmed a preferential option for the poor that can be reached philosophically and that must be affirmed if philosophy is to be fully consistent with itself. And it is also true that, as I become aware of the suffering, marginalized other, I become aware of my own fragile, suffering, vulnerable psyche. There is an internal link, I think, between self-appropriation and alterity, whether that be the poor, oppressed other or the other in myself, my own body and psyche.[31]

6. FROM *EXISTENZ* TO *AGGIORNAMENTO*

One of my favorite occasional essays by Lonergan is that published in *Collection*, "Existenz and Aggiornamento." In this essay Lonergan develops a distinction between substance and subject, between the being proper to a thing and the being proper to the subject, being conscious, intelligent, reasonable, critical, and responsible. One can as a human being and Christian live like or approximate living like a substance. I am obedient; I believe in Christ through an opaque faith; I know true propositions, meditate on them, make resolutions about them, and decide to commit my life to being a lay Christian or Jesuit. Insofar as this being in Jesus Christ is that of a substance, it is a being in love without awareness of being in love. The delicacy, the gentleness, the deftness, the continual operation of God's grace in us misses us.[32]

But insofar as being in Christ Jesus is the being of a subject, the hand of the Lord ceases to be wholly hidden. In ways that many have experienced, the substance in Christ Jesus becomes the subject in Christ Jesus. The love of God, being-in-love with God, can be as full and as dominant, as overwhelming and as lasting, an experience as human love. And being a subject in Christ Jesus rests upon a willingness and ability of the subject to take herself in hand, deliberate, and decide what she is going to make of herself. This making of oneself is open-eyed and deliberate and is opposed to all drifting, going along simply to get along.[33]

I take it that Lonergan is reflecting here on religious belief and commitment and conversion and their links to self-appropriation. Self-appropriation, we might say, is the first most fundamental form of contemplative praxis that then paves the way and leads up to the highest form, falling in love with God in the cloud of unknowing. Such contemplation is a faith, the faith that is the knowledge born of religious

---

31 Marsh, *Post-Cartesian Mediations*, 183-238. James L. Marsh, *Critique, Action, and Liberation* (Albany: SUNY Press, 1995), 174-75, 376-79, note 52. Doran, *Theology and the Dialectics of History*, 42-63, 232-53, 523-24.

32 Bernard Lonergan, "Existenz and Aggiornamento," *Collection*, ed. Frederick E. Crowe and Robert M. Doran (Toronto: The University of Toronto Press, 1967), 222-31.

33 Ibid., 222-24, 230-31.

love. The peak to which self-appropriation leads is a falling in love with God, an appropriation by God as the supreme Other. Once again we see the link between self-appropriation and alterity.[34]

Flowing from religious contemplative love is my involvement in the Church and the world, which Lonergan also considers in this essay. There is a way of being Christian and being human that is appropriate to the anguish and achievements of modernity, and there is a way of being that is not appropriate or that is less appropriate, being a subject as substance. The latter is not unacceptable or totally outside the pale or humanity and church, but it is less responsive and less comprehensive than the former. "There is the possibility of despoiling the Egyptians," Lonergan says, meaning by "Egyptians" secular modernity. "But that possibility will not be realized unless Catholics, religious, priests, exist, and exist not as drifters but creatively and authentically."[35]

In being Christian as substance, we keep our noses to the grindstone, obey the laws of society and church, attend conscientiously to our immediate families and neighborhoods, and do not rock the boat. In being Christian as subject, we reach out to that world in all of its complexity, anguish, and richness, learn from that world, and in turn bring something to that world, criticize it, and transform it. To engage in that work most fruitfully, we cannot be content just to remain on the level of immediate, intersubjective encounter, whether it is the kind discussed by Marcel and Buber earlier in the century or by Levinas and Derrida later. Authentic living includes authentic knowing, and eagerly human beings strive for the whole more than for the part. Nonetheless it remains that the authentic living of anyone reading this paper, though it must start at home, cannot remain confined within the horizons of the home, the workshop, the village. We are citizens of our countries, men of the twentieth century, members of a universal church. If any authenticity we achieve is to radiate out into our troubled world, we need much more objective knowing than men commonly feel ready to absorb.[36]

This quotation is, of course, from another essay in Collection, "Cognitional Structure," but it links up to "Existenz and Aggiornamento" in interesting ways. The Christian who has fallen in love with God

34 Lonergan, Method in Theology, 115-116.

35 Lonergan, "Existenz and Aggiornamento," 229.

36 Bernard Lonergan, "Cognitional Structure," Collection, 221.

and who has decided to exist as subject must, to be more effective, use and appropriate objective knowing based on and flowing from self-appropriation. Self-appropriation and the objective knowing to which it leads are not only the basis and starting point that lead to falling in love with God but also flow from it and are used by it, in a sense, to intervene in a troubled world. Self-appropriation and objective knowing are the basis of and consequence of the knowledge born of religious love.

Not only does Lonergan reflect on the role of the authentic Christian in the world, but he also invites us to reflect on the kind of Church that is required. There is a Church, he suggests, that is favorable to the flowering of the subject as subject, the Church of John XXIII and Paul VI and Vatican II, and there is a Church that is not so favorable, that is still more classicist than historical. Inspired by Lonergan, I am also inclined to suggest there is a Church that wishes, if not to repeal Vatican II, then at least to put the dampers on. Inspired by Lonergan, I am inclined to suggest there is a Church that favors the emergence of freedom, and there is Church that distrusts it and hearkens back to outdated notions of authority. There is a Church that plunges head-long prudently and courageously into the adventure of modernity, and there is a Church that tries to retreat from it, bury its head in the sand, move back into the thirteenth century, the greatest of the centuries, and loses its nerve before modernity.

What Lonergan says here inspires me to think creatively and prophetically about our Church as it has existed the last few decades under the reign of John Paul II and threatens to exist now under the new pope. Does this Church favor the emergence of the Christian as subject or Christian as substance? In any event, Lonergan leaves us in no doubt as to where he stands. The so-called sin of modernity, he says, is not a sin of frailty, a transient lapse, any lack of advertence or consent.

It is the full deliberate and permanently intended determination to be oneself, to attain the perfection proper to man, and to liberate humanity from the heavy hand of ecclesiastical tradition, ecclesiastical interference, ecclesiastical refusal to allow human beings to grow and be themselves.[37]

---

37 Lonergan, "Existenz and Aggiornamento," 228.

7. CONCLUSION

As a way of synthesizing and summarizing my reflections here, we might reflect on the various interrelationships uncovered by doing a brief phenomenology of self-appropriation in relationships and aspects of ordinary life. First of all, we note a reciprocal relationship between self-appropriation and ordinary life in general. Because of self-appropriation and the differentiated consciousness that accompanies it, I am able to negotiate more easily and more competently the various patterns of experience and the transitions between and among them. If there is a practical benefit of philosophy, even when it is pursued disinterestedly, this is certainly it or an aspect of it. And we are reminded here of Lonergan's claim in the Preface to *Insight* that "insight into insight and oversight is the very key to practicality."[38]

Not only does self-appropriation contribute to clarifying and enhancing practical life, but practical life realizes self-appropriation, makes it effective, and makes it fully real. The individual philosophical self, for example, that knows and chooses itself in self-appropriation expresses itself in an aesthetically and practically effective life style.

We can note, second, a relationship between self-appropriation and each of the sub-aspects of human life that I have laid out. When this philosopher goes for a walk, for example, he brings to that walk a desire to know already fully conscious of itself and, ready, therefore, to "shoot on the fly" insights which I bring back to the study in a way that enriches and deepens philosophical work. The sublime, revelatory power of a work of art can supply me with images and possible insights that enrich my theoretical work, and that theoretical work allows me to bring to the work of art greater depth, openness, and curiosity. Self-appropriation occurring in such a way that insisting on the conformity of doing to knowing leads me to expect and demand that of social, economic, and political institutions, to praise them when they live up to that demand, and to criticize them when they do not. The experience of protesting an unjust war can reinforce in me a sense of the relevance of critical thinking to concrete political practice. I have always thought that going to a demonstration and seeing signs like "no blood for oil" or "no justice, no peace" or "why die for Exxon?" enables one to experience on a concrete, lived, pragmatic level truths that are worked up more laboriously and abstractly in the classroom or study. Hence,

---

38 Lonergan, *Insight*, 8.

self-appropriation enables me to see more clearly and rigorously how religious commitment is essential to the full realization of personhood and how that commitment itself anchors and motivates self-appropriation. I am able to return to my study as a Christian in love with God, animated by the conviction that philosophy is my God-given vocation and that I am doing the work of God in the world.

Finally we can note the relationship between and among the sub-aspects of ordinary life and between them and practical life in general. The sub-aspects belong to that totality of daily life as parts to a whole. The intellectual relates to the aesthetic as a domain of human life that can stimulate reflection, and the aesthetic as a form of wonder is nourished by the conscious, articulate wonder of the intellectual and clarified by analytic and synthetic understanding and critical judgment. Taste is consciously formed, I think, not just by experiencing works of art but also by the reciprocal relationship between such experience and reflection. Art can inspire social, political insights that can enable me to be less narrow and ideological, and in turn a powerfully expressed, aesthetically appropriate symbol can inspire ethical, political action and resistance; think of Selma or Cantonsville or the Plowshares actions. Finally religious experience can be enhanced and deepened by art – consider the sublimity of Notre Dame and Chartres – and religious belief is a source of content for works of art, even modern works of art. The poetry of Gerard Manley Hopkins or T.S. Eliot or Denise Levertov or Daniel Berrigan comes to mind.

I conclude with a fuller quotation from Sertillanges on the intellectual going for a walk.

> Thus the wise man, at all times and on every road, carries a mind ripe for acquisitions that ordinary folk neglect. The humblest occupation is for him a continuation of the loftiest; his formal calls are fortunate chances of investigation; his walks are voyages of discovery, what he hears and his silent answers are a dialogue that truth carries on with herself within him. Wherever he is, his inner universe is comparing itself with the other, his life with Life, his work with the incessant work of all beings; and as he comes from the narrow space in which his concentrated study is done, one gets the impression, not that he is leaving the True behind, but that he is throwing his door wide open so that the world may bring to him all the truth given out in its mighty activities.[39]

---

39 Sertillanges, *The Intellectual Life*, 81.

THE FOURTH STAGE OF MEANING: ESSAY 44 OF THE SERIES FIELD NOCTURNES CANTOWER

Philip McShane

HALIFAX, NOVA SCOTIA

I. INTRODUCTION

Since this essay appears out of sequence it needs a preliminary identification. It is a part of a series of essays, *FNC 42 -117*, which aims at completing two previous series. The first series, monthly essays which began on Easter Monday, April 1, 2002, was intended to continue to December 1, 2011, and to contain 117 essays. It was named *Cantowers*, in reference to the *Cantos* of the poet Ezra Pound. It was interrupted in August 2005 at *Cantower 41* due to an opportunity to collaborate. That opportunity blossomed, in the following three years, into a collection of essays and two books. The final series of essays in that collection, running to 41 in number and to 300 pages in length, is titled *Field Nocturnes*.

The focus of *Field Nocturnes* is on that single powerful paragraph of *Insight* "Study of the organism begins ..."[1] The word *field* in the title is a direct reference to Lonergan's use of that word in *Phenomenology and Logic*. It may be taken elementarily as a colorful replacement of the word *being*.[2] *Nocturnes*, of course, is a reference to Chopin and John Field, but may be taken to point to dark searchings or searchers. The two series, *Field Nocturnes* and *Cantowers*, are made to converge after

---

1 Bernard Lonergan, *Insight: A Study of Human Understanding*, ed. Frederick E. Crowe and Robert M. Doran (Toronto: University of Toronto Press, 1996), 489 [464].

2 Bernard Lonergan, *Phenomenology and Logic, The Boston College Lectures on Mathematical Logic and Existentialism*, ed. Phil McShane (Toronto: University of Toronto Press, 2001). See the index under *Field*. This effort of Lonergan seems to me quite important. See my use of the shift and its mood in chapter 3 of McShane, *Lack in the Beingstalk: A Giant's Causeway* (Axial Publications, 2007).

41 essays in each case: so we arrive here at the third essay in the new series, with the general title given above.

The title is obviously a mesh of the two previous titles, but the mesh has a richer and more explicitly optimistic meaning. The 41 initial *Cantowers* and the works that followed lifted my searchings towards the core of a solution to the problem of history, "the real catch,"[3] in the emergence of a controlling regionalization called *The Tower of Able*.[4] The ongoing topologically-complex region is normatively a population of Field Nocturnes, people in functional collaboration within a genetically-shifting standard model of *Praxisweltanschauung*.[5] The optimism regarding a potentially effective solution to the problem of cosmopolis[6] is made quite explicit in the reading of the title as *Field Nocturnes Can Tower*. Previously I have mused over the character of the tower and the towering, but here I wish only to pause in a preliminary fashion over the origin and meaning of this essay's title.[7]

3 "The problem of general history, which is the real catch." Bernard Lonergan, "History," in *Topics in Education: The Cincinnati Lectures of 1959 on the Philosophy of Education*, ed. Robert M. Doran and Frederick E. Crowe (Toronto: University of Toronto Press, 1993), 236.

4 "History", the final chapter of *Topics in Education*, poses the problem complexly, but the manner in which Lonergan talks of regional history lends itself to envisaging the future sub-group of functional collaborators as constituting a peculiar complex topological region of the globe. The convenient image of the tower emerges from making the diagram on page 124 of *A Brief History of Tongue* into a three dimensional structure in which the cycle of collaboration spirals upwards. It belongs to my list of Metagrams, Wi. See *Prehumous 2* for a presentation of the list.

5 The enlarged view of functional collaboration is contained in two website books, *Method in Theology: Revisions and Implementations* and *Lonergan's Standard Model of Effective Global Inquiry*. The website is www.philipmcshane.ca

6 The problem of cosmopolis is posed in the concluding section to chapter 7 of *Insight*. The realization of its characteristics in the strategy of functional specialization is spelled out in *Joistings 22*.

7 The musing, of course, stretches back to my first essay of 1969 on the topic "Metamusic and Self-Meaning," which is chapter 2 of the 1976 website book *The Shaping of the Foundations*. It has been my central interest since Lonergan sketched the specialties for me in 1966.

It emerged as an affirmative answer to the question raised by a paper by John Dadosky, "Is there a fourth stage of meaning?"[8] That paper pushed towards an affirmative answer which I shall consider presently. In that consideration I attempt to show how both our struggles come towards the issue from different directions. My own searchings had led me to envisage a refinement of the definition of generalized empirical method that required a balance of attention to subject and object to a definition that would focus on the subject in a radical care mediated by an advanced comprehension of the object.[9] Dadosky pushed my searchings towards a fuller context.

But let us take our merging contexts in helpful stages. First, I consider Dadosky's question and answer. Then I turn to some of my own previous reflections. Third, I pay some attention to the sequencing of stages of meaning. Fourth, I pause over a parallel with the successful elementary science of physics, a paralleling that can aid us in coming to grips with future meanings. In the fifth place, I identify a central contemporary challenge.

2. DADOSKY'S SUGGESTION OF A FOURTH STAGE OF MEANING

Dadosky leads us towards an affirmative answer to his question regarding the existence of such a stage with a winning quotation from Catherine of Siena's *Dialogue*, "O dearest daughter whom I so love, you who are my bride. Rise above your self and open your mind's eye."[10] Catherine of Siena was a lady I met and cherished in the early 1950s, but now the "rise and open" were read by me in a recently freshened context of the luminous reading of a statement of Lonergan, "the pure

---

8 The paper was presented at the 35th annual Lonergan Workshop in Boston College June 21, 2008. When it becomes more available I shall add references. In the meantime, I give references here to the pages of the paper made available at the conference, with the paper referred to simply as **Dadosky**.

9 I give Lonergan's own definition at note 22 below. In *Joistings 21*, "Research, Communications, Stages of Method," I give an account of the first three modes of generalized empirical method. The fourth mode is considered in *Joisting 22*, "Reviewing Mathews' *Lonergan's Quest*, and Ours".

10 Catherine of Siena, "Dialogue 98," in *The Dialogue*, trans. Suzanne Noffke, OP, The Classics of Western Spirituality Series (New York and Mahwah: Paulist Press, 1980), 184.

334 MEANING AND HISTORY IN SYSTEMATIC THEOLOGY

desire to know is ineffable,"[11] coupled with a venturing into the reachings of the women mystics of the fourteenth century.[12] But Dadosky's reach was wider, into Lonergan's "Prolegomena to the Emerging Religious Consciousness of our Time,"[13] into Robley Whitson's *The Coming Convergence of World Religions*,[14] into Dadosky's own suggestions about a "genetic unfolding of *Insight's* cosmopolis with its theological correlate the Reign of God on earth."[15]

In later sections Dadosky weaves a more complex web of correlations that are certainly of concern here, but I wish to maintain a simple focus on the core pointing, symbolized by Catherine's invitation to rise, to open. Loving knowledge of self is in some way to be knowledge of God, "just as the fish is in the sea and the sea in the fish."[16] Is there something here of an edging towards a cherishing of God as "not an object"?[17] Might such an edging edge a community towards a new vulnerable openness to "being at pains not to conceal his tracks,"[18] and a "new sacralization to be fostered?"[19] I venture no fur-

---

11 I am quoting from thesis 12 of the unpublished translation, due to Charles Hefling Jr., of *De Verbo Incarnato*, which is to appear as volume 8 of the *Collected Works* as *The Incarnate Word*.

12 My series *Prehumous* contains five essays; numbers 4 to 8 are all titled *Foundational Prayer*. On fourteenth century mysticism, its place and transposition, see *Prehumous* 8, "Foundational Prayer V: Placing Mysticism."

13 Bernard Lonergan, *A Third Collection*, ed. Frederick E. Crowe (Mahwah, N.J.: Paulist Press, 1985).

14 Robley Whitson, *The Coming Convergence of World Religions*, (New York: Newman Press, 1971).

15 John Dadosky, "Sacralization, Secularization, and Religious Fundamentalism," *Studies in Religious/Sciences Religieuses*, 36.3-4 (Fall, 2007): 513–529.

16 Catherine of Siena, *Dialogue*, 112.

17 "On what I have called the primary and fundamental meaning of the name God, God is not an object." Bernard Lonergan, *Method in Theology* (Toronto: University of Toronto Press, 1971), 342.

18 *Method in Theology*, 193. Lonergan is making the point here about good historians. It is altogether more deeply true of the dialectic challenge built into the strategy of dialectic in the second half of page 250 of *Method*.

19 Bernard Lonergan, "Sacralization and Secularization," in *Philosophical and Theological Papers 1965-1980*, ed. Robert C. Croken and Robert M. Doran (Toronto: University of Toronto Press, 2004), 265.

ther into Dadosky's searchings but rather would have us pause over a single quotation from Lonergan which Dadosky considers as central: "So it is – as we shall attempt to show in the next chapter – that [humans] can reach basic fulfilment, peace, joy, only by moving beyond the realms of common sense, theory, and interiority and into the realm in which God is known and loved."[20] Is there a pointing here towards an overcoming of the catch of history already mentioned, towards, in Dadosky's words, "an ecclesiology of friendship" but in a fullness of global towering and its mediations?

3. THE LIFT GIVEN TO MY OWN PREVIOUS STRUGGLE

My own struggle of more than five decades has led me to some appreciation of Lonergan's suggestion of the two times of the temporal subject.[21] I came to consider these two times as separated by a long, perhaps more than five millennia long, axial period, identifiable mainly with the present shabby emergence of the second stage of meaning. In the third stage of meaning there is to emerge a luminous balanced turn to the subject. The turn is to be dominated by generalized empirical method in its second mode, specified by Lonergan thus: "generalized empirical method operates on a combination of both the data of sense and the data of consciousness: it does not treat of objects without taking into account the corresponding operations of the subject; it does not treat of the subject's operations without taking into account the corresponding objects."[22]

The past few years have pushed me towards envisaging a refinement of this second mode, given the obvious name of GEM3. The push came from a spread of efforts. There was a reach for a heuristics both of the *Eschaton* and of kataphatic prayer, and in that context there emerged the view both of paradise and prayer as *resting and questing in the real*.[23] Pilgrim Tower-prayer would reach for a normative

---

20 *Method in Theology*, 84.

21 Bernard Lonergan, *The Triune God: Systematics*, ed. Robert M. Doran and Daniel Monsour, trans. Michael Shields (Toronto: University of Toronto Press, 2007), 403.

22 *A Third Collection*, 141.

23 See McShane, *Prehumous 4*: "Foundational Prayer I," 3, and *Prehumous 6*, "Foundational Prayer III," 2.

fullness that would mediate a proto-possessive community,[24] living towards luminous resonance with the Word as God's Explanation,[25] the Theory of the Speaker. Speaker, Spoke, Clasp circumincessionally echoed in the cherishing and caring of the spiraling tower cycles of human's meaning – inwardly and in radiant symbol – history's chemical

---

24 This is a complex topic which I treated in an initial stumbling manner in *Cantower* 9, "Position, Poisition, Protopossession". In my struggles with the nature of foundational prayer, I moved to more light and precision on the matter of Proto-Possession, and usefully quote here note 8 of *Prehumous* 5, "Foundational Prayer: All Saints Reaching": "Ut homo studium deputet ad vacandum Deo et rebus divinis"(Thomas Aquinas, *Summa theologiae*, IIa IIae, q.24, a.8). Perhaps here is a good place to come to the heart of the matter, the topic that is to occupy us in the next several essays on foundational prayer. Thomas is dealing here with a high calling. But is not the global call of Faith seeking pragmatic understanding that high call globalized? And is not that the call of cosmopolis, identifiable now methodologically as functional specialization? "It would be unfair not to stress the chief characteristic of cosmopolis. It is not easy." (*Insight* 266 [241]). So I would claim, bluntly, that foundational prayer is the core of the challenge of cosmopolis, the heart of that collaboration mentioned 29 times in the second-last section of chapter 20 of *Insight*. It is to be "not only a new and higher collaboration of intellects through faith in God, but also a mystery that is at once symbol of the uncomprehended and sign of what is grasped and psychic force that sweeps living human bodies, linked in charity, to a joyful, courageous, whole-hearted, yet intelligently controlled performance of the tasks set by a world order in which the problem of evil is not suppressed but transcended." (*Insight*, 745 [723]). Are we not close to the mood of the appeal in the verse quoted at the end of the previous footnote? "Please come home. Please come home into your own body, / Your own vessel, your own earth. / Please come home into each and every cell, / And fully into the space that surrounds you." And there are the further pointers of notes 18-25 of *Prehumous* 5.

25 There are some very complex issues involved here, but it is important to advert to the simplest perspective, one that meshes with Lonergan's comments in "Mission and Spirit" (*A Third Collection*, 27) on Aristotle's ideal – "too high for man" – and on *theoria* in the Greek Fathers. Clinging in theology to descriptions, however rich, is a blocking of the mission of the processive Word. A more complex reach is to ask, as Lonergan does implicitly in *Insight* chapter 10, how we are called to lift into the best human analogue our wonder at the Word's containing of "The Secondary Component in the Idea of Being" (title of section 7 of chapter 19 of *Insight*).

zeal.[26] The practice of GEM2 would have at its neuroheart a focus on that echoing circumincession of the Circumcession.[27] The heartiness, a mustard seed, would be fostered by GEM3, a kataphatic cherishing of the loved subject. But would not this be a new stage of meaning,

---

26 I am pointing compactly here to the power of the second half of Lonergan's systematic treatment of the Trinity. "Speak, Spoke, Clasp" I find useful pastorally as a naming of the Trinity. The concluding paragraph of *Insight* 722 [700] adds a magnificent context, especially taken in the context of the chemical zeal of 13.7 billion years. Indeed, the paragraph is worth quoting here, with "good will" thought of within the reality of the Clasping Joy of the Spirit, Godswell: " Finally, good will is joyful. For it is the love of God above all and in all, and love is joy. Its repentance and sorrow regard the past. Its present sacrifices look to the future. It is at one with the universe in being in love with God, and it shares its dynamic resilience and expectancy. As emergent probability, it ever rises above past achievement. As genetic process, it develops generic potentiality to its specific perfection. As dialectic, it overcomes evil both by meeting it with good and by using it to reinforce the good. But good will wills the order of the universe, and so it wills with that order's dynamic joy and zeal."

27 We are here in the world of Thomas' and Lonergan's reflections. A text worth contemplating inward and onward is "For the glory of the Father is this, that just as he eternally speaks the Word in truth and through the Word breathes forth Love in holiness, so also in the fullness of time he sent his incarnate Son in truth so that by believing the Word we might speak and understand true inner words, and through the Word he sent the Spirit of the Word in holiness so that joined to the Spirit in love and made living members of the body of Christ we might cry out, Abba, Father." (*The Truine God: Systematics*, 521). It is as well to mention in this context the searchings of the mystics for inner and outer words of the Trinitarian reality. Kataphatic contemplation is to lift that anaphatic effort into a new luminosity of minding. I have written previously of problems of the anaphatic reaching, and it seems useful to repeat a note given in that context (note 15 of *Prehumous* 8) which comments on a quotation "the birth of the divine Word in the soul," from note 85, 423, of McGinn, *The Flowering of Mysticism*, Volume 3 of his *The Presence of God: A History of Western Mysticism* (Crossroads/Herder, New York, 1998). A fuller piece of McGinn's note reads: "This mystical theme of the birth of the divine Word in the soul, found in a number of Cistercian authors, such as Guerric of Igny (see *Growth of Mysticism*, 283-4), was richly developed by Meister Eckhart. For an overview, see Hugo Rahner, "Die Gottesgeburt: Die Lehre der Kirchenväter von der Geburt Christi aus dem Herzen der Kirche und der Glaubigen," in *Symbole der Kirche* (Saltzburg: Otto Mueller, 1964), 13-87.

even though ecologically meshed with varieties of all other stages, thus shabbily sequential?

4. SEQUENCINGS OF STAGES OF MEANING

Sequencing, whether ontogenetic or phylogenetic, is a general problem. One may ask what type of moral conversion, if any, can be expected to precede a certain type of religious reorientation. Here our interest is in sequencings of stages of meaning and of general types of generalized empirical method, each separately and also in their interweaving. Further, our interest here cannot be more than that of preliminary scientific description, and so we muddle along with crude genera.

It seems sufficiently accurate to claim that the four stages of meaning are roughly in the right order when we consider their emergence either in history or in the individual subject. But beyond the roughness we find exceptions. Both the Socrates of Plato and the Saint of Siena seem oddly close to what we name the fourth stage of meaning. The oddness invites us beyond the consideration of genera to an ecology of species and varieties. We must make do, in this short essay, with some few pointers. The question of the subject, or of "the subject as subject"[28] in Lonergan's uncomfortable expression, emerges in elementary ways, differently in different cultures. There is the way of Confucius, the way of Dogen, the way of the twentieth century existentialists that interested Lonergan when he coined his phrase, *subject as subject*. Husserl obviously figures in that interest for Lonergan and us, and it gives the opportunity to mention the distant achievement of a developed fourth stage of meaning that would give an ecology of Husserl, both of his achievements in specifying stages of the Calculus of Variation and of his muddled persistence in misreading his own activities of *is-ing*.[29] That ecology and the ecologies of Confucius or Catherine

---

28 See *Phenomenology and Logic*, 314, and the index under *Subject, as subject*. The word as is generally taken as abstractive, but Lonergan's push is towards the subject in full concreteness, a concreteness that I would relate to the subject's ineffable obedientiality.

29 In the next section I draw on a paralleling with Einstein's searching in Spacetime's understanding, but there is a large and fruitful paralleling to be had from Husserl's work on the stages of development of the Calculus of Variation, a thesis written in the early 1880s under Weirstrass. I develop this parallel in *Lack in the Beingstalk* , chapter 4, "A Calculus of Variation."

are to be patterned by what I call the Standard Model of the Tower
Community, a relatively mature context named UV + GS, where both
UV – a universal viewpoint – and GS – a geohistorical genetic systematics – have a richness of meaning rooted in a future century or so
of cyclically cumulative progressive results.[30] But all this is too much
for our present effort, indeed, for our present generation. I wish only
to make two broad descriptive points: that the sequencing and the related ecologies are massively flexible, and that nonetheless that there is
to be, as Lonergan would have it, a "normative pattern"[31] of cumulating
results. The flexibility is illustrated by a sort-of premature presence
of the fourth stage of meaning in the searchings of Socrates and the
sighings of Catherine. The normativity is embedded in my claim that
the Tower of Able is eventually to be a community alive in a mature
fourth stage of meaning that is generalized empirical method in its
third mode, mediated by the general and special categories of up-to-
date global culture, within the dynamic spiral of GEM4.

So I return to the concluding quotation from Lonergan given at the
end of section 2 above. Is there a normativity of some refined sequencing of the differentiations involved, which yet has a tolerant flexibility?

5. EXISTENTIAL ASSISTANCE FROM PHYSICS

It is important that we pause here over the parallel between GEM3
and the successful pursuit of a successful science, and the parallel I
would make is one that lurks in many of Lonergan's suggestions. It is

That parallel brings out better the anticipated subtle remoteness of a developed science of calculated care, since the calculus of variation has a long
history, starting from the Aenead's problem of maximizing an area and
moving towards the complexity expressed by such a text as I.M.Gelfand,
Calculus of Variation, Prentice-Hall, New Jersey, 1993. A parallel development in theology and in global inquiry is the object of our present fantasy,
reaching into later centuries of this millennium.

30 This is all too compact, expressing facets of the two books mentioned in
note 5 above. The heuristic conceiving of genetic systematics seems especially difficult for the present generation, especially when it is taken in a
spacetime fullness that would include geographic divergences, ecologies.
John of Antioch and Cyril of Alexandra were in different genetic snakings,
as were Dogen and Thomas in the 13th century. We need a heuristic and
scientific complexification of Lonergan's various suggestions about ongoing, overlapping, etc., contexts.

31 *Method in Theology*, 4.

the parallel with the most elementary science, physics. The first lecture of Lonergan I heard in 1961 gave a lead to my present pointing. He spoke of the lady who invited Einstein to tea. Midway through the tea she expressed her delight and went on, "I am fascinated by your work and would love to understand your theory of relativity. I would love you to explain it to me, just in my own simple words: I am no good whatsoever with equations."[32] He anticipates in this story the mood of his later comments on *haute vulgarization*,[33] a large topic to which I can only give footnote pointers, for here I wish us to focus in that mood, but sublationally, on Lonergan's meaning of stages, theoria, patterns, etc. General bias, molecularly possessive of all of us in this late stage of the longer cycle of decline, would have us shrink his meaning with gentle brutality. So it is useful to enlarge Lonergan's tale about Einstein into a definite paralleling of the two innovators.

Einstein was trying to envisage and initiate a lift in our understanding of space and time. There was the partial achievement, in 1904, of key elements expressed in his special theory of relativity. To that he added, eleven years later in 1915, a decent shot at the general theory that eventually blossomed into a present incomplete gauge theory.[34] The story of that blossoming cannot concern us here, although it is to be part of the Tower-stand against *haute vulgarization*. Let us simply leap descriptively and suggestively to Lonergan's efforts, exactly fifty years later.

---

32 I am recalling the first of six lectures on "Method and Science" given during Easter, 1961. We were not great at recording in those days. The remaining lectures are available in the Toronto Archives, but I am not sure whether we recorded the first lecture at all: I recalled points from it for those Archives.

33 See *The Ontological and Psychological Constitution of Christ*, 121, 155. There are also relevant refection in *Topics in Education*, 145, and in Lonergan's musings, in *Phenomenology and Logic*, on decaying schools of thought. In *Lack in the Beingstalk*, chapter 3, "Haute Vulgarization" raises the question of the transposition of popular exposition to a positivity that would be an ex-plane-ing, from a present plane of the Tower to the plain plane of common sense.

34 A relevant piece of an extended paralleling would be had from Lochlainn O'Raifeartaigh, *The Dawning of Gauge Theory* (Cambridge University Press, 1986), a brilliant critical work. There is need for a parallel work on the dawning of Lonergan's gauge theory although we are as yet not close to sun-up: a work, then, for the end of this century.

Lonergan was trying to envisage and initiate a lift in our understanding of neuro-space and neuro-time. There was the partial achievement, in 1954, of key elements that bubbled out of his special effort of *Insight*.[35] He was onto the core of progress in theology that could be controlled by the sharing of that special effort. Hear his burst of confidence, however opaque it sits in your neurospacetime: "The Method in Theology is coming into perspective. For the Trinity: *Imago Dei in homine* and proceed to the limit as in evaluating $[1 + 1/n]^{nx}$ as n approaches infinity. For the rest: *ordo universi*. From the viewpoint of theology, it is a manifold of unities developing in relation to one another and in relation to God."[36]

Eleven years later he broke through history's nudges to the core of the general character of the control of that sharing that is eventually to blossom into a global gauge of progress. He had solved, in principle, the larger problem lurking in the special theory, the problem of realistic efficiency.[37] And, in principle but not in expression, he had arrived at a general theory. GEM2 was to be weaved into a GEM4.

---

35 I would note that *Insight* in some ways is a light-weight book. Difficulties are described or passed over, even with such a comic turn as occurs at the beginning of the last paragraph of chapter 5: "The answer is easily reached." On the problem of a fuller axiomatics of "the position," (*Insight*, 413[388]) including axioms of intentionality, of infinity, of incompleteness etc, see *Prehumous 2*. Then there is the problem that *Insight* was the first of two volumes envisaged by Lonergan, the second having some such title as *Insight and Faith*. (This, from a letter to Eric O'Connor in 1952).

36 I quote from a letter of Lonergan to Fr. Frederick Crowe in May 1954, which he kindly made available to me decades ago. I consider the letter, and the problem implicit there of accelerating adult growth (see *Eldorede 4*), in *Field Nocturnes 4*: "Lonergan's 1954 View of Theology in the New Context."

37 I have all too often referred to the key text, line 16 of page 160 of *Topics in Education*, regarding the unity of a science to be found in its efficiency. Present global reflective concern, including present theology, is quite evidently "effete" (*Method in Theology*, 99). In the following *Field Nocturnes CanTower 45*, "Eau Canada" I shall attempt to illustrate this more concretely in relation to global care of water. The title of *FNC 45* is the title of a recent book edited by Karen Bakker, University of British Columbia Press, 2007. The title is an obvious pun, but it leads me to lift the reflection into another musical context, that of C. Hubert Parry's 1916 melody *Jerusalem*, with modern words "O world of God so vast and strange, profound and wonderful and strange, beyond the utmost reach of thought but not beyond

6. THE EXISTENTIAL CHALLENGE

The existential assistance that is touched on in the previous section is, alas, of real significance and of real assent, ascent, only if it assisted by patient involvement in the effort to climb a little in scientific understanding. This is an old thesis of mine, but it can be well documented from Lonergan's writings.[38] Perhaps, in this brief essay, the challenge might be intimated by focusing on the word *patterned* as I wrote it above and you read it there and here.[39] How did you read it? More broadly, how do you read the word *pattern* in *Insight* and *Method in Theology*? Einstein and his followers in gauge theory think and write of the patterns of planets and particles. Lonergan has written of a normative gauge of thinking of persons and patterns of consciousness. If the first group's reachings are incomprehensible to common sense, the second group's reachings are to be much more so.

---

our Maker's care." The issue of modern theology and care is, nonetheless, to push for that utmost reach, rise out of its shallowness, stop being "a titanothore, a beast with a three-ton-body with a ten-ounce brain .... It must glory in its deepening, in the pure deepening that adds to aggregate leisure, to liberate many entirely and all increasingly to the field of cultural activities ..... It must lift its eyes more and ever more to the more general and the more difficult fields of speculation, for it is from them that it has to derive the delicate compound of unity and freedom in which alone progress can be born, struggle, and win through" (*For A New Political Economy*, 20).

38 See Part three, chapter 1, of Pierrot Lambert and Philip McShane, *Bernard Lonergan: His Life and Leading Ideas*, a work in progress, to appear in English, French, and other languages. In that chapter I focus attention on Lonergan's ingestion of the perspective of Lindsay and Margenau, *Foundations of Physics*.

39 The word occurs in the sentence following that marked by note 29. It refers to patterning by the Standard Model. It is useful to note the two lengthy commentaries on components of this patterning that the series *Field Nocturnes* focuses on: the pattern of serious science described in the paragraph "study of the organism," talked about in that 300 pages, and the pattern of serious dialectic collaboration described on page 250 of *Method*, commented on previously in the 200 pages of the two series, SOFAWARDs and *Quodlibets*. One does not come to grips with the pattern of scientific inquiry from outside science or by reading *Scientific American*.

7. BUT IS THIS LATTER STAND YOURS?

The series of 41 essays titled *Field Nocturnes* was a 300-page invitation to exercises on the single paragraph "Study of the organism." One might thus come to the stand in question by savouring the distressing fact that patterns of human experience are not forms, but flexible circles of ranges of recurrence – schemes realized by acts of forms, those actual and active forms being forms of flexible aggregates of vastly complex neurochemical acts, and so on down to those particles which intrigue the practitioners of the elementary gauge theory of physics. The achievement of the stand removes one existentially from metaphysical myth-making,[40] from simplistic and distorted phenomenology, but above all from the *haute vulgarization*, mate of general bias, that haunts present Lonergan studies. The effective long-term remedy to that sickness is, of course, the slow global implementation of the Towering Enterprise of GEM4. But that circles us back to the million-word project of the 117 Cantowers, not something to be put in simple words without equations.

---

40 *Insight* 528 [505] speaks of "the substitution of a pseudometaphysical myth-making for scientific inquiry." *The Triune God: Systematics* puts the point in uncompromising terms: "Only in the intermediate scientific stage are relations divided into predicamental and transcendental and even in that state such a division is not very suitable" (725). Add to that the comment on page 199 of *Understanding and Being*: "We arrive at Aristotle's categories most simply by going into the woods, meeting animals, and asking, What kind of an animal is this? How big is it? What is its color? What relations does it have? And so on. They are categories of descriptive knowledge, and descriptive knowledge is science in a preliminary stage."

LONERGAN, GIRARD, AND CONFLICT

Kenneth R. Melchin

SAINT PAUL UNIVERSITY, OTTAWA

I. INTRODUCTION

It is a pleasure to be invited to contribute to this Festschrift in honour of Bob Doran. I have been an admirer of Bob's work for more than 25 years. More than this, I have been an admirer of Bob. As a scholar, as Director of the Lonergan Research Institute, and as a colleague and friend, Bob's efforts to keep theology connected to authentic living have always impressed me. Lonergan's work is intellectually demanding, yet it is also demanding existentially, for it calls the reader to reflect intensely and honestly on the coherence between one's theology and one's life. I believe we can discern in Bob's life and work both the intellectual and existential dimensions of the Lonergan Project. My short contribution to this volume explores one of the areas of Bob's work where these two dimensions come together in a way I find most compelling.

This paper arises from an invitation to respond to Bob Doran's presentation to the 2006 Colloquium on Violence and Religion.[1] Through the years, Bob has sought to build bridges between the works of Lonergan and René Girard. On this particular occasion, his paper explored a possible contribution that Lonergan's work might make to Girard's theory of mimetic desire. Girard has helped us understand with extraordinary lucidity the destructive power of mimetic desire: how it works; how it unfolds in human life; how it leaves so much suffering in its wake; and how its analysis illuminates so much of the

---

1 Robert Doran, "Imitating the Divine Relations: A Theological Contribution to Mimetic Theory," presented at the Conference on Violence and Religion, Saint Paul University, Ottawa, June 1, 2006. See Robert Doran "Summarizing 'Imitating the Divine Relations: A Theological Contribution to Mimetic Theory,'" in *Contagion: Journal of Violence, Mimesis, and Culture*, vol. 14 (2007); 27-38.

drama of human existence. In his paper, Bob Doran asked whether, alongside and in contrast to this destructive form of desire, there might exist an authentic form of human desiring, and whether this authentic desiring might be understood, following Lonergan, as an imitation of and a graced participation in the divine relations of the triune God. Bob does indeed find such an authentic form of desiring in Lonergan's work, and he speaks of this as the very self-transcending dynamism of human consciousness that is operative in genuine human curiosity, in the search for truth, in the pursuit of value, and in its fullest form, in the dynamic state of unrestricted being-in-love that Lonergan calls religious conversion.

I find Bob's analysis quite illuminating, both with respect to Girard's work and Lonergan's. A similar line of analysis is articulated by Rebecca Adams in a paper presented at the 1995 session of the Colloquium on Violence and Religion.[2] Like Bob Doran, she explores whether there might exist an authentic form of mimetic desire that arises in an encounter with a God who desires my own subjectivity, my own dignity, my own autonomy. Imitation of this act of divine love, then, gives rise in me to an opening to others, not as objects, but as subjects.

This paper is an illustration of what Bob Doran speaks of in contrasting the destructive forms of mimetic desire with an authentic desiring which Lonergan calls the transcendental desiring of the human spirit. This simple example is drawn from the field of conflict resolution and arises from work I have been doing with Cheryl Picard, applying Lonergan's *Insight* theory to the field of conflict and mediation.[3]

---

2 Rebecca Adams, "Mothers, Metamorphs, Myth and Mimesis: A Creative Reassessment of Mimetic Desire," paper presented at the Conference on Violence and Religion, Loyola University, June 2, 1995, subsequently published as "Loving Mimesis and Girard's 'Scapegoat of the Text': A Creative Reassessment of Mimetic Desire," in Willard M. Swartley, ed., *Violence Renounced: René Girard, Biblical Studies, and Peacemaking* (Telford: Pandora Press, 2000), 277-307. This text is cited in Vern Neufeld Redekop, *From Violence to Blessing* (Ottawa: Novalis, 2002), 259-271.

3 Kenneth R. Melchin and Cheryl A. Picard, *Transforming Conflict Through Insight* (Toronto: University of Toronto Press, 2008); Cheryl A. Picard and Kenneth R. Melchin, "Insight Mediation: A Learning-Centered Mediation Model," *Negotiation Journal* 23 (2007): 35–53; Cheryl A. Picard, "Learning About Learning: The Value of 'Insight'," *Conflict Resolution Quarterly* 20 (2003): 477–84.

2. APPLICATION TO CONFLICT RESOLUTION

The example is of a very ordinary conflict, not the violent, deep root-ed conflict we despair of ever resolving. It is the sort of small conflict that actually gets resolved often in life, particularly with the help of a good mediator. However, I believe we can gain insights from simple conflicts that can prove helpful in the more difficult cases. The me-diator strategies, in this illustration, come from the *Insight Mediation* method that is taught and practised at Carleton University, Ottawa.[4] The focus in this discussion is on the strategies used by the mediator to move the parties from a destructive pattern of interaction to one characterized by openness, curiosity, and mutual interest.

The conflict arises from an ordinary conversation and involves par-ties that have a relationship within a family, friendship, or workplace context. The parties are trying to say something important to each other, but they just do not seem to get it. The topic evokes strong feel-ings as both try explaining themselves to no avail. Soon the conversa-tion turns into a heated argument, and what begins to emerge is a pat-tern that is all too familiar. The issue of the original conversation stops being the issue, and something else takes over: a common dynamic that both have lived again and again in the relationship. It is a dynamic that evokes old feelings of anger and resentment, a dynamic structure that captures both and holds them in its grip until the relationship is reduced to a cold and bitter hostility.

This time, however, the parties are in the presence of a mediator, and she walks them through a process in which both are allowed to explore some of the deeper feelings that lie behind the issues. They are in an environment where they begin to feel safe, and by speaking to each directly and with affirmation, the mediator models a way of re-lating that allows both to explore what matters to them. In Lonergan's language, the mediator helps the parties explore the feelings in search of the values that lie behind the issues in the conflict.[5] The values are

---

4 See Cheryl A. Picard, Peter Bishop, Rena Ramkay, and Neil Sargent, *The Art and Science of Mediation* (Toronto: Emond Montgomery, 2004); and <http://www.carleton.ca/ccer>.

5 On feelings as intentional responses to values see Bernard Lonergan, *Meth-od in Theology*, 2nd ed. (Toronto: University of Toronto Press, 2003; orig. 1972), 30-34; see also Frederick E. Crowe, "An Exploration of Lonergan's New Notion of Value," in *Appropriating the Lonergan Idea*, ed. M. Vertin (Washington, D.C.: Catholic University of America Press, 1989), 51-70;

intended in the feelings, but the parties may never have understood or articulated what these values are about. Consequently, they remain hidden from both parties, even as they remain operative as drivers of the conflict. The mediator helps the parties along this road of exploration, offering encouragement and affirmation.

As the process unfolds, the mediator helps the parties gain insights into the values at stake in the conflict.[6] Moreover, she helps them articulate how they interpret the actions of the other as threatening these values. What comes out are underlying fears and feelings of threat that previously would not have surfaced in the conversation: feelings of expected humiliation; expectations that another's competence would result in harm to oneself; fears that the other's skills would necessarily bring hurt or grief. What she explores are the origins of these feelings of threat and the expectations that they need necessarily define the course of future events.

Of particular interest to the mediator are the parties' expectations of the *necessity* of a future defined by these anticipations of threat. Insight mediators probe the respective parties' feelings and values in search of assumptions about future patterns of events that parties believe will follow necessarily if the conflict is allowed to play out. At times these expectations arise from a past history of the relationship. At other times, they arise from earlier personal histories or experiences that pre-date the relationship. Regardless of their origin, however, it is the assumed *necessity* of these negative courses of events that keeps parties locked in patterns of interaction where they remain closed to the values of the other. The expectations of threat force parties into positions of defence, protection, retreat, retaliation, or attack. And their images of the other become dominated by these expectations of threat.[7]

---

and Kenneth R. Melchin, *Living with Other People* (Ottawa: Novalis; Collegeville MN: 1998), 31-33.

6 For a fascinating analysis of violent conflict that focuses on the role of values in shaping the sense of identity and threat of parties, see Daniel Rothbart and Karina V. Korostelina, eds., *Identity, Morality, and Threat: Studies in Violent Conflict,* (Lanham MD: Lexington Books, 2006).

7 Rothbart and Korostlina explore this dimension of certainty or assumed predictability in parties' future expectations about the Other in violent conflicts. They argue that this predictability is central to the way that axiological (value) differences shape the parties' sense of identity and thus the

At this stage in the process, the Insight mediator engages the parties in an exploration aimed at *de-linking* the threat.[8] She invites the parties to explore possible ways that the other's values can be affirmed and achieved without threatening one's own. It is the necessity or certainty of the expectations of a threat that lock the parties in conflict. As long as they remain certain about the future defined by the threat scenario, the parties cannot let go of their commitment to defence or retaliation. Once the mediator helps them move out of this certainty, however, something new emerges in them: interest, curiosity, and a willingness to explore alternative forms of engagement. What emerges is quite genuine. And it is this genuine spirit that replaces the distorted form of engagement that prevails when parties anticipate the other as threat.

The result is a shift in the pattern of conversation. One of the parties stops and listens. It is as if she were hearing the other's words for the first time. It is the necessity of the cycle of anger and threat that has been broken. Both now feel permitted to articulate and hold their respective values without invoking the cycle of reprisals that had dominated the conflict to this point. What arises is genuine curiosity about the values of the other. The other's story becomes interesting in a new way. Under the guidance of the mediator, the parties tentatively begin opening up to a new way of talking. The familiar pattern of conflict and argument begins to give way to a real conversation about things that matter.

I would like to suggest that what happens in this illustration is a shift from an inauthentic, dysfunctional form of desire to what Bob Doran has drawn on Lonergan to call the authentic dynamism of self-transcendence. I believe René Girard's work offers a great deal towards understanding the dysfunctional dynamics of mimetic desire. Bob Doran is correct in saying that Lonergan offers a very good understanding of what is at work in authentic desiring. Its most basic and common manifestation is curiosity and wonder. It is the human spirit raising and answering questions, getting insights, consulting evidence and making judgements, understanding and affirming values,

---

course of violent events in conflicts. See "Moral Denigration of the Other," in *Identity, Morality, and Threat*, 29-52.

8 On de-linking, see Melchin and Picard, *Transforming Conflict through Insight*, chap. 4.

350 MEANING AND HISTORY IN SYSTEMATIC THEOLOGY

and making good decisions. In its fullest form it is the human spirit in the dynamic state of being in love.

What is revealed in this illustration from *Insight Mediation* is the role of the inverse insight in breaking the grip of dysfunctional desire and releasing authentic desire.[9] When the mediator strategy of *de-linking* helps parties break out of the expectations of threat, it is the *necessity* of the expected negative future that gives way. It is the parties' *certainty* about this negative future that holds them in the conflict. The future envisioned by the parties in conflict is of a necessary intelligibility that they believe is certain if the other prevails. And this expected future necessity defines their stance in the present. It is the necessity of this expected intelligibility that is met with the inverse insight when the mediator is successful. This future is not necessary. It can be otherwise. What she invokes in the parties is a dialectical form of analysis in which future events are imagined differently. Things do not need to unfold in this pattern of hurt and reprisal. I suggest that what is at work here is similar to what is captured in Lonergan's chapter 20 of *Insight* where he speaks of the infused habit of charity as breaking the cycle of evil.[10] In more dramatic and violent conflicts, it is the refusal to require that a history of oppression be lived out in cycles of violent reprisal.

What arises in place of the typical patterned response in the conflict is a new form of engagement, animated by the dynamism of self-transcendence. Its humble beginnings are curiosity, a newfound interest, a desire to understand the other. What actually does matter to you? What do you care about so deeply in the midst of all this? In its fullest form, I suggest, it blossoms into the unrestricted desire of love that is the imitation of and graced participation in the divine relations of the triune God.

---

9 On inverse insights, see Bernard Lonergan, *Collected Works of Bernard Lonergan* vol. 3, *Insight: A Study of Human Understanding*, eds. Frederick E. Crowe and Robert M. Doran (Toronto: University of Toronto Press, 1992; orig. 1957), chap. 1. See also Philip McShane, *Randomness, Statistics and Emergence* (Dublin: Gill and Macmillan, 1970); Patrick Byrne, "The Thomist Sources of Lonergan's Dynamic World-View," *The Thomist* 46 (1982): 108–45; and Melchin and Picard, *Transforming Conflict through Insight*, chap. 3.

10 See Lonergan, *Insight*, chap. 20.

I have offered a very simple example of this process at work in conflicts. But I do want to say that experiences like this are quite common for mediators. I do believe they reveal something that can be observed in all of our lives. And I suggest they provide preliminary clues for exploring how to deal with the more difficult conflicts studied by Girard. Alongside and in contrast to the destructive form of desire elaborated by Girard, there can be observed an authentic form of human desiring. This authentic form of engagement is what Insight mediators seek to evoke in parties in conflict. Following Lonergan, this authentic form of desiring can be understood as the self-transcending dynamism of human consciousness that is operative in genuine human curiosity, in the search for truth, and in the pursuit of value. In its fullest form, it is the dynamic state of being in love that Lonergan calls religious conversion. I believe that Bob Doran is correct in saying that exploring this authentic desire can indeed contribute to Girard's mimetic theory. And I propose that the experiences of Insight Mediators offer a fruitful evidential base for advancing this line of research.

CLASSICAL RHETORIC AND THE CONTROL OF ELEMENTAL MEANING

Gilles Mongeau, SJ

REGIS COLLEGE, UNIVERSITY OF TORONTO

I. INTRODUCTION

Robert Doran's oeuvre can be characterized by a root concern for elemental meaning, its role in human living, and its place in theological method. It is possible to give an account of Doran's development as a theologian by tracing the development of his account of elemental meaning, beginning with the initial insights that lead to the discovery of psychic conversion and ending with his most recent proposals for empirical consciousness as reception in the realm of ordinary meaningfulness. Concomitant with this interest in understanding elemental meaning is a concern to develop theological method to include the control of elemental meaning, particularly in the functional specialty systematics. I propose to celebrate Doran's achievement in this essay, first by sketching out the elements of his account of elemental meaning, and then by using this sketch as a framework to bring to light how classical rhetoric functioned as the science of elemental meaning in the ancient and patristic world. This in turn will allow us to appreciate just how significant Doran's contribution to the rediscovery of elemental meaning in theology really is.

2. DORAN'S ACCOUNT OF ELEMENTAL MEANING

Doran's work on psychic conversion focused initially on elements related to the transformation of the censor such that it habitually releases into intentional consciousness those authentic symbols and phantasms that make available for insight and judgment the real demands of the underlying neural manifold. His early account is thus connected with questions of dreams, symbols, feelings (both intentional and non-intentional), the overcoming of scotosis and dramatic bias. The operator he uncovers is named a symbolic operator. But as he admits in a recent article, which we will discuss more fully in a moment, this early work was already motivated by a concern with "not being alienated from the stream of an empirical consciousness that receives data mediated by meaning."[1] The work on psychic conversion tried to bring attention to the "tidal movement that begins before consciousness, unfolds through sensitivity, intelligence, rational reflection, responsible deliberation, only to find its rest beyond all of these in being in love."[2] The sources of elemental meaning in this account are mainly operations of the subject and their psychological contents, symbols, conations, feelings, and so on.

From the beginning, however, Doran wished to dialogue with von Balthasar and Heidegger. As the conversation with von Balthasar develops, and as he addresses issues related to the scale of values, Doran shifts his account of the symbolic operator and begins to speak of an aesthetic-dramatic operator, including in his recovery of the sources of elemental meaning the work of art, the efforts of the subject to make of his or her own life a work of art, and the uncovering of meaning and value in the flow of life through culture – understood as a dialectic between ideal types of matrices of constitutive meanings.

In more recent years, this engagement with constitutive meaning and value at the level of culture has brought Doran into dialogue with René Girard. In the context of this conversation, his original concern for the psychic rift that needs to be healed, his quest for a "habitual being-at-home with, not being alienated from," the stream of empirical consciousness,[3] has expanded to include those distortions that arise from processes of communal self-alienation as a function of the habitual covering over of violence. In this new conversation, mutual self-mediation in its authentic and distorted forms has taken more of a central role, so that there is already an awareness of the communal making of elemental meaning that can impact the subject whose aesthetic-dramatic operator makes those meanings available to consciousness. Doran has written of authentic and distorted sacraliza-

---

1 Robert Doran, "Reception and Elemental Meaning: an Expansion of the Notion of Psychic Conversion," *Toronto Journal of Theology* 20/2, 2004, 152.

2 Doran, "Reception", 152, citing Lonergan in "Natural Right and Historical Mindedness," *Third Collection*, ed. F.E. Crowe (Mahwah, NJ: Paulist Press 1985).

3 Ibid.

tions and secularizations of the world. In this context he has explored the crucial significance of the incarnate meaning of Christ and the Law of the Cross, a meaning whose elemental meaningfulness cannot be captured by definition and could be one of the "permanently elemental meanings" to which Doran has sometimes alluded in his work, and which must be included *as elemental* in a systematics.

This brings me to the paper "Reception and Elemental Meaning: an Expansion of the Notion of Psychic Conversion," occasioned by a discussion with Sean McGrath in April 2004, first presented by Doran at a Lonergan Workshop in that same year, and subsequently published in the *Toronto Journal of Theology*. In this essay, Doran returns to the circumstances that first inspired the notion of psychic conversion, and expands that notion – in response to McGrath's analysis of Heidegger as a Scotist – to account for the Heideggerian *Verstehen* and *Befindlichkeit*, the Balthasarian "seeing the form" and the Wittgenstinian concern for what Lonergan calls ordinary meaningfulness. He proposes that we think of empirical consciousness as "reception" and the operations of empirical consciousness as not just aesthetic-dramatic but also as hermeneutical. There is a patterned elemental meaningfulness that reaches us from the ordinary meaningfulness that is essentially public and common; it shapes our own development and enables our reception of meaning, including elemental meaning; it is a function of the priority of the dialectic of culture over the dialectics of community and of the subject. Doran states:

> ...the relative dominance [of the dialectic of culture] means that the horizon of the subject in his or her world, a horizon constituted by meaning, along with the world that is correlative to that horizon, are prior to critical reflection on the part of the subject, largely a function of what Heidegger's language calls temporal and historical facticity, of being thrown into existence in the world at this particular time and with these particular people, with their own horizons similarly determined for them by historical dialectics over which at the outset they have no control.[4]

There is a mediated immediacy of empirical consciousness as reception of ordinary meaningfulness, including the already patterned elemental meanings at work in the culture. It is at this level that God enters into the world of human meaning, and it is at this level of el-

4 Ibid., 149.

emental meaning, "of the already given intelligibility of received data,"[5] that God's original meaningfulness in the Incarnate Word transforms our common meanings and therefore our personal meanings and values. Theology's responsibility to receive and mediate communally and historically-generated elemental meanings and values authentically is thus brought to the fore.

This short sketch of Doran's development with respect to elemental meaning articulates four areas of concern for theological method: the operations that originate elemental meaning in the subject, symbols, feelings, conations, etc.; the aesthetic-dramatic carriers and sources of elemental meaning beyond these operations, intersubjectivity, works of art, stories, saints and great persons, cultural matrices, and so on; the distortions and healing of cultures and persons by means of elemental meaning; and empirical consciousness as reception of already intelligently-patterned elemental meaning, i.e. as hermeneutical and the consequent responsibility of a critical theological method to "correct the major unauthenticity of the received tradition" when necessary, by "exercising the original meaningfulness that, under God's gift of grace, is the sole source and guarantee of such healing and creating in history."[6]

The question I wish to ask now is the following: given that 19th and 20th century Western Christian theology did not by and large pay attention to elemental meaning as elemental, was there ever a time in the history of Christian theology that theological method concerned itself with elemental meaning and exhibited a capacity to receive and mediate such meaning authentically in the way that our sketch describes? And if such a capacity existed, what tools did theology have at its disposal? What was the *scientia* that enabled it to do so?

3. THE CLAIMS OF RHETORIC IN
THE ANCIENT WORLD

Irénée Marrou, Marshall McLuhan and, more recently, Rita Copeland have traced the development of the three arts of the *trivium* (grammar, dialectic, and rhetoric) in the ancient world, showing that the scope and purpose of each of these foundational disciplines at any given time was determined by a complex set of relations: the domi-

---

5 Ibid.

6 Ibid., 155.

nance of one of the three, the one of the other two mainly in conflict with the dominant discipline, and the status of the third within that conflict.[7] Each of the three disciplines of the trivium claimed to be the foundational discipline, not just for the study of language and meaning, but for the scientific study of reality. Such claims were grounded in a shared cosmological doctrine of the Logos which, as McLuhan shows, treated reality as language-like:

> Inseparable from the doctrine of the Logos is the cosmological view of the *rerum natura*, the whole, as a *continuum*, at once a network of natural causes and an *ordo naturae* whose least pattern expresses analogically a divine message. The notion, already implicit in the Chaldean cosmology, is the very basis of Plato's *Timaeus*, the work of his which had the greatest influence of any of his works, both in antiquity and in the medieval times…. Nothing [other than the *Timaeus*] could make more clear than this the relationship which was held to exist between the order of speech and language and the order of nature…. The Logos or universal reason is at once the life and order which are in all things, and in the mind of man.[8]

Through much of the ancient and medieval period, grammar reigns supreme as the science that can explain this language-like reality, with occasional attempts by dialectic to assert itself. It is rhetoric, however, that throughout this period claims the widest competence in the realm of meaning: beyond claims to interpret the book of nature like grammar and dialectics, rhetoric claimed competence over politics and ethics. The Logos is also the bond of the State: "Society, ideally the cosmopolis or perfect world state, thus claimed the devotion of every virtuous man," and "political prudence is the noblest sphere in which to

---

7 Henri Irénée Marrou, *Saint Augustin et la fin de la culture antique* (Paris: Boccard, 1938) shows the complementarity and conflict between grammar and rhetoric in the ancient world leading up to Augustine; more recently, Rita Copeland, *Rhetoric, Hermeneutics and Translation in the Middle Ages* (Cambridge: Cambridge University Press, 1991) picks up the story of grammar and rhetoric, focusing on the particular case of translation into the vernacular. The most complete account of the historical development of all three disciplines in relation to each other is Marshall McLuhan's recently published 1943 dissertation, *The Classical Trivium* (Toronto: Ginkho Press, 2006).

8 McLuhan, *The Classical Trivium*, 20-22.

exercise" the foundational virtue of wisdom.[9] In addition, because human beings as rational are also speaking animals (the Greek concept of Logos was translated by the Latins as *ratio atque oratio*, "reason and especially discourse," to try to capture its full meaning), "wisdom and eloquence, virtue and practical political power" are "inseparable and simultaneous achievements of verbal verbosity."[10] Rhetoric thus claims to cover the totality of meaning and value in human living, and it is to an exploration of those claims that we now turn.

4. THE PHAEDRUS OF PLATO

Behind much of the Greek discussion of rhetoric stands the shadowy figure of the sophist, a catchall term that describes various kinds of teachers of eloquence. The Platonic and Aristotelian caricature of them as manipulative and arrogant teachers of verbal tricks is largely unfair, though it applied to some. Isocrates, a contemporary of Plato and Aristotle and the founder of an important school of rhetoric, "sought to condition students' moral behaviour so that they would think and speak noble, virtuous ideas and implement them in civic policy, thus providing a response to claims that rhetoric was an art of deception and flattery."[11] Nevertheless, Isocrates emphasized techniques of amplification and smoothness of style, where Plato and Aristotle emphasized the importance of dialectic and an adequate grasp of logical argumentation. Plato's *Phaedrus*, which along with the *Symposium* and parts of the *Republic* discusses matters of beauty, politics, and public speaking and was highly influential on subsequent developments in rhetoric, must be read in this context.

The first thing to note is that for all its emphasis on dialectic, the *Phaedrus* is one of Plato's greatest artistic achievements: he crafts a dialogue that relies heavily for its convincing power on setting a particular mood and presenting a vivid image of the discourse of the wise under the shade of the trees. The rhetorical craft behind the text is an important factor in its effectiveness and its continuing influence.

The dialogue begins with a review of a public speech by a certain Lysias, read to Socrates by Phaedrus who has greatly appreciated

---

9   McLuhan, 63.

10   Ibid.

11   George A. Kennedy, "Introduction," Aristotle's *On Rhetoric* (New York: Oxford University Press, 2006), 13.

hearing it and wants to memorize it so as to better his own rhetorical abilities. The speech is a series of examples calculated to arouse horror or fear in the listener, cumulatively highlighting the base madness of human love. These rhetorical arguments are contrasted with the reasonableness and freedom possible in friendships not rooted in human love. After Phaedrus has read the speech, Socrates critiques it for its focus on the delight it has engendered, to the detriment of its ideas: "....it struck me as an extravagant performance, to demonstrate his ability to say the same thing twice, in different words but with equal success."[12] This is, of course, precisely what Sophists claimed as teachers of eloquence, but in the mouth of Socrates it becomes an accusation.

Socrates offers to improve on Lysias' speech by exercising greater control of meaning through dialectics, and particularly by defining love according to genus and species. This first speech[13] begins with a prayer, an appeal to the Muses for inspiration, for the "divine madness" about which he will presently argue to touch him; in fact, the speech will turn out not to have been inspired, and Socrates will repudiate it. But the prayer is important because it is a rhetorical device that creates a story and an affective context for the speech. The speech begins with an exercise in dialectics, coming to a definition by genus and species, making love a particular case of the general definition; the speech, rather than an inductive series of examples, consists of one explanatory syllogism. But Socrates, even as he remains dialectical, becomes more "dithyrambic," building affect onto the logical argumentation to strengthen the conviction of the hearer. There follows a series of conclusions derived from the lover's self-centered quest for pleasure over the genuine good of the other, which makes love a poor basis for friendship. Twice during the speech, Socrates interrupts himself to flag the fact that he is being unnecessarily (embarrassingly?) rhetorical and poetic, breaking the affective spell.

Having "improved" on Lysias' speech by employing dialectical control of meaning, Socrates completely reverses himself and repudiates this first speech,[14] stating that he must now atone for sinning against

---

12 Plato, *Phaedrus* 235a5.

13 Ibid., starting at 237a9.

14 Cf 242e1 ff.

the truth of love. He then pronounces a second speech[15] that distinguishes between the madness that lowers one into pleasure, and the madness that elevates one to spiritual perfection. Love is a madness sent from heaven for the advantage of lover and beloved, fraught with the highest bliss. The goal of human life is the regaining of communion with divine truth which the soul had. By cultivating the virtues and true intellectual contemplation, the soul is perfected: "For a soul does not return to the place whence she came for ten thousand years, since in no less time can she regain her wings, save only his soul who has sought after wisdom unfeignedly, or *has conjoined his passion for a loved one with that seeking.*"[16] Beauty, particularly the beauty of the beloved, reminds us of the true forms, since beauty is the strongest memory we have of the divine glory we beheld before falling into a body; beauty is thus the strongest trigger to a life dedicated to wisdom. The whole process of befriending another in an authentic way serves the spiritual development of the lover. Interestingly, this paean to the supremacy of philosophical truth is an extended rhetorical allegory rather than a syllogism.

This second speech raises the question, "What makes for good or bad writing and discourse?" If dialectic can be used in a false speech and rhetoric in a true, what is the status of rhetoric and its claims to receive and mediate meaning and value authentically? It is not speech writing in itself that is shameful, but speaking and writing shamefully and badly. The dialogue proceeds to attack the claims of rhetoric to be an art at all: it is truth that persuades and not the "knack" that embellishes a speech. Dialecticians have the art of defining and bringing things under a single view, which gives speeches consistency and lucidity. Nevertheless, anyone

> ...who seriously proffers a scientific rhetoric will, in the first place, describe the soul very precisely.... And secondly he will describe what natural capacities it has to act upon what, and through what means, or by what it can be acted upon.... Thirdly, he will classify the types of discourse and the types of soul, and the various ways in which souls are affected, explaining the reasons in each case, suggesting the type of speech appropriate to each type of soul, and

---

15 Ibid., beginning at 244a1.

16 Ibid., 248e6. Italics added for emphasis.

showing what kind of speech can be relied on to create belief in one soul and disbelief in another, and why.[17]

The *Phaedrus* captures the conflict between dialectic and rhetoric from the point of view of dialectic, but Plato's discussion creates the agenda for much of the development that follows. His own idealized rhetoric is "intended primarily for one-on-one communication" and "is clearly highly unrealistic if applied to public address."[18] Nevertheless the dialogue connects rhetoric with questions of received patterns of meaning and value and how they give rise to feelings as apprehensions of that value. Though Plato wants to place the emphasis on dialectic as the source of access to truth, he crafts the dialogue with a clear awareness of the need to communicate through analogy, story, image, and appeals to affect in order to convince his audience. The discussion of material beauty and its ability to open us to truth shows an awareness of the aesthetic-dramatic operator's capacity to orient our human knowing and loving authentically, even if they can be misused by the orator.

5. ARISTOTLE'S ON RHETORIC

Scholars of late antiquity and during the Middle Ages tended to classify rhetoric as part of the *organa*, the methods and tools applicable to all study. They received this tendency from Aristotle, who tried in his *On Rhetoric* to "adapt the principles of Plato's philosophical rhetoric to more realistic situations" of public speaking.[19] For Aristotle, rhetoric is a mixture of things: it is partly a method; it is partly a practical art derived from ethics and politics; it is partly a *scientia* that yields the ability to discern the available means of persuasion in any given speech situation. The treatment of rhetoric is more positive than in the *Phaedrus*, and partly meets the exigences for a scientific rhetoric articulated by Socrates at the end of the dialogue. Aristotle's treatment is also progressive: he begins with a short account of rhetoric as method, followed by a treatment of the theoretical aspects of rhetoric; this is followed by an extended exploration of the practical aspects and ethical and political purpose of rhetoric, followed by a study of productive aspects for making speeches.

---

17 Ibid., 271a5 ff.

18 Kennedy, "Introduction", *On Rhetoric*, 15.

19 Ibid.

For Aristotle, discourse signifies by means of three forms of mediation: first, the content of the speech, its strictly formal meaning communicating ideas; second, the elemental power of words to cause emotional responses in an audience, either by their affective associations, their material qualities (for example, the beauty of their sound), or their cultural associations; and third, the ability of the orator to communicate his own moral goodness to the audience. We will take up each of these in turn, but it is important to note right away that Aristotle's concern moves beyond Plato's to discuss rhetoric's ability to control elemental meaning with respect to judgment: the judgments we come to when we are pleased and friendly are different from those we reach when we are angry and ill-disposed.[20] The orator, whether he is engaging in political or judicial discourse, seeks to help dispose his audience to make certain kinds of judgments and decisions for their own good or the common good of the *polis*.

One of the strengths of Aristotle's proposal for rhetoric is its focus on cultural intervention, political science and the common good, and questions of public and private justice. Book one, chapters four to eight, focus on deliberative rhetoric and outline the practical knowledge of political and ethical good and evil that the orator needs to be effective and help an audience make good judgments. Chapters ten to fifteen of the same book, which address judicial rhetoric, include a discussion of what gives people pleasure, and what pleasure itself is in the mind, in a way useful to speaking to jurors and judges.

It is in book two, chapters two to eleven, that we find the most extensive discussion of the link between speech and the emotional states of an audience. These emotions, Aristotle tells us, are "all those feelings that so change men as to affect their judgments, and that are also attended by pain or pleasure." Aristotle proposes to study the emotions under three headings, the state of mind of the one experiencing the emotion, the one towards whom the emotion is experienced, and on what grounds we experience the emotion.[21] This is followed in chapters twelve to seventeen with an extensive account of the types of human character, the relation of character to emotional states and to moral qualities, and how all of this relates to the communication of one's own moral goodness to the audience. The entire discussion from

---

20 Aristotle, *On Rhetoric* 1356a15.

21 *On Rhetoric* 1378a20-30.

book one through to the end of book two, chapter seventeen, is characterized as the "manner and means of investing speeches with moral character."[22] Book two ends with an exploration of the general "topics" or argument structures common to all forms of oratory. These are general structures of ordinary meaningfulness that can serve as lines of argument: Amplification (the greatness or smallness of goods), which is most useful in ceremonial address; the Past, most useful in judicial speeches; and the Possible and Impossible, most useful to political speaking.[23] This material is covered in chapters eighteen to twenty. We should pay special attention to chapter twenty-one, which explores the use of maxims in enthymemes (the rhetorical syllogism). A maxim is a statement of a general kind that reflects common opinion or is clear at a glance; it may require some kind of proof if it is controversial or the subject of dispute, but it is clearly an instance of ordinary meaningfulness. Aristotle's comments on the use of maxims are worth an extended citation:

> The use of maxims is appropriate only to elderly men, and in handling subjects in which the speaker is experienced. For a young man to use them is – like telling stories – unbecoming; to use them in handling things in which one has no experience is silly and ill-bred, a fact sufficiently proved by the special fondness of country fellows for striking out maxims, and their readiness to air them…. Even hackneyed and commonplace maxims are to be used, if they suit one's purpose: just because they are commonplace, everyone seems to agree with them, and therefore they are taken for truth.[24]

The importance of maxims is that

> …people love to hear stated in general terms what they already believe in some particular connection…. [Maxims] invest a speech with moral character. There is moral character in every speech in which the moral purpose is conspicuous: and maxims always produce this effect, because the utterance of them amounts to a general declaration of moral principles: so that if the maxims are sound, they display the speaker as a man of sound moral character.[25]

---

22 Ibid., 1391b21.

23 Ibid., 1392a4-8.

24 Ibid., 1395a3-12.

25 Ibid., 1395b5-17.

This analysis takes us well into the realm of the complexities of ordinary meaningfulness, its connection with intersubjectivity and with the incarnate and aesthetic-dramatic sources and carriers of elemental meaning.

Book three discusses the productive aspects of making or writing a speech. Here, we find out that there is such a thing as verbal beauty, which is carried "in the sound or in the sense" of words and phrases.[26] Aristotle also shows awareness, in his discussion of "urbanities" in chapter ten of book three, of the power of words to evoke images that produce insight. Urbanity is that quality of speeches that creates "quick learning in our minds." While this quality comes most readily from well constructed enthymemes, it can also come from making contrasts, from metaphor, by means of "bringing-before-the-eyes," that is, visualization or actualization.[27]

Aristotle's discussion of rhetoric, like Plato's, tries to link the control of meaning first to dialectic and formal meaningfulness, and only then to surplus elemental meaning as an adjunct to persuasion. Nevertheless, his exploration shows a concern to understand and make responsible use of many of the various sources and carriers of elemental meaning, including feelings, and is particularly sophisticated in the area of ordinary meaningfulness and its reception and transmission. Nevertheless, Kennedy points out, Aristotle fails to grasp that epideictic rhetoric, the rhetoric of praise and blame and of ceremonial speechmaking, also plays a key role "in the instilling, preservation, and enhancement of cultural values, even though this was clearly a major function" of rhetoric even in Greece.[28] It will be the contribution of Cicero to bring this function of public speech into the fold of rhetorical *scientia*.

6. THE CONTEXT OF ROMAN ELOQUENCE

Rome splits the tradition of eloquence it receives from Greece into two streams: that of the *rhetores*, the teachers of rhetoric whose art is generally depreciated, and that of the *oratores*, the great political orators and leaders of civic parties, whose art is understood to be elevated and refined in comparison with that of the rhetors. The Romans (and

---

26   Ibid., 1405b9.

27   Ibid., 1410b20 ff.

28   Kennedy, "Introduction", 22.

Cicero will be no different) believe that their culture, though dependent on the Greek achievements, is superior in that it is the culture of
the *citizen*, preparing men (and generally only men of the aristocracy)
for action in society. Such culture integrates *sapientia* and gives it a
meaning and a goal in history.[29]

Rome has created a civilization of *mores* rather than simply of arts.
Rome's wisdom resides in its laws and institutions. These are the essential constituents of its culture, and the orator's wisdom is drawn
from them, from the *mores* of the *civitas* as much as from the art of
the rhetors. There is a long development behind this. The *oratores belli*,
those charged with the solemn proclamation of war, are among the
earliest surviving examples of orators in Roman culture. Their role is
one of public ritual, bearing religious and juridical efficacy and meaning within the political and cosmological spheres.

Ambassadors negotiating peace or deciding war on behalf of the city
are likewise orators: "Herald, ambassador, the orator is also simply the
one who speaks in an official capacity…. In fact, one of the principal
functions of senators [in the republic] was that of the orator."[30] Being
an orator was a civic function acquired during one's civic formation:
after proving oneself as a warrior in the army and before becoming
a general and then a senator, one took the office of orator. This office included public prayer and public speaking during civic worship.
Cato was the first to link the functions and the art of the orator, in
his famous definition *orator est vir bonus dicendi peritus* (the orator
is a good man who knows how to speak):[31] the orator has mastery of
the techniques of public speaking but is first and foremost one whose
personal resourcefulness and moral quality directs his speaking to and
for the common good of the city and to and for its moral and religious
development.

From very early on, Roman civic culture was aware of and cultivated the social and religious role of literature and epideictic discourse.
There is a sacred literature by means of which Rome meditates on its

---

29 I am beholden, in much of this section and the next, to the work of Alain
Michel of the Sorbonne and his many works on ancient and medieval rhetoric in relation to Christian liturgy and poetics. Of particular relevance
here is his *Les rapports de la rhétorique et de la philosophie dans l'oeuvre de
Cicéron* (Peeters: Louvain, 2003) in its second edition.

30 Michel, *Les rapports*, 7. All translations are mine.

31 Michel, 11.

destiny. It is precisely this form of cultural meditation that Augustine will seek to displace in the *City of God*. For the Roman, eloquence serves both gods and human beings: the orator has juridical and religious roles uniting *fortuna* and *virtus*, pleading always before both gods and people.

6.1 CICERO'S QUEST FOR A SCIENTIFIC RHETORIC

In the years immediately prior to Cicero's public career, the Roman state suffered serious challenges to its republican ideal and saw the birth of the empire. The eloquence Rome prized so highly had facilitated the ascendancy of tyrants, and once these were overthrown, Roman society found it difficult to restore balance between the classes. In Cicero's day, the problem of eloquence takes a particular form, that of how to achieve peaceful and just relations between the people – particularly the equestrian class – and the Senate. We have the evidence of the *Rhetorica ad Herennium* for this. This anonymous work published just as Cicero was finishing his formal education, and once thought to have been penned by him, is one of the important sources for our understanding of both the self-questioning undertaken by the senatorial milieu on eloquence and public leadership and the state of rhetoric in Cicero's day. This text also has the earliest account of memory training which we possess. The account shows a great deal of sophistication in understanding how memory works and how the symbolic operator can be cultivated. There is also quite a developed understanding of the relationship between sounds and the receptivity of an audience to a message. There is the wonderful example, in book four, given as an example of the unpleasant collision of sounds: *O Tite, tute, Tati, tibi tanta, tyranne, tulisti* ("Thyself to thyself, Titus Tatius the tyrant, thou tookest those terrible troubles," from Ennius).[32] The author of the text is attentive to the whole complex of the production of meaning, well beyond the mere lexical meaning of words. Much of the latter part of Cicero's own *De inventione* is in the same vein.

One of Cicero's earliest questions was "How can it be that eloquence, which is made to preserve peace and is linked to wisdom, can have at times such destructive social effects?"[33] For Cicero, eloquence "is iden-

---

32 *Rhetorica ad Herennium*, bk IV, par. 18. Translated here by Warmington. Loeb Classical Library, 1954. Lacus Curtius, http://penelope.uchicago.edu/Thayer/E/Roman/Texts/Rhetorica_ad_Herennium/4A*.html

33 Michel, 49.

tical to wisdom. This means that it cannot be false and that it obeys the laws of reason. In this it imitates dialectics. But eloquence is more fruitful and better adapted to the passions of the soul."[34] Unlike Aristotle, Cicero does not believe that the passions modify or amplify dialectic; they condition its very means of expression. The passions have a double role in eloquence: they convey meaning through style and thought, context and form. With Cicero "the theory of the passions in oratory changes its character. It is no longer a question of juggling human passions, but rather of finding in them the truth that underlies the appearances. All passions are judgments about the beneficial," the beautiful, and the proper (the *honestus*).[35] With Cicero, the study of the passions in relation to language has the double purpose of "meaning" the good into existence in both speaker and hearer. The extensive classification of techniques of argument according to circumstances becomes an examination of the performative effects of language, elemental meaning in its dramatic and constitutive dimensions.

The *De Inventione* begins with an account of the way in which eloquence creates the political environment and brings about the basic institutions of the state, along with its function in the moral and social formation of citizens. This is followed with an account of why eloquence goes awry, namely that techniques of speech are acquired without wisdom: "and hence it arose, and it is no wonder that it did, when rash and audacious men had seized on the helm of the republic, that great and terrible disasters occurred."[36] This is followed by an extended discussion of the duty and end of eloquence. All this is a rather novel beginning, insisting on the moral status of both the speaker and the speaking, and discussing the pedagogical character of the art of eloquence. Cicero makes the purpose and character of the orator more central to the study of eloquence and firmly anchors the control of meaning, not in dialectic or grammar, but in the moral character of the speaker.

Cicero pursues the same stance in the *De Oratore*, written later in his career. This work in three dialogues seeks nothing less than a refounding of rhetoric as a science. It features three dialogues over three

---

34 Ibid., 238.

35 Ibid., 243.

36 Marcus Tullius Cicero, *De Inventione*, translated by C.D. Yonge (Kessinger Publishing Reprints, 2001), 7.

days, with Lucius Crassus taking over the role of Socrates from the *Phaedrus.* The Greek ideal of contemplation as a source of wisdom is replaced with the common quest for wisdom in the human converse made possible by hours of leisure: "What in hours of ease can be a pleasanter thing or one more characteristic of culture, than discourse that is graceful and nowhere *rudis?* For the one point in which we have our very greatest advantage over the brute creation is that we hold converse one with another, and can reproduce our thoughts in words."[37] Eloquence, not dialectic, is the foundation of human knowing and wisdom. Ethics, the branch of philosophy concerned "with human life and conduct... must all of it be mastered by the orator."[38] Law must be studied for similar reasons, as the science of social morality: "to have our passions in subjection, bridle every lust, hold what we have, and keep our thoughts, eyes, and hands from what is our neighbour's."[39]

Throughout the dialogues, Crassus models the essential virtues of the orator, particularly the diffidence and humility that distinguishes the genuine orator from the rhetor who sells his services: modesty bears witness to the speaker's integrity.[40] The one who knows the whole of rhetoric knows more than tricks; the orator knows the whole speech situation in all its terms and relations: "For the better the orator, the more profoundly is he frightened of the difficulty of speaking, and of the doubtful fate of a speech, and of the anticipations of an audience."[41]

Cicero mediates a second breakthrough – whether it is his or that of Roman culture is not relevant here – namely the focus of eloquence on *inventio*, the "conceiving of topics either true or probable, which make one's case appear probable."[42] For Cicero, this is the most important

---

37 Cicero, *De Oratore*, Loeb Classical Library (Harvard: Harvard University Press, 1948), 25. E. Sutton, the translator, renders *rudis* as "uninstructed", but this is too narrow: the *rudes* are the uncultured bumpkins whose existence is scarcely distinguishable, in the Roman mind, from that of brute animals, and thus the significant parallel with brute creation in the next sentence.

38 *De Oratore*, 51.

39 Ibid., 135.

40 See especially 81 ff.

41 Ibid., 85.

42 *De Inventione*, 11.

task facing the orator: discovering which form of argument best captures the situation. The form of argument here is not the outer word of delivery, but the inner grasp of the complex of terms and relations that makes the case in question meaningful.[43] *Inventio* is a process of inquiry to determine the facts, the name (or nature) of the issue, its importance or moral character, and the fittingness of pleading a case or not. It issues forth in a statement of the case. Some statements are simple, capturing one plain question; others are complex and summarize several questions or topics of inquiry, or involve comparisons. These require further inquiry, including a determination of the kind of reasoning required, either general or exegetical.[44] Cicero transforms the structures of argument into names for operations of inquiry that uncover meaning. He repeats this and makes it even clearer in the *De Oratore*, where in the context of the second book he has Marcus Antonius describe his own practice in "getting up a case."[45] We are presented with an extended inquiry into the operations of the subject as sources and carriers of meaning.

6.2 AUGUSTINE'S *DE DOCTRINA CHRISTIANA*

Augustine will develop Cicero's focus on the importance of *inventio* and devote three quarters of the *De Doctrina Christiana* (DDC) to the quest for uncovering meaning authentically, but "in the *DDC* what is being invented has changed and the circumstances and aims of the inventing have changed."[46] For Aristotle, *inventio* was concerned mainly with the discovery of the technical means of persuasion pertinent to the case at hand, be they logical, affective, or ethical. For Cicero, *inventio* is of those true or probable arguments that will make one's case plausible. When one treats documents, one is concerned to discover how best to argue about their interpretation, not "how to arrive at a true or

---

43 The *gestalt* in von Balthasar's sense.

44 *De Inventione*, 11-18.

45 *De Oratore*, book II, beginning at page 219. This presentation is quite long and proceeds in two large sections: from section 30-216 and then again from 290-306. Between 216 and 290, there is a long discussion of wit and witticisms which, while it is a partial digression into questions of style, is not completely separate from issues of *inventio*, since it has to do with aesthetic-dramatic operations in the speaker and the audience.

46 Gerald A. Press, "The Subject and Structure of Augustine's *De Doctrina Christiana*," *Augustinian Studies* 11 (1980), 119.

correct interpretation... Augustine's use of the gerundive *intellegenda* [in his treatment of *inventio*], however, affirms that there is such an interpretation, and that it is this that is to be discovered."[47] Where classical and particularly Roman rhetoric had first functioned in law courts, the senate, and the temple as a set of tools for going about society's business, and as a mechanism for transmitting social values, in later Roman antiquity it had become the basis for entertainment. "The aim of [Augustine's] rhetoric.... is to discover the truth in texts.... Thus rhetoric is reborn as an important social force. Christianity is self-consciously a new society, a new EKKLESIA; and like Judaism and Islam, a distinctly verbal religion based on a book. To propagate the religion is to extend the society and to do the society's business, because the essence and spirit of the new society is its religion."[48] We must understand the *doctrina* of the title very broadly: "*Doctrina* has a range of logically related meanings, of which the most general and inclusive is 'learning' as a cultural ideal, and.... Augustine, an accomplished rhetorician, deliberately and artfully uses that variety of meanings in order, at once, to refute the pagan ideal and construct a Christian version of it."[49] Christian *doctrina* is different from, opposed to and superior to the *doctrina gentilium*, "and its superiority is expressed as its sanity, its spiritual soundness.... The fundamental meaning of *doctrina* in the *DDC* is the most general among those mentioned earlier – the cultural ideal of 'learning', 'erudition', or 'knowledge' – but importantly, it is this ideal understanding as including the narrower meanings, that is, teaching activity, content taught, and discipline or school."[50]

This can be seen particularly in book one where Augustine treats the truth to be understood in the Scriptures. But he not only tells us what is to be understood by us in the treatment of the Scriptures, he also shows us *how God teaches us, particularly in the Incarnation,* giving us a model to imitate when we put across to others what we have understood. Augustine compares the Incarnation to a form of preaching; actually, he states that it *is* a form of preaching: "So why did [wisdom] come, when she was already here, if not because it was God's

---

47 Press, 120.

48 Ibid., 121-122.

49 Press, "*Doctrina* in Augustine's *De Doctrina Christiana,*" *Philosophy and Rhetoric* 17/2 (1984): 99.

50 Ibid., 111.

pleasure through the folly of the preaching to save those who believe? How did she come, if not by the Word becoming flesh and dwelling amongst us? It is something like when we talk; in order for what we have in mind to reach the minds of our hearers through their ears of flesh, the word which we have in our thoughts becomes a sound, and is called speech."[51] Thus, incarnate and intersubjective eloquence becomes foundational and underlies the texts to be interpreted.

Augustine makes *love* the goal of all understanding. In doing so, he shifts the entire goal of understanding towards choice, decision, and relationship. This is practical knowing in the Roman tradition, rather than pure speculation, and it makes the quest to discover the true meaning of the Scriptures a key moment in personal formation, in *eruditio* or "un-ruding." But now becoming cultured and eloquent means becoming loving as Christ was. Where Plato saw love as an adjunct to reason, Augustine makes it the goal, the very basis of authentic meaning and value in the world.

Augustine's shift of the focus of *inventio* to the task of finding, not just any interpretation, but the true interpretation of the scriptural text requires that he import into rhetoric insights and techniques from the discipline of grammar. This is the theory of signs and things: what distinguishes those things that are signs from those things that are not signs is the ability of particular natural or conventional things to trigger in the mind a relation of meaning to other things. This meaningful relation, in a text or in the world, can be of many kinds. The treatment of meaning remains rhetorical, even as rhetoric is made more "scientific" by tools appropriated from grammar. Here, for example, is Augustine's presentation of the evocative power of a metaphor in the Song of Songs, where he takes the beauty of the beloved's teeth as referring to the example of the lives of the saints in the Church: "I find it more delightful to contemplate the saints" and their work in the body of Christ through this metaphor, so that "what is not in dispute… is both that one gets to know things more enjoyably through such comparisons, and also that discovering things is more gratifying if there has been some difficulty in the search for them."[52] The strictly textual interrelations discovered by grammar are augmented by a consideration of the effects of meaning on the knower, including affect as

51 Augustine, *De Doctrina Christiana* (New York, New City Press, 1996), 111.

52 Augustine, *DDC*, 131-132.

apprehension of value. The full meaning of the passage is grounded in
the authenticity of the person, as for Cicero, but now the relation of
personal authenticity and external signification is grounded in a relation of inner and outer self, of an inner and outer word. Thus, through
an appropriation of Cicero's development of *inventio* and the centrality
of personal virtue with a more profound grasp of Platonic psychology,
insights gained from the Christian Scriptures into the role of divine
love and the Incarnation, and an importing of tools from grammar,
Augustine develops a Christian rhetoric that unites all of the sources
and carriers of elemental meaning in one view for the first time in antiquity.

7. CONCLUSION

Augustine's rhetorical program for the re-invention of Christian
culture sets the stage for subsequent developments in the Christian
appropriation of rhetoric as a science of elemental meaning. The teaching of the trivium, of course, remains the foundation of education in
the Middle Ages. Monastic practice will receive Cicero and Augustine
as a set of principles for the activity of making thoughts in prayer, as
Mary Carruthers has shown in her study of medieval monastic *lectio
divina*.[53] The university division of theological praxis into *lectio, quaestio*, and *praedicatio* will replicate the divisions of the trivium, but in the
hands of an Aquinas, for example, rhetoric will form part of the tasks
of a systematics under the sign of the *quaestio*, providing elemental
meaning with a key role within the *scientia* of theology.[54]

This essay has traced a line of development in rhetoric that begins
with Plato and culminates with Augustine's *De Doctrina Christiana*.
This line of development has moved towards holding all the sources
and carriers of elemental meaning in a single view, empowered by the
Christian worldview of the incarnate intersubjective meaning of Jesus the Christ as foundational for all elemental, linguistic, and textual
mediations of meaning. With Augustine, rhetoric becomes the methodological ground of what has often been called a sacramental world-

---

53 Cf *The Book of Memory* and *The Craft of Thought*.

54 Cf my *Embracing Wisdom: the Summa Theologiae as a Christoform Pedagogy of Spiritual Exercises*, dissertation (Regis College: 2003); see also the
groundbreaking study of arguments of *convenientia* as aesthetic-dramatic
arguments by Gilbert Narcisse, *Les Raisons de Dieu* (Fribourg: Editions
Universitaires, 1997).

view. This sacramental view remains the dominant Christian horizon through the whole of the Middle Ages. It moves into spirituality and spiritual theology after the great divorce between spirituality and systematics and flourishes in writers such as Ignatius of Loyola, Teresa of Avila, and other great spiritual writers. An author such as Saint Francis de Sales will attempt a reconciliation that proves to be ahead of its time.

Robert Doran, in the article on empirical consciousness as reception cited at the beginning of this essay, relates the story of a conversation he had with Lonergan when he first began puzzling over von Balthasar's notion of "seeing the form." To Doran's query about von Balthasar, Lonergan replies with a simple question: "You're Catholic, aren't you?" In light of our study of the development of ancient rhetoric as a method for the reception and responsible mediation of elemental meaning, we can appreciate how well Doran has replied to that question in *his* retrieval of elemental meaning for systematics.

BERNARD LONERGAN'S EARLY FORMULATION OF THE FOUNDATIONAL *NEXUS MYSTERIORUM* IN GOD'S SELF COMMUNICATION IN CREATION

H. Daniel Monsour
LONERGAN RESEARCH INSTITUTE

I. INTRODUCTION

There is ample evidence that Bernard Lonergan's proposal in Question 26 of *De Deo Trino: pars systematica* specifying the four immediate, formal external terms that are both conditions consequent upon the Father's sending of the Son and the Father and Son's sending of the Holy Spirit and created participations in or imitations of the four real divine relations can be traced back earlier than 1957, the year in which *Divinarum personarum*, the precursor to *De Deo Trino: pars systematica*, was published *ad usum audiorium*.[1] A document in the Lonergan Archives, LP II-30, A 205, contains a typed page-and-a-quarter in Latin in which Lonergan, in an almost incidental way, first makes what is recognizably the same proposal as that found in *Divinarum personarum* and repeated in *De Deo Trino: pars systematica* and then enlarges upon the *convenientia* of the proposal briefly – but still to an extent that is unmatched elsewhere in his writings. And what is perhaps even more noteworthy, in this document Lonergan is discussing directly neither the Trinity nor the divine missions but sanctifying grace.

---

1 See Bernard Lonergan, *The Triune God: Systematics*, trans. from *De Deo Trino: pars systematica* (1964) by Michael G. Shields, vol. 12 in Collected Works of Bernard Lonergan, ed. Robert M. Doran and H. Daniel Monsour (Toronto: University of Toronto Press, 2007), 470-73. The same Latin text that appears on pp. 470, 472 of *The Triune God: Systematics* appeared originally in *Divinarum personarum conceptionem analogicam evolvit Bernardus Lonergan S.I.* (Rome: Gregorian University Press, 1957), 214.

The document bears the title, *De Gratia Sanctificante. Supplementum.*[2] Lonergan and another Jesuit, Elmer O'Brien, taught a course called *De Gratia Sanctificante; De Virtutibus* at Regis College, Toronto, in 1951-1952. Evidence in the Lonergan Archives indicates that the over forty pages of unevenly spaced Latin text which make up the document are the notes Lonergan prepared for this course. The document, then, precedes the appearance of *Divinarum personarum* by at least five years. And as the same proposal that Lonergan makes in Question 26 of *Divinarum personarum* is contained in the document, we can conclude that he had the proposal in mind as least five years prior to its publication in *Divinarum personarum*.[3]

On the title page of *De Gratia Sanctificante*, Lonergan divides the discussion to follow into three main sections: a brief historical sketch on the development and subsequent distortion of the theological notion of habitual grace, considered primarily as "the first intrinsic principle whereby we become living members of the mystical body of Christ," temples of the Holy Spirit, "and are raised up to a new supernatural life, and are capable of acts that are meritorious in the sight of God"; a summary of the positive doctrine of the New Testament on the state of the just, presented by elaborating upon the various parts of an initially stated thesis[4]; a section entitled 'Intelligentia fidei' in which questions are raised about the nature of habitual grace and some answers are suggested. This last section has six parts. There are

---

2 In what follows, I make use of the 2003 translation of the document by Michael G. Shields. If a text from the document is quoted, I shall indicate in which section or in which part of a section it can be found.

3 It may be premature to claim as certain that *De Gratia Sanctificante. Supplementum* is the earliest place in Lonergan's surviving writings in which the foundational *nexus mysteriorum* in God's self-communication in creation proposed in Question 26 of *Divinarum personarum* and *De Deo Trino: pars systematica* is to be found. Indeed, it has yet to be established definitively that no one prior to Lonergan made the same or a similar proposal.

4 The thesis reads: "To those whom God the Father loves (1) as he loves Jesus, his only-begotten Son, (2) he gives the uncreated Gift of the Holy Spirit, so that (3) into a new life they may be (4) born again and (5) become living members of Christ; therefore as (6) just, (7) friends of God, (8) adopted children of God, and (9) heirs in hope of eternal life, (10) they come to a sharing in the divine nature." The aim of the thesis, Lonergan says, "to set forth clearly and synthetically the positive teaching on sanctifying grace."

some discrepancies between the headings of these parts as listed on the title page of the document and as they appear in the body of the text, but as listed on the title page the parts are headed: '*Problema*'; '*Notiones*'; '*Fundamentum ontologicum*'; '*Effectus formales et immanentes*'; '*Effectus formales et transcendentales*'; '*Corollaria.*' Not surprisingly, the aforementioned page-and-a-quarter is found in the third part of the third section, which in the body of the text is headed, '*De Fundamento Gratiae Ontologico.*'

2. THE FOUR PREEMINENT GRACES

In this third part of the third section of *De Gratia Sanctificante*, Lonergan identifies four graces "that are preeminently qualified to be called such": the grace of union, the light of glory, sanctifying grace and the virtue of charity. Every other grace, he says, is either a predisposition towards these graces or consequent upon them.

In an earlier document, *De ente supernaturali*, Lonergan distinguished between absolutely supernatural acts that are formally supernatural and absolutely supernatural acts that are virtually supernatural.[5] Second acts in the accidental order, operations, are absolutely supernatural if they exceed the proportion of any finite substance whatsoever. Such acts are also formally supernatural if through them one attains God as he is in himself and in his entirety, and so not merely as God is imitable outside himself and not just in some respect. There are two such acts: the beatific vision of the blessed in heaven,[6] and the act of charity, whether it be the charity that precedes the beatific vision or the specifically same charity that is consequent upon the vision.[7] The

5 This distinction is introduced in the first excursus to Thesis 3 of *De ente supernaturali*.

6 In the course of the discussion of Thesis 1 of *De ente supernaturali*, Lonergan writes: "The blessed in heaven have a direct intuitive vision of God as he is in himself. It is God they see, not any created thing; they see all of God though not exhaustively, that is, as perfectly as God sees himself." For more on this, see Thomas Aquinas, *Summa theologiae*, 1, q. 12, a. 7.

7 Lonergan refers to this "specifically same charity" that is consequent upon the beatific vision in *Collected Works of Bernard Lonergan*, vol. 3, *Insight: A Study of Human Understanding*, ed. Frederick E. Crowe and Robert M. Doran (Toronto: University of Toronto Press, 1992; reprint edition 2005), 747, when he speaks of the "charity [that is] the transport, the ecstasy and unbounded intimacy that result from the communication of the absolute love that is God himself and alone can respond to the vision of God."

proximate principles of such acts are, respectively, the light of glory, "the supernatural disposition ... added to the intellect," enabling the intellect to see the essence of God,[8] and the habit (*habitus*) or virtue of charity.

Besides proximate principles, there are also the remote principles of such acts, the principles that give rise to the proximate principles of the acts. Primarily, the remote principle of such acts, Lonergan says in discussing the first thesis of *De ente supernaturale*, is the grace of union, that is, the created, contingent reality through which one can truly say that this man Jesus Christ is God. In a secondary sense, the remote principle of such acts is sanctifying grace.

The distinction between remote and proximate principles, at least where sanctifying grace is being considered as a remote principle, draws on the analogy with nature that Lonergan calls 'natural proportion' or 'parity of relations.' Thus, one can argue that if substance stands to the act of existence as accidental potency stands to operation, then substance stands to accidental potency as the act of existence stands to operation.[9] Or, as Lonergan puts it in discussing the first thesis of *De ente supernaturali*, accidental potencies, the proximate principle of operations, arise from substance, the remote principle, as operation follows the act of existence.

The *order* among the remote principles is based on the fact that only Christ, as God and man, possesses both the beatific vision and charity by right. No one else can claim as a right the vision and love of God that attain God as he is in himself. Now those who exercise operations that attain God as he is in himself possess the proximate principles of these operations, namely, the light of glory possessed by the blessed in heaven, and the habit of charity. Equally, they possess the secondary remote principle of such operations, namely, sanctifying grace. Christ as man, however, having the grace of union, thereby possesses sanctifying grace by right, as the natural Son of God, as the beloved Son of the Father. All others who come to possess sanctifying grace, the secondary remote principle of operations that attain God as he is in himself, possess it as a *gift* on account of Christ. And on account of Christ, they are born into a new life to become living members of

---

8 See Thomas Aquinas, *Summa theologiae*, 1, q. 12, a. 5 c.

9 If A stands to B as C stands to D, then by *alternando* A stands to C as B stands to D.

Christ, righteous, friends of God, adopted children of God, heirs of eternal life in hope of sharing in the divine nature.[10]

The light of glory and the habit of charity are graces in a preeminent sense because they are the respective proximate principles of the two acts or operations that are both absolutely supernatural and formally supernatural: they are the two acts or operations in which rational creatures attain God as he is in himself and in his entirety. Sanctifying grace is also grace in a preeminent sense because in the just it is the proximate principle of the light of glory and the habit of charity and the secondary remote principle of the beatific vision and acts of charity. Finally, the grace of union, the created, contingent, finite reality required in order that this man Jesus Christ be really and truly God, is grace in a preeminent sense. For the vision and love of God, along with their remote and proximate principles, were his by right because he is the beloved Son of the Father by nature and not by adoption, and every grace given to the just is Christ's grace, from whose fullness we have received "grace upon grace" (John 1:16).

3. 'GRATIA UNIONIS' AND 'GRACE OF THE ESSE SE-CUNDARIUM INCARNATIONIS'

Lonergan mentions sanctifying grace, the light of glory, and the habit of charity in Question 26 of *Divinarum personarum*. He does not, however, mention the grace of union, at least not by that name. Instead, he speaks of the *esse secundarium incarnationis*, the secondary act of existence of the incarnation, a category introduced by Thomas Aquinas in the fourth article of the short work *Quaestio disputata de unione Verbi incarnate* and mentioned nowhere else in his writings.

The grace of union, Lonergan says at the beginning of the third part of section three of *De Gratia Sanctificante*, "is that finite entity received in the humanity of Christ so that it exists through the personal existence of the divine Word. This grace is therefore the extrinsic term whereby one may say, 'The Word was made flesh.'" Peter Lombard, it seems, was the first to speak expressly of 'gratia unionis' in reference to Christ, though Abelard and Gilbert of Poitiers, and their schools, taught the doctrine earlier. Among authors of the twelfth century, 'gratia unionis' commonly referred to God's activity in effecting the union of divinity and humanity in the person of the Son of God. But after

---

10 Here, I am echoing Lonergan's phrasing in his thesis from the second section of *De Gratia Sanctificante*. See note 4 above.

William of Auxerre's example, it seems that the term began to be used more and more to refer to the union so effected.[11]

After the twelfth century, 'gratia unionis' became an established category in Catholic theology. The 'esse secundarium incarnationis,' however, remained controversial, even among Thomists. For a considerable period, the authenticity of *Quaestio disputata de unione Verbi incarnate* was questioned, largely, it seems, because it was thought that what is affirmed in article 4 of this work contradicts what Thomas affirmed in parallel passages, such as *Summa theologiae*, 3, q. 17, a. 2, which are of undoubted authenticity. It has become increasingly apparent, however, that this brief work is authentic, and for some this fact only exacerbated the problem of reconciling what Thomas affirmed in article 4 of the work with what he affirmed in parallel passages. Some authors have concluded that Thomas's affirmation in article 4 is simply a mistake. Thus Albert Patfoort speaks of Thomas's '*faux pas*' in article 4 and of his '*redoutable inattention*' in the article to an essential element of the metaphysics that Thomas himself believed to be true.[12]

Three considerations, if taken together, provide, I think, a plausible explanation as to why Lonergan, when he makes the same proposal in Question 26 of *Divinarum personarum* as he had made in the third part of section three of *De Gratia Sanctificante*, shifts from speaking of '*gratia unionis*' to speaking of the '*esse secundarium incarnationis*.' First, a remark in *De constitutione Christi ontologica et psychologica* indicates that Lonergan was familiar with the aforementioned twofold use of the term '*gratia unionis*':

> ... because this secondary act of existence is absolutely supernatural, it is also a grace. However, it is not the grace of the hypostatic union as though constituting that union. The grace of union constituting the union is that sole constitutive of the union that is the infinite act of existence of the Word. Nevertheless, this secondary act of existence can be said to be the grace of union inasmuch as it is required by and consequent upon the constitutive cause of the union.[13]

11 See Walter Henry Principe, *William of Auxerre's Theology of the Hypostatic Union* (Toronto: Pontifical Institute of Mediaeval Studies, 1963), 105-106.

12 See A. Patfoort, *L'unité d'être dans le Christ d'après S. Thomas; a la croisée de l'ontologie et de la christologie* (Paris: Desclée, 1964), 185-86.

13 Bernard Lonergan, *The Ontological and Psychological Constitution of Christ*, trans. from the fourth edition of *De constitutione Christi ontologica*

Second, it is, I think, evident from Lonergan's discussion in *De constitutione Christi* that he would claim that if one distinguishes between the intrinsic constitutive reason and cause of the hypostatic union, on the one hand, and the appropriate created, contingent term required as a consequent condition for the truth of the contingent predication that the Word of God became man, on the other, the problem that weighs so heavily on Patfoort and others of reconciling what Thomas affirms in article 4 of *Quaestio disputata de unione Verbi incarnate* with what he affirms in parallel passages dissolves.[14]

Third, an accurate understanding of what is proposed in Question 26 of *Divinarum personarum* and *De Deo Trino: pars systematica* regarding the *nexus mysteriorum* in God's self-communication in creation requires that one distinguish in a precise way between that which constitutes a divine mission and the appropriate external term and consequent condition of that mission. Given the twofold use of 'gratia unionis' in theological writings, if one uses that expression when one is attempting to distinguish that which constitutes a mission from the consequent term of that mission, one runs the risk of obscuring for one's audience the very distinction one is attempting to make. The advantage, then, of speaking of the "grace of the *esse secundarium incarnationis*" instead of 'gratia unionis' is that thereby one avoids the danger of being misunderstood as referring to the gratuitous will of God which freely produces the union of divinity and humanity in the person of the Son of God. And it seems not entirely unlikely that this consideration, along with the fact that Lonergan fully endorsed Thomas's affirmation in *Quaestio disputata de unione Verbi incarnate*, prompted him in Question 26 of *Divinarum personarum* and thereafter to shift from his earlier formulation in *De Gratia Sanctificante* of speaking of

---

et psychologica by Michael G. Shields, vol. 7 in Collected Works of Bernard Lonergan (Toronto: University of Toronto Press, 2002), 148-49.

14 "No sole cause of this union [of one and the same being both God and man] have we found other than the sole act of existence that St Thomas and his followers have always recognized in Christ. Nor have we affirmed the existence of any term required by this constitutive cause other than that secondary, non-accidental act of existence that Aquinas seems to have acknowledged in his *Quaestio disputata de unione Verbi incarnati.*" Ibid. 154-55. See pp. 106-55 for Lonergan's discussion of the ontological constitution of Christ. For the role of the *esse secundarium incarnationis*, see 138-51. See also B. Lonergan, *De Verbo Incarnato*, 3rd edition (Rome: Gregorian University Press, 1964) 259-66, 323.

'*gratia unionis*' to speaking of the '*esse secundarium incarnationis*.' It was a shift in terminology for the sake of clarity and precision, not a shift in what was being proposed.

4. THE FOUNDATIONS OF THE
FOUR PREEMINENT GRACES

Lonergan is concerned in the third part of the third section of *De Gratia Sanctificante* to specify the ontological foundations of the four preeminent graces. "We have to explain, as far as possible," he writes, "why these graces are of such a high degree of perfection that they touch, in a way, subsistent being itself." In the first section of the document, and again at the end of the document, Lonergan criticizes a tendency to assume a confrontationist and conceptualist view of human knowing, which, he says, has been especially prevalent in theological writings since the period immediately prior to the Reformation. This view tends to ignore or overlook the differences between distinction and abstraction or separation and so, in practice, to eliminate that difference, and then be prone to assuming that if *B* can be distinguished from *A*, *B* can be understood without taking *A* into account. Referring to Thomas's *In Boethium de Trinitate*, q. 5, a. 3 c., Lonergan points out that although one can rightly distinguish *B* from *A*, it does not necessarily follow that *B* can be understood in abstraction or separately from *A*.[15] More particularly, although the various kinds of graces can each be distinguished from their intelligible nexuses, they cannot be properly understood apart or in separation from their intelligible nexuses, any more than foot can be understood apart or in separation from animal. Lonergan claims that at the beginning of the period he is referring to, habitual grace was frequently thought of simply an accidental spiritual entity placed in the soul by God and "separable from the whole economy of the New Testament and the whole order of re-

---

15 In another archival document, LP II-18, A 160, Lonergan explains slightly more fully the connection between conceptualism and what he calls illegitimate abstraction: "According to conceptualists, if there are distinct terms with different meanings, there are distinct concepts, and there are distinct concepts, there is a legitimate abstraction of one from the other. According to St Thomas, *In Boet.*, q. 5. a. 3 c., there is no legitimate abstraction when the line of intelligible connection is broken: father cannot be abstracted from son, because although they are two things adequately and really distinct from each other, a father is not father unless he has a child, and a son is not a son without a father."

ality" and that this mistaken position has had a detrimental influence on subsequent theological reflection.[16]

Next, Lonergan introduces the notion of exemplary causality. The divine essence can be considered as "the primary exemplary cause which absolutely every finite being, created or creatable, substantial or accidental, imitates in some respect or quality." Further, the divine essence can be also considered either as absolute and common to the three divine persons or as really identical with one or other of the real trinitarian relations, that is, with paternity, filiation, active spiration, or passive spiration.[17]

There follows Lonergan's early formulation of the proposal that one finds expressed later in Question 26 of *Divinarum personarum* and *De Deo Trino: pars systematica*:

> Prionde cum omnis substantia finita sit quaedam res absoluta, conveniens videtur dicere eam imitari divinam essentiam s[e]c[un]d[u]m quod illa essentia absolute sumatur.
>
> Cum vero quattuor gratiae eminentiores cum ipsa vita divina intime connectantur, conveniens videtur dicere eas imitari divinam essentiam s[e]c[un]d[u]m quod re identificetur cum hac vel illa reali relatione trinitaria. Et sic gratia unionis divinam paternitatem, lumen gloriae divinam filiationem, gratia sanctificans spirationem activam, virtus vero caritatis spirationem passivam imitantur et modo finito participant.

---

16 Thus, towards the end of *De Gratia Sanctificante*, in responding to a thesis he ascribes to B. Beraza, namely, that "by God's absolute power habitual grace and mortal sin can exist at the same time in the same subject," Lonergan remarks: "With regard to the ultimate basis of Beraza's opinion, see St Thomas, *In Boet de Trinitate*, 5, 3, on distinction, abstraction, and separation. There is certainly a distinction between an animal and the foot of an animal. But a foot apart from the animal is not a foot. Animal can be abstracted from foot, as the whole from the part, for an animal without a foot is still an animal. But foot cannot be abstracted from animal, for a foot apart from the animal is not a foot. Now grace in this order of reality is the grace of Christ. It is sheer incompetence and by no means an exercise in metaphysical profundity to try to understand grace as a physical entity apart from Christ the Head."

17 On this point, see Assertion 7 in Lonergan, *The Triune God: Systematics*, 256-67.

Now since every finite substance is something absolute, it seems appropriate to say that it imitates the divine essence considered as absolute.

But since these four eminent graces are intimately connected with the divine life, it seems fitting to say that they imitate the divine essence considered as really identical with one or other real trinitarian relation. Thus the grace of union imitates and participates in a finite way the divine paternity, the light of glory divine filiation, sanctifying grace active spiration, and the virtue of charity passive spiration.

There is no explicit mention of exemplary causality in Question 26, though perhaps one could argue that there is the suggestion of it in Lonergan's remark about the four very special modes that ground the 'external imitation' of the divine substance. In any event, in what follows, I shall argue that the notion of exemplary causality fits seamlessly into Lonergan's later discussion and that its explicit inclusion provides us with a small but nonetheless significant clarification of his proposal as we find it in Question 26.

First, in Questions 22-25 of *De Deo Trino: pars systematica* Lonergan argues on the basis of the teaching of the New Testament that the Father really and truly, and not by appropriation, sends the Son, and that the Father and Son really and truly, and not by appropriation, send the Holy Spirit.[18] If one accepts this teaching, then to be consistent in one's theological reflections one ought also to acknowledge that there are proper contingent predications regarding God. For in accepting the teaching one acknowledges that in the mission of the Son, the Father is really and truly, and not by appropriation, the one sending and not the one sent, and the Son is really and truly, and not by appropriation, the one sent and not the one sending. Again, in accepting the teaching one acknowledges that in the mission of the Holy Spirit, the Father and Son are really and truly, and not by appropriation, the ones sending and not the ones sent, and the Holy Spirit is really and truly, and not by appropriation, the one sent and not the one sending. And as all of these predications regarding the divine missions are said of the divine persons not as a matter of necessity but contingently, it follows that if one accepts the teaching of the New Testament on the divine missions, to maintain consistency one is required to acknowledge in one's theological reflections that there are proper contingent predications regarding God.

---

18 See ibid., 446-55.

Second, prior to Questions 22-25, Lonergan had argued in Assertion 16 of *De Deo Trino: pars systematica* that whatever is predicated contingently of the divine persons as regards divine cognitive, volitional, and productive operation is constituted by the divine perfection common to the three persons as both the principle-by-which and the principle-which, and therefore is attributed distinctly and equally to each divine person. A contingent predication, however, cannot be true if there is lacking a contingent reality, for then the entire correspondence required for truth would be lacking. The contingent reality is required not as constituting the truth of whatever is predicated contingently of the divine persons as regards divine cognitive, volitional, and productive operation but as a condition required for the truth of the predication. Further, the contingent reality is neither a prior nor a simultaneous condition, for that would imply that God's cognitive, volitional, and productive operation is somehow dependent upon the prior or simultaneous presence of something. Rather, the condition is consequent upon such operation. Thus, prior to Assertion 16, Lonergan had argued in Assertion 15 that what is truly predicated contingently of the divine persons has a consequent condition in an appropriate external term.[19]

Third, in the assertion that follows Questions 22-25, Assertion 17, Lonergan turns to a further issue, namely, the constitution of the divine missions. He distinguishes three opposed positions on their constitution and argues for the third position: the mission of a divine person is constituted by a divine relation of origin but in such a way that it requires an appropriate created term, again as a consequent condition.[20]

In outline, Lonergan argues as follows. *To be sending* and *to be sent* are opposites. Opposites are truly predicated of divine persons only according to relations of origin. For in God "all things are one except where there is relational opposition." Accordingly, *to be sending* and *to be sent* are really and truly said of the Father and the Son respectively only according to the relations of origin of paternity and filiation. Equally, *to be sending* and *to be sent* are really and truly said respectively of the Father and Son, on the one hand, and of the Holy Spirit,

19 For Lonergan's full argumentation for these two assertions, see ibid., 438-47. See also, Lonergan, *The Ontological and Psychological Constitution of Christ*, 98-99.

20 See Lonergan, *The Triune God: Systematics*, 454-55.

on the other, only according to the divine relations of origin of active spiration and passive spiration. Further, the real divine relations, being really identical with the divine essence, are infinite in perfection. But if the divine relations of origin are infinite in perfection, anything else proposed as constituting the mission of a divine person would be superfluous. Divine missions, then, are constituted by nothing other than the divine relations of origin.

Still, the divine missions are not necessary. So to affirm that the Father is the one sending the Son, that the Son is the one sent, that the Father and Son are the ones sending the Holy Spirit, and that the Holy Spirit is the one sent, is to make contingent predications. A contingent predication cannot be true where a contingent reality is lacking, for then the entire correspondence required for truth would be lacking. For these predications to be true, then, contingent realities appropriate to what is being affirmed must be included. However, they are not included as constituting the missions, for as contingent realities are realities of finite perfection they are superfluous where it has been established that realities of infinite perfection constitute the missions. A contingent reality required for the truth of a contingent predication but not constitutive of its truth is a *condition* of its truth. And so, as he had argued in Assertion 15, here too Lonergan argues that such conditions are neither prior nor simultaneous but subsequent.[21]

Fourth, as we have seen, in Assertion 15 Lonergan argues that what is truly predicated of the divine persons is constituted by the divine perfection itself and has a consequent condition in an appropriate external term. In Assertion 16 he argues that what is truly predicated of the divine persons as regards divine cognitive, volitional, and productive operation is constituted by the divine perfection common to the three persons as both the principle-by-which and the principle-which and so is attributed distinctly and equally to each divine person. In Assertions 17, he argues for the claim that as regards the divine mis-

---

21 "... this [appropriate external term] is required as a condition consequent upon the mission itself. For the person sending and also the person sent in no way depend upon a creature and therefore, although the term is a condition because it is necessary, still it cannot be either a prior or a simultaneous condition." Ibid., 467. "According to the third opinion, a term follows a mission, and therefore if there is a mission there is necessarily a term." Ibid., 463.

sions an appropriate external term as consequent condition is again required but that a divine mission is constituted by a divine relation of origin. These three assertions, I suggest, provide the context for the issue raised in Question 26: are the ways in which the appropriate external terms are consequent upon the divine missions the same or different from the ways in which the appropriate external term are consequent upon divine cognitive, volitional, and productive operation? To answer this question, Lonergan distinguishes the following: constitution in the active sense; constitution in the passive sense; creation in the active sense; creation in the passive sense.

Although Lonergan does not say so explicitly, the basis for the distinction between constitution in the active sense and constitution in the passive sense is to be found, I think, in Thomas's position that potency or power is an attribute one can truly and really predicate of God, and that 'potency' or 'power' predicated of God internally, that is, in respect to the notional acts – to the proper divine attributes expressed not by nouns or adjectives but by verbs, such as 'to generate,' 'to be generated,' 'to speak,' 'to be spoken,' 'to spirate,' 'to be spirated,' 'to love notionally,' 'to proceed as love' – signifies principally or directly the divine essence and divine relations indirectly.[22]

Lonergan mentions the issue in Assertion 9 of *The Triune God: Systematics*:

> Potency ... is predicated [of God] really according to the fact that internally to God one person proceeds from another, or that externally creation proceeds from God. ... As predicated internally, it is the potency to generate or to spirate. Inasmuch as potency is a principle, it refers directly to the divine essence.[23]

The brilliant statement on the issue, however, is found in *Verbum*:

> ... though the generation of the Son is 'per modum intelligibilis actionis,' though a proper name of the Son is the Word, still Aquinas did not conclude that the principle by which the Father generates is the divine intellect or the divine understanding. ... [I]n God substance, being, understanding, thought, willing are absolutely one and the same reality. Accordingly, Aquinas not merely in his commentary on the *Sentences* but also in his *Summa* makes the divine

---

22 See Thomas Aquinas, *Summa theologiae*, 1, q. 41, aa. 3-5.

23 Lonergan, *The Triune God: Systematics*, 358-59.

essence the principle of divine generation. ... The one divine essence is common to Father and to Son. As the Father's, the essence is the potency by which the Father generates; as the Son's the essence is the potency by which the Son is generated. The *potentia spirandi* is conceived in parallel fashion. ... [T]he divine essence is the principle by which the Father generates the Son and by which Father and Son spirate the Holy Spirit; that *potentia generandi* and *potentia spirandi*, while *in recto* they mean the same divine essence, still *in obliquo* connote different personal properties.[24]

Now the notional acts are necessary;[25] the divine missions are not. The Father, the Son and the Holy Spirit conceive and will that the Father sends the Son, and that Father and Son send the Holy Spirit. The Son, just as he has the divine nature communicated to him from the Father, so too from the Father he conceives and wills that he be sent by the Father. Similarly, just as the Holy Spirit has the divine nature communicated to him from the Father and Son, so too from the Father and Son he conceives and wills that he be sent by the Father and Son. This conceiving and willing is identical with the divine essence. In the active sense of 'constitution,' the constitution of the divine mission is this conceiving and willing that is identical with the divine essence and common to the three divine persons.

In the passive sense of 'constitution,' the constitution of the missions is proper to the one(s) sending and the ones sent. For "the Three conceive and will, not that three send and that three be sent, but that the Father send the Son and the Father and the Son send the Holy Spirit."[26] The Father, Son and Holy Spirit conceive and will: (1) the Father as the one sending the Son, as the one *from whom another* not only in the uncreated, eternal, and necessary sense but also in a created, temporal, and contingent sense; (2) the Son as the one sent by

---

24 Bernard Lonergan, *Collected Works of Bernard Lonergan*, vol. 2, *Verbum: Word and Idea in Aquinas*, ed. Frederick E. Crowe and Robert M. Doran (Toronto: University of Toronto Press, 1997; reprint edition, 2005), 216-17.

25 "It is inconsistent with the infinity of divine perfection to grasp that evidence is sufficient to speak a word and not speak that word; it is likewise inconsistent to grasp the infinite good and judge that that good ought to be loved by spirated love and yet not spirate that love." Lonergan, *The Triune God: Systematics*, 370.

26 Ibid., 469.

the Father, as the one *who from another*, also not only in the uncreated, eternal, and necessary sense but in a created, temporal, and contingent sense as well; (3) the Father and Son as the ones sending, as the ones *from whom another*, not only in the uncreated, eternal and necessary sense but also in a created, temporal, and contingent sense; (4) the Holy Spirit as the one sent by the Father and Son, as the one *who from others*, not only in the uncreated, eternal, and necessary sense but also in a created, temporal, and contingent sense.

Further, if there are proper contingent predications regarding God that are true, one cannot simply rest content with constitution in the active sense and dispense with constitution in the passive sense. For a proper contingent predication requires a proper constitutive. If one were to dispense with constitution in the passive sense, then, to take one example, one would assign the same constitutive for the proper contingent predications (1) and (2) above, namely, the divine perfection common to the three persons. But in the predications, the Father is the one sending and not the one sent, and the Son is the one sent and not the one sending. Sending is proper to the Father and being sent is proper to the Son. To assign only a common constitutive would assign neither the constitutive proper to the Father as the one sending nor the constitutive proper to the Son as the one sent.

Next, "... action is the denomination of the agent from the patient or receiver, and passion is the denomination of the patient from the agent. ... Hence it is possible that in creation...there are the relations of active and passive creation."[27] Now, whatever God understands as actually distinct from God, or wills to be actually distinct from God, or produces as actually distinct from God, is actually distinct from God. Creation in the active sense is God's cognitive, volitional and productive operation, identical with the divine essence and common to the three divine persons in accordance with the trinitarian order, as both the principle-which and the principle-by-which of everything else. Creation, taken passively, "is the appropriate external term itself as dependent upon its first efficient cause."[28]

Fifth, the four preeminent graces are external realities that are absolutely and formally supernatural. As external, they are instances of creation in the passive sense, and as such they are dependent on God's

---

27 Ibid., 545.
28 Ibid., 469.

cognitive, volitional, and productive operation, that is, on creation in
the active sense, "which is God's essence."[29] Now, in Assertion 16 Lonergan says that whatever is truly predicated of the divine persons as
regards divine cognitive, volitional, and productive operation is constituted by the divine perfection common to the three persons and attributed distinctly and equally to each divine person. Again, in Question 26 he writes:

> ...through their infinite and unlimited divine perfection, either
> common or proper according to the case, the Three really and truly
> constitute, are really and truly constituted as sending and sent, re-
> spectively, and the three persons really and truly equally create the
> appropriate terms.[30]

This remark by Lonergan occurs on the page before he makes his
proposal characterizing four absolutely supernatural realities as formal, external terms imitating the four real divine relations. In light of
the distinctions he has introduced in Question 26, his meaning can,
I think, be stated more expansively as follows. In truths we know regarding God, and in accordance with the particular truth being considered, the constituting divine perfection is to be taken either as common to the three divine persons according to the trinitarian order, or
as proper to one or other divine person but not to all three. Further,
in the case of proper predication regarding God, whether necessary
or contingent, the distinction between constitution in the active sense
and constitution in the passive sense obtains. For constitution in the
active sense is the divine essence as the divine perfection, and constitution in the passive sense is the same divine essence as the divine
perfection understood with a relation of origin, and the divine perfection understood with a relation of origin is required in the case of
proper predications regarding God, whether necessary or contingent.
In the quoted remark, Lonergan does not say or in any way imply that
the three persons really and truly equally create the appropriate terms
only if the case being considered demands that the divine perfection
be taken as common. Irrespective of whether in the case being considered the constituting divine perfection is to be taken as common or
proper, "the three persons really and truly equally create the appropri-

---

29 Thomas Aquinas, *Summa theologiae*, 1, q. 45, a. 3, ad 1.

30 Lonergan, *The Triune God: Systematics*, 469. See also note 27 on the same
    page, in which an editorial clarification of Lonergan's remark is offered.

ate terms." To suppose, then, that in making his proposal in Question 26 Lonergan is in any way relaxing or softening the doctrine that all *ad extra* activities of God are common to the three divine persons would be to suppose that he contradicts himself in the space of a page.

Nor are there grounds for supposing that there is any kind of logical tension between Lonergan's proposal and the doctrine that all *ad extra* activities of God are common to the three divine persons. At the end of Question 26, Lonergan mentions an objection to his proposal that implies that there is a logical tension. On the basis of the *ad extra* doctrine that God operates externally not according to the relations but according to the common nature, the conclusion is drawn in the objection that the real divine relations cannot be participated in along the lines that Lonergan proposes. Lonergan counters this conclusion by pointing out that God is not some natural agent confined to producing blindly something similar to itself. God is an agent acting through intellect, with the freedom to produce whatever the wisdom of the divine intellect freely ordains:

> ... the divine nature common to the Three is intellectual, and just as God by the divine intellect knows the four real relations, so also by the divine intellect, together with the divine will, God can produce beings that are finite yet similar [to the four relations] and absolutely supernatural.[31]

Note that in the line of production or of omnipotent efficient causality, Lonergan does not in his proposal say that each one of the four divine subsistent relations, operating alone, produces just that external, absolutely supernatural reality that participates in it or imitates it. Rather, in perfect accord with the *ad extra* doctrine, he says: "God can produce ...," which is to say that the three divine persons as one principle can produce ...[32]

Sixth, it is here that the notion of exemplary causality, which features in Lonergan's early formulation of his proposal, can be seen as providing a useful clarification. An exemplary cause is *id secundum quod aliquid fit*. Now, Lonergan remarks in *Insight* that "the range of

---

31 Ibid., 473.

32 For more on this issue, see Thomas Aquinas, *Summa theologiae*, 1, q. 45, a. 6.

divine wisdom is as large as the range of divine omnipotence."[33] Everything that God produces by way of efficient causality accords with divine wisdom. Included in 'everything' is the "mystery of his will ... that he set forth in Christ, as a plan for the fullness of time, to gather up all things in him, things in heaven and things on earth" (Ephesians 1: 9-10), the "plan of the mystery hidden for ages in God, who created all things" (Ephesians 3: 9). Now God is the primary exemplary cause of everything else, of every being by participation.[34] Earlier, I adverted to Lonergan's remark in the third part of the third section of *De Gratia Sanctificante* that absolutely every finite being imitates the divine essence as its primary exemplary cause and that the divine essence can be considered either as absolute and common to the three divine persons or as being really identical with one or other real trinitarian relation. Part of what is claimed in Lonergan's proposal is that in the plan of salvation, in which all things will be gathered up into Christ and the kingdom of God be handed by him to the Father (1 Corinthians 15:24), and in harmonious continuation of the actual order of this universe, God in his omnipotence, and as an agent acting through the wisdom of the divine intellect, has ordained that there be produced finite participations in, or imitations of, the divine essence as really identical with one or other of the real trinitarian relations of paternity,

---

33 Lonergan, *Insight*, 724. Here, Lonergan is echoing Thomas: "... since the power of God, which is his essence, is nothing else but his wisdom, it can indeed be fittingly said that there is nothing in the divine power which is not in the order of the divine wisdom; for the divine wisdom includes the whole potency of the divine power." *Summa theologiae*, 1, q. 25, a. 5 c. A similar echo is heard in Lonergan's remark in the first section of *De Gratia Sanctificante*: "According to St Thomas it is impossible for a world to be created by God unless it has been so ordered by infinite wisdom."

34 "... things made by nature receive determinate forms. This determination of forms must be reduced to the divine wisdom as its first principle, for divine wisdom devised the order of the universe, which order consists in the variety of things. And therefore we must say that in the divine wisdom are the types of all things, which types we have called ideas – *i.e.*, exemplar forms existing in the divine mind ... And these ideas, though multiplied by their relations to things, in reality are not apart from the divine essence, according as the likeness to that essence can be shared diversely by different things. In this manner, therefore, God Himself is the first exemplar of all things." Thomas Aquinas, *Summa theologiae*, 1, q. 44, a. 3 c.

filiation, active spiration, and passive spiration.[35] In this ordination, the exemplary cause, as distinct from the efficient cause, is the divine essence as really identical with one or other real trinitarian relation.

Lastly, we can now return to Question 26. The question asks, "In what ways is an appropriate external term consequent upon a constituted mission?"[36] Phrased thus, it would seem that in asking the question Lonergan is assuming that there are a number of 'ways' in which an appropriate external term can be consequent upon a constituted mission. The 'ways' can include differences among the external terms themselves. But the 'ways' can also include differences in the manner in which the terms are consequent when a divine mission is involved, as compared with the 'ways' in which appropriate external terms are consequent upon divine cognitive, volitional, and productive operation when a divine mission is not involved – otherwise, there would be no point to the four distinctions Lonergan makes at the beginning of the question. If one interprets the question so as to include among the 'ways' differences in the manner in which the terms are consequent, one places the question in the context of the previous three assertions. And from this perspective, the question asks: is the manner in which the appropriate external term of a divine mission is consequent just the same as the manner in which the external term of a divine cognitive, volitional, and productive operation is consequent?

In the line of efficient causality, there is no difference in the 'way' or manner in which an appropriate external term is consequent upon divine cognitive, volitional, and productive operation when a divine mission is not involved and the 'way' or manner in which an appropriate external term is consequent upon a divine mission. The divine perfection common to the three divine persons is the constitutive cause in both cases as the principle-by-which and principle-which of the terms. The constitutive cause is constitution in the active sense and creation in the active sense, and the terms are instances of creation in the passive sense, even if in the case of the missions they are very special instances.

In the line of exemplary causality, there is a difference in the 'way' or manner in which an appropriate external term is consequent upon

---

35 Towards the end of *De Gratia Sanctificante*, Lonergan speaks of the "economy of salvation (God's purpose, as Paul terms it)" as an "order of divine wisdom that has been freely chosen and willed by God."

36 Lonergan, *The Triune God: Systematics*, 466-67.

divine cognitive, volitional, and productive operation when a divine mission is not involved and the 'way' or manner in which an appropriate external term is consequent upon a divine mission. For in the case of the divine mission, the exemplary cause of the external term, the *id secundum quod aliquid fit*, is not the divine perfection as absolute and common to the three divine persons but the divine perfection as really identical with one or other real divine relation. This is constitution in the passive sense, which, as previously argued, cannot be precluded if one is seeking to determine the constitution of a divine mission. In the case of the divine missions, then, constitution in the passive sense must be included along with constitution in the active sense, and with this inclusion comes the difference in the 'way' or manner in which the appropriate term is consequent.

If for no other reason, then, Lonergan's early formulation of his proposal regarding the *nexus mysteriorum* in God's self-communication in creation retains an importance in that its explicit reference to the role of exemplary causality adds a small but nonetheless significant clarification of that proposal, as we find it expressed in Question 26.

The remainder of Question 26 is taken up with differences regarding what is constituted by the missions, differences among the immediate material external terms and among the immediate formal external terms, and differences in what is accomplished in the incarnation and in the giving of the Spirit. The question ends with the formulation of the proposal in an attempt to clarify the 'supernatural character' of the formal terms of the missions, followed by an objection against the proposal and Lonergan's answer, both of which were mentioned above.

5. SEVEN INDICATIONS OF THE PROPOSAL'S APPROPRIATENESS

On a number of occasions in *The Triune God: Systematics*, Lonergan refers to a statement found in *Dei Filius*, the Dogmatic Constitution from the First Vatican Council, that reason illumined by faith can with God's help attain a fruitful understanding of the mysteries of faith from the analogy of what is naturally known and from the interconnection of the mysteries with one another and with our last end.[37] Lonergan's proposal in Question 26 is clearly concerned with the foundational interconnections of the mysteries of faith with one

37 See, for example, Lonergan, *The Triune God: Systematics*, 18-19, where Lonergan quotes the relevant text from *Dei Filius*.

another and with our last end. In a primary sense, then, the 'appropriateness' of the proposal is measured by the extent to which it is successful in showing how at the foundational level the mysteries of faith are brought together and connected intelligibly with one another and how they work together to bring humankind to its last end: the attainment of God in the beatific vision and in the love that is consequent upon that vision. One could add that there are also indirect indications or signs of the proposal's appropriateness. Thus, if reliance on the proposal as a guiding principle in one's theological reflections were to continue to yield fruitful results in less foundational areas and not lead one into error, and if at the foundational level there are no available alternatives to the proposal that can claim an equal or better capacity to connect intelligibly the mysteries of faith with one another and with our last end, then one would have valuable indirect indications of the proposal's theological appropriateness.

Under what in some instances amount to little more than headings, Lonergan lists in the third part of the third section of *De Gratia Sanctificante*, immediately after mentioning his proposal, seven direct indications of the appropriateness of the proposal.

FIRST INDICATION

The first indication is Lonergan's very brief remark that the proposal "shows the nexus between these graces and God's own life." Perhaps we can enlarge upon this briefly, even at the risk of going beyond what Lonergan may have intended.

The graces Lonergan has in mind here are, of course, the four preeminent graces: the grace of union or the *esse secundarium incarnationis*, sanctifying grace, the habit of charity, and light of glory. The proposal says that the graces are created participations in or created imitations of, respectively, paternity, active spiration, passive spiration, and the filiation. Now the emanation of the Word from the Speaker is the origin of one living from a conjoined living principle, as also is the emanation of Love from both the Speaker and the Word.[38] Now independently of the proposal, grace is commonly thought of as involving regeneration or rebirth into a new life, indeed, as a participation in the

---

38 "The divine emanation of the Word is the origin of one living from a conjoined living principle ..." "The divine emanation of Love ... is the origin of one living from a conjoined living principle ..." Ibid., 203.

life of God.[39] If one were to accept that the four preeminent graces are participations in or imitations of the four real divine relations, as is put forth in Lonergan's proposal, one would have not merely an understanding of some kind of nexus between the graces and God's own life but, more significantly, a structured understanding as to why these graces are a rebirth into new life, and also why this new life is indeed a participation in the intimacy of trinitarian life.

SECOND INDICATION

Lonergan's second indication of the appropriateness of his proposal "is that it clearly and distinctly lays bare the root of absolute supernaturality." In discussing the second thesis of De ente supernaturali,[40] Lonergan writes: "that which exceeds the proportion of this or that nature is *relatively supernatural*; that which exceeds the proportion of any finite substance whatsoever, whether created or creatable, is *absolutely supernatural*, supernatural without qualification." In explaining this distinction, he says that a finite substance, being something absolute, that is, an essence that does not include in its proper definition a relation to something else, can only imitate the divine essence in its absoluteness – it can only imitate the divine essence in a way that prescinds from the real divine relations. The human intellect and will, however, which are unrestricted in their potency, could, in obedience to God's bidding, come to be actuated in such a way that in their actuation by God they participate in or imitate in a created manner the real divine relation. And if that were the case, these actuations would be created realities that exceed the proportion of any finite substance whatsoever. Now in Lonergan's proposal, each of the four preeminent graces is said to be a participation in or imitation of one or other of the real divine relations. Each of these graces, then, would exceed the proportion of any created substance whatsoever. Accordingly, if one has theological reasons independent of explicit reliance on Lonergan's proposal to affirm that these graces are absolutely supernatural, as Lonergan himself had in his argument for Thesis 2 of De ente supernaturali, then identi-

---

39 The theme of life pervades Lonergan's summary in thesis form of the positive doctrine of the New Testament on the reality that later became known as sanctifying grace. For the thesis, see footnote 4 above.

40 The second thesis states that the 'created communication of the divine nature exceeds the proportion not only of human nature but also of any finite substance, and thus is absolutely supernatural.'

fying these graces as created participations in or imitations of the real divine relations would indeed seem "clearly and distinctly" to assign the root of their absolute supernaturality.[41]

THIRD INDICATION

The third indication Lonergan cites supporting the appropriateness of his proposal is simply that the proposal assigns four different ontological foundations for the four preeminent graces. That is all he says, and one could, I suppose, take him to mean simply that as a matter of fact for each of the four distinct preeminent graces the proposal identifies a distinct ontological foundation. That would suffice as a weak indication of the appropriateness of the proposal. But even if this is all Lonergan had in mind here, his later formulation of the proposal in *Divinarum personarum* and in *The Triune God: Systematics* suggests that this consideration can be retained and reworked so as to provide a stronger indication of the appropriateness of his proposal.

The clue to the reworking is Lonergan's remark in his later formulation of the proposal that there are four absolutely supernatural realities, the secondary act of existence of the incarnation, sanctifying

---

41 Put briefly, Lonergan's argument in support of Thesis 2 of *De ente supernaturali* runs as follows: (1) if the created communication of the divine nature is of a higher ontological order than any finite substance whatsoever, then the created communication of the divine nature exceeds the proportion of any finite substance whatsoever and is absolutely supernatural; (2) the created communication of the divine nature is the created, proportionate, and remote principle of acts whereby God is attained in himself; (3) God is attained in himself if God is attained in his infinity;(4) therefore, if the created communication of the divine nature attains God as he is in himself, it attains God in his infinity; (5) any finite substance whatsoever is defined by reason of its being an external imitation of God and not by God as he is in himself – if a finite substance, as such, could be defined by God as he is in himself, it would not be finite but infinite; (6) therefore, no finite substance, as such, is of an ontological order such that it can attain God as he is in himself; (7) therefore, the created communication of the divine nature, the created, proportionate, and remote principle of acts whereby God is attained in himself is of a higher ontological order than any finite substance whatsoever; (8) accordingly, the created communication of the divine nature is absolutely supernatural. See also, towards the end of the discussion of Thesis 2, Lonergan's explanation of how the created communication of the divine nature, though it is a created reality, is also infinite, not simply, but "in a certain respect."

grace, the habit of charity, and the light of glory, that "are never found uninformed (*informia*)."[42] Lonergan seems to imply in this formulation that it is just these four created supernatural realities that have the 'supernatural character' of never being found uninformed,[43] and that this has some significance for what he is about to propose. If so, the question arises: what precisely is this significance? Or, to put it another way: why in connection with his proposal does Lonergan mention the fact that there are four created supernatural realities that have the 'supernatural character' of never being found 'uninformed'?

An answer is suggested if we recall what has been said about the theological equivalents of proper contingent predications regarding the divine missions,[44] namely, that they are resolved into a constituting divine subsistent relation of origin and demand or require an appropriate created term as a consequent condition.[45] A predication in which a divine mission is affirmed necessarily includes a created term.[46] Moreover, the created term must be appropriate to what is being affirmed. At the very least, the term must be immediately consequent and formal. Material external terms, such as the non-subsistent human nature, as in the sending of the Son, or a subsistent human

42 See Lonergan, *The Triune God: Systematics*, 470-73.

43 In partial support of this interpretation, one can cite Lonergan's remark in Excursus 1 of Thesis 3 of *De ente supernaturali*: "Only love is meritorious per se; the other virtues or their acts can be informed or uninformed. They are informed by sanctifying grace and love, and when grace departs they become uninformed and cease to be meritorious."

44 Lonergan himself does not use the term "theological equivalence," but in *Insight* (526-33) he does list three rules or canons of what he calls "metaphysical equivalence." These canons are concerned to clarify the relationship between the metaphysical elements, on the one hand, and the objects of true propositions, on the other. Now, like the canons of metaphysical equivalence, the various canons Lonergan formulates regarding propositions about God seek to coordinate what is affirmed in these propositions with realities. Perhaps, then, it is not entirely inappropriate to name these, *canons of theological equivalence*.

45 The appropriateness of a created term is, of course, not the same as the appropriateness of the proposal.

46 " ... a term follows a mission, and therefore if there is a mission there is necessarily a term." Lonergan, *The Triune God: Systematics*, 463.

nature, as in the sending of the Spirit, [47] are not sufficient (they are not 'appropriate'), for they are merely the requisite created realities for the appropriate terms. Again, the appropriate created formal term must be the immediate consequent condition and not simply a term derivative from the consequent condition and informed by it. Finally, the appropriate created formal term must be present in its integrity and not, say, in some deformed similitude of itself. For if the term is not present in its integrity but only in some deformed similitude of itself, again, it fails to fulfil the requirement of appropriateness.

In Lonergan's later formulation of his proposal, the four real divine relations can be considered as "four very special modes that ground the external imitation of the divine substance." The implication is that if God so chooses there can be external imitations of paternity, filiation, active spiration, and passive spiration. "Next," Lonergan says, "there are four absolutely supernatural realities, which are never found uninformed."[48] This statement, presumably, is meant to remind the reader of a commonly held position among Scholastic theologians, a position that Lonergan endorses in *De ente supernaturali* by singling out the acts that attain God as he is in himself and in his entirety, along with the remote and proximate principles of those acts, as being not only absolutely supernatural but also as being formally, absolutely supernatural.[49] Now, to say that the four absolutely supernatural realities are never found uninformed is to say that they are always found in their proper integrity or not at all.[50] But this fulfils a requirement for the consequent created term in a predication in which a divine mission is affirmed. And if the secondary act of existence of the incarnation, sanctifying grace, the habit of charity, and the light of glory are, indeed, the only created, absolutely supernatural realities that are never found

---

47 Ibid., 469, 471.

48 Ibid., 471.

49 A common example of a supernatural reality that can be found uninformed is lifeless faith, faith uninformed by charity. Faith is absolutely supernatural, but it is virtually, absolutely supernatural, not formally, absolutely supernatural. See, again, Lonergan's discussion of the degrees among the supernatural acts in Excursus I of Thesis 3 of *De ente supernaturali*. On lifeless faith, see Thomas Aquinas, *Summa theologiae*, 2-2, q. 4, aa. 4-5.

50 This, of course, is not to deny that sanctifying grace, the habit of charity and the light of glory are supernatural realities that admit of degrees.

uninformed, then they alone can be the required consequent created terms in predications in which the divine missions are affirmed.

FOURTH INDICATION

Lonergan's fourth indication of the appropriateness of his proposal is that it provides a foundation for the distinction and connection between sanctifying grace and the habit or virtue of charity. The proposal says that sanctifying grace is a participation in or imitation of active spiration and that the habit or virtue of charity is a participation in or imitation of passive spiration. Although the real distinction between sanctifying grace and charity remained a disputed question among Scholastic theologians, the more common position, following Thomas, was that the distinction is real.[51] In the fourth part of the third section of *De Gratia Sanctificante*, Lonergan cites Thomas's *Summa theologiae*, 1-2, q. 110, aa. 3-4 on the issue and agrees with Thomas that the distinction is real, and he offers his own clarification of the distinction by saying that the infused virtue of charity is an "immanent formal but secondary effect" of sanctifying grace. Now, active spiration is to passive spiration as principle to its resultant. If, as in Lonergan's proposal, sanctifying grace is a participation in or imitation of active spiration, and the infused habit or virtue of charity is a participation in or imitation of passive spiration, then there is a foundation for the commonly held theological positions that sanctifying grace and charity are distinct, that sanctifying grace is the principle and charity the resultant, that sanctifying grace and grace are inseparable, so that when charity ceases so too does sanctifying grace, that the measure of sanctifying grace in a person is the same as the measure of charity.

FIFTH INDICATION

Lonergan's fifth indication of the appropriateness of his proposal is that it provides a foundation for the connection between the Incarnation and the beatific vision. Thomas affirms that Christ as man possessed the beatific vision by right throughout his entire mortal life.[52] We merit glory to the extent that we are living members of Christ: as living members of Christ, we are co-heirs with him of God, sharers with him in his suffering that we may also share in his glory (Romans

---

51 See the brief discussion on this issue in Carolus Boyer, *De gratia divina synopsis scholastica* (Rome: Gregorian University Press, 1930), 191-94.

52 Lonergan refers here to *Summa theologiae*, 3, q. 9 aa. 2-3 and q. 10, aa. 1-4.

8:17). Earlier in the discussion, I mentioned Lonergan's position in *De ente supernaturali* that the primary remote principle of the two acts that attain God as he is in himself and in his entirety is the grace of union, and that in a secondary sense the remote principle of these acts is sanctifying grace. Christ, having the grace of union and as the natural Son of the Father, possessed sanctifying grace by right. All others possess sanctifying grace as a gift, on account of Christ. Now in God, paternity is the principle and filiation is the resultant. In the proposal, the grace of union or, as in Lonergan's later formulation, the *esse secundarium incarnationis*, is a created participation in or imitation of paternity, and the light of glory is a created participation in or imitation of filiation. The light of glory is the created grace through which the blessed in heaven know God as he is in himself and in his entirety in the beatific vision. Thus, just as in God paternity is the principle and filiation is the resultant, so in Lonergan's proposal the created participation in or imitation of paternity, the *esse secundarium incarnationis*, is the principle, and the created participation in or imitation of filiation, the light of glory through which the blessed in heaven know God in the beatific vision, is the resultant.

SIXTH INDICATION

Lonergan's sixth indication of the appropriateness of his proposal can be seen, he says, in the Incarnation itself. In God, "divine paternity is the divine intellect as speaking his Word and thus intellectually generating his own Son." In the proposal, the *esse secundarium incarnationis* is said to be a created participation in or imitation of divine paternity. If that is so, then one would expect there to be in the Incarnation a reality one could properly understand as a kind of generation. This is found, Lonergan says, not in the generation of a new person but in the fact that "a new nature comes to an already existing person." For in the Incarnation, the incarnate Word, by his divine act of existence is not only God but a man. Further, if, as is claimed in the proposal, the *esse secundarium incarnationis* imitates divine paternity, it would follow that it has a special relation to divine filiation. But the *esse secundarium incarnationis* "is a finite entity whereby a created humanity exists through the personal act of existence of the divine Word." Therefore, it has a special relation to divine filiation.

SEVENTH INDICATION

Lonergan's final indication of the appropriateness of his proposal is to be found, he says, in the light of glory. In a sense, this is the opposite of the consideration just mentioned. In the proposal, the light of glory is said to be a created participation or imitation of divine filiation, of the Word as spoken by the Father. If so, it would have a special relation to the Father as intelligent and intellectually generating. Now in the beatific vision, in which God is attained as he is in himself and in his entirety, God is known not through some similitude[53] but through the divine essence itself.[54] But the light of glory "is that finite entity by which a created intellect is disposed to receive the divine essence as an intelligible *species* and thus see God as he is in himself."[55] Further, for Thomas, the light of glory "establishes the intellect in a kind of likeness to God, a *deiformity* whereby the intellect is made capable of seeing God in his essence."[56] Now if the light of glory is, as the proposal claims, a created participation in or imitation of divine filiation, one has an explanation of the fact that the light of glory is a *deiformity*, a likeness to God. Moreover, one has an explanation why this likeness to God is such that is ordered to receiving "the divine essence as a species and the vision itself."[57]

---

53 "To say that God is seen by some similitude is to say that the divine essence is not seen at all." Thomas Aquinas, *Summa theologiae*, 1, q.12, a.2 c.

54 "... when any created intellect sees the essence of God, the essence of God itself becomes the intelligible form of the intellect." Ibid., a. 5 c. "Those who see the divine essence see what they see in God not by any likeness, but by the divine essence itself united to their intellect." Ibid., a. 9 c.

55 This is Lonergan's own statement, made in the third part of the third section of *De Gratia Sanctificante*.

56 "The faculty of seeing God ... does not belong to the created intellect naturally but is given to it by the light of glory, which establishes the intellect in a kind of *deiformity* ..." Thomas Aquinas, *Summa theologiae*,1, q. 12, a. 6 c. "... in order to see God there must be some similitude of God on the part of the visual faculty whereby the intellect is made capable of seeing God." Ibid., a. 2 c. "By this light [of glory] the blessed are made *deiform* – that is, like to God ..." Ibid., a. 5 c.

57 In Lonergan's own words in the third part of the third section of *De Gratia Sanctificante*: "... since the light of glory imitates divine filiation, the Word as spoken by the Father, it has a special relation to God the Father as

6. CONCLUDING REMARKS

At the beginning of chapter 6 of *The Triune God: Systematics*, Lonergan mentions the fact that the divine missions are discussed not
only in the treatise on the trinity but also in treatises on the incarnate
Word, on grace, on the church and on revelation.[58] This should come
as no surprise. The divine missions are God's self-communication
in creation. But besides the *immediate* formal terms of the mission,
there is the prolongation or continuation of the missions through the
terms that derive and develop from the immediate formal terms of the
missions, and these the immediate formal terms inform. The other
treatises Lonergan mentions deal with various aspects of God's self-
communication in creation, and among the terms they consider are
those that derive and develop from the immediate formal terms of the
missions. Just as the immediate formal terms of the mission inform
the terms that derive and develop from them, so the treatise dealing
with doctrine of the divine missions underpins and penetrates the
doctrines treated in all of the other treatises.

If Lonergan is correct in identifying the four immediate, formal
external terms that are conditions consequent upon the Father's sending of the Son and the Father and Son's sending of the Spirit, and if
he is also correct in identifying these terms as created participations
in or imitations of the four real divine relations, his proposal would
provide a core theological clarification not only of the doctrine of the
divine missions but of the doctrines treated in the other treatises he
mentions as well. Indeed, it would provide an integrating framework
or structure, a *nexus mysteriorum* holding together in intelligible interconnection all that is put forth in systematic theology, while at the
same time allowing for development in understanding of those doctrines. This, I suggest, is the overriding reason why Lonergan's proposal warrants close, sustained scrutiny and testing.

Among Lonergan scholars, I doubt if anyone can at present show
definitively that Lonergan's proposal is a fundamentally significant and
permanently valid contribution to theological reflection, and not just
a bright idea soon to be discarded and forgotten. I have not attempted
to justify the proposal but merely to clarify its meaning by placing Lo-

---

intelligent and intellectually generating. And thus is found the reception of
the divine essence as a species and the vision itself."

58 See Lonergan's passing remark in *The Triune God: Systematics*, 436-37.

nergan's later, published formulation of it within the context of his earlier formulation of it in the unpublished archival document *De Gratia Sanctificante. Supplementum.* I have argued, in particular, that the notion of exemplary causality, prominent in the early formulation, provides a small but significant clarification of the proposal, as we find it in Question 26.

From this perspective, Lonergan's seven indications of the appropriateness of his proposal, which are so briefly stated in *De Gratia Sanctificante,* can be considered as suggestive, initial lines of exploration and investigation, along which, perhaps, scrutiny and testing of the proposal may fruitfully proceed.

LONERGAN'S DEBT TO HEGEL AND THE APPRO- PRIATION OF CRITICAL REALISM

Mark D. Morelli

LOYOLA MARYMOUNT UNIVERSITY

I. INTRODUCTION

When I was my pursuing my graduate studies at the University of Toronto in the 1970s, the Thomists there were highly suspicious of Lonergan. Lonergan, despite his obvious dissatisfaction with Kant, acknowledges more concretely and more thoroughly than Kant the methodological primacy of the synthetic unity of apperception.[1] As Lonergan puts it in more familiar terms, if I weren't present to myself, nothing would be present to me.[2] Lonergan's affinity with Kant on this point is a violation of the Gilsonian proscription against getting involved in any significant way

---

1 Bernard Lonergan, *Collected Works of Bernard Lonergan*, vol. 3, *Insight: A Study of Human Understanding*, ed. F. E. Crowe and Robert M. Doran (Toronto: University of Toronto Press, 1992), 365 (Hereafter CWL 3): "Kant deduced or postulated an original synthetic unity of apperception as the a priori condition of the 'I think' accompanying all cognitional acts." CWL 3, 349: "Indeed, consciousness is much more obviously of this unity in diverse acts than of the diverse acts, for it is within the unity that the acts are found and distinguished, and it is to the unity that we appeal when we talk about a single field of consciousness and draw a distinction between conscious acts occurring within the field and unconscious acts occurring outside it."

2 Bernard Lonergan, *Collected Works of Bernard Lonergan*, vol. 5, *Understanding and Being*, ed. Elizabeth A. Morelli and Mark D. Morelli; Revised and Augmented by F. E. Crowe with the collaboration of Elizabeth A. Morelli, Mark D. Morelli, Robert M. Doran, and Thomas V. Daly (Toronto: University of Toronto Press, 1990), 31 (Hereafter CWL 5): "Moreover, there is a third meaning of 'presence': you could not be present to me unless I were somehow present to myself."

with Kant's Copernican Revolution.[3] But these Thomists were doubly troubled by Lonergan. Lonergan seemed to them to be not only
post-Kantian – that was bad enough – but also post-Hegelian, and
that was just too much. Lonergan's post-Kantianism made them suspicious, but in his post-Hegelianism they found the sufficient reason
for dismissing him.

If the Toronto Thomists were wrong to dismiss Lonergan, they were
right about his kinship with Hegel. Indeed, Lonergan is not merely
post-Kantian but also post-Hegelian. Obviously, this has not meant
to us what it meant for those Toronto Thomists because Lonergan's
post-Hegelian philosophy has not scared us off. Still, our sticking with
Lonergan despite his Hegelianism cannot be attributed to our having grasped fully the significance of Lonergan's Hegelianism, for little
work has been done on Lonergan's relationship to Hegel.[4] So if we are
unfazed by Lonergan's Hegelianism, it is probably for other reasons.
My own suspicion is that we are untroubled because we trust that Lonergan's philosophical position, however post-Hegelian it may be, it
is nevertheless still fundamentally Thomistic. The Toronto Thomists
were scared off by Lonergan's Hegelianism because it seemed to them
too far removed from their Thomism and incompatible with it; whereas, we stick with Lonergan, not because of the Hegelian elements in

---

3   See Gerald A. McCool, SJ, *From Unity to Pluralism: The Internal Evolu-
     tion of Thomism* (New York: Fordham University Press, 1992), 162. Re-
     porting Gilson's position, McCool writes: "For the Kantian who makes
     consciousness the starting point of his philosophy can never be led out
     into the extra-mental world by the force of logical argument ... No method
     that begins in consciousness, even precisively as Maréchal . . ., can ever le-
     gitimately emerge from consciousness. Direct and immediate realism is the
     only valid starting point for a realistic Thomistic metaphysics."

4   The single lengthy study of Lonergan's relationship to Hegel is Jon Mi-
     chael Nilson's Hegel's <u>Phenomenology</u> and Lonergan's <u>Insight</u>: A Comparison
     of Two Ways to Christianity, a doctoral dissertation written under the direc-
     tion of John S. Dunne at the University of Notre Dame in 1975. Nilson
     has a good number of insights into the relationship in particular of Hegel's
     Phenomenology of Spirit to Lonergan's *Insight*, but he tends to conceive both
     philosophies as 'systems.' However, I would argue this is true not in the
     ordinary meaning of 'system,' and his comparisons and contrasts remain
     for the most part descriptive and so underestimate the import of both the
     similarities and the differences between the two thinkers.

his thought, but rather in spite of them, because we regard him as still authentically Thomistic.

There is a bit of irony here, and it invites interesting further questions: How does the Aquinas of the Toronto Thomists differ from Lonergan's Aquinas? Why was the Aquinas of the Toronto Thomists so radically incompatible with Hegel? In what way is Lonergan's Aquinas compatible with Hegelian idealism? Does Lonergan's kinship with both Aquinas and Hegel have any implications for the appropriation of Lonergan's *critical realism*? It is impossible to address all of these issues adequately in a brief essay. Instead of attempting the impossible, I propose to focus here on Lonergan's relation to Hegel and on the bearing of his debt to Hegel upon the appropriation of his critical realism.

First, I shall offer one especially compelling bit of evidence of Lonergan's debt to Hegel. That debt is, as the Toronto Thomists rightly discerned, a large one. Secondly, I shall consider the implications of Lonergan's debt to Hegel for our understanding of Lonergan's well-known claim that idealism is the halfway house between materialism and his own critical realism. This claim is easily misinterpreted, and I shall summarize here an argument I have made elsewhere that the idealism of the halfway house through which we must pass on the way to critical realism is not a version of subjective idealism but is in fact the Hegelian Absolute or Objective Idealism. If I am correct, Lonergan's debt to Hegel has important implications for our appropriation of his critical realism. Thirdly, then, I shall turn from Lonergan's relation to Hegel to our relation to this relation and shall discuss briefly the fear of idealism associated with the discovery of the role of insight in human knowing. I shall distinguish an unreasonable fear of subjective idealism, on the one hand, that vanishes as inertial confrontationalist presuppositions are abandoned, and on the other hand, I will distinguish a reasonable fear of Absolute Idealism that takes hold only once the inertial confrontationalist presuppositions are overcome.

2. LONERGAN'S DEBT TO HEGEL: A BIT OF EVIDENCE

First, then, I present a bit of evidence of Lonergan's large debt to Hegel. It is easy enough to show that the Toronto Thomists' suspicions were well-founded, even if their subsequent dismissal of Lonergan was not. A single citation from *Insight* will suffice to show this. In the footnote on the last page of Chapter 12 on "The Notion of Being,"

Lonergan declares that "characteristic features in the very movement of [Hegel's] thought have their parallels" in *Insight*, and that the "whole argument" of *Insight* "proceeds from *an sich*, through *für sich*, to *an und für sich*," in the manner of Hegel's *Phenomenology of Spirit* and *System of Logic*.[5]

We must leave the exploration of the dynamic structural similarities between the argument of *Insight* and the very movement of Hegel's thought in his two greatest works for another occasion, for the issue is made complicated by divergent ideals and different terminologies. But we need only notice how deeply into Lonergan's argument in *Insight* Hegel penetrates to realize that Lonergan's debt to Hegel must have important implications for the appropriation of his critical realism. In order to bring those implications into focus, let us turn to Lonergan's claim in the Introduction to *Insight* that his standpoint of critical realism is reached by entering into and then going beyond the halfway house of idealism.[6]

3. ABSOLUTE IDEALISM AS THE HALFWAY HOUSE

There is more than one type of idealism, and Lonergan did not specify the type that characterizes the halfway house.[7] It is very tempting to assume that the idealism in question is the critical philosophy of Kant which Lonergan evidently seeks to counter in *Insight*.[8] But, as I have

5 CWL 3, 398.

6 CWL 3, 22.

7 It should be noted that Lonergan typically speaks of 'idealism' without qualification, and one must determine from the context which idealism – critical idealism or absolute idealism – he is criticizing. Moreover, Lonergan commonly emphasizes the implicit anticipations of the position in Kant, rather than the counterpositional commitments. This emphasis tends to blur the fundamental difference between critical idealism and absolute idealism by emphasizing their shared oversight of the role of judgment. A similar ambiguity afflicts his reference to 'idealism', without qualification, as the halfway house in the quotation from the Introduction to *Insight*. However, in *Understanding and Method* (1959), translation by M. G. Shields of *De Intellectu et Methodo* (first draft, unpublished) 1990, p. 109, (Lonergan Research Institute), Lonergan does actually distinguish between 'Kantian criticism' and 'idealism'. Both fail to appropriate judgment, but only in 'idealism' is truth decisive.

8 Lonergan borrows the image of idealism as the halfway house between critical realism and materialism directly from Maréchal. See CWL 5, 276-

argued elsewhere and at length, the idealism through which we must pass on our way to critical realism cannot be Kant's critical philosophy but must be the absolute idealism of Hegel to whom Lonergan owes the dynamic structure of the argument with which he undertakes to refute Kant.[9] I shall provide just the skeleton of my argument here and invite you to consult the longer article where it is fleshed out.

The idealism that serves as the halfway house between materialism and critical realism cannot be rooted in the basic counterposition.[10] If it is so rooted, it cannot be considered fundamentally superior to, or a significant advance beyond, incoherent realism. If it is to be properly-speaking a halfway house, it has to lie beyond immediate, confrontational realism, whether of the naïve sort or of the more sophisticated Scholastic sort. But Kant's critical philosophy remains rooted firmly in the basic counterposition, and so it does not differ fundamentally from confrontational realism.[11] Despite his "Copernican shift," Kant retains the ideal of knowing as immediate confrontation with an 'already-out-there-now-real', for it is Kant's discovery of the impossibility of realizing this ideal that leads him to restrict the human mind to knowledge of phenomena and drives him into the *cul-de-sac* that is the antinomy of pure reason. As Lonergan put it in *Insight*, Kant's Coper-

---

77. However, as I shall attempt to show in what follows, we should not jump to the conclusion that since Maréchal in his *Cahiers* was crafting a Thomist response to Kant, it is Kant's critical idealism that has the design and the furnishings required for an idealism that is to serve as the halfway house. The image also occurs in Leo W. Keeler's *The Problem of Error from Plato to Kant: A Historical and Critical Study* (Rome: Pontifical Gregorian University, 1934), 6, which Lonergan reviewed in the 1935 volume of *Gregorianum*. However, the image is not Keeler's but occurs in a quotation from A. E. Taylor's *Plato* and is used with reference to the Eleatic doctrine.

9 See my article, "Going Beyond Idealism: Lonergan Relation to Hegel," *Lonergan Workshop Journal*, Vol. 20, ed. Fred Lawrence (forthcoming). The paper was originally presented at The Boston Lonergan Workshop, Boston College, June, 2007.

10 CWL 3, 413 on the elements of the basic counterposition.

11 See CWL 3, 447-48: ". . . Kant's philosophy is not built in a way that is compatible with the fact that the decisive element is truth. Because, for possible knowledge, the criterion in Kant always is the possibility of connecting it with an intuition. And that is why you get into these logical difficulties in Kant. But they are only symptomatic."

nican Revolution was a half-hearted affair.[12] In Kant there is a residual empiricism; for him the level of experience, intuition, remains decisive, at least ideally.[13]

Hegel's absolute idealism, in contrast, is not rooted in the basic counterposition.[14] Hegel rejects the ideal of knowledge as immediate confrontation and pursues an ideal of knowledge as comprehensive and coherent understanding.[15] He rejects intuitionism and affirms the discursive, mediating, constructive nature of intellect as intelligence.[16] Hegel's *Phenomenology of Spirit* is, on one interpretation at least, an account of Spirit's transcendence of confrontationism's presupposition of a primordial subject/object dichotomy.[17]

Still, if Hegel has abandoned knowing as immediate encounter, appropriated the pure and unrestricted desire to know, and rejected objectivity as extroversion, he has nevertheless failed to appropriate, as Lonergan notes repeatedly, the grasp of the virtually unconditioned

---

12 CWL 3, 438.

13 CWL 5, 277-78.

14 CWL 3, 372.

15 The ideal of comprehensive coherence in Hegel corresponds to the ideal that is the good or end of the second level of cognitional operation in Lonergan: "Intelligence as such seeks a complete explanation of all phenomena: it aims at understanding everything. Hence it is constantly making distinctions in order to comprehend all these distinct realities in all their aspects. The end of intelligence is the whole complex of intelligible relations such that the universe may be understood in its unity." This good is the end of "systematic intelligence" which invites comparison with Hegel's notion of system: "In saying 'systematic' we do not mean to suggest some abstract system consisting of propositions from which everything can be deduced. 'Systematic' as we are using it is intended to connote an understanding of the whole concrete universe distinguished according to all its many aspects and the intelligible relations of each of its parts, hence an understanding of the entire universe as something that is one." *Understanding and Method*, 93-94.

16 See *Hegel's Philosophy of Mind*, trans. A. V. Miller (Oxford: Clarendon Press, 1971), 224: "Pure thinking knows that it alone, and not feeling or representation, is capable of grasping the truth of things, and that the assertion of Epicurus that the true is what is sensed, must be pronounced a complete perversion of the nature of mind."

17 Of course, Lonergan objects to Hegel's 'necessitarian' depiction of this process of superseding the subject/object dichotomy.

and judgment of fact. Hegel's notion of being may be comprehensive in connotation, but it is restricted in denotation.[18] Accordingly, on its ascent beyond incoherent realism absolute idealism stalls, so to speak, on the level of understanding, and it may be described as quasi-positional or transitional.

Hegel's absolute idealism, then, is not counterpositional; it is basically positional but nevertheless incomplete. The sign of its incompleteness, it should be noted, is not to be found in its abstractness because for Hegel, as for Lonergan, abstraction is not impoverishing but enriching. It is not the bloodlessness of Hegel's intellectual ballet that is the indicator of its incompleteness; rather, it is the superhuman poise required of the dancers. The quasi-positionality and transitional character of Hegel's absolute idealism is reflected in its notorious instability; it is a philosophy whose distinguishing feature is a too precarious balance that manifests itself most vividly in Hegel's so-called "speculative propositions." In Hegel's pursuit of an ideal of the union of union and non-union, of the identity of identity and difference, we witness a heroic but ultimately unsuccessful struggle to work out the epistemological and metaphysical implications of the discovery that intellect is intelligence.

Of course, Hegel did not regard his philosophy as transitional and only quasi-positional as Lonergan did. Despite its instability, Hegel regarded his philosophy as absolute. What I have described as the residual instability of a transitional philosophy Hegel took to be the intrinsic dialectical tension of the Absolute itself which has reached its fully self-conscious, explanatory self-expression in absolute idealism. For Hegel, this tension is ontological. But the plethora of highly precarious conceptions or mixed conceptual results that characterize Hegel's system have generated perduring controversies in Hegel scholarship.[19] That the "speculative proposition" in its various formulations

---

18 CWL 3, 398.

19 In Hegel's logic-in-motion, for example, Lonergan discerns such a mixed result: "True, the same concept is always conceived in the same way, and there is no movement in concepts considered logically. Nevertheless, if they are considered in a concrete way as they exist in the human mind, they undergo continual modification because concepts do not exist independently of the intending and the understanding of a concrete human being ....Hence, with a greater or lesser advance in understanding, concepts undergo greater or lesser development and change. To recognize this fact is to

generates these controversies, even among committed Hegelians, suggests that it does not in fact satisfy the immanent criterion of truth that is Hegel's own intelligent *Geist*.[20] This perduring spiritual discomfort has evoked valiant efforts to articulate a "Hegelian Middle" that remains nevertheless elusive, and it has led even the most astute readers of Hegel to tip the balance to the right, like Kierkegaard, or to the left, like Marx, and more recently, Alexandre Kojève.[21] From Lonergan's standpoint, these controversies are intractable within the closed circle of the Hegelian System and so provide fodder for unending commentary. Their resolutions require transcendence of the residual dialectical tension that perpetually threatens the integrity of

---

recognize the fundamental point in the solution of the problem of historicity" (*Understanding and Method*, 54). Again, Hegel's logic in its entirety, in virtue of the identity of thought and being, is a transitional *metaphysics* which, Lonergan claims, is *connotatively comprehensive* but *denotatively restricted*. The intending of the *Logic* is a hybrid of transcendental notion and determinate category. Lonergan writes in *Method in Theology*, ". . . (T)he most fundamental difference in modes of intending lies between the categorial and the transcendental. Categories are determinations. They have a limited denotation. They vary with cultural variations. . . . In contrast, the transcendentals are comprehensive in connotation, unrestricted in denotation, invariant over cultural change. . . . They are comprehensive because they intend the unknown whole or totality of which our answers reveal only part." See *Method in Theology* (New York: Herder and Herder, 1972), 11. In Lonergan's terms, Hegel's intending is transcendental inasmuch as it is comprehensive in connotation, inasmuch as Hegel finds the whole, the totality, in every part, but it is categorial inasmuch as there is only the single virtually unconditioned which is the Absolute.

20 Thus, for example, Hegel's philosophy provides evidence for both the 'epochal' and the 'absolutist' interpretations of his eschatology. Is Hegel's philosophy *its* time comprehended in thought, or is it *time* comprehended in thought? See Daniel Berthold-Bond, *Hegel's Grand Synthesis: A Study of Being, Thought, and History* (Albany: SUNY Press, 1989), esp. Ch. Seven.

21 See Emil Fackenheim, *The Religious Dimension in Hegel's Thought* (Boston: Beacon Press, 1967), 76: "From the outset and throughout, the Hegelian system seems faced with the choice between saving the claims of an absolute and therefore all-comprehensive philosophic thought, but at the price of loss of any actual world besides it, and saving the contingent world of human experience at the price of reducing philosophic thought itself to finiteness." See Ch. 4 on "The Hegelian Middle" and right- and left-wing interpretations.

the "speculative proposition" and whose opposing poles are the Hegelian System itself, which is a seamless fabric of internal relations, on the one hand, and discrete matters of fact, on the other. In short, their resolutions require a different ontology.

This is a serious limitation. But it is not attributable to the counterpositionality of Hegel's idealism. It is, rather, a consequence of its incompleteness. Hegel's absolute idealism shares with Lonergan's critical realism at least five noteworthy differences from Kant's counterpositional critical philosophy. First, while both credit Kant with the discovery of the primacy of the unity of apperception, both criticize him for failing to exploit fully the implications of this discovery.[22] Accordingly, in the second place, following J. G. Fichte, both reject Kant's postulation of the *Ding an sich* behind phenomena and his residual empiricism, and both affirm the enriching role of intellectual mediation. Thirdly, then, following Aristotle in the *De Anima*, both affirm the original unity of subject and object and the doctrine of knowing by identity.[23] In the fourth place, both affirm an immanent criterion of objectivity; the criterion of objectivity lies not outside human consciousness but within it.[24] Finally, both understand Kant's critique of

22 See CWL 5, 15. On Kant, See CWL 3, 365 and 362-66 for Lonergan's contrast of his position with Kant's.

23 See *Hegel's Philosophy of Mind*, 180-81: "However, the Knowing of truth does not itself, to begin with, have the form of truth; for at the stage of development now reached, it is still *abstract*, the formal identity of subjectivity and objectivity. Only when this identity has developed into an actual difference and has made itself into the identity of itself and its difference, therefore, only when mind or spirit steps forth as an immanently developed totality, not till then has that certainty *established* itself as truth."

24 In the Introduction to his *Phenomenology of Spirit*, Hegel writes: "But the essential point to bear in mind throughout the whole investigation is that these two moments, 'Notion' and 'object', 'being-for-another' and being-in-itself', both fall *within* that knowledge which we are investigating. Consequently, we do not need to import criteria, or to make use of our own bright ideas and thoughts during the course of the inquiry; it is precisely when we leave these aside that we succeed in contemplating the matter in hand as it is *in and for itself*. But not only is a contribution by us superfluous, since Notion and object, the criterion and what is to be tested, are present in consciousness itself, but we are also spared the trouble of comparing the two and really *testing* them, so that, since what consciousness examines is its own self, all that is left for us to do is simply to look on. For consciousness is, on the one hand, consciousness of the object, and on the other,

pure reason to be, not the critique of the human mind it purports to be, but a critique of a long dominant historical conception of the human mind and ideal of knowledge.[25]

Kant's Critical Philosophy is properly-speaking counterpositional and, from Lonergan's standpoint, in this regard it is fundamentally wrong. Kant did not know about insight, and because he did not know about insight, he remained a confrontationist.[26] In addition to being

---

consciousness of itself; consciousness of what for it is the True, and con-sciousness of its knowledge of the truth. Since both are *for* the same con-sciousness, this consciousness is itself their comparison; it is for the same consciousness to know whether its knowledge of the object corresponds to the object or not. The object, it is true, seems only to be for conscious-ness in the way that consciousness knows it; it seems that consciousness cannot, as it were, get behind the object as it exists for consciousness so as to examine what the object is in itself, and hence, too, cannot test its own knowledge by that standard. But the distinction between the in-itself and knowledge is already present in the very fact that consciousness knows an object at all. Something is *for it* the *in-itself*; and knowledge, or the being of the object for consciousness, is, *for it*, another moment. Upon this distinc-tion, which is present as a fact, the examination rests." *Hegel's Phenomenol-ogy of Spirit*, trans. A. V. Miller (Oxford: Oxford University Press, 1979), 53-54. See CWL 3, 659 ff. on the immanent source of transcendence.

25 CWL 5, 20. Lonergan remarks that Kant's critique (the KRV) "was not of the pure reason but of the human mind as conceived by Scotus ..." See *Collected Works of Bernard Lonergan*, vol. 2, *Verbum: Word and Idea in Aquinas*, ed. Frederick E. Crowe and Robert M. Doran (Toronto: Univer-sity of Toronto Press, 1997), 38-39. Philosophers after Kant may be sort-ed into two groups: those who believe Kant to have critiqued the human mind, and those who believe Kant to have critiqued an *historical conception* of the human mind or *a particular ideal of knowledge*. Hegel and Lonergan may be counted among those in the latter group. Hegel locates Kant at the limit of the standpoint of understanding in his *Phenomenology of Spirit*.

26 While Lonergan says in CWL 5 that "Kant, Aristotle, and St Thomas all knew about insight," he also immediately identifies a difference between Aristotle and Kant on this score: "The difference between Kant, on the one hand, and Aristotle and Thomas on the other, is this: Kant's a priori is ... absolutely independent of experience. ... In Aristotle and Thomas, on the other hand, the insight and the concept are distinguished, and the phantasm, the image, causes the insight. In Kant there is no talk of the insight, but only of the concept, the image, and the concept governing the image. Kant's synthetic a priori presupposes that the insight already exists and that the concepts are already formed. Given those presuppositions,

deficient in this fundamental way, Kant's philosophy is incomplete in other ways, the most notable being the absence from it of a doctrine of rational judgment. But it is not the missing doctrine of judgment in Kant's critical philosophy that precludes its serving as the halfway house on the way to critical realism; it is its counterpositionality.

Hegel's absolute idealism, on the other hand, is quasi-positional, and so it is a transitional position. It is not properly-speaking counterpositional, and in this fundamental respect it is not deficient, although it too remains incomplete. Hegel, to an extent sufficient to push him beyond Kant's critical philosophy into absolute idealism, knew about insight in the same unthematized way that Aristotle (as Lonergan asserted) knew about insight, even though neither Hegel nor Aristotle seems to have known about grasp of the virtually unconditioned and judgment.[27]

It is absolute idealism, then, that is to serve as the halfway house between the "two quite different realisms" distinguished by Lonergan. There is an incoherent realism that is half-animal and half-human, for which immediate intuitions, either sensitive or intellectual, are decisive; on the other hand, there is a coherent, fully human realism, for which rational judgment is decisive. Whereas incoherent realism is merely the static midpoint between materialism and idealism, absolute idealism is the halfway house, the transitional position, between materialism and the coherent critical realism beyond idealism. To reach Lonergan's critical realism, then, we must enter into and go beyond Hegel's absolute idealism. But the entry into and movement beyond absolute idealism is both a daunting intellectual challenge and a fearsome personal one.

4. INSIGHT INTO INSIGHT AND
THE FEAR OF IDEALISM

Recently, Richard Liddy published an account of his own gradual entry into the standpoint of critical realism.[28] It is the story of his personal struggle to appropriate Lonergan's position. For the title of his

one controls one's images, but the images do not cause the insight." See CWL 5, 31. In short, Kant knew about the consequences of insight but not about the event.

27 CWL 5, 18.

28 Richard M. Liddy, *Startling Strangeness: Reading Lonergan's Insight* (Lanham: University Press of America, 2007).

book Liddy borrowed the phrase "Startling Strangeness" that occurs in the very paragraph in the Introduction to *Insight* where Lonergan speaks of two quite different realisms and identifies idealism as the halfway house on the way to critical realism. In his autobiographical account, Liddy describes a fear of idealism that arose in him subsequent to his discovery of insight and of the mediative and constructive functions of conscious and intentional operations. In light of the requirement that we enter into and go beyond absolute idealism in order to reach the standpoint of critical realism, this fear of idealism and its relationship to the appropriation of critical realism warrant closer scrutiny.

It may seem odd or inappropriate to shift the focus from the idealism of the halfway house, its philosophical superiority to Kant's critical philosophy, and its residual incompleteness, to the experience of fear associated with the break with confrontationism. Surely of primary importance is the distinction between the two realisms and its philosophical implications; whether or not a fear is associated with this discovery may seem to be a minor issue. But we should recall that the critical realism that Lonergan promotes is not to be regarded as a system of mere concepts, nor even as a theory in the strong sense. The movement from incoherent to critical realism is not merely a change of mind or the adoption of a different *Begrifflichkeit* effected by the exercise of an isolated cognitive faculty; it is a personal transformation, a conversion of the concrete, existing subject.

While it may be premature to declare that the Age of Theory has ended – for even so-called 'postmodernism', far from being a positive alternative to classicism, is still in reaction against its failures – it is clear enough that the Age of Theory is on its last legs. Indeed, one might argue that the instability of Hegel's system is itself a consequence of his own futile attempt to find room in the static systems of conceptualism for the dynamic flow of the interior intellectual life. Hegel insisted that his absolute idealism is not to be regarded as another in the series of *philosophies of the understanding*, as he called them, but as an objectification of a self-developing dynamism, albeit of a dynamic *Begriff*. Similarly, Lonergan insisted that his critical realism not be viewed as yet another conceptual product of the Age of Theory, but as an objectification of the normative unfolding of concept-generating conscious intentionality. If Hegel nudged the Wolffian static, conceptual system, which found its ultimate criterion in the principle of non-contradiction, toward greater concreteness by insisting upon the dynamic flexibility of Kant's categories of the understanding, then, by regarding Kant's antinomies not as dead-ends but as signs of the need for a new beginning, Lonergan has pushed Hegel's peculiar logic-in-motion toward greater concreteness by nudging us beyond the flexible categories to their preconceptual generative principles. The critical realism Lonergan offers is not a self-conscious, self-mediating, dynamic system of interrelated concepts but the dynamic standpoint of a deliberate and methodical existential subject. When we treat the concrete fear of idealism that is said to accompany insight into insight as a marginal concern, we operate within a structure of relevance characteristic of the Age of Theory, with its faculty psychology, but no longer appropriate in the Age of Interiority, with its qualitatively differentiated conscious continuum that is the concrete unity of consciousness.

The fear of idealism arises as a function of the combination of insight into insight with horizonal preconditions. As it happens, many students of Lonergan seem to have arrived at their breakthroughs with three prior horizonal commitments, each of which, when combined with insight into insight, may generate the fear of idealism. The first is the prior commitment to confrontationism, often in a putatively Thomist guise, without which there would be no need for a breakthrough. The second is a prior commitment to Christian theism, usually in its specifically Catholic form. The third is a prior, inescapable respect for concrete fact. In combination with pre-existing confrontationism, insight into insight evokes one sort of fear of idealism that dissipates fairly quickly. In combination with either or both of the other two commitments, insight into insight evokes another sort of fear of idealism, one that initiates and qualifies a prolonged personal and intellectual struggle.

The first sort of fear is expressed as a fear of being trapped in one's own subjectivity. The roots of this fear do not lie in insight into insight, pure and simple, but in the combination of insight into insight with inertial confrontationist presuppositions. For insight into insight, by itself, entails the realization that knowing is not immediate confrontation, that objectivity is not extroversion, and that being is not a subdivision of the 'already out there now'. The fear of being trapped in one's own subjectivity, however, presupposes a *Gegenstand* or object standing over against or in opposition to the subject, an object of the type postulated by Kant, and it entails an epistemological "problem of the bridge." This first sort of fear of idealism is the one Liddy identifies as emerging with his discovery of insight, and he reports that it was dissolved when he realized that the idealism he was fearing, in his words, "still holds on to the idea of reality as 'out there'. . ." (206). Because he understood the idealism he feared was just as counterpositional as the incoherent realism he was leaving behind, his fear dissipated.

This first sort of fear, then, is in its most vulgar form an unreasonable fear of solipsism. In its most sophisticated form, it is an unreasonable fear of Kantian critical idealism. The realization of its unreasonableness and its dissipation, then, do not signal either an entry into or a passage beyond the halfway house on the way to critical realism. The dissipation of this unreasonable fear of counterpositional idealism merely clears the way, I would say, for the emergence of a second sort of fear of a different sort of idealism – a fear of the quasi-positional, transitional, Hegelian absolute idealism of the halfway house. That is to say, insight into insight does not propel one through and beyond the halfway house of absolute idealism; on the contrary, it merely situates one at its threshold.

This second fear is a reasonable one, and as such, it is not so easily alleviated. Now, either the pre-existing commitment to theism joins with insight into insight to evoke the fear that a real distinction cannot be drawn between divine and human subjectivity, or the pre-existing respect for fact combines with insight into insight to elicit the fear that being is just a tissue of internal relations, or both join with the discovery to elicit a fear of the implications of absolute idealism. One now confronts the precarious balance, the instability and the mixed results of the transitional position, and the residual dialectical tension between the ideal of comprehensive coherence and concrete and discrete matters of fact. The pseudo-problem of gaining access to being from without is replaced by the real problem of dividing being from within. That is to say, a pseudo-problem of objectivity, previously framed imaginatively in terms of 'inside' and 'outside', is replaced by a genuine problem of objectivity framed now in terms of unimaginable immanence and transcendence. The unreasonable fear of counterpositional idealism is gone, but a reasonable fear of quasi-positional idealism remains, and it should remain. It is this fear that initiates and qualifies the prolonged personal and intellectual struggle to go beyond idealism.

As Lonergan observed in 1958 in his first set of lectures on *Insight*, "[I]f you frankly acknowledge that intellect is intelligence, you discover that you have terrific problems in epistemology."[29] These terrific problems arise as a consequence of insight into insight. That is to say, insight into insight evokes them; insight into insight does not solve them. Moreover, these terrific epistemological problems are not safely quarantined within an isolated cognitive faculty. They infect the concrete, existing subject. So it is that when Lonergan discovered insight in the summer of 1930 while reading Stewart's *Plato's Doctrine of Ideas*,[30] he did not immediately declare himself a critical realist but found himself at the threshold of the halfway house of absolute idealism, and he feared he was becoming an idealist. Again, Lonergan reports that he sought assurance that he was not an idealist when he "got hold of the idea that knowledge is discursive,"[31] and the fear that

---

29 CWL 5, 19.

30 Lonergan reported his discovery by way of Stewart in the question session that took place on June 19, 1979, at Boston College. "Aristotle and Thomas held that you abstracted from phantasm the *eidos*, the *species*, the idea. And my first clue into the idea was when I was reading a book by an Oxford don by the name of J. A. Stewart who in 1905 had written on Plato's myths and in 1909 on Plato's doctrine of ideas. And he explained the doctrine of ideas by contending that for Plato an idea was something like the Cartesian formula for a circle...and that exemplified an act of understanding to me, and the idea was getting what's in behind the formula for the circle. So you have something in between the concept and the datum or phantasm. And that is the sort of thing that you can't hold and be a naïve realist..." The transcription of the tape-recording of the question session is held by the Lonergan Research Institute in Toronto and was done by Nicholas Graham. On Lonergan's relation to Stewart, see my book *At the Threshold of the Halfway House: Bernard Lonergan's Encounter with John Alexander Stewart* (Chestnut Hill, MA: The Lonergan Institute at Boston College, 2007).

31 *Caring About Meaning: Patterns in the Life of Bernard Lonergan*, ed. Pierrot Lambert, Charlotte Tansey, and Cathleen Going (Montreal: Thomas More Institute Papers, 1982), 110. Also in *Caring About Meaning*, 108, Lonergan remarks that, while Husserl's "account of knowledge was never purely constructive," his is. "It is all construction. Saying it is all construction enlarges the notion that human knowledge is discourse. When I say 'critical realism is not a half-way house between materialism and idealism but idealism is the half-way house between materialism and critical realism,' it is the same thing again."

he might be an idealist was still present, by his own admission, years after his discovery of the act of understanding, when he was arriving at the conclusions he set forth in *Insight*.[32] In the Preface to *Insight* Lonergan alludes to his twenty-eight-year search, from the beginning of his philosophical studies in 1926 until the completion of *Insight* in 1953. I think it is fair to say that the last twenty-three-and-one-half years of that twenty-eight year search – from his discovery of insight in the summer of 1930 while reading Stewart until the completion of *Insight* in 1953 – were spent in the halfway house of idealism, engaged in the terrific epistemological struggle required to move beyond it.[33] As Lonergan remarked in the Halifax Lectures, "The intrusion of epistemological problems in a real, significant way is a disturbing event."[34]

So it is that despite the essential role of insight into insight in the appropriation of his critical realism, Lonergan regarded his doctrine of judgment as his greatest contribution to philosophy. Insight into insight may dispel the myth of confrontationism and dissipate the fear of counterpositional idealism. But with the elimination of that myth and the abating of that unreasonable fear, there come to light terrific epistemological problems, and there emerges another reasonable fear. The epistemological problems are finally resolved, and this reasonable fear is finally alleviated, only with the discovery of the virtually unconditioned and judgment of fact. As one's entry into the halfway house of idealism is occasioned by insight into insight, and as one's dwelling in the halfway house is characterized by a struggle with a genuine problem of objectivity, so one's passage beyond the halfway house of idealism is accomplished only with the discovery of the grasp of the virtually unconditioned and judgment.

By way of conclusion, let us return briefly to the irony with which I began this essay and the questions it evoked. Why is the Aquinas of the Toronto Thomists so radically incompatible with Hegel? I would say it is because Hegel breaks with confrontationism and they, like Kant, do not.[35] Therefore, their Aquinas is radically incompatible with

32 Ibid., 110-111.

33 On Lonergan's reading of Stewart's book on Plato's doctrine of ideas, see *At the Threshold of the Halfway House.*

34 CWL 5, 351.

35 See Bernard Lonergan, *Collection*, Collected Works of Bernard Lonergan, Vol. 4, ed. Frederick E. Crowe and Robert M. Doran (Toronto: Uni-

Hegel who breaks completely with confrontationism. In what ways is Lonergan's Aquinas compatible with Hegelian idealism? Lonergan's Aquinas, like Hegel, breaks with confrontationism, and both, following Aristotle, affirm the doctrine of knowledge by identity.[36] Does Lonergan's kinship with both Aquinas and Hegel have consequences for our appropriation of Lonergan's critical realism? I think it has important and far-reaching consequences. It requires that we distinguish an unreasonable fear of idealism that is to be dismissed from a reasonable fear of idealism that is to be appropriated. That reasonable fear of idealism initiates and qualifies our pursuit of solutions to the terrific epistemological problems that follow upon the discovery that intellect is intelligence. It ushers us into and beyond the halfway house of Hegel's absolute idealism. It abates only with the completing achievement of a doctrine of the grasp of the virtually unconditioned and judgment that is the final moment of the ascent to the rationally self-conscious standpoint "above the clouds" that is Lonergan's critical realism.

---

versity of Toronto Press, 1988), 192 ff. for Lonergan's discussion of Kant and Gilsonian Thomism.

36 CWL 3, 372 for Lonergan's acknowledgement of Hegel's rejection of confrontationism. Hegel evidently derives his understanding of knowing by identity from Aristotle's *De Anima*. See in this connection, Alfredo Ferrarin, *Hegel and Aristotle* (Cambridge: Cambridge University Press, 2001). In his *History of Philosophy* Hegel gives no attention whatsoever to the positions of Aquinas. See his extensive treatment of Aristotle in his *Lectures on the History of Philosophy, Vol. 2: Plato and the Platonists*, trans. E. S. Haldane and Frances H. Simson (Lincoln: University of Nebraska Press, 1999), 117 ff. Compare his one-paragraph treatment of Aquinas in his *Lectures on the History of Philosophy, Vol. III: Medieval and Modern Philosophy*, ed. Robert f. Brown, trans. R. F. Brown and J. M. Stewart, with the assistance of H. S. Harris (Berkeley: University of California Press, 1990), 58.

UNMASKING THE CENSOR

Elizabeth A. Murray
LOYOLA MARYMOUNT UNIVERSITY

I. INTRODUCTION

In his major work *Theology and the Dialectics of History*,[1] Robert Doran provides a masterful study of the problem of sustained development. He writes of the 'movement of life,' the natural internal dynamism that would move us to further development and creativity, and the various obstacles to this dynamism. The dialectical obstacles to growth are both socio-historical and psychological. The subject develops in an inherited, socio-historical context already riddled with the effects of bias and the surd of sin. Insofar as one inadvertently adopts the inauthenticity of one's world, one's psychological development may be similarly distorted. The psychological aberration of dramatic bias disorients and stultifies the movement of life. It is within the complex framework of these dialectical obstacles that Doran introduces the concept of *psychic conversion*. He focuses on the role that psychic conversion has in conjunction with the 'healing vector' of God's love in liberating the immanent 'creative vector.'

Doran works out the concept of psychic conversion in the context of Lonergan's thought including Lonergan's notions of conscious intentionality, dialectic, and conversion. In *Method in Theology* Lonergan defines dialectically differentiated horizons as distinguished by the presence or absence of three forms of conversion: religious, moral, and intellectual. Lonergan defines conversion as a free act of will, as a decision or a choice:

> It is a decision about whom and what you are for and, again, whom and what you are against. It is a decision illuminated by the mani-

---

1 Robert M. Doran, *Theology and the Dialectics of History* (Toronto: University of Toronto Press, 1990). From now on, I will refer to this work as *TDH*.

fold possibilities exhibited in dialectic. It is a fully conscious decision about one's horizon, one's outlook, one's world-view.[2]

Doran argues for the addition of a fourth conversion, the conversion
that takes place on the psychic level. The psychic level underlies the
spiritual levels of conscious intentionality, the level of intelligent consciousness, rational consciousness, and rational self-consciousness or
moral consciousness. At the same time, this level supervenes and organizes the underlying and unconscious neurological level. The psychic
level, which is the level of sense, perception, imagination, memory, desires, and feelings, is partly conscious and partly unconscious. Because
of the primitive nature of the psychic level, conversion on this level
does not fit the same pattern as conversion on the higher levels of conscious intentionality. Doran does not define this form of conversion as
a decision, which would be an act of rational self-consciousness on the
fourth level; rather, he defines psychic conversion as a transformation
of a psychic component on the first level of consciousness:

> …Psychic conversion affects the first level. Psychic conversion is a
> transformation of the psychic component of what Freud calls 'the
> censor' from a repressive to a constructive agency in a person's de-
> velopment.[3]

The censor as originally conceived by Freud is a psychic component
operating on the border of the unconscious and the conscious mind.
Similarly, the censor in Doran's sense is an element of the psychic
level operating on the unconscious neural level. The transformation
of the censor is a more or less spontaneous process which issues in
psychic appropriation.[4] One must choose to engage in this process and
to reorient oneself by turning one's attention to the contents of one's
psyche – one's dreams, fears, desires, spontaneous images, memories,
etc. This process may also require the decision to seek the collaboration of a therapist or analyst. Yet psychic conversion is not conceived
in the same sense as Lonergan's other three conversions. While it may

---

2   Bernard Lonergan, *Method in Theology* (Toronto: University of Toronto
    Press, 1990), 268.

3   Doran, *TDH*, 59.

4   Doran, *TDH*, 142.

require conscious decisions, it itself is not a conscious decisive act, but the transformation of a preconscious psychic function.[5]

In defining psychic conversion as primarily a transformation of the censor, Doran is using the familiar term first coined by Freud in his pivotal work *The Interpretation of Dreams* and later employed by Lonergan in his account of the elements in the dramatic subject in *Insight*. Lonergan and Doran incorporate Freud's concept even though it has come under blistering attack from twentieth century critics such as Sartre and Ricoeur. The psychic function of censorship is inherently problematic. Before we examine what Freud, Sartre, Lonergan, and Doran mean by the censor, let us consider in a preliminary way an inherent difficulty with the very concept of psychic censorship.

We will see that the censor for Lonergan and Doran can have a dual function as constructive and repressive. As repressive, the censor blocks from consciousness the affect-laden images which would lead one to a disturbing or painful realization. How is it possible for the censor in its repressive role to block from consciousness the images that would give rise to an unwanted insight, if one does not already have some apprehension of the insight which one then does not want? This question, incidentally, is the converse of Meno's sophistical complaint to Socrates regarding the impossibility of arriving at knowledge:

> How will you look for something when you don't in the least know what it is…how will you know that the thing you have found is the thing you didn't know?[6]

The problem with the censor is how to account for the proleptic apprehension of an understood which the censor blocks us from understanding. We can highlight the difficulty more sharply by reaffirming with Lonergan the unity of the developing, existing subject.[7] The higher levels of conscious intentionality on which I question and understand are not more 'me' than the underlying psychic level:

> Nor are the pure desire [to know] and the sensitive psyche two things, one of them 'I' and the other 'It.' They are the unfolding on

---

5 Bernard Lonergan, *Collected Works of Bernard Lonergan*, vol. 3, *Insight: A Study of Human Understanding* (Toronto: University of Toronto Press, 1992), 218.

6 Plato, *Meno*, 80d.

7 Lonergan, *Insight*, 495.

different levels of a single, individual unity, identity, whole. Both are 'I,' and neither is merely 'It.'[8]

The censor, then, cannot be conceived of as a psychic function, distinct from me, which stands guard at the gate separating me from the rest of the unconscious. The I who desires to know and to understand is the I who interferes with the images that would enable me to understand. This unity which I am seems both to desire to know and to flee understanding. That the one same subject would have conflicting desires is not in itself a problem. It is a manifestation of the fact that the subject is, according to Lonergan, a unity in tension.[9] The difficulty is that the concept of the censor requires that one apprehend and understand and neither apprehend nor understand the same thing at the same time.

2. FREUD'S CENSOR

In his *The Interpretation of Dreams* (1899), Freud primarily developed a theory of dreams and secondarily suggested a general theory of the mind or psyche. After three decades Freud still viewed this book as a pivotal achievement. He wrote in the preface to its third and final edition: "Insight such as this falls to one's lot but once in a lifetime."[10] The key insight into dreams revealed through the laborious work of their interpretation is that "a dream is a fulfillment of a wish."[11] The concept of the censor emerges in Freud's account of how repression operates in dreaming and in other psycho-pathological structures. In his summary of the psychology of repression in *On Dreams*, Freud describes two "thought-constructing agencies" – one has free access to consciousness and its contents, the other is in itself unconscious and can only reach consciousness through the former consciousness. The censor functions on the borderline between these two agencies:

> On the frontier between the two agencies, where the first passes over to the second, there is a censorship which only allows what is agreeable to it to pass through and holds back everything else. Ac-

8 Ibid., 499.

9 Ibid., 494-504.

10 Sigmund Freud, *The Freud Reader*, ed. Peter Gay (New York: W. W. Norton & Company, 1989), 129.

11 Freud, "The Interpretation of Dreams," in *The Freud Reader*, 142.

cording to our definition, then, what is rejected by the censorship is in a state of repression.[12]

In dreams the strict control of the censorship, which Freud likened to the Russian political censorship of his day,[13] is somewhat relaxed, allowing certain impulses and desires to be expressed in dream representations. This enables contents of the unconscious a circuitous way into consciousness. Yet while the censorship is relaxed in sleep, it is not completely eliminated. Thus, dreaming involves a systematic process of distortion and disguise which renders the content of a dream obscure. For example, a dream content can be disguised by the use of its opposite. The fundamental pattern for the generation of dreams is "repression – relaxation of the censorship – the formation of a compromise."[14] The intentions of one agency (the conscious mind) and the demands of the other agency (the unconscious mind) arrive at a compromise in the obscure dream representations. One vital function of the disguise of the dream contents is to enable the dreamer to remain asleep. When the dreamer awakens, the censor regains its strength and can eliminate any trace of the revealed, previously unconscious contents. Freud surmises that this is one explanation for the complete or partial forgetting of dreams.

Freud readily acknowledges that the psychology of repression that he outlines is but a crude hypothesis based on a simile:

> We have gathered an impression that the formation of obscure dreams occurs *as though* one person who was dependent upon a second person had to make a remark which was bound to be disagreeable in the ears of this second one; and it is on the basis of this simile that we arrived at the concepts of dream-distortion and censorship.[15]

Yet he is confident that further research into the two opposing psychic agencies will ultimately confirm it. Of one thing he is sure, that "the second agency controls access to consciousness and can bar the

---

12 Freud, "On Dreams," in *The Freud Reader*, 166.

13 James Hopkins, "The Interpretation of Dreams," in *The Cambridge Companion to Freud*, ed. Jerome Neu (Cambridge: Cambridge University Press, 1992), 113.

14 Freud, "On Dreams," in *The Freud Reader*, 166.

15 Ibid.

first agency from such access."[16] The second agency, as was indicated above, is that which has free access to consciousness and its contents; the first agency is wholly unconscious. In attributing the control of the access to consciousness to the second agency, he is characterizing the censor as a function of consciousness. But in what sense is the censor conscious? Am I responsible for the censorship? Must I be continuously vigilant to guard the gates of consciousness? To determine in what sense the censor is conscious, let us examine what Freud means by the unconscious.

In the course of systematizing psychoanalysis, Freud developed two typologies of the psyche. His accounts of the nature and role of the unconscious and the censor evolve with the revisions to his metapsychology. First, it should be noted that the unconscious has two senses: a descriptive sense in which simple awareness is its criterion and a systematic sense, the main interest of psychoanalysis, in which the unconscious is seen as the source of motivation and psychic conflict.[17] The latter is the unconscious as uncovered through the clinical phenomena of resistance and transference, and as manifested in dreams and in certain waking parapraxes, such as slips of the tongue, misreadings, slips of the pen (typos), bungled actions, etc.[18]

The first typology was initially one of regions or systems: the unconscious, the preconscious, and the conscious. As Ricoeur notes, this typology tended to be abstract and solipsistic insofar as it dealt with psychic phenomena without consideration of their interpersonal genesis and context.[19] The first typology was one of rather static locations. In *The Interpretation of Dreams*, dream thoughts, for example, are described as *in* the unconscious. The censor, as we have seen, is placed at the border between the unconscious and the conscious. In his later essays in metapsychology, the typology of static places is gradually replaced by a dynamic economics of psychic forces. In *The Unconscious* (1915), Freud differentiates the preconscious from the unconscious

16 Ibid.

17 Sebastian Gardner, "The Unconscious," in *The Cambridge Companion to Freud*, 137.

18 Freud, *The Pelican Freud Library*, vol. 5, *The Psychopathology of Everyday Life*, trans. Alan Tyson, ed. James Strachey (New York: Penguin Books, 1976).

19 Paul Ricoeur, *Freud and Philosophy: An Essay on Interpretation*, trans. Denis Savage (New Haven and London: Yale University Press, 1970), 62.

and the conscious and he elaborates the complexity of the unconscious:

> In general a psychical act goes through two phases as regards its
> state, between which is interposed a kind of testing (censorship). In
> the first phase the psychical act is unconscious and belongs to the
> system Ucs.; if, on testing, it is rejected by the censorship, it is not
> allowed to pass into the second phase; it is then said to be 'repressed'
> and must remain unconscious. If, however, it passes this testing, it
> enters the second phase and thenceforth belongs to the second sys-
> tem…Cs. But the fact that it belongs to that system does not yet
> unequivocally determine its relation to consciousness. It is not yet
> conscious, but it is certainly *capable of becoming conscious*… . In con-
> sideration of this capacity for becoming conscious, we also call the
> system Cs. the 'preconscious'. If it should turn out that a certain cen-
> sorship also plays a part in determining whether the preconscious
> becomes conscious, we shall discriminate more sharply between the
> systems Pcs. and Cs.[20]

The Unconscious in the systematic sense is not merely what we
would describe as unconscious. It is differentiated into that which is
initially or temporarily unconscious and may become conscious and
that which is repressed and cannot become conscious. Similarly, the
Conscious in the systematic sense includes what we might describe
as conscious, what we are aware of, as well as that which has been repressed, which we are not presently aware of, but yet still may become
conscious if not again repressed (the Preconscious). It is clear in the
above passage that these three psychic systems are differentiated not
so much by our awareness of the acts or contents, but by the process
of repression and the agency of repression, the censor.

As Freud's psychology expanded to include a theory of society and
culture, he developed a typology that was a kind of 'personology'.[21] It
was not conceived of in terms of places but rather in terms of roles of
the individual. In his later works rather than divide the psyche into the
Unconscious, the Preconscious, and the Conscious he now develops
the familiar triad of the Ego, the Id, and the Superego. Freud did not
abandon the earlier elements of the first typology, but he saw them as
less critical in his definitive statement of the structure of the psyche.
There is not a simple correlation between the respective elements of

---

20 Freud, "The Unconscious," in *The Freud Reader*, 578.

21 Ricoeur, 181.

the two typologies. The Ego is not to be identified with the conscious because it starts out as preconscious and the preconscious remains its nucleus.[22] Further, the Ego is in part unconscious because it is not sharply separated from the Id. The lower portion of the Ego, the basic passions, merges into the Id. Not only are the nether reaches of the Ego unconscious, even the highest intellectual and critical operations of the Ego can be unconscious as, for example, when a difficult intellectual problem is resolved during sleep. Similarly, while the Id and the Superego are generally considered to be unconscious, the conscious extends into the Id insofar as the repressed becomes a part of the Id: "The repressed is only cut off sharply from the ego by the resistances of repression; it can communicate with the ego through the id."[23]

Notwithstanding the reciprocal contamination of the unconscious Id and the conscious Ego, Freud reasserts that the division of the psychical into what is conscious and what is unconscious is fundamental to psychoanalysis.

Freud speaks of the process of repression and the repressed in delineating the Ego and the Id. How does the agent of repression, the censor, function in the context of the second typology? In each individual there is found "a coherent organization of mental processes" which Freud defines as the Ego. He further characterizes the Ego as that to which consciousness is attached, as the agency in control of the individual's operations with the external world, and as the mental agency capable of supervising all of its conscious mental activity. In this last role of the self-conscious agency in control of its own mental operations and contents, the Ego is the source of all repressions. "Even [when it sleeps] it exercises the censorship on dreams."[24]

Reviewing the two typologies of Freud's metapsychology has brought us closer to the nature of the censor in his thought. In the first typology, the censor stands as the guard or tester on the border between the Unconscious and the Conscious, and also on the border between the Preconscious and the Conscious. He describes the censor as a function of the second thought-constructing agency, that which has access to consciousness. In the second typology, the role of the censor is attributed to the Ego, to which consciousness is primarily attached

---

22 Freud, "The Ego and the Id," in *The Freud Reader*, 631-635.

23 Ibid., 635.

24 Ibid., 630.

but which at its outer edges is also unconscious. The function of the censor, then, is closely associated with consciousness in both typologies, that is, throughout the development of Freud's metapsychology. Yet whether the process of censorship is consciously controlled by the self-conscious ego remains unresolved. While guarding and protecting consciousness and functioning as an agent of consciousness in that sense, it nevertheless seems that censorship itself takes place behind the back of the conscious ego.

3. SARTRE'S CRITIQUE OF FREUD'S CENSOR

The critique of the psychoanalytic hypothesis of the censor found in Sartre's *Being and Nothingness* is an integral part of his denial of the unconscious. His denial of the unconscious is one of the most striking aspects of Sartre's philosophy of consciousness especially in light of the fact that he proceeds towards the end of the same work to develop an existential psychoanalytic method. Without examining fully what Sartre means by 'consciousness,' we can at least recall that he distinguishes between prereflective and reflective consciousness. It should be noted, however, that these are not to be understood as distinct, co-existing regions of the human psyche:

> Sartre views consciousness as all of a piece, without compartments or spheres. Reflective consciousness is simply prereflective consciousness turning and making an object of its own (past) actions, feelings, and gestures – instead of being directed toward the world, consciousness is now directed toward the self.[25]

While prereflective consciousness and reflective consciousness are not to be understood as parts of consciousness, the nature of reflective consciousness does introduce the possibility of self-deception.

As consciousness turns on itself in reflection, a gap is introduced in the unity of consciousness – a duality is introduced in consciousness. The duality in the unity of consciousness is what makes possible the self-deception that Sartre calls 'bad faith.'[26] Reflective consciousness and the duality it introduces do not necessarily create bad faith,

---

25 Betty Cannon, *Sartre and Psychoanalysis: An Existentialist Challenge to Clinical Metatheory* (Lawrence, Kansas: University Press of Kansas, 1991), 38.

26 Jean-Paul Sartre, *Being and Nothingness*, trans. Hazel E. Barnes (New York: Washington Square Press, 1966), 86-116.

just the conditions for bad faith. While not absolutely ineluctable, bad faith can be so durable and long-lasting that it is assumed to be the normal mode of existence. The fundamental goal of bad faith is: "'To cause me to be what I am, in the mode of 'not being what one is,' or not to be what I am in the mode of 'being what one is.'"[27] Authenticity is possible, according to Sartre, but only as a recovery from the inauthenticity of being in bad faith.[28]

The psychoanalytic theory which posits a conscious ego and an unconscious id, Freud's second typology, is itself an exercise in bad faith, an instance of meta-psychological self-deception. Rather than contend with the self as lying to itself in reflective consciousness, Freud's theory introduces into the psyche an intersubjective structure which renders the analysand as much a passive (and thereby guiltless) spectator as the analyst:

> Thus psychoanalytic theory substitutes for the notion of bad faith, the idea of a lie without a liar; it allows me to understand how it is possible for me to be lied to without lying to myself...; it replaces the duality of the deceiver and the deceived, the essential condition of the lie, by the "id" and the "ego."[29]

Freud further complicates the theoretical deception by introducing a third agency – the censor. Sartre characterizes Freud's censor as "a line of demarcation with customs, passport division, currency-control, etc."[30] If the censor is in control of the distortion and obfuscation in my consciousness, then I need not realize nor take responsibility for my own self-deception. However, the problem of bad faith is not thereby eluded because "in order to overcome bad faith, it has established between the unconscious and the conscious an autonomous consciousness in bad faith."[31]

The censor functions as a second duality placed between the duality of the ego and the id. The id is seen by Freud, according to Sartre, as a blind libidinal force, and the ego, specifically the analysand, as a passive spectator of the psychic phenomena brought to light. The

---

27 Ibid., 110.

28 Ibid., 116, fn. 9.

29 Ibid., 92.

30 Ibid., 90.

31 Ibid., 94.

agency responsible for the deception now becomes the censor. The same duality that must operate in self-deception, the deceiver and the deceived, is relocated in a condensed form into the censor (a kind of autonomous 'mini-me'). In order for the censor to effectively repress it must know what it is repressing:

> How could the censor discern the impulses needing to be repressed without being conscious of discerning them? How can we conceive of a knowledge which is ignorant of itself?[32]

In fact, the censor must not only be aware of that which it is repressing, it must also choose what to repress. It allows acceptable desires and impulses, even sexual, into consciousness, and incarcerates those that are unlawful.

Freud's censor, then, for Sartre does nothing to alleviate the philosophic and moral problem of bad faith. The philosophic difficulty of how one can know and not know the same thing at the same time is not resolved but displaced. Similarly, the moral problem of taking responsibility for one's own desires, impulses and feelings is passed off to another, a fictitious conscious agent who chooses for me. The very hypothesis of the censor, for Sartre, is an exercise in bad faith.

4. LONERGAN'S DEVELOPMENT OF FREUD'S CENSOR

In light of Sartre's seemingly devastating critique of Freud's censor, we might question why Lonergan would employ this conception in Chapter Six of *Insight*. His acceptance of the essential meaning of the censor becomes understandable if we consider two significant differences in Lonergan's and Sartre's interpretations.

First, Lonergan does not deny the existence of the unconscious, but this does not manifest naïveté on his part. By the unconscious, Lonergan does not mean a region of the psyche (the human mind), but rather the underlying neural level. The fact that Lonergan acknowledges the reality of brain functioning as providing materials for psychic integration manifests his acceptance of the self's embodiment, which some later Sartreans also develop.[33] In *Method in Theology*, Lonergan articulates a second meaning of the unconscious: "This twilight

---

32 Ibid., 93.

33 Kathleen Wider, *The Bodily Nature of Consciousness* (Ithaca, New York: Cornell University Press, 1977).

of what is conscious but not objectified seems to be the meaning of what some psychiatrists call the unconscious."[34] However, in Chapter Six he uses the term 'preconscious' for that of which we are only dimly aware or only potentially aware insofar as it is receives no advertence. Lonergan's 'preconscious' in *Insight* correlates with Sartre's 'prereflective consciousness.' Both of these terms roughly correspond to Freud's notion of 'the preconscious' which he articulates in his first typology although neither Sartre nor Lonergan conceive of the preconscious or the prereflective as a region of the psyche coexisting with consciousness.

Secondly, Lonergan does not hypostasize the censor as an autonomous consciousness, which Sartre claims that Freud does. In the multi-level metaphysics of human development developed through Lonergan's genetic method, we find supervening levels each governed by their proper laws and the proper subject matter of distinct sciences:

> In man, there is intellectual development supervening upon psychic and psychic supervening upon organic....In the organism both the underlying manifold and the higher system are unconscious. In intellectual development both the underlying manifold of sensible presentations and the higher system of insights and formulations are conscious. In psychic development the underlying neural manifold is unconscious and the supervening higher system is conscious.[35]

Further, on each level of integration we find a network of correlative terms defined by the laws of that level. Lonergan calls such explanatory terms 'conjugates.'[36] Rather than acting as some kind of existing, autonomous agent, the censor in Lonergan's account functions as an explanatory conjugate of the psychic level on a par with impulses, affects, images, behaviors, dreams, and the processes of repression and inhibition. That censoring is not an operation experienced by the conscious subject is not an argument against its role on the psychic level. The explanatory conjugates of the sciences (and Lonergan does consider psychology, including the area of depth psychology, to be a science) are commonly beyond our direct experience.

---

34 Lonergan, *Method in Theology*, 34 fn. 5.

35 Lonergan, *Insight*, 492.

36 Ibid., 102-105.

Lonergan appropriates the essence of Freud's account of the censor in its repressive role as barring certain psychic materials from becoming conscious: "[T]he function that excludes elements from emerging in consciousness is now familiar as Freud's censor."[37] He also agrees with a number of auxiliary points Freud makes about the censor, for example, that it is relaxed in sleep, allowing materials to arise in dreams that it would normally reject in waking life.[38] However, Lonergan views the repressive role of the censor to be only half of the story. He considers the primary role of the censor to be constructive. The constructive role of the censor is a function that neither Freud nor, consequently, Sartre in his critique of Freud's censor stresses.

In order to understand Lonergan's censor as primarily constructive and as aberrantly repressive, we should review the elements and interplay of the underlying, unconscious neural level and the supervening psychic and intellectual levels of consciousness. Lonergan's remarks about the censor are found in his account of the psychic level of the subject in the dramatic pattern of experience. As dramatic, the self finds itself in an interpersonal context in which its own living is a creative work of art: "Such artistry is dramatic. It is in the presence of others, and the others too are also actors in the primordial drama that the theatre only imitates."[39] The effort to maintain oneself in this social context requires insights into oneself and one's interpersonal relations, and it can involve, as well, the avoidance of those realizations that would disrupt the status quo of one's dramatic achievement to date.

Three interrelated levels of operation are at play in the dramatic pattern of experience. First, there is the underlying, unconscious level of neural stimuli, patterns, and processes which demand some representation and integration on the supervening level of psychic consciousness. The neural demand for psychic representation is a significant requirement of the healthy subject: "The demand functions of neural patterns and processes constitute the exigence of the organism for its conscious complement; and to violate that exigence is to invite the anguish of abnormality."[40] Lonergan terms the neural demands for

37 Ibid., 214.
38 Ibid., 218.
39 Ibid., 211.
40 Ibid., 214.

conscious expression 'neural demand functions' because their need for higher integration can be met in a variety of ways, primarily in the affects and images of the psychic level of consciousness. Imaginative representations are required for an act of understanding; insights are into images not into affects per se. The next higher level of consciousness, the level of intelligent consciousness, which is the level of seeking understanding, having insights, and formulating those insights, supervenes and integrates the underlying psychic material that has already emerged into consciousness. The unfettered desire to know will penetrate the underlying psychic level and even the neural level positively to seek out the patterns and images required for insight. On the other hand, the fears and biases of the dramatic subject can function to thwart the emergence into consciousness of the images that would give rise to unwanted insights: "Besides the love of light, there can be a love of darkness."[41] In its constructive role, the censor selects and arranges materials that emerge in consciousness in such a way that an insight could occur. In its repressive role, the censor blocks the emergence into consciousness of those images which would likely give rise to insight.

The avoidance of unwanted insights into oneself can be conscious and deliberate or "prior to conscious advertence" and spontaneous.[42] The former is the root of individual bias; the latter is the root of dramatic bias. When the refusal to recognize something about oneself is conscious, it is not a refusal to understand but normally a deliberate shift of one's focus and preoccupation. One will simply change the subject in a conversation or put the book down when things hit too close to home. In fact, the more one consciously denies something and seeks to overlook it, the more likely it is that one will continue to advert to it. There is no interference with or lasting influence on the underlying psychic level, and consequently the imaginative representations required for the insights will readily emerge. But in the case of repressive censorship, schemes that would suggest the unwanted insights are blocked from emerging into consciousness. The resulting aberration can play havoc with the normal satisfaction of neural demand functions. On a very primitive, preconscious level, patterns

41 Ibid.

42 Ibid., 216

and arrangements of psychic materials are distorted and excluded.[43] The consequent aberration of repression and inhibition interfere with one's conscious performance in the dramatic sphere and not uncommonly in one's other spheres of performance, in the biological, artistic, intellectual, and mystical patterns of experience. For an example of the effect of repression on the subject as biological, we need only recall Freud's remarkable discovery of the aetiology of very serious physical disorders, such as temporary blindness and partial paralysis. Through his various psychoanalytic methods of releasing repressed psychic materials, he was able to reverse these psychosomatic symptoms in his analysands.[44]

We find in Lonergan's Chapter 6, then, an account of the censor that articulates both its positive and its possible negative function:

> The liberation of consciousness is founded on a control of apprehensions; as has been seen, the censorship selects and arranges materials for insight, or in its aberration excludes the arrangements that would yield insight.[45]

Lonergan's focus in his account of the censor is on its role in aiding or thwarting the emergence into consciousness of the images that would lead to insight. This emphasis on the role of understanding in relation to psychopathology is not found in the works of many depth psychologists. William Stekel is an exception. In his work he finds that repression is linked to a refusal to understand, and psychotherapeutic advance is linked to a "lightening flash of illumination."[46] In both its positive and its negative functions, the censor for Lonergan is correlated to the level of intelligence. The censor prepares the psychic materials into which we have insights, and its selection is influenced by the desire to understand or by the dread of understanding, which penetrates to the underlying psychic and neural levels. While Freud

---

43 Ibid., 216. Lonergan actually uses the term 'unconscious' in this passage; however, the discussion is about the censorship and aberration that are "operative prior to conscious advertence," which I understand to mean the preconscious.

44 Freud, "The Aetiology of Hysteria" in *The Freud Reader*, 96-110.

45 Lonergan, *Insight*, 218-219.

46 Ibid., 224. Lonergan is quoting here from William Stekel, *Technique of Analytical Psychotherapy*, trans. Eden and Cedar Paul (New York: Liveright, 1950).

tends to restrict identity the 'real' drives of the psyche exclusively to the libidinal and instinctual drives of the Id, Lonergan acknowledges and stresses the pure desire to know as the finality of human existence become conscious and intelligent.

> ...[A]n acknowledgement that the real is the verified makes it pos-
> sible to affirm the reality no less of the higher system than of the
> underlying manifold. The chemical is as real as the physical; the
> biological as real as the chemical; the psychic as real as the biologi-
> cal; and insight as real as the psychic....[T]he latent content of the
> dream, so far from revealing the 'real' man, now merely exhibits po-
> tentialities that are rejected not only by waking but also by dream-
> ing consciousness.[47]

In Lonergan's emphasis on the act of understanding and the pure desire to know, he parts company not only with Freud, but also with Freud's critic, Sartre.

The censor, for Lonergan, is conscious but not objectified. It is not wholly conscious in the sense of intelligent and rational, nor is it a blind unconscious neural function. It is preconscious in the sense of functioning prior to our advertence. It is interesting to note that Sartre also refers to Stekel's work in order to establish that the phenomena of psychopathology are conscious and, therefore, ploys of bad faith. He quotes the following from Stekel's *La femme frigide*: "Every time that I have been able to carry my investigations far enough, I have established that the crux of the psychosis was conscious."[48] For Sartre, all knowing is conscious and self-conscious, and so the censor, if there were such an agency, would have to be conscious and self-conscious in order to have the knowledge to select and reject materials. As we have seen, Sartre rejects the censor as *de trop*; its machinations can be carried out by the conscious self in bad faith. For Lonergan, the censor is an explanatory conjugate of the psychic level of consciousness. It functions in correlation to the neural demands of the underlying un-conscious level and to the intelligent and rational (or obfuscating and biased) intentionality of the higher levels of intelligent and rational consciousness.

---

47 Lonergan, *Insight*, 230.

48 Sartre, *Being and Nothingness*, 95.

5. THE CENSOR'S PRECURSORS IN
RATIONAL PSYCHOLOGY

For Freud the censor is a repressive psychic agency which functions in an unconscious dimension of the conscious ego. For Sartre the censor is a fiction. Any censoring is actually carried out prereflectively by the self in bad faith, that is, as engaged in self-deception. For Lonergan, Freud's censor, as an element of the psychic level of consciousness, can be resurrected but with qualifications. Its primary function is constructive and only as aberrant is it repressive. The primacy of the censor's constructive role points to its possible precursors in previous faculty psychologies.

The role of the *vis cogitativa* in St. Thomas and in Lonergan's *Verbum* bears striking similarities to the constructive role of the censor.[49] In *Verbum*, Lonergan asserts that without the *cogitativa* there would be no act of insight;[50] however, in *Insight* and his later works, in which he employs the language of intentionality analysis, there is no mention of this power. Lonergan does not make explicit what element in intentionality analysis would replace the role of the *cogitativa*.[51] Let us

---

49 Elizabeth Murray, "Wolves, Fingers, and Radii" presented at the West Coast Methods Institute, Lonergan Conference, Los Angeles, California, 2006 [unpublished].

50 Lonergan, *Collected Works of Bernard Lonergan*, vol. 2, *Verbum: Word and Idea in Aquinas*, ed. Frederick E. Crowe and Robert M. Doran (Toronto: University of Toronto Press, 1997), 44.

51 Lonergan remarked on the *cogitativa* in a letter to Fred Crowe in 1955: "Incidentally, re anxiety, what the Freudians call the Super-Ego is Aquinas' cogitativa: just as the little birds know that twigs are good for building nests and the little lambs know that wolves are bad, so little human beings develop a cogitativa about good and bad; it reflects their childish understanding of what papa and mamma say is good or bad. [I]n adult life it can cause a hell of a lot of trouble." This is quoted from the 13th of 129 communications of Lonergan to Crowe (unpublished) cited from Philip McShane, "*Vis Cogitativa*: Contemporary Defective Patterns of Anticipation," in *Humus 2*, http://www.philipmcshane.ca/humus-02.pdf. My hypothesis is that the censor in its constructive capacity is like Aquinas's *cogitativa*. In this quote Lonergan likens Freud's super-ego to the *cogitativa*. Insofar as the super-ego plays a repressive (censoring) function, Lonergan's remark adds some weight to the idea that Freud's censor is related to Aquinas's *cogitativa*. I am grateful to John Dadosky for bringing this material to my attention.

return to his account in *Verbum* to explore the possibility of a connection between the *cogitativa* and the censor.

In *Verbum* when Lonergan first introduces the *cogitativa*, he distinguishes the activity and the object of the cogitative sense by comparing the knowledge of the technician and the person of experience:

> In other words, the technician knows the abstract universal, which is an inner word consequent to insight. But the man of experience merely knows the *universale in particulari*, and that knowledge is not intellectual knowledge but exists in a sensitive potency variously named the *ratio particularis, cogitativa, intellectus passivus*. It carries on comparisons of particulars in virtue of the influence of intellect.[52]

Lonergan here describes the sensitive nature of the *cogitativa*, the nature of its object – the universal in particulars, and the influence it receives from the intellect. Lonergan follows Thomas in distinguishing this particular sensitive faculty from the other five senses and from the imagination.[53] This faculty is found in animals and in humans. In animals it is called the estimative sense, and in humans, the cogitative sense. In both animals and man, the object of this sensory power is the individual thing as existing in a common nature, that is, the universal in a particular. However, in animals the apprehension of these sensory objects is restricted to the object qua beneficial or harmful. In humans, the object of the *cogitativa* is not so restricted; the object of the cogitative sense is any universal in a particular.

Lonergan views the *cogitativa* as leading to and necessary for the act of insight. In describing human intelligence as process and as non-angelic, he writes of "the experience we all have of working from, and on, a sensible basis towards understanding."[54] In the process of reasoning towards an understanding, the intellect is dependent on sense for its object. In the case of coming to understand what a circle is, to employ Lonergan's familiar example from Chapter One of *Insight*,[55] we rely either on a visible diagram or an imagined diagram. The act of insight into the meaning of a circle comes as an increment in a process that involves imagining spokes, rims, and hubs, imagining the spokes

52 Lonergan, *Verbum*, 43-44.

53 St. Thomas Aquinas, *In II de Anima*, lect. 13, #398.

54 Lonergan, *Verbum*, 45.

55 Lonergan, *Insight*, 31-37.

reduced to fine lines, reduced to invisible radii. Further, the intellect relies on what he calls a "preparatory elaboration of its object."[56] These radii must be aligned properly: they must emanate from the center out to the perimeter; they must be of equal length; they must lie side by side; they must be so numerous as to be uncountable; etc. The *cogitativa* makes possible the imaginative manipulation of the radii. Prior to multiplying and moving radii in our imagination, we must apprehend each radius qua radius. Only through such apprehension and comparison can we imagine one radius to be longer and one to be shorter or two to be equal. It is the cogitative preparation of the phantasm that prepares us for insight.

In fact, according to Peghaire in his work on the cogitative sense, the preparatory role of the *cogitativa* is to be found in the very process of reasoning itself. In order to follow an argument, the elements of the reasoning process must be placed serially so that thought can move more easily from one to the other to arrive at a conclusion.[57] Kant uses a strikingly similar example in arguing for the necessity of a transcendental faculty of imagination:

> For experience as such necessarily presupposes the reproducibility of appearances. When I seek to draw a line in thought, or to think of the time from one noon to another, or even to represent to myself some particular number, obviously the various manifold representations that are involved must be apprehended by me in thought one after the other. But if I were always to drop out of thought the preceding representations (the first parts of the line, the antecedent parts of the time period, or the units in the order represented)…a complete representation would never be obtained…."[58]

Kant describes this synthetic work of the imagination as a "blind but indispensable function of the soul, without which we should have no knowledge whatsoever, but of which we are scarcely ever conscious."[59] Kant's account of this non-conscious faculty seems very close to Thomas's *cogitativa*; however, we should note that Thomas

---

56 Ibid., 44.

57 Julien Peghaire, "A Forgotten Sense, The Cogitative according to St. Thomas Aquinas," *The Modern Schoolman*, Vol. XX, November 1942, 136.

58 Immanuel Kant, *Critique of Pure Reason*, trans. Norman Kemp Smith (New York: St Martin's Press, 1929), (A) 102, 133.

59 Ibid., (A) 78, (B) 103, 112.

carefully differentiates the *cogitativa* from the imagination.[60] If we take an example of an animal sensing the presence of a predator, the color, shape, and sound are given by the external senses; the combined image of an approaching figure is provided by the internal senses of imagination and the common sense; and the sense of danger is provided by the estimative sense.

In the human subject, the *cogitativa* and the intellect are interrelated. The *cogitativa* provides the necessary elaboration of the representations upon which the intellect depends for its insights, and the intellect influences through its questions and its prior understanding the apprehension of the *cogitativa*. How is the *cogitativa* distinct from the act of insight itself? The cogitative sense apprehends the universal in the particular. Insight is not an apprehension of the universal, but the abstraction of the universal. "Abstraction," Lonergan writes, is "the elimination by the understanding of the intellectually irrelevant because it is understood to be irrelevant."[61] Whereas "knowing the universal in the particular, knowing what is common to the instances in the instances, is not abstraction at all," it is merely the operation of the *cogitativa*.[62] The act of insight, then, is an abstractive act that presupposes the cogitative act which apprehends the universal in the particular. Let us consider for illustration an insight into a 'thing,' as such, which is a grasp of a unity, identity, whole in data taken in their concrete individuality.[63] What does the insight into the thing add to the apprehension of the universal in the particular? The contribution of the act of understanding is the abstraction of the thing's unity, its identity across change, and its relation to its parts. Preliminary apprehensive comparison by the cogitative faculty is necessary for any of these aspects of a thing to be grasped. For the identity to be grasped, for instance, there must be a seriating and comparison of sensory apprehensions. In *Insight*, Lonergan distinguishes human knowing from animal knowing. The former involves intelligence and rationality; the latter is primarily a matter of sense and imagination. Animal knowing in us, however, is influenced by intelligence and provides the underlying manifold for intellectual and rational operations.

---

60 St. Thomas, *In II de Anima*, lect. 13, # 398.

61 Lonergan, *Verbum*, 53.

62 Ibid.

63 Lonergan, *Insight*, 271.

Much interpretive work remains to be done in this area, but I suspect that the preconscious censor in its constructive capacity corresponds to Thomas's *vis cogitativa* as that which provides the "preparatory elaboration of its [the intellect's] object." The preparation of representations by the *cogitativa* is necessary for an act of understanding and for the process of reasoning. As sensory, this operation is spontaneous and natural rather than intelligent and deliberate; it is an instance of animal knowing as defined by Lonergan. An equally controversial possibility is that the censor in its constructive capacity corresponds to Kant's transcendental synthesis of the imagination. Notwithstanding the fact that Kant identifies this synthetic function with the imagination rather than with the cogitative faculty, the accounts of the faculties are strikingly similar. For Kant, the synthetic work of the imagination is necessary in order for thought to take place at all, and it is unconscious. For Lonergan in *Insight*, the materials that emerge in consciousness are already subject to the preconscious selection and patterning of the censor. This arrangement of the materials results from the dialectical interplay of underlying neural demands and conscious interests and orientations. There is some process or operation that takes places preconsciously (for Lonergan), unconsciously (for Kant), instinctually (for Thomas), which selects, patterns, synthesizes, or arranges the materials that emerge in consciousness under the influence of and for higher level operations.

6. THE PARADOX OF THE CENSOR

There is an inherent philosophical difficulty with the notion of the censor which Sartre clearly articulates. How is it possible for a consciousness, even as prereflective or preconscious, to know and to not know the same thing in the same regard at the same time? How can the censor select material which is to be repressed without apprehending that material? If one has already apprehended the material in the process of censoring it, in what sense is it rendered unconscious? The unity of the self, the unity of consciousness, exacerbates the difficulty. As we have seen above, Lonergan does not identify the self more with intelligent and rational consciousness than with the sensitive psyche: "They are the unfolding on different levels of a single, individual unity, identity, whole. Both are 'I,' and neither is merely 'It.'[64] Similarly, for Sartre consciousness is a unity:

64 Ibid., 499.

By the distinction between the "id" and the "ego," Freud has cut the psychic whole into two. I *am* the ego but I *am not* the id....Psychoanalysis...introduces into my subjectivity the deepest intersubjective structure of the *mit-sein*.[65]

The problem posed by the repressive function of the censor is that we cannot blame its resulting scotoma on some agency apart from ourselves.

The similarity of the censor and the *cogitativa* may contribute to solving the difficulty of how the same self both knows and does not know in censoring the contents of its consciousness. As Lonergan points out, there are two kinds of knowing: animal and human. Animal knowing is not knowing in the strict sense for Lonergan, but it is a kind of pre-intellectual, pre-conceptual apprehension of sensory representations (bodies). The object of the *cogitativa* is the universal in the particular. There is a primitive recognition of the same in the many instances. This, as we have seen, does not require intelligence; it is a sensitive capacity we share with animals. Thomas distinguishes the cogitative sense in humans from the cogitative sense in animals, the estimative, inasmuch as the object of the human cogitative sense is not restricted to the harmful and the beneficial. Nevertheless, the fact that the cogitative sense in us is capable of apprehending any particular does not mean that we do not also still apprehend the harmful and the beneficial. As animals in a habitat we too are instinctively aware of what is a threat to or conducive to our well-being. Not only must the human organism be alert to positive and negative possibilities in its "external" habitat, it must also be on guard against "internal" threats to its psychic integrity. Strictly speaking, all sensory and imaginative representations arise prior to the distinction of inner and outer, but we can distinguish, after the fact, between biological and social threats and neural impulses and demands. As I can recognize in the periphery of my vision and react spontaneously to swat away a spider crawling near (whether it is an actual spider or the result of mistaken perception or a hallucination), so I can swat away from conscious advertence an imaginative representation that threatens my self-image.

How does one recognize the image or representation as having the potential to provide material for the insight into oneself that one does not want? The intention of the understanding is already at work on

---

65 Sartre, *Being and Nothingness*, 91-92.

the underlying levels. The desire to know helps guide the selection of materials for questions for which it seeks answers. Fear and insecurity, on the other hand, also influence the selection of materials. We avoid and block those images that would lead to unwanted insights into oneself or one's situation. The preliminary sense that there is something of a threatening nature that could be understood creates the psychic distance to block the image prior to its emergence in consciousness. The sensory cogitative act is an apprehension of a type (universal) in the representation, and it is simultaneously the apprehension of the harmful, some felt-danger to oneself.

The primitive schematizing of psychic materials seems to be the locus of the censorship both in its constructive and its repressive capacities. This censoring does not require knowing in the full, human sense of intelligence and reason, let alone rationally self-conscious choice; it simply requires an animal apprehension of possibilities. The selection and arrangement of psychic materials takes place preconsciously. In the terminology of *Method*, the censorship is unconscious – "conscious but not objectified."[66] We should no more blame a person for his/her repression and subsequent *scotoma*, than we should praise them for spontaneous reflexes, such as, a sudden movement of the head to avoid being hit. As a reflex action occurs consciously but normally without one's advertence or choice, so the censorship proceeds without need of our conscious advertence and deliberate control.

7. A FINAL NOTE ON MORAL RESPONSIBILITY

As we have seen above, Doran defines psychic conversion as the transformation of the censor from primarily repressive to primarily constructive. The constructive function of the censor on the psychic level is so fundamental to all higher operations of consciousness that it must operate continuously. Similarly, even the healthiest psyche does not enjoy pure transparency. Thus, the censor must be always constructively selecting, which simultaneously is a rejecting, and unfortunately, it is commonly repressing. For this reason, Doran qualifies the conversion as a matter of degree, of moving from "primarily" repressive to "primarily" constructive. The labor of appropriating one's own affectivity and gradually transforming the censor is not only arduous and painstaking, it also requires resolute courage.

66 Lonergan, *Method*, 44.

First, one must appropriate the "creative vector" which moves from below upwards through five levels of conscious intentionality.[67] One must identify and appropriate the pure desire to know manifested successively as wonder, doubt, and conscience. The pure desire to know gives rise to the questions that evoke the images which can lead to insights. The creative vector is the core of the self-transcending process of intentional consciousness, and it is operative in our dreaming as well as in our waking consciousness. Secondly, one must contend with the powerful resistances to the appropriation of one's own psyche:

> But a second and equally necessary step entails the depth-psychological discovery and healing of the affective obstructions to creativity constituted by certain compositions of psychic energy that create sources of resistance to the search for direction.[68]

Psychic conversion requires attention to the stream of waking sensitive consciousness and communication with oneself through attention to the feelings and images of one's dreams.[69] The patience and fortitude required for such redirection of our attention is undermined by commonsense and academic devaluation of the psychic level. Further, internal resistance to releasing repressed materials, as Freud has amply shown, can be even more effective than societal pressures in interfering with the psychotherapeutic process.

One aspect of Doran's account of psychic conversion that may be effective in helping us to overcome resistance is his articulation of the *victimization* of the psyche. He explains:

> The point is that *psychic spontaneity as such is not morally responsible for its disorder*....Disordered complexes are the victims of history: of significant others, of social situations emergent from the distorted dialectic of history, of derailed cultural values, of one's own freedom, or of some combination of these various sources.[70]

In this passage, Doran does include reference to one's own freedom. We are responsible to some degree for the disorder of one's censorship, for dramatic bias, but there are other factors at work in the formation of one's psychic integration. It may be difficult or even impossible to

---

67 Doran, *TDH*, 222.

68 Ibid., 227.

69 Ibid., 85.

70 Ibid., 232.

discern in oneself where passive victimization leaves off and bad faith takes over. While Sartre would have the self in its radical freedom thoroughly responsible for its psychic disorder, Doran argues for a more complex interpersonal, moral reality. Doran's articulation of the psyche as, in a sense, the victim of history and circumstances encourages a compassionate and patient approach to oneself without denying the fact of original and basic, personal sin. Still, by taking an attitude of compassion towards oneself, one is in line with the "healing vector," God's love operating from above downwards to penetrate all the levels of human conscious intentionality.[71] In Lonergan's words:

> Where hatred reinforces bias, love dissolves it, whether it be the bias of unconscious motivation [dramatic bias], the bias of individual or group egoism, or the bias of omnicompetent, shortsighted common sense.[72]

Self-hatred, as manifested in the destructiveness of an over-zealous superego, could amplify feelings of guilt for one's psychic disorder. The weight of such presumed moral responsibility could lead to a hopelessness that resists any transformation. An authentic self-love, on the other hand, would appropriate the creative vector and work with the healing vector to approach the work of psychic conversion with some compassion.

---

71 Ibid., 222.

72 Lonergan, "Healing and Creating in History," in *The Lonergan Reader*, ed. Mark D. Morelli and Elizabeth A. Morelli [Murray] (Toronto: University of Toronto Press, 1997), 573.

CHARLES TAYLOR IN CONVERSATION WITH
LONERGAN AND DORAN:
ON UPPER AND LOWER BLADES

NEIL ORMEROD
AUSTRALIAN CATHOLIC UNIVERSITY

I. INTRODUCTION

A recent attempt to run a conference on the work of Charles Taylor in Australia brought his impressive corpus of writings to my attention. A colleague of mine had challenged a presentation I had given on which I drew heavily on the work of Robert Doran by suggesting that Taylor presented a better account of the problem I was examining. That problem concerned the long term falling away of belief in the provability of God's existence, and my analysis drew on Doran's notions of cosmological and anthropological cultures.[1] My colleague's challenge and the looming possibility of a specialized conference on Taylor's work led me to begin the task of reading Taylor's then major work, *Sources of the Self*.[2] I was even more interested when his most recent work, *A Secular Age*, which more directly addresses the sort of issues I had raised in my presentation, emerged.

My reading of Taylor's *Sources of the Self* left with me the impression that his project was highly intelligible within a Lonerganian framework. Taylor's narrative of the move from external and/or metaphysical identity constructions to more internal sources is congruent with Lonergan's identification of a cultural shift from the second to the third

1 The paper was subsequently published. See Neil Ormerod, "In Defence of Natural Theology: Bringing God into the Public Realm," *Irish Theological Quarterly* 72 (2007): 227-41. The article anticipates the central concern raised by Taylor in his latest book although the analysis is somewhat different.See Charles Taylor, *A Secular Age* (Cambridge, Mass.: Belknap Press of Harvard University Press, 2007).

2 Charles Taylor, *Sources of the Self: The Making of the Modern Identity* (Cambridge, Mass.: Harvard University Press, 1989).

stage of meaning. The third stage of meaning involves a shift to interiority and it seemed to me that Taylor's work was a detailed mapping of the philosophical and social impact of that shift from Descartes (with anticipations in Augustine) to our present age.Taylor's mastery of the rich tapestry of philosophical texts was impressive, to say the least, but it lacked what Lonergan would call a developed "upper blade" for ordering his materials.[3] There are hints of a dialectic operating, but these are not explicated, and so the work remains largely descriptive.

In his more recent work on the rise of the secular in the West, *A Secular Age*, the move to interiority is further developed in relation to its impact on the place of God in society. Again Taylor presents a very fine-grained narrative of the move away from a publically accepted belief in the existence of God, to our more modern denials and agnosticism. However, this time there are more explicitly developed "upper blade" elements, theoretical constructs by which he seeks to order the material. The first of these comes from the writings of Victor Turner and involves Turner's dialectic of *communitas* (sometimes referred to as anti-structure) and structure in human communities.[4] The second element is Taylor's own construction of three ideal types that he calls the *ancien régime*, the age of mobilization, and the age of authenticity, which he uses to characterize larger scale historical epochs.

In this paper I would like to explore these elements of an historical upper blade that Taylor deploys in his recent work. In particular I would like to explore them through a conversation with the writings of Bernard Lonergan[5] and Robert Doran.[6] I believe that Doran's work is a genuine development of Lonergan's positions, particularly

---

3 Lonergan develops the image of upper and lower blades in *Insight*. The lower blade involves the collection and shifting of the data, the upper blade refers to the *a priori* anticipations of the investigator into which the data is structured.See Bernard J. F. Lonergan, Collected Works of Bernard Lonergan, vol. 3, *Insight: A Study of Human Understanding*, ed. Frederick E. Crowe and Robert M. Doran (Toronto: University of Toronto Press, 1992), 87, 114-15, 337-58, etc.

4 For an exposition of Turner's account and its application to ecclesiology, see Carl Starkloff, "Church as Structure and *Communitas*: Victor Turner and Ecclesiology," *Theological Studies* 58 (1997): 643-68.

5 In particular, Lonergan, *Insight*.

6 In particular, Robert M. Doran, *Theology and the Dialectics of History* (Toronto: University of Toronto Press, 1990).

in relation to an emerging theology of history. I would like to suggest that Taylor's position would benefit greatly from such a conversation, and it is somewhat ironic (and sad) that he seems so unaware of the achievements of his fellow Canadian thinker, Bernard Lonergan.

2. TAYLOR AND SECULARIZATION

Before considering the two upper blade elements present in Taylor's work, it is worthwhile spelling out the nature of his argument in *A Secular Age*. Taylor is seeking to write a response to two distinct readings of the rise of secularism. He begins his account with a carefully nuanced account of secularism, distinguishing three distinct meanings that can be given to the term. Secularism is defined as: (1) the withdrawal of God from "public spaces", for example, through the separation of Church and state; (2) a decline in religious practice; and (3) "a move from a society where belief in God is unchallenged and, indeed, unproblematic, to one in which it is understood to be one option among others, and frequently not the easiest to embrace."[7] As Taylor notes, a society can be secular in the sense of #1 but still have relatively high rates of religious practice, as for example in the USA, and so not display secularization in the sense of #2. However, what is of most concern for his analysis is the third sense: "the change I want to define and trace is one which takes us from a society in which it was virtually impossible not to believe in God, to one in which faith, even for the staunchest believer, is one possibility among others … Belief in God is no longer axiomatic. There are alternatives."[8]

Of course, many readings of secularism are less differentiated than this and tend to lump different elements together. One such reading views the rise of secularism as a clear sign of decline, a falling away from religious belief and practice, and a collapse into moral relativism and social and cultural decay. This type of reading is common among Church figures who seek to promote a return to the past, where religious belief went hand in hand with strong moral and cultural norms. They tend to focus on the decline of God's presence in the public sphere and bemoan the falling away of religious practice. The opposite reading can be found among the proponents of secularism who view it as a narrative of progress, a sloughing off of the constraints of

---

7 Taylor, *A Secular Age*, 3.
8 Ibid., 3.

MEANING AND HISTORY IN SYSTEMATIC THEOLOGY

the past, particularly the religious constraints which are viewed as so much superstition, ignorance, and fanaticism. The dead hand of tradition is replaced by the march of progress driven by science and technology. These focus on the decline in religious practice as a natural consequence of science and modernization. Taylor refers to these as "subtraction stories," stories which view the rise of the modern world in terms of liberation from "certain earlier confining horizons."[9]

Taylor rejects both these readings of the rise of secularism and develops a different narrative for the rise of secularism as involving elements both of decline and progress. He wants to uncover the moral core at the heart of the rise of secularism, a moral core which itself emerges from within the Christian tradition. Far from being an alien growth, the progressive elements in the rise of secularism have deeply Christian roots. In this way he seeks to counter a reading which views the present simply in terms of decline. On the other hand, he argues against subtraction stories of modernity by noting that decline in religious practice is not uniform and is not a necessary consequence of the emergence of modern science. Neither condemnation nor outright praise is appropriate: rather, what is needed is a nuanced account of the dynamisms which have led to the present and will continue to shape our future.

A central issue that emerges from Taylor's account is the question of what constitutes human flourishing. Going hand in hand with the rise of secularism is the emergence of what Taylor refers to as "exclusive humanism". This is a position which limits the horizon of human flourishing to our present mortal existence. It presents us with a closed horizon and requires that we be satisfied with that. He argues that the closure of this horizon is not necessitated by the "immanent frame" of modernity (what Lonergan would speak of as the emergence of the third stage of meaning). Rather, both open and closed horizons remain possible, and both require a "leap of faith" which goes beyond the evidence.[10] Taylor expends considerable energy engaging "CWS" (closed world systems), analyzing the structure of their arguments, and countering their philosophical and epistemological moves. From

---

9 Ibid., 22.

10 In this sense Taylor remains skeptical of the possibility of proving the existence of God through reason.

Lonergan's perspective, Taylor is seeking to overcome the truncated subjectivity that dominates our post-Kantian culture.[11]

3. TAYLOR AND TURNER: A SOCIAL DIALECTIC

As part of his reconstruction of the emergence of modern secularism, Taylor takes us back to the beginning of the modern era and the breakdown of the social and cultural system referred to as Christendom. With the Reformation we find a valorization of ordinary life, a growing suspicion of religious virtuosi, and the notion that the reform of life that Christianity entails is enjoined upon all peoples.[12] This reform tended to judge harshly the earlier medieval traditions of "popular religion," of festivals and feast, and particularly of "carnival," "feasts of misrule … in which the ordinary order of things is inverted." Such carnivals were necessary as a "safety valve. The weight of virtue and good order was so heavy … that there had to be periodic blow-outs if the whole system were not to fly apart."[13] The long term suppression of carnival, and growing disdain at what it signified, forms one element of Taylor's narrative of the rise of secularism.

In seeking to analyze the importance of carnival (and its equivalents), Taylor evokes the work of Victor Turner and his dialectical construction of structure and *communitas*. For Turner "the order we are mocking is important but not ultimate; what is ultimate is the community it serves; and this community is fundamentally egalitarian." Principles of order and of community are complementary, mutually necessary, opposed but linked contrary principles. "All structure needs anti-structure."[14] Structure refers to "patterned arrangements of role-sets, status-sets and status sequences consciously recognized and regularly operative in a given society"[15] while *communitas* "is the intu-

---

11 See Bernard J. F. Lonergan, "The Subject," in *Second Collection*, ed. William Ryan and Bernard Tyrrell (Philadelphia: Westminster, 1974), for an account of the truncated, immanentist subject.

12 This is a rejection of what Taylor refers to as "two tiered" Christianity where some select group of religious virtuosi live a fully Christian life while the rest of humanity settles for a more nominal adoption of Christian belief and practice. Taylor, *A Secular Age*, 62-66. See also Taylor, *Sources of the Self*, 13-14.

13 Taylor, *A Secular Age*, 45-6.

14 Ibid., 47.

15 Ibid.

ition we all share that, beyond the way we relate to each other through our diversified coded roles, we also are a community of many-sided human beings, fundamentally equal, who are associated together."[16] Clearly we have elements here of what Lonergan would call a dialectic, of linked but opposed principles of change.[17]

Clearly Taylor finds Turner's construction useful, and he refers to it often as his narrative unfolds. Both Turner and Taylor have their strengths in the gathering and intelligent exposition of the range of data they are investigating, what Lonergan would speak of in terms of the lower blade of their discipline. And any intelligent worker in such fields will seek out and develop theories about the patterns they find in their data. In this regard, both Turner and Taylor are working *a posteriori*, finding or utilizing a pattern they have found in the social data. The question is for us whether this is an adequate pattern, a proper upper blade for organizing the data? I would like to suggest that it is not, or at least not quite.

It is of interest then to compare Turner's dialectic of structure and *communitas* with Lonergan's dialectic of spontaneous intersubjectivity and practical intelligence. For Lonergan spontaneous intersubjectivity is the primordial basis for human community, but it is constantly transformed by the demands of practical intelligence with its technological, economic, and political specializations.[18] Lonergan conceives of the dialectic as one of transcendence and limitation, the normatively ordered transcendence of practical intelligence and the basic principle of social limitation in our spontaneous intersubjective identification with the other. Both are values to be held in tension, though the operator (of practical intelligence) ruthlessly transforms the integrator (of spontaneous intersubjectivity).[19]

There are similarities and differences with Turner's account here. Both clearly have a communal aspect at one pole of the dialectic and a more structural pole at the other. But there are differences, and they are important. For Turner the structural pole is fixed and static in contrast with the inherently chaotic dynamism of *communitas*. For Turner new structure emerges from *communitas* in an almost spontaneous

---

16 Ibid., 49.

17 Lonergan, *Insight*, 242.

18 Ibid., 237-244.

19 Ibid., 501.

fashion. *Communitas* is the source of social creativity. This is in fact very different from Lonergan's account. For Lonergan creativity in the social order is to be located in the work of practical intelligence. Spontaneous intersubjectivity is a fundamental principle of limitation which must be respected by practical intelligence, but this intelligence remains the operator which transforms the social order.

There are metaphysical and cognitional parallels to the type of approach Turner is suggesting. In some forms of process thought, an equivalent of Aristotle's prime matter provides a source of creativity in a universe that would otherwise be dominated by the necessary consequences of a necessary divine being acting in the universe.[20] Turner's *communitas* plays a parallel role to prime matter in the process account; in fact it is a form of social "prime matter." As Taylor puts it, "order needs chaos."[21] Without a principle of chaos, order produces static, fixed, and ultimately life-destroying system, Weber's "iron cage" leading to endless repetition of the same boring order forever. *Communitas* breaks through the order and gives us an alternative vision of social possibilities. The cognitional parallel can be found in modern popular accounts of the role of imagination which is said to stand in contrast to reason, which again is portrayed as fixed, static, and life-denying,

Behind each of these, I suggest, lies a conceptualist understanding of the operation of reason. The conceptualist focuses on what is most obvious in the reasoning process: concepts, clear and distinct ideas, propositions. For Turner what are most obvious are the social orderings, status-sets, and institutions which structure the social order. Faced with the limitations of concepts (static and fixed), others have sought refuge in imagination as a way of identifying something that is creative; similarly Turner is seeking a source of social creativity in the unstructured flow of *communitas*. What both miss is the creativity of (practical) intelligence which must work with imagination (or spontaneous intersubjectivity) to create an intelligent (social) system. Lonergan's intellectualist approach breaks through conceptualism through

---

20 Process thought seems caught in the idea that a necessary being must create "necessarily" which is then identified in terms of a mechanistic determinism. Contingence and hence creativity and novelty must come from some other source. For a critique of process thought in this regard see Neil Ormerod, "Chance and Necessity, Providence and God," *Irish Theological Quarterly* 70 (2005): 263-78.

21 Taylor, *A Secular Age*, 47.

its recognition of the pre-conceptual nature of insight into phantasm. In the social order, social orderings and institutions, as Lonergan states of concepts, also have dates, that is, they begin at a certain place and time in history.[22]

Indeed one can find tensions in Taylor's use of Turner's dialectic which arise from these problems. As I have already noted, at one stage he refers to *communitas* and structure as "contradictory principles" so that "order needs chaos."[23] Later he will refer to *communitas* as a principle of limitation. He writes of the growing power of conceptions of social order which no longer "acknowledge limits in any opposing principle of chaos...there is a limit to the malleability of people."[24] Here *communitas* is not portrayed as a principle of novelty but of limitation. But then where does the novelty of new conceptions of social order come from? In the terms that Doran develops, one may ask, Is the dialectic of *communitas* and structure a dialectic of contraries or of contradictories? When they are referred to as structure and anti-structure they sound more like contradictories, to which one can only reasonably say "yes" to one and "no" to the other. When referred to as structure and *communitas* they may be thought of as contraries, to which we can say "both/and."[25]

A similar tension can be found in Taylor's evaluation of the moral significance of *communitas*. Again as I have noted in his early reference to it, he speaks of an intuition that we are "a community of many-sided human beings, fundamentally equal, who are associated together."[26] Later he will refer to anti-structure as "raw savage nature" which "resists civility".[27] I would argue that this tension reveals a further lacuna in Turner's construction, that is, the conflation of two distinct elements in human consciousness. One the one hand there is the elemental and instinctual basis for our spontaneous intersubjectivity,

---

22 Lonergan once noted, "Concepts have dates" as a counter to the notion that concepts are somehow universal. See Bernard J. F. Lonergan, *Collected Works of Bernard Lonergan*, vol. 4. *Collection*, ed. Frederick E. Crowe and Robert M. Doran (Toronto: Toronto University Press, 1988), 310, note i.

23 Ibid., 47.

24 Ibid., 125.

25 Doran, *Theology and the Dialectics of History*, 10.

26 Taylor, *A Secular Age*, 49.

27 Ibid., 125.

which can in turn be both savage and nurturing, brutal and tender. On the other is an emerging intentional response to the value of human community, which takes delight in the good of human community and recognises the value of each person in that community. This emerging moral response should not be confused with spontaneous intersubjectivity grounded in our instinctual mammalian nature.

My conclusion to this section is that Lonergan's dialectic of spontaneous intersubjectivity and practical intelligence is a better "upper blade" for ordering the data Taylor is considering than that offered by Turner's dialectic of *communitas* and structure. I do not think this is a fatal flaw in Taylor's narrative, though I do think his work would benefit from adopting Lonergan's upper blade in this regard.

4. TAYLOR'S THREE IDEAL TYPES

As a dialectic in the social order, the considerations above have a more short-term impact, though they are important in shaping long term social and cultural options. However, the second element that Taylor deploys concerns a more large scale and longer term movement in the narrative of the rise of Western secularism. He evokes Weber's notion of "ideal types" to provide "an outrageously simplified potted history of the last two-and-some centuries, the move from an age of some elite unbelief (the eighteenth century) to that of mass secularization (the twenty-first)."[28] The three ideal types that Taylor develops are the *ancien régime*, the age of mobilization, and the age of authenticity.

Taylor identifies the characteristics of the *ancien régime* as follows.[29] It displays a pre-modern order of hierarchical complementarity grounded in the Divine Will. This order is present both in the larger society and the microcosm of the village. Collective rituals and elements of "folk religion" are evident. Taylor rejects criticisms of such folk elements as simply a pagan undercurrent yet to be overcome. Rather, there was "generally a real symbiosis," a transformation of pagan practices by Christian belief. There is a close connection between Church membership and being part of the community: "this connection was cemented in part by the coexistence of official orthodox ritual and prayer, on the one hand, with, on the other, ritual forms concerned

28 Ibid., 437.
29 Ibid., 438-440.

with defense, luck and warding off evil."[30] The connection was so close that any deviation from orthodoxy was viewed as a threat to the whole community. Taylor describes this connection between Church and society as "Durkheimian" "in the sense that church and social sacred are one – although the relation of primary and secondary focus is reversed, since for Durkheim the social is the principal focus while [here] the opposite is true."[31]

Personally I find Taylor's use of the term *ancien régime* a little confusing because of its association with the French revolution and the efforts of restorationism in that country. Clearly the roots of the phenomena he is highlighting go back to Christendom and so pre-date the eighteenth century by some time. Of course the phenomena do extend beyond the breakdown of Christendom, particularly in Catholic countries which resisted the modernizing trends more than their Protestant counterparts did. Moreover, the Reformation is a major contributor to the undermining of the *ancien régime*. The Reformers were very critical of the elements of popular religion in Catholicism, and so this critique moved out of the cultural elites and into the mainstream. Reform "put a brutal end to a great deal of popular religion."[32] As well other powerful social forces – the growth of democratization, urbanization, and industrialization – all contribute to the breakdown of a system where the very fact of change could not be acknowledged because the social order was meant to reflect the Divine Will.

This breakdown leads to a new era, what Taylor calls the age of mobilization. If the social order is no longer a matter of divine fiat but is a human construction, then human beings need to be mobilized into the task of that construction:

> it designates a process whereby people are persuaded, pushed, dragooned, or bullied into new forms of society, church, association … they are induced through the actions of governments, church hierarchies, and/or other elites, not only to adopt new structures, but also to some extent to alter their social imaginaries, and sense of legitimacy, as well as their sense of what is crucially important in their lives or society.[33]

---

30 Ibid., 440.

31 Ibid., 442.

32 Ibid., 441.

33 Ibid., 445.

Rather than having a fixed social order in which each person can find his/her place, we are now called into the construction of a new social project. For some that might mean working to restore what they feel has been lost. But that very fact means that what would be restored would never be what was lost, for previously it was held as a divinely willed order, but now it would be a human achievement (even if "a society which plainly follows God's design"[34]). Taylor links the age of mobilization with what he calls the "Modern Moral Order." This moral order starts with individuals "and doesn't see these as set a priori within a hierarchical order, outside of which they wouldn't be fully human agents." Rather they are "disembedded individuals who come to associate together … [in] a society structured for mutual benefit, in which each respects the rights of others, and offers them mutual help of certain kinds."[35]

Taylor notes that "all Western societies have trodden the path out of the *ancien régime* form into the Age of Mobilization … but the ride was much bumpier and more conflictual in old Europe."[36] A clear indication in church life is denominationalism where a denomination "is not a divinely established body …but something that we have to create – not just at our whim, but to fulfill the plan of God."[37] On the Catholic side he notes movements such as "Catholic Action." Much of the mobilization in fact had a religious motivation, but in a sense that motivation was killed by its own success. Taylor argues that the Age of Mobilization was highly successful in bringing about major social and moral reforms in the general population. He credits it with creating a rise in the level of public civility unmatched by the earlier era. But this very success led to the situation where people take that achievement for granted and no longer associate it with its initial religious inspiration.[38]

There are many nuances in Taylor's account of the Age of Mobilization which go beyond what I want to highlight here. What I shall single out is the shift in the relationship between the social and the

---

34 Ibid., 447.

35 Ibid.

36 Ibid., 448.

37 Ibid., 450.

38 Though Taylor does not mention the word, there is an incipient Pelagianism in the Age of Mobilization once it is cut off from its religious roots.

individual. In the *ancien régime* each one asks, "What is my place in society?" In the Age of Mobilization the question becomes, "What is to be my contribution to the building of society?" Of course such mass mobilization can go horribly wrong as in the mass movements of fascism and communism in the twentieth century. The disillusionment that arose from these failures can perhaps help us understand the emergence of a new age, the Age of Authenticity.

Taylor's choice of designation of the era as an age of "authenticity" rather than the more common term "post-modernity" is, I think, indicative of his attempt to put a more positive slant on this modern phenomenon.[39] This age is characterized by a "widespread 'expressive' individualism."[40] Within this culture of authenticity, "each one of us has his/her own way of realizing our humanity, and that it is important to find and live out one's own, as against surrendering to conformity with a model imposed on us from outside, by society, or the previous generation, or religious or political authority."[41] An appeal to authenticity holds out the promise to overcome "inner divisions, like reason against feeling, and social divisions, like between students and workers, as well as divisions between spheres of life, like work/play."[42] While Taylor acknowledges the potential for a moral trivializing (doing your own thing) in the name of authenticity, he insists that there is also a profound moral core to this new age. An appeal to authenticity is almost inevitable once moral sources are interiorized. And appeals to external authorities have been problematized by a hermeneutic of suspicion. Taylor wants to correct the excesses of the age by an appeal to its own inner convictions, its own inner logic. On the other hand "root and branch attacks on authenticity help to make our lives worse, while being powerless to put the clock back to an earlier time."[43]

Again Taylor's account of the Age of Authenticity is highly nuanced and detailed, and this is not the place to provide a thorough account of it. As with the Age of Mobilization, I want to focus on the relationship between the social and the individual. In the *ancien régime*

---

39 See, for example, his argument in Charles Taylor, *The Ethics of Authenticity* (Cambridge, Mass.: Harvard University Press, 1992).

40 Taylor, *A Secular Age*, 473.

41 Ibid., 475.

42 Ibid., 476.

43 Ibid., 481.

each one asks, "What is my place in society?" In the Age of Mobilization the question is "What is to be my contribution to the building of society?" In this new era the question is "How does society assist me in achieving authenticity?" In the *ancien régime* the individual is ordered to society and society to a cosmologically conceived order, while in the Age of Authenticity, society is ordered to the individual who is on a personal quest for authenticity. The Age of Mobilization is a type of half-way house between these two competing conceptions of the social-individual relationship.

Those who are familiar with the writings of Robert Doran will recognize that my account of the difference between the *ancien régime* and the Age of Authenticity is influenced by Doran's account of cosmological and anthropological cultures. Building on Lonergan's notion of dialectic and the scale of values and Eric Voegelin's accounts of culture, Doran develops a cultural dialectic between two permanently valid sources of meaning and value, which he designates as cosmological culture and anthropological culture.[44] Fundamental to Doran's description of cosmological culture is that the individual is ordered to the society and the society to some cosmologically conceived order. Human destiny is viewed as subject to cosmic forces that are beyond our control, and human flourishing requires our conformity to the cosmic order. Alternatively in an anthropological culture, the society is ordered towards the individual and the individual to some world transcendent source of meaning and value. Rather than conforming to society, society is measured by its responsiveness to the individual. As I have explored elsewhere, the question that arises for any anthropologically oriented society is the precise nature of a world transcendent source of meaning and value and, indeed, the very existence of such a source.[45] In this way we return to the question raised by Taylor in his recent study.

As with the previous section we have some similarity between Taylor's construction of an upper blade, his three ideal types, and Doran's account of the cultural dialectic. Taylor's *ancien régime* bears some resemblance to Doran's account of cosmological culture, his Age of Au-

---

44 Doran, *Theology and the Dialectics of History*, 500-526. For a more compact account see Robert M. Doran, "The Analogy of Dialectic and the Systematics of History," in *Religion in Context*, ed. T. Fallon and P. Riley (Lanham, MD: University Press of America, 1988), 35-57.

45 Ormerod, "In Defence of Natural Theology."

thenticity to Doran's account of anthropological culture, and his Age of Mobilization seems to hold the two poles in some tension. What Doran's account has, which Taylor's lacks, is some sense of normativity in the structure. For Doran a breakdown in the dialectic tension between the pole in limitation (cosmological culture) and the pole of transcendence (anthropological culture) is a manifestation of cultural evil. For Doran one could say that both the *ancien régime* and the Age of Authenticity represent a breakdown in the cultural dialectic, one in the direction of limitation and the other in the direction of transcendence. In this sense the Age of Mobilization as a culture represents a better approximation to maintaining the dialectic tension than the other two ideal types Taylor considers.

Further, one could argue that the moral core that Taylor identifies in the Age of Authenticity is strongly linked to the emergence of anthropological cultural elements which the Christian tradition has fostered. And indeed it is a moral core because it is, as Doran claims, a permanently valid source of meaning and value. However, increasingly cut off from cosmological culture (a process Taylor refers to as disenchantment), anthropological culture itself becomes distorted, as the critics of the present age have noted. One symptom of that distortion, as I have argued elsewhere,[46] is the collapse of a cultural horizon in which the existence of God is taken for granted.

Again I think Taylor's work would not need major revision to take into account the type of dialectic Doran has developed. Taylor's three ideal types become more transparent in the light of Doran's analysis of the cultural dialectic, and the strengths and weaknesses of the types becomes more apparent. We also, I would suggest, get a sense of the historical flow from one pole of the dialectic dominating to the other pole taking precedence. Taylor's account is merely descriptive whereas Doran provides an explanatory framework.

5. CONCLUSION

I began by noting the challenge posed by a colleague that Taylor's account of a certain cultural shift was a better account than one I had developed drawing on the dialectical constructs of Lonergan and Doran. I have no doubt that Taylor's account is more fine-grained than I could achieve and that the nuances he uncovers are far richer than I had attended to. But this is still largely a matter of lower blade work,

46 Ibid.

of assembling and categorizing the data. In terms of the upper blade, however, I am still convinced that the dialectics developed by Lonergan and Doran have an explanatory power which is simply not present in Taylor's work.

'LET US BE PRACTICAL!':
THE BEGINNINGS OF THE LONG PROCESS TO FUNCTIONAL SPECIALIZATION IN THE ESSAY IN FUNDAMENTAL SOCIOLOGY

MICHAEL SHUTE
MEMORIAL UNIVERSITY OF NEWFOUNDLAND

"It may be asked...what is the value of abstract ideas applied to the situation? Let us be practical! The answer is that the abstract ideas have, indeed, a greater possibility of being wrong than the concrete ideas. Also, they work out for good or evil far more rapidly. But, whether we like it or not, the world has got beyond the stage where concrete problems can be solved merely in the concrete. Economics supplies us with the most palpable example: you have to have some economic theory in conducting the state and changing from one to another with every change of government is neither intelligent, fair to the people, or fair to the wide world which has to have an [sic] universal solution to the problem or go to pieces. Politics supplies us with another example. The modern state does not think in terms of the past, of its merits or demerits in being what it is; it thinks in terms of the future and if it foresees that it is being put out of the running by those with more economic power and more diplomatic skill, then it simply turns berserk in the name of Odin, Thor, or what you please. The sum and substance of the whole issue is that ideas in the concrete will build you a shanty but not a house and still less a skyscraper. The modern situation demands that questions be settled not in the concrete, not by the petty minds of politics who think of grabbing all they can because they can and make a virtue of not doing what they know either to be unprofitable or impossible, but in terms of pure reason. Physical reality functions perfectly in blind obedience to intelligible law. Humanity must first discover its law and then apply it: to discover the law is a long process and to apply it a painful process but it has to be done. The alternative is extinction. And practical minds are oriented towards extinction just as much whether they realize the point or not." (*Essay in Fundamental Sociology*, 1934)[1]

I. INTRODUCTION

A profound practicality informed Lonergan's intellectual quest. As Frederick Crowe puts it: "From start to finish of his career Lonergan was orientated and guided by a deep-lying pastoral concern."[2] Lonergan, however, did not often stress the point in his published writings. But at the very end of *Insight*, reflecting on his own encounter with Aquinas, he writes: "I would say that it is only through a personal appropriation of one's own rational consciousness that one can hope to reach the mind of Aquinas, and once that mind is reached, then it is difficult not to import his compelling genius to the problems of this latter day."[3] Did he mean practical problems here? In the preface of *Insight* he writes:

> There remains the question, what practical good can come of this book? The answer is more forthright than might be expected, for insight is the source not only of theoretical knowledge but also of all its practical applications, and indeed of all intellectual activity. Insight into insight, then, will reveal what activity is intelligent, and insight into oversights will reveal what activity is unintelligent. But to be practical is to do the intelligent thing, and to be unpractical is to keep blundering about. It follows that insight into both insight and oversight is the very key to practicality.[4]

---

1 Bernard Lonergan, *Essay on Fundamental Sociology*, unpublished, 193, 124-25. [Hereafter *EFS*.] Available from the Archives of the Lonergan Research Institute, Regis College, Toronto. [Hereafter LRI]. Page references are to the original typescript. The essay in its entirety appears in Michael Shute, *Lonergan's Early Economic Research* (Toronto: University of Toronto Press, forthcoming).

2 Frederick Crowe, "Bernard Lonergan as Pastoral Theologian," in *Appropriating the Lonergan Idea*, ed. Michael Vertin (Washington: The Catholic University of America Press, 1989), 132.

3 Bernard Lonergan, *Collected Works of Bernard Lonergan*, vol. 3, *Insight: A Study of Human Understanding*, ed. Frederick E. Crowe and Robert M. Doran (Toronto: University of Toronto Press, 1992), 770 [748]. Hereafter *CWL3*. References in brackets are to the original edition.

4 *CWL3*, 7-8.

And in the introduction to *Method in Theology* he writes: "Method...is a framework for collaborative creativity. It would outline the various clusters of operations to be performed by theologians when they go about their various tasks. A contemporary method would conceive those tasks in the context of modern science, modern scholarship, modern philosophy, of historicity, *collective practicality*, and *coresponsibility*."[5]

Being practical did not mean being a pragmatist. In *Insight* Lonergan warns vigorously about the general bias of common sense and its contribution to the longer cycle of decline. Common sense practicality "entertains no aspirations about reaching abstract and universal laws. It is easily led to rationalize its limitations by engendering a conviction that other forms of human knowledge are useless or doubtfully valid."[6] He was more blunt in 1934: "Practical minds are oriented towards extinction just as much whether they realize the point or not."[7] So "humanity must first discover its law and then apply it: to discover the law is *a long process* and to apply it a painful process but it has to be done."[8]

Lonergan began the long process of discovery in the student work *Essay In Fundamental Sociology*, which began this article. In this essay I will examine that first step. Fr. Doran discovered it after Lonergan's death among his private papers and sent a copy to me because he thought it relevant to my work. Reading the essay changed the direction of my own research, and for that I am grateful. What follows, then, is a return to the subject of my dissertation done under the direction of Fr. Doran. Further, what follows should shed light on the relationship between theology and the human sciences – a central theme of Doran's own work.

2. PRELIMINARIES

Lonergan's bent was theoretical. As a young student at Heythrop College he considered studying physics but found economics to be the more challenging problem. He comments: "I [had] studied a bit of economics during philosophy year [at Heythrop] on the side. We

---

5 Bernard Lonergan, *Method in Theology* (London: Darton, Longman & Todd, 1972), xi. Hereafter *Method*. Emphasis added.

6 *CWL3*, 251 [226].

7 *EFS*, 125.

8 Ibid.

had five hours of physics – a waste of time because it wasn't physics it was just simplification – and I always felt the study of physics would be fine, but in 1926 it was passé – I was interested in economics."[9] At Heythrop he was also 'awakened to the problem of knowledge,'[10] and the Blandyke Papers written at this time chronicle his interest in the foundations of logic and the beginnings of his justly famous exploration of cognitional process.[11] However, as William Mathews tells us in *Lonergan's Quest*, Lonergan was still undecided about his intellectual vocation: "Although he admitted that philosophy was his 'fine frenzy' he was seeking advice about a future academic life in classics or mathematics."[12] Soon his direction became clearer. When he returned to Canada from England in 1930 the country was in the terrible grip of the Great Depression.[13] "I got back to Canada and the depression was on and the rich were poor and the poor were out of work and there were a lot of economic theories floating about and I became interested in figuring out what was wrong with them."[14] The experience, I believe, shifts Lonergan's focus. He did not abandon the problem of knowledge, but his approach widened. Current political and economic issues occupied him as he developed a deepening sense of the *crisis* of the times. He took an interest in Catholic action.[15] History

---

9 From a typescript of an interview of Lonergan with Luis Morfin, SJ. July 11, 1981 available from LRI. [Hereafter Morfin].

10 William Mathews, *Lonergan's Quest*, chapter 3.

11 The article "The Form of Inference," *Thought* 18: 277-92 (1943) is a product of this early work. The essay also appears in *Collected Works of Bernard Lonergan*, vol. 4, *Collection*, ed. Frederick E. Crowe and Robert M. Doran (Toronto: University of Toronto Press, 1988).

12 William Mathews, *Lonergan's Quest: A Study of Desire in the Authoring of Insight* (Toronto: University of Toronto Press, 2005), 48.

13 Canada was especially hard hit by the depression. Its economy relied heavily on exports, so the general collapse of world trade worsened its effects. Many businesses were wiped out. At the depths of the depression in 1933, the unemployment rate in Canada reached 27%, and national production was at less than 60% of the 1929 levels. Those who were employed often worked fewer hours. The province of Quebec where Lonergan lived was among the hardest hit areas.

14 Morfin.

15 Patrick Brown explores this theme in Lonergan's work in an unpublished essay "The Task of 'Aiming Excessively High and Far': Catholic Social

and economics become major zones of inquiry. In 1930 Lonergan read Dawson's *The Age of the Gods*, which, he writes "introduced me to the anthropological notion of culture and so began the correction of my hitherto normative or classicist notion [of culture]."[16] The emergence of the question of history was significant, so much so that he would later characterize his life's work as the effort to introduce history into theology.[17]

In an article on Chesterton from 1931 he writes: "Karl Marx had German Materialism, the industrial revolution, reasonable publicity, a wild theory of value and an outrageous conception of history. That originator of a great experiment on civilization is not a unique example of noble sentiment and addled thought uniting to form a monstrosity. Democracy is faced with the alternative of teaching thought or meeting its decline and fall."[18] This brief statement articulates a concern that drives his work over the next 13 years: How do we preserve democracy in the face of totalitarian alternatives? Lonergan recognized the devastating effects of secularist ideologies: "abstract ideas have, indeed, a greater possibility of being wrong than the concrete ideas. Also, they work out for good or evil far more rapidly."[19] He knew the challenge of such ideologies had to be met at the level of ideas: "whether we like it or not, the world has got beyond the stage where concrete problems

Thought and the Question of Method." The full original title of the 1935 essay published as "*Pantôn Anakephalaiôsis* (Restoration of All Things)" in *Method: Journal of Lonergan Studies* 9/2 (October 1991): 139-72 is "*Pantôn Anakephalaiôsis*: A Theory of Human Solidarity, A Metaphysic for the Interpretation of St. Paul, A Theology for the Social Order, Catholic Action, and the Kingship of Christ in Incipient Outline."

16 "*Insight* Revisited," in *A Second Collection*, ed. William F.J. Ryan and Bernard J. Tyrell (London: Darton, Longman and Todd, 1974), 264.

17 From an interview in *Curiosity at the Center of One's Life: Statements and Questions of R. Eric O'Connor*, ed. J. Martin O'Hara (Montreal: Thomas More Institute, 1984), 427. See especially, Frederick Crowe, "'All My Work Has Been Introducing History into Catholic Theology,'" *Lonergan Workshop* vol. 10, ed. Fred Lawrence (Boston: Boston College, 1994), 49-81; reprinted in *Developing the Lonergan Legacy: Historical, Theoretical, and Existential Themes*, ed. Michael Vertin (Toronto: University of Toronto Press, 2004), 78-110.

18 Bernard Lonergan, "Gilbert Keith Chesterton" *Loyola College Review*, 1931, 8.

19 *EFS*, 124.

can be solved merely in the concrete."[20] The pressing scientific problem was in the field of economics. The standard model in economics
could neither explain why the depression occurred nor concur on how
to correct the problem.[21] Lonergan took on the creative challenge of
establishing economics as a science.[22] The more general issue for Lonergan was the influence of competing secular philosophies of history.
In response, Lonergan asserted the need for a *summa sociologica* or
metaphysic of history that would make explicit the implicit Catholic
social philosophy needed to meet the crisis.[23] The *Essay in Fundamental Sociology* was his first attempt to address this need.

3. ESSAY IN FUNDAMENTAL SOCIOLOGY: THE POSSIBILITY OF AN EFFECTIVE PHILOSOPHY

In youthful enthusiasm Lonergan described his *Essay in Fundamental Sociology* as "a Thomistic metaphysic of history that will throw
Hegel and Marx, despite the enormity of their influence on this very
account, into the shade."[24] We do not have the entire essay; only the
last quarter on the philosophy of history survives. Nonetheless, it is
clear the problem it tackles is the social disorder of the times. In the
frontispiece of the essay Lonergan placed the 'philosopher-king' passage from Plato's *Republic*, signaling the themes of the essay.[25] In the
essay itself he writes: "Philosophy emerged with the assertion of its

---

20 Ibid.

21 The standard model was the so-called 'great theory' whose general thesis
was an economy of perfectly competitive full employment in stationary (or
better) timeless equilibrium. At the time Lonergan took up economics, he
was not alone in either challenging elements of the model or seeking alternative approaches. See George Shackle, *The Years of High Theory* (Cambridge University Press, 1967).

22 See Michael Shute, *Lonergan's Discovery of the Science of Economics* (Toronto: University of Toronto Press, forthcoming).

23 Lonergan writes: "Catholic social theory has existed since the middle ages
but the degree to which Catholics were conscious of the importance of
social philosophy has been small almost up to the present time." EFS, 125.

24 From a letter to his superior Fr. Keane dated January 22, 1935. Available
from the LRI.

25 Lonergan saved in his files the last section on the Philosophy of History
and a front page with the quote from the *Republic* V 473d handwritten in
Greek.

social significance. 'Men and cities will not be happy till philosophers are kings' is the central position of Plato's *Republic*, and the *Republic* is the center of the dialogues."[26] Lonergan grasped a parallel between the problem Plato tackles in the *Republic* and the contemporary situation characterized by the rise of competing secularist philosophies of history, the dominance of *Realpolitik*, and the economic disaster of the Great Depression. The modern sophistry was liberalism. Liberalism proclaimed the principle of *liberty*, meaning by this that individuals could pursue their self-interests. In practice, however, this policy favored the interests of the powerful. Liberalism denied the need for a higher order beyond the calculus of individual interests, instead asserting naïve faith in an automatic progress propelled by a free market and a politics of the balance of power.[27] He writes: "What Plato longed for, the liberal threw away."[28] Marxists responded to the liberal disorder by suppressing individual liberty, proclaiming the virtues of naked power and declaring class war in the name of social order. In either case, 'might is right.'

It was Lonergan's view that the Catholic philosophy had the resources to meet the liberal thesis and the Marxist antithesis. In this respect, the metaphysic of history he developed in the *Essay in Fundamental Sociology* aligns with orthodox Catholic salvation history. There are, however, two elements in the essay that are original. The first is his account of the fundamental dynamics of history, including his account

---

26 *EFS*, 103.

27 In "*Questionnaire on Philosophy: Response*", Lonergan writes: "[W]hat the self-interest of the capitalist must have is profit, for the alternative to profit is loss, and sustained loss means bankruptcy. In such a context enlightened self-interest easily comes to mean really profitable self-interest. And when the mathematical economists draw up their design for utopia, the best of all possible worlds is seen to result from maximizing profits. In this fashion an ambiguous term betrays capitalist enterprise into complicity with the forces of decline. Profit as a criterion encourages the egoism of individuals and of groups; individual and especially group egoism is a bias that generates inattention, obtuseness, unreasonableness, and social irresponsibility; what initially appeared to be a 'scientifically' efficient and efficacious motivation has turned out to be an engine of decline." *Collected Works of Bernard Lonergan*, vol. 17, *Philosophical and Theological Papers 1965-1980*, ed. Robert C. Croken and Robert M. Doran (Toronto: University of Toronto Press, 2004), 368-369.

28 *EFS*, 103.

of historical stages. The second is his sublation of the metaphysic of history into a theology of the mystical body of Christ.[29] The first highlights an advance in philosophy. The second situates this advance in its theological context.

Lonergan frames the philosophical problem in terms of the relationship between *internal* acts of individual consciences and shared *external* action. He imagines the relationship in terms of a dynamic flow of acts; what he seeks are the 'differentials' of the flow that, like the differential equation in calculus, organizes an underlying material flow. His desire is to make sense of the whole process, that is, to discover a higher order or viewpoint beyond a liberal aggregate of competing individual interests. However, the order that he affirms must, unlike totalitarian responses, preserve the personal liberty that is at the heart of democracy. The solution arrived at is an application of Aquinas' metaphysics. The elements included are Aquinas' account of intellect and its relationship to will, the concept of pre-motion, and his account of sin and its restoration through the theological virtues.[30] There are five steps in the philosophical elements of the solution.

First, Lonergan differentiates between a *material cause* in the flow of external action and a *formal cause* in the emergence of intellectual forms.[31] The intellect is *one* act relevant to *many* actions in the material

---

29 There had been a re-discovery and development of the Pauline conception of the Mystical Body in Catholic theology in 1920s and 1930s culminating in Pius XI's 1943 encyclical *Mystici Corporis Christi*.

30 It is not, however, a Thomist application. In the Keane letter from 1935 Lonergan writes: "The current interpretation of St. Thomas is a consistent misinterpretation." Lonergan works from an intellectualist version of Thomas, a position for which he eventually argued in his detailed interpretation of Thomas in the *Verbum* articles. See *Verbum: Word and Idea in Aquinas*, volume 2, *Collected Works of Bernard Lonergan*, ed. Frederick E. Crowe and Robert M. Doran (Toronto: University of Toronto Press, 1997).

31 The individual receives the external flow *as given* in the sensitive flow in experience. Intellect orders the flow of experiences, which are given in the sensitive flow. Lonergan writes that material change is "sensible in consciousness, physical in the subconscious and the physical world" (*EFS*, 95). In individuals, then, we locate the material cause in the psycho-sensitive flow of change.

flow. It is a higher organization of the flow which, if the will cooperates, acts to intelligently direct the material flow.[32]

Second, intellect is dynamic; it develops *over time* from potency to act: "a potency does not leap to its perfect act but goes through a series of imperfect acts on its way to attaining a perfect act."[33] Implicit in this formulation is the notion of knowing as a self-correcting process. *Progress* is possible because of the emergence of new intellectual forms.

Third, the concept of *pre-motion* establishes the link between internal acts and the external flow of history for *quidquid movetur ab alio movetur*. One the one hand, everything that individuals do is premoved by the action of other things. Internal acts are in response to the environment or sensitive flow presented to us: "What you think about depends upon the mentality you have imbibed from an environment of home, school, university, and the general influence of others."[34] Lonergan stresses the dominance of community over individual.[35] Positively, "intellectual achievement is the achievement of the [human] race, of the unity of human action; the individual genius is but the instrument of the [human] race in its expansion."[36] On the other hand, internal acts are directed outward in actions: this pre-motion

---

32 Lonergan's account of Aquinas on intellect in the essay is sketchy, especially in light of subsequent work. The writing in the essay has the feel of a recent discovery and, as he acknowledges, would require a much fuller exposition to be entirely convincing. For example, while he differentiates experience and understanding, he conflates judgment to understanding. Nonetheless, Lonergan is able to work out many of the elements of his notion of the dialectic of history in the essay, suggesting that he was on the right track. On the development of the basic position of this essay, see Michael Shute, *The Origins of Lonergan's Notion of the Dialectic of History* (Lanham, Md.: University Press of America, 1993), chapter six.

33 *EFS*, 100.

34 *EFS*, 95.

35 In *Insight* he writes: "…[T]he dialectic of community holds the dominant position [over the dialect of the dramatic subject], for it gives rise to the situations that stimulate neural demands, and it molds the orientation of intelligence that preconsciously exercises the censorship." The dominance is not, however, absolute, "for both covertly and overtly neural demands conspire with an obnubilation of intelligence, and what happens in isolated individuals tends to brings them together and so to provide a focal point from which aberrant social attitudes originate." (*CWL3*, 243[218]).

36 *EFS*, 100.

extends to the intellectual field and constitutes the pre-motion of the will. Thus, will is the *efficient* cause of human action. Pre-motion connects intelligence and will and connects both to the external material flow.[37] If this is so, then the present historical situation is pre-moved by the past action. History, then, is "the flow of human acts proceeding from one human nature, materially individuated in space-time, and all united according to the principle of pre-motion."[38] The fact of pre-motion constitutes the unity of human action and thus the solidarity of the human species.

Fourth, as noted, the immanent control of history stems from acts of intellect and will. However, the will can opt to follow or not follow human understanding. Insofar as the will follows intellect, human beings attain their proper end or *energeia* of their personality.[39] Otherwise, human beings are pre-determined by the physical flow. Failure to follow the dictates of intelligence is the source of sin (evil) and ultimately, because of the solidarity of the species, results in the reign of

---

37 The argument from pre-motion here anticipates the notion of a *scheme of recurrence* as it links the material flow, physico-sensitive flow, emerging forms, and human will to external actions which enter into the material flow as a continuous set of acts.

38 *EFS*, 98. The reference to 'space-time' here shows Lonergan's familiarity with Einstein's theory of relativity and points ahead to the pivotal chapter 5 of *Insight*. To make the transition from the physical and life sciences to a scientific theory of common sense, one must eventually grapple with the physics of space-time.

39 The term 'energeia' translates as 'energy-power' and is an equivalent term to act or operation. See *CWL2*, 111-114 where Lonergan variously translates the term as either act or operation. In his discussion of operation in *Verbum*, Lonergan writes: "In an operation there is no assignable instant in which what is occurring stands in need of something further that later will make it specifically complete. A similar general contrast occurs in the *Metaphysics*. There is a difference between action (*praxis*) distinct from its end and action coincident with its end. One cannot at once be walking a given distance and have walked it, be being cured and have been cured, be learning something and have learned it. But at once one is seeing and has seen, one is understanding and has understood, one is alive and has been alive, one is happy and has been happy. In the former instances there is a difference between action and end, and we have either what is not properly action or, at best, incomplete action – such are movements. In the latter instances action and end are coincident – such are operations" *CWL2*, 112.

sin (social surd).[40] Given the solidarity of the species, the fact of free will makes possible both progress and decline. Progress occurs when intelligence and will cooperate to creatively respond to problems. Decline is the obfuscation of the creative process through bias and sin.

Fifth, Lonegan distinguishes between practical intelligence and theoretical intelligence and, on the basis of the distinction, develops a dialectic account of historical stages. There is the dialectic of fact, the dialectic of thought, and the absolute dialectic. Practical creativity rules the first stage, the dialectic of fact. Its development is automatic, meaning that it follows the spontaneous course of practical creativity. Invention meets the challenges presented by the environment. Human beings create new technologies, economies, political organizations, and so forth to organize their survival. The second stage is the dialectic of thought. Where practical thought is the spontaneous manifestation of intelligence in response to specific situations, theory is general and speculative. In the dialectic of thought, developments proceed from theoretical to practical. For example, Newton's physics produces a whole plethora of practical applications. The absolute dialectic is the historical development of dogma that counters the regressive tendencies in the first two dialectic stages.

The dialectic of thought arises out of the shortcomings of practical thought. Practical intelligence can deal only with the immediate and practical. Moreover, given the fact of sin, social organizations developed in the first stage are inevitably distorted. Lonergan gives as an example the bureaucracy of the Mesopotamian city-states. Theory emerges to intimate a higher viewpoint. The sciences seek what is true in all instances. Philosophy provides the general *critical* stance to deal with the particular distorted social organizations that emerge in the automatic phase of history. Thus, in the *Republic* Plato makes a claim for a way of living, an *idea*, beyond a social ranking based on power, beyond the horizon of particular cities and empires. Plato's hope was for a transformed polis. The philosopher's 'form of the good' is the core vision for the 'new polis'. The practical tool was the conversational dialectic that would educate and persuade citizens by argument. In the *Republic* Plato's dialogue reveals the contradiction in Thrasymachus' claim that 'might is right' and demonstrates that it is better to suffer

---

40 Sin and the reign of sin are theological equivalences for evil and social surd. What is evil in the human sphere *pre se* is theologically an offence to God.

injustice than to inflict it. The dialectical conversation leads him to a revelation about the intelligible form of the good. Knowing the 'form of the good' makes known its absence; this gave him the power of social criticism. Plato rightfully criticized the Greek gods and goddesses and "sought to make education his ally by purifying it of its manifest corruptions."[41] Knowledge of the forms was "an irreducible something, the emergence of a new light upon experience that can not be brought back and expressed in terms of experience."[42]

Lonergan writes: "Plato's greatness lies in his fidelity to the social problem in its most acute form. His *Republic* like Kant's *Kritik* set a perfect question but utterly failed to answer it."[43] Part of the problem lay with Plato's proposals for reform: the abolition of the family, his 'material communism,' and 'the education of the guardians in a school of mysticism.'[44] More generally, there was the gap between the philosophical idea and effective practice. One the one hand, philosophy seeks to solve problems, to erect synthesis, to embrace the world in a single view. On the other hand, in the practical world of common sense human beings are more like animals living in a habitat. They are interested in survival and advancement, moved by dreams and symbols, and committed to the experiential objectivity presented by extroverted sensibility. While Plato developed a blueprint for reform, he could not translate the philosophical idea into effective practice within the Athenian polis. Plato eventually renounced the 'philosophy project' in the *Laws*. The ghost of Plato's failure has haunted philosophy ever since. The moral idea of the just republic becomes a rhetorical tool for politicians on the stump. Machiavelli's *Prince* and Marx's *Communist Manifesto* have been the real influence on affairs of state. Both rejected the moral quest in favor of the practical expediency of power. In the world of *Realpolitik*, it is Thrasymachus' position that has the legs. For good or ill, in the second phase of history, theory directs practice and so bad theories can produce devastating results. To put it another way, "abstract ideas have, indeed, a greater possibility of being wrong than the concrete ideas. Also, they work out for good

---

41 *EFS*, 107.

42 *EFS*, 106.

43 Ibid., 108.

44 Ibid., 107-108.

or evil far more rapidly."[45] Creative developments emerge only to fall into the hands of powerful interest groups who would block future developments to preserve present power and who would use theory to justify and enforce self-interests or class interests. In short, in the second stage distorted theory accelerates decline.

Nonetheless, Lonergan believed in the social significance of philosophy and, by implication, for theory, to paraphrase Newman, 'a thousand difficulties do not make a doubt.' The problems of social order generated in the first phase of history were real, and philosophy possessed the power of criticism because it "enables man to express not by symbol but by a concept the divine."[46] What was required was a sound philosophy and good theories. The reversal of the downward spiral of the modern world required a modern 'turn to the idea,' a shift towards system that could be effectively implemented in the contemporary situation.[47] His application of Aquinas to the question of history provided him with a critique of liberal and Marxist theories of history. Liberalism and Marxism contributed to the longer cycle of decline and were in fundamental contradiction to human conscience. Politically, the liberal state depends on a precarious balance of power. Economically, the modern liberal state is subject to global economic factors that go beyond its capacity to control. The domination of 'the great powers' and the promotion of nationalism are to the detriment of culture. Liberalism includes both error and evil in the data for its theory and on this basis cannot operate on an intelligent principle. Truth cannot be made consistent with error nor wrong made consistent with right. Therefore, truth and value are distorted to maintain consistency. Bolshevism is not concerned with truth at all. It asserts the order of power and accelerates the decline. In opposition to both is the Church, whose foundation is in the conscience of persons. The metaphysic of history needed to reverse the effect of the longer cycle of decline would make explicit the implicit Catholic social philosophy needed for the effective direction of Catholic action. Such a metaphysic would of necessity

---

45 *EFS*, 100.

46 *EFS*, 106.

47 See Patrick Brown, "System and History in Lonergan's Early Historical and Economic Analysis," in *The Journal of Macrodynamic Analysis* 1 (2001): 32-76.

have to include elements that transcend the deformation of human nature in liberalism and bolshevism.

4. ESSAY IN FUNDAMENTAL SOCIOLOGY: THE SUPERNATURAL VIEWPOINT

There was a larger issue. While philosophy emerged to meet the shortcomings of common sense, given the fact of sin, theory is also confounded and, as we have seen, when deformed theory accelerates, decline and sin become not simply the incidental waywardness of individuals but a deformation of the social order; a reign of sin occurs.[48] Certainly, the solution required sound philosophy "for only sound philosophy can establish the conviction necessary to reassure men, can eliminate false theories in a purely natural sphere, can give positive guidance in… 'technical matters'"[49] However, sound philosophy could not *on its own* counter the modern reign of sin. In *Insight* Lonergan develops this theme more fully:

> The problem is not to discover a correct philosophy, ethics, or human science. For such discoveries are quite compatible with the continued existence of the problem. The correct philosophy can be but one of many philosophies, the correct ethics one of many ethical systems, the correct human science an old or new view among many views. But precisely because they are correct, they will not appear correct to minds disorientated by the conflict between positions and counterpositions. Precisely because they are correct, they will not appear workable to wills with restricted ranges of effective freedom. Precisely because they are correct, they will be weak competitors for serious attention in the realm of practical affairs.[50]

In other words, intelligence is not enough. The effective solution depends upon the appearance of a higher supernatural viewpoint than can meet the source of the deformation of the reign of sin in the conscience of individuals. Thus, while correct theory is an essential component for the reversal of the modern crisis, an effective solution depends upon the emergence of a higher supernatural viewpoint and its corresponding integration with concrete living.

---

48 It is this insight that informs Lonergan's latter distinction of minor and major authenticity. See *Method*, 80.

49 *EFS*, 118.

50 *CWL3*, 654 [631-32]. Hard comfort indeed!

There must be both a development of mind and a change of heart that works to restore human history to its proper ends. Lonergan writes: "The hope for the future lies in a philosophical presentation of the supernatural concept of social order."[51] The higher viewpoint is necessary because of sin. Its appearance in history is possible because of the solidarity of the human species through the fact of premotion. It is actual because of the Incarnation. Historically the higher supernatural viewpoint re-establishes all things in a new movement in Christ. The many sins of humankind are brought under a higher control by virtue of the justification of Christ. Christ is the *one* head who restores through actual grace the *many* persons in the mystical body. The movement of the mystical body is the higher synthesis that meets the liberal thesis and the Marxist antithesis. We grasp the full meaning of history in the salvation drama of creation, fall and redemption. "It is an ever fuller manifestation of Eternal Wisdom in which 'evil is permitted merely that good may more fully abound.'"[52] Of the doctrine of the mystical body he later writes: "Because it is a supernatural doctrine, the relevant viewpoint...is the viewpoint of God himself, so that, while from books and lectures we can learn many things about the Mystical Body, still it is only in prayer and contemplation that one really comes to know and appreciate it."[53] Thus the meaning of history, and of human practicality, is ultimately beyond history. Our understanding of this is an 'intelligible mystery' whose meaning we reach only analogously. Nonetheless, it is the transcendental measure of all human achievement and the source of the criticism of any finite good: "[A]nything that exists and is good by participation is finite....[I]t is not good in every respect, ... it can be criticized."[54] In this respect, the notion of the Mystical Body is a Christian analog to Plato's form of the good. It is the invitation to a creative participation with the divine mystery in the making of the finite good in history. In *Essay in Fundamental Sociology*, the progress of the Mystical Body in history consti-

51 *EFS*, 118.

52 *EFS*, 127.

53 Bernard Lonergan, "The Mystical Body of Christ." Domestic exhortation given at the Jesuit Seminary, Toronto, 1951. Available from LRI.

54 Bernard Lonergan, *Collected Works of Bernard Lonergan*, vol. 10, *Topics in Education*, ed. Robert M. Doran and Frederick E. Crowe, revising and augmenting the text prepared by James Quinn and John Quinn, 1993 (Toronto: University of Toronto Press, 1993), 32.

tutes a third stage of history, the absolute dialectic whose function is to reverse the deforming effects of sin on human actions. The Church is the social form of this movement. On the one hand, the church assimilates the world to itself by means of the gospel message and in the development of doctrine, culminating in a new apostolate informed by a scientific sociology – i.e. a *summa sociologica* and missiology.

The philosophy of history Lonergan developed in this essay aims to provide the scientific sociology for the new apostolate of Catholic action. It was not simply the discerning of the implicit social philosophy in the Catholic tradition. What he attempted was a massive overhaul of the tradition meant to reconstruct the social order. As Patrick Brown notes: "A careful examination of those texts reveals that, to use a favorite phrase from John Courtney Murray, Lonergan undertook the task, not just of "discerning the growing end of the tradition," but of "massively accelerating and transposing it as well."[55]

5. FROM A METAPHYSICS OF HISTORY TO FUNCTIONAL SPECIALIZATION?

While *Essay in Fundamental Sociology* was Lonergan's first attempt at a metaphysic of history, many ideas found in *Insight* and *Method in Theology* have their beginnings in the essay. His ideas on bias, dialectic, and the longer cycle of decline all have their origins there. In his appropriation of Aquinas' conception of pre-motion to link internal acts and the external material flow, we recognize the beginnings of his notion of schemes of recurrence. His three level account of stages of history become, with considerable modification, the stages of meaning. His ideas will undergo considerable development as will his understanding of the modern crisis itself.

A year later, in "*Pantôn Anakephalaiôsis* (Restoration of all Things)" he returns to the same theme. Soon after, however, Lonergan begins to divide up his intellectual tasks. He shifts attention to the purely theoretical component of the solution, which developed into the analytic concept of history; the practical matter of Catholic action receded from view. The essay "Analytic Concept of History" is purely philosophical with minimal reference to the historical situation; there is no mention of Catholic action. His work in economics was entirely theoretical; the only practical directives that emerged were general precepts

55 Patrick Brown, ""The Task of 'Aiming Excessively High and Far': Catholic Social Thought and the Question of Method," 11.

related to economic phases. For example, in a surplus expansion the precept is "thrift and enterprise."[56] He did not address the issue of how his economic theory should be applied in the concrete case.

The work of *Essay in Fundamental Sociology* made its way into *Insight* particularly in chapters six and seven on common sense intelligence. The supernatural component of the philosophy of history is addressed in chapter twenty. In the epilogue Lonergan locates the Church's response to the rise of secular philosophies of religion in "calls to Catholic action, by a fuller advertence to collective responsibility, and by the deep and widespread interest in the doctrine of the mystical body."[57] Also in the epilogue, Lonergan addresses the relationship between theology and the social sciences. The practical gist of his position is this: The specifically Christian contribution to the social sciences is the exhortation to effective charity. If one is to love one's neighbor then we must acknowledge his real needs and work towards their recurrent supply. To apply moral exhortation without an understanding of how human systems function is an empty gesture. Moral theology needs the social sciences in order to be moral, for one cannot be truly responsible without reference to the related science.

In the *Essay in Fundamental Sociology* Lonergan had averted to the significance of 'technical matters' in Christian praxis. He did not change his view in *Insight*. As late as 1976 he writes: "There is needed up-to-date technical knowledge of economic and political theory and their respective histories; perhaps the great weakness of Catholic social thought is its apparent lack of awareness of the need for technical knowledge."[58] The development of the human sciences is part of the creative vector in human history. To ignore it is to stagnate, or worse, to hand over our liberty to the forces of totalitarian control. This is the force behind Lonergan's remark that "If Catholics had spent some of their time in the British Museum...we might have a good answer to Marx."[59]

---

56 We may note the similarity with the transcendental precepts of generalized empirical method: be attentive, be intelligent, be reasonable, and be responsible. In both cases the advice is *completely general*.

57 *CWL3*, 764 [743].

58 Bernard Lonergan, "Questionnaire on Philosophy: Responses by Bernard Lonergan." *Method: Journal of Lonergan Studies*, 2 (1984), 14-15.

59 Pierrot Lambert, Charlotte Tansey, and Cathleen Going, eds., *Caring About Meaning: Patterns in the Life of Bernard Lonergan*, Thomas More

Similarly, the social sciences need theology. Certainly social scientists can do research proper to their field without reference to theology. However, once thought turns to practical application then moral questions arise where the context is concrete human living. With this we encounter the problem of the social surd which lay at the heart of the problem in *Essay in Fundamental Sociology*. In the epilogue of *Insight* Lonergan writes:

> ...the development of the empirical human sciences has created a fundamentally new problem. For these sciences consider man in his concrete performance, and that performance is a manifestation not only of human nature but also of human sin, not only of nature and sin but also of a de facto need of divine grace, not only of a need for grace but also of its reception and of its acceptance or rejection. It follows that an empirical human science cannot analyze successfully the elements in its object without an appeal to theology.[60]

The issue is implementation of the best ideas. Social theory no less than philosophy needs more than the right answers; it needs a way to turn ideas into good practice. Lonergan continues: "Inversely, it follows that if theology is to be queen of the sciences, not only by right but also in fact, then theologians have to take a professional interest in the human sciences and make a positive contribution to their methodology."[61] This means the human sciences are part of theological foundations and that theology is relevant to the implementation of social theory. This does not mean that the human sciences collapse into theology. The point assumes that there is an adequate differentiation of consciousness. Each field has its proper tasks and ends. However, adequate differentiation also means a corresponding integration of results. A conscientious economist, for example, can neither ignore the real economy, nor the relevant moral questions, nor the demand for charity. The key question is this: What is the contribution of the economist or any scientist to realizing this demand for effective charity? The answer is good ideas informed by sound theory. And how are these ideas implemented? Lonergan writes: "Christian praxis is the dynamic of human creativity and freedom in which individually men

---

Institute Papers 82 (Montreal: Thomas More Institute, 1982), 163.

60 *CWL3*, 765 [745].

61 Ibid.

[and women] make themselves and collectively they make the world in which they live."⁶²

Lonergan's comments on the relationship between theology and the human sciences in the epilogue of *Insight* affirm the collaborative nature of the higher integration he envisaged. While "the problem [of evil] is not primarily social[;] it results in the social surd. It receives from the social surd its continuity, its aggravation, its cumulative character. But its root is elsewhere. Hence it is that a political revolution can sweep away old evils and initiate a fresh effort; but the fresh effort will occur through the same dynamic structure as the old effort and lead to essentially the same results."⁶³ The solution involves a favorable shift in probabilities resulting from the acceptance and implementation of the supernatural conjugates by persons and communities. Their acceptance is a change of heart in persons that shifts the meaning of communities. In *Insight* Lonergan writes: "The antecedent willingness of charity has to mount from an affective to an effective determination to discover and implement *in all things* the intelligibility of universal order that is God's concept and choice."⁶⁴ Lonergan had not abandoned his quest for a foundation for Catholic action. However, as Philip McShane observes: "*Insight* was a splendid solitary foundational work, written as a pedagogical moving viewpoint from a viewpoint that lacked the key insight into modern academic culture. It is in need of multiple elevations to shift the probability-schedules of hope."⁶⁵

The implementation of the metaphysics in *Insight* requires massive collaboration, not just in its practical task but also in the division of theoretical labor. Lonergan, of course, was well aware of this. In "For A New Political Economy" he addresses the question of the implementation of his economic theory. He writes: "The task will be vast, so vast that only the creative imagination of all individuals in all democracies will be able to construct at once the full conception and the full real-

---

62 Bernard Lonergan "Questionnaire on Philosophy: Response," in *Philosophical and Theological Papers 1965-1980*, 370.

63 *CWL3*, 654 [631].

64 *CWL3*, 747-48 (726). Emphasis added.

65 Philip McShane, "Implementation: The Ongoing Crisis of Method," in *Journal of Macrodynamic Analysis*, Vol. 3 (2003), 15.

ization of the new order."⁶⁶ In *Insight* his vision of cosmopolis is the possibility of an authentic higher viewpoint directing human collaboration. Yet he writes: "Cosmopolis is not Babel....This is the problem. So far from solving it in this chapter, we do not hope to reach a full solution in this volume."⁶⁷

After *Insight* Lonergan pushed ahead on the question of implementation that had remained unsolved in *Insight*. A full solution had to deal with the fragmentation of the modern world and in particular the fragmentation of the modern academy.⁶⁸ The result was his discovery of functional specialization in 1965. With functional specialization he found a general method for theoretic collaboration and in its feedback system a way of implementing that idea in history. The discovery was the culmination of the 'long process' in search of the 'law' – an adequate theory of Catholic action – that began with his response to the economic and political crisis of the 1930s and which he first articulated in *Essay in Fundamental Sociology*. With functional specialization, Lonergan had found the collaborative structure for directing the "painful process" of applying it – the alternative of which is extinction.

Finally, by the time functional specialization was discovered in 1965, Lonergan's understanding of the situation of Catholic action had shifted. In 1934 the context is Western civilization and "Christianity was at once a symbol and a trans-philosophic higher control."⁶⁹ But in *Method in Theology* and in his post-*Method* writings he writes about the common infrastructure that grounds the world religions.⁷⁰ He acknowledges the thrust towards world community in the contemporary consciousness, and he points to a role for Catholic theolo-

---

66 Bernard Lonergan, *Collected Works of Bernard Lonergan*, vol. 21, *For a New Political Economy*, ed. Philip J. McShane (Toronto: University of Toronto Press, 1998), 37.

67 *CWL3*, 267 [242].

68 On the problem of the fragmentation in specialization see, for example, the work of physicist David Bohm, *Wholeness and the Implicate Order* (London; Routledge, 1980). Bohm hits the problem on the nose, but his brilliant effort to solve the problem would benefit greatly from functional specialization.

69 *EFS*, 123.

70 See *Method*, chapter 4, especially 108-111.

gians in cooperating with the coming convergence of world religions.[71] Certainly, his meaning for 'global' and 'catholic' and 'collaboration' had developed. Perhaps Lonergan envisaged a strategic importance for this particular collaboration in the building up of the mystical body of Christ?

---

71 Lonergan adopts the phrase from the title of R. E. Whitson's *The Coming Convergence of World Religions* (New York: Newman, 1971). This is a significant theme in a number of late essays including "Prolegomena to the Study of the Emerging Religious Consciousness of our Time," "A Post-Hegelian Philosophy of Religion", and the three essays of his "Lectures on Religious Studies and Theology." These essays are collected in A *Third Collection: Papers by Bernard J.F. Lonergan, S.J,* ed. F. Crowe, SJ. (Mahwah, NJ: Paulist Press and London: Geoffrey Chapman, 1985).

CULTURE BUILDING IN KENYA: EMPLOYING ROBERT DORAN'S THOUGHT IN PARISH WORK

GERARD WHELAN, SJ

GREGORIAN UNIVERSITY, ROME

I. INTRODUCTION

It is a pleasure for me to contribute to this festschrift for Robert Doran under whom I studied during doctoral studies in Toronto between 1992 and 1995. Although I am Irish, I have worked for a number of years as a missionary in Africa. In this article I offer an account of how I tried to employ the heuristic structure offered by Bob's theory of the dialectics of history during my responsibility as pastor of St. Joseph the Worker Parish, a poor parish in Kangemi on the outskirts of Nairobi, Kenya.[1]

My account of this pastoral experience needs to begin, as does all pastoral reflection, with an analysis of the situation in which the Christian ministry finds itself. In this respect, I find Doran's analysis of the analogy of dialectic between the levels of social value, cultural value, and personal value to be illuminating. Next, when I analyze the effectiveness of pastoral ministry in the parish where I worked, I find it especially helpful to keep in mind Doran's notion of how ministry

---

1 In this article I assume a certain familiarity with Doran's thought on the part of readers. Elsewhere I have offered accounts of my understanding of Robert Doran's thought. (See my contribution in the forthcoming publication of proceedings of the Lonergan Workshop 34, 2007: "Unfinished Business in *Insight*: the Dialectics of History in Bernard Lonergan and Robert Doran".) I have written elsewhere on efforts to apply Doran's methodology to the task of pastoral decision-making, although never so directly about my experience in Kangemi. [See "Robert Doran and Pastoral Theology: Reflections From Nairobi, Kenya," also awaiting publication in the proceedings of the Lonergan Workshop 34, 2007; see also: "Theological Reflection and the Slums of Nairobi" in *The Slums: A Challenge to Evangelisation*, ed. F. Pierli and Y. Abeledo, Tangaza Occasional Papers, No.14 (Nairobi, Pauline Publications Africa, 2002), 77-98, 142-151.]

should facilitate a mediation of soteriological values, i.e., first to healing the integral dialectics within a Christian community and then to
helping a network of such communities discover a similar healing history at large so as to facilitate the emergence of a "world-cultural humanity."[2]

2. THE DIALECTICS OF KENYAN HISTORY

As I move into an analysis of the situation in Nairobi and Kenya
using the heuristic categories of Doran, there are certain basic points
that in fact apply to most parts of sub-Saharan Africa and can be dealt
with in this broad way. Above all, one needs to register certain truths
concerning how the imperialism of the nineteenth and twentieth centuries affected the dialectics of the history of that continent.

2.1 COLONIALISM AND CHRISTIANITY IN AFRICA

Most experts hold that the emergence of the human species occurred in Africa – indeed, probably in the Great Rift Valley of East
Africa. For reasons that have largely to do with the climate and ge-
ography, some human societies outside Africa advanced more rapidly
beyond the stage of undifferentiated consciousness that characterizes
primal culture. So it was that modernity emerged in Europe and was
exported to the other continents through the instruments of military
conquest and empire. Writers such as Arnold Toynbee trace how trau-
matic was the change introduced to primal cultures such as those of
Africa under this experience. The cultural developments that took
thousands of years to emerge in Europe were now introduced virtually overnight in such societies. What resulted was a domination of
the European at the level of infrastructure and a profound alienation
of local inhabitants at the level of cultural superstructure. I believe
that it is important to analyze this alienation in a manner that is both
genetic and dialectical.

The genetic point is that a transformation of ideas and values occurs
only gradually and that there was an inevitable trauma when primal
cultures – cultures in which a cosmological worldview was predomi-
nant – were compelled to accelerate to a cultural state where cosmological culture existed in tension with the kind of sophisticated anthro-

2 In referring to Doran's thought I primarily use *Theology and the Dialectics of History* by Robert M. Doran (Toronto: University of Toronto Press,
1990).

pological culture that could govern the kind of economic and political infrastructure introduced by the modern colonizers. A cultural alienation was perhaps inevitable, but this problem was compounded by a further reality that needs to be studied dialectically: the imperialists themselves exhibited a form of cultural decline that was especially antagonistic to primal cultures. So it was that the Europeans who arrived as overlords in Africa were themselves in denial of their own need to hold an integral dialectic of culture where cosmological culture was held in tension with anthropological. Thus, as they sought to educate local inhabitants about the countries of their empires, they imposed a notion of culture that was both foreign to those inhabitants and was itself in decline.[3]

A further point that needs to be acknowledged is that the main expansion of Christianity in Africa occurred during this colonial period and that its impact was ambiguous. Of course, Christian missionaries brought much that was positive to Africa, not least of which was the soteriological value of knowing Jesus Christ. However, they participated in the normative notion of culture held by their fellow Europeans and, however unwittingly, missionaries themselves contributed to the cultural alienation of Africans. A related point here is that through the schools and hospitals of their mission stations, the missionaries were often the most proximate carriers of the new cultural forces to the African.

Finally, we can trace how this pattern of cultural alienation was carried forward into the post-independence African nation-states and had tragic consequences for the quality of governance exercised by many of Africa's ruling elites. In some respects, it is best to turn to the work of African novelists to appreciate the pain that was inflicted on Africans at the level of personal and cultural values and the manner in which patterns established during colonial times continued to afflict the emergent independent states of Africa from the 1960s onwards.[4]

---

3 "An exclusively anthropological determination of culture is productive of that distortion of the dialectic of culture that is internally constitutive of modern imperialism," in Robert M. Doran, *Theology and the Dialectics of History* (Toronto: University of Toronto Press, 1990), 479.

4 One African novel read today by primary students across the continent is tellingly entitled "Things Fall Apart" (Chenua Achebe, *Things Fall Apart*, New York, Anchor Books, 1994, [1958]) and describes the results of the arrival of Christian missionaries in an Igbo village of modern-day Niger-

Kenya certainly participated in this general pattern of cultural alienation, and I now turn to note some characteristics of Kenyan history which give particular character to the manner in which Kenyans lived out this reality.

2.2. SOME PARTICULARS OF KENYA

A first particular point to note about Kenya is that it enjoys greater ethnic diversity than almost any other African country. Consequently, building a Kenyan patriotism that could unite its citizens was always going to be especially challenging.

Kenya is a zone of convergence for some of the largest and most different ethnic, or what is often called racial, groupings. These include the Bantu-speaking peoples, who are the most numerous in Africa, as well as Nilotic, Hamitic, and Semitic groupings. Another point that concerns diversity is that a major distinction exists among the cultures of pastoralist and agriculturalist peoples and that Kenya has a particularly high proportion of pastoralists. Agriculturalist peoples have tended to adapt more readily to the Western ways introduced by colonialism and so an unequal development has been evident in Kenya between its agriculturalist and pastoralist communities.

Another characteristic particular to Kenyan history is that the colonial power found it a particularly attractive country in which to live. Consequently, from early on, the British government began to invite European farmers to migrate to this colony and to settle permanently there. For related reasons, the numbers of Christian missionaries who came to work in Kenya were also larger than in some other African colonies. These facts had a number of positive consequences: the British invested relatively heavily in roads, railways, and economic institu-

---

ia. Another novelist of international stature is the Kenyan author Ngugi Wa Thiong'o. In his first novel, *The River Between* (London, Heinemann, 1964), he describes a situation where the education that young people receive from mission schools had little respect for the values of cosmological culture and so a kind of deep wound was inflicted in the local community and in the self-esteem of young Kenyans. At the same time, in this and in later novels, Ngugi traces how, if the young adapt themselves to some degree to the anthropological values being promoted, there were real material gains to be had. Ngugi describes a kind of cultural schizophrenia that comes to characterize young educated Africans; he also traces how this cultural confusion would bode ill for the behaviour of the elites that would come into power in the newly independent states of the 1960s.

tions such as banks and agricultural development agencies. Similarly, the preponderance of mission stations meant that, at independence, Kenya had systems of formal education and health care that were more advanced than most other African countries.

However, we now turn to one implication of the desire of the British to remain in Kenya for the long term that had profoundly negative consequences for both the infrastructure and superstructure in Kenya: the land issue.

2.3 THE LAND ISSUE

We have mentioned how at an early stage of the colonization process the British government made a decision to invite large numbers of British farmers to settle in Kenya. In order to facilitate this process of colonization by white farmers, the British colonial administration took some radical steps of land expropriation from local inhabitants. Beginning with the "Foreign Jurisdiction Act" in 1890, and enacting a more elaborate legislation in 1939, the colonial administration divided the land of Kenya into two major categories: "government land" and "trust land." Government land was any area that was likely to be valuable to the government for creating public utilities or for settling white farmers. Huge swathes of the best agricultural land were designated as government land. Land of lesser value was called trust land and assigned formally to different ethnic communities.

In practice, however, large proportions of the local ethnic communities continued to live on government land, but they now did so without rights before the law to do so. During the 1950s, there was a rebellion against colonial rule, and this "Mau Mau rebellion" was ruthlessly put down by the government. At this time, the British government started allocating trust land to selected Africans whom they trusted to be loyal to them and not to the Mau Mau rebels.[5] This pattern of using land allocation to ensure political loyalty set an example that, sadly, would be imitated by leaders of the newly independent Kenya. By the 1960s, the British government had changed its plans for a long-term stay in Kenya. After Prime Minister Harold McMillan made his famous "Winds of Change" speech, plans for granting independence to Kenya were be-

---

5 The historian M.P.R. Sorrenson explains the purpose of this land policy: "Land consolidation would create a class of land-owners that would refuse to have any truck with the nationalist politicians." *Land Reform in the Kikuyu Community* (Oxford, Oxford University Press, 1967), 250-251.

gun. In 1963 it was President Jomo Kenyatta, a former Mau Mau sup-
porter, who became the first leader of the independent nation.

A point of crucial importance for subsequent Kenyan history is that
the Kenyatta government chose not to change land law when it came
to power, and so the new government found that it had vast tracts
of much of the best land in the country at its disposal and began allocating land to its own loyalists. Throughout the Kenyatta era, those
receiving these gifts of land were usually prominent members of the
Kikuyu community, not the least of whom were President Kenyatta's
own family.

In 1978 President Kenyatta died and his successor was chosen from
one of the Kalenjin communities. President Daniel Arap Moi was a
compromise candidate from within the single ruling party in which
ethnic tensions were already evident among several of the other larger
ethnic communities. President Moi felt the need to secure his power
and accelerated the practice of bestowing gifts of land upon political
supporters – this time usually to his own community. This ethnic
community of Kalenjin were traditionally pastoralist and resented
the fact that significant numbers of agriculturalist settlers had already
been allocated land in the areas that had formerly belonged to them.
What resulted, then, was not only the allocation of land to prominent
Kalenjin families in various other parts of Kenya, but also a process
of ethnic cleansing of non-Kalenjin inhabitants from traditionally
Kalenjin lands. The worst of such incidents occurred in the Rift Valley in 1992 when 1,500 people were killed.

2.4 URBANIZATION, INEQUALITY AND SLUMS

It need not surprise us that with such injustice prevailing in rural
areas regarding the distribution of land, a rapid increase of migra-
tion to the cities should occur. In fact, in economic activity other than
the agricultural, a pattern of political patronage and favouritism also
existed, and Kenya climbed to the unenviable position of being the
fourth most unequal country in the world regarding the distribution
of wealth. It also climbed high in the ranking of countries where corruption was endemic.

The inequality of life in Kenya became most visible in cities such
as Nairobi where the majority of the population lives in poverty near
some of the most prosperous suburbs to be found in Africa. On this
note, there is a satellite photograph of Nairobi that highlights a re-

markable phenomenon. Within the city limits, slums with a population totalling 3 million are equal in area to a series of about six golf courses. One slum in Nairobi, Kibera, has received a certain amount of international media attention. With about one million inhabitants, it is the biggest slum in Africa, and by some measures, it offers living conditions that make it one of the worst slums in the world. Kibera is located beside a golf-course that is the private property of the President of the Republic.[6]

Given our account of Kenyan history, it is not surprising that slum-dwellers in the Kenyan cities are not only keenly aware of the economic inequality that exists in their country, they also feel that this is related to unjust policies related to land-grabbing and that this kind of corruption has an ethnocentric edge.

3. ST. JOSEPH THE WORKER PARISH, KANGEMI, NAIROBI: ANALYSIS OF A PASTORAL STRATEGY: 1985-2000

In the early 1980s Jesuits were new to Kenya but planned to build a large regional theologate to form their young men from all over Africa who were preparing for priesthood. In tandem with their arrival in the city, they communicated with the Archbishop of the diocese, Cardinal Maurice Otunga, offering to take responsibility for any parish he recommended in a poor area. As an exercise in good diocesan planning, the Cardinal invited the Jesuits to found a parish at the periphery of the city as it was already showing signs of a rapid population growth. The parish of Saint Joseph the Worker is located in the township of Kangemi and is 12 kilometres from the centre of Nairobi along the main road leading west out of the city. When the Jesuits helped found the parish in 1985, the population of the town was about 35,000. By the time I worked there during 2000-2006, the population was closer to 100,000.

3.1 KANGEMI, EXAMPLE OF A NAIROBI SLUM

Kangemi suffers from a lack of basic infrastructural services such as sanitation and clean water. Until recently there were few government

---

6 This photograph can be found by entering the three keywords "golf courses," "Kenya" and "slums" in a number of Internet search engines. See http://maps.grida.no/go/graphic/nairobi-interesting-neighbours-golfcourses-and-slums, downloaded 12/26/2008.

services. Education and health services were minimal as were formal employment opportunities. In terms of ethnicity, the area is striking for being characterised mostly by inhabitants from two ethnic groups, each of which comprises about 40% of the population. The first is the Kikuyu, and this is not surprising as this was originally an area inhabited by the Kikuyu community. The second is that of the Luhya, one of the other large ethnic groups of Western Kenya. This community tends to cluster in and around Kangemi whereas other ethnic groups cluster in other slums of the city.

Recent years have seen some modest improvements in the economic and political environment of Kenya. The advent of multi-party democracy during the 1990s and especially the departure from the political scene of President Moi in 2002 made for an unprecedented environment of freedom of expression. Some moderate improvement in the economy is evident, and the provision of public services in the area is moving in the right direction. While improved progress is to be discerned in the infrastructure of Kangemi, so also is the persistence of, and new manifestations of, decline at this level. There is trade in illegally brewed alcohol and drugs in Nairobi; contraband commodities arrive in bulk in the Kangemi area from the western agricultural regions and then get redistributed to the rest of the city. From this results a higher than average incidence of organized crime in our area as well as addiction. Kangemi is also a truck stop where vehicles on the large highway stay overnight, and one result of this is a particularly high incidence of HIV and AIDS.

3.2 PASTORAL STRATEGY IN KANGEMI: 1985-2000

The founding team of St. Joseph the Worker Parish began work in 1985 and developed a two-prong strategy for the parish they would build in Kangemi: building pastoral life on the basis of small Christian communities (SCCs) and initiating a number of development projects.

The first pastoral strategy had very much the character of the recent Jesuit General Congregation which had stressed the link between faith and justice. This Jesuit option fitted well with one taken by the bishops of Eastern and Southern Africa in a declaration they had made in the 1970s that SCCs should be the foundation of pastoral strategy in their region. The idea for SCCs was borrowed from that of "basic Christian communities" in Latin America and was associated with theologies of liberation.

SCCs function as follows: groups of twenty or thirty people meet in the house of one of the members. They elect their own leadership and meet once a week for about one hour and a half. These meetings devote about half of their time to shared prayer and about half to "talking business." The shared prayer is usually based on the Gospel of the next Sunday and adopts a "See, Judge, Act" approach to relating prayer to daily life. The "act" dimension of the prayer leads into the "business" part of the meeting and concerns itself with activities of service of the broader community that are usually ongoing. In Kangemi each Sunday, one SCC takes responsibility to animate the liturgies in the central parish Church. These liturgies are well known in the archdiocese for the vitality of their singing and dancing. We have a large church that can house a congregation of up to 4,000. A priest also arrives to say a house-Mass in each SCC once a month.

The second component of the early strategy of the parish was to establish a wide range of development projects to substitute for the absence of other development institutions in the area. These included a primary school and a remedial centre for street children; a vocational training centre that included a computer department; a furniture factory and a printing press; a medical clinic; a women's savings cooperative; and a women's handicraft factory. Development projects were built up in this Jesuit parish with unusual haste. As we will see, it was not always clear that the two aspects of this pastoral strategy proceeded in perfect coordination.

3.3 A FIRST EVALUATION OF ACHIEVEMENTS: 1985-2000

In the 1990s, the Kangemi Catholic parish came to be well-known in Kenya and even further afield as a model parish for implementing the bishops' priority for the SCC pastoral strategy. One result of Catholic parish strategy was the stimulation of a wide level of general community activism in Kangemi. Similarly, the development projects run by the parish also made a significant contribution to the area.

While many successes were evident, the passing of the years also started to reveal certain problems in parish functioning that raised questions about initial strategies. A kind of crisis of management capacity befell the institutions of the parish in the late 1990s. A number of the development projects experienced financial problems, and tension became apparent between parish priests and certain members of the pastoral council. These prompted a process of re-evaluating the parish pastoral strategy.

When consulted, some parishioners acknowledged that the Jesuits had perhaps initiated too many development projects too quickly. Some parishioners explained that individuals could on occasion aspire to join SCCs to obtain positions of leadership in the parish pastoral council and thus have access to financial benefits accruing from the development projects. This could then produce tension at election time within the SCCs and the pastoral council when some parishioners put themselves forward for the wrong reasons. Another evident pattern in the parish was that leadership continued to be firmly Kikuyu, often from the original farming families of Kangemi. Large numbers of Catholic Luhyas seemed to be leaving the Catholic Church after they migrated to Kangemi, choosing to practise their faith instead in ethnic-specific "African Initiated Churches."

So it was that when I arrived as parish priest in 2000 with an assistant Jesuit priest and a Jesuit brother, our team was set specific goals by our Jesuit Provincial superior: we needed to take steps to restore the parish to financial viability and to improve the formation of lay leadership. I was told that I could expect to be the last of the European missionaries to be pastor of this parish and that the changes I would introduce should make the parish more manageable for an African successor.

3.4 GENETIC AND DIALECTICAL ANALYSIS: 1985-2000

As I began work in the parish in the year 2000, I had no doubt that the recommendations of my Provincial superior were well judged and should set a pattern for the years that I would spend in the parish. However, in my Doran-influenced manner, I felt that a deeper analysis could be made of the situation that would produce yet more specific policies.

I became convinced that some fascinating if sad truths were to be acknowledged about the history of parish policy-making in Kangemi. A first conclusion was, in a certain sense, that the two Jesuit priests who had founded the parish had introduced policies that did not entirely cohere with each other. The approach to initiating development projects was admirable in many ways but also had a kind of pre-Vatican II paternalism about it. Weaknesses in the manner in which development projects were initiated and managed started to have a negative impact on the pastoral development of the parish. It would normally be assumed that SCCs would be associated with self-sustaining, co-operative kinds of economic initiatives as well as with political action that addressed deeper causes of poverty, and that their stress on the importance of lay ministry should not lead to dependency upon a priest. However, just such patterns of dependency occurred in Kangemi parish. The thought could occur to one that that in Kangemi parish a kind of pre-Vatican II strategy with regard to economic development projects interfered with a post-Vatican II strategy of promoting SCCs.

While there is some truth in this insight, it seemed to me that yet further analysis was warranted concerning the manner in which SCCs were initiated and developed in their own right, irrespective of influences from some problematic development projects. When one examined the kind of formation that had been offered to members of SCCs and to their leaders, one found that there seemed to be a stress on social justice activism that outweighed other dimensions of how to live as an SCC. From the point of view of the scale of values, a heavy stress seemed to be placed on trying to address issues of social values *ad extra* in Kangemi and more broadly in Kenya. Insufficient attention seemed to have been given to the values that need to be embraced *ad intra* to the parish before this *ad extra* mission could be undertaken. Above all, *ad intra* values that seemed to have been neglected were those of religious, personal, and cultural values.

A sad conclusion of our analysis was that the results of the pastoral praxis by Jesuits in Kangemi between 1985 and 2000 had been ambiguous; while real successes had been registered, so also had some failures. This pastoral praxis had produced the degree of dependency syndrome that offered a sad echo of the wider history of the ambiguous effects of missionary activity in Kenya, not to mention in Africa as a whole. Instead of empowering a cultural progress that was both Christian and modern, it had the effect, at times, of contributing to cultural alienation. A further irony is that weaknesses in the post-Vatican II strategy of promoting social justice had remarkable similarities to weaknesses of pre-Vatican II strategies. Both tended to take a reductionist approach to the scale of values and to promote social values without sufficient attention to the prior need for an integrated development of religious, personal, and cultural values. A pre-Vatican II approach did this by building non-self-sufficient development projects;

a post-Vatican II approach did this by attempting to train immature Christian communities in social justice activism.[7]

In light of this analysis, an obvious option for parish planning in the next era was to stress the formation of religious, personal, and cultural values *ad intra* to the parish, and only subsequently and with caution would we be ready to promote a transformation *ad extra*. In this latter dimension of mission we would need to be aware of the distinction between cultural values and social values, and of the priority of the former. Of course, such a proposal was easier stated than implemented. The following section traces the broad lines of how I, along with others on a pastoral team, attempted to implement such a strategy from 2000 to 2006.[8]

---

7 With regard to this imbalanced formation of SCCs, I believe we witness an example of what Doran has written about in terms of the ambiguity of the phenomenon of liberation theology. In *Theology and the Dialectics of History* (224-239) he offers an impressive analysis of the thought of a representative of this movement: Juan Luis Segundo. While he is full of praise for Segundo's commitment to a theology that informs Church praxis as historically transformative, he criticises Segundo's neglect of the distinction between superstructure and infrastructure and Segundo's apparent option of a kind of political action that seems close to the notion of Karl Marx's revolutionary praxis: "Ideology becomes a function and agent of the collapse or imbalance of the integral scale of values, through the elevation of the political into the superstructure, and through the consequent evacuation of cultural values from the position of determining the cognitive and existential orientations according to which economic systems and technological institutions are to be constituted" (*Dialectics*, 436). A more immediate link between the Jesuits who founded SCCs in Kangemi and liberation theology lies in their direct employment of the thought and methodology of the educationalist Paulo Freire. Doran conducts an analysis of Freire's thought in *Dialectics* (38-41). This analysis is more brief than that addressing Segundo and is entirely positive. I suspect that a more comprehensive analysis of the thought of Freire would support criticisms similar to those Doran makes of Segundo. At any rate, in Kangemi, the kind of use made of Freire in the forming of SCCs fell into the mistake of "elevating of the political into the superstructure."

8 On the question of employing the scale of values as a measure of the effectiveness of ministry *ad intra* to the Church, I make use of a development of Doran's thought on ministry by Neil Ormerod in "System, History, and a Theology of Ministry," in *Theological Studies* 61(2000): 432-446.

4. PASTORAL EXPERIENCES: 2000-2006

I was assigned to St Joseph the Worker Parish in 2000 together with a team that comprised a second Jesuit priest and two Jesuit brothers – all younger than I and local to East Africa. There was also a congregation of sisters who were active in the parish and who formed a pastoral team in the parish together with the Jesuits. Together we set about a process of planning for the next time period.

I explained above how there were two dimensions of the pastoral strategy that founded the parish: development projects and SCCs. Correspondingly, as we sat down to plan for the future in 2000, our planning followed these two major directions. In what follows I speak less of the details of the management of the development projects than of pastoral activities, but address this management issue first.

4.1 DEVELOPMENT PROJECTS: 2000-2003

I mentioned above how the parish ran development projects in areas of health, education, and income generating activities. As parish priest, I found myself to be the legal employer – under the Archbishop of Nairobi – of eighty people. Being experienced in such managerial and financial problems that were being experienced in the development projects, I began a process of separating these activities from the pastoral activities of the parish. I invited assistance from an Italian Catholic NGO (Non-Governmental Organization) to assist me in building a structure of management for our projects that would free priests for pastoral work. In effect, we created a new organization that resembled an NGO and that managed all our development projects. Two volunteers came from Italy to build up this structure and to become its first managers. This new organization, "The St. Joseph Development Programme," increasingly took care of its own fundraising needs and thus freed the priests of the parish to devote time to pastoral work.

4.2 PASTORAL STRATEGIES 2000-2002: PROMOTING RELIGIOUS VALUES

On the question of pastoral strategies, in a certain sense our policy was simple: we would begin by placing a priority on the formation of religious and personal values *ad intra* to the parish and hope for results that would enable us to discern how to proceed "downwards" with time. This central stress on promoting religious and personal values continued for about two years. It included organizing weekend retreats for members of each of our fifteen SCCs; in addition, we offered more intensive and ongoing formation seminars for the leaders of these communities who were expected to lead prayer using scripture in the weekly meetings of these groups.

In seeking to facilitate religious conversion, I worked from two sets of resources. The first was a training in spiritual direction according to the tradition of Ignatian spirituality; the second was the conversions and differentiations derived from studying the work of Lonergan and Doran. Regarding the latter skill-set, as a European missionary I became immediately aware of the importance of understanding that I was involved in an exercise of cross-cultural communication. The average level of formal education of my parishioners was that of primary school, and the differentiation of consciousness was that of common sense. I was struck by how close our parishioners were to the primal cultures of their ethnic origins and of the prominence of cosmological cultural ideas and values in their world. A related point here is that our retreats were being held in the Swahili language where orientations to this common sense differentiation of consciousness and cosmological cultural orientation were reinforced.

4.3 CONFLICT AND THE ELECTION OF THE "SPIRITUAL PARTY"

After about two years of promoting the kind of formation described here, some remarkable developments occurred that can be understood as a development from above, i.e., where graced transformation of religious and moral values began to affect the cultural and social structural realities of the parish.

A first point to note is that the shift of policies I initiated in the parish began to produce, perhaps inevitably, a backlash in certain quarters. Above all, those who felt that I had unjustly removed them from responsibilities in the parish development projects began to speak ill of me in the SCCs and in the pastoral council. This criticism extended to requests for my removal from the parish to the Archbishop of Nairobi and to my Jesuit Provincial. I came to recognize that the heuristic principle that explained this phenomenon was the "Law of the Cross." It had perhaps been inevitable that those taken up by ways of decline in the ethos of the parish would react in this way. This was typical of the way in which decline was defended in the culture at large, and we

could not expect that our parishioners would be free of such tempta-
tions.

At any rate, as the months went by it became clear that I was not
alone in wanting to promote the changes in priorities that we had begun to implement. After two of my years in the parish, the custom-
ary time arrived to elect or re-elect leaders in the SCCs, in the Parish
Pastoral Council, and to a five-person executive of this council. Un-
beknownst to me and to members of our pastoral team, parishioners
who had attended the retreats and other formation activities began to
organize themselves into what they called the "spiritual party" so as to
oppose what they called the "projects party" within these elected bodies of the parish. During the elections, a clear victory was attained for
the "spiritual party," and those of us on the pastoral team only began to
catch on to what had happened when we saw a large number of new
faces appearing in the leadership of these different groups. I recognized a number of the individuals who had been evidently most graced
on our retreats appearing in these ranks. It was also evident that a
greater diversity of economic and ethnic background was appearing in
our leadership.

4.4 FORMING CULTURAL VALUES AD INTRA
IN THE PARISH: 2002-2004

One can imagine what joy these developments brought to us on the
pastoral team. By the advent of year three of my time in Kangemi parish, it was clear that our efforts to promote transformation at the levels
of religious and personal values had had positive results. It was time to
concern ourselves with the integrity of the dialectic of culture.

Clearly, the basic logic of the scale of values and of the importance
of development from above was perfectly comprehensible to our parishioners. Given the growing authenticity of our communities, the
process of moving to prioritize cultural values *ad intra* to the parish
could now be performed in a highly consultative manner. When asked
what might be the ideas and values in which our parishioners most
need to be formed, members of SCCs pointed to two areas: family life
and ethnic inclusivity. During the two years that followed, the stress
was now placed less on retreats and scripture courses and more on
formation activities appertaining to these two themes.

Formation of these kinds tended not always to occur in SCCs
but also in specialised groups. We followed a principle that had been

established at the time of the founding of the parish: that no associations or Catholic movements that competed with the basic activities of SCCs would be welcomed into the parish. Indeed, we added that parishioners who might wish to be members of additional clubs or movements within the parish should first be active within their SCCs. Remarkably, many of our parishioners were ready to comply with these conditions.

This issue of a continuing commitment to different groups was especially relevant when it came to the delicate question of ethnicity. We initiated an association of Catholics that came from the Western Province of Kenya, the heartland of the Luhya community. This group had particular needs such as the formation of a savings and welfare cooperative which extended structures of solidarity from home villages to urban life. An important dimension of this solidarity was the need for assistance in the removal of the bodies of those who died in Nairobi so that they could be buried in their homesteads – something of the highest importance within Luhya culture. Members of this new association understood perfectly how regrettable it would be if their new association began to become a mono-ethnic "church within a church" and they continued to be loyal members of their SCCs. In fact, they became the backbone of door-to-door recruitment drives in the territories of each SCC to invite lapsed Catholics to return to active engagement in the parish.

In our efforts to assist the deepening of family values, it also became clear that much formation could best be done in discrete groups where members had much in common with each other. We were reminded that traditional African cultures tend to differentiate gender and age roles in a clear manner, and we initiated a range of special groups under the rubric of promoting family values. One such group was a "fathers' group" where men could meet in a safe environment and speak of the challenges they found in understanding what role they should play in their family in the changing cultural environment of today. In a similar manner we initiated marriage encounter groups where couples could be helped in communication skills and in understanding marriage as a Christian vocation. Another group we founded was a single-mothers group, and we discovered that a majority of active members of our SCCs were in fact of this status. Finally, we founded one group at the recommendation of our active youth group; it was called the "young adult" group, and it welcomed young couples who were living

together but who, for a variety of reasons, often financial, were not able
to marry.

4.5 PARISH MINISTRY AD EXTRA: 2004-2006

By the final two years of my time in the parish had arrived, we felt
that we were operating in a pastoral environment of a "virtuous circle."
We felt that our promoting of religious, personal and cultural values
were leading to a mutual reinforcement of all of these levels with progress being made in each of them. Logically, the next step would have
been to address issues of social and organizational structures within
the parish. However, for the most part, we found that the structures
of SCCs, of a limited number of additional groups and movements,
and of the parish pastoral council, founded from the beginning of the
parish, served us well. What had been crucial in my first years in the
parish was to "breathe life," as it were, into these structures by making
sure that religious, personal, and cultural values were being attended
to. Now that we were confident that the integrity of the scale of values
ad intra to the parish was being attended to reasonably well, the time
seemed to have arrived to address ourselves to ministry *ad extra* to the
parish.

A happy convergence with these events occurred with respect to the
development projects of the parish. It was becoming clear that our
new managerial structures within the St. Joseph Development Programme (SJDP) were resulting in a smooth running of the projects for
which it had responsibility. In fact, we had closed certain activities and
opened others. So it was that when we began a parish-wide consultation process about what were the greatest cultural and social problems
in the Kangemi area in general, we had social workers employed in
the SJDP available to visit the SCCs and to help animate this process
of reflection. As a result of this consultation, parishioners identified
three main problems in the area and assigned an order of priority in
the urgency of the need to address them: crime, addiction to alcohol
and drugs, and HIV/AIDS. In our pastoral planning for the years
2004-2006, we organized ourselves around the need to both act and
to be seen to act on each of these three issues. Our attentiveness to the
distinction between superstructure and infrastructure helped us pay

due attention to the value and attitudinal dimensions of each of these problems.[9]

The story of how we took action on each of these issues is a complex one, and I will stress only a few points. A first point is that we engaged these issues in a manner that was collaborative with other institutions beyond our Catholic parish. These included above all other Christian ecclesial communities in Kangemi, but we also sought to collaborate with local government and police. Another point to note here is that our efforts met with some success. We found that we could mobilize large numbers of Kangemi residents – Catholic and non-Catholic – around our three priority issues. One example was a march against the selling of illegally brewed alcohol; it attracted many thousands of participants and gained national media attention.

4.6 PARISH EXPANSION AND THE DIALECTIC OF COMMUNITY

One final issue began to emerge with particular clarity towards the end of my time in Kangemi: the need for us to start multiplying the numbers of pastoral structures in the parish and to begin the process of creating a second parish in the area. Actually, this can be understood as a call for us to attend to issues of social value *ad intra* to the parish. This exigency led to a process of us first increasing the number of our SCCs and then buying land for, and developing, a second "outstation" church within Kangemi. These activities occurred at the same time as our efforts to address our three parish priorities *ad extra* to the parish as we have just described.[10]

---

9 A topic for a further article would be a dialogue between notions of community development current in social science literature and one emerging from a Doran-based use of the analogy of dialectic. One methodology that our SJDP was required to employ with some donors was one based on "participatory rural development"; this is an impressive and widely used methodology and can by investigated by entering it as a keyword in most internet search engines. Key questions that we might ask would include how clearly this methodology distinguishes cultural from social values and how open it is to the role of religion in community development (another related methodology could be investigated under the keywords "log frame" and "project management)."

10 It is also worth making another point at this stage of my account. In this context of a virtuous circle of many fruitful activities in the parish, my use of the heuristic structure of the scale of values needed to become more

Regarding proposals to expand the numbers of our SCCs, I encountered some surprising reactions that I only later came to understand.
In a parish where so many positive developments now seemed to be
converging, the pastoral council and I came up against a remarkable
resistance from members of SCCs when we proposed this expansion.
We came to recognize that what we were encountering was an essentially healthy phenomenon: the resistance of intersubjectivity to the
dictates of practical intelligence. SCC members had developed strong
bonds of loyalty and friendship over recent years and did not take
kindly to the thought that some of their best friends might soon be
praying in a different SCC from their own. To be frank, I believe that
in some cases there continued to be an element of this resistance that
appertained to issues of class and ethnicity. There was little doubt that
the changes of structure we were proposing would bring advantages,
above all, to recent migrants to the area who tended to be poor and
more ethnically diverse than the more permanent members of the parish.

For me the value of employing the heuristic method in addressing
this challenge was that it helped me to be most patient with the resistance being demonstrated.[11] We initiated what turned out to be a
process which took a year of catechesis in order to communicate the
reasons for the proposed change. Eventually, we became convinced
that a large majority of SCC members were now ready to accept this
costly expression of living a Christian life. We initiated the process of
dividing every SCC in the parish into two. We took care to employ the
vocabulary of a cosmological culture in this and never actually spoke

---

flexible and more sophisticated. So it was that it seemed to make sense
to prioritize both ministry *ad extra* and an expansion of social structures
within the parish at the same time.

11 It seems to me that there is a lesson here for a number of dioceses in
Europe and North America who are trying to plan for the contraction of
parishes – an opposite process to the expansion we undertook in Kangemi.
Some dioceses in the North may perhaps be trying to implement rational
proposals of parish "clustering" too quickly. Patience and understanding
needs to be shown with the resistance that loyal Catholics demonstrate to
these proposals. Similarly, understanding needs to be demonstrated to the
psychological reality that the call to respond to these new policies is occurring at a time when intersubjective bonds between hierarchy and people
have been damaged by a series of sexual abuse scandals involving priests
and bishops.

of "division"; rather, we spoke of every SCC as a parent "giving birth to a child."

What resulted was a successful multiplication of our SCCs where, in fact, the pastoral team of the parish did not have to get very involved. The many and complex decisions involved in this major change of parish structure were made in and between the parent SCCs. Now, instead of working against the changes, so to speak, the mass and momentum of intersubjectivity was supporting the changes. Finally – again aware of the dialectical way we respond to values, and so of the important role of symbol and ritual – we took care to finalize this multiplication process by inviting the Archbishop to "baptize" the new SCCs in a Sunday liturgy that took three hours and was filled with processions and exchanges of gifts.

5. A POSTSCRIPT FROM 2008

In June of 2006, I came to the end of my time in St. Joseph the Worker Parish. I was sad to leave but also aware that in a certain sense the big test of the effectiveness of the decision-making in which we had been involved for six years lay in the ability of the structures we had created to endure through a change in personnel. With much pleasure I witnessed a change in the Jesuit community in Kangemi and the formation of a new team. This new team included two young Kenyan Jesuit priests. Since this time the new team has no doubt become aware of the weaknesses as well as the strengths of their predecessors. However, what brings me much satisfaction is to hear that all goes well in the parish and that exciting new decisions continue to be made. The St. Joseph Development Programme continues to function as a managerial structure that frees priests for pastoral work, and a temporary structure has been erected in the outstation plot where Mass is now celebrated every Sunday. And what brings me not the least pleasure, our increased number of thirty SCCs continues to exist.

Readers may be aware that from January to March of 2008 Kenya was wracked by ethnic violence. The causes of the violence were complex but related to the matters explained in the second part of this paper. The immediate cause was irregularities in a national election. This is a great sadness as it appears that the government dating from 2002, whose policies I have partly praised above, refused to preside over a free and fair election. A clear perception was received that this was a Kikuyu centred coalition government, and old resentments were ignited amongst some other ethnic communities. As we saw, these resentments had been fuelled over years by what was perceived to be land-grabbing across the country and consequent economic inequality. In the course of this violence, deep and long-term damage was inflicted both on the cultural superstructure and the economic infrastructure of the country. The healing of historic hurts will be made far more difficult by these recent ruptures. However, it does seem that a reasonably just political agreement, at least, was made at the end of this period. One can hope that a real shift of power relations has occurred in the country after this agreement and that it is the basis for a longer term restoration of the cultural dialectic of the country.

At any rate, the need for the Church to build up a world-cultural humanity in Kenya through policies that include well-formed SCCs has taken on a new urgency. I am happy to report that Kangemi remained relatively untouched by the violence that erupted in certain other locations. Sadly, one centre of violence was the nearby Kibera slum which featured in most international news coverage of the events. Reasons for the relative peace of Kangemi are various, but we like to think that our efforts at addressing issues of ethnicity within our Catholic parish, as well as our ecumenical efforts to address social problems in the area, made some contribution to the less violent atmosphere in Kangemi.

6. CONCLUSION:
RELIGIOUS AND CULTURE BUILDING IN KENYA

When one reads Robert Doran's *Theology and the Dialectics of History*, one is struck by his repeated return to the theme that one of the greatest lacks in modern and post-modern reflection on social affairs is proper attentiveness to the important influence that cultural superstructure brings to bear on the infrastructure of economics, politics, and intersubjectivity. I find this theme to be verified in the experiences upon which I have been reflecting in these pages. First of all, we notice that the cultural alienation of Africans that began during colonial times and that continues in many ways today is key to explaining much of the dysfunction at the level of infrastructure that so afflicts the continent. Similarly, and sadly, the weaknesses of the missionary endeavour of the nineteenth and twentieth centuries are often best understood as characterised by blindness to what was occurring at the level of superstructure in the African communities being evangelised. Finally, and I have to say most fascinating for me, I became convinced that certain progressive, post-Vatican II strategies of evangelization in Africa demonstrated a similar neglect of issues of superstructure. In the example of how SCCs tended to be promoted in the early days of Kangemi parish, I believe I witnessed the manner in which the ambiguities of liberation theology can lead to some negative consequences for Church praxis.

However, despite being an astute critic of Karl Marx, Doran agrees with him and with those liberation theologians who assert: "The point is not to understand the world but to change it." And here again I have found the tools provided by Doran's analysis of history to be of immense practical value. In this paper I have tried to outline how an attentiveness to the principles of ministry as mediating development from above bore concrete results in Kangemi parish. And this is the main message to which I want to testify regarding the not-easy-to-appropriate heuristic structure proposed by Robert Doran: it works!

INDEX

A

Abelard, Peter, 161-163, 379

Absolute Idealism, 407-411, 413, 415-416, 418-419, 421

active meaning, 5, 217-219, 225-226, 237

active spiration, 102, 105, 167, 383-384, 386, 393, 395, 399-400

aesthetic experience, 319

aesthetic-dramatic operator, 354-355, 361

affective response, 223

Africa, 487-490, 492-494, 497, 499, 508

age of authenticity, 450, 457, 460-462

age of mobilization, 450, 457-462

aggiornamento, 205, 218, 226, 325-328

already-out-there-now, 265, 267-268, 276-277

ancien régime, 450, 457-462

Anselm, Saint, 147-152, 155-164, 286, 308

anthropological culture, 60, 461-462, 488

apprehensions of value, 222

Aristotle, 46, 94, 114-115, 117-118, 122, 135, 142, 160, 201, 212-213, 232, 270, 275-277, 288, 297, 313, 336, 343, 358, 361-364, 367, 369, 413-415, 419, 421, 455

art, 5, 25, 36, 57, 113-114, 117, 126-127, 132-137, 139-144, 173, 188, 226, 244, 247-248, 259, 272, 317, 319-321, 328-329, 347, 354, 356, 358, 360-361, 364-365, 367, 435

artistically differentiated consciousness, 246

Augustine, Saint, 77, 115, 146, 192-194, 197-198, 200-201, 208-209, 221, 257, 264-265, 270, 274, 276, 280, 285-286, 357, 366, 369-373, 450

authentic desiring, 346, 349, 351

authentic subjectivity, 197, 208, 211, 223, 321

authenticity, 48, 69, 107-108, 130, 183, 197, 223-225, 231, 234, 239, 262-263, 269-270, 327, 372, 380, 432, 450, 457, 460-462, 478, 501

B

bad faith, 431-433, 438-439, 447

bearers of values, 25-26

being-in-love, 58, 75-76, 78, 87-88, 105, 157, 325, 346

Boff, Clodovis, 54-55, 63-64, 281

Bultmann, Rudolf, 260-264, 270, 272

Bush, George W., 322

C

Cage, John, 248, 455

Calculus of Variation, 338-339

Carruthers, Mary, 372

cartwheel, 146

Catherine of Siena, Saint, 79-82, 333-334, 339

Catholic action, 459, 468, 477, 480-481, 483-484

CELAM, 52-53

censor, 6, 353, 423-440, 443-445

Christ's constitution, 151, 153-154, 164

Christology, 54, 98-99, 106, 110, 146-147, 151-153, 164, 166, 283, 297, 303, 309